Reactions to
Voices in the Wilderne.

MW01005584

......posers

"I've received and just finished reading your *Voices in the Wilderness*—what an extraordinary book! . . . . I found it to be a thorough and fascinating read. You've done a tremendous service and it would be wonderful if the schools of music around our country would embrace this book and make it required reading for all college music courses." **Gerard Schwarz, Music Director, Seattle Symphony Orchestra**

"As a work of music criticism, *Voices* is as close to a model of its kind as anything I have ever read. . . . Simmons's introduction, in which he lays out the case for reconsidering these composers and the reasons for their neglect, is worth the price of the book by itself. . . . Simmons is adept at sketching out the musical structure of a composition without descending into the kind of labored technical jargon found in many CD booklets. . . . The very hardest thing for a music critic to do is to put in words the "meaning" of a piece of music. Simmons is particularly gifted in doing this, and it is what makes *Voices* so valuable." **Robert Reilly, author of *Surprised by Beauty***

"[Simmons's] introduction offers an impressively clear summary of the various ways in which the history of musical modernism is in need of correction and revision. His largely non-technical descriptions of the music discussed in *Voices in the Wilderness* are models of accessibility." **Terry Teachout, *Commentary***

"In this persuasively argued and passionately committed book, musicologist Walter Simmons . . . has done an inestimably important service in making a cogent case for the Neo-Romantic Aesthetic." **Thomas F. Bertonneau, *The University Bookman***

"Simmons is both vivid in his own descriptions of the music and level-headed in his judgements. He is unafraid of challenging opinions he deems ill-considered . . . or of pointing out when his pet composers are not at their best." **Ken Smith, *Gramophone***

"The value of this book is in its evangelisation through knowledge and reticence. It lacks excesses and overt advocacy. We are not told what to think. We are made curious, intrigued." **Rob Barnett, *Classical Music on the Web***

"Simmons writes clearly and even eloquently, , , , Furthermore, he pulls off the neat trick of providing both an introduction for the novice and a deeper instruction for someone already acquainted with the music." **Steven Schwartz, *Classical Net***

The Music of William Schuman, Vincent Persichetti, and Peter Mennin

Voices of Stone and Steel

Walter Simmons

ROWMAN & LITTLEFIELD
Lanham • Boulder • New York • London

Published by Rowman & Littlefield
A wholly owned subsidiary of The Rowman & Littlefield Publishing Group, Inc.
4501 Forbes Boulevard, Suite 200, Lanham, Maryland 20706
www.rowman.com

Unit A, Whitacre Mews, 26-34 Stannary Street, London SE11 4AB

British Library Cataloguing in Publication Information Available

Library of Congress Cataloging-in-Publication Data

Simmons, Walter, 1946-
  The music of William Schuman, Vincent Persichetti, and Peter Mennin : voices of stone and steel / Walter Simmons.
    p. cm.
  Includes bibliographical references and index.
  ISBN 978-0-8108-5748-3 (cloth : alk. paper) — ISBN 978-1-5381-0383-8 (pbk. : alk. paper) — ISBN 978-1-5381-0384-5 (electronic)
  1. Schuman, William, 1910–1992—Criticism and interpretation. 2. Persichetti, Vincent, 1915-1987—Criticism and interpretation. 3. Mennin, Peter—Criticism and interpretation. 4. Music—United States—20th century—History and criticism.
  5. Composers—United States—Biography. I. Title.
  ML390.S615 2011
  780.92'273—dc22

                                    2010023899

♾™ The paper used in this publication meets the minimum requirements of American National Standard for Information Sciences—Permanence of Paper for Printed Library Materials, ANSI/NISO Z39.48-1992. Printed in the United States of America

This book is dedicated to my wife, Ronnie Halperin. Her support—both emotional and editorial—her consistent generosity of spirit, and her unwavering belief in the value of this project were indispensable in enabling me to bring it to fruition.

Contents

Acknowledgments

Like *Voices in the Wilderness: Six American Neo-Romantic Composers*, this book is the result of many years of research, listening, analysis, and reflection. But throughout the period during which this volume has been in preparation, I was the beneficiary of many forms of encouragement, assistance, and support from both colleagues and friends. I would like to express my appreciation to Nicholas Tawa, Mark Lehman, Anthony Sbordoni, and Joseph Greco, who have provided welcome encouragement and support of my efforts for many years. I would also like to thank Barry O'Neal of Carl Fischer Music, and Judith Ilika and Daniel Dorff of the Theodore Presser Company, who made scores and other material available to me that greatly facilitated my research. I am indebted to Donald A. Morris, Karl Miller, David Shaw, and Jana Holzmeier for providing me with rare and valuable materials that were of great benefit in helping me to achieve the thoroughness that was my goal. I am deeply grateful to Georganne Mennin, Phillip Ramey, Larry Bell, Andrea Olmstead, Elizabeth Bell, and Michael White for sharing their unique recollections and perspectives. For valuable professional advice I thank Isidore Silver and Nancy Kramer. And I owe a special debt of gratitude to Carson Cooman, who provided much valuable feedback and ongoing assistance throughout my years of work on this project.

1

Introduction

Conventional accounts of the history of American concert music throughout most of the twentieth century typically begin with Charles Ives—his rebellion against the timid Eurocentric epigones who comprised his teachers and their peers, his American Transcendentalism, and his anticipation of innovations later adopted by the European avant-garde. This is often followed by a discussion of the development of jazz and the appeal it held for European sophisticates during the 1920s, as well as for American composers like George Gershwin and others, who sought ways of incorporating its spontaneity, its rhythmic vitality, and its unmistakable "Americanness" into traditional "classical" forms. The quest for an independent national musical identity might then be juxtaposed against the "crisis of tonality" said to beset European music around the time of the First World War. Tonality refers to the tendency of conventional music to gravitate toward a particular home note, or "tonic." But more than just a musical center of gravity, tonality was developed by the Austro-Germanic classical masters into the fundamental organizing principle of large-scale works. Symphonies, sonatas, and string quartets were structured according to relationships among subordinate tonal regions to a primary tonal center, all of which were presumably audible and comprehensible to the listener. Around the turn of the twentieth century, Arnold Schoenberg and others asserted that Richard Wagner and his followers (including Schoenberg himself) had exhausted this system upon which music had been predicated for centuries.

This alleged "crisis" led composers to explore a variety of radical new paths: Igor Stravinsky liberated dissonance from its historical role as an expression of harmonic tension requiring resolution. Instead, dissonance was exalted as a legitimate, independent class of harmonic sonority in its own right. The element of rhythm also assumed greater importance, equivalent to harmony and melody rather than subordinate to them. Some composers, like the Hungarian Bela Bartók, turned to their own indigenous folk melodies to revitalize their music and infuse it with an authentic—rather than refined and romanticized—national flavor. These new directions were part of an avant-garde movement that contributed to the development of "Modernism," an aesthetic perspective that influenced all the arts during and after World War I in reaction to the alleged extravagance of Romanticism in its later manifestations.

The Modernist position in music held that the emphasis placed on subjective experience by the Romantics—especially, the grandiose distortions and exaggerations that resulted from excessive self-absorption—had become narcissistic and self-indulgent. New areas of cultural inquiry appeared—areas that turned attention outward toward social and political issues and toward developments in science and technology that promised to take on increased importance in the years to follow. In order to reflect these trends, entirely new forms of musical expression were said to be needed.

Around 1920 Schoenberg devised an alternative to the organizing principle of tonality, proposing a means of systematizing the *absence* of tonality. His concept became known as "twelve-tone composition," later developed into a more comprehensive approach known as "serialism." The serialists argued that abandoning the system of tonality required dispensing with classical forms as well, as these were felt to be inseparable from the principle of tonality as a unifying force. Therefore, new forms were needed, specifically tailored to the premises of serial composition.

Although Schoenberg saw in twelve-tone composition a means of perpetuating the supremacy of the Austro-Germanic musical aesthetic, many of its proponents promoted their system as "international," scorning the provinciality of more nationalistic approaches. A number of American composers, such as Wallingford Riegger and Roger Sessions, were attracted to the twelve-tone approach as a means of dispelling the impression of provincialism and of distinguishing themselves from those who were embracing vernacular elements in their music.

Other innovative approaches to musical composition that arose as alternatives to traditional tonality and flourished in the United States during the middle decades of the twentieth century included indeterminacy, microtonality, and the use of electronic sound sources. The proponents of these new approaches to composition were often at odds with each other, many of their tenets being essentially mutually exclusive. But all were in fundamental agreement that tonality was no longer a viable principle in the creation of music as a serious art form. The American music-loving public, however, never accepted the music composed in the wake of the tonal system. In fact, many of those composers, roughly contemporary with Schoenberg, who did not embrace his notions of an exhausted tonal system—Ravel, Puccini, Richard Strauss, and Rachmaninoff, for example—achieved tremendous popular success. (For more elaborate discussions and analyses of these developments and those that follow, see Nicholas Tawa's *A Most Wondrous Babble* [1987], *American Composers and Their Public* [1995], and *The Great American Symphony* [2009].)

During the 1930s, the period of the Great Depression, another nationalist trend emerged in America, this time under the guise of populism, influenced to some extent by the Soviet aesthetic known as "socialist realism," which extolled the virtues of art for the masses and regarded avant-garde intellectual innovations as "elitist." This populist trend attracted many composers who were sympathetic to socialist ideology, as well as others who were simply unwilling to limit their work to a small esoteric audience. The quest to create an American symphonic repertoire dated back to the mid 1800s, but it was not until the 1930s and 1940s that a distinctive American symphonic school of composition emerged. Most of the composers who participated in this movement—Aaron Copland, Roy Harris, Morton Gould, Elie Siegmeister, and others—were eager to find an appreciative audience for their work and attempted to evoke a sense of the "American character" or the "American experience" in a way that would be discernible to the untrained listener. Many incorporated explicitly American vernacular elements in their work. Other composers, among them Howard Hanson, Samuel Barber, Vittorio Giannini, and Paul Creston, were more interested in adding their voices to the traditional classical music heritage than in creating a distinctly American "sound." Still others, such as William Schuman and David Diamond, sought to reconcile some of these competing ideals by seeking a recognizably American identity without resorting to vernacular sources by creating a "modern" sound while retaining a connection to tonality, and by rejecting the language of Late Romanticism without forfeiting accessibility to general audiences. These composers too enjoyed a period of attention, as well as popular and critical favor. Some—Copland and Barber, for example—developed prominent reputations that outlasted the brief period when these trends were in vogue.

However, by the mid 1950s the Modernist aesthetic had been largely co-opted by the European serialist movement, which had begun to establish influential power bases in the music departments of Princeton, Columbia, and other major American universities, where composers were freed from the responsibility of having to win acceptance for their creative fruits in the marketplace of music lovers. Touting its "internationalism," this approach, as articulated by provocative, outspoken European advocates like Pierre Boulez

and Karlheinz Stockhausen and by Americans like Milton Babbitt, successfully preempted the American symphonic school. Boulez had written in 1952,
"I . . . assert that any musician who has not experienced . . . the necessity for
the dodecaphonic (i.e., twelve-tone) language is USELESS. For his whole
work is irrelevant to the needs of his epoch."[1] (On the other hand, Tawa quotes
composer-critic Paul Turok as having pointed out, "European artists are for
internationalism, so long as they come out on top."[2]) With an abundance of
theoretical writing to elaborate its principles and support its claim of providing a comparable alternative to the organizing power of tonality, serialism lent
itself to the academic propensity for abstract rationalization, aligning itself
with subjects like mathematics, linguistics, and philosophy. Conservatories,
the traditional centers for musical study and less eager to embrace this point
of view, were disparaged by spokesmen for the avant-garde as trade schools
for the training of musical artisans. Scholars who embraced the Modernist
view of musical history propagated it in their teaching and writing, and, by
suppressing or discrediting alternative interpretations, succeeded in achieving
intellectual hegemony. Composers like Elliott Carter and even Copland, who
had embraced the nationalist-populist aesthetic during the 1940s, began to
incorporate aspects of serialism into their work during the 1950s.

Anthony Tommasini recalled the "fractious decades after World War II"
in an article in the *New York Times*, describing how university composers
"seized the intellectual high ground and bullied their colleagues and students
into accepting serial procedures as the only valid form of modernism. All
those fusty holdouts still clinging to tonality were laughably irrelevant, the
serialists argued. And if beleaguered audiences and even many critics re-
coiled from 12-tone music, well . . . that was their problem."[3] The contemptuous attitude of Modernist composers was crystallized in a notorious article,
published with the title "Who Cares if You Listen?" by the serial composer
Milton Babbitt.[4] The result of force-feeding nontraditional musical styles to
a public that became increasingly uncertain of its own reactions and insecure
in its own tastes was a gradual estrangement of the audience from the music
of its own time.

The piece of the truth that was suppressed during this aesthetic fiat was
that there continued to be many American composers for whom the crisis
of tonality was not a central issue, nor was the development of a distinctly
American musical style or the other issues that concerned the Modernists.
Few of the conventional accounts of American musical history included any
but the most prominent of these figures, except in the lists of miscellaneous
"others" typically found at the ends of chapters. Usually such composers
were dismissed as shallow, unoriginal, or derivative, academic journeymen of
limited talent, panderers to commercial interests, or guilty of some other defi-

ciency of character or artistry. By 1979, serialist composer Charles Wuorinen conceded patronizingly, "the tonal system, in an atrophied or vestigial form, is still used today in popular and commercial music, and even occasionally in the works of backward-looking serious composers," adding, "it is no longer employed by serious composers of the mainstream," having "been replaced or succeeded by the 12-tone system."[5]

The disparagement and suppression from about 1955 until about 1975 of new music that retained a connection to tonality was reflected in critical attitudes, frequency of performance, and frequency of recordings. The most celebrated figures, such as Aaron Copland and Samuel Barber, had admittedly enjoyed sufficient public exposure and popular success to ensure their works a foothold in the repertoire durable enough to withstand critical condescension. And others—Walter Piston, William Schuman, Vincent Persichetti, and Peter Mennin, for example—who had achieved substantial reputations as a result of their positions as administrators or highly regarded pedagogues were accorded the nominal respect typically associated with such positions. But the works of even these figures, not to mention those with less prominent reputations, were simply disregarded, their contributions denigrated and relegated to the periphery of the musical arena.[6]

During the 1990s a music theorist named Joseph N. Straus attempted to refute the claim that advocates of serialism and related approaches successfully marginalized American composers who pursued more traditional, tonal musical styles. He designed what purported to be an objective, statistically based investigation of the issue and concluded that tonal composers dominated the musical institutions of the post–World War II years, reporting his findings in an article called "The Myth of Serial 'Tyranny' in the 1950s and 1960s."[7] However, Straus's study did not consider such variables as prestige of venue, forum, or platform, which are less susceptible to objective quantification. Furthermore, the categorization of composers he used in compiling his statistics is open to question, as are many of the other indicators from which he derived his results.

The Music of William Schuman, Vincent Persichetti, and Peter Mennin: Voices of Stone and Steel and its companion volume, *Voices in the Wilderness* (2004), challenge the Modernist interpretation of musical history, along with many of the assumptions on which it is predicated. For example, I reject the view that the fundamental significance of tonality is its function as a macrostructural organizing principle; this view of tonality applies chiefly to the Austro-Germanic line of musical evolution and the aesthetics that developed alongside it, but it does not apply to the styles of music that developed in Italy, France, England, the Slavic countries, or—to focus on the subject of this book—in the United States, except insofar as composers in these countries chose to adopt the Austro-Germanic aesthetic. I reject the assumption that the evolution of the tonal system proceeded according to a linear progression that led inevitably to the dissolution of tonality altogether. More broadly, I reject the view that music is fruitfully studied as *any* sort of linear progression, with some hypothetical goal toward which all contenders are racing, the prize going to the one who gets there first.

By the late 1970s, Modernist attitudes had begun to lose ground. Discouraged by the unwavering hostility and indifference of audiences to their works, an increasing number of composers, including such erstwhile proponents of atonality in its myriad guises as George Rochberg, Jacob Druckman, and David Del Tredici among the most prominent, were beginning to question the linear musico-historical imperative that had served as their aesthetic premise. Many also addressed some of the consequences and hidden psychosocial agendas of the avant-garde and its public posture and began to seek ways of achieving a rapprochement with audiences by accommodating their creative work to the perceptual frameworks of the general listener. Meanwhile, composers like Philip Glass and Steve Reich had been developing a defiantly tonal, if not simplistic, approach that became known as "minimalism." A radical repudiation of the intellectual complexity of serialism, minimalism aroused an astonishingly enthusiastic response from audiences. However, most of the composers who had maintained their commitment to traditional tonality all along were now largely forgotten. While the music of a figure as prominent as Samuel Barber was soon heard widely again, he was identified more as an anachronism than as the most prominent example of a significant aesthetic alternative.

Since the late 1980s, however, a number of performers and commentators have begun to reconsider the composers who have been languishing in the footnotes of mainstream textbooks. Many dismissive judgments made decades ago are being questioned. It is this revival of interest that has made a serious survey of traditionalist composers both timely and necessary.

This book and its predecessor argue that the marginalization of these "alternative" figures deprived the listening public of an important and rewarding repertoire. I assert that the value of music lies in the myriad temperaments, personalities, perceptions, and perspectives on life-and-the-cosmos reflected in it; that the most interesting composers are those whose music reveals the most rewarding perspectives and does so through the means that convey them most effectively and convincingly. Furthermore, I claim that the compositional languages adopted by the traditionalists of the twentieth century allowed for a richer, subtler, more varied range of musical expression than ever before in history. That is, the renunciation of tonality as a fundamental structural principle—without its being replaced by an arbitrary system like serialism—freed tonality to function within itself as an expressive parameter of the greatest nuance, in conjunction with other parameters like melody, rhythm, tone color, and so on.

These books argue and demonstrate that the most distinguished traditionalist composers created substantial bodies of work notable for their richness, variety, accessibility, and expressive power; that their music revealed distinctive individual features, recognizable stylistic traits, consistent themes and attitudes, as did the acknowledged masterpieces of the past; that much of this music had—and still has—the ability to bridge the gap between composer and audience, to enrich a musical repertoire that has become stagnant with the endless repetition of the tried and true, and to engage the enthusiasm of those seeking the adventure of discovering new creative personalities and their masterpieces rather than merely the reassurance and soporific comfort of the overly familiar. It is to bring the most rewarding of these voices to greater public awareness—as well as to the awareness of younger composers whose ignorance of the accomplishments of their forebears has often resulted in their "reinventing the wheel"—that these studies have been written.

A common reaction to the courses and lectures that have led to the writing of these books has been the bewildered question: How can music as appealing and rewarding as this have been ignored for so long? Or: How could a composer with so much creative vision and expressive breadth be so little known? Some of the reasons are discussed in this introduction; other, more individual reasons are presented in the chapters that follow. But, ultimately, there is no *adequate* answer, just as there is no *adequate* answer to the question: If the American Declaration of Independence states "All men are created equal," then how could the institution of slavery have flourished? It is our hope that this study and others that follow will begin to increase awareness of this repertoire among scholars and performers, as well as general listeners.

The Music of William Schuman, Vincent Persichetti, and Peter Mennin: Voices of Stone and Steel and its predecessor offer serious examinations of those composers who created significant, artistically meaningful bodies of work without abandoning traditional principles, forms, and procedures. Rather than dwelling on polemical diatribes concerning aesthetic abstractions, I highlight the most significant compositional figures, discussing their importance through biographical overviews and comprehensive critical assessments of their outputs, including both strengths and weaknesses, and identifying their most important and representative compositions, their distinguishing stylistic features, and their identities within the broader sociomusical context.

The term *traditionalists* is used in these works to refer to those composers who embraced the continuing viability of tonality as well as the musical forms and developmental principles on which the body of Western classical music has been based. These were composers who were more concerned with their own individual expressive purposes than with novel compositional procedures. Some continued along the stylistic lines of nineteenth-century European music; some followed the lead of Igor Stravinsky, who himself attempted to find an alternative to the grandiloquence of Late Romanticism without renouncing tonality and other traditional techniques; still others attempted in a variety of ways to "Americanize" the European musical tradition in order to give it greater meaning and relevance for the domestic public.

Another term that requires some clarification is *tonal*, as a lack of unanimity in its usage has led to considerable confusion. The "strict constructionist" uses the term *tonal* to describe music composed according to the paradigms that developed chiefly in eighteenth-century Austria and Germany and dominated the music of those countries until the turn of the twentieth century. In this music, a primary tonal center serves as an overall organizing principle, unifying all other, subordinate aspects of a composition. The "loose constructionist" uses the term *tonal* to describe all music in which tension/resolution expectations rooted in tonal harmony play a role in the expressive impact of a composition. The confusion to which this lack of unanimity has given rise has been further complicated by the advent of additional terms—*atonal, nontonal, pan-tonal, pan-diatonic, twelve-tone, serial*, and others—in efforts to provide clarification, but these have in some cases perpetuated the confusion. In adopting the loose construction of the concept of tonality, these studies acknowledge the use of "atonality" as an expressive device within a tonal composition, in passages where the subjective experience of a tonal center is largely absent, even though a theoretical tonic may be adduced through elaborate objective analysis.

The previous volume, *Voices in the Wilderness*, dealt with six American composers who pursued a Neo-Romantic approach. Further studies in the series are being contemplated. These may include American Neo-Classicists, American Opera Composers, American Nationalists and Populists, and American Traditionalists—the post-1930 generations. The volume at hand discusses three Modern Traditionalists—composers who embraced aspects of Modernism without renouncing traditional structural and developmental principles.

MODERN TRADITIONALISTS

In addition to such traditionalist subgroups as Neo-Romantics, Neo-Classicists, National Populists, and so forth, there is another subgroup of American composers that might be termed "Modern Traditionalists." ("Modernist Traditionalists" would be more precise but less graceful.) Unlike the Neo-

Summary

dissussion on serialism, European tonality, Morderism, Marginalizing neo-classisism as backwards lookers.

Romantics, these composers were not primarily concerned with the expression of personal moods, feelings, and emotions, nor with the representation of narratives, nor was their musical language a direct outgrowth of Late Romantic harmonic and tonal practice; unlike the Neo-Classicists, these composers did not represent a return to eighteenth-century musical values, such as conceptual simplicity, textural clarity, formal symmetry, or expressive restraint; and unlike the National Populists, they did not turn to jazz, folk, or popular music to appeal to a broader array of less sophisticated listeners or to create an explicitly American "sound." But in contrast to the composers most closely associated with Modernism—the serialists and various subgroups of avant-garde experimentalists—these composers did not reject tonality as a dynamic expressive parameter, nor did they reject traditional forms such as the sonata, symphony, or concerto, nor such techniques as counterpoint, motivic development, or metrical rhythm. Instead, embracing musical features similar to those found in the works of such early Modernists as Stravinsky, Bartók, and Hindemith, the Modern Traditionalists preferred generic forms to literary or other extramusical hybrids while rejecting many of the conventions associated with the classical forms that no longer seemed relevant. They embraced a fluid notion of tonality while rejecting its macrostructural functions and de-emphasizing its use in suggesting emotional states through analogy; and they embraced harmonic dissonance for its value as sonority, rather than as part of a subtle tension-release mechanism, and often adopted a significant level of dissonance as a harmonic baseline.

The Modern Traditionalists were not as concerned as the National Populists with creating an identifiably American "sound." But they were more conscious of contributing to the development of a native symphonic repertoire than were the Neo-Romantics, whose roots in the languages of European composers and whose expression focused on more subjective feelings resulted in less of a concern with creating a collective American identity. During the 1930s and 1940s, when these issues were frequent subjects of public discussion, numerous attempts were made to identify specifically American expressive traits. Optimism, adventurousness, individualism, exuberance, brash vitality, emotional directness and innocence, syncopated or other irregular rhythmic patterns, and emphasis on winds and percussion relative to strings are just a few of the temperamental and musical traits held to be "typically American."[8] Many of the Modern Traditionalists—consciously or unconsciously—cultivated some of these qualities in their work, along with the other Modernist usages noted above, as points of distinction from the music of their recent European predecessors such as Sibelius, Rachmaninoff, Strauss, and others. As a result, much of the music of the Modern Traditionalists has been characterized as recognizably American.

The importance of formal and structural matters relative to expressive content is another issue that distinguishes the Modern Traditionalists from the Neo-Romantics. While the Neo-Romantics typically gave primacy to emotional expression, often adopting formal processes and templates inherited from their European predecessors as useful blueprints, many of the Modern Traditionalists sought to update classical forms and procedures, tailoring them to suit the needs of specific musical material in more streamlined, efficient, and individualized ways. Thus, for many Modern Traditionalists, the use of such forms as sonata and symphony did not require such a work to fall into three or four movements or to embrace *sonata-allegro* form, with its two contrasting themes and its sequence of exposition/development/recapitulation. The result is a relatively equivalent balance between structural and expressive concerns.

Although American traditionalist composers have been divided into subgroups for the purpose of these studies, neither critics nor the general public have endeavored to discriminate with this degree of specificity. As was discussed in *Voices in the Wilderness*, the American Neo-Romantics represent the subgroup that probably faced the harshest censure from the critical and musicological establishment because of their blatantly reactionary stylistic orientation, their obvious roots in the works of their European predecessors, and their concern with audience appeal. Of course, those very factors also resulted in their finding favor with the music-listening public—at least during the 1930s and 1940s, when their music first achieved prominence. However, the Modern Traditionalists initially escaped some of this critical opprobrium but failed, for the most part, to win approval from the public. For example, the music written by Aaron Copland upon his return to the United States in 1924, after several years of study in Paris with Nadia Boulanger but before he began to infuse his work with nationalist and populist elements, might be said to exemplify the Modern Traditionalist approach. However, at that time his work was regarded as quite avant-garde. (One recalls Walter Damrosch's remark, made after conducting the 1925 premiere of Copland's Symphony for Organ and Orchestra, that if a young man "can write a symphony like this at 23, within five years he will be ready to commit murder!"[9]).

But if one sought to cite a single work as initiating the Modern Traditionalist approach in American music, that work is likely to be the *Symphony 1933* by Roy Harris, although the body of this composer's work merits discussion more appropriately among the National Populists. Harris, born in Oklahoma in 1898, spent his youth and young adulthood in California. Moving to the East Coast in 1925, he became acquainted with Copland, who persuaded him to pursue his musical study in Paris with Mlle. Boulanger. Shortly after Harris returned to America in 1929, Copland, who was very impressed with the qualities he found in Harris's work, introduced him to Serge Koussevitzky, who suggested that Harris compose "a big symphony from the west."[10] Harris took the suggestion, and the result was the *Symphony 1933*, which Koussevitzky introduced with the Boston Symphony Orchestra in January 1934. The work made a remarkable impact on both critics and listeners, but perhaps even more significantly, on other young composers as well. Harris soon became a figure of national importance, and the *Symphony 1933* became the first American symphony to be recorded commercially. Harris further refined his approach in his Symphony No. 3 of 1939, also introduced by Koussevitzky in Boston. This work made an even greater impact, appealing to audiences as well, and was for many years regarded as the quintessential American symphony of the first half of the twentieth century. Ultimately, Harris's talent and skills proved insufficient to support a meaningful body of work, and many of his works that initially attracted attention failed to sustain enduring interest. However, Harris's greatest importance—especially from the standpoint of this study—lies in his articulation of a viable structural alternative to the classical symphonic template. Though the Neo-Romantics may have expanded this prototype, altering its proportions and modifying points of emphasis, they nevertheless retained it as a formal blueprint, for the most part. Harris introduced his thematic material via a gradual and seemingly spontaneous coalescence that he called "autogenesis." In this manner he gave voice to a different kind of symphonic rhetoric—lofty, expansive, and open-ended rather than symmetrical—and somehow indisputably American, yet without recourse to vernacular material. It is a music of assertion, speculation, and reflection rather than of dialectical dynamism or melodic/harmonic progression. This new approach captured the imagination of many younger composers, some of whom were especially gifted and subsequently achieved a consummation that Harris had never anticipated. Reflecting on the impact of Harris's work on his own development, William Schuman later commented, "For me the sounds were like no others I had ever heard—his whole 'autogenetic' concept of form, the free and strong orchestration, the extraordinary beauty and sweep of the melodic material. He was a new voice."[11]

By the 1940s the number of American Modern Traditionalists was growing, and their music continued to win the approval of critics while finding favor with some of the more adventurous members of the listening public as well. It was at this time when the American symphony was becoming a genre with an identity of its own. Although this blossoming new repertoire included entries from the Neo-Romantic, Neo-Classical, and National Populist camps, it was largely the Modern Traditionalists whose contributions shaped the identity of the genre. And it was during this period when the reputations of many of these composers were forged. Perhaps the next milestone—a symphony in the Modern Traditionalist vein that catapulted its composer into the national spotlight—was the Symphony No. 3 of William Schuman. Composed in 1941 and introduced that year—also by Serge Koussevitzky and the Boston Symphony Orchestra—the work won the first New York Music Critics' Circle Award the following year. It is perhaps not an oversimplification to observe that the success of his Third Symphony led to Schuman's winning the first Pulitzer Prize in music in 1943, his attaining the influential position of director of publications for the major music publisher G. Schirmer in 1945, and his appointment to the presidency of the Juilliard School. Two years later he invited such other Modern Traditionalists as Vincent Persichetti and Peter Mennin to join the faculty. Yet somewhat ironically, it was during the 1950s and 1960s, when the American symphonic genre went into eclipse, displaced by musicological enthusiasm for the more radical serial approach, that many of the greatest works of the Modern Traditionalists were composed.

Among other American composers who might be described as Modern Traditionalists, as defined here, are William Bergsma, David Diamond, Roger Goeb, Ezra Laderman, Benjamin Lees, Ray Luke, Gardner Read, and Stanley Wolfe. Some of the works of Aaron Copland fall within this category, though not, of course, those associated with Americana. Furthermore, the Modern Traditionalist approach has proven to be the stylistic basis for many of the most prominent and successful composers among more recent generations of American composers, such as Ellen Taaffe Zwilich, John Harbison, Paul Moravec, Christopher Rouse, and many others. And, as was the case with the Neo-Romantics, there are many European composers whose work may be seen as analogous to that of the American Modern Traditionalists: Edmund Rubbra, Benjamin Britten, and Michael Tippett in England, Henry Barraud in France, Frank Martin in Switzerland, Bruno Bettinelli in Italy, Hendrik Andriessen in Holland, Hilding Rosenberg in Sweden, Joonas Kokkonen in Finland, Vagn Holmboe in Denmark, Andrzej Panufnik in Poland and England, and Miloslav Kabeláč in Czechoslovakia, to name just a few.

For the purposes of this study, the lives and works of three American Modern Traditionalists will be examined: William Schuman (1910–1992), Vincent Persichetti (1915–1987), and Peter Mennin (1923–1983). The careers of these three figures shared much in common, most notably their close association with the Juilliard School: Schuman was the president of Juilliard from 1945 until 1962, when he left to head the Lincoln Center for the Performing Arts; Persichetti joined the faculty in 1947, serving for four decades, as chairman of the Composition Department from 1963, and of the Literature and Materials Department from 1970 until his death; Mennin, who had served on the faculty from 1947 to 1958, returned to Juilliard in 1962, succeeding Schuman as president until his own death. However, this volume makes only passing reference to the history of the Juilliard School. Other books (e.g., Andrea Olmstead's *Juilliard: A History*) have dealt with the school and its history, and the reader seeking such a historical study is advised to seek them out. The focus of this book is on Schuman, Persichetti, and Mennin as composers and, to some extent, as people; Juilliard was simply a common element that linked their lives together for a period of time. On the other hand, it can be argued persuasively that that period—1947 to 1958—represented the most fertile and productive years of all three composers—not only from the standpoint of quantity but also from the standpoint of quality: It was during this period that each composer produced most of his finest and most distinctive music. The following list itemizes the most outstanding works written by each composer during this twelve-year period:

1947	Mennin	Symphony No. 4
1948	Schuman	Symphony No. 6
1949	Schuman	*Judith*
1950	Schuman	String Quartet No. 4
	Mennin	Symphony No. 5
1951	Persichetti	*Harmonium*
	Mennin	String Quartet No. 2
1952	Persichetti	Concerto for Piano, Four Hands
1953	Schuman	*The Mighty Casey*
	Persichetti	*Little Piano Book*; Symphony No. 5
	Mennin	Symphony No. 6
1954	Persichetti	Piano Quintet
1955	Schuman	*Credendum*
	Persichetti	*Hymns & Responses*, Vol. I; Piano Sonata No. 10
1956	Persichetti	Symphony No. 6
	Mennin	Sonata Concertante for Violin and Piano
1957	Persichetti	Serenade No. 10; Emily Dickinson Songs
	Mennin	Piano Concerto
1959	Schuman	Violin Concerto
	Persichetti	String Quartet No. 3
1960	Schuman	Symphony No. 7
1962—	Schuman	Symphony No. 8

It is my opinion that of these compositions, Schuman's Quartet No. 4, Mennin's Quartet No. 2, and Persichetti's Quartet No. 3 are among the greatest of all American string quartets; and that Schuman's Symphony No. 6, Mennin's Symphonies Nos. 5 and 6, and Persichetti's Symphonies Nos. 5 and 6 are among the greatest American symphonies.

However, because their careers were thus intertwined, the three composers have often been grouped together, along with others, as if interchangeable. For example, as recently as 2005, critic David Hurwitz lumped Vincent Persichetti together not just with Schuman and Mennin but also with Giannini, Creston, Barber (identified within this series as Neo-Romantics), Harris (a National Populist), and Piston (a Neo-Classicist) as all "[belonging] to a fairly well-defined school of American neo-classicists that sometimes display more of a corporate identity than they do individual character." He then singles out Persichetti, "whose use of traditional forms and pungent harmony now comes across as very much 'of its type.'"[12] It is partly to dispel just such misleading oversimplifications that this series—and the present volume, in particular—has come into existence. For while the music of Schuman, Persichetti, and Mennin may belong to the category of Modern Traditionalism, and while their professional lives may have been intertwined, their actual musical outputs and the temperaments that produced them were dramatically different.

Certainly the three composers did share a number of musical attitudes and values in common: All demonstrated a deep commitment to the symphony as a viable form for a uniquely twentieth-century statement. Based on the familiar principle of motivic development as a unifying procedure, a symphony by Schuman, Persichetti, or Mennin is usually a large, serious statement—unmistakably modern and unmistakably American in its vigor, assertiveness, and absence of either sentimentality or uncertainty. Although their periods of creativity were linked together, Schuman, as the oldest, clearly saw himself as an important influence on his colleagues. "Mennin and Persichetti were obviously very much influenced by me. Vincent used to joke with me, saying, 'Don't dare listen to my Third Symphony—it's note-for-note *your* Third.' I went down to hear it and it *was*, note-for-note. And that's not important—that's how music evolves."[13] Persichetti certainly had great admiration for Schuman, as will be clear in this study. However, Persichetti was a modest fellow and generous in his praise of others. On the other hand, when the subject of a video documentary comparing the work of the three composers was proposed to Schuman, he bristled and snapped, "I will not be placed on a par with my disciples."[14] Furthermore, anyone who compares the Third Symphonies of the two composers will be forced to acknowledge that a "note-for-note" identity is rather an overstatement, as discussed in the section on Persichetti's Third.

But despite such similarities, the music of the three composers reflects their profoundly distinct personalities. Schuman worked with much larger gestures and a more expansive perspective than Persichetti, and his outlook was more detached and balanced than the frenzied Mennin. Closest in aesthetic lineage to Roy Harris, Schuman favored broad planes of sound, while Persichetti focused on small details, revealed through transparent textures. By comparison, Mennin's textures are almost compulsively contrapuntal. But the music of all three is characterized, each in quite a different way, by a strong sense of rhythmic energy. Schuman's approach was somewhat hard-edged, with nervous, spasmodic bursts of rapidly syncopated figurations in brittle sonorities. Persichetti's was more effervescent and playful, with lean, actively syncopated figures dancing freely within a background pulsation. For Mennin, rhythm—along with tempo, density of texture, and degree of contrapuntal complexity—was a means of regulating emotional intensity, with irregular punctuations interjected into the constant flow, driving kinetic energy to the outer limits of human tolerance. It is this pervasive rhythmic vitality that is the chief area of overlap among the three. This characteristic was commonly acknowledged by critics and other commentators, whether they viewed it as a virtue or a weakness. Words like "muscular," "athletic," and "jazzy" appeared frequently. (Composer Douglas Moore described Schuman's works as "gymnasium music."[15]) But most felt that these composers created an unmistakably "American" impression, though their music rarely drew upon vernacular idioms. On the whole, Schuman lacked the comprehensive scope and limitless technical facility of Persichetti, nor did he display the intense concentration and expressive urgency of Mennin. But he was, nevertheless, a serious, highly individual symphonic thinker who, in his best works, pursued an approach derived from Harris into boldly original directions, while developing a musical personality of his own.

Schuman seemed to come naturally to the role of public statesman: a grand visionary with progressive ideas and unwavering confidence in his ability both to articulate them and to implement them. Drawn to "serious" music at the relatively advanced age of twenty, having begun as a writer of pop tunes, he never developed great competence on any musical instrument. However, he embraced large musical forms from the start. His substantial and varied musical output touched upon most standard forms and media, but its backbone comprised ten symphonies, of which the first two were withdrawn. Although he wrote some significant chamber music, he tended to favor large, grandiloquent statements.

Persichetti, on the other hand, was barely out of infancy when he began to play and write music, absorbing instruction like a sponge. Although he too was attracted to the symphonic genre, completing nine (of which his first two, like Schuman's, were withdrawn), the preponderance of his work favors epigrammatic forms and calls for relatively small performing forces. His musical output was large and encompassed a stylistic range—from diatonic simplicity to atonal complexity—broader than that of any composer of his generation. A prodigious pianist with the entire Western musical heritage at his fingertips, he was renowned for his lecture-recitals, in which he would illustrate the vast range of twentieth-century compositional techniques at the keyboard, offering wry, witty comments with a peculiar nervous, deadpan delivery.

Mennin's career and musical persona contrasted with those of both Schuman and Persichetti. He too began composing during early childhood, but never developed professional proficiency as a performer. His personality was dominated by an intense sense of focus and a remarkable seriousness of purpose. His musical output is relatively small, comprising nine symphonies (of which the first two, coincidentally, were withdrawn), and fewer than two dozen additional works. Most of these, however, are large in scale and severe in character, pursuing a highly individual mode of expression along a consistent course of increasing intensity and complexity. Deviations from this path are rare. Not naturally gregarious, Mennin turned to musical administration because he found it less disruptive to his own composing than was teaching. His public pronouncements paralleled his compositions in their uncompromising commitment to the highest standards in traditional artistic values and in their avoidance of the frivolous and the meretricious.

However, common to all three composers, in addition to a predilection for the symphonic genre, is that, as Modernists, they viewed their music as abstract. That is not to say that they were unconcerned with "expression" but, rather, that the expression resided in the music, not in the composers. Unlike the Neo-Romantics, for these Modern Traditionalists music was not an analogue to personal experience: They were more concerned with the abstract drama suggested by their treatment of the musical elements than with depicting a "human drama." They viewed their works as wholly autonomous and self-sufficient formal entities.

Yet while the three composers focused largely on abstract musical forms, each produced one theatrical or stage work that (a) embodied the essence of his musical language; (b) embodied a central theme within his personality; and (c) presented in allegorical form the manifestation of a concern of particular significance to him, often suggested, implied, or otherwise indicated in more abstract works. What is especially curious is that each of these works proved, at least initially, to be unsuccessful with both critics and the public, perhaps because each, to one extent or another, is fundamentally pessimistic. The works in question are William Schuman's opera *The Mighty Casey* (1953), Vincent Persichetti's opera *The Sibyl* (1976), and Peter Mennin's *cantata di virtute*, *The Pied Piper of Hamelin* (1969).

Baseball was a central theme throughout Schuman's life. Like so many boys, he entertained the dream of becoming a professional ballplayer himself, and continued to enjoy the game throughout his adulthood. But on a deeper level, the story of *Casey* involves the hubris of overconfidence and the defeat of a heroic ideal via public humiliation. Schuman's own biography was one of supreme confidence and heroic success. But one suspects that driving this ambitious quest for outstanding achievement was an inner fear of public failure. Though he sought to conceal its details, reframing them in a more positive light, Schuman's forced departure from the presidency of Lincoln Center was a form of public humiliation and a failure of excessive self-confidence. (The fact that this failure took place years after the composition of *Casey* does not invalidate its significance as a personal theme.)

Persichetti described *The Sibyl* as "an ecological opera," suggesting that its concern was the destruction of the natural environment. But the composer's own libretto, based on the story of Chicken Little, suggests a good deal more than that, using the children's tale as an allegory portraying the human tendency to become absorbed in mundane concerns while remaining "in denial" regarding profound dangers that threaten humanity's continued existence. To present this serious allegory via a children's tale, with animals as speaking characters and musical material drawn from pieces written for elementary instrumentalists, is highly characteristic of a composer who said, "People and animals are the same to me," and composed some of his most poignant music for children.

Mennin also drew upon a favorite children's story in producing his allegory. Notoriously secretive to an extent described by some who knew him as "paranoid," Mennin maintained a stern, unyielding demeanor and staunchly maintained positions advocating diligence and self-discipline while scorning shortcuts or easy answers, and his own music exemplified his commitment to such principles. His adaptation of the story of the Pied Piper into a brutal cantata of morality in which reneging on a promise is met by the most merciless and cruel retribution is fulfilled musically by the same sorts of materials and developmental procedures found in his abstract symphonic and chamber works, which seem to imply such ruthless dynamic forces on a cosmic level.

Each of these works is discussed in greater detail in the chapter devoted to its respective composer.

Also common to all three composers, beginning in the mid 1960s and continuing for the remainder of their respective lives, was an attempt to accommodate within their own individual styles some of the techniques and devices that were at the forefront of the "new music" scene in America. All three maintained a firm position against serialism on the grounds of its dogmatism as a "system" of composition. Nevertheless, each began to devise thematic material that included all twelve tones, and, while they did not treat these musical ideas according to the precepts of serialism, the use of such material led to a "free chromaticism" that often strained the bounds of tonality. While their works may have been vaguely "tonal" in theory and may have even ended with tonal cadences, the general impact they made upon initial exposure was of an atonality indistinguishable to many listeners from the music of the staunch serialists. Other avant-garde devices and techniques that appeared in their works included the obscuring of audible metric pulse, widely disjunct melodic lines, fragmentary gestures, "sound masses" and the use of texture as a primary thematic element, along with other techniques found in the music of such Eastern European contemporaries as Penderecki, Lutosławski, and Ligeti. However, rather than winning praise for embracing such innovations, their efforts tended to be regarded by the cognoscenti as quintessentially "academic," as belated attempts by representatives of "the Establishment" to "jump on the bandwagon," while more conservative listeners failed to distinguish their work from that of the avant-garde and viewed such efforts as "selling out." As a result, from the 1970s on, all three composers found their work increasingly marginalized, to a greater or lesser extent, and supported by a dwindling number of advocates. Furthermore, since that time their reputations have remained essentially dormant, aside from minor ripples of incidental attention, while other, more conservative figures, such as the Neo-Romantics, have enjoyed more positive reappraisals.

The year 2010 was the hundredth anniversary of William Schuman's birth. The previous year, *American Muse: The Life and Times of William Schuman* was published by Amadeus Press. This, the first comprehensive biography of the composer, was written by Joseph Polisi, Peter Mennin's successor as president of the Juilliard School. Partly to commemorate this anniversary, Juilliard presented a weeklong festival, organized by Joel Sachs, entitled *Focus! 2010: Music at the Center—Composing an American Mainstream* in January 2010. Daily concerts presented the music of the leading Modern Traditionalists of the second third of the twentieth century. Every concert presented a work of Schuman's, while one piece each by Persichetti and Mennin was included. The *New York Times* heralded the festival with an article by Anthony Tommasini entitled "Championing the Music of Neglected Traditionalists."[16] "The battles within contemporary music during the middle decades of the 20th century are long forgotten," he writes, and then adds, "But residues of that contentious time linger." He notes that Sachs suggests that "the centrists from the mid-20th century, composers like William Schuman [et al.], are unjustly overlooked today. [In this festival] Mr. Sachs is championing the forgotten traditionalists, as he called them in a program note for the opening concert. . . . But to describe these American composers as traditionalists suggests that they played it safe, in stylistic lock step." The remainder of his article goes on to illustrate the inaccuracy of this assumption.

The function of this book is to illustrate the inaccuracy of that assumption in greater detail, and, especially, to help guide general listeners into an appreciation of Schuman, Persichetti, and Mennin, who (with the addition of Samuel Barber) produced what is arguably the finest, most durable American music of the 1940s and 1950s. However, because their music tended to avoid extramusical associations—and, as Modernists, much of it embraced a high level of harmonic dissonance while stretching the bounds of tonality—general listeners may well find some of their works to be impenetrable when encountered at random. As most listeners prefer a familiar musical language, the body of work created by these composers remains largely misunderstood today, if known at all. It is hoped that a discussion of each composer through an overview that outlines his work according to style-periods and other relevant points of distinction—and that identifies those compositions that are strongest, those that are weakest, those that are most representative of each individual, as well as those that might serve as the most optimal points of entry into their creative worlds—will entice new listeners and help them to grasp and appreciate each composer's unique artistic personality.

As was the case in the preceding volume, much of the information included in this study has never been presented in print before. My own conceptualizations of this music have been facilitated and enriched in some cases by direct personal contact with the composers themselves and/or with others close to them, as well as by access to unpublished manuscripts and recordings. This contact was sought as an outgrowth of my own interest in their music and of my frustration with the lack of available recordings and published information concerning their lives and work. My understanding of their music was enhanced by intermittent personal contact with William Schuman in 1980–1982, intermittent personal contact with Vincent Persichetti from 1968 until his death in 1987, one interview with Peter Mennin in 1982, and frequent personal contact with Georganne Mennin since 1983.

ORGANIZATION AND USE OF THIS BOOK

Each composer featured in this study is discussed through a biographical overview, followed by a comprehensive survey of his compositional output. Their works are reviewed with an eye toward identifying the distinctive stylistic features of the three composers, the evolution of their creative "voices" over the course of their careers, their most important and most representative works, and their compositional strengths and weaknesses. The reactions of critics and commentators are also included, drawn from reviews of early performances and recordings as well as from commentaries written after the passage of time has provided an opportunity for reflection. It is hoped that these critical comments will illuminate the way the cultural climate responded to this music at various points during the composers' careers, as well as the shifts that have taken place in conceptualizing their contributions during the years following their deaths.

An effort has been made to structure the book in such a way as to be useful to students, scholars, and performing musicians, as well as to serious music lovers and collectors of recordings, and in different ways at different times. It is not expected that everyone will read and absorb the surveys of each composer's entire output from beginning to end. The biographical portions of each chapter present narrative overviews of each composer's career and attempt to capture something of his character, personality, and the context in which he lived. The sections addressing the composers' outputs begin with general discussions of their styles and of the natural subdivisions of their work into chronological periods or performance media, as applicable. The comprehensiveness of each chapter has been influenced not only by the varying availability of information but also by my own judgment regarding the relative importance of the totality of each composer's contribution. A list of each composer's most representative and fully realized works is provided before the works are discussed in greater detail.

The question of how much analytical detail is appropriate for a book of this nature is difficult to answer. An effort has been made to provide descriptions that might guide and enhance listening and understanding, without indulgence in excessive detail. Nevertheless, some readers may find the descriptions of individual compositions tedious and irrelevant—especially if they are not familiar with the work in question—while others may well find them superficial and insufficiently detailed. A decision was made to avoid musical notation and minimize the use of specialized terminology, which will be a relief to some readers but perhaps frustrating to others.

NOTES

1. Pierre Boulez, *Notes of an Apprenticeship* (New York: Knopf, 1968), 148.

2. Nicholas Tawa, *The Great American Symphony: Music, the Depression, and War* (Bloomington: Indiana University Press, 2009), 202.

3. Anthony Tommasini, "Midcentury Serialists: The Bullies or the Besieged," *New York Times*, 9 July 2000.

4. Milton Babbitt, "Who Cares if You Listen?" *High Fidelity* (February 1958).

5. Charles Wuorinen, *Simple Composition* (New York: Longman, 1979), 3.

6. Walter Simmons, "Contemporary Music: A Weekend of Reflections," *Fanfare* (May/June 1981): 22–23.

7. Joseph N. Straus, "The Myth of Serial 'Tyranny' in the 1950s and 1960s," *Musical Quarterly* (Autumn 1999): 301–43.

8. Virgil Thomson, *American Music since 1910* (New York: Holt, Rinehart, and Winston, 1970), 18–19.

9. Aaron Copland and Vivian Perlis, *Copland: 1900 through 1942* (New York: St. Martin's/Marek, 1984), 104.

10. Neil Butterworth, *The American Symphony* (Brookfield, Vt.: Ashgate, 1998), 82.

11. Butterworth, *The American Symphony*, 84.

12. David Hurwitz, Review, *Classics Today*, 2005, http://www.classicstoday.com/review.asp?ReviewNum=9456 (accessed 24 January 2010).

13. William Schuman, interviewed by Jack Stamp, 5 March 1990 (compact disc Klavier K11155, 2005).

14. Conversation with Walter Simmons (24 February 1982).

15. Douglas Moore, quoted in Joseph W. Polisi, *American Muse: The Life and Times of William Schuman* (New York: Amadeus Press, 2008), 144.

16. Anthony Tommasini, "Championing the Music of Neglected Traditionalists," *New York Times* (25 January 2010).

SELECTED BIBLIOGRAPHY

Babbitt, Milton. "Who Cares If You Listen?" *High Fidelity* (February 1958): 38–40, 126–27.

Butterworth, Neil. *The American Symphony*. Brookfield, Vt.: Ashgate, 1998.

Olmstead, Andrea. *Juilliard: A History*. Urbana: University of Illinois Press, 1999.

Simmons, Walter. "Contemporary Music: A Weekend of Reflections." *Fanfare* (May–June 1981): 22–23.

Simmons, Walter. *Voices in the Wilderness: Six American Neo-Romantic Composers*. Lanham, Md.: Scarecrow Press, 2004.

Tawa, Nicholas. *American Composers and Their Public*. Metuchen, N.J.: Scarecrow Press, 1995.

———. *A Most Wondrous Babble*. Westport, Conn.: Greenwood Press, 1987.

———. *The Great American Symphony*. Bloomington: Indiana University Press, 2009.

Tommasini, Anthony. "Midcentury Serialists: The Bullies or the Besieged." *New York Times* (9 July 2000).

William Schuman

During the 1960s, William Schuman was considered "probably the most powerful figure in the world of art music" and "the most important musical administrator of the 20th century," according to the *New York Times.*[1] He was also one of America's most highly regarded composers throughout the middle third of the century. The story of his rapid ascent to a position of such eminence was legendary during his lifetime. He was an "all-American boy," born in New York City, who spent his childhood consumed with baseball. He later formed a dance band, for which he wrote a host of popular songs, many of them with lyrics by his friend Frank Loesser. Classical music meant nothing to him until, at the age of twenty, he was dragged reluctantly by his sister to hear Toscanini conduct the New York Philharmonic. The sound and appearance of the symphony orchestra was a revelation to him: The next day he dropped out of business school and decided then and there to become a composer. Amazingly, nine years later his Symphony No. 2 was performed by Koussevitzky and the Boston Symphony. At the age of thirty-five, he became president of the famed Juilliard School, revamping the entire faculty and curriculum; seventeen years later he became president of the brand-new Lincoln Center for the Performing Arts, shaping it into a world-famous institution that influenced all performing arts centers to follow.

However, by the 1960s Schuman's reputation as an administrator had overshadowed his importance as a composer. To the younger generation this erstwhile exponent of musical Modernism had become the very embodiment of the musical Establishment. And although his music continued to increase in complexity, his refusal to embrace the serial approach to composition set him apart from the vanguard. "It was a different environment," noted Joseph

Polisi, Schuman's biographer. "Although it didn't make any sense I think it was perceived in the later '50s, the '60s, and the '70s, that there was an intellectual rigor to serialism [that was missing from] tonal music."[2] "If you didn't write using that technique, you were perceived as old-fashioned or intellectually barren or questionable in terms of your motives."[3] Schuman's stature as a composer has never really recovered from that period of eclipse. While he never became a proponent of serialism, much of his music was quite dissonant, thereby alienating both the academic avant-garde and also more conservative general listeners. Although he completed ten symphonies, two operas, and numerous choral, orchestral, and chamber works, most of which had been performed and recorded by the world's leading soloists, conductors, and ensembles, by the time he died in 1992, little of that music was performed with any regularity. And during the years since then, his reputation as a composer has rested chiefly on three pieces, two of them based on material by other composers.

BIOGRAPHY

William Schuman was born in New York City on 4 August 1910 into a German-Jewish family that had immigrated to the United States before the Civil War. His father, Samuel, had developed a modestly successful printing business, allowing the family to maintain a comfortable standard of living, even during the Great Depression. Staunchly patriotic, he named his son William Howard Schuman after William Howard Taft, who was the nation's president at the time of the boy's birth.[4] Schuman later described his father as "a combination of Walt Whitman and the Chamber of Commerce."[5] Like many German Jews of his generation, Samuel was a firm believer in assimilation and did not foster a strong sense of ethnic identity in his family. (William was to follow his father's precedent in this regard, often omitting this aspect of his heritage from autobiographical notes. Even K. Gary Adams's *William Schuman: A Bio-Bibliography* [1998] makes no mention of his Jewish background. Interestingly, in his later years, Schuman would poke fun at Jews who changed their names in order to hide their origins.[6]) Billy's mother, Rachel, maintained a stronger sense of her Jewish heritage but deferred to her husband's assimilationist views in managing the household. Billy was the second of three children, preceded by a sister, Audrey, and followed by a brother, Robert. (Robert was developmentally disabled and was institutionalized from childhood until his death in 1957. Schuman rarely visited him and did not publicly acknowledge his existence until the 1980s.[7])

Young Billy attended public elementary schools in Manhattan. Like many Jewish boys of his generation, he took music lessons—first the piano, then the violin—but displayed no serious interest. Both his mother and his sister played the piano, so informal musicales occurred frequently when the family was together. As he approached adolescence, Billy was identified as intellectually gifted and sent to the Speyer Experimental Junior High School for Boys. During those years his greatest love was baseball. ("It was not a matter of my being interested in baseball as a youth. It *was* my youth."[8]) Entrepreneurial at an early age, he established a child-care "business" on his own. He also began to develop an interest in theater: He wrote a play, arranged for a school production, and soon envisioned a career as a theatrical producer. He also developed a fondness for poetry, but he kept this passion, unseemly for an adolescent boy, largely to himself. His Speyer school yearbook indicates that he was voted "best orator" of his class.[9]

When he was twelve, Billy began attending Camp Cobbossee, a summer camp in Maine that provided him with valuable opportunities to pursue his interests and develop his talents. During the summer of 1925 he and some of his schoolmates received a modest grant from the French government to visit Paris for several weeks. Later that year he entered George Washington High School in Manhattan, where he managed to excel without expending much effort. But most of the summers of his teenage years were spent at camp, where he indulged his enthusiasm for baseball and theater and, in 1926, composed his first piece: *Fate*—a tango.

It was at Camp Cobbossee that Billy met Eddie Marks, son of the music publisher Edward B. Marks. Eddie became one of his closest friends, and the two collaborated on a musical comedy, which they presented at camp. In 1926, Billy formed a jazz band, "Billy Schuman and His Alamo Society Orchestra." Although barely literate musically, Billy wrote the music and Eddie the lyrics for more than a hundred popular songs. Billy sang, played fiddle and banjo, and even managed to get around on the clarinet, saxophone, double bass, and piano. He served as the band's business manager as well, and they were fairly successful, playing for weddings, bar mitzvahs, proms, and the like. Billy had also become acquainted with Frank Loesser when both were students at the Speyer School. He enlisted Loesser as a lyricist as well, and the two wrote some forty songs, well into their twenties. (Loesser went on to write *Guys and Dolls*, *The Most Happy Fella*, and other Broadway successes.)

During his teens Billy became aware of a physical difficulty that seemed to prevent him from developing any real proficiency on an instrument. This condition was later diagnosed as progressive muscular atrophy, a deteriorating neurological condition somewhat related to Lou Gehrig's disease. At one point a normal life expectancy was not anticipated, but, fortunately, his case was very slow in progressing.[10]

In 1928 Bill graduated from George Washington High School and, for want of a better idea, entered the NYU School of Commerce. He had a half-hearted notion of building a career in advertising but was generally unmotivated and did rather poorly.[11] He maintained an active social life, pursuing what has been characterized as a "Fitzgerald-like 'roaring twenties' lifestyle."[12]

Everything changed on 4 April 1930, when his sister found herself with an extra ticket to hear Toscanini conduct the New York Philharmonic. She invited her younger brother to accompany her, and he accepted rather reluctantly. The program included Schumann's "Rhenish" Symphony and "Siegfried's Funeral Music" from Wagner's *Götterdämmerung*. It proved to be a "conversion experience" that transformed his life forever. As he later recounted, what impressed him was not so much the music itself but the enormous range of expression of which the symphony orchestra was capable, as well as the disciplined synchrony of the string players all bowing together. The next day, exhibiting the impulsiveness that would become a lifelong pattern, he quit his advertising job and dropped out of school (with the somewhat skeptical approval of his father). Supposedly on the same day, as he was walking pensively uptown, he encountered the Malkin Conservatory, a small local music school. He walked in and told the receptionist that he wanted to become a composer and asked what he should do. She suggested that he begin by registering for a course in harmony with the Russian-born and trained Max Persin. Interestingly, Persin's approach focused on the study of scores rather than on completing exercises, anticipating Schuman's subsequent development of the "Literature and Materials" concept. Persin also encouraged Schuman's creative efforts, while the student attempted to make up for lost time, devouring the symphonic repertoire voraciously and attending live performances as often as possible.

In 1931 Schuman met Frances Prince, a woman three years younger than he, and the two began dating seriously. Though sharing his German-Jewish background, she came from a somewhat more cultured family and was extremely intelligent, graduating from Barnard College at age nineteen.[13]

The following year Schuman added counterpoint to his curriculum, which he studied with Charles Haubiel (1892–1978), a more rigid and formal pedagogue. In 1932 and 1933 he took further theory courses as a nonmatriculating student at the summer program of the Institute for Musical Art (later absorbed by the Juilliard School) with Bernard Wagenaar (1894–1971) and Adolf Schmid (1868–1958). At this point he began to take a serious interest in "classical" composition, although he continued to write and promote popular tunes with his friend Frank Loesser.

In 1933 Schuman enrolled at Columbia University's Teachers College. There he was exposed to the pedagogical ideas of John Dewey, who opposed authoritarian dogma and rote learning, advocating guided experience as a better teaching method. It was at Teachers College that he began to develop his own strong convictions about music education. Meanwhile he began to feel constrained by the limitations of Tin Pan Alley and its overriding commercial concerns. He began to lose interest in popular music and soon gave it up altogether. It was about this time that Schuman heard a performance of Roy Harris's *Symphony 1933*, which proved to be another transformative experience. He heard in this work a spirit that spoke personally to him and suggested a direction that he might follow.

In 1935 Schuman graduated from Teachers College with a BS in music education. That summer he enrolled at the Salzburg Mozarteum, where he studied conducting with Bernhard Paumgartner, an experience that left him convinced that his talent did not extend to that activity.[14] However, while he was in Salzburg he worked intensively on a symphony of his own, which he completed later that year. Back home, in addition to composing, he became consumed with developing his own ideas for a more "progressive" approach to music education and surveyed college catalogs in search of schools that might be receptive to such an approach.

Schuman's quest led him to Sarah Lawrence College, which was then just seven years old. He requested an interview with the president and attempted to persuade her to invest in his idealistic notions of a more individualized approach to music pedagogy, rather than the standardized curricula that generally prevailed. Although she and her administration were initially resistant to the untested assertions of this brash twenty-five-year-old, they were eventually won over by his enthusiasm, self-confidence, and persistence. When the Rockefeller Foundation announced that it was funding a new program for colleges called "Exploring the Arts," Schuman was invited to initiate it at Sarah Lawrence that September (1935).

Now established in a responsible position, Schuman and his fiancée Frances, or "Frankie" as she was called, decided to get married. The event took place in March 1936 in a traditional Jewish ceremony. The couple bought a house in Larchmont, New York, not far from Sarah Lawrence. Their son Anthony was born there in 1943. Frankie would prove to be an ideal mate for Bill. She was sympathetic and supportive of his ambitions as a composer; she was also very protective and did her best to shelter him from the emotional stresses and challenges of family life.[15]

Schuman's tenure at Sarah Lawrence provided him with a "laboratory" in which to test, elaborate, and refine his ideas on arts pedagogy. He felt that it was possible to devise a curriculum for each individual student, tailored to that student's needs and interests, rather than starting with a fixed syllabus to be imposed on every student. In addition the school provided him with the opportunity to develop his skills as a public speaker. Given the responsibility of conducting the school's chorus, he enjoyed this role and fulfilled it more successfully than his experience at Salzburg might have suggested. In addition to initiating a program to commission new works, he raised the group's performance level and arranged for tours. (These efforts culminated in 1943 in a performance of Debussy's *La Damoiselle Élue* at Carnegie Hall.)

In 1936 Schuman submitted his Symphony No. 1 for the Bearns Prize, a significant award administered through Columbia University. The work did not win and was subjected to harsh criticism by Columbia's department chairman, the notoriously reactionary Daniel Gregory Mason.

Schuman learned that Roy Harris would be teaching in Juilliard's summer program that year. At the time, Harris was, along with Aaron Copland, America's most prominent composer. Having been so deeply impressed by Harris's *Symphony 1933*, the young composer decided to enroll in three courses with him. This gave Schuman the opportunity to show his symphony to Harris, who, like Mason, found much to criticize in the work but nevertheless took an encouraging posture toward his new student. Harris was living and teaching in New Jersey at the time, so after the summer classes, Schuman continued studying with him privately for the next two years. Schuman was greatly influenced by Harris's music, as well as by his ideas. Harris introduced his talented student to the church modes, to his own adaptation of *organum* (a form of interval parallelism developed during the Middle Ages), and most of all, to his notion of "autogenesis," an open-ended approach to developmental form, in contrast to the more symmetrical classical forms. Autogenesis proved to be a strong influence on many younger composers at the time. For his part, Harris's endorsement of Schuman's creative gifts in influential circles helped to draw attention to his student's work, although as Schuman's reputation grew, Harris's advocacy diminished. Despite the fact that Harris's own reputation had dropped precipitously by 1950, Schuman continued to defend his contribution for the rest of his life, although he realized that his mentor's excessive egotism in its various manifestations had prevented him from fulfilling his creative potential.[16] An alternative explanation for Harris's eclipse is Schuman's mastery of many of Harris's compositional principles and devices: His craftsmanship soon outdistanced that of his teacher to such an extent that Harris's work paled by comparison.

In October 1936, Schuman's Symphony No. 1 and his String Quartet No. 1 were performed in New York City at the Composer's Forum Laboratory, one of a number of arts projects sponsored by the Works Progress Administration (WPA) during the Depression. These concerts featured the music of a young composer, who would then respond to questions and comments from the audience. The symphony was performed by the Gotham Symphony Orchestra, conducted by Jules Werner. The response to Schuman's music was quite negative, and he subsequently withdrew both works. However, he enjoyed the experience of responding to questions from the audience and began to see that he had a particular gift in this area as well.

Undaunted by the failure of his initial efforts, Schuman committed himself to a rigorous daily regimen of composition and immediately began work on another symphony, which he completed in 1937. It was in this year that he was introduced to Aaron Copland, as well as the year in which he earned a master's degree from Columbia Teachers College, with a thesis that expounded the approach to arts pedagogy that he had been developing.[17] This degree completed Schuman's formal higher education.

Gaining the attention of Aaron Copland proved to be a most auspicious turning point in Schuman's career. Reviewing a concert that included one of his pieces, Copland, then thirty-eight years old and one of America's most influential composers, wrote in the highly regarded journal *Modern Music*, "Schuman is, so far as I am concerned, the musical find of the year. There is nothing puny or miniature about this young man's talent. If he fails he will fail on a grand scale. . . . [I]t seems to me that Schuman is a composer who is going places."[18] Copland was on the panel of judges, along with Wallingford Riegger, Roger Sessions, and Bernard Wagenaar, of a composition contest sponsored by the Musicians' Committee to Aid Spanish Democracy. Schuman entered his Second Symphony into the competition, and it won. In June of that year the work was performed by the WPA Greenwich Village Orchestra, and soon after was broadcast over CBS radio in a performance by the station's resident orchestra, conducted by Howard Barlow. Again the music failed to make a positive impression. One listener wrote to the composer, "Your symphony made one lose faith in the power of the aspirin tablet."[19] Notwithstanding its poor reception, Copland introduced Schuman's Second to Serge Koussevitzky in 1938, and the conductor decided to perform the work with the Boston Symphony Orchestra in February of the following year. Again both the audience and critics responded unfavorably to the work. Nevertheless, Koussevitzky said to the disappointed composer, "You must hear a great orchestra and conductor play your music, and I want you to write something more for me, and everything you write I will play."[20] (Years later, Schuman said about his unconventional compositional maturation, "I really learned how to be a composer by composing symphonies. I didn't fool around. I wanted to run before I could creep."[21]). Despite the many negative reactions to the Second Symphony, two who attended the Boston performance defended the work: the influential Modernist critic Paul Rosenfeld and a brash young twenty-year-old, Leonard Bernstein. Nevertheless, Schuman eventually withdrew the Second Symphony, as he had the First.

Encouraged by Koussevitzky's statement of support, Schuman immediately began another orchestral piece, which he planned to offer to Koussevitzky for performance at an American Music Festival in Boston. Koussevitzky agreed to perform the work, entitled *American Festival Overture*, with the Boston Symphony in October 1939. This proved to be Schuman's biggest audience success thus far in his career. However, Koussevitzky's comment was, "Fine! Now you must begin to hate Roy Harris."[22]

Also in 1939 Schuman was awarded a Guggenheim Fellowship, which enabled him to take a leave of absence from Sarah Lawrence and concentrate on composition. The fellowship was renewed for a second year. During this period Schuman composed his String Quartet No. 3, which had been requested by the League of Composers—his first commission. He also completed a Third Symphony, which he planned to offer to Koussevitzky. However, he began to realize that he wasn't content to be a full-time composer. He had an appetite for other challenges: to develop and promote his pedagogical ideas and, in general, to take an active role in American musical life as a spokesman and advocate.

During the late 1930s and early 1940s, like so many other artists and intellectuals, including Aaron Copland, Schuman was attracted to somewhat left-wing political sentiments—especially the idealization of "the common man." But while this sentiment led other artists to construct nostalgic visions of a mythical America of the past, Schuman's populism took a different form. "He chose to celebrate the metropolis over the heartland, the present day over yesteryear. And his decisions resulted in critical and popular acclaim that, at the very least, remind us that in the late 1930s and early 1940s, simplicity and nostalgia were but one avenue open to the American composer who sought and found an audience." Schuman's populism extended to a belief in musical participation and appreciation among nonprofessionals, and his effort to appeal to "the masses" even won praise in *The Daily Worker*.[23] However, Schuman was adamant that accessibility should never be sought at the expense of quality. And while leftist organizations may have viewed him as a sympathizer, Schuman was concerned more with creating an exciting and broadly appealing repertoire of fine music that would inspire the participation of student musicians and amateurs than with harnessing music to a political agenda. As left-wing causes became a focus of national controversy during the "red scare" just a few years later, Schuman was careful not to associate himself with any socialist or communist groups. Employing the strategy of "going right to the top" that he had initiated in his pursuit of the Sarah Lawrence position—a strategy he was to follow throughout his life—he wrote to Secretary of the Interior Harold Ickes to request support for a plan to encourage "our best composers and writers who would agree to turn out material which would deal with the vital issues in the life of people living in a democracy and include as well a real educative message as to the genuine threats to the democratic way."[24] Throughout his career Schuman maintained his commitment to compose pieces that could be played by students and/or laymen, and used his gift for public speaking to help audiences understand, follow, and appreciate some of the more challenging approaches found in contemporary music.[25]

The next quantum leap in Schuman's career took place in October 1941, when Koussevitzky led the Boston Symphony in the premiere of his Symphony No. 3. Finally he had successfully reached both audience and critics with a major work. The tremendous positive impact made by this symphony catapulted his reputation to a new plateau (and it remains one of his most popular compositions). The Third Symphony won the first New York Music Critics' Circle Award as "the best orchestral work of 1941." The president of the prominent music publisher G. Schirmer was at the time Carl Engel, whom Schuman had met in 1938; Engel now offered the young composer a monthly stipend in exchange for the first option to publish each of his new works. Engel became an outspoken supporter and advocate for the remaining years of his life.

When the United States entered the Second World War, Schuman attempted to join the Army. However, his neurological condition ruled out his active participation—a considerable disappointment. In compensation, he tried to involve himself through musical organizations, such as the Sarah Lawrence chorus, in aiding the war effort, but he was unable to bring these efforts to fruition. However, he did write several compositions on behalf of the struggle against fascism: *A Free Song* (1942), *Prayer in Time of War* (1943), as well as the score to a film called *Steeltown* (1944), which had been commissioned by the Office of War Information.

During the war years Schuman's reputation as a composer continued to grow, as one success followed another, each premiere followed by performances by other major conductors, orchestras, and ensembles. He completed a Fourth Symphony, commissioned by the Cleveland Orchestra, before the Third was even performed. Its premiere, under the direction of Artur Rodzinski, took place just three months after the premiere of the Third. In January 1943, an all-Schuman concert at New York's Town Hall introduced his Piano Concerto, in a performance by Rosalyn Tureck. Several choral works were presented at the same concert in performances by the Collegiate Chorale conducted by Robert Shaw—his debut appearance. Perhaps Schuman's most auspicious success in 1943 was winning the first Pulitzer Prize ever given for a piece of music: in this case, *A Free Song*, a patriotic work with a text taken from Walt Whitman, for chorus and orchestra, which Koussevitzky had premiered earlier that year. All this success began to liberate Schuman from the constraints of modesty, false or otherwise, and he began to speak his mind freely. By this time his music had been heard not just in the United States but in other countries as well. While much of the response to it was favorable, there were also strongly negative reactions.[26] Schuman had no compunction about confronting well-known conductors or critics who challenged his creative judgment, employing his spontaneous verbal facility in public displays of defiance, arrogance, or disrespect. At one point, the far more circumspect Copland, witnessing such an incident, cautioned Frankie, "You must do something. Bill simply can't get up and speak that way."[27]

In 1944 Schuman was approached by the prominent choreographer Antony Tudor, who solicited the composer's interest in writing a work for the dance. Tudor was a notoriously demanding collaborator, very precise in his requirements and ruthlessly critical and manipulative in his efforts to elicit what he viewed as essential to his work. Despite Schuman's own tendency toward highhandedness, he tolerated Tudor's specific demands and made every effort to accommodate them, which indicates the importance he placed on achieving a successful collaboration with someone of the choreographer's stature. The result was called *Undertow*. Not only was the work a critical success, but it also engendered a new level of expressive and psychological depth from the composer and led to a number of subsequent choreographic works from his pen. He later recalled the Tudor episode as "one of the most productive and satisfying artistic experiences of my career."[28]

By 1945 Schuman was becoming somewhat restless and bored with the repetitive routines of his teaching position. The previous year, Carl Engel, Schuman's staunch supporter at G. Schirmer, had died suddenly. At the recommendation of Koussevitzky, Schirmer offered Schuman the position of director of publications. So he decided to resign from the Sarah Lawrence faculty, effective June of that year, and accepted the offer from the publisher, signing a three-year contract. However, he hated the job almost immediately, finding Gustav Schirmer himself to be unscrupulous in his business dealings and, in general, "a vulgar and horrible man."[29] He managed to break his contract and resigned after two months. Nevertheless, relishing the opportunity to decide which American composers Schirmer would represent, he agreed to remain as "publications advisor" until 1951.

The month after his resignation from Sarah Lawrence went into effect, Schuman began to receive exploratory contacts from the board of directors of the Juilliard School, who were undertaking a search for a new president. His initial reaction was to decline emphatically, stating that he had little regard for the way the arts were being taught in America at that time. He wouldn't even consider such a position unless he was assured of complete authority to reshape the institution according to his own ideas and principles.[30] Invited to attend a meeting and present to the search committee some of his views on arts education and the role of an arts institution in society, he accepted with the understanding that he was not a candidate for the position. Given this assurance, he wasted no time in expressing to the search committee his belief that Juilliard's approach to theory and composition was "incompetent and without any relationship whatsoever to the study of music."[31] Schuman's coyness bore fruit when, to his surprise, the board offered him the position of president after all. Despite all his demurrals, the thirty-five-year-old firebrand accepted, with the warning, "There will be a revolution!"[32]

Schuman assumed his new position in October 1945 and soon moved his family into a house in New Rochelle, large enough for the entertaining that would be expected of him in his new role. During the next few months, he undertook an extensive restructuring of the entire institution, according to the principles he had been developing. Despite considerable opposition, he announced a plan to merge the Institute of Musical Art and the Juilliard Graduate School into a single entity. At the suggestion of violinist Robert Mann, he decided to form a resident string quartet; the Juilliard String Quartet soon developed international renown. He devised plans to increase the attention paid by the school to contemporary music of all styles. And perhaps most notably, he hired twenty-eight new faculty and staff, including Norman Lloyd (a former colleague from Sarah Lawrence) as director of education and Mark Schubart (a close friend who had worked at the *New York Times*) as director of public activities and, later, as dean. These were men who he knew were in sympathy with his ideas and would help him to implement them. Among the others he enlisted immediately were composer William Bergsma, conductor Robert Shaw, cellist Leonard Rose, and violist Milton Katims.

In May 1947, Schuman unveiled what was perhaps his most significant innovation at Juilliard: The Literature and Materials of Music, a revolutionary curriculum that sought to integrate music history and the various components of music theory (ear-training, harmony, counterpoint, formal analysis) into a single course of study. The essential idea behind the "L&M" approach (as it came to be known) was that theoretical principles ought to be derived from the study of great works of the repertoire—not through exercises created by theorists that abstract and isolate specific usages solely for the purpose of analysis and repetitive drills. The approach advocated a curriculum tailored to each student's individual interests and abilities; also, contemporary music was to be understood within the context of the other arts and within contemporary society in general. Schuman initially developed this concept together with

Norman Lloyd but eventually hired a number of talented individuals—mostly composers—to implement it, including Richard Franko Goldman, Vincent Persichetti, Peter Mennin, Vittorio Giannini, and Robert Ward. After its first semester, an anonymous poll of the student body found 80 percent in favor of the new curriculum.[33] The L&M approach represented a dramatic innovation in music pedagogy, generating a great deal of attention and controversy within the field of music education, as conservatories and music departments throughout the country—and even in Europe—began to emulate or adapt it for their own use. In view of all the attention and controversy, Schuman decided that a book should be written that would outline the L&M program, as well as its underlying principles. He assigned this task to Richard Franko Goldman. *The Juilliard Report on Teaching the Literature and Materials of Music* was published by W. W. Norton in 1953. But despite the initial enthusiasm that greeted the L&M approach, with the passage of time Schuman's idealism proved insufficiently responsive to the needs of the students as *they* perceived them, while demanding so much preparation and dedication from the faculty that by the late 1950s enthusiasm for the program began to wane among both quarters, and aspects of it were eventually diluted.

During the summer of 1946 Schuman had received an invitation to compose the music for another choreographic work—this time from Martha Graham, who had in mind a piece based on the Oedipus myth. He did not meet the famed choreographer until the following year, when he encountered her backstage after a performance they both happened to attend. He later recalled that when she looked at him and said, "Mr. Schuman, your music *moves* me," the penetrating intensity of her gaze made him want to "run from the hall and scream, 'Mama!'"[34] Their collaboration resulted in a work called *Night Journey*. Although he missed the emotional specificity that guided him while working with Tudor, Graham provided him with a detailed scenario, which he found helpful in a different way. The premiere of *Night Journey* took place at Harvard in May 1947. Schuman hoped for another opportunity to work with Graham, and this materialized in 1949, when she invited him to compose the music for a solo choreographic work. Graham later described this project, based on the Old Testament story of Judith, as "the most difficult assignment I have ever set myself,"[35] while Schuman's score proved to be one of his finest musical achievements.

During the early 1950s, Schuman consummated his lifelong devotion to baseball with an expansion of the once-popular mock-tragic-heroic poem *Casey at the Bat* by Ernest L. Thayer (1863–1949) into an opera. He enlisted advertising executive Jeremy Gury to write the libretto, and the result was entitled *The Mighty Casey*. Schuman was unable to generate much enthusiasm for the work and had to be content with a premiere at the Hartt School of Music in Hartford, Connecticut, in 1953. Although it was not well received, and there have been few subsequent productions, the composer always maintained his conviction that the work had merit but had yet to find its audience.

Meanwhile, Schuman was continuing to make far-reaching changes at Juilliard. In 1951 he formed a Dance Division, hiring Martha Graham, Antony Tudor, José Limon, and Agnes de Mille, all of whom would work under Martha Hill's direction. Among the other important innovations during Schuman's tenure at Juilliard were a revival of the Opera Theater, and the institution of a curriculum that would lead to a bachelor of science degree. Reactions to Schuman's administrative approach were mixed. Many were impressed by his combination of visionary idealism, decisiveness, and gift for practical implementation, while others expressed concern about a tendency toward impetuousness, such as arriving at conclusions prematurely and taking action without sufficient reflection. But all recognized his consistent commitment to the principle that high artistic standards must not be compromised by financial considerations.

During the 1950s Schuman was enlisted to contribute to America's Cold War propaganda when the State Department selected him to represent American music at a UNESCO-sponsored conference of creative artists in Venice in 1952. Schuman emphasized the fundamental importance of artistic freedom, warning of the vulnerability of the arts to exploitation on behalf of political issues. In 1955 the U.S. National Commission for UNESCO requested a musical work from Schuman—the first time an orchestral work was ever commissioned by an agency of the U.S. government. The result was *Credendum: Article of Faith*, which proved to be one of his most expressive and affecting compositions. Naturally inclined to the role of "advocate," Schuman espoused the importance of governmental support of artistic expression as a matter of national policy and sought ways to use Juilliard as a means of promoting democracy, and, more specifically, as a vehicle for seeking and highlighting commonalities among different cultures. This effort came to its richest fruition in 1958, when Juilliard alumnus Van Cliburn won the gold medal at the first International Tchaikovsky Competition in Moscow (six months after the United States had been embarrassed by the Soviet Union's launch of Sputnik, the first man-made space satellite). Cliburn became a national celebrity virtually overnight, and his connection to Juilliard was publicized.

During those years of general affluence, the Schumans maintained an upper-middle-class lifestyle typical for southern Westchester County, the suburban area north of New York City. In a sense, his own career paralleled the meteoric rise to success enjoyed by many of his contemporaries in the business world. Indeed, in his personal manner Schuman was rather like the CEO of a large corporation, displaying boundless enthusiasm and creative energy. In addition to their son Anthony, the Schumans now had a daughter, Andrea, whom they had adopted as a five-month-old in 1949. As in many such families during that period, Frankie concentrated on parenting and managing the household, which included protecting her husband's freedom to work. Schuman was largely preoccupied with his professional responsibilities. Since these included maintaining his creative productivity as well as fulfilling his responsibilities to Juilliard, he worked constantly, six days per week. It would have been seven had Frankie not insisted that Sunday be devoted to family activities.[36] Summer vacations were often spent at a relative's retreat on Martha's Vineyard. Schuman's children have recalled him as rather remote, except for their Sunday outings. Like many men of his generation, he avoided discussing feelings and would respond to intrafamilial squabbling with, "Let's not have any unpleasantness."[37] As a parent Schuman perpetuated his own father's suppression of their Jewish identity: The children had not celebrated their bar (bas) mitzvah, the family did not attend temple or synagogue, they displayed a Christmas tree, and they celebrated Easter with a ham dinner.[38]

In order to remain creatively productive in the face of endless administrative responsibilities, Schuman imposed strict discipline on himself. "I had determined that if I were able to devote between 800 and 1000 hours a year to composition, I would be able to write as much as I wished. I kept a diary detailing the number of hours I spent writing each day. . . . I would start writing first thing in the morning, at home, and go into the office later."[39] Unlike many composers, Schuman always composed a work from beginning to end, without jumping ahead or back and forth.[40]

Around 1950 Vincent Persichetti was invited by Schuman to write a book on his life and works, to be published by G. Schirmer. When Persichetti presented his final draft, Schuman rejected the biographical portion, saying that it was "too close to the irreverent style of *New Yorker* magazine 'Profiles.'"[41] Schuman then asked Flora Rheta Schreiber (1918–1988) to rewrite the biographical portion. (She was later to win considerable attention for her bestselling book *Sybil* [1973], about a woman with multiple personality disorder.) *William Schuman* was published by Schirmer in 1954.

Although the book was not a critical success, Schreiber presented a vivid characterization of Schuman at this time in his life. She observed that his restless sense of urgency about his creative productivity was essential in compensating for his "late start as a composer. . . . Time is a commodity to be hoarded, an enemy to be conquered, a friend to be cultivated. Schuman himself is a personality seldom in repose. Roy Harris put it this way: 'I can't imagine Bill's spending one minute contemplating a rose.'" Schreiber also noted that his late start left him free of two of the most baffling problems confronting artists—a sense of isolation from average people, and an ineptitude in the conduct of practical affairs. . . . [H]e is . . . the very reverse of the popular picture of the artist as long-haired, gauche, living a life of penury, beating ineffectual wings. Though musically he became a radical, he clung to conservative manners. Schuman is relatively free of introspection and of psychic conflict. He was able to change the whole course of his life without wasting much energy in self-reproach or foreboding. But nonetheless the restlessness that spurred his ambition remains to deprive him of simple quietude. . . . Schuman is a pragmatist. His pragmatism is a way of asserting his ego effectively in the world of practical affairs and it is also a form of altruism, the altruism of promoting causes. It is a pragmatism strongly colored by moral and ethical convictions. . . .

Schuman knew that he himself could not become an effective artist unless he freed himself from economic worry. His solution was to become his own patron through teaching so that his music could be free of commercial . . . dictates. . . . [If an artist] is to earn a living, he must cultivate skills and behavior patterns that are acceptable. To live within the given, one must make peace with the Philistines, and to make peace one must make all unimportant concessions. One can do this and yet remain uncompromising on the real issues.[42]

Schuman also seems to have developed a remarkable capacity for denial, along with reinterpretation or rationalization of unpleasant or disturbing issues that threatened to interfere with the achievement of his goals. This quality was to play a significant role in his retrospective assessment of his subsequent experience at Lincoln Center.

Schreiber acknowledged that some resented Schuman's apparent ease in managing the various roles he filled. "His integration strikes them as sterility, his ability to get along with people of different types, as Philistinism."[43] Noting his interest in remaining informed regarding world affairs, she identifies his political sympathies as leaning toward the liberal side, but without strong party affiliation.[44] She describes him as intolerant of dilettantism, as well as of pretentiousness. "Unrelenting is his contempt for a certain brand of intellectualism which he considers pretentious and arty. In his definition music becomes pretentious when it crosses the line between a direct expression of human emotion and a devious expression of an affected attitude toward life."[45]

As Schuman's power within the music world grew, he became increasingly intolerant of those who did not share his view of his own importance. In 1952 he was able to negotiate a more advantageous arrangement with BMI, the performing rights organization, and thus transferred his affiliation from ASCAP. He felt that G. Schirmer was not promoting his music adequately, and began to exert pressure on Hans Heinsheimer, then director of publications, to take more aggressive action. His outrage and indignation reached the point where he finally dissolved his relationship with Schirmer in 1955. He was able to negotiate more favorable terms with Theodore Presser, and the following year signed a contract with them through their subsidiary, Merion Music. (He would retain this affiliation for the rest of his life.) Perhaps most astonishing was the squabble he had with his boyhood friend and songwriting partner Eddie Marks, who was then managing his father's music publishing company. Schuman insisted on receiving an advance against royalties on the songs they had written together, before he would agree to renewing their copyright, despite the fact that these songs, written almost thirty years earlier, had never earned any money.[46]

In 1956 Schuman was invited to speak at a general session of the Music Educators National Conference, held that year in St. Louis. His talk proved to be remarkably condescending and insulting to the large group of music teachers in attendance: He accused them of mediocre artistic standards, general ignorance, and inadequate professionalism, and expressed contempt for the sort of music pedagogy that was typically part of the curriculum of teacher education. Despite such a broadside, Schuman's stature at the time was such that the membership accepted his diatribe with respect and chastened humility.[47]

During the mid 1950s, plans were underway for an ambitious new performing arts complex in New York City. The site, on the west side of midtown Manhattan, had been proposed by Robert Moses. At one time the neighborhood had been known as "Hell's Kitchen," although more recently the less pejorative "Lincoln Square" had been adopted. The planned complex was to be called the Lincoln Center for the Performing Arts, and Schuman had been actively involved in discussions with the exploratory committee, led by John D. Rockefeller III, virtually from the beginning. In fact, it has been said that Schuman coined the term "performing arts."[48] The proposed center would include a large concert hall, an opera house, and additional halls, as well as a public library devoted to the arts, and an educational institution. Schuman was determined that Juilliard would be that educational institution, enabling it to become, in Joseph Polisi's words, "the pre-eminent school of its type in the nation and perhaps the world."[49] Schuman's plan met with considerable resistance; a strong contingent favored the creation of a school for the performing arts ancillary to Columbia University.[50] Persuading the planning board that Juilliard was the better choice taxed Schuman's skills in diplomatic negotiation to the utmost, although in February 1957 he finally prevailed. However, in addition to music and dance, a division devoted to drama would have to be created, its source of funding remaining vague.

The official groundbreaking for the construction of Lincoln Center took place in May 1959. There was an auspicious ceremony, with speeches by President Eisenhower, John D. Rockefeller III, Mayor Robert Wagner, and

Robert Moses. Initially General Maxwell Taylor was appointed to the presidency of the center, but in 1961 he was forced to leave abruptly to investigate the fiasco involving the U.S.-sponsored attempt to overthrow the Cuban government (known as the "Bay of Pigs Invasion").

In September 1961 the presidency of the center was offered to Schuman. He accepted the offer almost immediately, although many of those closest to him (including his wife Frankie and Leonard Bernstein) advised him against it, viewing his decision as a compromise of his creative life on behalf of his own personal aggrandizement.[51] But he insisted that he could never envision a life solely as a composer. "I'd go out of my mind and my publisher would go broke." He later recalled, "I never regarded the other things as appendages to my music. It was always one: It's all been part of a creative life in music."[52]

The same month Schuman announced his resignation from Juilliard and was promptly asked to submit a list of recommended successors. Among those he proposed were William Bergsma, Vincent Persichetti, Richard Franko Goldman, and Norman Lloyd. Conspicuously absent from his list was Peter Mennin, reflecting an enmity between the two that had been developing for several years. (Possible explanations for this enmity will be pursued in the chapter on Mennin.) However, the board of directors settled on Mennin. Schuman commented, "[H]e didn't seem to have the attributes you think of in an administrator . . . [but] at the end it was felt, and I concurred, that he was the best candidate, but nobody was excited about it."[53]

On 1 January 1962 William Schuman began his tenure as president of the Lincoln Center for the Performing Arts. The years to follow may be said to have represented the apex of his career, as "the most prominent arts leader in America."[54] In a sense, Schuman represented the spirit of post–World War II America, especially as it extended into the Kennedy and Johnson years—a period characterized by great prosperity, high ideals, and the confidence that these ideals were within reach. At this time Harold Schonberg wrote,

Schuman has a combination of pragmatism and imagination that puts its mark on everybody he meets. About 90 per cent of the people who have anything to do with him automatically describe him as an "unusual combination," two words Schuman must be heartily sick of by now. The other 10 per cent do not make snap judgments. They think deeply and describe him as a "rare combination." Those who respect him and also like him tack on words like "practical visionary" or "an artist who gets things done." Those who respect him but do not know him too well call him an administrator with a fine cultural background. Those who respect him but do not like him call him a super-salesman of a politician with Madison Avenue in his blood. But one thing all are agreed upon: the man can speak with the fervor, hypnotism and eloquence of Gielgud on one of his better days.[55]

Upon assuming the presidency, Schuman eagerly began to set forth his vision of what the Center could accomplish, and immediately delved into the many challenges that faced him. "My mind seethes with ideas and projects . . . I can see them flowing past in my mind."[56] Philharmonic Hall, the new home of the New York Philharmonic and the first of the center's constituents to open, was inaugurated in the fall of 1962. For the opening concerts, the orchestra had commissioned a new symphony from Schuman—No. 8—which was conducted by Leonard Bernstein. In 1963 the Schumans sold their house in New Rochelle and moved into an elegant apartment on Manhattan's upper Fifth Avenue. The following year they built a house in Greenwich, Connecticut, as a weekend retreat.

Although Schuman always maintained a shrewd eye toward maximizing the financial return on his own work—both creative and administrative—and, as has been illustrated, could be rigid and demanding, he was quite cavalier about spending the money of others in order to fulfill his ambitious plans. During his years at Juilliard, Schuman had become accustomed to the unquestioning support of his faculty, staff, and board of directors, as well as to the acceptance of his initiatives on behalf of the school's artistic standards and its impact in the community. He was not prepared for many of the challenges that faced him in his new role: He was no longer free to implement his "visions" without regard for their cost, or for their impact on the other constituent members of the center, all of which competed for money, attention, and prestige. Finances, in particular, became a continual focus of tense negotiation and conflict. Now he was faced with many channels to negotiate and fiscal guardians he had to cajole and win over.

Over the years Schuman had developed a direct, somewhat haughtily confrontational manner, whose impact he had learned to cushion through his wit and charm but without compromising his essential demands. However, this style was not viewed sympathetically by the experienced, hard-nosed, financially sophisticated overseers led by John D. Rockefeller III. The center faced numerous problems, from basic issues concerning the construction of new buildings, to the notorious acoustical problems of Philharmonic Hall, to difficult negotiations concerning the move of the New York City Opera and the New York City Ballet to Lincoln Center from their previous quarters at the City Center. And, of course, Schuman fervently expected Juilliard to play the major educational role. For this purpose he hired his longtime friend Mark Schubart from Juilliard to direct Lincoln Center's educational program (although this never really got underway until after Schuman left the center). But he now had to switch his loyalty from Juilliard to the center as a whole. Ever since Schuman's half-hearted support of Peter Mennin as his successor, the two men had been on bad terms. Now, with Juilliard and Lincoln Center competing for funding from the same sources, more serious antagonisms began to develop.[57] The lack of clarity as to the source of funding for Juilliard's projected drama division and the disputes that ensued eventually precipitated a major rift between the two men. (The drama division was not realized until Mennin's tenure as president.)

In December 1966 Schuman gave a talk at Princeton University that addressed the economic problems facing the performing arts. He stated, "Nonprofit institutions in the performing arts compromise their reason for being in direct proportion to the programs and policies which are adopted for fiscal reasons extrinsic to artistic purpose. . . . The success or failure of our enterprise cannot be measured in the plusses and minuses of ledgers, but in philosophy and mission, and in the clarity and conviction with which they are given life in our theaters, in our concert halls and in our classrooms."[58] Such a public pronouncement, issued against a backdrop of intense financial negotiations behind the scenes, was received by Rockefeller and his associates as brazenly defiant.

During the later 1960s, social discontent stemming from widespread opposition to the war in Vietnam, seething racial tensions in America's urban centers, and the cultural polarization that resulted attracted a great deal of attention. Foundation money that might otherwise have been directed to the arts was now channeled into addressing social problems. This increased the tension between Schuman and the board of directors regarding the funding of the projects he envisioned, while ongoing friction between the boards of directors of the center and of Juilliard became a constant source of exasperation.[59] Schuman's refusal to compromise his ambitious demands and his propensity for provocative public statements (e.g., "Far from having any hope of making money, our task is to lose money wisely"[60]) aroused considerable animosity among the board members.[61] Furthermore, these social and cultural issues, exacerbated by a much-publicized "generation gap" between college students and their parents, engendered conflict between Schuman and his children as they did in many middle-class families of the period, despite Schuman's aversion to "any unpleasantness" within his household. Creating further anxiety and uncertainty was the discovery that Frankie was suffering from breast cancer, which was ultimately treated successfully. Although it was often stated that "even in his busiest times at Lincoln Center, he composed a minimum of 600 hours a year,"[62] Schuman admitted that, in fact, during his Lincoln Center years, the number had dwindled to 300, with a corresponding diminution of output. In May 1968, during stressful negotiations concerning the formation of the Chamber Music Society and shortly before the wedding of daughter Andrea, Schuman suffered a major heart attack.

Schuman returned to work that September, clearly in a weakened state. But he relentlessly continued to pursue the projects on his agenda. Finally, demoralized by the constant emphasis on "the bottom line" by the board of directors, he felt compelled to submit his resignation, effective 1 January 1969.

Long delayed by numerous complications, the grand opening of the new Juilliard School at Lincoln Center finally took place in October 1969. Schuman attended the opening ceremonies, which were televised, but was not invited to speak, a slight he greatly resented. In his remarks Peter Mennin made perfunctory acknowledgment of Schuman's role. Among the distinguished personages who did speak was Leonard Bernstein. Mennin reportedly modified Bernstein's script to limit the attention given to Schuman. However, at the event, Bernstein went off script and heaped extravagant praise on his longtime friend and colleague.[63]

During the years that followed, Schuman continued to maintain the position that Rockefeller and his colleagues lacked sufficient "artistic understanding" to make the decisions he felt were necessary for Lincoln Center to fulfill its potential. Polisi aptly notes that Schuman "saw himself as taking the high road, with art trumping the ubiquitous power of money. . . . His belief that he could prevail in an arena of budget deficits, construction overruns, and enormous egos could also be fairly called naïve."[64] Nevertheless, when one considers Schuman's accomplishments during his tenure as president and the sources of much of the squabbling—the founding of the Great Performers series, formation of the Chamber Music Society of Lincoln Center, the Lincoln Center Film Society, the Lincoln Center Institute, the Promenade series, followed by the Mostly Mozart Festival (although some of these did not actually materialize until after Schuman left the center)—his vision seems largely to be vindicated. Most of these programs continue to function to this day, and many are internationally recognized as distinguished contributors to America's cultural life. On the other hand, perhaps what Andrea Olmstead described as "Schuman's bull-in-a-china-shop style" exacerbated tensions that might have been mollified by more effective diplomacy.[65]

The public explanation for Schuman's resignation as president of Lincoln Center was that he wanted to devote more time to composition. Not only had his productivity been dwindling, but it was during the 1960s that his stature as a composer began to wane. During that tumultuous decade, Schuman emerged as the very embodiment of the East Coast Artistic Establishment, and that was anathema to the anti-Establishment spirit of the times. This was the period when the serial approach to composition had seized the intellectual high ground, its advocates dismissing as trivial any music that did not adhere to this dogma. As challenging and intellectually sophisticated as Schuman's music may have been, he was nevertheless a traditionalist, composing symphonies with themes and motifs that were developed along conventional lines, and maintaining an allegiance to tonality, no matter how tenuous. This was the litmus test of acceptability among the proponents of "New Music," and it was a test that Schuman failed.

In an interview during the 1960s, asked to name the American composers he felt had made the most significant contributions, Schuman maintained his long-standing admiration for Roy Harris. He described Harris as

> one of the most original minds ever to appear in music. He is greatly under-estimated as a composer even today. The reason for this is that his technique never advanced in terms equal to his fantastic talent. The music he has already given the world is quite exceptional. It is rather absurd that everybody discovers Charles Ives and lets Roy Harris wither on the vine. Ives was a great originator but he is vastly overrated in every way except as an originator. But his poor technical achievement will eventually do him in. At this time, these are very extreme views because there is an Ives vogue. Ives is remarkable, absolutely original, but originality does not make a composer. This is only one element of being an artist.[66]

In 1967 Schuman was commissioned on behalf of Eugene Ormandy and the Philadelphia Orchestra to write a symphony, his No. 9. Subtitled "Le Fosse Ardeatine," the work commemorated the 1944 massacre of 335 Italians by the Nazis. Schuman had been deeply moved upon visiting the site the previous year. Determined to draw as much attention to the work as possible, he had begun urging RCA to record it before he had even submitted the score to Ormandy, much to the latter's embarrassment.[67] (He also had made a point of mentioning to a writer for the *New York Times* that the symphony took him 306 hours and 25 minutes to compose.[68]) Ormandy conducted the premiere in January of 1969. After the first performance Schuman had supposedly commented to one of the Philadelphia critics that the orchestra gave "a satisfactory reading enough, at least, to get an idea of how the music sounds."[69] When Ormandy saw this comment in print, he was reportedly livid and wrote an enraged letter to the composer. Schuman denied having made the remark and wrote a letter to the *Philadelphia Inquirer*, asserting that the performance was "nothing short of phenomenal."[70] After much effort, Schuman extracted a half-hearted agreement from RCA to record the work. He felt that he could elicit a firmer commitment if he could raise some money to contribute to the recording costs. He succeeded in persuading the original commissioning foundation to provide some additional funding, but RCA continued to withhold its commitment, while the orchestra made clear that they had no intention of subsidizing the recording in any way. Brimming with self-righteous anger and indignation, Schuman wrote a letter to the orchestra in a tone similar to the one he had so often used with the Lincoln Center board.[71] But this time he managed to succeed in negotiating his desired outcome, and the symphony was recorded by RCA.

As he had so often pointed out, Schuman could not be satisfied with a life as "just a composer." Now, as he entered his sixties, he approached the new decade with a restless search for projects in which to involve himself. Without an employer for the first time in many years, one concern he faced was obtaining health insurance for himself and his wife. He was able to persuade BMI to grant him the status of an "employee," which qualified him for that and other benefits. He began to explore some of the new technologies under development and considered ways they might be adapted and applied to education and the arts. He took consulting positions with some of the companies interested in applying these technologies, joined the boards of a host of arts organizations, and served as chairman of the Videorecord Corporation of America, a short-lived enterprise. In 1971 he even accepted an invitation to undertake comprehensive evaluations of the Puerto Rico Conservatory and Symphony Orchestra. During this period he relied on Frankie as his chief advisor, as well as his main source of emotional, intellectual, and social support.

Schuman had served for many years on the board of the Naumburg Foundation, an organization whose mission is to discover and support new musical talent. Elected president of the foundation in 1959, he was forced to resign when he took on the presidency of Lincoln Center. Peter Mennin was elected president in 1964. In 1971 Schuman set about unseating Mennin through an invidious series of public humiliations, and once again his efforts were successful,[72] although Polisi conceded that Schuman's actions were "very aggressive and probably inappropriate . . . clearly an overstepping of bounds."[73]

During this period a number of his friends and colleagues urged Schuman to capitalize on his gift for public speaking by launching a series of lucrative lecture-tours. He considered this seriously but soon realized that the appeal of public speaking for him was rooted in his desire to promote projects or causes in which he fervently believed. He had little enthusiasm for lecturing on more abstract subjects. However, for the remainder of his professional life he continued to accept invitations to speak on special occasions, often making pointed comments that he softened with his customary cleverness and wit. In these talks he often returned to the theme that had obviously been gnawing at him for many years, especially after the Lincoln Center period: how to maintain high standards in the arts within a profit-oriented society.

In 1974 Schuman became chairman and (together with Frankie) principal fund-raiser of the MacDowell Colony in Peterborough, New Hampshire. He held this post until 1977, then again from 1980 until 1983. In 1975, he was invited by the Norlin Corporation, America's largest musical instrument company, to help establish a foundation to reward excellence in music. As chairman of the Norlin Foundation, he conceived a variety of ways that technology might be utilized to improve music education. He was also invited to serve on the board of the National Humanities Center as the only representative from the world of the arts.

As early as 1966 Schuman had begun to plan "Project 1976," which was to be his contribution to the American bicentennial celebrations. He had in mind a large-scale work of full-evening's length for soloists, chorus, and orchestra. "I regard this as a culminating effort of a life's work," he asserted grandly.[74] In 1972 he began to seek financial support but was unable to raise funds of sufficient magnitude to finance a project of such scope. Ultimately, he was forced to compromise his plan to something much smaller in scale: a concert in Washington, D.C., given by the National Symphony Orchestra with the Westminster Choir, conducted by Antal Dorati. The program featured three premieres: *The Young Dead Soldiers*, for soprano and chamber orchestra, set to a text by Archibald MacLeish; his Symphony No. 10, subtitled "American Muse" (both works commissioned by the National Symphony Orchestra); and a somewhat shortened cantata version of his critically unsuccessful opera from the early 1950s, *The Mighty Casey*, given the new title *Casey at the Bat: A Baseball Cantata*, with soprano Rosalind Rees and baritone Robert Merrill as soloists. The adaptation was funded by a $25,000 grant from the Norlin Foundation (of which Schuman was chairman).

In 1980, a fifty-four-page brochure was published jointly by Theodore Presser and G. Schirmer, entitled *William Schuman: Documentary*, in honor of the composer's seventieth birthday. Enlisted to write the document was Christopher Rouse, noted composer and an enthusiastic admirer of Schuman since adolescence. It consists of a biographical essay, catalogue of works, discography, and bibliography, with an introduction by Leonard Bernstein. (Schuman held the copyright to the brochure.)

Interviewed around this time, Schuman conveyed the impression that he had much composing left to do: "I have more ideas than I'll ever live to execute. I simply can't imagine not having the prospect of writing music. What I do find is that composing gets more difficult, which really has nothing to do with age. That's because you find you've been everywhere, so to speak, before. You have to be careful not just to repeat yourself."[75] Reflecting back on his years at Lincoln Center, he commented,

The musical life of our country is . . . based on the fight for funds. And [therefore] the programming has become timid. I do not believe a country has a musical culture if it just has brilliant performers. We do have a body of compositions in this country that actually succeeds with audiences, but it isn't being played.

. . . You're always fighting something in this country, because serious music doesn't make any money. And if it doesn't make money here, it isn't honored very much. . . . Progress is only made when there are people who will fight for their ideals, and people like that are always in short supply. The Bernsteins and the Koussevitzkys, people who care deeply about American music, don't come along in bunches. I think it's a *moral* issue, not just an esthetic issue, to care about the music of your own country. But I don't like to pause to *think* about these things too much. I *act* on them, through organizational pursuits, to try to change the situation.[76]

Answering questions posed by composer Phillip Ramey at a preconcert lecture at that time, Schuman commented revealingly on his life as a composer:

I adore being a composer when I'm in my studio writing music. But once the work leaves the studio it's all downhill. If I'm lucky there will be a great performance, but then I have to go through hardly anybody understanding the music and getting a bad press. There are some intelligent critics, but mostly they're not on newspapers. . . . What red-blooded American boy would choose a career nobody likes and that you can't make a living at? You have to be a pragmatist and do something else or go into a corner and cry and live in poverty. I don't cry, nor do I live in poverty. Next question?[77]

During the 1980s Schuman received countless awards and honors. In 1981 Columbia University established the William Schuman Award, a $50,000 prize to a composer for lifetime achievement. Its namesake was honored as the first recipient. In 1984 he received a letter from Martha Graham, in which she stated, "I hold you in great esteem, both as a composer and as a man with whom I have worked so magically. You have contributed so unbelievably much to my life and I deeply treasure you."[78] The following year he was awarded a Pulitzer Prize Special Citation in honor of his lifetime achievements. Perhaps Schuman's most treasured award was the gold medal he received from the American Academy and Institute of Arts and Letters. The medal was presented to him by Leonard Bernstein, whose speech overflowed with extravagant praise.

In 1982 Schuman formed the American Music Recording Institute for the purpose of financing recordings of significant American music. He succeeded in raising modest funding, but not enough to fulfill his original conception. Eventually he was able to gain the cooperation of Juilliard and succeeded in arranging for the release of three recordings through New World Records. However, the project was dropped after Schuman's death.

During the early 1980s, Schuman became consumed with developing and promoting a plan to facilitate philanthropic donations to not-for-profit organizations. His plan, which he elaborated in excruciating detail, was quite complex and would require modifications in the tax code, and therefore faced considerable resistance. A voluminous correspondence developed as he attempted to enlist the cooperation and support of corporate executives, leaders from the world of finance, and political representatives. Eventually he gained the satisfaction of having an article on the subject published in *Philanthropy Monthly*.[79] Undaunted by cardiac bypass surgery in 1983, he continued to pursue his idea with the same persistence and zeal that he demonstrated on behalf of the many other projects that engaged his interest throughout his career. However, this plan ultimately came to naught and he was forced to admit defeat.[80]

Meanwhile, Schuman continued to monitor and attempt to influence the directions taken by some of the Lincoln Center institutions, especially the Film Society and the Chamber Music Society, both of which he had been instrumental in founding. As always, his involvement was vigorous and contentious. Schuman had originally appointed Charles Wadsworth to head the Chamber Music Society in 1968. But now he felt that Wadsworth had diverged from Schuman's original conception, so he undertook an aggressive campaign to have him removed.[81] However, Wadsworth—perhaps sensing that despite his haughty attitude, Schuman no longer had the power over the board that he once did—held his ground, while accommodating some of Schuman's criticisms, and stayed on until 1989. In 1985 the Chamber Music Society marked Schuman's seventy-fifth birthday with an entire concert devoted to his music.

With Peter Mennin's unexpected death in 1983, Juilliard suddenly had to find a new president. Schuman evidently seized the opportunity and promoted Joseph Polisi, whose father had taught bassoon at Juilliard for years, for the position. Schuman knew the family, and Olmstead quotes W. McNeil Lowry, former vice-president of the Ford Foundation, as saying that Schuman "knew he could control Polisi. He also knew that Polisi would have a kind of revisionist treatment of Schuman's role. . . . Schuman, after twenty-two years away from the School, was apparently again calling the shots, this time through his young protégé. He began using the title 'president emeritus,' never previously used in Juilliard publications."[82]

In 1984 Schuman accepted a large commission from a consortium of major orchestras, led by the New York Philharmonic together with the Crane School of Music at the State University of New York (SUNY) at Potsdam, to write a major work in commemoration of the hundredth anniversary of the Statue of Liberty. He decided on a large choral work, which provided him with the opportunity to create the sort of composition he had hoped to write for the American bicentennial. He selected poet Richard Wilbur to write the text, and the result was entitled *On Freedom's Ground*. The premiere was given in October 1986 by the New York Philharmonic and the Crane Chorus. Zubin Mehta conducted, and Sherrill Milnes was the baritone soloist.

In 1986 the adventurous Glimmerglass Opera Company revived *The Mighty Casey* for a production in Cooperstown, New York, home of the Baseball Hall of Fame. The performance at such a symbolically significant site was very gratifying and somewhat vindicating for Schuman, whose belief in the opera had never wavered. One of the work's difficulties was its eighty-minute duration, which is a little short for an evening-length production. However, encouraged by the success of this performance, Glimmerglass commissioned Schuman to write a companion work. While he was looking for a subject, Frankie suggested to him a short story by Roald Dahl, called "Taste." The story appealed to Schuman, and, after much consideration, he selected poet J. D. McClatchy as librettist. The resulting one-act opera, *A Question of Taste*, proved to be Schuman's last major work. Together with *The Mighty Casey*, it was introduced by the Glimmerglass Opera in June 1989 as part of the fiftieth anniversary celebration of the Baseball Hall of Fame.

Schuman's neurological condition was worsening, and he was eventually diagnosed with Parkinson's disease. As a result of the lucrative positions he had held and the shrewdness with which he had managed his money, he was able to spend his final years in considerable material comfort, enjoying the companionship of his large group of friends, which included many from the business world as well as from the world of the arts.[83] In 1989 he was presented with the Kennedy Center Award for his lifetime of achievement in the arts. (Noting that other recipients that year were Harry Belafonte and Mary Martin, he commented, "Only in America could you mix all these things."[84])

On 15 February 1992, immediately following hip surgery, Schuman died of a pulmonary embolism. As he had specified, his body was cremated, and there was no religious service. Two months later a memorial ceremony was held in the Juilliard Theater. Selections of his music were performed, and the speakers included Joseph Polisi, Christopher Rouse, Morton Gould, and his son, Anthony Schuman. The service ended with the deeply moving finale of his beloved *Casey*, accompanied by the projection of his portrait.

William Schuman was an intensely complex individual, driven by an unflagging energy that could be perceived as noble, idealistic, altruistic, and visionary, but also as arrogant, greedy, and self-aggrandizing. One's own impression typically depended on the degree of one's familiarity with him and on the nature of one's interactions with him. Some have characterized him as a master manipulator, ruthlessly driven by a quest for power—power that he sought for the purpose of achieving objectives, many of which involved the enhancement of his own reputation. In so doing he could be surprisingly petty and shockingly disloyal to friends and admirers, manipulating situations behind the scenes, often at the expense of those toward whom he was publicly magnanimous. Phillip Ramey recounts an occasion when he commented to his close friend Aaron Copland on Schuman's personal charm; Copland responded, "Yes—so long as he sees a purpose to it."[85]

On the other hand, in an obituary that appeared in the *San Francisco Chronicle*, the distinguished critic Robert Commanday wrote, "On the exterior, he was smooth, polished, well-turned out, smiling, genial and jocular. At the functioning level of the executive, he was purposeful, systematic and efficient. . . . The governing quality in that life was a dedication to principle, a mental set that underlay the craft and purpose of his music no less than it informed his attitude, philosophy and performance as educator and executive. This made him seem large and to an outsider, imposing, his public statements polished and grand. That's what it took to serve at the center, as a leader, the elder statesman of American music."[86]

MUSIC

"Whatever meaning my life has is to be found in the music itself."[87] This often-quoted statement of Schuman invites a consideration of his significance solely as a composer. As stated in the introduction to this book, William Schuman was, along with Roy Harris and Aaron Copland, one of the American founders of what is termed in this volume "Modern Traditionalism." However, in the late 1930s both Harris and Copland altered their compositional styles by embracing—to varying extents—both vernacular and explicitly national elements in an effort to shape identities as distinctly "American" composers. On the other hand, Schuman, whose compositional persona has always been perceived as American to the core, achieved this identity without recourse to such facile devices. Schuman's "Americanness" is embedded within the very tone and spirit of his expression, which may be described as bold and brash, declamatory, self-confidently assertive, tense, aggressive, nervously edgy, and, at times, contemplative, lofty, and even oratorical. Many of these are qualities often associated with the American character. His music has frequently been described as "optimistic," and this is true of many of his works; but equally salient is a vein of tragedy that runs through a comparable number of compositions.

In his study of Schuman's music through 1950, Vincent Persichetti wrote, "If there is more of one ingredient than another in the rich mixture of William Schuman's music it is the strong-flavored energy that generates a constant boil of movement. There is motion stirred by boldness and intensity, movement that pushes forward resourcefully and seriously and beneath even the quietest pages a restless current that will eventually surface in a rush."[88]

Schuman was always drawn to large forms, large forces, and large statements. Most of his work retains some discernable connection to tonality, although this connection is often tenuous in his later compositions. He maintained a fondness for jagged, brittle gestures, often in counterpoint, as well as major-minor juxtapositions that create a recognizable harmonic identity, even when chordal structures are more complex than mere triads. As Persichetti noted, "The harmonies that result from this contrapuntal movement . . . weave a pattern of similar chordal structures with matching textures suited to the mood and personality of the musical statement."[89] Many have commented on Schuman's frequent use of polytonality, within both harmonic and melodic contexts. But, according to Persichetti, "The much mentioned polytonality in Schuman is not polytonality but polyharmony. Triads of kindred tonalities joining to form one resonant five- or six-note chord result in a harmony enriched by overtones and belonging to one key. He is fond of these chords and can manipulate them by adjusting the dissonant relationship of the chord-members to acquire any texture he needs."[90]

Persichetti emphasized that in addition to innovations in harmony, Schuman developed his own approach to rhythm, form, and melody. "His modernism is distinctively individual and unique. In his song-plugging days he heard few of the serious works that were either grafted to jazz idioms or forced into a dissonant shell by experimentalists. He built his own path of dissonant thinking and his ideas were already crystallized by the time he was fully exposed to new trends. He invariably found merit in techniques far removed from his own creative channels, but . . . [h]e never became infatuated with the twelve-tone style."[91]

Schuman devised a characteristic approach to rhythm, especially in rapid passages—breathlessly nervous, irregular, and highly syncopated, with a fondness for "chattering" patterns often in intensely contrapuntal interaction. Phrases often begin with a silent downbeat, followed by an accented off-beat, which Persichetti considered "a derivation of jazz." He felt that this element is what gave Schuman's music its "American" flavor.

As Roy Harris once pointed out, Europeans think of rhythm in its largest common denominator, while we are brought up with a feeling for its smallest units. Jazz players are chained to symmetrical dance rhythms but continually break into cross-rhythm variations. This superimposing of rhythm has entered the American blood stream. Schuman has a way of writing these rhythms without meter changes. The fundamental pulse-beats remain regular for long stretches while the metric patterns above this beat shift constantly. . . . Unlike the music of some Americans whose sources of style can be traced to jazz, Schuman's reveals jazz elements as an integral part of his thinking; they never obtrude as foreign bodies.[92]

In 1971 Aaron Copland stated, "In Schuman's pieces you have the feeling that only an American could have written them. . . . You hear it in his orchestration which is full of snap and brilliance. You hear it in the kind of American optimism which is at the basis of his music."[93] Some two decades later, in his comprehensive study *The American Symphony*, the English musicologist Neil Butterworth wrote, "Without ever resorting to folksong or jazz, Schuman is the epitome of an American composer. The boldness of gesture, a willingness to take risks and the elaborate rhythmical complexities owe nothing to European influences."[94]

Perhaps the most notable element of Schuman's language and the one most often commented upon is his creation of simultaneous planes of activity—often distinguished according to instrumental family—the music of each plane seeming almost unrelated to the others. That is, strings may be engaged in a sustained lyrical passage, while high woodwinds are chirping nervously, and the brasses offer jagged punctuations—each with different tonal implications. "It has the musical effect of tectonic plates grinding over and against each other."[95]

Schuman frequently ended his compositions with triumphant major triads, often reiterated with octave leaps, and with the fifth of the chord in the top voice, at times in dissonant relationship with the bass note, and often reinforced by generous tattoos of percussion. Although the exuberance of this triumphant gesture was tempered somewhat in his later compositions, he never really abandoned it. Even later pieces that were dark and pessimistic in character or those largely atonal throughout—for example, *The Young Dead Soldiers*—typically ended with major triads, though without necessarily implying a sense of triumph. Perhaps a mannerism more than a stylistic trait, these major-triad conclusions persisted into his last compositions. One can only speculate as to the meaning of this practice for the composer. Was it a statement of loyalty to tonality? An inability to relinquish hope, or a spirit of optimism? As his language became increasingly atonal and dissonant, these triadic endings appeared more and more incongruous and peculiar, rather like musical *dei ex machina*.

Schuman frequently insisted that his music was fundamentally melodic and that melody was the element that determined the course of a composition. However, as composer Irving Fine pointed out, "[Schuman] knows how to sing, but rarely sings highly formal tunes—those models of symmetry in which antecedent and consequent phrases balance off so neatly."[96] Many of Schuman's best works do display long, flowing, if angular melodic lines, but these became increasingly austere and remote as time went on.

"The sound he created is unmistakable," wrote Robert Commanday. Most perceptively he described it as "a music of solid sonorities, triadic chordal structures moving about freely, the instruments typically treated by family in choirs, something like the 'Big Band' manner applied to the symphony. The rhythm in fast movements is typically feverishly off-balance. . . . There were dark intensities in his music, not highly personalized, romantic emotion, but emotion unmistakably."[97] Critic Mark Lehman enthused, "No one surpasses Schuman for contrapuntal sophistication, dazzling orchestral brilliance, supremely confident brio, and sheer symphonic drama. No listener forgets those springy rhythms that generate immense kinetic energy, those magniloquent chromatically-enriched chorales, those sinuous string cantabiles punctuated by brassy, percussive outbursts."[98]

Persichetti aptly described the music prior to 1950:

> The result is a forward-moving mass of sound in unorthodox treatment that is as unfamiliar to some ears as it is peculiar to the Schuman idiom. This music, without structural gaps and recurring cadences, can easily be mistaken for the misguided wanderings of a fundamentally conventional mode of writing. . . . Enthusiasm, drive, and bite in a melodic frame give Schuman's music its power of projection. This huge-sounding music is made for billboards rather than newspapers. Boldness, freshness, and intensity of feeling are prominent; yet there is some grace and charm. Most of Schuman's music is about something big. . . . Only short periods of time are allowed for personal retrospection, and as contrast, the contemplative is overshadowed, or even swallowed, by surrounding passages.[99]

At its best, Schuman's music displays a lofty eloquence, a highly charged kinetic vigor, and perhaps the deepest musical insight into the distinctive American character ever accomplished through purely abstract means. (Michael Steinberg referred to him as the "great Public Orator among America's composers"[100]). However, his weaker works reveal long, barren passages of brooding that seem devoid of compelling content, dry compositional activity lacking expressive meaning, with a tendency to recycle devices already explored, with no new creative purpose apparent.

As a true traditionalist, Schuman placed little importance on originality. "If you have to worry about originality or think about it, you're not original. And if you're a composer you are original in the sense that you're writing what you are, you're writing your personal profile, and if you don't have a personal profile, you're not a composer. You're someone who's merely schooled in the techniques of composition."[101] Persichetti noted, "He does not seek aid from out-of-the-way experiments, those obvious attempts to lure the public to a work by way of an unheard-of combination of instruments or an extra-musical association. The press is never able to hail or propagandize a coming Schuman event; they can only announce it. . . . One attends the performance and finds the excitement in the music."[102]

However, what *was* important to Schuman was individuality. "I think a composer is someone who has a profile. . . . [U]nless he has something that sets him apart then he's like Telemann, a writer of yardage music. However, I don't think stylistic consistency is terrifically important, at least not from piece to piece. It never occurs to me to strive for that. I simply get involved in the ambience of each work as I'm composing it."[103] As early as 1950, Persichetti noted, "Though a young man, he has, in a surprisingly short space of time, developed a personal style. His rhythmic and harmonic gestures are easily distinguished from those of his contemporaries, and his melodies contain unmistakable Schumanesque trade-marks."[104]

According to Persichetti, "Schuman thinks in long-range terms, plotting the course of a large-scale work before the writing actually begins. . . . The material selected takes form as a more or less complete organism before reaching paper. . . . Occasionally, certain aspects of the music are sketched in rough. A kind of 'dummy' music is written to get the feel of the piece."[105] The "ambience," or "emotional climate," was another aspect that was important to Schuman. "Above all, when composing I must be sure of the emotional climate of the music at every single moment."[106] "Then, when I have the emotional climate quite firmly in mind, . . . I make tentative plans as to how I think this work is going to proceed. However, these tentative plans can all be junked as I go along writing because I retain flexibility."[107] Sometimes Schuman referred to this "emotional climate" as "atmosphere."

> Writers on music have commented on my use of [the clash of major and minor triads]. The reason you find this device goes back to my preoccupation with atmosphere, because I do not use harmony as a device for musical progression, but as an environmental factor for the kind of horizontal sounds that I am interested in at that particular moment. Sometimes contrapuntal lines will go through harmonic structures, but more often they will not. They will be independent contrapuntal lines, but always forming some specific kind of overall harmonic effect. However, it is not harmony of progression. If harmonic progress is heard, it is incidental, not intentionally there.[108]

Fine made some perceptive observations about Schuman's treatment of the harmonic element: "The harmonic materials . . . have little to do with classical tonal harmony. The basis for Schuman's harmony is the triad, (1) connected in parallel; or (2) in homorhythmic passages connected in such a way as to obtain the maximum possible number of cross relations; or (3) combined bitonally with another triad. The very simplicity of this harmonic palette assures the music of a certain crude strength."[109]

Roy Harris's concept of autogenesis deeply underlay Schuman's approach to form and development. Persichetti noted,

Characteristic figures resulting from the development of one section's material generate the thematic constituents of the next. Therefore, all elements that make up a piece are related to each other and form a tight structure, free of loose ends. This approach insures uniformity of design and accounts for the clear shape of his long works. It leaves no room for impressionistic scattering of ideas, or annoying breaks that let in fickle cadenzas. No vague harmonies are needed to glaze a page spattered with odds and ends of themes.[110]

Also influencing the development of Schuman's symphonic style were Harris's tendency to integrate several sections into a single movement, his propensity for treating the instrumental choirs of the orchestra separately, and his fondness for parallelism, for quartal harmony, and for lumbering rhythmic *ostinati*.

Schuman was concerned with coherence and consistency.

[A]s I invent each character I listen to the qualities of that character, and it must tell me where it goes from there. I do not like to superimpose my own judgments. . . . [As a literary analogy], sometimes you feel when you read a novel that is not entirely successful, that the author has created a character which is not developed logically from the character invented. The author has superimposed his/her own ideas as to where that character should go. The same thing applies to music. . . . If I were to choose one word to describe my preoccupation, my objective preoccupation, it is the word clarity—clarity of architecture. . . . Form is basically what happens next. If what happens next does not have a basic human truth, it will not succeed in the long term.[111]

Schuman recounted that his composing process began with deciding upon a tempo; he would set his metronome to that speed and then let his thoughts flow freely. Unlike many composers, he did not compose at the piano, nor begin with a piano sketch, to be orchestrated as a later step. He wrote directly on the orchestral score and did relatively little rewriting.[112] "When I compose an orchestral piece, I think in a totally orchestral way. I never think of a melody and then assign it to an oboe; I think of an oboe melody. I wouldn't know how to sit down and sketch something in the abstract that I would then score for orchestra—I write for the orchestra immediately. For me, orchestration is one of the most exciting things of all."[113]

Public acceptance was important to Schuman. "The greatest achievement that a composer can have in a lifetime is to somehow create works that enter the mainstream."[114] Some years later he said, "My job is to write the best music that I can write, and there are always people around who will evaluate it. It might be flattering or demeaning, but it doesn't matter, because in the long pull there's a body of opinion that creates a consensus. There's nothing much you can do about that. It's rather a comforting thought."[115]

But Schuman found the question of "communication" somewhat baffling. "How and what a composer communicates to his listeners is an interesting question." Noting that some people claimed that his music lacks humor, that it is consistently melancholy, he commented,

> Certainly, I know that my exterior demeanor is not one of melancholy, and in my appearances as a speaker I am not known to be without wit. . . . Anyone who runs the Lincoln Center has to have a sense of humor. I can tell you that! But this question of communication between the composer and his listeners interests me because, apparently, you give out a certain feeling through your compositions which I am forced to believe does not reveal the whole gamut of your character. . . . [A] person's art, contrary to what psychologists tell us, probably does not reveal everything. It reveals things that the person is able or wishes to say in his/her art. . . . I guess that there are parts of your nature that you do not want to reveal, that you cannot reveal, or that are not germane to the medium. This, I feel, follows through in all the arts.[116]

A number of commentators (Rouse et al.) have identified three creative periods into which Schuman's music can be subdivided, preceded by an early exploratory period (from which most of the works were subsequently withdrawn by the composer). The first period begins in 1939 with the *American Festival Overture* and extends through 1944 with the *Circus Overture*. The music from this period shows the strong influence of Roy Harris and tends to exude an exuberant sense of optimism. The second period begins with the music for the ballet *Undertow* in 1945 and lasts until the completion of the final version of the Violin Concerto in 1959. (Rouse's conceptualization concludes this period one year earlier.) This period represents the emergence of Schuman's own mature creative voice. The music from this time reveals more emotional depth and complexity, and a greater variety of expression, as well as more elaborate formal structures. This period corresponds roughly with Schuman's Juilliard years, and it was during this time that most of his greatest works were composed. The third and final period begins in 1960 with the Symphony No. 7 and lasts until the end of his composing career. The works from this period show a somewhat less consistent level of quality: There is an attempt in some works to give nodding acknowledgment to the newer compositional approaches being explored by a younger generation of composers—chiefly, more attenuated tonality and a fuller use of the percussion section in orchestral pieces. Some of these works maintain the high standards of the previous period; others seem to exhibit a "pseudo profundity," with serious subject matter and solemn gestures but inadequate musical substance; still others seem to repeat concepts and devices already used sufficiently in previous works.

Although his music embraced increasingly high levels of vertical dissonance as he grew older, Schuman never embraced the twelve-tone system—
especially its pretense as an international style representing the intellectual
"cutting edge" in musical composition. From Polisi's standpoint, "To adopt
the system, as Copland did in his later years, was a rejection of the American
ethos that was so much a fundamental element of Schuman's music. . . . The
Eurocentric orientation of America's musical intelligentsia at mid-twentieth
century was anathema to everything in which Schuman believed."[117]

As one considers Schuman's compositional output as a whole, one genre
is notably unrepresented: religious music. Aside from a few trifling choral
pieces with routine texts, sacred works are conspicuously absent. While
Schuman attempted to downplay his Jewish heritage, he certainly made no
pretense in the direction of Christianity either. He had clearly decided to define his creative identity as wholly secular in nature.

MOST REPRESENTATIVE, FULLY REALIZED WORKS

Symphony No. 3 (1941)
Symphony No. 4 (1941)
Symphony No. 6 (1948)
Judith (1949)
String Quartet No. 4 (1950)
The Mighty Casey/Casey at the Bat: A Baseball Cantata (1953; 1976)
Credendum: Article of Faith (1955)
Violin Concerto (1947–1959)
Symphony No. 7 (1960)
Symphony No. 8 (1962)
Symphony No. 9, "Le Fosse Ardeatine" (1968)
Concerto on Old English Rounds (1973)
Symphony No. 10, "American Muse" (1975)
American Hymn: Orchestral Variations on an Original Melody (1981)
On Freedom's Ground (1985)

Schuman composed approximately eighty works. Among them are the two
short operas, the ten symphonies (of which the first two were withdrawn),
along with choreographic works, concertos, and other miscellaneous orchestral pieces, numerous choral works, a small number of chamber works, and a
host of occasional pieces, some of which reappeared in other, more ambitious
compositions. Because of the large number of pieces in Schuman's output of
relatively minor import and questionable musical significance, and because,

unlike the cases of Persichetti and Mennin, much has already been written and discussed concerning Schuman's music, the following survey addresses primarily the works of major substance and significance.

Exploratory Phase

The compositions of William Schuman's "exploratory phase" comprise those works he composed between 1932 and 1938, when he was searching for a voice and a language of his own. This period embraces his early composition studies at the Juilliard summer school, his period of study at Columbia University Teachers College, where he earned his bachelor's and master's degrees, his first years on the faculty of Sarah Lawrence College, and the beginning of his apprenticeship with Roy Harris. During this time he composed two symphonies, two string quartets, and several pieces for chorus. He also began work on a piano concerto, not completed until 1942. Most of these pieces were subsequently withdrawn and are not part of his active body of work.

The development of Schuman's compositional voice differed considerably from what might be regarded as the norm. Unlike many composers, his childhood was not spent absorbing music history and its repertoire of masterpieces. First "discovering" classical music at the age of twenty, then beginning to compose at twenty-two, he embraced in his initial efforts (disregarding the pop tunes he had written during his teens) an angular, dissonant language with few discernible roots in the music of the past, instead reflecting more of what his elder colleagues were exploring at that time—especially Roy Harris. During the 1930s Harris's music struck the cultivated American public as the embodiment of what American symphonic music should sound like, and his music seemed to capture Schuman's imagination more than did that of any other composer.

One piece from this period that Schuman did *not* withdraw was his String Quartet No. 2, making it the earliest work of significance in his canon. Although he devoted relatively little attention to producing chamber music, at each stage of his development Schuman was drawn to the string quartet, a medium with a long tradition of distillation, concentration, economy, and understatement, producing a series of substantial and ambitious works that display his central compositional concerns at the times he composed them. Discounting the Quartet No. 1, each of the four extant string quartets falls respectively into one of Schuman's style-periods.

The Quartet No. 2 was completed in 1937; its three movements (entitled *Sinfonia*, *Passacaglia*, and *Fugue*) reveal an attraction to modern applications of Baroque formal concepts, inherited from Harris. "Despite its ambitious formal scheme," noted critic Mark Lehman retrospectively, "it has (in the light of Schuman's later music) an embryonic quality, its gestures and forms not quite as fully developed as they would soon become."[118] The fifteen-minute work is severe in tone, chromatic in its linear unfolding, and relatively dissonant in its harmonic orientation, with an angular, crabbed quality that would be ironed out in the next style-period. Despite the dissonant chromaticism of the opening movement, there are periodic affirmations of tonality. There is much unison writing, although there is also considerable contrapuntal activity. The influence of Harris is seen in the frequent use of parallelism. The second movement—twice the duration of each outer movement—is even drier overall than the first, although some lyrical moments emerge. The fugal finale is based on a subject whose angular contour and varied rhythmic patterns anticipate the character of themes yet to come. On the whole, the quartet is somewhat ungainly in its articulation, with a gray coloration of harmonic language and little distinctive melody.

As Persichetti aptly noted,

> In his early works Schuman lacked an objective approach. He was terribly anxious to write and loved his measures so fiercely that he was unable to evaluate them fairly. Inferior stuff was mixed with exciting, original material and carried by continuous drive to make the passage come off. Delighted with his ability to produce a variety of colors by combining fourths, he set out to build whole sections and sometimes pieces on these chords by fourths. The harmonic background became pale and tension monotonous, so that there was a drain on his rhythmic and formal resources which sapped the quality of the output.[119]

Schuman's Quartet No. 2 was first performed in New York City in the spring of 1938 by the string quartet of the Composers Forum. It did not appear on recording until 1994, when the Lydian String Quartet included it on a compact disc, together with Quartets Nos. 3 and 5.

Shortly after finishing his second String Quartet, Schuman completed a second symphony. Although he eventually withdrew the work, it had a number of auspicious performances during its short lifetime, prompting considerable discussion and drawing a good deal of attention to the young composer. The symphony was introduced in May 1938 by the WPA Greenwich Village Orchestra, conducted by Edgar Schenkman. Four months later a performance was broadcast on CBS radio, featuring the CBS Symphony under the direction of Howard Barlow. Five months after that, Serge Koussevitzky included the work on a program of the Boston Symphony Orchestra. And that was not its last performance.

The Symphony No. 2 (1937) comprises a single multisectional movement. Perhaps its best-known detail is the C with which the trumpet begins the work; this note is sustained (through judiciously alternated breathing among the section members) for some eight minutes. Against this held note an angular line begins to take shape, soon to become the faster, more rhythmic theme of the *ostinato* section that follows, against which slow, chromatic lines are heard, often in unison. Finally dispensing with the C, a slower section featuring the woodwinds in sequence is followed by the entrance of the brass choir and then of the strings. A *pizzicato* passage is accompanied by stentorian brass unisons, returning then to a variant of the *ostinato* heard earlier. The work concludes with a Harris-like peroration, as pulsating timpani are heard against a chorale in the brass.

Although the work must have seemed very bold and adventurous at the time, it now seems constructed more through abstract artifice than from personal conviction. Perhaps this is what Elliott Carter was referring to when he wrote that it suffered from too obvious a plan, "filled with ideas often of no very great interest."[120]

Schuman himself later recollected, "I had . . . written the piece at a very slow tempo, not only because I heard it that way, but also because the slower the tempo, the fewer the pages, and the lower the copying costs." Referring to the sustained trumpet note, he added, "What I didn't know, in my inexperience, was that the audience was going crazy with that note that wouldn't go away."[121] Most of the critics had something to say about that note. "The striking trick about the score is the almost constant iteration of the note C," wrote the reviewer from the *Boston Monitor.* "The persistent sounding of this note, set off by chords totally unrelated, constitutes a violent assault upon the sensibilities. It is this assault of monotony aggravated by dissonance that marks the score, rather than its adventures in contrapuntal writing."[122] "When in the course of the single movement this pedal tone, mostly carried by a trumpet, is dropped, the listener experiences a blessed sense of relief, as when a dentist removes his drill."[123] Another critic wrote that the note "continued with a fine disregard for whatever else the rest of the orchestra was doing until it beat into the ears of the listeners like the voice of conscience. At a point where it seemed about to cause a mass reaction in the audience the note changed, and an audible sigh went up from all parts of the hall. As an experiment in mass psychology it was extremely interesting, but had that single trumpet blast gone on much longer it might easily have worked a serious effect on an unstable mind."[124]

However, not all the notices were negative. Another critic for the *Baltimore Evening Sun* praised the "sustained 'C' in the trumpet, a note that becomes like a bright object held in a hypnotist's hand, holding one's attention to the point that the rest of the orchestration is heard only as in a haze."[125] Most notable was the reaction of Paul Rosenfeld, a prominent advocate and spokesman of the artistic avant-garde.

In the Second Symphony [Schuman's] structural style has energy and grandeur. The effects are large and ample, the feeling is elevated. . . . The raucous and sensuous sound reflects the world of mechanism and industrial techniques; its closer parallels are in Varèse and Chavez; but it is clear and firm in its own way. One hears it in the lowing, groaning ox-horn-like onset of the piece and the jagged principal subject. The Symphony testifies to the presence of something primitive in the composer's feeling, a fierceness and an earthiness. Indeed, a fixed and almost murderous vehemence seems to express itself in the *ostinato* of the initial movement. . . . To be sure, this seventeen-minute work has been found lacking in rhythmic vitality. . . . The tempo, it is true, is preponderantly *larghissimo*. Still, . . . the little work perfectly deserves its title. Its material appeared to be unified and its effects to converge: it seemed to sustain and fully release, through three contrasting and complementary sections, the tension established by the initial impact. While the *ostinato* of the opening movement has an almost painful insistence, it differs thoroughly from that of Ravel's *Boléro*; there is continual melodic contrast and development. . . . And while there seem to be a couple of repetitious measures in the *finale*, the movement builds strongly to the end. One has the sense of some force, originally fixed and deadly, which is subjected to a new incarnation, and finally moves joyously and with a gesture of embrace out toward life.[126]

However, it appears that Schuman finally agreed with those who were dissatisfied with the work.

Early Style-Period

It is astonishing to note the extraordinary progress that took place in Schuman's compositional development within the two years that separated the Symphony No. 2 from the works of his early style-period. These works reveal both a tremendous increase in competence, as well as a commensurate sense of self-confidence. Moreover, in a work like the *American Festival Overture*, which may be said to have initiated this period in 1939, many of the characteristic devices and stylistic traits that can be traced throughout his compositional career are already apparent: the fondness for polychords; the nervously irregular rhythmic patterns, often based on an oscillation between two adjacent notes, but with irregular accents; simple, driving, dotted-note rhythmic *ostinati*; rapid and abrupt modulations; much use of parallelism, especially at the interval of the fourth or fifth (Harris's adaptation of the ancient principle of *organum*), or of tonally unrelated triads; and copious use of percussion for emphasis. The distinctively brash, bold, and identifiably "American" character emerged as well—but urban rather than rural, distinguishing it from both Harris and Copland. Some might hear in it the spirit of New York City at the time. Compared with the exploratory works described above, thematic material is diatonic and clearly tonal rather than chromatic, and there is a far greater fluency of utterance.

In attempting to characterize Schuman's music at this time, musicologist and critic Nathan Broder made a number of perceptive observations:

> In the period from about 1937 to about 1941 Schuman was so fond of parallel fourths and fifths that their use became a mannerism. . . . As with most of the outstanding composers of this century, harmony is not, as a rule, a structural element in Schuman's large forms; that is to say, he does not normally employ key relationships as a means of binding large sections together. . . . [P]olytonality [is] a favorite device with him. . . . Some pieces . . . end polytonally, but most of them end in a consonant triad. . . . Schuman's rhythms are extremely varied, and while the fundamental pulse-beat may remain regular for long stretches, particularly in slow sections, the metric patterns above this beat shift constantly. . . . He is especially fond of accented off-beats. . . . Since . . . key-relationship has been abandoned as a means of achieving structural coherence, its place is taken by thematic repetition, either in entirely free forms or in free adaptations of old forms. . . . His orchestral colors are usually fresh and sharp, bold and clear, a favorite method being to treat the three main choirs—strings, wood-winds, and brasses—as separate blocks of color. . . . Its most prominent traits are boldness, originality, freshness, resourcefulness, and intensity of feeling. The fast movements are full of an exuberant energy.[127]

Schuman composed the *American Festival Overture* in response to Koussevitzky's encouragement that he continue composing orchestral music, with the assurance that the Boston Symphony would perform it. The title is a reference to a short festival of American music that Koussevitzky had planned for the 1939–1940 concert season. He led the orchestra in the premiere of the overture in Boston, in October 1939. The piece is based entirely on a simple motif that Schuman identified as a familiar boys' street call. Sung to the syllables "wee-awk-eee," the motif consists of three notes, the first falling a minor-third, and the third a return to the original note. This motif, along with a sequence of perfect fourths, thoroughly permeates the overture. Persichetti noted, "Schuman wanted to write . . . music that stemmed directly from the American idiom; he probably wanted to write a piece and summon a public at the same time."[128] Schuman himself later stated, "The *American Festival Overture* is obviously a piece that could only have been composed by someone in his/her twenties or maybe thirties, but not an older person. This overture is a musical pep talk, brash and all those things."[129] Except for a brief passage of reflection, the work is vigorously rousing and emphatically exuberant. Despite its extroverted character, it is saturated with a profusion of brilliant developmental activity. Although much of the melodic articulation is diatonic, there is a great deal of quartal harmony, which imparts a bristling, modern surface. A recording of the overture, featuring Hans Kindler and the National Symphony Orchestra, was released by RCA Victor in 1940, making it the first work of Schuman's to be recorded. Several additional recorded performances have appeared over the years.

American Festival Overture was generally well received by the critics. Olin Downes found it "a lusty piece, full of vitality, and fearless."[130] A twenty-three-year-old Leonard Bernstein noted perceptively "an energetic drive, a vigor of propulsion which seizes the listener by the hair, whirls him through space, and sets him down at will. This involves a buoyance and lust-for-life which I find . . . wholly American."[131] More recently, Edward Seckerson commented concerning the overture, "Schuman's is both music of the land— gritty, pioneering, open—and of the first cityscapes: iron and steel, always reaching outwards and upwards."[132]

The other major work that Schuman completed in 1939 was his String Quartet No. 3. Commissioned jointly by the League of Composers and New York City's Town Hall, this was the composer's first work for hire. The premiere was given by the Coolidge Quartet in February 1940. The first of the work's three movements is entitled "Introduction and Fugue." It begins with a soulful, modal-flavored melody that creates a lonely, searching mood that anticipates the opening of the second half of the Third Symphony. After some contrapuntal elaboration of this melody, the texture becomes homophonic, and a gestural motif is introduced that proves to be the central unifying idea of the entire quartet: a note repeated several times, then, falling on an accented downbeat, resolves down a major-second, in a "scotch-snap" rhythm, as an augmented-fourth resolving to a major-third, within a triadic harmonization. The lively fugue that follows fails to maintain the same level of interest. In the second movement, "Intermezzo," largely diatonic lines are treated in dissonant counterpoint, which again resolve in homophony. The third movement, "Rondo-Variations," combines the essence of those two forms, although, as Nathan Broder pointed out, "each time the rondo theme returns it takes on a different shape, and towards the end there are no episodes at all, but an avalanche of repetitions of the theme in ever new guises."[133] The main theme is unmistakably Schumanian in its contours. Some of the material from this movement was reused two years later in the last movement of the Symphony No. 4.

The generous use of parallelism in the quartet points to the ongoing salient influence of Harris. The work has compelling moments, but many extended developmental passages seem to lack purpose or direction. The severity, introspection, and abstraction of the quartet medium do not allow for the instrumental color and flashy excitement that give so much of Schuman's orchestral music its direct appeal. The work's critical reception has always been mixed, though it has had its admirers. As early as 1946 it found its way onto recording, with a performance that featured the Gordon Quartet, while as recently as 1994, Mark Lehman observed that "the immediately identifiable Schuman *elan* is in full display, with expansive, slowly unfolding adagios leading to propulsive and brilliant allegros."[134]

This Is Our Time: Secular Cantata No. 1, a work for chorus and orchestra, represents Schuman's contribution to the brief trend of socialist realism, American-style, which flourished in the arts during the late 1930s and early 1940s. Though drawn from the writing of socialist poet Genevieve Taggard (1894–1948), the text is quite innocuous, if quaintly naïve and idealistic, with lines like "This is our day,/Our own, our only time./Together we make/Today" and "The idle are the sad./Our day has work to do." The half-hour piece comprises five sections, entitled: "Celebration," "Work," "Foundations," "Questions," and "Fanfares." The second section features only male voices with the orchestra, while the fourth features only female voices. The other three movements utilize the entire chorus. In July 1940 Alexander Smallens conducted the premiere of *This Is Our Time* at the Lewisohn Stadium, at the time a favorite summer music venue in Harlem; the New York Philharmonic was joined by the People's Philharmonic Choral Society, "made up of iron workers, painters, carpenters, workers in shoe factories, housewives and white-collar workers."[135]

Rather than being motivated by a political agenda, Schuman was more concerned that America's finest composers produce music that could be performed by students and amateurs, that is, *Gebrauchsmusik* with no apology. Schreiber quotes Schuman as saying, "Music which the layman can perform is essential if we hope to reach a wide audience."[136] In this work Schuman simplified his language in the interests of facilitating execution for a chorus and orchestra of amateurs. The choral writing is mostly homophonic, with a generous amount of unison, aside from a Handelian fugue in the third section. While the chorus is active, the orchestra tends to be much less active, and vice versa. Revealing little of Schuman's musical personality while avoiding recourse to vernacular elements, the result is remarkably uninteresting from a musical perspective, although, to its credit, the work largely avoids the pitfall of banality. The fourth and fifth sections are probably the most musically inventive, and the work ends with a triumphant exhortation to community cooperation.

The cantata was very well received at the time and enjoyed several additional performances. To critic Henry Simon it celebrated "the American people's time to work, build foundations, laugh and dance. The music . . . says exactly that as well as the words, and the workers' chorus sang it just as hard as it could. The thunderous applause showed that the idea got across, no mistake."[137]

But it was to the symphonic genre that Schuman was drawn most strongly. For him the symphony was a powerful vehicle through which to explore the developmental possibilities of a musical idea, in a manner predicated on the late works of Beethoven, but imbued with a distinctly American vision inspired by the precedent set by Roy Harris. The result was a kind of symphony geared toward the highest standards of absolute music, as defined by the great European works of the past, but expressed in a language filled with terse gestures, brittle sonorities, and jagged rhythms that gave the music a distinctly American and unquestionably modern tone.

In 1941 Schuman composed the masterpiece of his early period—a work that launched him virtually overnight into the pantheon of leading American composers, and remains today his most frequently performed major work: the Symphony No. 3. In reflecting upon its masterly formal complexity, its brilliantly inventive treatment of the orchestra, and the utter self-confidence reflected in the forthright assertiveness of its gestures, one cannot help but agree with critic and archivist Karl Miller, who wrote, "It is incredible to think that this work was written by a man who had heard his first symphony concert only eleven years before."[138] Furthermore, while the symphony is thoroughly rooted in the compositional principles and rhetorical approach of Roy Harris, Schuman applied them with a fluency, an incisive dramatic sense, and an eye to structural economy that exceeded the capabilities of his mentor. A comparison of Harris' Third Symphony (1939) with Schuman's Third makes readily apparent both the latter's adoption of the older man's compositional approach and the vastly greater ease and competence he displayed in achieving its artistic fulfillment. By the age of thirty-one he had already attained a level of sophistication and polish that eluded Harris, whose music never shed the ungainliness that was perhaps its greatest weakness.

Schuman's Third Symphony is scored for a large orchestra and bears a dedication to Serge Koussevitzky. Its four movements are grouped into two parts: "Passacaglia and Fugue" and "Chorale and Toccata." Unlike traditional symphonic music of the prior generation, musical ideas are developed not so much through the analogue of a drama as through variations in rhythmic energy and bodies of sonority. It is pure, abstract music, without any extrinsic reference. Part I begins as the noble *passacaglia* theme is introduced by the violas (highly reminiscent of the opening cello theme of Harris's Third Symphony). This wide-ranging theme strongly suggests a tonic of A, although that implication is soon negated as the "Passacaglia" unfolds. The intervals that comprise the theme, as well as its overall contour, serve as the basis of the entire work. Initially it is treated in canon, with seven entrances, each a half-step higher than the previous one, although the texture never exceeds four voices. This canonic treatment compels one's attention to the dimensions and facets of the theme, while pressing forward with increasing sonority. Four additional variations follow, against variants of the repeating *passacaglia* theme. Each variation introduces a new type of pattern: For example, the first variation introduces an emphatic triplet pattern, contradicted by accents on alternate notes, in the strings. (This sort of forcefully repeated rhythmic pattern is another device inherited from Harris, as are the prevalence of the interval of the fourth, used both melodically and harmonically, and the frequent use of parallelism.) The second variation introduces a gripping harmonic sonority that is a Schuman trademark: an A major triad over a C–G open fifth in the bass, with clashing C-natural against C-sharp. Above this the woodwinds pursue a further variant of the theme. (This variant is similar to one heard in the previous variation; it is characterized by a note followed by one a step lower, then by the first note again, then by one a step lower than the second one. This motivic pattern, whose length may vary, recurs in so many of Schuman's works, especially during this period, that it warrants an identification of its own. In this study it will be identified as "motif WS-a.") The third variation presents a continuous running pattern in the cellos, later joined by the violas, while the violins introduce a free variation of the main theme, beginning very slowly but gradually increasing via faster note-values. A resting point is reached briefly on a similar polychord, A major over C major, before the fourth variation is underway. This passage features an interlocking dotted-rhythm pattern in the strings—another Harris device—while the trombones play a version of the main theme in four-part harmony.

The tension mounts, culminating in the presentation of the subject of the swaggering, boisterous "Fugue," which maintains enough of an intervallic similarity to the *passacaglia* theme to feel at first as if it is simply the next variation. Paralleling the "Passacaglia," the exposition comprises seven entrances of the subject, each a half-step higher than the preceding one. By the seventh entrance, the contrapuntal texture has become so active and complex as to project a near-manic exuberance. An intricate *stretto* featuring only the four trumpets follows, reducing the volume of sonority and leading to a calm episode in striking contrast to the foregoing. This episode, which highlights the woodwinds, is derived from motif WS-a from the "Passacaglia." The muted strings follow with Harris-like parallel triads, at first maintaining the tranquility, but then accumulating energy again, building toward the final section of Part I, heralded by a vigorous timpani solo. The strings enter, picking up an insistent dotted rhythm from the timpani solo. Against this driving rhythmic background the horns enter, blaring out a variant of the *passacaglia* theme in rhythmic augmentation, while retaining elements of motif WS-a. The woodwinds then enter with this line, in shrill canon with the horns. The bass instruments reiterate a pedal E-flat throughout, while other instruments contribute reminiscences of motivic elements, in another manic maelstrom of contrapuntal activity. Finally, the texture begins to solidify as a triumphant D-major tonic over a low B-flat gradually emerges into view. This culminates in the first instance of a trademark (or mannerism) noted earlier, in the general comments on Schuman's style: A reiterated tonic chord (enriched by whatever dissonance), with the fifth in the top voice emphasized through octave leaps. However, in this case, after much reinforcement of the D tonic, the chord suddenly jumps away to a B-major triad as a "stinger."

As Part II begins, the "Chorale" is prepared by the lower strings in gentle modal polyphony, evoking a lonely, nocturnal mood, while suggesting fragments of the chorale theme to follow. In what is perhaps the most beloved trumpet solo in the American symphonic repertoire, the chorale theme is stated, revealing an intervallic affinity with both the *passacaglia* and fugue themes from Part I. This melody is elaborated in a leisurely manner by the trumpet and later by the flute against a background of non-tonally related triads in the strings. This movement, one of the most poignant Schuman ever composed, proves to be something of a "chorale prelude," as a series of variations on the chorale theme follows. The first violins and cellos pursue the theme, against an eighth-note pattern in parallel fifths by the inner string voices, derived from the gentle woodwind episode (motif WS-a) from the "Fugue." A second variation treats the theme in a forceful statement in the woodwinds and strings, in polytonal harmony. An English horn solo leads to the third variation, which features the four horns in solemn two-part counterpoint. A brief trumpet duet brings the "Chorale" to a quiet close.

In one of many striking orchestral touches found in this symphony, the "Toccata" begins with the rhythm of its main theme played quietly on the snare drum. This is answered in quasi-fugal style by a full statement of this lively theme by the bass clarinet, while the snare drum continues in rhythmic counterpoint. The wide-ranging *toccata* theme, which again bears an intervallic affinity with the *passacaglia* theme, spans virtually the entire compass of the instrument. This theme is soon picked up by the remainder of the woodwinds, sometimes in parallelism, as they toss the idea playfully back and forth. There is a more subdued passage as the oboe presents a variant of the theme in augmentation, while the timpani maintains a restless undercurrent. The energy returns as the woodwinds, now reinforced by xylophone, continue the theme in communal interaction, before receding once more. The cellos in unison now introduce a Harris-like interlude. Very flexible in tempo, this passage, in *divisi* strings, has the feeling of a cadenza, largely focused on that woodwind motif from the "Fugue." A rapid, energetic section follows, as the strings develop first the chorale melody in nervous spurts, and then a variant of the fugue subject in a bold statement. The bass instruments join in with an augmented variant of the *toccata* theme, while the strings continue with odd jabbing gestures. A trumpet fanfare and a flurry from the *toccata* theme lead to a texture of busy triplet figures in the strings. Suddenly the accompaniment simplifies into a driving, galloping rhythm, enriched by the piano, as the music breaks into what sounds like a cowboy chase, replete with rim-shots mimicking gunshots, as fragments of the various motifs of the symphony are tossed back and forth, building toward a grandly triumphant peroration.

The premiere of Schuman's Third Symphony was given by the Boston Symphony Orchestra under the direction of Serge Koussevitzky in October 1941. After the Boston performance, the orchestra took the work to New York. The initial response was extraordinarily enthusiastic. Olin Downes called it "the best work by an American of the rising generation,"[139] and it won the first New York Music Critics Circle Award. It was recorded in 1951 by the Philadelphia Orchestra, conducted by Eugene Ormandy, and in 1961 by the New York Philharmonic under the direction of Leonard Bernstein. In 1942, Bernstein had written, "Almost as exciting as hearing the music itself is to observe how Schuman's progress is manifested in the *Third Symphony*—a progress alive, radiant, optimistic. It is, in fact, all one piece—his development and his music—a pattern of health and youth, and work, and hope."[140] Bernstein had also helped Koussevitzky prepare the 1941 premiere and maintained a proprietary attachment to the work for the rest of his life.

From the perspective of some three decades later, Peter G. Davis wrote,

The Third Symphony marked [Schuman's] arrival as a major creative force in contemporary American music. [It] contains all of his stylistic fingerprints, and at the first performance, its muscular power bowled over just about everyone. Even now, the Symphony's aggressive nature and coiled energy can set an audience on its ears. Here for the first time, Mr. Schuman found a format that best suited his penchant for spinning long themes pregnant with developmental possibilities, rhythmic vitality and hard-edged orchestral brilliance. [The work's structure is] a crafty manipulation of Baroque forms filled out with the sort of extravagant optimism, feisty dissonance and forward drive that seemed so much a part of American symphonic music in those days. If the Symphony's rhetorical vision finally has a slightly hollow mechanistic ring, that too was apparently very much a part of the era in which it was written.[141]

On the other hand, Alfred Frankenstein saw this last point somewhat differently: "If historians of the future really want to know what the era of Franklin D Roosevelt was like—its optimism, its energy, its sense of purpose—they ought to go to such works as this."[142]

Steve Swayne points out that both Schuman's Third and Fourth Symphonies "emerged at a time when [he] felt that American composers were obligated to reach the widest audience possible with the highest quality music imaginable, all in order to strengthen the spirit of the American public when world events worked to enervate that spirit. And he did so without drawing upon folk material or nostalgic images of America."[143]

Noted American music scholar H. Wiley Hitchcock wrote of the Third Symphony, "This is *positive* music, music that never wheedles, that asserts rather than implies, that lets you know where it stands, that says, 'Take me or leave me,'"[144] while Mark Lehman, in a survey of American symphonies, wrote of Schuman's Third, "There isn't a more exciting piece in the repertoire."[145]

While noting the close affinity between Schuman's Third and the Third of Harris, Neil Butterworth states, "Schuman's Third Symphony is a remarkable achievement, a totally American work of considerable integrity." In discussing Part I of the work, he asserts, "Schuman has packed an extraordinary amount of material, closely argued development entirely derived from the Passacaglia theme by means of extensive transformation. This is no abstract intellectual exercise but an expression of changing moods and emotions, generating excitement and ecstasy at the climactic points."[146] He adds that the symphony was so successful that Schuman's subsequent works often failed to stand up to the inevitable comparisons.

Schuman's Third Symphony is a landmark in the history of American orchestral music—one of the first native symphonies that might be said to embody the values of Modern Traditionalism. It is not the first, because it was preceded by Copland's Symphony for Organ and Orchestra (1924), Sessions's Symphony No. 1 (1927), and Harris's Symphony 1933 and his Third Symphony. However, Schuman's is the first to display both the compositional skill and communicative appeal to transcend its time and place, so that it maintains its stature to this day.

Schuman completed his Symphony No. 4 in August 1941, two months before the much-heralded premiere of the Third Symphony, so nothing about this work can be attributed to the reception accorded its predecessor, although it has never prompted anything comparable to that response and has remained in the shadows ever since its premiere. Comprising three separate movements, it is about one third shorter in duration than No. 3.

The first movement, which falls into two sections, begins with a slow duet between the English horn, playing a lonely, plaintive, wide-ranging melody, most notable for its repeated first note, and the solo double bass, which reiterates a one-measure ground bass in quarter-notes throughout the section. The texture of this spare opening gradually fills out as several instruments, then whole instrumental sections, join in, in a grand, sweeping line, thickened by Harris-style *organum*, with its perfect intervals in parallel motion. This builds to a sudden *Vigoroso con spirito*. This rapid section is highly contrapuntal. Its main motivic ideas are the *fugato* motif, a falling major-third followed by a rising major-seventh (intervallically related to the ground bass motif), the repeated note idea derived from the English horn solo, and the ground bass motif itself. This section is both brash and contrapuntally active, the repeated-note idea becoming characteristic Schumanian "chatter," offset by more subdued passages. Here is found an early example of the separate, independent planes of sonority that became one of the composer's most distinctive devices, as the strings "chatter" away, while the brasses and bass instruments continue with stately, long-breathed, lines, tenuously related tonally to the other elements. The movement finally culminates in a grand stentorian statement of the *fugato* motif, ending on a major triad. As a whole, the movement is quite complex and has its compelling moments but lacks the strong sense of focus found in the opening section of the Third Symphony.

The second movement, marked, "Tenderly, simply," is the expressive core of the symphony, and its elegant, dignified beauty reaches the listener with great immediacy. Its scoring omits the lower brasses and percussion. The muted first violins play a wide-ranging, lyrical melody clearly based on the *fugato* motif, against repeated minor triads played *pizzicato* by the muted cellos. This "strumming" effect is another favorite Schuman device, used in some of the most profound moments in his music to create a somber, dirge-like effect. The repeated-note idea also plays a role, as the haunting melody is developed among different subgroups of the ensemble. In the contrapuntal woodwind passage that follows there are also reminiscences of motif WS-a from the Third Symphony. A variant of the ground bass from the first movement is then developed in parallel triads in the strings. This is an especially clear example of Schuman's use of consonant triads, unrelated tonally to each other or to the fragments that appear in the flutes and clarinets. A climax is reached as the strings play in unison, against strong repeated notes in the horns. This leads to a return of the poignant ideas from the opening of the movement, but with the addition of material derived from the *fugato* motif, as the movement concludes with quiet gravity.

The third movement opens with material taken in toto directly from the third movement of the String Quartet No. 3, although it diverges from its treatment there after the main motifs have been stated. (This is an early example of Schuman's incorporating and reworking material from an earlier piece within a later one—a practice that he pursued increasingly throughout his career.) These motifs—including the repeated-note idea from the first movement—are then developed through a series of free variations; toward the middle of the movement a rather elaborate *fugato* is introduced, based on all the motifs stated thus far. A timpani solo leads to the forceful final section, which pulls together the motivic material into a fuller, simpler texture. The movement, which has provided little sense of tonal center throughout, finally gravitates to an emphatic finish in C major.

There is no question but that Schuman's Fourth Symphony offers nothing like the concentrated focus, formal clarity, or sheer excitement of the Third. The finale of No. 4 is especially episodic, rambling, and discursive, with a sense of being "forced" through development procedures as a matter of course, rather than conviction. On the other hand, though still reflecting the strong influence of Harris, Schuman's own voice is beginning to emerge, and there is much about the work that represents an inevitable step forward from its predecessor.

The premiere of Schuman's Symphony No. 4 took place in January 1942—just six weeks after the bombing of Pearl Harbor. The Cleveland Orchestra, which had commissioned it, was conducted by Artur Rodzinski. After the tremendous success of No. 3, a more subdued response to the new work was both predictable and inevitable, and, indeed, the general critical response was that it was something of a let-down. Virgil Thomson noted with supercilious condescension: "I found it vague and more than a little diffuse. . . . [Schuman] writes pleasant little exercises in free counterpoint that go along nicely but that lack definition. . . . I should like to put him to work writing incidental music for plays or doing ballet scores. I fancy the necessity of making music say something briefly and clearly and simply might be a valuable experience for him. He has an agreeable kind of boisterousness, also, that should be fun to dance to."[147]

Nearly forty years later, in his brief retrospective study, Christopher Rouse commented that the symphony "lacked the monolithic monumentality and heroic grandeur—not to mention the fascinating structural cohesiveness—of its predecessor, and it remains to this day less popular."[148] In his study of the American symphony, Butterworth noted acutely,

> The Fourth Symphony has several features in common with its predecessor, the Harris-like non-functional triadic harmony, the frequent segregation of the separate orchestral groups, and the long non-repetitive cantilenas symptomatic of Schuman's freedom in melodic manipulation. What is missing is the single-minded unity of form and material that is the strength of the Third Symphony. The vital sense of inevitability is absent where thematic development is diffuse with little feeling of spontaneity. For example, the fugue for strings in the middle of the finale is contrived, more an academic exercise than natural symphonic argument. Too often the composer relies on his own formulae when inspiration flags. Nevertheless there are some fine passages, the curious opening wind dialogue over a walking bass, the lush sonorities of the chorale in the slow movement and the bold writing for brass throughout the symphony.[149]

On the other hand, in 2003 Mark Lehman expressed his conviction that the work "has all of the composer's trademark elements—springy syncopations, propulsive and brightly-scored polyphony, chromatically enriched chorales, and brassy, percussion-laced outbursts setting off or superimposed on slow, sinuous, string-dominated cantabiles."[150]

Schuman's Symphony No. 4 did not appear on recording until 1969, when an LP was issued featuring the Louisville Orchestra, under the direction of Jorge Mester. There have been several additional recordings of the work since then, including a CD reissue of the Louisville reading.

Schuman had completed a piano concerto in 1938, but he wasn't pleased with it and continued to modify it until 1942, when it finally reached a state that satisfied him. The work is scored for a small chamber orchestra; some early commentators identified the influence of jazz, although this may have simply been the reaction to hearing syncopated rhythms on the piano. Uncharacteristically neoclassical in effect, the outer movements are lean in texture, and brusque, acerbic, and feisty in character, with none of the grandiosity so central to Schuman's mature compositional personality. Its origin in 1938, during the composer's "exploratory phase," probably accounts for the concerto's unusual character and its divergence from the kind of music he had been composing at the time of its completion. It is not the sort of work generally described as "pianistic"; that is, it does not draw upon the instrument's richness of sonority but rather treats it as a pitched percussion instrument, for the most part playing a single line, although this line is often reinforced by another line in parallel motion. The first movement, "With energy and precision," is essentially based on two simple, straightforward ideas: The first is a syncopated motif, introduced by the piano alone at the outset; the second is a stepwise motif, in contrary motion (or "mirror-writing"), presented by the orchestra immediately after the first. These two ideas are subjected to intense development with much rhythmic interplay.

The slow movement, "Deliberately," is again the high point of the work, with moments of haunting, poignant contemplation. The opening is clearly derived from the first motif from the opening movement. Here the piano's contribution is often quite dissonant, in contrast to the straightforward, diatonic material presented simultaneously by the orchestra. The expressive content of the movement is dramatic, and, at times, rather beautiful, in "romantic" ways that were less than natural to Schuman, and hence a little awkward. On the other hand, Lehman found the second movement to be "the least persuasive movement . . . a chorale that builds relentlessly to a big, chordal, heavily-treading climax before subsiding into a wistful, Coplandesque coda."[151]

The second movement leads directly, *attacca*, into the third, a rapid, nervous, *toccata*-like movement based on a two-measure motif that turns back on itself rhythmically, in a mirror-like fashion, and the stepwise motif from the opening. Contrary motion is a pervasive aspect of this movement. The roles of the piano and the orchestra at times seem unrelated to each other. Lehman writes, "The piano part in this concerto is unusual but effective: it's chunky and tough sounding, like a squat local hoodlum."[152]

The Piano Concerto is not one of Schuman's more successful works, having found favor with few soloists. It does not reveal a personal voice of its own, nor does it share the qualities that were beginning to form his musical personality during the early 1940s. The premiere took place at an all-Schuman concert in New York City in January 1943. The soloist was Rosalyn Tureck (soon to be known as the "High Priestess of Bach"), and Daniel Saidenberg conducted the Saidenberg Sinfonietta. The first recording of the concerto was released in 1978, with Gary Steigerwalt as soloist. David Epstein conducted the MIT Symphony Orchestra.

A work with an unusual history is Schuman's *A Free Song: Secular Cantata No. 2*. After the composer's long-standing neurological disorder prevented him from joining the Armed Forces during World War II, he decided to make his patriotic contribution through music. This work, composed in 1942, and a short orchestral piece, *Prayer in Time of War*, written the following year, represent the fruits of this effort. Scored for chorus and orchestra, *A Free Song* was based on poems from Walt Whitman's "Drum Taps," texts that inspired the creativity of a number of American composers at that time.[153] The work is in two parts. The first, based on "Too Long, America," and "Look Down, Fair Moon," introduces the work's main motif: the interval of the second, both major and minor. This section identifies the current situation: After years of peace, we must now face "crises of anguish." Much of the choral writing is declamatory and unison. Purely musical values seem not always to be paramount; the dominance of text thus achieved resembles other creative works of populist patriotism from that time, giving the work a dated, heavy-handed quality from a later perspective. At one point a baritone solo, "Look down, fair moon, and bathe this scene," is accompanied by quarter-note chords in the lower strings, *pizzicato*, creating the dirge-like "strumming" effect noted in the discussion of the Fourth Symphony.

Part Two opens with a rather elaborate fugue whose perky subject, based on the interval of the second (and with a subtle reminiscence of motif WS-a), is introduced by the bass clarinet, and taken up in turn by the remaining clarinets, before being joined by the other woodwinds, then the strings, then the horns. This is perhaps the most musically interesting portion of the work. If Part One served as a statement of the current plight, Part Two, a setting of "Song of the Banner at Daybreak," points to the goal of victory. After the fugue, the voices enter with, "O, a new song, a free song," treated contrapuntally. As in many of Schuman's choral works, words are used as rhythmic gestures in a characteristic way that might be described as "percussive." The work ends with an affirmation that in the "jubilant shouts of millions of men, we hear Liberty!"

A Free Song was introduced in Boston in March 1943, with Serge Koussevitzky conducting the Harvard Glee Club, the Radcliffe Choral Society, and the Boston Symphony Orchestra. The work seems to have achieved its exhortative purpose, immediately prompting a positive audience response, and winning the first Pulitzer Prize given for music, although one suspects that this award was based on patriotic, rather than musical, considerations.[154] However, other professionals were (perhaps envious, perhaps not) less enthusiastic. The day after the premiere, which had been broadcast widely, Copland wrote to Schuman, "Typical Schuman in conception and orchestration; full of imagination on the instrumental side . . .;—but the choral writing not my dish, giving the whole a somewhat forced impressiveness."[155] A few days later, Schuman wrote back, "It can't possibly sound forced because it isn't. Take it from me Aaron it's a swell piece and it would have swept you right along [if you had heard the live performance rather than a broadcast]."[156] Shortly thereafter, the typically dour composer and sometime-critic Arthur Berger wrote to Copland, "Schuman has achieved a real low in his Free Song."[157] On the other hand, in 1985, Karl Miller described *A Free Song* as "a positive statement inspiring patriotism."[158] The work has been revived sporadically during the ensuing years, but it has never been recorded and remains a work that is cited more often than it is heard.

In the summer of 1943, Schuman completed his Symphony No. 5, which he subtitled "Symphony for Strings." Commissioned by the Koussevitzky Foundation, it is a relatively short, concise work in three movements with a total duration of less than twenty minutes. The first movement, *Molto agitato ed energico*, is brisk and vigorous. Much of its character is shaped by a repeated-note figuration and by the use of continual hemiola, that is, three-against-two rhythmic interactions. The main thematic idea—a lengthy twelve-measure statement presented by the violins in unison—comprises several motifs: a rapid repeated-note idea, a slower three-note figure whose intervals shift frequently, and the familiar motif WS-a. The movement has something of a *sonata-allegro* feeling, although there is no real Theme II. (Persichetti identifies a Theme II, or "B," as he calls it, but it is clearly derived from the main theme.[159]) The exposition explodes with energy, as the various elements of the theme are elaborated contrapuntally—and often canonically—without regard for the bracing dissonances that result. The rhythmic drive finally comes to rest on a series of long-held polychords. This ushers in a more homophonic treatment of the material, followed by further contrapuntal development. There is a modified recapitulation, with still more development, until the movement gradually pulls together triadically, reaching a solid conclusion on a unison.

The slow movement, *Larghissimo*, is the longest and most deeply affecting movement of the symphony. It opens in characteristic fashion with full polychords played by the muted strings. The outer voices of the chords move stepwise but in contrary motion, the lower chords presented in second inversion. The violins then present a melodic line in which the interval of the fourth plays a dominant role, accompanied by tonally unrelated triads in the lower strings. Their juxtaposition creates a poignant effect. This all proves to be introductory to the doleful, dirge-like body of the movement, accompanied by slowly "strummed" chords in some of the cellos, while the others hold sustained triads. Over them a heartfelt melody unfolds, based on both the stepwise upper voice from the opening, and the violin melody that followed. As this develops, the second violins enter with the melody in canon, while the first violins continue contrapuntally. Then the violas enter in canon with the same melody against the two violin lines, while the cellos continue their "strumming" accompaniment. The mood begins to shift as the first violins begin one of those Harris-like persistent rhythmic *ostinati*. They then continue the melody, doubled two octaves lower by the cellos, while the inner voices pursue a busy sixteenth-note pattern. This finally builds to a broad climax on the polychords with which the movement opened, after which the energy recedes in a quiet, dissonant chorale reminiscent of the introductory melody, as the movement comes to a quiet close.

The finale, *Presto*, is not one of Schuman's stronger movements, although it opens impressively with one of the first appearances of the sort of urgent, breathless rhythmic pattern that was to become one of the composer's most distinctive traits. The movement is in *rondo* form, and it is the episodes that suffer from an uncharacteristic banality. The "refrain," or *rondo*, is based on the interval of the second. Within a consistent 2/2 meter are subsumed a variety of other metrical patterns, as skittish motivic fragments are tossed around in unpredictable rhythms. *Pizzicato* passages bound up and down from one instrumental section to another, in a way that some have likened to the third movement of Tchaikovsky's Fourth Symphony, although the similarity ends there. The first episode, though derived from the major-second, presents a baldly diatonic major-key melody played by the first violins, in a skipping rhythmic pattern suggesting an American folk dance, while the *pizzicati* continue underneath. In the second episode the violas introduce a pentatonic-flavored melody, answered canonically by the cellos. As the other instruments enter with flowing counterpoint, some continue to coincide on the beat while others shift to off-beats, which creates a muddy effect unless played with impeccable precision. Finally, the *rondo* material returns, now joined by reminiscences of the episodes. An extended passage in hemiola follows, which is soon consolidated into a simpler texture, driving the music to a decisive and affirmative conclusion.

Schuman's Fifth Symphony was introduced in Boston in November 1943, once again by the Boston Symphony Orchestra conducted by Serge Koussevitzky. The initial response was extremely positive, as illustrated by Rudolph Elie Jr., who wrote, "It is evident that William Schuman is well on his way to becoming the foremost American-born composer of the day."[160] The symphony was heard frequently thereafter, and a recording appeared in 1947, with Edgar Schenkman conducting the Concert Hall Symphony Orchestra, followed by several others during the ensuing years.

In 1980 Rouse attempted to place the work in context, stating, "As taut and concise as the Symphony No. 3 is expansive and majestic, the Fifth Symphony remains one of Schuman's most popular works, representing at its best his early dynamically affirmative style."[161] Lehman noted similarly, "It is a beautifully shaped and sustained work, more compact and classical in structure than the Third, replacing a little of the freshness and exuberance of the Third with deeper, more introspective emotion in its expressive central Larghissimo."[162]

However, Michael Fleming's contention that the Fifth is "by general consensus the best of Schuman's 10 symphonies"[163] is preposterous. Enthusiasm for the work has not been unanimous. After its first performance in London, Malcolm Barry dismissed it, stating that it had "just enough spice to make the piece sound modern, enough notes to demonstrate the players' techniques, but also enough disposability to make the piece completely forgettable."[164] Aside from the eloquent, long-breathed slow movement, much of the work is routine, relying on devices—polychords, themes dominated by the interval of the fourth—used so frequently as to verge on mannerisms. The prolific American music scholar Nicholas Tawa finds the symphony both erratic and unconvincing.[165] Perhaps even Schuman was aware that his work needed to grow broader and deeper, lest he fall into a rut.

Middle Style-Period

In 1945 (the year he assumed the presidency of the Juilliard School), William Schuman entered a new phase in his creative work, with his score to Antony Tudor's ballet *Undertow*. The principles of composition that he had learned from Roy Harris had been absorbed and integrated into his creative thinking. No longer was he expressing himself through his mentor's musical language; he had his own voice now, somewhat analogous to the "International Style" in architecture—bold, urbane, and confident, with clashing metallic sonorities, hard-edged planes of sound, and nervous, tightly coiled rhythms. His music was no longer so relentlessly exuberant and affirmative; it became more reflective as well as more complex, and began to explore a fuller range of human emotion, including tragic feelings. Most of Schuman's greatest works appeared during this period.

Schuman had been commissioned in 1944 by the celebrated choreographer Antony Tudor to create the music for a new ballet he was conceiving. Polisi provides a fascinating account of the evolution of their collaboration.[166] Tudor's scenario was concerned with

> the emotional development of a transgressor. The choreographic action depicts a series of related happenings, the psychological implications of which result in an inevitable murder. The hero is seen at various stages, beginning with his babyhood when he is neglected by his mother who leaves him hungry while she seeks the embrace of her husband. The frustrations engendered by this episode are heightened during boyhood and adolescence by his sordid experiences in the lower reaches of a large city. He encounters prostitutes, street urchins, an innocent young girl, a gay bridal couple, carousing dipsomaniacs, and a visiting mission worker whose friendship and care he seeks. The emotions aroused in the abnormal youth by these episodes—revulsion, rage, terror, loneliness, fear of domination—result in climax after climax, reaching a peak in his murder of a lascivious woman. It is only when he is apprehended for this crime that his soul is purged by the tremendous relief that . . . he will no longer be called upon to endure the anguish of being a misfit and an outcast among his fellow men.[167]

Tudor was remarkably specific in identifying the kinds of scenes and emotions he wanted Schuman to evoke, and did not hesitate to express his dissatisfaction when he felt that the results did not suit his needs. However, Schuman—perhaps realizing that his collaborator was setting a higher standard than he had encountered before and that he stood to learn a great deal from this experience—tolerated Tudor's ruthless criticism and made every effort to meet his demands. In retrospect, the often haughty composer regarded their collaboration as "one of the most productive and satisfying artistic experiences of my career."[168] Whether it was the experience of working with Tudor that led the composer to discover within himself a deeper range of musical expression or simply that Tudor had approached him at a time when he was ready to try something new and different is hard to determine.

For concert use, Schuman condensed the material into a symphonic suite, which he entitled *Undertow: Choreographic Episodes for Orchestra*. This music is subdivided into three sections, which follow one another without pauses: "Prologue: Birth and Infancy," "The City: Adolescence and Manhood," and "Epilogue: Guilt." Persichetti notes that this concert version "succeeds in shaping [the music] for symphonic requirements independent of the ballet. [Schuman] contracted the music with such ingenuity that a completely new form evolved."[169] Persichetti then proceeds with a detailed analysis of the score.[170] However, as probing as his analysis may be, it does not describe the music in a manner that corresponds to what the listener is likely to perceive without benefit of intensive score study.

But what is unmistakable to the listener is the entirely different realm of expression that Schuman had entered in this work, in comparison to his earlier efforts. Not only had his musical language itself become more dissonant and its approach to tonality more ambiguous, but it was less focused on purely abstract formal processes and more on evoking the moods and emotional states indicated in the attached scenario, and among them are feelings new to Schuman's expressive palette: desolation, great anxiety, violence, and so forth. The chief musical elements of the work are the interval of a minor-third, and a simple, diatonic hymn melody that appears toward the middle and recurs several times. This melody is anticipated toward the beginning of the work by a motif built from the tonic, the note a fourth below it, and the note a fourth above it. However, despite Schuman's effort to create an autonomous musical structure, the score, though compelling in many ways, does not achieve a natural fluency and sense of coherence. At many points it sounds like a sequence of "tracks" strung together from the score to an intense, gripping film noir from the 1940s. *Undertow* proved to be something of a first attempt for Schuman; he would accomplish a true, musically autonomous choreographic work within a few years.

The premiere of *Undertow* was given by Ballet Theatre at New York's Metropolitan Opera House in April 1945. The conductor was Antal Dorati. Apparently the work as a whole received a mixed reception, although Schuman's music was well received. Perhaps most notably, the influential critic Virgil Thomson, who had been quite disparaging of Schuman's earlier efforts, felt that this new work represented a breakthrough. In a devastating recapitulation of the composer's earlier efforts, Thomson wrote,

> His workmanship is skillful, individual, striking. His expressivity has always been tenuous, timid, conventional. His serious works have shown a respectable seriousness of attitude without much private or particular passion, while his gayer ones have expressed either a standard American cheerfulness or the comforting bumptiousness of middle-quality comic-strip humor. . . . [H]is music has been, on the whole, reticent, has communicated to the public little about himself or about anything else.

However, after hearing the music to *Undertow*, Thomson described Schuman as "a man of high, of spectacular expressive gifts who has been constricted by the elegant abstractions of the American concert style."[171] The first performance of the concert version of *Undertow* was given in November 1945 by the Los Angeles Philharmonic, under the direction of Alfred Wallenstein. The first recording was released in 1951, with the composer himself conducting the Louisville Orchestra.

Reviewing the concert suite without having seen the ballet, composer Normand Lockwood found the music to be "positive and exciting. It contains satire and characterization . . . ; and even where the music does not clearly underline any specific action or topic, it is always expressive of one mood or another. It is especially arresting in its orchestration which, in spite of the orchestra's size, is economical and taut."[172]

Commenting on a recording of *Undertow* that appeared in 1954, Irving Fine wrote, "The music easily matches the story in neurotic intensity. When I saw the ballet in Boston sometime during its first season, I must confess I found it quite unpleasant. My prejudices against shock art were considerably stronger in those days than they are now. However, I remember also being somewhat irritated by what I felt was a certain pretentiousness and facile intellectualism in the idea behind the ballet." But, hearing this recording of the musical score alone, he continued, "Schuman has traveled a great distance since *Undertow*. . . . And although he continues to grow in stature, it is good to see how well his early works stand the passage of time. In many ways they sound even better today than they did before."[173] As late as 1985, Karl Miller described *Undertow* as "almost an American equivalent of Bartók's *Miraculous Mandarin*. Schuman, like Bartók, explored some of the darker sides of human experience and produced a stark score that forcefully supports the ballet scenario."[174]

Not long after the completion of *Undertow*, Schuman was approached for another musical score to accompany choreography, this time by Martha Graham, then at the height of her eminence. Commissioned by the Elizabeth Sprague Coolidge Foundation, she was developing the scenario for a work based on the Oedipus myth. Impressed by what she had heard of Schuman's music, she solicited his interest in her project. Aware that she had worked with many of the most important composers of the day, he was eager for such a collaboration. After his experience with the demanding Tudor, he expected much the same specificity from Graham. But he was surprised to receive from her a detailed scenario in which she elaborated her choreographic conception, but without explicit indications of mood or emotion. However, he found that by prodding her, he was able to elicit what he felt he needed. She proved to be somewhat more flexible than Tudor, and expected a fluid mutual influence between the two of them. Schuman later acknowledged that she had exerted an influence on the actual music he composed.[175]

Printed in the score is a program note, in which Schuman wrote,

In *Night Journey*, Martha Graham's dramatization of this myth, it is not Oedipus but Jocasta who is the protagonist. The action turns upon that instant of Jocasta's death when she relives her destiny, sees with double insight the triumphal entry of Oedipus, their meeting, courtship, marriage, their years of intimacy which were darkly crossed by the blind seer, Tiresias, until at last the truth burst from him. The chorus of women who know the truth before the seer speaks it, vainly try to divert the prophecy from its cruel conclusion.[176]

The premiere of *Night Journey* took place in May 1947 during a symposium on music criticism held at Harvard. Graham herself took the role of Jocasta, while Erick Hawkins represented Oedipus. The orchestra was conducted by Louis Horst, and the set was designed by Isamu Noguchi. Initially, the work as a whole was not well received, but gradually its stature grew, and it has remained an active part of the Graham repertory. Schuman did not prepare a concert version of his music until 1981, when *Night Journey: Choreographic Poem for Fifteen Instruments* was published. Scored for woodwind quintet, piano, and strings, this version, approximately 25 percent shorter in duration than the music as choreographed, eliminated elements required for theatrical presentation.

The concert version of *Night Journey* suggests a stark, gripping fatalism, achieved with an incisive sense of intimacy. It represents a further step in the direction initiated in *Undertow*: dark and introspective, with an increasing degree of harmonic dissonance and tonal ambiguity. Although still somewhat episodic and overextended, it is more successful as an autonomous, integrated musical structure than *Undertow*. Its main motivic elements are the horn line—descending with a turnaround at the end—that begins the work, and an ascending line with a turnaround at the end, first played by the oboe a few moments later. These are heard in several variants throughout the work, most notably in combination with each other, the first motif tagged onto the end of the second. These serve more as anchors of familiarity than as generative material. But in addition to these motifs are harmonic sonorities and conceptual gestures that serve as structural elements—a direction the composer would continue to pursue in subsequent works. The most prominent conceptual gesture is the tension produced by the two motifs heard simultaneously, in contrary motion, in alternation as the ascending lines move off the beat while the descending lines change on the beat. Related to this is a pattern of dissonant, rapidly ascending and descending lines in similar motion, and irregular meter. Perhaps the most notable recurrent harmonic sonority is the striking consonance of a sustained minor triad in the strings, heard against the descending motif on pitches in sharp tonal conflict with that triad. It is through such devices that Schuman developed his often-noted presentation of discrete planes of simultaneous activity.

The first performance of the concert version of *Night Journey* was given in Albany, New York, by the Endymion Ensemble, conducted by Jon Goldberg, in February 1981. This same group made the first recording of the work in 1984. Typical of the unsympathetic dismissals of Schuman's music common during the 1970s and 1980s, Joshua Kosman found *Night Journey* to exemplify the composer's "characteristically bland, unobjectionable style."[177] However, to Schuman champion Karl Miller, this was among the composer's "most introspective works . . . a stark score of unnerving intensity."[178]

Schuman completed his Symphony No. 6 on the last day of 1948. Commissioned by the Dallas Symphony Orchestra and its conductor Antal Dorati, the work represents a remarkable advance in both expressive range and symphonic technique, relative to the Symphony No. 3, written just seven years before. It is also the first of Schuman's symphonies to reveal full emancipation from the dominating influence of Harris. By general consensus it is the greatest of Schuman's symphonies,[179] and justifiably so (although a convincing case can also be made for the Symphony No. 9). The most serious and demanding piece he had composed thus far, it is a continuation along the same lines as his other recent works: extremely serious, thoroughly abstract in its concerns, with little perceptible tonal focus, and a constantly high level of harmonic dissonance. The Sixth explores the outer reaches of the composer's expressive range, resulting in a harsh vision of searing intensity.

The work comprises six discernible sections, all integrated into a single movement. In a deeply penetrating commentary, Persichetti identifies the work's thematic elements: the somber series of chords with which it opens, which functions as the basis of a *passacaglia*; a chromatically rising melody first heard in the violins before the previous idea has been stated fully; and a rapid, filigreed theme introduced by the flute several moments later.[180] The development of these elements builds a coherent, thoroughly integrated musical structure, although the thematic ideas themselves are too complex, and their treatment too dense, for most listeners to grasp initially. Rather, the listener first approaching the work encounters an opening *Largo*, as several snarling, menacing chords built around major-minor conflict, give rise to a series of variations. These variations are characterized by an ever-increasing melodic intensity, articulated with severe restraint, to display an icy beauty. During this section, the third idea, heard in the flute, flutters far above the slowly unfolding *passacaglia* variations, as if inhabiting another affective realm altogether. The second section, *Moderato con moto*, is marked by an increase in the level of motoric energy, while the counterpoint continues to build in density, punctuated by interjections of dissonant chords that increase the sense of rhythmic drive. A timpani solo serves as transition to the third section, *Leggieramente*, which is lighter in texture and fleeter in tempo, with characteristically nervous, irregular rhythmic patterns abounding. This is followed by the dolorous *Adagio*, a reminder of the frigid eloquence of the melodic counterpoint heard in the opening section. A violin solo of rarefied beauty takes on a dirge-like quality as Schuman's familiar pulsating chords, strummed *pizzicati* in the lower strings, serve as accompaniment. The fifth section, *Allegro risoluto; presto*, is the most aggressively active—even violent—part of the symphony. The percussion play a major role, setting off Schuman's frantically edgy rhythms, with rapid jumps among the various orchestral choirs, and some extremely difficult instrumental writing. A searing melody in the strings, heard over jagged brass dissonances, ushers in the concluding *Larghissimo*. The energy recedes during this final section, bringing the work to a quiet, somber close on a major-minor chord, much as it began, before gradually fading away. Despite the largely atonal impact of the symphony as a whole, this conclusion anchors the work in tonality.

Antal Dorati led the Dallas Symphony Orchestra in the premiere of Schuman's Sixth Symphony in February 1949. In a program note, Dorati wrote: "It has to be said here that to this writer the construction of the work seems fundamentally new; pointing more to the future than leaning on the past. At the same time, it is put forth with extreme assurance and clarity, void of any trait or feeling of experimentation"[181] However, the Dallas premiere did not go well, and the work was so poorly received that there was talk of withholding part of the commissioning fee.[182] Schuman was very disappointed by the performance itself and badly stung by the poor reception.

However, Eugene Ormandy took an interest in the work and performed it in Philadelphia two years later. Speaking to the audience before a public rehearsal, Schuman acknowledged the work's disastrous reception in Dallas but explained that it "really sounds the way I want it to sound, that I am well aware that hearing it for the first time presents formidable problems with which I am most sympathetic, but which I do not have the power to change." He urged the audience to try to "understand" the work, but explained, "By understanding I do not mean . . . technical understanding. . . . I mean that at each point in the course of listening there is absence of aural chaos and realization of the presence of coherent musical expression."[183]

Schuman's clearly articulated comments raise an important question that has plagued Modernist music throughout the past century: If a work requires multiple hearings before it begins to "make sense" and if the listener fails to be captivated by anything about the work on an initial hearing, why would the listener choose to hear it a second time? This is a question prompted repeatedly in this study, despite the fact that the three composers discussed are generally held to be "traditionalists."

However, the fact remains that Schuman's Sixth Symphony enjoyed repeated performances, as well as a stunning recording by the Philadelphia Orchestra under Ormandy's direction, released in 1955, which made the work available to a wide audience. Although the symphony has never become a favorite among general listeners, it has attained a stature over the years—especially among composers and other professionals—that might not have been anticipated at the time of its initial presentation.

One of the first to recognize its merit was composer-critic Charles Jones, who was initially impressed by its "musical architecture," which he found to be "the key to the whole work. A passacaglia, a set of variations, a fugue, and a cadenza for timpani are some of the shapes in which the form of the piece is cast." But he was aware that most listeners do not approach an unfamiliar work by focusing on its structure. "I think that even without this understanding the piece may be able to take over on its own, for it is full of the sort of high-powered orchestral sound that pleads its cause from the very edge of the footlights. On the other hand, a work so strongly and urgently stated cannot be accused of facile audience appeal, and major cities should be given a chance to hear it. Its demands are too great both for more modestly equipped orchestras and their conductors."[184]

The initial critical reactions reveal an awareness of the challenges posed by the symphony. Nathan Broder described it as

> one of Schuman's finest works, powerful and passionate. More subtle and complex than his earlier symphonies, it does not yield all of its secrets on one or two hearings. Once one becomes acquainted with the themes, following what happens to them becomes an exciting adventure. . . . The writing is primarily linear, yet the principal lines are now set against others of equal vitality and almost equal interest, and the result is a rich, live texture. The idiom, as usual with this composer, is a dissonant one (simultaneous major and minor thirds play an important part here) and steadfastly declines to lull the ear, yet there are many passages of a pungent beauty and the final pages are exquisitely poetic.[185]

As the Sixth became more familiar, positive reactions were encountered more frequently. Published comments stated, "The Symphony is beautifully written—superlative in craftsmanship."[186] "Here is a sincere and serious work, a craggy composition in a style that is individual in its romanticized neo-classicism. It is a composition tightly wrought in its rhythmic impulses and astringent in its harmonies."[187] "In terms of stylistic range, extremes of dynamics and color, contrapuntal and rhythmic virtuosity, and general demands made on the executant capacities of the orchestra, there is nothing quite like this work in the annals of mainstream American symphonism. . . . The dramatic impact of the piece can be described only as shattering."[188]

Although the symphony fell victim to some of the anti-Schuman sentiment that developed during his later years, as voiced by Michael Fleming who patronizingly dismissed the work as "the product of a diligent workman with a second-rate talent,"[189] the Sixth continues to be held in awe for the most part—especially among Schuman's admirers. Louis Blois felt that the work "summarizes the Schuman-American experience of the 1940s," finding it "a feast of impassioned cantilena, and bracing, syncopated exchanges between orchestral groups. Almost every moment boasts a virtuoso event: the cowpoking orchestral fugato, the apocalyptic declamation for solo tympani, the radiant adagio, the ecstatic accumulation of the finale."[190] Miller described it as "perhaps, Schuman's most profound musical statement."[191] While acknowledging that the work may be "rough listening for some," he predicted that

it may end up being one of the most moving listening experiences you will ever have. . . . Schuman's harmonic style is perhaps at its most dissonant in his Sixth Symphony. That constant crossrelation of major versus minor within the context of a polychordal harmonic structure provides an almost constant tension throughout the work. . . . Upon reflection one might see Schuman's Sixth Symphony as a commentary on the horrors of war, but on one occasion when I pressed him to discuss this implication the composer responded, "I wrote the first measures and I was on my way. The entire piece is derived from those opening measures." While much of his music is filled with such optimism, this work stands out amongst his entire oeuvre as almost being defiant, perhaps even contemptuous, filled with anger, yet ending with a profound sense of remorse.[192]

Butterworth writes of Schuman's Sixth,

Probably the finest of the cycle of symphonies, it contains dark brooding music with aggressively vigorous passages of rhythmical energy. Although it earned warm approval, the Sixth Symphony never achieved wide popularity, probably on account of its overriding pessimism. In its compact single movement form, [it] covers a vast gamut of moods, from dark despair to wild exertion, similar in some features to the symphonies of one of Schuman's contemporaries, Shostakovich, but achieved with totally different musical means. The gloomy pessimism and sheer ferocity of utterance that characterize the music have mitigated against its popular acceptance. Live performance would have both a disturbing and invigorating effect upon players and audience; the Sixth is not a comfortable or comforting work. It is, however, because of, not in spite of, the uncompromising language that Schuman's Sixth Symphony occupies a major position in the symphonic output of American composers this century.[193]

One may readily infer from these comments that Schuman's Sixth strikes many as somewhat cold, dry, and impersonal. But those who feel an affinity for Schuman's language and overall mode of discourse are likely to find its brilliant concentration of content and tautness of energy both convincing and compelling, despite a harmonic language that is largely atonal in effect, if not in theory.

Listeners who find the Sixth Symphony too abstract and detached may find a more accessible point of entry into the heart of Schuman's work in *Judith*, a "Choreographic Poem" commissioned by the Louisville Orchestra for Martha Graham, and conceived as a work for solo dancer and orchestra, somewhat along the lines of a "concerto," and completed in 1949. While it is less austere and complex than the symphony, it is much more fluent formally than *Undertow*. As composer William Bergsma observed, despite an impressively "grand design" of great technical difficulty, "its importance lies in its content of rich, controlled emotion."[194] Persichetti noted, "This dramatic and mature work contains numerous episodes and outbursts that are tightly integrated by potent thematic material."[195] It may be argued that in this work Schuman optimized the balance between expressive intensity and formal unity and concision more profoundly and successfully than in any other work he had composed thus far—and perhaps more than in any he would compose in the future.

The subject matter of *Judith* is the episode from the Apocrypha in which a beautiful Israelite widow saves the Jews from the tyrannical Holofernes by charming him into a drunken stupor and then cutting off his head. The music itself has a dramatic, narrative quality that suggests a "symphonic poem." Its vividness readily prompts the listener's imagination to envision the story and its loftiest implications through a succession of five compelling sections that seem to evoke moods of enraged dignity, violence, lamentation, and triumph. Therefore one may be surprised to learn that Schuman composed the music before Graham had decided on the subject matter, beyond a general theme of archetypal womanhood. The two had discussed the structure and character of the music in only the most abstract terms.[196]

Conveying the sense of narrative are the most distinctive features of the composer's mature language: free-flowing, highly chromatic contrapuntal lines stabilized by a foundation of nonfunctional triads—major, minor, and major-minor; instrumental choirs moving in separate and sometimes seemingly incongruous textural and tonal planes; an eerily effective use of polytonality; angular melodic lines that culminate in a highly personal, jagged counterpoint; brittle, nervously irregular rhythms; and passages of hard-bitten hocketing in the woodwinds and brasses. In this work usages abound that soon found their way into the music of many other American composers.

The first section of *Judith*, marked *Adagio*, introduces the two main motif-groups. Opening with a characteristic harmonic sonority—a major-minor triad with the minor-third in the bass and the major-third on top—the first, motif (a), is simply a vacillating half-step up and down. But this simple activity is but the top line of a series of chords: triads over a dissonant bass line. The elaboration of this motif eloquently evokes a threatening sense of portent. The passage builds in intensity to a ferocious, hard-bitten outburst in the trumpets and trombones that finds release in the proclamation of a major-ninth, the central interval that unites the work. This interval is reiterated more obviously by the horns (A > B over a powerful C-sharp-minor triad), ushering in a thorough presentation by the strings, *dolce*, of motif-group (b), which appears in several variants, as noted by Persichetti.[197] It is heard first as simply a major-ninth, then as a major-ninth preceded or separated by a note approximately midway between them, and several sequences in which the ninth is camouflaged by other intervening intervals. As this passage unfolds, a sinuous, tightly woven counterpoint develops, becoming increasingly distressed and distraught, while seeming untouched by stern triads that continue underneath.

The second section, *Moderato con moto*, is something of a *scherzo*, introduced by the double-reeds, who, after a reminiscence of motif (a), present motif-group (c), an ascending or descending line in which perfect-fourths figure prominently. This section features characteristically nervous, irregular rhythms jumping back and forth among the woodwinds, which lead to contrapuntal byplay between the first and second violins, soon joined by an *espressivo* melody in the cellos that seems oblivious to the violins. Other instruments enter, creating the Schuman multiplanar effect, until a conflict develops between the strings in strident counterpoint and the trumpets, trombones, then remaining brasses snapping and pecking in syncopated, accented chords. This section concludes with a clear statement by the horns of the most significant variant of (b), comprising the intervallic pattern 5 > 1 > 9 (b¹).

The third section, *Tranquillo*, begins as woodwinds explore motif (c) in its descending form, followed by subdued reminiscences of motif (a). These reminiscences suddenly explode in hard-bitten brass exchanges as heard in the first section. Motif (a) is then pursued stealthily by strings *pizzicato*, doubled by the xylophone—a most effective instrumental combination—before concluding with a restatement of (b¹) by the solo violin.

The fourth section, *Presto*, is the central developmental focal point of the work and is a striking compositional tour de force, revealing not only a counterpoint of lines within textural planes but also a counterpoint among those planes themselves. First, against motif (b¹) in syncopated timpani figures, violins and oboe pursue (b¹) in slow rhythmic values, not unlike a *cantus firmus* in music of the Renaissance. This long line unfolds, transferred from one instrumental group to another through smooth elisions, in what proves to be a canon with distant entrances. Against this are irregular rhythmic patterns in *pizzicato* strings supported by bassoon. A tense figure of two sixteenth-notes is added to the long line, as more instruments join the *pizzicato* figures. Frequently used by Schuman, this device conveys a sense of stealth and danger, and was adopted by Leonard Bernstein to heighten suspense in his score for the film *On the Waterfront*, not to mention *West Side Story*. The texture gradually becomes fuller as another contrapuntal line embraces the two-sixteenth-note figure, and additional instruments are added. The *pizzicato* figures are now replaced by the lower brass, marked "*secco, stridente,* incisive and clearly audible," while the strings continue in dense counterpoint, and the horns maintain the slow *cantus firmus*. Suddenly all drop out but the brass and double-basses in a stunning passage of jagged hocketing. The texture swells again, as woodwinds, xylophone, and piano are added. A series of pyramid effects finally culminates in another stentorian statement of (b[1]) by the violins and upper woodwinds, and then a series of sharp, violent chords recalling motif (a), which then recede.

The final section, *Andante*, begins as a lament, with a slow melody in the first violins accompanied by those familiar strummed *pizzicato* triads in the cellos, while a countermelody in the second violins, then English horn, provides reminders of the motif (b) variants. Rather abruptly—too abruptly, one might argue—the tempo accelerates, pressing forward to a triumphant conclusion, reinforced by percussion, in an unequivocal C major.

The premiere of *Judith* took place in January 1950, in Louisville, Kentucky. The Louisville Orchestra was conducted by Robert Whitney, and Martha Graham herself was the solo dancer. The performance was repeated soon afterward in New York City, and the commissioning orchestra and conductor made a recording of the work, released in 1951.

The initial reception was generally positive. Robert Sabin described the work as "music in blacks and greys, music of understatement and tremendous restrained power."[198] Hans Kuppenheim noted, "The music is tragic, somber, highly emotional, full of tension and of beautiful melodies, and abounds in technical difficulties."[199] William Bergsma commented on Schuman's use of polytonal planes, each of which may be diatonic, but in combination, can be quite dissonant. "[T]herefore Schuman can have a diatonic strength and direction to his line without sacrificing dissonance. Contrapuntally, the work is lithe and strong, gaining an emotional perspective by the opposition of ideas and textures." He felt that with this work Schuman entered a new "perspective. . . . [O]n its merits of strength and humanity, *Judith* stands among the best scores of today."[200] Perhaps the most perceptive and insightful reaction was expressed by Richard Franko Goldman, who wrote,

Judith has the virtues of Schuman at his best. The obvious fact about Schuman is that he is a big composer, vehement, self-confident, and emphatically positive. He is, in a sense, a musical Walt Whitman: he has the same athleticism, the same exuberance, the same love of sound, and also the same capacity for the elegiac and the poignant. Schuman, like Whitman, is sometimes too much himself, in the sense that he will use a machine-gun to kill a mosquito and be happy about it because the gun makes such a nice loud rat-tat-tat. . . . [*Judith*] is well-knit and well-proportioned in every respect. It is forceful, dramatic, imaginative, and brilliantly written for orchestra, not merely "orchestrated." Its economy of material makes for coherence throughout the multi-sectional structure . . . Schuman's orchestral imagination is certainly superior to that of any other American composer. The display of virtuosity is sometimes such that it dazzles, or even distracts, rather than beguiles the listener. . . . A good deal has already been written about the restless, nervous, emphatic quality of rhythmic activity in Schuman's music. The score of *Judith* is characteristic in this respect, but there is a satisfactory balance of quieter elements, giving not only relief in the simplest terms of lessening of tension, but making much more effective, through well-conceived proportioning, the excitement produced by the complex counterpoint of rhythm and timbre. It is in this way, among others, that *Judith* seems one of the most wholly satisfactory of Schuman's scores. . . . [A]s concert music it will stand with the best American scores of the past many years.[201]

Although *Judith* enjoyed a number of successful performances as a choreographic work, Graham eventually dropped it from her repertoire, feeling that it was stronger as a piece of music than as a dance work. Yet despite its favorable reception, the music itself was somehow overshadowed by other, more highly publicized works, and *Judith* has remained on the sidelines, as of this writing.

The original performers released a second recording of *Judith* in 1960, but no further recording appeared until the 1980s. At that time David Hall praised the work for its "sheer brilliance and drama," while noting that it adds "to [Schuman's] already impressive orchestral and rhythmic prowess an element of harmonic flexibility that has remained an integral part of his music language."[202]

During the 1950s the United States witnessed a burgeoning interest in music for wind band. (This phenomenon will be discussed in greater detail in the section of this study dealing with Vincent Persichetti.) Although most of America's leading composers eventually contributed to this medium, William Schuman was one of the first, with his *Newsreel*, a lighthearted trifle he had written in 1941. However, his most important work for band was *George Washington Bridge*—An Impression for Band, composed in 1950, and first performed that summer by the National Music Camp Band in Interlochen, Michigan.

Aspects of Schuman's music—its brash, self-confident assertiveness, the harsh solidity of its polychordal harmony, and its nervous, irregular rhythmic drive—have often impressed listeners as evoking the spirit of New York City—at least, the New York City of the mid-twentieth century. This connection is explicitly suggested by the title, *George Washington Bridge*, in addition to being suggested by the music. The blunt forthrightness of the polychords that open the work seems to suggest the strength and solidity of this mighty structure that links the borough of Manhattan to the state of New Jersey.

The following comments are taken from the composer's program note: "There are few days in the year when I do not see the George Washington Bridge. . . . Ever since my student days when I watched the progress of its construction, this bridge has had for me an almost human personality, and this personality is astonishingly varied, assuming different moods depending on the time of day or night, the weather, the traffic and, of course, my own mood as I pass by. . . . It is difficult to imagine a more gracious welcome or dramatic entry to the great metropolis."[203]

Not surprisingly, the short work (less than ten minutes in duration) is structured in a symmetrical arch form (ABCBA) that parallels the expanse of the bridge. The first section is based on a virile four-measure statement of fully scored polychords—all quarter-notes and half-notes but with a syncopated "kick" in the third measure. This section emphasizes brass and percussion. The second section, which jumps back and forth between the woodwinds and the brasses, with percussion punctuation, offers the contrast of Schuman's familiar "chirping" in jagged, irregular rhythmic patterns. Further contrast is provided by the third section, which is lyrical in gesture, but a lyricism that is rather dry and impersonal. This is followed by an altered return of the second section, followed by a dramatic, altered return of the opening material, which brings the work to a decisive conclusion.

The first recording of *George Washington Bridge* was an auspicious one. In 1953 the newly formed Eastman Symphonic Wind Ensemble, under the leadership of Frederick Fennell, included the work on the first of a series of commercial recordings made by the ensemble for Mercury Records. The widespread exposure thus afforded this piece, written by one of America's foremost composers at the time, resulted in its recognition as a classic of the wind ensemble repertoire, a status it holds to this day. Schuman's name is associated with other works for wind band, but, aside from *Newsreel*, they are either transcriptions or adaptations of compositions originally intended for other media.

In 1950 Schuman was commissioned by the Elizabeth Sprague Coolidge Foundation to compose a string quartet to commemorate the founding of the Library of Congress. That summer, while vacationing on the island of Martha's Vineyard, off the coast of Massachusetts, the composer injured his leg during an impromptu softball game and was house-ridden for much of the summer. In a burst of industry, he took the opportunity to work on the quartet, completing it between late June and early August. Mark Lehman probably had the Quartet No. 4 in mind when he noted that "Schuman's mature quartets are almost symphonic in their richness of sonority and breadth of statement. Like the symphonies they also show the evolution of Schuman's art as it outgrew his early indebtedness to the . . . spacious 'American-sounding' textures of Roy Harris to become more idiosyncratic, more cosmopolitan, more chromatic, and more searching."[204]

Schuman's Fourth String Quartet comprises four discrete movements with a duration just under half an hour. A number of commentators have observed the work's similarity to the Symphony No. 6. Persichetti linked the two works together "at the top of [Schuman's] output. No longer is one conscious of technique or devices in [his music]."[205] The two compositions share the most complex structures of any music written by Schuman up to that time. Both maintain a high level of harmonic dissonance and create a largely atonal impression throughout, although subtle tonal references are present, especially at structural junctures. Both make considerable demands upon the concentration of the listener, as they offer little in the way of local felicities, their impact based primarily upon abstract conceptual relationships that only become clear with increased familiarity and over long spans of structural time. And, perhaps most of all, both works are pervaded by the dominating influence of the triad with both major- and minor-thirds. However, the most relevant distinction between them is that the Sixth Symphony has at its disposal the instrumental variety and potential for visceral dramatic effects available to the symphony orchestra, while the string quartet must sustain interest through the limited sonorities of this more abstract medium.

The first movement of the quartet, *Adagio*, introduces a mood of deep, searching contemplation, as the viola and first violin introduce a highly chromatic two-part counterpoint. Shortly the cello enters, echoing the viola line, promptly followed by the second violin, as the loosely imitative four-voice counterpoint proceeds. The sense of animation gradually increases slightly, by means of shorter note-values and more symmetrical rhythmic balance. There is a modified return of the opening material, as the movement fades out, ending with a G-major-minor sonority.

The second movement, *Allegro con fuoco*, stands in marked contrast to the first, although there is some motivic connection with that movement, especially through an emphasis on the intervals of the major- and minor-seventh. This movement highlights Schuman's distinctive treatment of rhythm at rapid tempos. The music is vigorous and aggressive, with irregular, highly syncopated rhythmic patterns, and a wide range of dynamic activity, although actual rhythmic patterns are often in unison among the members of the quartet. Much of the instrumental articulation creates a skittish effect. A central section is somewhat more gentle and lyrical, as it focuses on the development of a brief motif that highlights the intervals of the perfect- and augmented-fourth. There is a return to the spirit and some of the material from the opening, which becomes increasingly wild and agitated as the music presses forward to an intense conclusion.

The *Andante* is the longest and perhaps most elaborate movement of the quartet. An A-major-minor triad introduces a chorale of rich, polychordal double-stops in each instrument, creating a haunting, bittersweet effect. This leads to a freely contrapuntal passage in the violins, heard over quarter-note chords in the viola and cello. The counterpoint becomes increasingly dense as the viola joins in over *pizzicato* triple-stops in the cello (a brief reminiscence of Schuman's "strumming" effect). Further intensity is generated as the upper voices introduce a more active figuration, while the motivic attention focuses on an atonal melody in the cello. This gradually builds to a stunning climax on a succession of pure triads, stabbed by heartrending major-minor conflicts. The energy gradually recedes as the music fades away on an E-major-minor triad.

The finale, *Presto*, illustrates—perhaps even more clearly than the second movement—Schuman's mature treatment of rhythm at fast tempos. Drawing upon the motif heard in the central portion of the second movement, the music displays a breathless sense of urgency as it tears forward, exploiting a number of notable instrumental effects, such as a series of alternating, overlapping four-voice *pizzicato* chords in all four instruments. A lyrical but atonal melody is introduced by the viola, in the midst of the frantic contrapuntal activity. This melody is picked up and pursued by the cello, juxtaposed against ideas in the other instruments that at times stand in striking contrast, or even seem altogether unrelated to the surrounding activity. There is a return to a variant of the movement's opening material, which presses forward *prestissimo* with increasing frenzy. Finally a series of slashing polychords in quadruple-stops among all four instruments carries the music to a surprisingly innocuous and unambiguous conclusion in G major.

Schuman's String Quartet No. 4 was introduced by the Hungarian String Quartet in October 1950 at the Library of Congress in Washington, D.C. Present at the premiere, Olin Downes described the work as "ultra-modern . . . a score of a highly progressive composer who is well acquainted with the modern literature of music, knowing his Bartók, Hindemith, Schoenberg and Berg as well; able to adapt their idioms at will to his own esthetic needs."[206] Afforded the opportunity for greater reflection, the composer's staunch advocate Aaron Copland commented,

A composition like the Fourth String Quartet makes one understand why Schuman is generally ranked among the top men in American music. Even a single hearing made it evident that this is one of Schuman's most mature works. A second hearing confirmed the impression. This is music written with true urgency: compact in form, ingenious in its instrumental technique, quite experimental as to harmony. In some ways it is typical of the composer, in others it seems to be composed from a new premise. . . . I cannot remember another work of Schuman that strikes so somber a note. . . . [A] more tentative expressivity has taken over; a darker, more forbidding tone that seems far different from the basically optimistic—sometimes boyishly optimistic—tone of his earlier music. . . . [One has the sense] that a new (for Schuman) expressive content rendered the old formulas inadequate, leading him in a direction that is likely to enrich his style.[207]

Schuman's Fourth Quartet was recorded in 1952 by the Julliard Quartet, under the composer's supervision. That recording was most highly regarded at the time—a tour de force of virtuosity. However, close study of this extremely challenging work reveals how much of its expressive power remained untapped by the Juilliard reading. Impeccable precision and coordination at times were achieved at the expense of breadth, power, and dynamic range. It is possible that Schuman realized that the expressive content of this work could not be contained or projected by merely four string players, when he decided to incorporate and rework the quartet's last two movements into the Symphony No. 8 some twelve years later.

Also, the question must be raised once more: Who is the intended audience for a work that demands such intense concentration while offering so little to the casual or less sophisticated listener? More than fifty years have elapsed since the quartet's sole recording, now long out of print, was first issued; no quartet or record company has been motivated to take up the challenge. In this work, perhaps more than any other he had yet composed, Schuman entered the limbo of a language too dissonant and atonal for the general concertgoer to appreciate in a single hearing, yet one that refused to conform to the serial method that was being afforded a protective intellectual defense by influential spokesmen for that approach.

Almost as if he were responding to the implications of the previous paragraph, Schuman next turned his attention to his one major effort in musical populism: *The Mighty Casey: A Baseball Opera,* based on the iconic poem, "Casey at the Bat," by Ernest Lawrence Thayer (1863–1940). For much of the twentieth century, this poem, a mock-tragic epic about a baseball hero who fails at the crucial moment, was a classic of humorous verse, its protagonist an American legend. Thayer was a Harvard philosophy student who had also been editor of the *Harvard Lampoon.* After college he accepted an invitation from his schoolmate William Randolph Hearst to write a weekly humor column for his newly acquired newspaper, the *San Francisco Examiner*. Thayer accepted the position, which he held for several years. "Casey at the Bat" was his contribution to the edition of June 3, 1888.

The poem might have soon disappeared into oblivion had it not come to the attention of a popular entertainer, William DeWolf Hopper (1858–1935), several months later. Hopper memorized the poem and recited it at one of his performances. The reception proved so enthusiastic that "Casey" became part of Hopper's permanent repertoire, and as a result the poem began to appear in print throughout the country. (Hopper later estimated that he had recited the poem more than ten thousand times.)

Many have attempted to explain the enduring popularity of Thayer's poem. Perhaps the notion of a great hero failing at the moment of truth, in the presence of his peers, touches a particularly sensitive nerve in the American collective unconscious. In his memoirs, DeWolf Hopper speculated,

> The crowds do not flock into the American League parks . . . solely in anticipation of seeing Babe Ruth whale the ball over the center field fence. . . . There always is a chance that the Babe will strike out, a sight even more healing to sore eyes, for the Sultan of Swat can miss the third strike just as furiously as he can meet it, and the contrast between the terrible threat of his swing and the futility of the result is a banquet for the malicious, which includes us all. . . . There are one or more Caseys in every league, bush or big, and there is no day in the playing season that this same supreme tragedy, as stark as Aristophanes for the moment, does not befall on some field.[208]

Somehow a tale concerning a popular national pastime, presented in a tone of mock portentousness, with an implicit sense of metaphysical allegory, captured the public imagination and preserved Thayer's poem as an enduring element of American popular culture. Two silent film versions of the "Casey" story were made during the early years of the twentieth century. In the 1940s, Walt Disney created an animated cartoon version. But in *The Annotated Casey at the Bat*, Martin Gardner asserts that the musical adaptation by William Schuman and librettist Jeremy Gury is "the most important continuation and elaboration of the Casey story."[209]

Like so many men of his generation—especially those with a passion for baseball—Schuman maintained an enduring affection for Thayer's poem. Having become acquainted with Jeremy Gury, creative director of the Ted Bates advertising agency, Schuman managed to interest Gury in developing a libretto for an opera based on "Casey." Gury accepted the challenge, and work on the project began in 1951. Although the collaboration proved contentious, Schuman was ultimately pleased with the final libretto.[210] They expanded Thayer's poem into a seventy-five-minute opera, adding romantic interest in the form of a girlfriend and a Watchman who serves as commentator, while linking the various elements together into "a vivid portrait of small-town America. It is about the fall of a village small-town hero—who, like Prufrock, sees the moment of his greatness flicker—and his redemption through love." Tim Page felt that Schuman and Gury's expansion added a dimension reminiscent of Thornton Wilder's *Our Town*.[211] It is tempting to speculate further that for a man like Schuman, the core of whose personality hinged on notions of heroism, of facing the most difficult challenges with an appearance of confident aplomb, and of achieving great success in the eyes of one's peers, the character of Casey bore an especially personal meaning (a meaning whose prophetic implications would not be realized for another fifteen years).

While the notion of a "baseball opera" may call to mind the ridiculous prospect of overweight and/or effeminate singers—mostly European— dressed in baseball garb, solemnly declaiming incongruously atonal vocal lines, such a characterization couldn't be further from the reality of Schuman and Gury's work. *The Mighty Casey*, completed in 1953, is guilty of no such unintentional pomposity or incongruity—to the point where the term "opera" raises the questions of genre also prompted by works like *Porgy and Bess* and *West Side Story*. The general musical style is lightweight and accessible, although it doesn't quite reach into the language of the Broadway musical to the extent that Leonard Bernstein, for example, did in his musical shows. In truth, its chief claim to being an "opera" lies in its brilliant, thoroughly integrated construction, based on the simple interval of a descending half-step. Aside from that, the work owes little to the tone or style of European music-drama. Although Schuman rarely drew upon vernacular musical idioms, from the breathtakingly exciting overture he displayed in this work an exuberant "popular" side that may surprise listeners accustomed to his hard, angular, "serious" side, yet is authentically and recognizably his own. Most characteristic is the virile, aggressive, and nervously syncopated treatment of rhythm rooted in American speech patterns and totally appropriate to the subject matter. The use of the chorus is especially effective in rendering this element. The tone of mock heroism, suspense, and tragedy that gives life to the poem (recited by the Watchman in bits and pieces throughout the work) is retained and developed in this expansion. Indeed, the finale, "Oh, Somewhere," is a classic Schuman lament, with a tragic eloquence that places it among some of the composer's finest moments. There are a couple of pretty melodies—"Kiss Me Not Goodbye," in particular, might have become a "hit." For the rest of it, catchy tunes, such as the title song, choruses reminiscent of American hymnody, exciting rhythms, consonant triadic harmony, and a robust, vigorous flow of energy keep the music direct and appealing. Nevertheless, the melodic lines are occasionally atonal, with much use of parallel major-thirds, chromaticism, and the whole-tone scale, all of which militate against a strong sense of tonality.

Schuman and Gury had perhaps unrealistically high expectations for *Casey*. They anticipated its success to reach far beyond the "chic Menotti audiences," to the professional baseball world itself. Schuman pressured Hans Heinsheimer of G. Schirmer to promote the work accordingly, blaming his lack of success on the German's utter ignorance of America's "national pastime."[212] There were attempts to arrange for a Broadway production, which never materialized. Greatly disappointed, the creators had to settle for a premiere at the Hartt College of Music in Hartford, Connecticut, in May 1953. The conductor was Moshe Paranov.

Although the reviews were far from raves, they were not devastating either. However, the emotional investment the two had made in the work's triumph as a national apotheosis seemed to have led them to find anything less than that to be utter failure. Harold Schonberg, notorious for his use of irony and sarcasm to convey an impression of ridicule without providing any actual, substantive criticism, fulfilled his reputation in his notice. However, aside from the gratuitous sarcasm, Schonberg's chief point seems to have been that "Mr. Schuman, one feels, tries too hard. His dry, often jerky melodic line, with all of its major-sevenths and -ninths, his austere harmonies and his rhythmic intensity somehow do not fit this pleasant little fable. . . . [W]hat is missing is the folkish flavor and the genial musical outlook of a practiced hand at operetta."[213] But, as Martin Gardner retorted in his introduction to *Casey at the Bat*, "Pleasant little fable, indeed! *Casey* is neither pleasant nor little, it is tragic and titanic. Perhaps Schuman's intense music is not so inappropriate after all."[214] Whether one agrees with Schonberg or not, his snide comments do not amount to condemnation. On the other hand, the often vicious composer-critic Arthur Berger wrote, "The harmonies are, for my taste, too colored, at times, for the . . . appropriate simplicity of the melodies. But Schuman is very, very expert, indeed, in his technical handling, his orchestration and his general ease."[215] *Time* magazine commented, "Musically, the opera was ingenious if not immortal—though at an hour and 20 minutes, it was about 20 minutes too long. Nonetheless, the Hartford audience seemed to like most of it, and gave the composer a rousing hand at the end."[216]

Two years later *Casey* enjoyed a nationwide telecast on CBS-TV's "Omnibus" series. Schonberg reiterated his earlier comments, adding that Schuman "decidedly does not have the light touch."[217] Paul Hume remarked on the technical difficulties entailed in performing the work. The most consistent and probably most justified criticism involved its length. "[T]he action is too often interrupted for too long. This becomes increasingly disturbing as the climax is neared. When, finally, we have to wait so long between the final, fateful three strikes, it gets into the realm of music too much for the good of its subject. Schuman's love of baseball is clear, but his over-riding love of music smothers our national sport a bit."[218]

The work continued to enjoy occasional performances. It wasn't produced in New York City until August 1967, when it was presented by the Theater Workshop for Students, sponsored by the City Parks Department. The reaction of *New York Times* critic Allen Hughes was more favorable than that of his predecessor. He felt that the work got "a fair amount of entertainment mileage out of a rather slender story idea," noting that it "might be better described as a musical pageant than an opera. The music itself has a Broadway flavor, but there is some characterization in it and it does provide opportunities for serious singing."[219]

As part of an all-Schuman program presented in April 1976, in Washington, D.C., by the National Symphony Orchestra, in connection with the American bicentennial, Schuman was commissioned to create a "concert version" of *Casey*. Entitled *Casey at the Bat: A Baseball Cantata*, this version was shorter, and the cast was reduced to a baritone singer-reciter and a soprano, plus chorus and orchestra. With only two soloists and optional staging suggestions, this version was obviously more practical to perform, and, in fact, even led, in some cases, to stagings of the original opera.

In 1980, an educational publisher, EAV, proposed to Schuman a plan to create a sound-filmstrip representation of *Casey* for use in schools, but this would require considerable further abridgment. At first the composer dismissed the notion, but when presented with a "mocked-up" version of a twenty-six-minute condensation, which was surprisingly effective, he consented to the project, accepting an invitation to recite the poem as distributed throughout the work. The resulting audiovisual product was well received, and remained on the market until the sound-filmstrip medium was gradually supplanted by videotape and other more advanced media.

In 1986 *The Mighty Casey* was presented by the Glimmerglass Opera Company in Cooperstown, New York, home of the Baseball Hall of Fame. This production was so well received that it was revived there again three years later, in honor of the fiftieth anniversary of the Hall of Fame. Now the critical response was more positive, critic Leslie Kandell going so far as to call Cooperstown "the Bayreuth for performances of *The Mighty Casey . . .* William Schuman's endearing one-act opera." To her the work "looks and sounds something like a golden-age Broadway musical."[220] Bernard Holland noted, "There is buoyant bright light here—the orchestra wind- and brass-heavy like a Broadway pit band. The rhythmic interest is considerable, and Mr. Schuman's simple harmonic language fits." While acknowledging that portions of the exposition of characters are overextended, he found the actual game sequence "an utter delight—imaginatively tongue-in-cheek but never descending into self-parody."[221]

A production at the Juilliard School in 1990, conducted by Gerard Schwarz, was executed proficiently enough to be released commercially on recording in 1994. There is no question but that *Casey*—in both versions—has been slow to catch on, but its unusual qualities are gradually being recognized. In his entry on Schuman in the *New Grove Dictionary of Opera*, Harry Haskell wrote of *Casey*, "The composer's imprint is evident in the athletic rhythms, leaping vocal lines, major-minor chords and use of ostinatos and semitonal clashes to produce tension. He later recast the work as a cantata, making minor adjustments to the score, enlarging the orchestra and eliminating the spoken dialogue."[222]

In 1977 Schuman had said of *Casey*, "I love that work more than anybody else does. . . . I still believe that one day [it] is going to find its mark."[223] Over the years he devoted a good deal of time and energy in attempting to rationalize its failure to achieve the level of success he had envisioned. Any number of possible explanations can be adduced to account for this. But perhaps the most convincing explanation is that the work is simply too sophisticated musically to win over an audience of the size Schuman and Gury were anticipating. Nevertheless, *Casey* displays so many of the distinctive features of Schuman's mature style within a framework that is far easier to grasp and appreciate than most of his major works that it may yet prove to be one of his most enduring compositions among Schuman admirers, but it may be the cantata version rather than the opera that achieves this.

Although Schuman did compose a substantial piano concerto, as a solo instrument the piano seemed not to engage his imagination. Indeed, there is only one such work of significant dimension: a group of five abstract character pieces, composed in 1953 on a commission from the Sigma Alpha Iota sorority. Apparently, shortly after completing the work, he asked Martha Graham to listen to it and suggest a title. Not only did she have a title to propose—*Voyage*—but she also asked him to orchestrate it and offered to choreograph the result. He accepted her offer, scoring the music for chamber orchestra, with the title *Voyage for a Theater*. Only after hearing the work performed in New York, in May 1953, did titles for the individual movements occur to him: "Anticipation," "Caprice," "Realization," "Decision," and "Retrospection." After several performances with Graham's choreography, all the principals agreed that the resulting work was not successful, and further performances were canceled. Schuman later withdrew his chamber orchestration. As per the original commission, the piano version had its premiere in Chicago, in August of that year. The pianist was Lillian Steuber. This sequence of events led to the often-repeated misconception that the work was originally scored for chamber orchestra, but the piano version was planned and completed first.[224]

The first, third, and fifth sections of *Voyage* are rather slow in tempo, while the second and fourth move quickly. Perhaps the most intriguing aspect of the work is that while Schuman had tended to avoid the medium of piano solo, his close colleague Vincent Persichetti had devoted a great deal of attention to it, having completed nine sonatas and many other individual pieces for the instrument by the time the older composer had reached the point of addressing it. The key point of interest is that the harmonic language of *Voyage*, not to mention the overall approach to writing for the instrument, shares a great deal in common with the piano music Persichetti had been composing for the past decade. The similarity is most noticeable in the first movement, where a shapely, lyrical melodic line establishes an emotional remoteness by avoiding consonant harmony or tonal implications; the similarity is also especially apparent in the fourth section, which is driven by vigorous rhythmic syncopations and irregularities that are rife throughout Persichetti's piano works. There is a great deal of evidence in Persichetti's music—not to mention his copious writings on the subject—that the younger composer was intimately familiar with the work of Schuman. *Voyage* is one of the few instances in the latter's work where his familiarity with the music of his younger colleague appears to have influenced his own.

Voyage is a reasonably satisfying work in its own right, drawing upon a personal, introspective side of Schuman's personality that did not often emerge in his music. There is much, in the three slow movements especially, that has a reflective, improvisatory feeling, although aspects of the harmonic language sound somewhat synthetic. The third movement may be seen as an exploration of harsh harmonic sonorities, while the final movement achieves a quiet serenity. On the other hand, the second movement—the most immediately appealing one—is unmistakably Schuman, with its fleet, breathless rhythmic urgency, while the fourth is quite exciting.

Nathan Broder recognized in the work "the intensity and the rhythmic virtuosity that one expects in Schuman but [it] does not seem to stand as firmly, away from the ballet-stage, as do Undertow and Judith."[225] Frederick Sternfeld felt, "Harmonically, the music seems more taut and chromatic than earlier works of Schuman heard in the concert hall. Some of the moods evoked are distinctly tragic, if not tortured. The piece . . . is held together by a secure sense of style."[226]

Voyage appeared on recording in 1955, in a performance by Beveridge Webster. In 1971 Schuman created a version for full orchestra, which he called *Voyage for Orchestra.* It will be discussed later in this chapter, where it belongs chronologically.

If *Voyage* represented a rather unusual direction for Schuman, his next work was in a sense a musical crystallization of the "presidential" persona that he had been cultivating as a public figure and with which he was becoming identified in the minds of those who followed American culture. This was *Credendum: Article of Faith*, composed in 1955 on a commission from the State Department on behalf of the U.S. National Commission for UNESCO. This was the first time a musical work was commissioned by an agency of the U.S. government, and Schuman was inspired by the ideal of free cultural exchange among countries, so it was a natural opportunity for him to express his public persona in musical terms. Commentator John Proffitt cited *Credendum* as "one of Schuman's most important, and characteristic, orchestral works," stating that it captured the composer's "humanistic faith in the power of Education, Science, and Culture to shape mankind for the better."[227] It was also a statement of educated postwar America's view of the values to be reflected through our arts.

Coming soon after some of Schuman's most profound and challenging works, *Credendum* is perhaps the most accessible orchestral representation of the distinctive features of his mature style, making it an ideal point of entry into his output as a whole. Scored for an especially large orchestra, with augmented percussion, the work comprises three sections, separated from each other by the rather simplistic device of a sustained major triad. The first section, "Declaration," is brash and brassy, virile and extroverted, with bold percussion punctuations and characteristically syncopated rhythms. The thematic material, centering on a four-note motif comprising two pairs of the interval of the second, is more straightforward and simple in gesture than in other recent works. The second section, "Chorale," is based on a solemn—even poignantly sad and longing—hymn introduced by the strings. It is one of the most beautiful passages Schuman ever wrote, capturing something of the feeling of the Chorale from the Symphony No. 3. The mood of the music is broadened through a series of clearly defined, increasingly polyphonic variations, which build in volume and intensity to a climax, before receding to the mood of the opening. If the first two sections serve as something of a "theme 1" and "theme 2," the "Finale" may be seen as development, recapitulation, and coda. This section subjects the thematic material to Schuman's exciting, characteristically jumpy, irregular rhythmic development, along with polytonal harmony, searing counterpoint, and cumulative pyramid effects. Finally, a grand orchestral statement of the Chorale is combined with the developmental proceedings, all culminating in a virtually manic affirmation of unashamed grandiloquence, punctuated by clanging bells and other percussion.

The first performance of *Credendum* took place in Cincinnati in November 1955. Thor Johnson conducted the Cincinnati Symphony Orchestra. The work was well received and has enjoyed many subsequent performances. Paul Hume found it to be "music of immense beauty, built with sure knowledge into a work of convincing power."[228] English commentator Denis Stevens felt that "It [was] as if Schuman had warmed spontaneously to his task, creating a deeply felt work of original cast and powerful design."[229]

The reliably perceptive and thoughtful composer-critic Henry Cowell penned an elaborate commentary on the work, in which he captured many essential features of Schuman's style:

> *Credendum*'s introduction is ejaculatory. There are many short motifs and snatches of music that end in exclamation points. . . . Schuman uses the direction "legato, but with sustained force." . . . The style in which this is needed returns in the Chorale section; and it is indeed a symptom of the sustained fervor of religious feeling. It is based on hymn-singing, in spite of the employment of more modem harmony and part-writing and wider melodic leaps. The lyric side of Schuman's style—and he possesses a very definite style—is a recognizable development of church counterpoint into a 20th-century manner through contemporary means. The result of such an approach is that melodies and fundamental chords may be quite simple, but with some added aspects.

Noting that wide leaps often occur within Schuman's lyrical melodies, Cowell adds that while they

> are sometimes used to break up a sense of melodic continuity, Schuman preserves such a sense here. . . . The second aspect of Schuman's style consists of chattering repetitions of tones and chords, usually highly dissonant, rapid and syncopated. . . . It splutters and stutters, but agreeably, and induces a sort of static excitement which is a great contrast to the long lyric lines of the other side of the Schuman style. One method of development is through a rhythmic expansion consisting of placing more rests between the repeated notes, as well as subjecting them to new syncopated off-beat accents. . . . The Chorale opens with sustained strings in a rather simple counterpoint which unexpectedly slips in some independent chords in perfect fourths. These are integrated into the close, well-webbed fabric rather unnoticeably, but of course the fourths are given a fundamental character totally opposed to their use in older systems of polyphony. The idea of repeated tones in syncopation is brought back quietly and slowly at first, but with increasing liveliness. There is effective use of sectional scoring, the whole string body answered by the whole wind bodies. Another effective bit of scoring occurs at the opening of the Presto, in which all the strings are divided so that the same parts are played both *pizzicato* and *arco*. This enhances the feeling of the indicated *leggiero*, which is made more lightsome. . . . The work as a whole shows much formal relationship between the parts, but is not hampered by over-systematization. It achieves a natural flow of rhythmical asymmetry which is impelling, but not artificially induced

by following a preconceived plan; rather it is the result of a certain freedom of relationship. The scoring is expert, although sometimes wide leaps make it hard for the inexperienced listener to follow easily. One might wish for more sustained flow in some parts—there are often too many small climaxes and too many interpolations of change of pace, as if the author became afraid of boring his listeners if he followed his ideas through to their conclusions. This is an unimportant matter, however. The total work is impressive, large-scaled, Schuman's *magnum opus*.[230]

While perhaps not Schuman's magnum opus, *Credendum* is definitely quintessential and contains some of his finest writing. However, not all the responses to the work have been so positive. Critic Peter G. Davis felt that it was "perhaps the worst piece of music I have ever heard."[231] And even Polisi feels that its thunderous peroration "drive[s] this work to the edge of good taste."[232]

The first recording of *Credendum* appeared in 1957, with a stunning performance by the Philadelphia Orchestra, conducted by Eugene Ormandy. The work has become one of Schuman's most frequently performed compositions.

The composer's next work was commissioned by conductor Andre Kostelanetz, who often turned to America's most highly regarded composers for pieces of a lighter, more popular slant. In this case he asked Schuman for an accessible work on an American theme. The composer's original plan was a composition based on *The Legend of Sleepy Hollow*, but Kostelanetz rejected the idea as too similar to pieces already in existence.

Around 1940, when Schuman was conducting the chorus at Sarah Lawrence College, he had become acquainted with the choral anthems of William Billings (1746–1800), an amateur New England composer whose hymns served as inspiration during the period of the American Revolution. Schuman later stated that in examining Billings' music, he encountered "feelings which I recognized as being wholly akin to my own."[233] Still later he elaborated these feelings as a "sinewy ruggedness, deep religiosity and patriotic fervor."[234] In 1943 he had composed a work entitled *William Billings Overture*, a series of variations on three Billings tunes: "Be Glad Then, America," "When Jesus Wept," and "Chester." Although the overture enjoyed a premiere in February 1944 by the New York Philharmonic under the direction of Artur Rodzinski, followed by subsequent performances, Schuman stated that he was never fully satisfied with it.[235]

So, in attempting to satisfy Kostelanetz's request, Schuman proposed an expansion of the *William Billings Overture* into a concise, three-movement composition that would be based on the same three hymns. Kostelanetz was enthusiastic about the idea, and the work, completed in 1956, was finally named *New England Triptych*. In the process, Schuman withdrew the original overture altogether.

In his program notes for the work, Schuman stressed that what he was attempting was not a "fantasy" on themes of Billings but, rather, a "fusion of styles and musical language," although the actual difference between these two notions seems purely semantic. However, the result is a work of great immediate appeal, in which Billings' tonal, diatonic hymn melodies are subjected—especially in the first and last movements—to Schuman's own brand of melodic fragmentation, rhythmic dislocation, and abrupt harmonic shifts, not to mention his brilliant orchestration. The beautifully moving second movement remains closer in both spirit and musical structure to the Billings original. The rousing finale, which acknowledges the hymn's dual function as both religious and martial, concludes with Schuman's trademark octave leaps on the fifth of the tonic chord.

The premiere of *New England Triptych* took place in October 1956. Kostelanetz conducted the University of Miami Symphony Orchestra. The following week he presented the work with the New York Philharmonic. Schuman's brisk, exhilarating treatment of Billings' diatonic materials immediately proved successful with both critics and audiences, and has continued to be a favorite throughout the years. After one of its first performances, Rose Widder described it as "music of great appeal and fascinating construction. It was heartily applauded by the audience."[236] Daniel Webster noted that "Schuman's music bursts with an invigorated optimism."[237] Other critics have praised its "raw grandeur,"[238] and its "thorough craftsmanship and richness of musical invention,"[239] finding it "a beautiful, superbly well-crafted tribute to William Billings."[240]

Shortly after completing the work, Schuman produced a version of "Chester"—the third movement—for wind band. However, this is not—as is often claimed—simply a transcription but rather an elaborate recomposition, using the same materials, into a piece approximately twice as long as the original. (This version was transformed into a work for piano solo—*Chester Variations*—in 1988, as a test piece for the Van Cliburn International Piano Competition.) Eventually Schuman completed an entire band arrangement of the *Triptych*.

The first recording of *New England Triptych* was released in 1959, in a performance by the New York Philharmonic under Kostelanetz's direction. Numerous additional recordings have appeared throughout the years.

New England Triptych soon became Schuman's most popular original work, to an extent that the composer eventually came to resent.[241] Like Samuel Barber's *Adagio for Strings*, it has become the first resort of unimaginative programmers looking for a "sure-fire hit" to place on a program honoring

American composers or celebrating a national holiday. Though it displays brilliant ingenuity and is a delightful piece of music, it is nevertheless peripheral
to the mainstream of Schuman's output, and its popularity is no doubt partly
attributable to its basis in diatonic hymn-tunes, its picturesque title, and its
modest duration. This would not be the last time that Schuman would subject
materials from a distant historical context to his own distinctive treatment.

Schuman composed choral music throughout his career. In fact, in 1963,
Robert Sabin named Schuman as "the most original and forceful" American
composer of choral music in the twentieth century.[242] Yet most of Schuman's
choral works are slight diversions and therefore will not be discussed here.
However, one of his most important works for chorus is *Carols of Death*,
frequently performed *a cappella* settings for mixed voices of three poems
by Walt Whitman, commissioned for the Laurentian Singers of St. Lawrence
University, who gave the premiere in Canton, New York, in March 1959. The
three poems are "The Last Invocation," "The Unknown Region," and "To
All, to Each"—poems that have inspired settings by a number of composers.
Schuman recalled that these poems "haunted me for years, because I think
they're absolutely beautiful, and I never could find the music that I felt was
right to go with them" until 1958, when he made these settings.[243] In view of
the composer's statement, expressed late in life, that "I am not and have never
been morbid about death. I always think that death is one branch of life,"[244] it
is illuminating to observe his sober confrontation with Whitman's reflections
on the subject, from the perspective of the forty-eight-year-old composer.

The three movements are largely slow and somber in character, capturing
the profound sense of mystery and awe evoked by Whitman. The first setting
is quite grim and is largely limited to two-voice counterpoint, doubled at the
octave, with many open fourths and fifths, which evoke a somewhat archaic
flavor. The setting is largely block-like and syllabic, so that the counterpoint
is controlled vertically, with limited rhythmic independence of the voices.
The first portion of the second section moves quickly and is decidedly jazzy,
displaying some of the intricate rhythmic interplays commonly found in
Schuman's fast music. In fact, there is a phrase or two of that section that
would not be out of place in *The Mighty Casey*. This is the most musically
interesting setting of the three. The third poem, which begins, "Come lovely
and soothing death," offers some comfort. The largely syllabic settings facilitate the aural comprehension of the text, which was obviously important
to the composer. There is much use—especially in the outer movements—of
a device in which the chorus sustains a single note in unison, from which
half the group splits off in a stepwise fashion, while the other half holds the
original note constant or moves independently. This is a technique found
frequently in American choral music.

The *Carols of Death* have been generally well received, for the most part. Joseph McLellan wrote, "Schuman's choral writing is brilliant. The music is always at the service of the text, and clarity is a prime virtue, but the range of expression is wide and the colors are almost as vivid as in his orchestral music,"[245] while Bernard Holland observed that Schuman gives Whitman's poetry "a musical underpinning, a foundation in sound that allows every word to come through. Textures are adjusted for verbal clarity more than for musical effect; rhythm and meter follow the words rather than lead them."[246]

A contrary view is provided by an English critic, who, in the process, reveals an "outsider's" perspective on the composer:

> The received critical image of William Schuman . . . seems to be that of the archetypal thousand-kilowatt American composer, his technique as masterly as a steamroller, furiously communicating nothing. It's not entirely just—there are pleasant, unpretentious pieces in his *oeuvre*, and the power of the earlier symphonies is not merely rhetorical—but certainly in recent years Schuman's supreme professionalism seems to have frozen into mannerism. The *Carols of Death* . . . contrive to go through outwardly fascinating motions of harmony and texture without expressing much. Perhaps the most interesting movement, simply as a musical object, is the second: a rapid scherzo on "Toward the Unknown Region" which suggests no parallel with Vaughan Williams. Sadly, it suggests nothing that one can identify as a response to Whitman's words, either.[247]

The first recording of the *Carols of Death* was released in 1965. Gregg Smith conducted an expert performance of the work with his eponymous chorus.

The final work from Schuman's middle style-period is his Violin Concerto, a composition that gave him a great deal of trouble and went through a series of major revisions before reaching its final form. In 1946, the composer was approached by Stravinsky's friend Samuel Dushkin, who was interested in commissioning a violin concerto that he hoped to introduce with the Boston Symphony under Koussevitzky. The commission entailed a provision that Dushkin would have an exclusive right to perform the work for three years. Without ever having heard Dushkin perform publicly, Schuman accepted these terms, finishing the work in 1947. Soon after, when he did hear Dushkin play in recital, Schuman realized that the violinist was not adequate to the task of performing such a difficult concerto, although by then he had received the full commissioning fee. Furthermore, Koussevitzky agreed to give the premiere, but not with Dushkin as soloist. So Schuman was faced with the difficult task of presenting this situation to Dushkin. The violinist was reportedly enraged and insisted somewhat spitefully on maintaining his exclusive right to the work, so that no one else could perform it for three years.

Finally, the three years having elapsed, the premiere of the concerto took place in February 1950, with Isaac Stern as soloist with the Boston Symphony, then under the direction of Charles Munch. Although the work met with a generally positive reception, Schuman felt that Stern, accustomed to the shallow showpieces that comprise most of the violin virtuoso's repertoire, failed to plumb the depths of his work. But, perhaps more important, he was bothered by structural problems within the work itself that he felt he had not resolved adequately. So he undertook a significant revision of the concerto, completing it in 1956. He offered Stern another opportunity to present the concerto, this time with the Juilliard Orchestra, conducted by Jean Morel, in February 1956. But after this performance Schuman still had reservations about the work. After making further revisions, in 1959 he reached the point where he was satisfied, and this version was presented at the Aspen Music Festival in August 1959. Roman Totenberg was the soloist, and the orchestra was conducted by Izler Solomon. It is interesting to note that the final version of the concerto retained about 80 percent of the original version.[248]

In its final form, the Violin Concerto, comprising only two elaborate, multisectional movements, is, in the words of conductor José Serebrier, "one of Schuman's most powerful works. Emotionally packed, it could almost be considered a symphony for violin and orchestra. . . . The work is indeed extremely theatrical, evoking powerful emotions in a highly charged romantic atmosphere." Its sense of tremendous expressive urgency is conveyed from the first measure. As Serebrier aptly describes, "The first movement starts bluntly, as if the theatre curtain had gone up and the stage lights went on all at once."[249] The opening theme itself, marked *Allegro risoluto*, together with its accompaniment, is one of Schuman's most inspired and pregnant themes. Critic Harold Schonberg once commented that Schuman conveyed "a quality of quivering suppressed excitement, something like that of a leashed Doberman pinscher who sees a rabbit in the distance."[250] This opening theme vividly evokes that image. The violin enters with its motif, in strong half-notes and quarter-notes, "*ben legato*, with full broad strokes of the bow," while the accompaniment responds with *staccato* chords at irregular intervals, the combination of the two compelling the listener's attention instantly, as the violin line begins to spin off subsidiary motifs immediately. (One of these subsidiary motifs consists of an ascending tritone, followed by an ascending half-step, which some may recognize immediately as the main motif of Leonard Bernstein's score for *West Side Story* [1957]). Schuman described the concerto as "very Romantic." Although it is certainly powerful, bristling with a barely containable vigor and dynamism, it is romantic only in an abstract sense, rather than suggesting the rhetoric of nineteenth-century music, which it resembles in only the most conceptual sense; and, aside from the presentation of the main theme, the harmonic language of the work as a whole is too dissonant even to be considered Neo-Romantic. On the other hand, there is virtually no precedent in Schuman's work for a theme of such urgent emotional expression.

The first movement falls into a number of sections, but they are clearly discernable: the elaboration of the opening theme, which propels the several contrasting sections of the fifteen-minute first movement without a moment's flagging of interest; a contrasting section of exquisite poignancy and fragile lyricism, marked *Molto tranquillo*, in which the violin engages in a dialogue with the clarinet, then joined by the flute; a brief development during which the opening motif is heard in the strings *pizzicato*, against rapid triplets in the solo violin; a cadenza, in which the various ideas presented thus far are reviewed by the soloist with the customary virtuosic demands; a short section that recapitulates the spirit and character of the opening, though the material played by the solo violin is closer to the lyrical motif than to its predecessor; and, finally, a coda that brings the movement to a conclusion of considerable excitement and brilliance.

It was the second movement of the concerto that proved so elusive to Schuman, and, although he eventually arrived at a result that satisfied him, this movement continues to suffer from a lack of focus, with too many shifts in attitude and tempo, some of which are of questionable interest or necessity. The movement opens very dramatically, with a series of extremely dissonant chords in the brass and strings, punctuated by much activity in the timpani. The violin enters with a highly chromatic but lyrical line reminiscent in character of the second section of the first movement. This is followed by a string *fugato* introduced by the cellos on a subject derived from the opening theme of the first movement. It is after this *fugato* that the movement begins to lose focus, interrupted by brief cadenza-like fragments and empty virtuoso noodling. Interest returns for two passages in which the solo violin is accompanied by the three trombones; the second of these again recalls the opening theme of the first movement. An *Adagietto* follows, offering more opportunity for the soloist to pursue cadenza-like material. At last, the final section, marked *Pressing forward*, recapitulates much of the previous material in a powerful orchestral *tutti*, with interjections from the solo violin, until the work comes to a hair-raising conclusion, heralded by Schuman's obligatory and increasingly incongruous major triads. In spite of the waywardness of portions of the second movement, the concerto is one of Schuman's most compelling and exciting works, and ranks among the most important American violin concertos.

Interestingly, the concerto was received well in all three phases of its evolution. Immediately after the first premiere in Boston, an article in *Time* reported,

The first movement, full of vigor, speed and spirit, gave listeners a slice of "bread & butter"; there was a broad theme to hold on to, although in periods of paraphrase and pyrotechnics it sometimes slithered out of the average listener's grasp. In the second movement, an *andantino* "interlude," the violin sang a beautifully simple song. Composer Schuman split the furious pace of the last movement with a long brassy chorale. To one listener the concerto seemed "somewhat like a surrealistic painting—with familiar and beautiful forms in unfamiliar relationships and in a dreamlike atmosphere." Another subtitled it "The id in search of itself." One Boston critic found it "crabbed and harshly dissonant"; another "wanting likability" and "without heart." But beaming Conductor Munch thought that "with Bartók, Berg and Bloch, it is one of the most important concerti." Bill Schuman himself . . . was mighty pleased with 2½ minutes of applause.[251]

Of course it is the final version that it has been most frequently played and recorded, and its reception has been consistently favorable—more so than for any other work of Schuman, except perhaps for the Symphony No. 3. Composer-critic Lester Trimble called it a "magnificent work, with some of the most compelling and deeply affecting music, particularly in its slow, philosophical sections, that I have heard in any contemporary piece, by a composer of whatever nationality. It is a big opus, a half-hour long, and aims for the broadest possible statement."[252] Edward Seckerson commented perceptively,

Schuman comes straight to the point. Spurred on by chiselled syncopations in the orchestra, his soloist is caught in urgent flight from the first bar. As ever, this tough, energizing music is impatient to move on, loathe to be idle for so much as a second. Even the stillnesses, the long lyrical departures (and there are many) move inwardly, restlessly—primarily in the solo line, which is charged and rhapsodic. One instinctively feels Schuman's symphonic thinking throughout this big work: the lyric interludes are so clearly the natural product of those powerful motoric *tuttis* and vice versa: the hazy *tranquillo* which grows out of the agitated opening dialogue and finds the soloist in moody partnerships with clarinet and flute, is already pointing us in a new direction. There are landmarks to watch out for: typical Schumanesque touches, like the craggy fanfares proclaiming the second movement—timpani characteristically to the fore and still uneasily active as the brass subside under a pedal bass of strings. And there is one stunning release of energy, an eruption of whooping brass and sidedrum rim-shots when the end is in sight.[253]

Richard Schneider found it "a nervous, agitated, anxious, work, filled with nuclear jitters and cold-war paranoia, and yet there are moments of lyric repose and consolation, even the naïve euphoria which Schuman finds so irresistible as an expression of ultimate optimism."[254]

Even the commentators who noted the concerto's weaknesses viewed them as minor blemishes.

> This Schuman Concerto deserves to be planted firmly in the repertory. It's bold, romantic and contains some of the most personal and tender music Schuman ever wrote for orchestra. . . . With dominating attack, the violinist establishes a theme that takes hold and provides the substance for engrossing development and regeneration. There is character in this stuff, with phrases and lines of inspired breadth and shape. . . . The material eventually outstays its welcome. The concerto's one big weakness is exposed: The ending is trumped-up razzmatazz, sounding as a glued-on send-off. Disappointing yes, but the total piece overcomes it.[255]

Other enthusiastic commentators praised the concerto's "eloquence, power, and visceral excitement,"[256] and described it as "a masterpiece,"[257] "a terrific piece, full of high-energy lyricism . . . abundant in character, open, generous in emotion and high spirits";[258] "comes from the very top drawer of that eminent symphonist's output";[259] "one of the finest works to be composed in this format during the second half of this century";[260] "combines the rock-em-sock-em style of his early symphonies with some of his most lyrical writing. . . . [T]he concerto strikes this listener as a unified work which could not part with a single note."[261]

Still others added:

> The music has muscle and thrust and lyricism and imagination that make it one of the best of concertos galore for violin and orchestra by American composers since World War 2 (if you wonder, by the way, where Leonard Bernstein collected a whole portfolio of ideas, lend an ear). The *molto tranquillo* section five minutes into the opening movement is extraordinarily poetic, with the soloist playing *con sordino*. But then the music heats up again, and by the end of the second movement, you've been on a trip that included everything from turbulence to haute cuisine with champagne to a drop in cabin pressure to sudden changes in altitude.[262]

> The work can be stark, tender, delicately dancing but always on the edge of the abyss. There is a comforting big city loneliness about this music as well as some awed perspectives on mortality. . . . The end of the work is one of the most adrenaline-exciting yet substantial among all violin concertos—rushing, clamant, breathless, triumphant, defiant.[263]

Late Style-Period

As noted earlier, Schuman appeared to enter a new style-period in 1960 with his Symphony No. 7. For some time his music, as well as that of many other modern American symphonic traditionalists, had been characterized as "muscular" or "athletic," to the point where it had become a meaningless cliché. These terms were perhaps applied more aptly to Schuman than to most of the others. But Schuman also had an introspective side, and during his late period this side assumed increased prominence within his work, although at times it seemed to lack a convincing sense of the depths it was straining to plumb. Compared to the works of his middle period, these later works are somewhat less consistent in quality: At times Schuman seemed to be acknowledging some of the newer compositional trends, exhibiting less dependence on tonal centers, while exploring a higher level of harmonic dissonance, as well as an expanded treatment of the percussion section. Some listeners and critics were able to follow these directions along with him, but others parted company with him at this point. Furthermore, some compositions betray a sense of redundancy, as devices and techniques found in earlier pieces are recycled anew. Although some of his new works continued the process of creative evolution and development over the course of the years, others were marred by lapses into mannerism, self-quotation, a rather artificial grandiloquence, and a pseudo-profound orotundity, with grave moods and solemn subject matter, unsustained by compelling musical substance.

As noted earlier, Christopher Rouse identified essentially the same three phases to Schuman's compositional career as does this study, although he dated the beginning of the third period a year or two earlier than is done here. Rouse attempted to make the most positive case for these later works, referring to this phase as Schuman's "rhetorical" period, noting that these works are

> increasingly dramatic. Textures are simplified, and complex polyphony occurs less frequently. Harmonic rhythm . . . becomes noticeably slower, and the ratio of slow music to fast becomes markedly greater. If the mood of the "expressionistic" works can be described as introspective or introverted, these later scores are often threnodial and monolithically anguished. The composer's use of dissonance becomes freer, and the dissonant harmonies themselves become even more pungent.[264]
>
> These more recent scores . . . are more stoic, almost ritualized in their sense of tragedy. I say "tragedy" rather than "gloom" because Schuman's music, however serious, is never morbid; his music speaks more of resignation than of surrender . . . but now the language is more dissonant still than in an earlier piece such as the Third Symphony, and the grandeur is more often tempered by a contemplation of other concerns.[265]

Joseph Polisi views the increased complexity, greater harmonic astringency, and textural density of Schuman's later music as a response to the disparagement of his work after 1960 by the "New Music" partisans. "So he's perceived as being this populist out of Americana. . . . I often think that he was driven to more chromaticism, to more complexity of rhythm, to more dissonance, because of that. . . . And it's not audience accessible on first listening. You have to really study it and understand where Bill is going. Then it's deeply compelling. But for an uninitiated audience to hear his Eighth Symphony is a challenging experience."[266]

Regarding some of these matters, Schuman commented,

> In my own music, I tried to follow the dictates of my own tastes. The only thing that's a serious mistake on the part of any composer is to try to be "with it," because if he tries to be with it, he's out of it. You only have your own thing to say in your own way. I have never written a note of music in my life that was not deeply felt. I am always absolutely certain in my own mind what the *emotional character* of a piece is going to be. My music has changed over the years—the harmonic language has gotten more complicated, for one thing. But I don't think the actual idiom is of any importance, as long as the composer has something to say. I don't work with key centers, but the music is melodic, and it has a sense of line. My music can always be *sung*. . . . I think the symphony orchestra is one of the superb creations of man.[267]

The first work of Schuman's late style-period is his Symphony No. 7, commissioned by the Koussevitzky Music Foundation in commemoration of the seventy-fifth anniversary of the Boston Symphony Orchestra. Schuman completed the work, which incorporated material from a documentary film score he had composed for Time-Life, Inc., and expanded ideas from the second of his Three Piano Moods—music he had composed just before the symphony—in 1960.

Schuman has been widely quoted as saying, "My own general feeling is that my Seventh, Eighth, and Ninth Symphonies are somehow connected in my mind, perhaps because they represent the efforts, more or less, of a single decade."[268] On the other hand, the Seventh may be seen as following fairly closely the line of evolution displayed by its predecessor of some twelve years earlier: pushing to expand the boundaries of Modern Traditionalism and challenging the tolerance of his listeners by introducing greater expressive and structural complexity, as well as achieving a fuller emancipation from tonality, as it is perceived by the general concert-going public. The result is abstract in expression, with virtually no reference to classical forms: a drama of gestures that looms as the chief source of coherence—to the extent that he was successful in achieving this. Those who were sympathetic to his new direction praised its profound introspectiveness; those who were less so found the music dull and empty. Nowhere was this divergence of opinion among both audiences and critics more apparent than in reactions to the Seventh Symphony, although it has persisted throughout the ensuing years.

Half an hour in duration and scored for a large orchestra, the symphony comprises four movements, following each other without pauses. Reminiscent of some of Shostakovich's middle-period symphonies, Schuman's Seventh opens with a lengthy slow movement. In fact, the two longest movements are slow, while the two shortest are fast, resulting in a preponderance of very slow music. This fact alone probably contributes to its being perhaps the most difficult to penetrate of all Schuman's symphonies. The first movement, *Largo assai*, introduces a dense background texture through a slow-moving sequence of menacing, darkly brooding, dissonant, thickly scored chords, moving from one to the next via lurching dotted rhythms. These chords include a melodic line, so to speak—a gradually ascending series of notes that comprise all twelve tones. Soon the trumpet introduces what is perhaps the symphony's main motif: a rising major-third, followed by a rising perfect-fifth, outlining a major-seventh. Energy gradually accumulates as multiple bands of parallel thirds interact contrapuntally, further intensifying the dense web of dissonance. This configuration changes markedly as the bass clarinet plays a nagging, highly chromatic solo cadenza, punctuated by brass chords, and is soon joined by the soprano clarinet in contrary motion. The movement as a whole does not lend itself to easy characterization.

The clarinet duet leads directly into the second movement, *Vigoroso*, a three-minute *scherzo* based on the ascending motif introduced by the trumpet in the first movement. This is the familiar, readily identifiable side of Schuman: lively, with his distinctive, urgently syncopated rhythmic patterns. Although the material is very dissonant, and densely contrapuntal, the overall concept is relatively simple.

The third movement, *Cantabile intensamente*, is the expressive heart of the work. Scored for strings only, the movement develops a dense counterpoint based on motifs derived from the symphony's opening melodic line. The movement builds to an almost unprecedented level of agonizing intensity, although it seems to lose focus after the climax, wandering aimlessly to its conclusion.

The finale, *Scherzando brioso*, proves to be a second *scherzo*, also based on the opening line from the first movement. This is again familiar Schuman territory, with running passages in the strings and twittering woodwinds juxtaposed against pugnacious, hard-bitten punctuation in the brasses, and lots of percussion; a *legato* melody toward the middle offers a modicum of contrast. Finally, the ending is near, signaled as this largely dissonant, atonal music gradually gives way to the approach of a major triad, which finally comes fully into view—fifth on top once again—accompanied by much percussion clatter, in an incongruously triumphant peroration. Whether the four movements of this work—connected though they may be—comprise a convincingly coherent statement has remained an open question since its first performance.

The premiere of Schuman's Symphony No. 7 was given in October 1960 by the Boston Symphony Orchestra, conducted by Charles Munch. Critical reactions were mixed at best. The notoriously outspoken Winthrop Sargeant wrote, "Nobody, as far as I could make out, approached the other night's performance expecting it to slake a deep thirst for emotional experience, and nobody left the hall with his heart aflame or with his brain set tingling by intellectual stimulation. The new symphony, like many of its kind, was not so much a work of art as what is nowadays called a status symbol."[269] Harold Schonberg wrote, "Mr. Schuman has his own style of melody, and it's not to everybody's taste. . . . The harmonic dissonance that underpinned it sounded too tense and, even, rather dated."[270] On the other hand, Paul Hume found it "a piece of unmistakable power."[271] Leopoldo Frias commented, "The music is both lean and lusty, altogether 'American' in its dynamism and brass component. But Schuman clearly understands that volume must serve rhetoric, and he handles his forces convincingly."[272] One English critic wrote, "It was the opening *Largo assai* of Schuman's Symphony No. 7 (1960) which first convinced me that hitherto I had under-rated this composer, and this piece . . . shows him near his best. . . . [T]he self-confidence of the leaping phrases and open, brusquely-rhythmed textures and the sureness of the music's formal processes, are attractive in themselves. Sometimes, as during the second movement, the drive is nearly overwhelming, the athletic energy seeming, at first hearing, too much at variance with the dark introspection of the *Largo* and *Cantabile.*"[273] But another English critic, writing for the journal *Music and Letters* differed sharply: "William Schuman's symphony is tough going. Gritty and aggressive, it does not try to persuade but to batter one into acceptance. I, personally, refuse to be so battered, but others may enjoy the masochistic experience and win through to some sort of understanding."[274]

Composer and American music scholar Karl Kroeger was quite harsh in appraising this new work, and offered a stinging indictment:

William Schuman's Seventh Symphony . . . is, like its predecessors, a large, complicated, and serious work. . . . One cannot deny that the score has some moments of brilliance, and even inspiration . . . however, so much of the material has been heard so many times before in so many other Schuman works that it is no longer either appealing or interesting. The incisive dotted rhythms of the first movement, the trumpet calls and rim-shots of the second movement, the complex counterpoint of the third movement, and the fast rhythmic exchanges between the woodwinds, brass, and strings of the fourth movement, have become such familiar parts of Schuman's orchestral music that they are now only bland stereotypes. Moreover, one tires of hearing the major-minor triad used to death. Though Schuman does use other harmonic combinations, tone-clusters and the like, he seems always to fall back on this sound that is so hackneyed, and of which one tires so quickly. Frankly, one wishes that a composer of Mr. Schuman's distinguished reputation would recognize the fact that it is not sufficient simply to rewrite, over and over, the same piece with minor variations. If one's music is to live it must be reborn with every work. As it is, the Symphony was old-hat before the ink dried on the page.[275]

In *The American Symphony*, Butterworth expressed much the same reaction as Kroeger:

> Of the complete symphonic canon [the Seventh] is the most conventional, lacking few truly memorable moments; the composer's characteristics have become mannerisms. . . . [In the first movement] there is a debilitating overuse of thick scoring of multiple parallel triads in a very slow tempo that inevitably leads to a monotonous tonal texture. . . . [In the second movement] heavy orchestration and lack of melodic development never allow the music to generate momentum or excitement. The third movement . . . is the only part of the Seventh Symphony with any distinct personality. . . . [In the fourth movement] nagging irregular rhythms never escape the treadmill repetition, again seriously weighed down by hefty orchestration. The mind-numbing impact of the full forces, including an unrelenting percussion section, merely serves to underline the lack of significant development of the initial material.[276]

The first recording of the Symphony No. 7 was released in 1971, in a performance featuring the Utah Symphony Orchestra under the direction of Maurice Abravanel. In her program notes for this recording, Sheila Keats was a fervent advocate. While bearing in mind that liner notes for a recording constitute paid advertising for that recording, one can readily perceive how differently she views this work, as she enthuses that it

> reveals in full maturity the emerging romanticism, increasing profundity, and deepening introspection evidenced by [recent works], while retaining all of his earlier orchestral glamour, kinetic energy, and rhythmic verve. . . . The opening . . . supplies the work with an intense and brooding introduction. . . . The prevailingly dark sonority, . . . and most significantly, the bass clarinet, is . . . used here as a harbinger of the affirmation to come later in the work. . . . With [the] second movement . . . we emerge from the conflict and dark intensity of the opening. Here is unrestricted, joyful affirmation. . . . . [In] the third movement . . . the intensity here is tempered by an expressive tenderness. . . . Rhythmic excitement and brilliant orchestral color provide the basic materials for the finale . . . . The initial rhythmic statement expands into the movement's true principal theme, a brisk and cheerful syncopated dance motif.[277]

Polisi too considers the Seventh to be "an extraordinary composition that projected an exceptional pathos."[278] However, he also recounts an anecdote supposedly overheard after a performance of this work: An elderly woman in the audience was expressing some surprise to her husband, remarking that the work didn't sound to her like "Schumann." Her husband calmly explained that this work was composed shortly before the German Romantic went insane.[279]

The last work Schuman composed before leaving Juilliard to take on the presidency of Lincoln Center was a commission from the Ford Foundation, on behalf of cellist Leonard Rose. In 1944 Schuman had composed a setting of "Orpheus with His Lute," as incidental music for a production of Shakespeare's *Henry VIII* that never actually materialized. At one point Vincent Persichetti had suggested that the song, a largely diatonic setting with some unexpected harmonic touches that create a remarkable poignancy, was a promising theme for a set of variations. As he pondered how to proceed with the new work, Schuman recalled Persichetti's suggestion. But instead of a classical theme with variations, Schuman decided on a freer, more spontaneous form. The result, completed in 1961, was *A Song of Orpheus: Fantasy for Cello and Orchestra*. Schuman scored the work for an orchestra without brasses (except for French horns) or percussion; both the English horn and the harp, suggesting Orpheus's lute, play an important role throughout much of the piece.

The work begins with a complete statement of the original song by the cello, unaccompanied at first. In the score Shakespeare's words are printed under the cello part, so that the soloist has a sense of the song's original meaning. (The composer also specified that the words be printed in the program notes.) Schuman later commented,

> As I began to compose *Song of Orpheus*, I decided to open with a statement of the theme by the cello. I soon found myself enjoying the freedom to interrupt the song with harmonic statements, little things which gave atmosphere, and enjoying the business of interpreting the song in a different way than I had done before. As the variations unfolded, they evolved into very unconventional variations which centered around one or two segments of the melody. . . . I did not call it a concerto because I think of it as a fantasy with a simpler approach.[280]

After the cello has presented a solemn rendition of the song in D-sharp minor, the solo oboe takes over the song melody while the solo cello begins to launch the fantasy by spinning a somber, austere, chromatic line in polytonal counterpoint, while the strings play sustained chords, soon joined by strummed chords in the harp. Orchestrated with haunting subtlety, the music gradually builds intensity until the orchestra drops out, leaving the solo cello to reflect on the material in a brief cadenza. This proves to be a transition to a much faster, more playful section, with skittering woodwinds in parallel thirds, while the cello plays rapidly, but seems oblivious to the orchestra. Then the cello drops out for a powerful *tutti* passage, replete with the composer's favorite orchestral devices. After the horns assert their own blaring developmental passage, the cello rejoins the proceedings, but only briefly, before the orchestra drops out again, leaving the cello to embark on an elaborate, virtuosic cadenza, with only occasional comments from the ensemble. After the cadenza the opening mood of somber gravity returns, and the music moves in a more diatonic direction, as the English horn plays a portion of the song melody, leading to a striking iteration of the first part of this melody by the cello in harmonics, accompanied by flutes and harp. The music trails away with ineffable sadness as the cello plays a few notes of the song once more, before the work comes to an unresolved conclusion, the cello sustaining a B, against the tonic D-sharp-minor triad in the orchestra. (It is noteworthy that such a subdued ending is exceedingly rare—especially up to this point—among Schuman's major works.)

A Song of Orpheus must be regarded as a mixed success. The opening and closing portions in particular are extremely and hauntingly beautiful, and much of the developmental activity is compelling throughout. However, the lengthy cadenza that comprises the central portion of the work is drastically overextended, with much empty, gratuitous passagework. Alan Rich described it as "a beautiful work, slow and quiet for most of its 20-minute length. Harmonically quite diatonic, the work really sings. The scoring, for winds and strings, is clear and open allowing the soloist to wander in and out of the texture with considerable freedom." He concluded by citing it as "one of the most eloquent American compositions to appear in some time."[281] On the other hand, the English critic Peter Dickinson found it to be "unfortunately the kind of work a busy and enlightened musical administrator might be expected to produce. It falls back on facile formulas in bitonality or parallel intervals, and offers the cellist disappointingly conventional fare. The composer is better equipped for logical discourse than rhapsodic fantasy, which has caused vacillations of idiom in this work."[282] This review is especially notable as an early instance in which Schuman's administrative activities were used to disparage his prowess as a composer. This perspective was encountered with increasing frequency during the years that followed.

The premiere of *A Song of Orpheus* took place in Indianapolis, Indiana, in February 1962. Leonard Rose was the cellist with the Indianapolis Symphony Orchestra, conducted by Izler Solomon. The first recording of the work was released in 1964; Rose again was soloist, this time with the Cleveland Orchestra, under the direction of George Szell.

Philharmonic Hall (now Avery Fisher Hall) opened in the fall of 1962, the first constituent of Lincoln Center to begin functioning. Schuman had been commissioned by the New York Philharmonic to provide a new work for its opening concerts. The result was the Symphony No. 8, whose premiere took place in October 1962. This was not just the public presentation of a major new work by one of America's foremost composers; it was also a symbol. As a new creative effort by the recently appointed president of Lincoln Center, the symphony was a virtual statement of artistic identity for the new arts complex; it also highlighted the orchestra in its new home, as well as Leonard Bernstein, music director of the New York Philharmonic and a champion of Schuman's music for more than twenty years. So this premiere was an auspicious occasion, and Schuman was no doubt fully aware of its significance within his career, as well as its being a milestone for Lincoln Center itself. A recording of the work, featuring the same performers, was released the following year.

During the 1960s, as serial music took center stage as the dominant approach within "New Music" circles, composers frequently accompanied their latest works with elaborate program notes that described the techniques used in their creation. These descriptions were often long and detailed, written in an esoteric technical jargon that was largely meaningless to an audience of nonprofessionals, except as an indication of the "advanced," complex procedures involved. So when Schuman was asked by the orchestra's program annotator for some comments on the work, his response was a political, not just a personal, statement.

> Frankly, over the years I have become increasingly resistant about issuing play-by-play accounts of my own music. Perhaps I'm making a minor protest against the elaborate essays which these days so often accompany the launching of new works. Complicated polemics for particular aesthetic creeds of compositional procedures may be of value to scholars, but they confuse laymen. Techniques, after all, are work methods, which, in the mature artist, cannot be isolated from his creative process. . . . That is not to say that it is not desirable to help an active listener hear more in his first exposure to a new work . . . Certainly, a writer can supply helpful guideposts and I am all for it, provided he sticks to the music and avoids philosophical meandering. In time, the music will be judged by its inherent worth. Fortunately, no propaganda, however skillfully contrived, can, in the final analysis, substitute for genuine criteria any more than prose explanations can substitute for musical clarity.[283]

On the other hand, Schuman did acknowledge that exposure to the music of younger composers opened his eyes and ears to new approaches to orchestration—particularly regarding a much more varied and prominent use of percussion instruments. This is readily apparent in the Eighth Symphony.

Schuman's Eighth Symphony, scored for a large orchestra, comprises three movements, each of which is subdivided further into sections. The first movement, *Lento sostenuto; Pressante vigoroso; Lento*, opens with an unforgettably rich, dense harmonic texture—a D-major-minor triad, scored for woodwinds, pitched percussion, two harps, piano, and strings (*pizzicato*, on downbeat only). A series of more dissonant chords follows, built around the ubiquitous major-minor triad, creating an ominous mood. Superimposed over this texture is an extended French horn solo—solemn and searching—that uses all twelve tones, while introducing the minor-third, major- and minor-sevenths, and tritone as intervallic motifs that will figure significantly throughout the work. This horn melody is largely atonal, despite occasional brief moments of tonal implication. It is followed by an extended oboe solo that continues in a similar manner, accompanied by trumpets and trombones, and is then passed to the violins for further development. This finally culminates in an angst-laden outburst in which the melody continues in the strings, against chattering woodwinds, and stern, jagged chords in the brass, which eventually move to the forefront in a kind of manic hysteria. There is a return to the opening mood, but now with a more menacing impact.

The second movement, *Largo; Tempi più mosso; Largo*, follows on the heels of the first, and is, like the first, mostly slow. It is largely a reworking of the third movement of the String Quartet No. 4, although its impact in orchestral garb is considerably richer than that conveyed by a small chamber group. The longest of the three movements, it is an austere, largely atonal lament that gradually builds in intensity through grinding harmonic dissonances. A passage suggesting the tread of footsteps leads to an expansive melody in the lower instruments, against hard-bitten dissonances in the brass, creating the familiar Schuman effect of multiple planes of simultaneous but seemingly unrelated activity. The intensity continues building to a climax, followed by a decline in the energy level, then succeeded by an agitated undercurrent of triplets. This section builds to another large climax and then recedes. A slow-moving chordal passage is heard in the lower strings and lower woodwinds, while the flutes and clarinets chatter nervously and unrelatedly above. The texture thickens, as additional instruments gradually join one or the other of these elements. The horns enter, taking over the melody, while the other brasses offer jagged punctuation. As the movement draws to a close, there is a striking instrumental effect in which the piano and two harps strum an arpeggiated accompaniment to the woodwinds. There is a reference to the opening of the symphony before the movement ends on a major-minor triad.

The finale, *Presto; Prestissimo*, provides a marked contrast to the preceding movements. Roughly suggesting *rondo* form, it is a tour de force of orchestration, with much percussion activity that places an emphasis on bell sounds, including a notable solo for the vibraphone. Its flamboyant orchestration is notable in view of the fact that this movement is a reworking of the Quartet No. 4 finale, although it is barely recognizable as such when presented in such flashy instrumental dress. The movement is typical of the composer's fast music, with its syncopated rhythms, rapid leaps back and forth among the instrumental choirs, long *legato* melodies juxtaposed against irregular running figures, and barely suppressed nervous agitation. Although the movement is largely atonal throughout, a pedal G is heard, signaling the ending and a possible tonic, while additional percussion piles on. A triumphant G-major triad is heard, but C-major, F-major, and B-flat-major triads are added to it immediately, building to a noisy, strident conclusion.

With its brilliant orchestration, highlighted by bell-like sonorities, this symphony is a major showcase for William Schuman's most distinctive techniques, identified during the foregoing description. Yet once again listeners' reactions seem to be divided between those who perceive the work as a profound abstract statement and those who hear it as a work straining to sound profound. Some commentators again expressed impatience with the composer's overuse of his own familiar devices. As with most of his late compositions, there are parts that are stunning in their impact and others that seem to be setting the backdrop for something striking that never occurs. The preponderance of slow music—in this case, two consecutive movements—may be seen by some as self-indulgent, especially passages in those movements that seem inflated to no purpose.

Critical reactions to the symphony reflect such ambivalent feelings. *Time* found it to be "a typically Schuman-crafted product: powerful, impetuous, rhythmically complex and grindingly dissonant—a work more notable for its vigor and blaring momentum than for charm or lyric effect."[284] The *New York Times* critic called it "tragic and intense," adding, "It has two slow movements and a swift finale, which for all its rhythmic difference from the earlier movements, seems very much part of them. Indeed, the whole work hangs together remarkably well and one gets the sense of a piece dominated by a single broad-arched, rather mournful melody. It was unfailingly expressive and one was struck by the mastery shown in the use of interesting instrumental color to communicate what seemed the symphony's essential intent."[285] Alfred Frankenstein described it as "one of the most somber, profound, monumental and moving symphonies in recent years. Following none of the academicisms of contemporary music, this work is, like most of Schuman's music, ingeniously complex, altogether original in form, and wonderfully orchestrated."[286]

A more penetrating commentary, though one perhaps overly influenced by the attitudes of the times, was offered by conductor, critic, and former colleague Richard Franko Goldman, who was

[surprised] . . . to realize how fundamentally conservative Schuman's Eighth proves to be, not only in its evident concern with tonality and its handling of melodic ideas, but in its structural concepts and its implicit esthetic. It is a big, romantic work, not unlike a Tchaikovskyan symphony, having many of the same virtues and possibly a few of the same faults. The orchestral handling is, of course, assured and brilliant; the opening pages in particular, are stunning in sound. These pages are, in all respects, the most impressive of the entire work. The Symphony is in three lengthy movements, of which only the last is at a fast tempo. . . . The texture of the first movement is fairly thick, as is that of the second; as a result the final movement seems oddly lighter and not entirely relevant or successful. As with all of Schuman's large works, there are pages of astonishing power and beauty. But one cannot say that interest is sustained at an equal level throughout. Technically, the Eighth reveals little change from Schuman's other works of recent years. The basic harmonic trademark is still the major-minor triad in wide-open position; the melodies are still more notable as "tunes" than as themes or motifs; and the rhythmic bounce and restlessness, the energetic punctuation of brass and percussion are still stylistically characteristic. In the Eighth Symphony, one feels this latter element of the Schuman style to be more of an overlay than it has appeared to be previously.[287]

Perhaps the most incisive and telling point was penned by the noted British critic Hugh Ottaway, who remarked,

Neither avant-garde nor unadventurous, such music tends to fall between the acclamation of the few and the acceptance of the many. Nobody has much to say about it, less still a determination to perform it. . . . Composed for a large orchestra, this symphony is certainly "big-intentioned," but I find it hard to discover what the intentions really are. There is a great deal of conscientious manipulation of motives, in a way that seems to fidget rather than further the musical argument, and all too little well-directed movement capable of generating a large-scale dramatic structure. Schuman's many big gestures are self-defeating, partly as a result of his habitual overscoring, but also because the music never really develops a convincing momentum. This is academic modernism, with a vengeance.[288]

When the symphony was heard in Philadelphia some twenty years later, critic Daniel Webster commented that it "sounds somber and insistent. Despite its large instrumentation, it seems to be a series of arias for solo instruments against the background blocks of sound from brass, strings or woodwind. The oboe, horn, bassoon, violin all have their chance to sing in this work, but for all the singing the music is dark, the kind of thing that invites publishers to add the word 'Tragic' to the title."[289]

Attempting to revive Schuman's posthumous reputation, some more recent commentators display a revisionist advocacy:

The Eighth Symphony is an orchestral tour de force. From the opening chords you . . . are confronted with distinctive, and quite original orchestration for the accompaniment of a long solo in the french horn. The dissonant quality of the harmonic vocabulary is heightened by a relatively conventional harmonic rhythm usually associated with a less strident harmonic structure. Relative dissonances are offered on strong beats with the use of brass and percussion strengthening the intensity. The entire first movement has the character of lament tinged with bitterness. The second movement is in the nature of an orchestral song. The finale is difficult to describe. The metaphor that comes to mind is a moto perpetuo from hell. The pace is almost unrelenting as it screams along the way. I would find it difficult to imagine anyone not being affected for there is a level of intensity that one rarely finds in music. While there is strength in the thematic material, it is clearly the scoring that brings out the emphasis. This becomes clear when one listens to the finale as it was originally conceived, as the last movement of his 4th String Quartet. This Symphony is not an easy listen but the conventional formal structure and rhythmic style, with plenty of references to jazz, including a vibraphone solo, provide a clear sense of direction and drama. There are few works that come to mind that convey such an overwhelming sense of power.[290]

By the time Schuman wrote his Eighth Symphony . . . his emotional and harmonic palette had darkened considerably; and the first two of the symphony's three very substantial movements are predominantly slow (though with active central sections that collapse into despair) and very somber indeed. But what a velvety lush and sonorous gloom Schuman calls forth in those tolling, richly orchestrated chordal dissonances, wide-spanning horn cantilenas, tormented strings that rock back and forth in lament, and grimly defiant outbursts of brass and percussion. Even at his darkest Schuman is theatrical, and for the presto finale he lets out all the stops, bringing this so-far doom-laden symphony to a rhythmically super-charged conclusion.[291]

The most often-performed composition associated with Schuman—perhaps even more popular than *New England Triptych*—is his orchestration of Charles Ives's impishly satirical *Variations on "America,"* originally composed for organ in 1891. Schuman made his transcription—without changing any of the actual music—in 1963, on a commission from BMI. The result was first performed by the New York Philharmonic, conducted by Andre Kostelanetz in May 1964, and it has been a hit with audiences ever since. Although its success is well deserved, as the transcription is delightful, maintaining the appropriate tone of levity, it is also somewhat ironic, as Schuman had considerable reservations about the music of Ives, which he considered "vastly over-rated."[292] "I've rarely been moved by Ives' music and, despite a few lovely pieces . . . would venture to guess that the percentage of his output that will prove viable, that will enter the repertoire, will be quite small. . . . But if I've not often been moved by Ives, I have been intrigued. What I love is the *idea* of Ives—that eccentric character, that insurance man, getting all those crazy, innovative ideas. He had a great and original creative urge, and I have an extraordinary admiration for him."[293]

During the 1940s Schuman had become acquainted with Marion Jones Farquhar, a tennis champion who was also a translator of librettos and other music-related texts. She had introduced him to a number of old English rounds, which he found fascinating; they were to play significant roles in some of his later compositions. The one that affected him most deeply was "Amaryllis." So when Schuman was commissioned by the Elizabeth Sprague Coolidge Foundation some twenty years later to provide a work to be performed at the Library of Congress, he composed *Amaryllis: Variations for String Trio*, completing it in 1964.

The twenty-five-minute piece begins as the complete melody of the round is played very slowly in unison at the octave by the viola and cello, both muted. As with *A Song of Orpheus*, the words to the round are printed in the instrumental parts together with the actual notes, so that the player can "project the melody with the clarity of a singer." After this first statement, the violin enters, playing the complete melody, while the viola provides a modern but stylistically congruent line of counterpoint, the cello maintaining a tonic drone. After four measures, the viola joins the violin in unison two octaves below, while the cello then enters with the round melody. The trio continues with the round for several repetitions, embellished by increasingly anachronistic modifications. This then leads into a series of four variations.

Abandoning any semblance of the Elizabethan style, the first variation features a process of individual, overlapping notes played on the three instruments, within a chromatic, angular language, in which the relationship to the theme may be more apparent on paper than it is perceptible to the listener. The second variation is very fast and much lighter in texture, as the violin and cello play *staccato* fragments in a manner that suggests both hocketing and canon, and even bebop jazz, while the viola continues in long rhythmic values in the manner of a *cantus firmus*. But there is no actual canon, nor actual *cantus firmus*, nor any perceptible relation to the theme. The third variation begins very aggressively, and in rhythmic unison. The dynamic level drops quickly, as the three instruments pursue a highly angular, dissonant counterpoint with only the most remote connection to the main theme. The fourth variation is again very fast, the instruments playing in rhythmic unison; there is some inconsistent unison of pitch as well. This variation bears some relationship to Schuman's typical "fast music." A pointillistic transition leads to a running contrapuntal passage, followed by an even faster passage with much imitative counterpoint. After reaching a climax of sorts, the energy recedes, bringing the variations to a quietly subdued conclusion.

At this point there is a surprise, as three solo sopranos appear and, over a tonic pedal in the cello, proceed to sing the entire round in its original form. As they continue, the string trio enters, one instrument at a time, reinforcing the vocal counterpoint with a sort of heterophonous canon of their own, having returned to the tonal, diatonic style of the opening section. This section is very moving, if perhaps somewhat overextended. A merging of the two styles then brings the work to a quiet conclusion.

Although the opening and closing sections of *Amaryllis* are quite beautiful, the variations are most unsatisfactory: Their atonal, disjointed language appears abruptly and without sufficient preparation; their relationship to the theme is tenuous; and the high level of harmonic dissonance is especially abrasive in view of the overlapping registers of the instruments, so that the intervallic juxtapositions are often very close together. Polisi attributes the exceedingly harsh language to the tension and stress that Schuman was experiencing in his position at Lincoln Center.[294] Another, perhaps more cynical explanation is that this may have been an example of Schuman's attempting to update his musical language by incorporating the kinds of fragmentary gestures, continuous vertical dissonance, and indistinct rhythmic pulse that were favored by the post-Webernian serialists then in fashion.

The premiere of the work was given by the New York String Trio at the Library of Congress in Washington, D.C., in October 1964. There has been no recording thus far. The response of critics was mixed. Composer-critic Robert Evett observed that the surprise appearance of the three sopranos at the end "was the only note in a protracted work that could be construed as an attempt at levity." He continued,

> The music is a set of variations on an Elizabethan round. The theme is long and slow in any case, longer and slower as exposed by Mr. Schuman, and tonal in the most unyielding sense of the word. The exposition takes several minutes. The segments that occupy the lengthy middle of the piece are non-tonal . . . The long and solemn coda . . . is a colorful restatement of the original materials. . . . For me, the juxtaposition of tonal and non-tonal materials was unsettling, and the obscurity of the theme in the variations was confusing. Nonetheless, the seriousness of the piece and the brilliance of the string writing were impressive, and the New York String Trio put on a dazzling show.[295]

The critic from the English journal *Music and Letters* found the work representative of

> the traditional style of tonal music but treated in a harmonically most astringent manner. The four variations are based on the old English round "Turn Amaryllis to thy swain," stated in the introduction in a modal G# minor, and are in the nature of "character" pieces, each projecting a different mood and a different texture. . . . The speed increases from variation to variation up to *prestissimo* and thus adds to their cumulative effect. The ending brings a surprise in that the

round is now sung in canon at the unison (in a modal A minor) by three sopranos; there is an alternative instrumental conclusion in case voices are not available. This is highly resourceful music, notably in the way the theme is subjected
to variation technique, and written with great economy.[296]

In June 1967, on a trip to Rome, Schuman and his wife visited the site of a
1944 massacre by the Nazis of 335 Italians—Jews as well as Christians—in
retaliation for the killing of thirty-two German soldiers by Italian partisans.
To conceal the deed, the Germans had blown up the site, burying the bodies of the Italians in the rubble, subsequently known as Le Fosse Ardeatine,
where a monument was later erected. This encounter moved Schuman so
deeply that he decided to memorialize the site—and the incident—in his next
work, commissioned on behalf of the Philadelphia Orchestra. This would
be his Ninth Symphony, which he subtitled "Le Fosse Ardeatine"—the first
of his symphonies to be given a subtitle or to be associated with any extramusical element. Interestingly, in light of his remarks concerning program
notes with regard to his Eighth Symphony, Schuman prepared an elaborate
commentary for the Ninth that he insisted be printed whenever the work is
performed. In them he explained that the symphony, completed in 1968, was
an expression of his feelings upon confronting the site of the massacre and
learning of the event. He wrote,

> The mood of my symphony, especially in its opening and closing sections,
> is directly related to emotions engendered by this visit. But the entire middle
> section, too, with its various moods of fast music, much of it far from somber,
> stems from the fantasies I had of the variety, promise and aborted lives of the
> martyrs. . . . The work does not attempt to depict the event realistically. . . . My
> reason for using the title is not, then, musical, but philosophical. One must come
> to terms with the past in order to build a future. But in this exercise I am a foe of
> forgetting. Whatever future my symphony may have, whenever it is performed,
> audiences will remember.[297]

The Symphony No. 9, "Le Fosse Ardeatine," is one of the most profoundly
affecting works of Schuman's late style-period. Despite its extrinsic source of
inspiration, the work itself is as abstract and structurally autonomous as any
of his other symphonies; as in No. 7, its movements—three in this case—are
played without pause. However, what distinguishes this work is the intensity
of its expression. Schuman acknowledged that his emotional reaction to the
historical incident affected him throughout the composition of the symphony;
it is perhaps for this reason that it is far more compelling than Nos. 7 or 8,
joining Nos. 3 and 6 as his most fully consummated works in that genre. With
a palpable sense of horrifying drama and almost unbearably intense emotion,

not to mention more sheer musical activity than either of its predecessors, the Ninth is gripping from beginning to end. This is music based on varying degrees of inner tensile energy. Here Schuman's distinctive use of several simultaneous planes of activity, seemingly unrelated to or independent of each other, is taken to its extreme as widely divergent types of activity occur concurrently; perceptible tonality has by now all but disappeared. Yet despite its consistently grim, harsh character, the music is remarkably eloquent.

Although Schuman named the three sections of his Symphony No. 9 "Anteludium," "Offertorium," and "Postludium," the score does not indicate where one section ends and the next begins. However, the listener can discern the changes in mood and level of activity. "Anteludium" begins as a canon, played very slowly, and introduces a long, wide-ranging melodic line comprising all twelve notes played in unison by the muted first violins and cellos, at a distance of two octaves. (The interval of the tritone figures significantly in this theme and will become the work's most important motivic element.) As in the Third Symphony and other works, the second entrance—by the second violins and violas—begins a half-step higher than the first, creating a highly dissonant imitative counterpoint. The strings are then subdivided, providing the third entrance, an additional half-step higher than the last. After this entrance is complete, the piercing canon continues in the strings, while the woodwinds interject rapid, chirping figures that emphasize the tritone. At first the woodwinds play in unison, but then they too subdivide, becoming increasingly active, their clipped gestures in stark contrast to the flowing but highly dissonant counterpoint in the strings. All four horns then enter, blaring the original canon theme, now added to the already-dense texture. The remaining brasses, joined by active percussion, enter in canon, while the strings now pursue an angular line that emphasizes the tritone. This complex texture builds to an intense level of dissonance, proclaimed with considerable power and aggression. After it has reached its climax, the music begins to calm down, in transition to the second section.

The "Offertorium" is the longest section of the work. A stunning, brilliantly orchestrated sonic showpiece, it is fast in tempo and very active, with many changes of mood and character. It is also the movement that is most "old-fashioned" within the context of Schuman's stylistic evolution, although it is almost completely atonal. (It is noteworthy that in his later works the composer explored unprecedented levels of harmonic dissonance, while his approach to rhythm remained generally similar to his previous practices, thereby providing an anchor of familiarity for the listener.) This movement may be seen as a rowdy fantasy in which Schuman exploited to the hilt all his favorite devices—jagged, twitching rhythmic patterns;

frequent passages in parallelism, especially at the interval of the third; and individualized treatment of the different sections of the orchestra, often simultaneously, in an almost Ivesian juxtaposition of drastically different types of activity. The section begins softly and stealthily in the strings until the woodwinds enter, twittering playfully, against sustained chords in the brass. An extended bass clarinet solo introduces a long polyphonic passage for woodwinds only. There is a brief return to the character of the beginning of the movement, now with strings *pizzicato*, before the music goes off in further different directions, in which the piano plays an important role, while the large, active percussion section frequently erupts explosively. A brief lyrical section toward the middle of the movement offers some relief in the midst of this counterpoint of wildly chaotic activity. As did the first section, this one builds to a dissonant climax of tremendous aggressive power before moving toward a subdued transition into the final section.

The final section, "Postludium," returns to the mood of the opening, while reviving materials from both preceding movements. This is the most hauntingly beautiful section of the symphony, evoking a scene that is both gloomy and extraordinarily bleak. Contributing to the ominous mood is the quietly menacing, nearly constant activity in the percussion, augmented by large tone-clusters in the piano. A striking effect is produced when the strings return to the atonal opening statement of the symphony, now accompanied by a triadic chorale in the lower brasses. The strings then play the theme, altered to become a near-tonal hymn, as if glimpsed from afar, against chirping woodwinds, and interrupted by occasional explosions of percussion. Evocatively atmospheric, this passage soon recedes into the distance, leaving a chilling feeling of impending peril, dominated by the tritone. Finally, an explosive twelve-note chord, described by some as resembling a scream, brings this disturbing symphony to an end.[298]

Eugene Ormandy conducted the premiere of Schuman's Ninth Symphony with the Philadelphia Orchestra in January 1969. Four days later the same forces presented the work to New York audiences, and recorded it shortly thereafter. That recording was released in 1971. Despite the extreme emotional intensity of the symphony, the critical response was generally favorable. Philadelphia critic Daniel Webster commented, "Its structure is firm, its statement direct and its somber mood pervading . . . . [T]here are subtle colors, powerful, even thunderous climactic moments, highly innovative use of usually inarticulate instruments like the cymbals."[299] Interestingly, Ronald Eyer described Schuman as "mainly a cerebral composer who could touch only remotely and fleetingly the emotions of his listeners." However, he found the new symphony to be "fruit of a different vintage and it speaks far more directly and passionately to the listener than anything that went before it. . . . The music has a warmth, born of anger, tenderness, outrage and simple humanity, which could fit any programmatic design."[300] Harold Schonberg, never a great admirer of Schuman's music, described the Ninth as "a serious work written in his sharp, clear, busy style. It also has the typically buoyant kind of orchestration that is characteristic of his music. . . . Everything is skillfully put together, but the melodic impulse flickers low, and the symphony sounds more like a professional paste job than anything that stems from a deep impulse. . . . Certainly the audience received it warmly enough to drown out a few boos."[301]

However, some commentators have had difficulty penetrating its forbidding language. Louis Blois felt that the work failed to have "the staggering emotional impact that was probably intended," although he acknowledged that the "Offertorium" highlights "the composer's new tonal austerity with dark and dazzling sonorities. The lean, atmospheric texture is punctuated with anguished gestures of strong rhythmic profile. . . . The outer sections reinforce the framework of funereal bereavement."[302] David Hurwitz bluntly called it "a dud," before elaborating that he found the piece "both ugly and pedantic, as Schuman increasingly became as his career progressed. Monochrome string writing predominates: the winds noodle aimlessly, with brass and percussion making noisy exclamations at climaxes. The lapidary treatment of texture is boringly predictable, the relentless lack of thematic appeal ultimately irritating. As his style veered toward the atonal . . . much of his late music sounds gratuitously unmotivated, with a huge gap between evident expressive intent and the means employed." He concluded, "Atonal music is like any other kind: there's good and bad. Schuman's is bad."[303] Veteran critic Roger Dettmer displayed a little more candor and humility, acknowledging, "It is not 'easy' music to listen to, but is gripping and grows on one as the work is heard and reheard. One can argue that Schuman in his later 50s . . . had emerged a greater composer than the popular—and to an extent populist—composer of the Third and Fifth Symphonies."[304]

Schuman followed the Ninth Symphony with another "difficult" work. Having been commissioned by the New York Philharmonic to compose a piece to mark the orchestra's 125th anniversary, he initially planned to write something lighthearted. However, in April 1968, the Rev. Dr. Martin Luther King Jr. was assassinated, and two months later Senator Robert F. Kennedy was as well. In between these two devastating events, Schuman himself had suffered a serious heart attack. These developments left the composer in a far more serious state of mind. It was during the summer of 1968, while he was regaining his health, that he composed *To Thee Old Cause*, subtitled "Evocation for Oboe, Brass, Timpani, Piano, and Strings." The title came from Walt Whitman's *Leaves of Grass*—these lines in particular:

Thou peerless passionate, good cause,
Thou stern, remorseless, sweet idea,
Deathless throughout the ages, races, lands,
Thou seething principle!

These fervently idealistic lines may seem incongruous with the grim, doleful cast of the work's expressive content. But considered in conjunction with the recent events just cited, the piece may be viewed as an exhortation—not just to the audience, but to the composer himself—not to abandon one's commitment to long-held ideals, despite severe setbacks that may occur along the way.

Structured as one continuous, multisectional movement of about fifteen minutes' duration, the work begins very slowly with a harmonic texture, as favored by the composer ever since the Symphony No. 6. In this case the texture is created by tolling, dissonant chords in the brass, with broken chords in the piano, above which a long line is played by the solo oboe, based largely on the interval of the second, in one form or another. As if focused on some distant point, this solo recalls the long-breathed, atonal melody played by the French horn toward the beginning of the Symphony No. 8. The oboe drops out, as a subdued, dissonant chorale in the strings, also highlighting the interval of the second, is heard, while the tempo doubles. The texture begins to expand and subdivide into several modes of activity, the original motivic material now embedded within the dissonant harmony. The brasses treat the same material repetitively, then drop out. As the tempo is doubled again, the strings are heard alone, developing the initial idea in nervous, irregular rhythms, when the oboe reappears, introducing the tritone as a new motivic element. The tempo halves, as muted strings, in dialogue with the horns, pursue both intervallic motifs in parallel thirds. While the upper strings continue in a sustained manner, the double-basses, piano, and lower brass offer jagged interjections, while the horns and upper trombones pursue a line of their own, characterized by quarter-note triplets, all of which combine to create Schuman's multiplanar effect. The strings continue their rhythmically irregular treatment of the intervallic motifs, against a chorale-like passage in the brass, who soon loudly take over, interrupted by a *pizzicato* passage in the strings. The brasses continue, encouraged by activity in the timpani. The oboe reenters, in the same speculative vein that has been its role throughout the piece, continuing its focus on the interval of the second, as the slow tempo of the opening returns. Then, while the strings softly pursue a wide-ranging line, the brasses intone a dissonant chorale based melodically on the interval of the second, as heard in the strings at the work's beginning. Here it is fit to the rhythm of Whitman's words, which are printed in the instrumental parts to encourage clarity of articulation. The music builds to an intensely strident climax, which comes to rest rather surprisingly on pure triads in the brass. The music then gradually becomes quiet, with suggestions of Schuman's familiar "strumming" lament, as pure triads are combined with dissonant gestures. Led by the oboe doubled by solo violin, the music gradually drifts away. A tonal ending is finally suggested as the solo oboe rests on a C-sharp, while the strings bring the work to a quiet, Mahlerian cadence in F-sharp major.

To Thee Old Cause is like a "tone poem," in the sense of an abstract narrative, dramatic in character. Schuman's treatment of the modest instrumental ensemble is brilliant, with many striking effects. But in order to appreciate the drama as it is portrayed, the listener must be able to discern the music's inner dynamics within a language that is—until the characteristically incongruous tonal cadence—essentially atonal and unremittingly dissonant. Within this context, the passage specifically connected to Whitman's words is quite ineffective, because there is no attempt to set it off harmonically in any way. So Whitman's exhortation to remain true to one's ideals is sacrificed by Schuman's unyielding severity.

To Thee Old Cause was introduced in October 1968. Leonard Bernstein conducted the New York Philharmonic, and Harold Gomberg played the demanding—if somewhat thankless—solo oboe part. The work was recorded at that time by the same performers, although it was not released until 1970. The initial critical response was generally positive, although the work has not been a favorite among listeners. Schuman himself acknowledged that even his admirers were not happy with it.[305] Harold Schonberg called it a "threnody" and found it "an ingenious piece of writing that seems to metamorphosize a chord. It has the superb feeling for sonority that Mr. Schuman displays in all his music; his use of brass instruments is especially characteristic. Even in so mournful a work the typical bright sound is encountered." However, he added, "Less striking are the materials proper. Mr. Schuman's attempts at lyricism have always been among the least convincing part of his arsenal. The tunes flap around but do not fly."[306] Years later the Internet critic Jon Yungkans offered some perceptive observations. Describing the work, as did Schonberg, as a threnody, he noted that the two assassinations left many with the feeling that "the candle of optimism that burned during John F. Kennedy's presidency was finally snuffed out, the light of Camelot . . . no longer aglow." Comparing the music to that of Samuel Barber, he continued, "*To Thee Old Cause* will at first seem more thorn than rose. But listen often and carefully and the bud of this dusky flower unfolds its petals of passion as well as pain, sweet memory along with bitter loss. The word 'haunting' is used superficially too often . . . , but that is exactly what this score is—haunting, lingering in the memory to be meditated upon, pondered, and weighed as a reminder of the price of mortality."[307]

In March 1969, the noted artist Ben Shahn died. Schuman had met Shahn casually on a few occasions. But when several of Shahn's friends approached the composer with the notion of commissioning a work in the artist's memory, Schuman—now retired and facing "free time"—agreed immediately. Reflecting on one extended conversation between them, the composer later commented, "I was struck immediately by the artist's ebullience, far-ranging social interests and insights, and, most of all, by his optimistic embrace of life. . . . Shahn, it seems to me, combined a contrasting yet wholly compatible duality—unabashed optimism and a searching poignancy."[308] Schuman completed *In Praise of Shahn: Canticle for Orchestra* during the course of the next few months. The work is very different in tone from those he had most recently composed. In contrast to the sober and sometimes anguished introspection of his other works of the 1960s, the new composition was something of a return to his "public" celebratory manner—extroverted and jubilant—although its approach to tonality and harmonic dissonance is updated, relative to the language he had used fifteen years earlier.

The work opens with an extended fanfare—a "clarion call" Schuman calls it—for brass and percussion. This hard-edged, raucous opening introduces two intervals—the second and the tritone (a most significant interval in the composer's later works)—that will figure prominently in the work. Strident trumpets and pugnacious percussion, and later, woodwinds, compete aggressively with atonally linked major triads in the lower brass. This section builds in volume and tempo, culminating unequivocally in F-sharp major, followed by a sudden, unexpected entrance of the strings alone on a richly voiced, reiterated G-major triad. The strings continue with a slowly brooding, dissonant chorale, based on the intervals of the second and the tritone. This proves to be an introduction to the work's main melodic idea, first heard in the violins, violas, and clarinets—mournful, lyrical, even beautiful, yet atonal, harmonized poignantly with minor triads that convey bittersweet implications of tonality. The melody is then repeated by the oboes, second violins, and piano, while the clarinets and first violins introduce a dissonant contrapuntal line. After another variation the melody shifts to the woodwinds and brass, against a chromatically moving line in the first violins. Further variations follow, as seemingly incongruous contrapuntal lines are added, creating increasingly dense, even congested textures. Suddenly the fast tempo returns, and with it an array of Schuman's familiar orchestral and rhythmic devices—some of which date back to the 1940s—but also more fragmentary gestures, presented within a freely atonal, dissonant harmonic language that sounds more "modern" as well as more aggressive. This section combines material from the opening "clarion call" as well as from the central lyrical portion, all culminating in the composer's most celebratory manner—hard-hitting and dynamic, while avoiding a sense of tonality until the last few seconds, then finally ending with a tonal cadence in C major.

In Praise of Shahn may readily be viewed as a modernized version of *Credendum—Article of Faith*, which had been composed in 1955. The raucous brass-only opening section, followed by a more subdued, lyrical central section featuring the strings, and concluding with a return to the brash material from the opening, combined with some of the material from the central section, is conceptually a virtual paraphrase of the earlier work, while the fast passages parade Schuman's most familiar techniques. On the one hand, the piece may be dismissed as a true "pot-boiler"—a shameless reiteration of the devices he had used throughout his career, modified superficially in order to sound up to date. On the other hand, while it may not represent his most profound inner searching, *In Praise of Shahn* is a grand, colorful, and exciting tribute to a fellow artist. Another point warranting mention is the fact that the opening brass salvo is identical to a short occasional piece called *Anniversary Fanfare*, which had been commissioned for the centennial of the Metropolitan Museum of Art. The *Fanfare* was composed about the same time as the Shahn work, but it is not clear whether this material was taken from one piece and reused in the other, or whether Schuman realized from the start that the same material could serve both purposes. Although Polisi seems to look askance at such flagrant "double-dipping,"[309] this sort of pragmatic economizing has been practiced routinely by composers for the past five centuries and is especially understandable when one of the pieces was written for a specific occasion and was not likely to have much of a life of its own.

In Praise of Shahn had its premiere in January 1970 by the New York Philharmonic, conducted by Leonard Bernstein. A recording of their performance was released later that year. Not surprisingly, the work made a favorable impact on audiences, although critics were increasingly divided about the merits of Schuman's creative output at this point in his career. Raymond Ericson found it to be "a strong, varied, well-constructed composition." He noted that while the piece was supposedly based on Shahn's personal traits, "it comes out sounding more like Schuman than anyone else. It has the composer's characteristic use of orchestral choirs as opposing units, thick polyphony and healthy extroversion." Though "[i]ts main section begins with a quite beautiful melody . . . [t]he beginning and end are loud and rhetorical. As a whole, the music proceeds at white heat. Compressed within a 15-minute span, it is indeed a hymn of praise, a celebration, somewhat noisy but impressive for all that."[310] Richard Swift, reviewing the printed score rather than the performance event, expressed a similar, if more specific, reaction: "Admirers of Mr. Schuman's music will find all the familiar traits: parallel fifth movement, rhythmic unisons, straightforward pitch relations, freely dissonant counterpoint and simple but lush scoring. For others, the work will seem thin, one-dimensional, and more than a little gaudy. The score . . . includes the lengthy program note that the composer asks to be printed when the work is played."[311]

English critic Paul Griffiths has long been an outspoken opponent of the traditionalist wing of twentieth-century composers. His comments are included as a representative example of the sort of snide disparagement that contributed to the post-1960 disregard of the music discussed in this book: Having attended the first English performance of the work, he wrote,

> Schuman intended the piece to represent something of [Shahn's] personal qualities. The opening . . . forms a sort of extended, lumbering fanfare, that finally reaches the last of its climaxes to be followed by a "dramatic" entry of the full strings. A string *Adagio* is followed by the entry of the work's main theme . . . an enigmatic and twisting melody. Various appearances of this, coupled with recalled lumps of the fanfare, steadily accumulate to the conclusion in a movement of coagulated diatonic harmony. *In Praise of Shahn* leaves an impression of heaviness rather than depth, of self-importance and inconsequence.[312]

More recently, Jon Yungkans found the work to be "as knotty a listening experience as *To Thee Old Cause* with its sharply dissonant but still tonal vocabulary. Schuman said he wanted to capture artist Ben Shahn's 'contrasting yet wholly compatible duality. . . .' He does so brilliantly, with two festive episodes flanking a core of probing introspection."[313]

A remarkably thoughtful commentary was offered by English musicologist Simon Harris, who made a provocative comparison between *In Praise of Shahn* and the Ninth Symphony upon the publication of both scores. Although his remarks suggest perhaps limited familiarity with Schuman's output as a whole, his observations warrant consideration while providing an excellent example of cogent criticism free of spite or malice. After noting that both works are memorial in intent, he continues,

> Both are serious, rather aggressive works (*fff* is a common dynamic), distinguished by a flamboyant, often brassy orchestration, insistent repetitions and a melodic style whose grand gestures and recitative-like shapes are at times reminiscent of early twentieth-century Vienna. Schuman's style, however, is forceful and direct, and avoids the currently fashionable harmonic complexities without sounding out-of-date. Despite a difference in scale . . . , there is a close similarity between the two works. . . . [E]ach work is in three sections contrasted from each other in tempo, the third providing a return to the material and tempo of the first. The tempo pattern of each work, however, is the reverse of the other, that of "In Praise of Shahn" being fast-slow-fast, that of the symphony slow-fast-slow. Music in the same tempo in the two works is closely similar.

The opening section of the symphony and the central section of "In Praise of Shahn" for instance are both passacaglia-like, consisting of a series of uninterrupted repetitions at different pitches of an extended opening melody based on a twelve-note series. And a comparison between the opening of the central section of the symphony with that of the final section of "In Praise of Shahn" will show a similar correspondence between the fast tempo sections. . . . Schuman's music is therefore both distinctive and consistent in these works, but I find it difficult to avoid one reservation about them: they seem to me devoid of what the eighteenth century called "art." The slow sections, for instance, involve a process of mechanical and cumulative repetition ending in exaggerated climaxes and excluding nearly all variety or contrast. Similar passages can be found in the fast sections where variety and contrast are in any case limited by the frequent resort to ever more emphatic reiterations of the same ideas. Deliberate textural contrasts are periodically introduced in both fast and slow sections, but these, like the climaxes, tend to be overdramatic and lead to a situation where textures in between changes of this kind are held in a series of straight-jackets characterized by block orchestration for woodwind, brass, strings or a combination of two of these. The result is a type of music that seems both crude and the product of enormous effort, producing a kind of mechanical Romanticism that is as much a result of the exigencies of achieving coherence as it is of the emotions the composer says were engendered by the subjects of the works.[314]

Whether or not one agrees with Harris's points—which depends to some extent upon the listener's sympathies—his thoughts certainly merit some consideration.

In 1971, when the Eastman School of Music offered Schuman a commission for an orchestral piece, he decided to return to his solo piano work from 1953, *Voyage*. At the time he had also done a chamber orchestration for use in conjunction with choreography by Martha Graham. But that endeavor was deemed unsuccessful by all participants, and Schuman withdrew his orchestration. Now, in returning to the work, he decided to rewrite it for full symphony orchestra.

It is interesting to compare the orchestral and piano versions: While the orchestral version retains the basic structure and thematic material of the earlier work, each section is somewhat expanded, some only minimally, others—the fourth, in particular—more extensively. But throughout, the harmonic textures are thickened and made more dissonant, relative to the piano version, while the orchestra offers the composer the opportunity to augment the work with contributions from his beloved percussion section. Some of the expansions enlarge and enhance the impact of particular sections, while at other points, the music seems overextended to the point of tedium. The result is a work comparable in duration to the Ninth and Tenth Symphonies, between which it fell chronologically, but perhaps more severe in expression than either of them, while the improvisatory quality of the original version tends to vitiate a true symphonic focus. In this work Schuman seemed to be adopting gestures associated with emotional expression—including his own familiar strumming of *pizzicato* chords in the cellos—while carefully avoiding tonal resolutions or consonant harmony, until the very end, an unambiguous tonal cadence. The work is thus pervaded by a sense of emotional "holding back," resulting in a relatively weak impact.

The premiere of *Voyage for Orchestra* was given by the Eastman Phil-harmonia conducted by Gustav Meier, in October 1972. The work has never been recorded.

Early in 1972 Schuman was approached by violist Donald McInnes, who hoped to interest the composer in writing a viola concerto for him. Schuman later recalled, "I told McInnes that my schedule wouldn't permit it. The truth is that I just didn't want to do anything for viola."[315] But the violist persisted, eventually persuading Schuman to listen to a tape of his playing. Schuman agreed to do so and was promptly won over by the instrument's unusual qualities, as well as by McInnes's artistry. A Ford Foundation commission was arranged, and Schuman agreed to accept the challenge. However, he did not have a conventional concerto in mind. "In my mind's ear I began to hear a viola and an orchestra with a women's chorus—the viola under the chorus, through the chorus, on top of the chorus. I just imagined that that would be a stunning sound, and I think it is."[316]

Not finding a suitable text, Schuman returned to those old English rounds he had learned from Marion Farquhar, one of which, "Amaryllis," had been the basis of the eponymous work he had composed in 1964. Now he returned to "Amaryllis," using it for the opening and closing sections of the *Concerto on Old English Rounds*, and selecting three others as well: "Great Tom Is Cast," "Who'll Buy Mi Roses?" and "Come, Follow Me." Schuman treated the rounds much as he had the Billings hymns in *New England Triptych*, altering them in accordance with his own musical language so that a sort of stylistic fusion was achieved. However, this new work is far more elaborate and far less immediately accessible than the earlier work. Schuman conceived the chorus as a "separate and sometimes solo element. I think of the chorus as being another choir of the orchestra, similar to the woodwind, brass, or string choir. It's part of the general sound, but like the other choirs it's occasionally heard by itself (there is a whole *a cappella* section)."[317]

The result, completed in 1973, is a most unusual and impractical work: a concerto for viola, women's voices, and orchestra, with a duration of forty-five minutes. Although Vaughan Williams's masterpiece *Flos Campi*—a much shorter work—calls for a similar combination of forces, Schuman's *Concerto* is highly original, with moments of considerable beauty. It is also the fullest elaboration of the technique Schuman developed for weaving pre-existing thematic material into a contemporary work in his own style. The overall approach uses the women's voices largely for more straightforward presentation of the rounds or for elaborations that retain their general harmonic style; the viola chiefly comments improvisationally on the musical material of the rounds but often in a highly chromatic, atonal manner—and often simultaneously with the more tonal, consonant material sung by the chorus; the orchestra mostly offers support to the other two elements, only occasionally emerging to the forefront. It is the drifting back and forth along the spectrum between pure, consonant tonality and virtual atonality and intense dissonance, along with their simultaneous juxtapositions, that makes the work so distinctive. Often these juxtapositions create an effect that is strikingly ethereal, poignant, even otherworldly; but there are also times when the technique seems arbitrary and contrived, as if Schuman combined elements without actually knowing just what the result would sound like. The *Concerto* is certainly one of the most interesting and compelling works of the composer's later years, as well as one of his most unusual conceptions. During the process of composition, McInnes worked closely with Schuman, commenting not only on details of the viola part but offering musical suggestions as well. It is noteworthy that while he was composing the *Concerto*, Schuman also completed *To thy Love: Choral Fantasy on Old English Rounds* for women's choir, which uses the same material. And in 1976 he composed *Amaryllis*, a short work for strings, based on the opening and closing portions of the *Concerto*.

The first movement, "Amaryllis—Introduction and Variations," opens as the muted viola very softly introduces the first phrase of the somber, modal round melody, answered by a dissonant pyramid in the woodwinds. The next two phrases follow similarly. Then the altos hum the first phrase of the round, doubled by the clarinets, while the viola veers off into an eerie descant. Thus the first few moments of the work present its primary thematic material, its overall tonal-harmonic range, and the performing forces in their distinctive roles. As the viola continues its commentary, the voices gradually present more of the round melody, eventually in full canonic polyphony, thereby concluding the "Introduction." A short cadenza-like passage for the solo viola then leads to two cheerful, sprightly variations, characterized by some of the composer's most familiar devices, although their connection to the original melody is often remote. The first variation initially features the chorus; then, as the voices drop out, the viola enters with its commentary. A short viola cadenza leads to the second variation, which features the strings in characteristic parallel thirds, while the theme is heard in the winds, disguised by extensive rhythmic dislocations. The viola reappears, continuing its pseudo-improvisatory commentary with light orchestral accompaniment;

they are eventually joined by the voices, who repeat their motif from the first variation. All three elements now press forward toward an elision with the following movement.

The second movement, "Great Tom Is Cast," is based on another round melody. As its text is "Great Tom is cast, and Christ church bells ring one, two, three, four, five, six, and Tom comes last," the chimes play a prominent role in this movement. The movement begins as the chimes are joined by dissonant chords in the brass, followed by a strange dialogue between chimes and the solo viola playing triple-stops *pizzicato*. After some elaboration by the viola and orchestra, the choir introduces the simple round in full canonic counterpoint, while the viola continues its commentary. Additional instruments enter and the round is taken through several modulations. The horns then loudly introduce a variant of the "Great Tom" melody. This too is developed canonically and taken through several modulations. The character changes when the simple melody is then treated polytonally by the brass, followed by the rest of the orchestra. This builds to a substantial climax, culminating in a wild passage ad lib by the chimes, and then subsides. An elaborate and angular commentary from the solo viola follows, against sustained chords in the strings and voices—a striking effect.

The viola is *tacet* during the short third movement, which has the character of a *scherzo*, in which the chorus plays the dominant role. Anticipating the tunes to follow, a simple, lighthearted idea is introduced by the orchestra. The voices then present the two remaining rounds, "Who'll Buy Mi Roses" and "Come, Follow Me," which are heard in alternation and in contrapuntal elaboration in an extended choral passage with orchestral accompaniment. An *a cappella* passage brings the movement to an end, eliding directly with the next movement.

The fourth movement, "Combinations," offers each of the performing elements an opportunity to explore the rounds in various juxtapositions. Picking up directly from the preceding movement, the chorus *a cappella* joins three of the rounds contrapuntally. This is followed by an extended solo cadenza, in which the viola treats all four of the rounds in elaborately virtuosic fashion. Finally the orchestra enters tentatively, initially treating the material of the rounds contrapuntally within a consonant harmonic context. Then, as additional instrumental forces enter, the language expands harmonically into a massive, dissonant orchestral *tutti*, the most forceful in the entire work.

The final movement, "Amaryllis—Recapitulation," is the high point of the *Concerto*, and contains some of the most beautiful music Schuman ever composed. It opens as the orchestra presents a rich—but stylistically congruent—harmonization of the "Amaryllis" theme, followed by an equally lovely treatment by the voices. During this the solo viola softly enters, this time with an *obbligato* that is somewhat more tonally congruent with its surroundings. Finally, all three elements slowly and gradually drift away, as if into the ether, the voices continuing their polyphonic treatment of the melody, the orchestra offering gentle support, while the viola comments wistfully. The emotional impact of this conclusion is extraordinarily powerful.

The *Concerto on Old English Rounds* was first performed in Boston in November 1974. Donald McInnes was the viola soloist, with the Boston Symphony Orchestra and the Radcliffe Choral Society, under the direction of Michael Tilson Thomas. A recording led by Leonard Bernstein, featuring McInnes with the Camerata Singers and the New York Philharmonic, was issued in 1978. Critical response was mixed, a number of commentators objecting to the mixture of styles within the work. Typical is the reaction of Paul Kresh, who found the *Concerto* to be "a piece of considerable ambition and high technical gloss that is in the end overwhelmed by the very skill that went into constructing it."[318] On the other hand, Ben Pernick observed, "Schuman's idiom is mellower in the Concerto, less spiky and dissonant than usual and really very accessible. . . . Four rounds dating from the late 17th century . . . form the nucleus of the five movement work."[319]

A most provocative commentary was offered by violist and critic Michelle Dulak, who found the concerto to be

one strange piece. We violists tend to have an exhaustive and not entirely healthy knowledge of our smallish repertoire, so that if someone says, for example, "it's for viola solo and orchestra, but there's a chorus," we'll immediately say, "Oh, *Flos Campi*"; in the same way, "it's a viola concerto based on old folk songs" returns "Sure, *Der Schwanendreher*." Schuman's concerto has the chorus *and* the folk songs and isn't either of the above, though it's a heck of a lot closer to Hindemith than to Vaughan Williams. And, frankly, a little dose of *Flos Campi* might have done it some good. Given the strikingly original idea of combining a viola and a women's chorus, it's disappointing how little Schuman lets them really interact with one another. And how little fun he has with the rounds, too. He lets them run *as* rounds in a few places (most notably in a big set-piece for the chorus about two-thirds of the way through the work . . .). Otherwise they are merely mined for their melodic ideas, which aren't especially strong or memorable, and surrounded by rather drab orchestral commentary and a lot of violistic rumination. Hindemith squeezed a lot more out of his German folk-songs in *Schwanendreher*.

All in all, she found it "a peculiar and not really satisfactory piece."[320]

With the approach of the American bicentennial in 1976, Schuman was hoping for the opportunity to create a significant statement of major proportions. But by that time the composer's name no longer had the cachet that it had wielded twenty years earlier, and no such opportunity was offered to him. Ultimately he had to content himself with an all-Schuman concert at Washington, D.C.'s Kennedy Center. The program, which took place in April 1976, featured the National Symphony Orchestra under the direction of Antal Dorati. The program would consist of two new works commissioned by the National Symphony Orchestra—*The Young Dead Soldiers* and the Symphony No. 10—along with the first performance of the concert adaptation of the opera *The Mighty Casey*, entitled *Casey at the Bat: A Baseball Cantata*.

Schuman completed the symphony, scored for a large orchestra, early in 1975, giving it the subtitle "American Muse." He intended the work as a tribute, "dedicated to our country's creative artists, past, present and future. . . . This work . . . is for my colleagues, with gratitude for their achievements and joy in the identification of being one of them. . . . I trust that overall the music emerges as an expression of affirmation."[321] In composing such a work, Schuman assumed a role that was both comfortable and familiar to him, and in which he had been enormously successful throughout much of his career: that of musical statesman—a spokesman and advocate for artistic life in America. Thus, as with many of his works, there is a feeling of public oratory to the symphony, and in it he reverted to a number of musical devices familiar from his more extroverted earlier works while also retaining the high level of harmonic dissonance he had been pursuing in his later works. In its noisy exuberance, the symphony—the first movement, in particular—resembles the recently composed *In Praise of Shahn*.

The first movement of the Symphony No. 10 is marked *Con fuoco* and utilizes some of the same material found in *Prelude for a Great Occasion*, a short, celebratory piece for brass and percussion Schuman was composing around the same time. The brief first movement opens with a veritable avalanche of sound, brutally dissonant and scored to the hilt, reinforced by a blazing array of percussion. Bristling with unflagging sonic energy and a taut, bracing sense of affirmation, the movement introduces two significant motivic elements: a descending minor scale and an alternation between two notes a step apart. Melodies in parallel thirds abound, not only in the first movement but throughout the entire symphony. Despite its consistently aggressive dissonance, major triads begin to emerge toward the end of the movement, which concludes characteristically with a triumphant triad in root position, fifth at the top. In fact, the ending is so decisive that Dorati expressed a concern that it was too definitive for a first movement.[322]

More than twice the duration of the first movement, the second movement, *Larghissimo*, is the emotional core of the symphony, conveying a bleak, solemn, contemplative beauty. An unusual device heard toward the beginning of the movement, and again toward the end, is a series of long, downward *portamenti* in the strings, lending a touch of Mahlerian poignancy. Another key element of this movement is a pulsating texture of extreme dissonance, which serves as a backdrop. One of Schuman's characteristically slow, lofty, long-lined, and wide-arching melodies emerges, accompanied initially by triadic harmony. However, chromatic lines of counterpoint are added, seemingly without regard for the resulting harmony, creating a very thick, dissonant texture. An unusual duet between solo flute and solo trumpet follows, in which the former pursues a florid series of flourishes, while the latter moves slowly and simply. Out of this develops another long, slow melody in the strings at tenor level, while flutes and oboes flutter rapidly in parallel thirds above, in apparent obliviousness, gradually building to a tremendous climax highlighted by the brasses. A somber lamentation in the violins and clarinets follows, heard over the familiar *pizzicato* strumming of the cellos. This melody too builds through the addition of dissonant contrapuntal lines, which then gradually dwindle down to piercing high notes in unison. The movement ends with the sudden, inexplicably gratuitous appearance of a major triad scored for full orchestra.

The final movement, *Presto; Andantino; Leggiero; Pesante; Presto possible*, is less successful than the first two: Subdivided into many sections, it bounces in too many directions and becomes somewhat incoherent in the process. It is almost as if Schuman were trying to pack into this one movement all the devices and techniques that had appeared in his symphonies over the years, some harking back as far as No. 3. There is a *fugato*, examples of multiplanar writing, and numerous passages of parallel thirds. Nevertheless there are also some striking new orchestral effects, most notably a recurring passage that features celesta, harp, vibraphone, chimes, crotales, glockenspiel, and piano—all playing together. Finally, after extended passages of crunching dissonance and every attempt to avoid tonality, all elements come together in the composer's final triumphant symphonic peroration, with a sustained tonic triad, pressed forward by percussion fireworks.

At this point in his career, Schuman was no longer a power broker, nor was he at the forefront of contemporary American musical composition. Hence he became fair game for a younger generation of critics, who viewed him as a member of the established "old guard." John Rockwell found the Tenth Symphony to be "determinedly, blissfully old-fashioned. . . . Mr. Schuman writes his music in calm contradiction of nearly every avant-garde musical fashion of the last 40 years. . . . [H]is anachronistic qualities sound as if he simply hasn't been listening to the music of his time."[323] This inane comment illustrates that as late as 1979, some critics were still implying that a new piece of music "should" somehow conform to musical fashions prevalent at the time—a continuation of the sort of anti-Traditionalist propaganda encountered most toxically during the 1960s. The first sentence—obviously an overstatement—might even be regarded as positive; its sneering tone becomes apparent, however, with the subsequent remark. Shortly after this review appeared, musicologist Joseph Machlis wrote to Schuman, "The idiot who passes for a critic on the *Times* was sure you wrote the way you did because you had not heard what's being done these days. Did it never occur to him that you wrote the way you did precisely because you HAD heard what people are doing nowadays?"[324]

Several years later, Tim Page commented on a subsequent performance of the work. "It begins with a celebratory and virtuosic proclamation. For this listener, Mr. Schuman is at his weakest in such moments. Everything seemed busy and overstated, as if a writer, asked to make a paragraph stronger, were to add an exclamation point to the end of each sentence. The second movement, however, is masterly; a long, haunted nocturnal procession, superbly orchestrated and deeply compelling."[325]

American music scholar and critic James Wierzbicki was surprisingly condemnatory of this work and of the composer in general. Reviewing a performance by Leonard Slatkin and the St. Louis Symphony, prior to their first recording of the work, which was released in 1992, he seized upon a note in the program that identified Schuman as "the Great American Symphonist."

> I hope that's taken with a grain of salt by anyone who heard . . . Schuman's 1975 "Symphony No. 10" in Powell Hall on Saturday evening. This most recent of Schuman's symphonies is bottom-of-the-barrel stuff, an aimless bluster that would probably get a failing grade if it were submitted as a doctoral thesis at a respectable music school. And it is not significantly inferior to most of Schuman's other symphonic essays. The 81-year-old Schuman is a politically important figure, which in part explains why Slatkin and company will commit the meager "Symphony No. 10" to disc next week. And to be sure, over the course of his long career Schuman has often shown that he is a composer whose skill and talent count for something. Still, his real successes have all come with music that is either overtly programmatic or relatively small in scale. . . . A listener who wants to find the Great American Symphonist should explore the music of Howard Hanson and Roy Harris, or—more to the point—of Roger Sessions and Walter Piston.[326]

Even Butterworth, who refers to Schuman as "an epitome of the American composer" in his book on the American symphony, was disappointed with the Tenth: "Slabs of sound, unrelentingly heavily scored dissonant chords with multiple doublings soon prove wearisome to both listeners and players. The ear longs for some dynamic variation and a little contrapuntal relief amid the indigestible textures. Even the central *Larghissimo*, beginning on muted strings, is anchored to the ground by repeated triadic chords covering the whole orchestral range."[327]

Also completed in 1975 for performance at the April 1976 bicentennial concert in Washington, D.C., was *The Young Dead Soldiers*, subtitled "Lamentation for Soprano, French Horn, Eight Woodwinds and Nine Strings." At the time when Schuman was working on this composition, the highly controversial war in Vietnam was coming to an end. During the preceding years, most of America's intelligentsia were united in vehement opposition to the war, and works of art expressing that opposition—at various levels of abstraction—were encountered frequently. For this composition Schuman chose a deeply moving poem published in 1948 by Archibald MacLeish. Its essence is captured by the lines, "Our deaths are not ours; they are yours; they will mean what you make them. . . . We have died. Remember us."[328]

The fifteen-minute work begins with an extended unaccompanied duet: a soprano vocalise intertwined with the French horn, as both elaborate one of those long, slow, searching, atonal melodies, not unlike that played by the oboe in *To Thee Old Cause*, the Schuman piece that this one most resembles. Again one encounters the downward *portamenti* that had been so effective in the slow movement of the Tenth Symphony. With a primary focus on the soprano and the horn, the instrumental ensemble plays a relatively small role in this work. When it finally enters, it is with one of the composer's dissonant harmonic sonorities. Schuman said of this opening chord, "[T]he whole trick of that chord is in the scoring, because it uses all the notes, but all the instruments are in thirds, and so they all sound consonant with each other within families of instruments, which is something that has always intrigued me."[329] At this point the soprano introduces the words of MacLeish's poem. Other striking harmonic sonorities appear briefly throughout the work. Schuman's atonal treatment of the voice was characteristic of much vocal music composed during the 1960s and 1970s—a miscalculation that violated the nature of the singing voice and resulted in countless premieres of compositions rarely, if ever, heard again. In this work, more than any other he had composed thus far, Schuman seemed to be acceding to the climate of the times—with regard to music, as well as to politics. Not only is the vocal line hard-edged and inexpressive, but it is so strenuous for the singer that the clarity of the text is inevitably compromised, although any relationship between music and text is tenuous at best. Eventually the work ends softly with a sustained E-major triad—a device that became increasingly pointless as his language became more dissonant and severe. The work is one of the composer's weakest efforts and does an injustice to the heart-breaking clarity of MacLeish's poem.

At the Washington, D.C., premiere, the soprano soloist was Rosalind Rees, whose impeccable sense of pitch made her a favorite of Schuman's as soloist for his late, atonal vocal works. The critical reaction to the work was mixed, although one suspects that some of the positive comments were rooted in both political and musico-political sympathies. Having attended the bicentennial concert, Robert Parris wrote, "*The Young Dead Soldiers . . .* had a lovely air about it; quiet, cool, elegant, but like most of Schuman, distant and unmoving."[330] Noting the similarity to *To Thee Old Cause*, Rouse called it "austere and unremittingly bleak," adding that it "may best be described as a single fifteen-minute melody over a dissonant chordal accompaniment. The textures remain simple, and except for occasional two-part writing for the soprano and horn, the work contains virtually no counterpoint. There is an asceticism in *The Young Dead Soldiers* unusual to Schuman, and in this regard it is unique, standing apart from his other scores."[331]

The work was recorded in 1980 by Rosalind Rees, with Robin Graham, French horn, and the White Mountains Festival Orchestra conducted by Gerard Schwarz. Reviewing this recording, Roger Dettmer wrote, "Muted, without theatricality or concessions to popular taste, a plea rather than a patriotic exhortation, *Soldiers* isn't likely to have a frequent performance record." The music "summoned up for me the graveyard scene that opens the last act of *Our Town*, and in essence summed it up—haunting music, softly but insistently incantatory, powerfully expressive without raising its voice."[332] Eric Dalheim wrote, "Schuman's individual way with expressive atonality and a lyrical vocal line thoroughly captures the elegiac essence of the poetry even though he states in the disc-jacket notes: 'In setting words so complete within themselves, a composer cannot hope to enhance but rather to bring that special unspoken meaning which alone is the province particular to music.'"[333]

The second half of the National Symphony Orchestra's all-Schuman program featured the first performance of the shortened "concert version" of the opera *The Mighty Casey*, entitled *Casey at the Bat: A Baseball Cantata*. (See earlier discussion of the opera.) This performance featured soprano Rosalind Rees along with the renowned baritone and baseball fan Robert Merrill, and the Westminster Choir. No complete recording of this version has yet appeared.

Schuman's next major work was commissioned by the Chamber Music Society of Lincoln Center—the organization he had labored so hard to bring into existence—in honor of its tenth anniversary. For this new work, entitled *In Sweet Music: Serenade on a Setting of Shakespeare*, the composer returned to "Orpheus with His Lute," the song he had composed in 1944 for a production of *Henry VIII* and that served as the basis of his 1961 *Song of Orpheus* for cello and orchestra. This new work, completed in 1978, shares much in common with two other previous works as well—most notably *Amaryllis: Variations for String Trio* (1964) and the *Concerto on Old English Rounds*

(1973)—as the pseudo-Elizabethan "Orpheus with His Lute" provides the opportunity for stylistic juxtapositions much as the English rounds did.

Nearly half an hour in duration, *In Sweet Music* is scored for flute (alternating with alto flute and piccolo), viola, voice, and harp. The score indicates the desired arrangement of the musicians on the stage, and even when the singer is to sit or stand. The work comprises three main sections: a slow opening that examines the "Orpheus" song from a number of perspectives; a rapid middle section along the lines of a variation fantasy on the song, not unlike the middle section of the *Song of Orpheus* or of the *Amaryllis* variations; and a final section that returns to the song in the slow, somber character of the opening.

The work begins as the voice slowly sings the words "in sweet music," accompanied by open fifths in the harp. Then, unaccompanied, the alto flute plays the modal opening phrase of the "Orpheus" song, eliding with a slightly dissonant response from the viola that immediately recalls the relationship between chorus and viola in the aforementioned *Concerto*. The alto flute then presents the second phrase of the song, to a warm, triadic accompaniment by the harp, again followed by a more wayward response from the viola. The third phrase follows similarly, and then the fourth, as the contributions from the harp become increasingly chromatic, elaborate, and dissonant. The singer then hums the entire melody against chromatic contrapuntal activity in the viola and harp, then the flute and harp, and then with all three. For the final phrase, the voice is directed to sing nonsense syllables. This leads to a cadenza-like passage for flute and viola, which serves as a transition into the second section, a fast, typically Schumanian treatment of the various motifs embedded within the "Orpheus" melody. Sometimes the relationship to the melody is very clear—at others, rather tenuous. There is much nervously sputtering rhythmic dislocation and considerable focus on the lower mordent (a note followed by the note below, returning to the original note). The mordent is a very common feature of Schuman's fast developmental passages but is justified here motivically as the opening of the second phrase of the song. Similarly, the scale passages found in the song's first phrase are singled out for extensive development as well. Throughout this entire section, the score suggests nonsense syllables to be sung in the manner of the "scat-singing" practiced by jazz vocalists. The singer's role during this section is actively integrated with the other instruments of the ensemble, eventually building to a frenetic climax. A transition to the final section is signaled by a cadenza-like passage for piccolo and harp, followed by viola alone, and then viola with harp. The slow tempo returns as the singer hums a recognizable variant of the "Orpheus" melody within a contrapuntally active, polytonal treatment by the entire ensemble. The first two phrases of the melody are next heard in the alto flute; it is continued by the viola in harmonics—exactly the same eerie treatment that occurs (in the solo cello) toward the conclusion of *Song of Orpheus*. The instrumental ensemble continues the actively polyphonic, chromatic, and polytonal variant until the voice, accompanied by the harp, sings the words "in sweet music." Then the entire "Orpheus" song follows, only now the text is sung against the poignant polyphony of the three instruments, all gradually fading away into an ethereal D minor.

The first performance of *In Sweet Music* was given at Lincoln Center's Alice Tully Hall, in October 1978. Jan DeGaetani was the mezzo-soprano with members of the Chamber Music Society of Lincoln Center. The overall critical response was largely favorable. Rouse considered this work to be "Schuman's chamber music masterpiece,"[334] and Polisi described it as "one of Schuman's most masterly and moving chamber works."[335] However, some listeners felt that despite the work's passages of considerable ethereal beauty, the novelty of its conception is mitigated by Schuman's having used such a similar approach—and more effectively—in previous works. Nevertheless, the use of the humming voice and saving the song text until the end are certainly unusual features. Perhaps it is not surprising that the most moderate reaction came from Harold Schonberg, who commented, "There were some sweet, lyrical things in the piece, but there also was a good deal of mechanical padding."[336]

On the other hand, Joseph McLellan was much less reserved in his reaction to a subsequent performance, noting that Schuman's "setting of a Shakespeare song is preceded by a long, wordless meditation on its melody. [Last night's performers] made one wish the melody would never end."[337] Eric Dalheim described it as a

> finely wrought, highly expressive piece of chamber music. . . . The instrumental writing is skillfully idiomatic; the lyrical viola contributes effective harmonics and double stops, the versatile flute also supplies the rich timbre of the alto flute as well as brilliant imitations of nature on the piccolo, and the harp, ranging over five octaves, serves as a catalyst for the entire musical texture. The composer requires the musicians to employ a wide dynamic range, much use of *messa di voce* in sustained passages, sharply contrasted vocal and instrumental registers, and the keenest sense of ensemble playing. . . . *In Sweet Music* establishes for Schuman a firm position in the mainstream of twentieth-century vocal chamber music.[338]

In Sweet Music was released on recording in 1980, in a performance featuring Rosalind Rees, soprano, with the Orpheus Trio.

During the late 1970s, the New York Philharmonic was engaged in a project to commission works that would highlight some of the orchestra's first-chair players. As part of this project, William Schuman was invited to compose a work to feature French horn player Philip Myers. He completed the work in 1979, entitling it *Three Colloquies*. Its three sections, linked without pause, are "Rumination," "Renewal," and "Remembrance." In describing the composition, Schuman explained that he viewed the *Colloquies* as dialogues between the solo horn and the orchestra. He stated, "I knew that it was not a concerto I would compose, for my goal was not a priori to exploit all the technical resources of the instrument as a display piece. Rather, I hoped to create music which required a solo French horn to realize its intentions."[339] The French horn is notoriously unpredictable, even in the hands of a master, and extended passages of showy writing are treacherous. Schuman's work challenges the virtuosity, reliability, and composure of the soloist, as it calls upon the instrument's full range of technical effects—alternating rapidly between "stopped" (muted with the hand) and "unstopped" or open passages, in particular. *Three Colloquies* is scored for orchestra minus the brass section (except for three trumpets).

"Rumination" begins—as do so many of Schuman's late pieces—with a dissonant harmonic sonority, initially sustained by woodwinds and metallic percussion, promptly joined by the strings. There is no perceptible sense of meter, so that the gradual emergence of the horn against this texture creates the illusion of a spontaneous improvisation. The intervals of the third and the second dominate the horn part as well as the orchestra, although later the tritone assumes comparable importance. After this atonal, free-form opening, the tempo quickens, while the rhythmic character of the music becomes clearer as the horn negotiates a passage characterized by repeated notes. The music builds to a modest climax of metallic sonority, then quiets and slows down, leading directly into the next movement.

"Renewal," marked *Leggiero*, is somewhat *scherzo*-like in character, and opens with an extended *tutti* passage, featuring strings *pizzicato*, woodwinds, and piano, in irregular rhythm, creating Schuman's familiar "stealth" effect. The other main motivic elements here are grace notes, as well as the intervals of the tritone and the perfect fourth. The trumpets soon enter with their own dissonant harmonic motif, characterized by a distinctive rhythmic idea. Finally, the horn enters with a series of trills, before picking up the "stealthy" motif. The horn becomes increasingly agitated, at which point the orchestra takes over with a *tutti* interlude, highlighted by brilliantly deployed percussion. The horn returns, with repeated notes that lead back to the grace-note motif, now in counterpoint with the clarinets, while the other instruments sustain long dissonant chords. The energy subsides somewhat, for the appearance of a "trio" section with the character of a dissonant, atonal, yet lyrical, waltz. A *tutti* interlude, with prominent percussion activity, leads to an extended passage for the horn featuring repeated notes and much rapid alternation between stopped and open phrases, heard against the slow-moving strings. The *scherzo*-like character then returns in another *tutti* passage, as the strings play sustained chords, with the woodwinds chirping, and the trumpet, doubled by cellos an octave lower, playing a slow melody. The horn enters, continuing with a variant of the *scherzo* material, joined by the rest of the orchestra. Woodwinds and percussion take over, leading to a dialogue between horn and trumpets. The full orchestra builds to a brief climax, then recedes, as a roll on the cymbal leads directly into the third and final movement.

This section, "Remembrance," begins with a duet between the horn and the solo cello, against a background of throbbing chords in the strings. Once again the intervals of the second and the third are dominant throughout this slightly more tonal, lyrical passage. The horn enters into a dialogue with the first violin, accompanied by the harp; then the violins drop out, as the celesta enters. Perhaps in the most literal example of "colloquies," melodic lines are offered by the solo flute, answered by the horn, then in dialogue with the trumpet. A brief orchestral passage leads to a further dialogue between horn and trumpet. Suddenly and unexpectedly, the woodwinds, joined by the strings, play a series of richly spaced—but nontonal—parallel major triads, while the horn's line moves in a free but diatonic direction. The horn continues searching, and while the orchestra finally settles softly on F-major triads, the horn sustains a B, a tritone away, then finally moves down to a still-unresolved B-flat.

Schuman's *Three Colloquies* represent a major addition to the repertoire of works for horn and orchestra. However, it is of somewhat lesser significance within the composer's output. Furthermore, its predominantly slow tempo and its largely atonal language offer little to focus the attention of listeners. Polisi acknowledged that the work provides "a less than gratifying role for the soloist," noting that "most of the work is introspective in character, [lacking] the heroic quality of the French horn heard in the concertos of Strauss or the symphonies of Mahler."[340] The work was introduced in January 1980 by horn virtuoso Philip Myers, with the New York Philharmonic conducted by Zubin Mehta. A recording by these performers was issued in 1985.

Critical opinion concerning the *Colloquies* was again strongly divided. Harold Schonberg described it as "a 'color piece.' Mr. Schuman in this work seems intensely interested in contrasting sonorities. The first movement is full of block harmonies set against violent percussion, against which the horn breathes long-phrased notes. The second movement is typical Schuman—bracing, with peppy rhythms and a hint of jazz. The finale has the horn in long, quiet melodies, ending with a chorale in almost traditional harmonies (much of the previous writing had been tonal but dissonant)." Schonberg perhaps captured the feelings of most listeners when he wrote, "These three 'Colloquies' are representative of Mr. Schuman's compositional expertise, especially in orchestration. The music is even slick. But it does not really have much nourishment. The gestures sound a bit tired and routine, and the big tune of the last movement is one of those fabricated melodies that is forgotten as soon as it is heard."[341] Reviewing the recording, Michael Walsh noted, "A tired essay in Schuman's '50s style, the piece is only occasionally brightened by some pretty noises and adept writing for the solo instrument. Perhaps in response, Mehta turns in a slack reading."[342] Edward Tatnall Canby found it "competent in every technical sense but somehow chilly and academic."[343]

On the other hand, there were some positive reactions. Niall O'Loughlin wrote, "[I]n the first [movement] the horn emerges unobtrusively from numerous long-held chords, and in the last it is complemented by various ghostly counterpoints from different instruments in turn. The central scherzo is a spectral piece with thin textures and plenty of rhythmic variety. Although it does not use new instrumental techniques but keeps to fairly traditional rhythms and harmonies, the work impresses through memorable material and its imaginative handling."[344] Susan Feder described the work as "a bold and bright piece,"[345] while Leighton Kerner found it "not terribly complex or challenging, but less grayly anonymous than most of [Schuman's] middle-period pieces and, in sum, full of motives and colors that consistently please the ear."[346] Stephen Ellis considered it "one of the best of the few American horn concertos. It brings technical brilliance and musical adventure to a genre so often mired in pastoral mustiness."[347]

For his next major work Schuman returned to a concept that seemed increasingly fruitful for him: revisiting an earlier, tonal melody—in this case, his own—and subjecting it to developmental variations that drew upon more recent expansions of his language. In 1956 he had composed a moving setting of a hymnlike poem, "The Lord Has a Child," which Langston Hughes had written at Schuman's request.[348] Offered a commission from the American Brass Quintet to write a new work, he returned to the Hughes setting, approaching it in much the same way as he had "Orpheus with His Lute." In 1980 he completed *American Hymn*, which consisted of variations on this song setting, for brass quintet. In 1981 he arranged that work for band, in response to a commission from the American Bandmasters Association and the U.S. Air Force Band, entitling it *American Hymn: Variations on an Original Melody.* When the St. Louis Symphony Orchestra requested a new work in commemoration of its centennial, Schuman expanded that piece by nearly 300 percent. He completed *American Hymn: Orchestral Variations on an Original Melody* toward the end of 1981. (Interestingly, his very last piece, composed in 1990, was a setting for chorus and brass ensemble of *The Lord Has a Child.*)

While acknowledging that the new orchestral work "uses some ideas from the earlier versions . . . it is an entirely new concept, and the main body of its large form consists wholly of new material." The composer emphasized that in this work only the melodic aspect of the song was subject to variation, describing it as "a continuum—a huge arc, encompassing six discernible sections—that goes from the first note to the last without interruption."[349] As in most of Schuman's late orchestral works, the percussion section is large and varied, and its role is prominent throughout.

The work begins with an almost celestial introduction, highlighted by metallic percussion. This introduction, in the composer's words, "serves to set the aural ambiance" but "has no relationship to the melody." However, listeners familiar with the original song will note that this section draws upon its harmonic language in evoking the mood. When the song melody is finally introduced in the second section, it is played on the cornet, a more mellow-toned relative of the trumpet, which lends it an especially "small-town America" flavor. It is accompanied initially by major triads in the strings that bear a polytonal relationship to the song melody itself, producing an eerie effect. Variations on the melody begin immediately in a continuing developmental series. After these continuing variations, an *accelerando* leads to the third section, *Allegro con spirito*. Here the melody is developed according to the composer's usual approach to fast variations, with rhythmic dislocation of melodic fragments and presentation of material in parallel thirds, punctuated by pyramid effects in the brass. As it continues, the development moves farther and farther from the original melody. Suddenly, with no letup in the tempo, a smooth melody in thirds is heard in the strings against a soft oompah accompaniment, reinforced by light bass drum taps and brushes on the snare drum—an engagingly dance-like effect, novel for Schuman. This leads to a fast waltz with melody in the first violins, and a frolicsome countermelody in the solo cornet, before the rapid oompah material returns. The tempo increases even more in the fourth section, which features a continuous eighth-note pattern that alternates among the various instrumental groups as the music builds to a climax, heightened by drums and metallic percussion—what Schuman called "a sounding sea of steel." The music then slows down for the fifth section, *Adagissimo*. The strings play a solemn, drooping melody, picked up by solo woodwinds, as the cellos strum *pizzicato* triads in repeated quarter-note rhythm, creating the familiar dirge-like effect. The strings play a sustained melody, against which the bass clarinet offers rapid, atonal, and seemingly unrelated arabesques. Then, while the brasses play in chorale style, the strings and piano offer a dense, busy accompaniment in parallel thirds, producing a multiplanar effect. Heralding the final section, the song melody suddenly returns, now harmonized in a manner closer to its original 1956 setting but with some contrapuntal elaboration. Two cornets play the song melody again, and as the work gradually comes to an end, the strings with celesta present ethereal triads, followed by motifs from the song shared by several instrumental groupings. Then the strings play the original song melody in rhythmic augmentation over dirge-like pulsations. The work finally comes to a soft, subdued ending on a D-major triad that gradually fades away.

The premiere of *American Hymn: Orchestral Variations on an Original Melody* took place in September 1982. Leonard Slatkin conducted the St. Louis Symphony Orchestra. It was recorded the following year by the same forces, and released one year after that.

The orchestral version of *American Hymn* is one of the late Schuman works that generates a sense of freshness and excitement. Although many of the composer's familiar devices reappear, there are passages—especially during the faster portions—that are new to the composer, while the ingenious deployment of an array of percussion creates a glistening aural sheen.

However, this view has not been shared by all commentators. Polisi feels that it "lacks the imagination, rhythmic energy, and pathos typical of Schuman's earlier work.... Even the orchestration is surprisingly colorless.... The music seems the product of a diminished man."[350] Generally unsympathetic to Schuman, John Rockwell was relatively restrained, referring to the composer as "America's most visible and determined symphonist." As for the piece itself, he felt that it had "its quietly affecting moments, and betrays throughout the craftsmanship that has defined Mr. Schuman's oeuvre. But it also sounded bland and self-importantly empty, the folkish simplicity comprised of ingenuity, yet not really attaining to genuine complexity."[351] James Wierzbicki similarly felt that the work was "not compelling music," despite "evidence of the craftsmanship that has characterized the music of the seventy-two year old Schuman."[352] On the other hand, Richard Dyer found it to show "the composer in characteristic form. The variations . . . exploit various potentialities of the orchestra, perhaps a little too systematically, but the best of the piece shows the composer's awareness of the eloquence of plain-speaking."[353]

As noted earlier, Schuman had hoped for a commission that would enable him to produce a major statement of large proportions on an American subject for the bicentennial celebration in 1976. But such an opportunity did not arise. However, in 1984 he was approached by the New York Philharmonic, exploring the possibility of a commission for a major work commemorating the hundredth anniversary of the Statue of Liberty. Schuman suggested that a consortium commission be arranged. That way each organization would be responsible for a smaller fee, while the new work would enjoy a number of performances, rather than just one. (And, of course, in such a case, Schuman would receive a larger fee than a single commissioner could offer.) Ultimately nine organizations agreed to participate—believed to be the largest number of institutions ever to have participated in a single commission up to that time—and Schuman received a fee of $75,000.[354]

For this large commission, Schuman had in mind a work for chorus and orchestra. Once the terms were settled, the composer had to decide upon a text. After a fruitless search through the most likely resources, he requested that a new text be written for the occasion. After much further literary research, he invited Richard Wilbur (b. 1921) to collaborate with him on the project. (Several years later Wilbur would be named America's poet laureate.) Schuman described to the poet exactly what he was seeking in a text, specifically warning against excessive sentimentality or mawkish patriotism. Wilbur enthusiastically agreed to work with Schuman, urging him to be candid and direct in reacting to the poet's efforts. Ultimately the collaboration proved to be congenial and fruitful, and Schuman accepted Wilbur's text with few alterations.[355]

On Freedom's Ground: An American Cantata was completed early in 1985. In an article published several months before the premiere, Schuman was quoted as saying, "Basically, the subject is America, all the things that are right about it and some that are wrong. It is a land with the possibility of change. It is about immigrants." Nan Robertson, writer of the article, reported that the composer "said the moods in the five-movement work ranged from contemplative to rousing, from solemn to cheerful. He called the third movement . . . a 'requiem' and a 'mourning for those who died for this country.' The fourth, he said, invokes various popular dance tunes, among them the jig, the schottische and the Lindy." Robertson noted that when he was first invited to write the poem, Wilbur recalled, "I hesitated. I thought, Great God! What a wealth of clichés are suggested by this theme." She added that he found the project "a 'true collaboration' involving many consultations with Mr. Schuman—'not just a matter of one person writing first, and another one following along later' to set a completed text to music. 'I've never worked in this way before,' Mr. Wilbur said. 'It was give and take all the time, with never a harsh word.' He added that 'On Freedom's Ground' could be read 'as a suite of short poems, but I thought of it always as words for music.'"[356] Wilbur's text is quite moving in its own right and was published in a collection entitled *New and Collected Poems* that resulted in the poet's second Pulitzer Prize.[357]

The forty-minute work, scored for baritone solo, mixed chorus, and orchestra, comprises five sections. The first, "Back Then," opens at a very slow tempo with a sustained dissonance in the strings, above which a solo trumpet intones a theme—clearly tonal but freely chromatic, and strophic in a manner suggesting poetry. This "main theme" serves as a central unifying element that recurs in a different guise in each movement. The theme is restated by the orchestra and developed somewhat until the chorus enters with the poem, which sets the scene of a virgin America, before the arrival of settlers. The choral writing is largely syllabic. Although the orchestra is lightly scored, focusing chiefly on individual instrumental choirs, the overall harmonic language creates an effect of undifferentiated dissonance, until the final chord—a major triad that serves as a springboard into the second section.

"Our Risen States" begins with an extended orchestral *tutti* at a rapid tempo, enlivened by much active percussion. The interval of the second is prominent in this section. (Interestingly, this entire movement is reminiscent in many ways of the manager's protest song ["Listen, listen"] from *The Mighty Casey*.) During this *tutti* section the orchestra breaks into much the same sort of melody with rapid oompah accompaniment as was heard in the recent *American Hymn*. In this case the melody, played by the woodwinds, later joined by the strings, is the main theme from the first movement. This *tutti* passage lasts for several minutes, before the chorus enters, with no slowdown of tempo. The text for this section deals with the idea, emanating from England, of a government rooted in the consent of the people, although America had to fight a war with England, with the help of the French, in order to achieve this ideal. The French then went on to fight for the same ideal, inspired by America's example. The choral presentation of the text shares much in common with the choral treatment in parts of *The Mighty Casey*, with much repetition of words for their effect as rhythmic gestures. But again, most of the choral material is uninteresting harmonically, except when the main theme reappears within a totally triadic—though barely tonal—harmonization.

The third movement, "Like a Great Statue," is the most serious portion of the cantata—indeed, its emotional core—at least with regard to its intentions. It accounts for almost 40 percent of the duration of the entire work. Wilbur's text for this movement is especially touching in addressing "the dead who died for this country." After an orchestral introduction, the solo baritone declaims the text, which develops this idea, while the orchestra provides rather dry musical support. After some elaboration, the baritone sings, "Say that they mattered alive and after/That they gave us the time to become what we could." Then there is a shift in the focus of the text. As the bass clarinet contributes one of those seemingly unrelated *obbligati*, the baritone continues, citing the sins of America:

> Grieve for the ways in which we betrayed them,
> How we robbed their graves of a reason to die;
> The tribes pushed west, and the treaties broken,
> The image of God on the auction block
> The immigrant scorned and the striker beaten,
> The vote denied to liberty's daughters.
> From all that has shamed us, what can we salvage?
> Be proud at least that we know we were wrong,
> That we need not lie, that our books are open.

Only then does the chorus enter, continuing the verse. The solo baritone then resumes his declamation. The chorus returns, the continuing text set to music based on its previous entrance. Finally, the chorus sings the words, "Lord God Almighty, free/At last to cast their shackles down/And wear the common crown/Of liberté, of liberty"—words that have a special resonance to all Americans—set to the work's main theme. This is followed by an extended orchestral *tutti*, grim in character, underscored by much activity among the drums. The movement comes to an end, settling into a solemn, funereal peroration, the drumbeats gradually fading away into silence. Despite the emotional weight of this movement—indeed, the section elevates the entire work above the level of mere patriotic chauvinism—its power must be attributed to Wilbur's profoundly moving poetry more than to Schuman's music, which does little more than provide an appropriate mood and a structure through which to present the text.

The following section, "Come Dance," offers a dramatic contrast to what has preceded it. With a primary focus on the orchestra, it is essentially a medley of dance tunes recalling the popular styles of the previous century. The tunes are treated much more gently than Schuman's typical handling of preexisting musical material. Instead of his usual "updating," he leaves the tunes largely untouched, aside from some abrupt modulations. Toward the end of the movement, the chorus enters with some light verse in keeping with the music's focus on popular dances, set to freely triadic harmony, with some suggestion of the main theme. But with the verse beginning, "But end it with the John Paul Jones/Invented in this land,/That each of us may circle 'round/And take the other's hand," the chorus, supported by the brass section, sings the main theme in a fresh, triadic harmonization. This line is picked up by the strings *pizzicato*, joined by other instruments, while the chorus provides a counterpoint of rhythmic speech, bringing the movement to a quiet conclusion.

The final movement, "Immigrants Still," follows on the heels of the preceding section. In a very slow tempo, the solo baritone, reinforced by a solo cello, declaims the final verses, which extol the Statue of Liberty ("our lady") as a steadfast beacon overseeing the changes that have taken place throughout the years. The chorus then enters, with a beautiful harmonic setting of the words,

> To our free eyes the gulls go weaving now
> Loose wreaths of flight about our lady's brow,
> And toward her feet the motions of the sea
> Leap up like hearts that hasten to be free.

The baritone declaims the following lines, soon joined by the chorus. The tempo quickens, and the energy increases, as the chorus and soloist continue in unison with the words, "We are immigrants still, who travel in time,/Bound where the thought of America beckons;/But we hold our course, and the wind is with us." Against this the orchestra provides a dissonant chordal accompaniment, with much percussion, including clusters in the piano. The tempo continues to quicken, as the chorus repeats its final lines against the main theme played by the orchestra in rhythmic diminution. As the final words are repeated, the orchestra builds to a triumphant conclusion on a major triad. Without implying any suggestion of "borrowing," one cannot help but note a similarity with the finale of Howard Hanson's valedictory Symphony No. 7 for chorus and orchestra, which ends with Whitman's "Joy, shipmate, Joy!" Both endings evoke the desperation of a man at the end of his life, attempting to summon a sense of hearty optimism toward the future.

As noted, *On Freedom's Ground* is a mixed success and owes much to the quality of Wilbur's verses. The work's premiere took place in New York in October 1986, a hundred years to the day following the original dedication of the statue. The baritone soloist was Sherrill Milnes, and the New York Philharmonic was joined by the 200-voice Crane Chorus from the State University of New York at Potsdam. The conductor was Zubin Mehta.

Not surprisingly, the reaction to the cantata was mixed. Polisi expressed his belief that the work "actually fulfilled Schuman's hope to write a work that would reflect the American dream."[358] However, in a less formal context, the writer noted, "*On Freedom's Ground* is another case where Bill stretches it out way too long for this commemorative idea. But the middle movement is quite moving. He's running out of ideas and energy, but he wants to keep composing. He never gives up."[359] John Rockwell was predictably negative, but in this case his criticisms were not without some justification. He noted that

> Richard Wilbur . . . suggests in his text that Americans derived their idea of liberty from the English. Mr. Schuman's 40-minute score struck this writer as similarly English, akin to those grand, empty, ceremonial pieces with which English composers of this century have favored us. Most of the time, Mr. Schuman sets a massed chorus to thick, tuneless proclamations. Sherrill Milnes's solos also emphasize the stentorian. . . . The score is at its most successful in its instrumental interludes, especially the quiet patter of percussion at the end of the third part and the witty dance music at the outset of the fourth. But for most of the time, this is a work more noble in its patriotic intentions than its esthetic realization.[360]

On the other hand, Joseph McLellan wrote,

> On Freedom's Ground" is nearly the ideal celebratory cantata—public music, not notable for deep personal feeling but well wrought, highly communicative in its gestures and instantly comprehensible and enjoyable. It is a carefully bal-

anced blend of verbal and musical rhetoric by two artists who are masters of
their respective crafts and who worked closely together. Its most immediately
enjoyable movement is probably the fourth, a sort of scherzo in which the spirit
of dancing is invoked amid a colorful sequence of varied dance rhythms. The
deepest feeling is in the third movement, an evocation of the dark side of the
American experience.[361]

John von Rhein felt that the work was "in many ways a musical embodiment of that same American vigor and optimism, a spirit that seems to burn
almost as brightly in the recent works of our musical elder statesman as in the
works he composed in his younger years."[362]

For his penultimate major work, Schuman returned to the string quartet, a
medium into which he had last ventured in 1950. As noted earlier, each of the
composer's string quartets belongs to one of his style-periods. Thus representing his late period is the String Quartet No. 5, dedicated to the memory of Vincent Persichetti, who had died five days before the date of completion printed
in the score. Whether Schuman had his younger colleague—who had been
suffering with cancer for more than a year—in mind while he was writing the
quartet, or whether the dedication was simply an acknowledgment of the passing of one whose career had been closely linked with his own, or whether the
work was in some way a contemplation of his own approaching end is open
to conjecture. The quartet was commissioned for the New York International
Festival of the Arts, with funding from Chase Manhattan Bank.

Completed in August 1987, the Fifth Quartet comprises two substantial
movements, each subdivided into sections. The first movement is identified "Introduction—Monody—Coda"; the second, "Variations—Epilogue."
Marked *Larghissimo*, the brief "Introduction" is only fourteen measures
long: muted strings in sustained harmonic dissonance, and a moving line
in the viola, then the cello, which droops the interval of the ninth, set a
severe mood. The long *portamenti* that Schuman began to employ in such
contexts during the late 1960s appear frequently in this work. The tempo
slows even further for the arrival of the "Monody," perhaps the most compelling music in the entire quartet. This section finds the composer in one
of his most lofty and visionary states of mind. A nine-measure melody of
quietly mournful, icily austere beauty, marked *cantabile dolce, quasi par-
lando*, is introduced by the first violin against a backdrop of parallel minor
triads moving in slowly treading half-notes. After an initial statement, the
chromatically searching melodic line moves to the second violin, which—
reviving a technique that dates back to the Third Symphony—enters a half-
step higher than did the first violin, while that instrument continues with a
high countermelody, and the viola and cello quietly pursue more active and

dissonant contrapuntal lines. The viola then enters with the melodic line, a half-step higher than the previous entrance, against dissonant counterpoint in the violins and minor triads played *pizzicato* by the cello. The harmony is harsh and the texture somewhat congested, as the cello presents the somber melodic line another half-step higher, in direct counterpoint with a much more rhythmically active, chromatic line in the first violin, while the second violin and viola sustain dissonant chords. The tempo suddenly quickens *più mosso*, while the melodic line returns to the viola (another half-step higher) but in rhythmic augmentation, so that, functioning like a traditional *cantus firmus*, it remains at roughly the same speed as in the preceding entrances. Meanwhile, the violins pursue rapidly skittering *staccato* figurations in parallel thirds, producing Schuman's multiplanar effect, while the cello adds a *pizzicato* line that soon becomes triple-stops, then quadruple-stops, as the section reaches a frenzied climax, then comes to a halt, as a series of harsh chords recalls the "Introduction." Returning to the slow tempo, the viola reviews the melodic line, played against *pizzicato* minor triads in the cello, in regular quarter-notes (the strummed dirge effect), while the violins offer contrapuntal reminiscences of the melody. The brief "Coda" recalls the "Introduction" with sustained dissonances and angular unisons, until a series of long-held E-flat-major triads brings the movement to an end.

The previous year Schuman had composed a duo for clarinet and violin based on a seventeenth-century Dutch carol called "Awake Thou Wintry Earth." For the second movement of his Quartet No. 5 he decided to compose a series of variations on this rather insipid melody. Although substantially longer than the first movement, the second presents considerably less musical interest. Much like the many sets of variations on diatonic themes Schuman composed during the latter part of his career, these begin with an initial presentation and elaboration of the theme in its own harmonic context, followed by subjection to a variety of techniques that wrench it into more contemporary rhythmic, harmonic, melodic, and tonal guises. The theme can be readily identified in most of the variations, although some range quite far afield from the original tune. In addition to the tediousness of this set of variations, a preponderance of writing for the violin in its highest register becomes a gnawing irritation. Tolerable in an impeccable performance, it can be quite unpleasant in a less refined reading. The quiet "Epilogue," marked *Tranquillo*, is an interesting attempt to fuse together most of the elements of the foregoing proceedings: the Dutch tune, the "Introduction" from the first movement, the theme of the "Monody" in its form as a "strummed lament," and the first-movement "Coda," finally concluding as the Dutch tune gradually resolves into the reiterated E-flat-major triad that ended the first movement.

Schuman's String Quartet No. 5 was introduced by the Orford String Quartet in June 1988, at the 92nd Street Y in New York City. A performance by the Lydian String Quartet was released on recording in 1994.

The critical response to the quartet was generally positive, but with some reservations. British critic Peter Dickinson commented,

> The prevailing mood is the rapt stillness of many of Schuman's Adagios—a kind of frozen, elegiac intensity which is impressively maintained. . . . [T]he tension is not completely resolved in the rich E flat major chords at the end of both movements. The second movement provides apparent contrast with a set of variations on the Dutch carol, *Awake thou wint'ry earth*. . . . As with Schuman's other variations on existing material—English rounds or Billings, for example—he benefits from poignantly audible references to the tune and its tonal harmony. But this movement also stems from the private world of Schuman as opposed to the élan of his rumbustious symphonic epics or the busy public life of his middle years.[363]

Mark Lehman's reaction is characteristically eloquent:

> The first [movement] is a bleak elegy of icy but anguished intensity. Its slow-moving melodic line maintains a keening lament without interruption for the entire 13 minutes—one eerie episode by a grief-stricken viola that continues obliviously under the frantic mockery of nervously skittering paired violins. II—at 18 minutes an even longer movement—begins in sharpest contrast to its grim predecessor: a cheerful 17th-Century Dutch carol . . . is sung out in airy counterpoint and warm harmony. This is then subjected to an elaborate series of variations, and the cold gloom of the first movement elegy slowly regains its power, finally reasserting its presence in an epilogue of haunted sorrow only faintly mitigated by a final soft reminiscence of the original tune.[364]

Schuman's last major work proved to be a one-act opera, commissioned by the Glimmerglass Opera Company and funded by the Eugene V. and Clare E. Thaw Charitable Trust. What may be viewed as his final effort to win acceptance for *The Mighty Casey*, this new work was intended as a companion piece to that work, so that together they might provide a full evening's entertainment. It was Frankie Schuman who suggested the short story "Taste," by Roald Dahl, as a subject. The idea appealed to her husband, who approached Richard Wilbur as a possible librettist. After Wilbur respectfully declined, Schuman turned to J. D. McClatchy (b. 1945).[365] Although he had grown up in a household steeped in opera, McClatchy had never written a libretto before. (However, he has written a number of them—some quite successful—since then.) When Schuman proposed the idea to the poet in 1987, McClatchy was unfamiliar with Dahl's story, but once he read it, accepted the composer's invitation and began to devise ways of expanding and deepening the story, resetting the time period, and attempting to "make an anecdote into a fable," and writing the libretto in rhymed verse to "give the right tone and pace to a dramatic comedy, [while] poetry's concise amplitude allowed me . . . to charge the story with thematic significance it lacks in its original version."[366]

In its final form, *A Question of Taste* revolves around a nouveau-riche businessman aspiring to acceptance as a sophisticate; his eligible daughter Louise, who is deeply in love with Tom, a young man her father does not find suitable; and an older man, a refined wine connoisseur named Phillisto Pratt. Pratt is smitten with Louise and attempts to use a wine-tasting wager with the girl's father as a means of winning her hand. Pratt devises a trick to manipulate the bet, but his chicanery is revealed by the housekeeper. Mc-Clatchy reset the opera in 1910 (the year of Schuman's birth) in an elegant New York brownstone. Though handicapped by a number of serious medical problems, Schuman worked very closely with his librettist, as he had on previous collaborative projects. He completed the vocal score in 1988, and the orchestration early in 1989.

The new work was to be unveiled by the Glimmerglass Opera Company in Cooperstown, New York, together with *The Mighty Casey*, as part of the festivities surrounding the fiftieth anniversary of the Baseball Hall of Fame in June 1989. As the new work was being prepared, a number of Glimmerglass executives were concerned that the music was too difficult for a general audience, although as they became more familiar with it, their fears were somewhat mollified. However, Schuman's physical exhaustion was apparent, and he strongly resisted making the kinds of changes that typically suggest themselves during the preparation of a new opera.[367]

Although the circumstances of the premiere generated a certain amount of excitement, the opera itself did not make a significant impact. Musically, the work revolves around a waltz-like idea that calls to mind similar passages in the operas of Gian Carlo Menotti, although its syncopations and melodic parallelisms are unmistakably the work of Schuman. The orchestral introduction presents this delightfully infectious idea, which recurs throughout the piece, somewhat like a *ritornello*. The overall tone is slick, elegant, and urbane— just the sort of thing at which Menotti excelled. However, unlike the way his Italian-American contemporary might have handled it, Schuman's vocal writing consists of wooden and inanimate declamation. Truthfully, the work is a series of missed opportunities: McClatchy provided texts for a poignant aria for Louise ("I feel so hopeless"), an ardent aria for Tom ("No man is rich who's not in love"), a love duet ("Our wealth is our love"), and a finale that begins as a duet, and gradually expands to a quintet. But Schuman was unable to provide the lyrical lines that these moments require; his efforts are almost amateurish in their obvious intervallic expansions and contractions to reflect rises and falls in emotional expression, while the harmonic language is consistently polytonal, and often unrelated tonally to the vocal lines. And despite his attempts to improve the story's "tone and pace" and develop the character of the housekeeper, McClatchy's scenario fails to give her crucial revelation the appropriate dramatic weight.

Reviewing the premiere, Bernard Holland felt that the opera "begins with some promise," but was soon undone by the libretto.

> There is villainy and virtue, love and contempt—but no people. Rather we are given characters who wear their one-idea identities like name tags at an auto dealer's convention—the ardent lover from the wrong side of the tracks, the daughter he loves, the matriarchal servant, the blustering upwardly mobile father. Phillisto Pratt is an oenophile villain of moustache-twirling proportions; making him a bass only deadens the load of his obviousness. . . . There are a few ponderous jokes inserted here, and a plot twist at the end, but this is basically a humorless text.[368]

A subsequent production at the Juilliard School, conducted by Gerard Schwarz, was described as "merely bland" by John Rockwell, who concluded that "Mr. Schuman has little real theatrical instinct." While he felt that neither libretto nor music interfered with Dahl's original story, "they don't add much either."[369] A recording of this performance was released in 1994.

CONCLUSION

As has been noted, during his later years Schuman's work was often discussed dismissively by commentators. But as an "elder statesman" of distinction, he was typically treated with deference when he received awards or attained milestone birthdays, which were usually documented in feature articles in newspapers and magazines. And there were certainly many—particularly among his professional peers—who continued to hold him in unreservedly high esteem. In 1971, when presenting him with the medal of the MacDowell Colony, Aaron Copland stated, "Whenever I think of [Schuman's music], I think of it as being the work of a man who has an enormous zest for life . . . and that zest informs all his music. . . . His music represents big emotions!"[370] In 1980, at the time of Schuman's seventieth birthday, composer Jacob Druckman, who had been a Juilliard student during Schuman's tenure as president, recalled his early reactions to his music,

The sense of an irresistible force was . . . totally tied in with my feelings about Schuman's music. It was shocking, not because the sounds were new. . . . But it was the incredible level of energy with which the music plunged forward that was and is shocking. That and the unabashed passion. To ears more used to European circumspection and complexity, it seemed a music without guile, with all its nerve ends exposed, singing and shouting without stopping to breathe, knowing exactly where it had to go and charging there relentlessly and shamelessly. . . . He was not only a mover and a doer but also a visionary. The forward motion was not just the overflow of nervous energy but a very carefully considered thrust toward clear and worthy goals.[371]

In 1990, in an article marking Schuman's eightieth birthday, conductor Leonard Slatkin, who also studied at Juilliard, remarked,

The first thing to remember is that Bill qualifies as one of the handful of true [American] symphonists who produced an extraordinary body of works trying to maintain the performance structure of the classic symphony. . . . Where Bill differs from his colleagues is that he has a highly urban style of writing. It smacks of city life. There's an urgency, even though there's great lyricism. You can't go two or three bars without recognizing Bill's voice. That's what I think will stand him in good stead as the years go by. There are certain signature moments—using a bass clarinet solo, a timpani solo, the use of percussion as an independent force. He writes in a kind of block style with the brass, woodwinds and strings having separate musics for the most part, and when they engage constantly with each other, they tend to be as opposing forces rather than unifying ones. The style and the sound are very recognizable, and that's what should carry them very well in terms of the totality of history, not just of American music but of all music.[372]

On the other hand, as illustrated throughout this chapter, there has always been a contingent of voices who were unmoved by Schuman's music, and one can glean certain common themes in the most thoughtful of their remarks. German composer and musicologist Peter Jona Korn (1922–1998), who commented astutely on American music, wrote during the 1960s,

[Schuman] has an affinity for sharply clashing sonorities, although his basic harmonic structures are entirely tonal. He is a brilliant orchestrator, a knowledgeable composer completely in command of every aspect of contemporary technique. Withal, there is a certain synthetic quality about his music, outside the realm of verbal definition; it leaves an impression of having been conceived in a spirit of emotional detachment, it is a music of symphonic gestures rather than of symphonic content. Something that is often said—incorrectly—of Walter Piston is true for William Schuman: he is the prototype of an academic composer.[373]

Critic Tim Page has noted,

[Schuman's music] is characterized by a restless, muscular propulsion, with colorful, sharply defined orchestration, including a liberal and inventive use of percussion instruments, and angular melodies that climb and balance with wiry grace. There is a certain hardness to his work, a hardness that rarely admits sentiment but does not preclude beauty. At times, Mr. Schuman's expertise works against him. One occasionally senses the presence of a superb craftsman going about his business, rather than a composer with an urgent message to convey.[374]

Even in a memorial article written less than a month after the composer's death, Edward Rothstein commented,

In [his] symphonies, and in much of Schuman's other music, there is a sense of comfort, of achievement without undue effort. The music is handsome, honest, well managed; projects undertaken are projects completed. It is music of a fluent public speaker. It is easy to follow; it is declamatory; it contains much variety. But often, I am afraid, it is not that interesting. It has passions within it, but it is not music of passion; it contains elements of sentiment, but not of deep feeling. It is never less than professional, but it rarely seems much more. . . . But Schuman's music, like everything he undertook, had a purpose. It was music by someone who made his living serving the art and its listeners. And one way to serve the art was to participate in its creation, and to offer it, in all humility, to the public. Schuman's music served, without pandering or posturing, to make him a composer. That gave him the vision to play a more influential role as a leader of the art, its public statesman. Accomplished composers are a rarity, but Schuman's accomplishments are rarer still. His public role will not soon be filled.[375]

Schuman's compositional output is, indeed, uneven, and most listeners, familiar with only a random sample, base their judgments on those works they have heard. A number of Schuman's compositions do display a cold, mannered, artificial quality that is probably responsible for alienating some listeners. Some offer long barren stretches in the guise of profundity; some recycle devices he had used for decades. However, his ten or fifteen finest works reveal a unique musical personality characterized by a brash, exuberant, but hard-edged optimism balanced by a deep, solemn contemplativeness, defining one of the most eloquent creative voices of his generation—a voice that is distinctively and unmistakably American, without recourse to vernacular references. As Neil Butterworth noted, "His eight surviving symphonies are a cornerstone of mid-twentieth century symphonic achievement."[376]

Schuman's death on 15 February 1992 was noted on the front page of the *New York Times* the following day; within the paper was a lengthy obituary by Bruce Lambert. It began, "William Schuman, a composer whose distinctly

American style won two Pulitzer Prizes and guided him as the founding president of Lincoln Center and the president of the Juilliard School, died yesterday at Lenox Hill Hospital in Manhattan." However, the fact that the obituary continues—inaccurately and uncorrected by the editorial staff, "Mr. Schuman incorporated American jazz and folk traditions into his works" indicates the extent to which his identity had already become a matter of general reputation rather than actual first-hand knowledge.[377]

After the memorial tributes had come and gone, Schuman's music, as well as his reputation, receded from the contemporary musical scene. Two recordings of his work appeared later in the year of his death: one featuring the St. Louis Symphony under Leonard Slatkin, the other featuring the Seattle Symphony under Gerard Schwarz. Both these recordings included the *New England Triptych* and Schuman's orchestration of Ives's *Variations on "America."* On those infrequent occasions when Schuman's music was performed, the pieces chosen were usually either of these two relatively minor entries or the Third Symphony. The remainder of his output was rarely played, and recordings virtually ceased. One may suppose that, as a Modern Traditionalist—like the two other composers featured in this volume—much of his later music, though based on traditional principles and thus not au courant, embraced Modernist approaches to harmony and tonality that were not appealing to most listeners.

This virtual moratorium on Schuman's music ended in 2005, when Naxos American Classics, an ambitious series of recordings that promised a comprehensive overview of American classical music, inaugurated a complete survey of Schuman's symphonies, as performed by the Seattle Symphony Orchestra, conducted by Schuman-champion Gerard Schwarz. These recordings were well received and served to some extent to revive interest in his music. As but one example, when the first entry in this series was released, Jerry Dubins wrote, "William Schuman (1910–1992), no less than Charles Ives, Samuel Barber, Aaron Copland, and Leonard Bernstein, is, in my opinion, one of America's greatest 20th-century composers, an American icon. It is therefore puzzling to me that his music, once championed, seems to be falling from grace. A quick perusal of the current Schuman discography reveals fewer entries than for any other of the aforementioned composers, and fewer even (this is the distressing part) than there once were."[378]

The next significant development was the publication in 2008 of *American Muse: The Life and Times of William Schuman*, written by Joseph W. Polisi, then president of the Juilliard School. Though many feared that Polisi, Schuman's choice to succeed Peter Mennin as president, was too beholden to the Schuman family to provide an objective perspective, the book proved to be a fascinating and enormously informative study (of great value in preparing the volume at hand), while presenting a candid and balanced picture of the man.

At the time of this writing, further studies of Schuman are reportedly in progress, in recognition of his hundredth birthday. Yet it is remarkable that in 2009, when his String Quartet No. 4 was performed, along with works by Babbitt and Carter, at the Juilliard School, *New York Times* critic Vivien Schweitzer devoted only about one fifth of the review to Schuman, almost all of which was spent in explaining just who William Schuman was.[379] And in April 2010, when Leonard Slatkin conducted the Juilliard Orchestra in an all-Schuman concert, which included the Third Symphony, *Times* critic Steve Smith identified it as "an early work from 1941," as if it were a new discovery. He "constantly marveled at the brave, unorthodox strokes in its structure and orchestration—like an extraordinary bass clarinet solo . . . and at the soaring optimism it conveyed. That American orchestras can neglect so vital a creation in favor of any number of second-shelf European works seems criminal."[380]

Perhaps it is appropriate to conclude this chapter with the reflections of J. D. McClatchy, librettist of *A Question of Taste*. Two years after Schuman's death, the poet recalled the experience of working with him:

> He was a man almost *driven* to happiness: an outsize life and career, the innovations and institutions he started, the buoyant optimism of his personality and convictions, the dramatic flair of his music. Underneath it all—and this is true of every great artist—was a strong, serious, stubborn streak that knew what he wanted, that listened to the voice he'd had in his mind's ear since childhood, and that time and again cannily found ways to let that voice sing out.[381]

NOTES

1. Edward Rothstein, "A Composer with Many Public Faces," *New York Times*, 3 March 1992.

2. John Clare, "Joseph Polisi on American Muse," 21 November 2008, http://vimeo.com/2307903?pg=embed&sec=2307903 (accessed 4 February 2010).

3. Frank J. Oteri, "A Conversation with Joseph W. Polisi," *New Music Box*, 11 March 2009, http://www.newmusicbox.org/article.nmbx?id=5903 (accessed 4 February 2010).

4. Andrea Olmstead, *Juilliard: A History* (Urbana: University of Illinois Press, 1999), 143.

5. Quoted in Joseph W. Polisi, *American Muse: The Life and Times of William Schuman* (New York: Amadeus Press, 2008), 5.

6. William Schuman, conversation with Walter Simmons, 29 February 1980.

7. Polisi, *American Muse*, 11.

8. Quoted in Christopher Rouse, *William Schuman: Documentary* (New York: G. Schirmer and Theodore Presser, 1980), 1.

9. Polisi, *American Muse*, 15.

10. Polisi, *American Muse*, 69.

11. Polisi, *American Muse*, 22.

12. Flora Rheta Schreiber and Vincent Persichetti, *William Schuman* (New York: G. Schirmer, 1954), 6.

13. Schreiber and Persichetti, *William Schuman*, 13.

14. Polisi, *American Muse*, 32.

15. Polisi, *American Muse*, 11.

16. Polisi, *American Muse*, 43.

17. Aaron Copland and Vivian Perlis, *Copland: 1900 through 1942* (New York: St. Martin's/Marek, 1984), 281.

18. Aaron Copland, review, *Modern Music* (May/June 1938): 245–46.

19. Neil Butterworth, *The American Symphony* (Brookfield, Vt.: Ashgate, 1998), 116.

20. Quoted in Polisi, *American Music*, 53.

21. Quoted in Polisi, *American Muse*, 62.

22. Quoted in Schreiber and Persichetti, *William Schuman*, 19.

23. Steve Swayne, "William Schuman, World War II, and the Pulitzer Prize," *Musical Quarterly* (Summer/Fall 2006): 274–75.

24. William Schuman, letter to Harold Ickes, 6 August 1940, quoted in Swayne, *William Schuman*, 277–78.

25. Swayne, *William Schuman*, 282.

26. Schreiber and Persichetti, *William Schuman*, 28.

27. Quoted in Polisi, *American Muse*, 85.

28. Quoted in Polisi, *American Muse*, 153.

29. Quoted in Olmstead, *Juilliard*, 147–48.

30. Schreiber and Persichetti, *William Schuman*, 29.

31. Quoted in Polisi, *American Muse*, 86.

32. Quoted in Olmstead, *Juilliard*, 149.

33. Olmstead, *Juilliard*, 160–62.

34. Quoted in Polisi, *American Muse*, 155.

35. Quoted in Polisi, *American Muse*, 159.

36. Polisi, *American Muse*, 106.

37. Quoted in Polisi, *American Muse*, 107.

38. Polisi, *American Muse*, 108.

39. Quoted in Polisi, *American Muse*, 141.

40. Polisi, *American Muse*, 142.

41. Dorothea Persichetti, *Vincent Persichetti's Music* (unpublished monograph, May 1960), 58; Persichetti Archive at New York Public Library, JPB 90–77, Box 103, Folders 17–18.

42. Schreiber and Persichetti, *William Schuman*, 36–37.

43. Schreiber and Persichetti, *William Schuman*, 39.

44. Schreiber and Persichetti, *William Schuman*, 40.

45. Schreiber and Persichetti, *William Schuman*, 44.

46. Polisi, *American Muse*, 187–88.

47. Polisi, *American Muse*, 125–27.

48. Rothstein, "A Composer with Many Public Faces."

49. Polisi, *American Muse*, 129.

50. Jack Beeson, conversation with Walter Simmons, 5 February 2009.

51. Olmstead, *Juilliard*, 169–70.

52. Quoted in John Rockwell, "William Schuman—'The Continuum Has Been Composition,'" *New York Times*, 3 August 1980.

53. Quoted in Polisi, *American Muse*, 203–4.

54. Polisi, *American Muse*, xv.

55. Harold C. Schonberg, "Man to Orchestrate Lincoln Center," *New York Times*, 31 December 1961.

56. Quoted in Ved Mehta, "An Enclave," *The New Yorker* (17 February 1962): 27.

57. Olmstead, *Juilliard*, 183.

58. Quoted in Polisi, *American Muse*, 244–45.

59. Polisi, *American Muse*, 269.

60. Quoted in Rouse, *William Schuman*, 21.

61. Richard F. Shepard, "Schuman Quitting Lincoln Center Post," *New York Times*, 5 December 1968.

62. Bruce Lambert, "William Schuman Is Dead at 81; Noted Composer Headed Juilliard," *New York Times*, 16 February 1992.

63. Polisi, *American Muse*, 280.

64. Polisi, *American Muse*, 283.

65. Olmstead, *Juilliard*, 189.

66. Robert S. Hines, "William Schuman Interview," *College Music Symposium* (Fall 1995): 144.

67. Polisi, *American Muse*, 290–91.

68. Richard F. Shepard, "Schuman Finishes His 9th Symphony," *New York Times*, 9 April 1968.

69. *Philadelphia Enquirer*, 9 February 1969.

70. Polisi, *American Muse*, 293.

71. Polisi, *American Muse*, 294–95.

72. Polisi, *American Muse*, 310–11.

73. Oteri, "Conversation with Polisi."

74. Quoted in Polisi, *American Muse*, 314.

75. Phillip Ramey, "William Schuman at Seventy: A Talk with the Composer," *Ovation* (September 1980): 17.

76. Rockwell, "William Schuman."

77. Quoted in Phillip Ramey, untitled autobiography (unpublished manuscript, 2010), 230.

78. Martha Graham, letter to William Schuman, 13 July 1984, quoted in Polisi, *American Muse*, 162.

79. William Schuman, "An Advance Bequest Certified Deposit Is Simple as ABCD," *Philanthropy Monthly* (May 1983): 28–9.

80. Polisi, *American Muse*, 338–40.

81. Polisi, *American Muse*, 342–45.

82. Olmstead, *Juilliard*, 268–69.

83. Polisi, *American Muse*, 374.

84. Polisi, *American Muse*, 352.

85. Ramey, untitled autobiography, 230.

86. Robert Commanday, "An American Original, Composer William Schuman Celebrated the Country in His Works," *San Francisco Chronicle*, 20 February 1992.

87. Quoted in Polisi, *American Muse*, xvi.

88. Schreiber and Persichetti, *William Schuman*, 49.

89. Schreiber and Persichetti, *William Schuman*, 49.

90. Schreiber and Persichetti, *William Schuman*, 58.

91. Schreiber and Persichetti, *William Schuman*, 66.

92. Schreiber and Persichetti, *William Schuman*, 67–68.

93. Aaron Copland, upon presenting Schuman with the MacDowell Colony Medal, Summer 1971, quoted by Oliver Daniel, "William Schuman" (BMI brochure).

94. Butterworth, *The American Symphony*, 131.

95. Nick Barnard, review, *Music Web International*, 2010, www.musicweb-international.com/classrev/2010/Jan10/Schuman6_8559625.htm (accessed 19 March 2010).

96. Irving Fine, review, *Musical Quarterly* (October 1954): 624.

97. Commanday, "An American Original."

98. Mark Lehman, "Overview of American Symphonies," *American Record Guide* (July/August 2007): 46.

99. Schreiber and Persichetti, *William Schuman*, 50.

100. Michael Steinberg, CD liner notes, Deutsche Grammophon 419 780–2 (1987), 3.

101. Polisi, *American Muse*, 379–80.

102. Schreiber and Persichetti, *William Schuman*, 51.

103. Ramey, "William Schuman at Seventy," 20.

104. Schreiber and Persichetti, *William Schuman*, 52.

105. Schreiber and Persichetti, *William Schuman*, 71.

106. Ramey, "William Schuman at Seventy," 20.

107. Hines, "William Schuman Interview," 135–36.

108. Hines, "William Schuman Interview," 140.

109. Fine, review, 623.

110. Schreiber and Persichetti, *William Schuman*, 73.

111. Hines, "William Schuman Interview," 136–37.

112. Schreiber and Persichetti, *William Schuman*, 46.

113. Ramey, "William Schuman at Seventy," 20.

114. Hines, "William Schuman Interview," 138.

115. Vivian Perlis, "A Life Spent on One Musical Path," *New York Times*, 12 August 1990.

116. Hines, "William Schuman Interview," 142.

117. Polisi, *American Muse*, 372.

118. Mark Lehman, review, *American Record Guide* (November/December 1994): 188.

119. Schreiber and Persichetti, *William Schuman*, 50.

120. Elliott Carter, review, *Modern Music* (November/December 1938): 37.

121. Quoted in Polisi, *American Muse*, 50.

122. L.A.S., review, *Boston Monitor*, 18 February 1939.

123. Warren Storey Smith, review, *Boston Post*, 18 February 1939.

124. R. B. C., review, *Baltimore Evening Sun*, 4 March 1940.

125. W.W., review, *Baltimore Evening Sun*, 4 March 1940.

126. Paul Rosenfeld, review, *Musical Quarterly* (July 1939): 380–81.

127. Nathan Broder, "The Music of William Schuman," *Musical Quarterly* (January 1945): 19–22.

128. Schreiber and Persichetti, *William Schuman*, 86.

129. Hines, "William Schuman Interview," 141.

130. Olin Downes, review, *New York Times*, 26 November 1939.

131. Leonard Bernstein, "Young American: William Schuman," *Modern Music* (Winter 1941–42): 97.

132. Edward Seckerson, review, *Gramophone* (May 1993): 51.

133. Broder, "Music of Schuman," 21.

134. Mark Lehman, review, *American Record Guide* (November/December 1994), 188.

135. Schreiber and Persichetti, *William Schuman*, 20.

136. Schreiber and Persichetti, *William Schuman*, 20.

137. Henry Simon, review, *PM*, 3 December 1940.

138. Karl Miller, "William Schuman at 75: An Appreciation," *Symphony* (June/July 1985): 30.

139. Olin Downes, review, *New York Times*, 22 November 1941.

140. Bernstein, "Young American," 99.

141. Peter G. Davis, review, *New York Times*, 23 November 1980.

142. Mark Lehman, review, *American Record Guide* (January/February 1998): 172.

143. Swayne, "William Schuman," 280–81.

144. H. Wiley Hitchcock, "William Schuman: Musical All-American," *Keynote* (August 1980): 15.

145. Lehman, "Overview of American Symphonies," 46.

146. Butterworth, *The American Symphony*, 120–22.

147. Virgil Thomson, review, *New York Herald Tribune*, 8 April 1942.

148. Rouse, *William Schuman*, 10.

149. Butterworth, *The American Symphony*, 122–23.

150. Mark Lehman, review, *American Record Guide* (July/August 2003): 147.

151. Lehman, review, *American Record Guide* (July/August 2003): 147.

152. Lehman, review, *American Record Guide* (July/August 2003): 147.

153. Swayne, "William Schuman," 296.

154. Swayne, "William Schuman," 273–320.

155. Aaron Copland, letter to Schuman, 27 March 1943, quoted in Swayne, "William Schuman," 310.

156. William Schuman, letter to Copland, 31 March 1943, quoted in Swayne, "William Schuman," 310.

157. Arthur Berger, letter to Copland, 12 April 1943, quoted in Swayne, "William Schuman," 310.

158. Miller, "William Schuman at 75," 30.

159. Schreiber and Persichetti, *William Schuman*, 103–6.

160. Rudolph Elie Jr., review, *Boston Herald*, 13 November 1943.

161. Rouse, *William Schuman*, 10.

162. Mark Lehman, review, *American Record Guide* (January/February 1998): 173.

163. Michael Fleming, review, *St. Paul Pioneer Press*, 17 October 1992.

164. Malcolm Barry, review, *Music and Musicians* (October 1974): 56.

165. Nicholas Tawa, *The Great American Symphony* (Bloomington: Indiana University Press, 2009), 71.

166. Polisi, *American Muse*, 146–54.

167. Antony Tudor and William Schuman, *Undertow: Choreographic Episodes* (New York: Associated Music Publishers, 1945), 4.

168. Quoted in Polisi, *American Muse*, 153.

169. Schreiber and Persichetti, *William Schuman*, 109.

170. Schreiber and Persichetti, *William Schuman*, 109–13.

171. Virgil Thomson, review, *New York Herald Tribune*, 29 April 1945.

172. Normand Lockwood, review, *MLA Notes* (June 1947): 362.

173. Fine, review, 624.

174. Miller, "William Schuman at 75," 161.

175. Polisi, *American Muse*, 155.

176. William Schuman, *Night Journey* (Philadelphia: Merion Music, 1947).

177. Joshua Kosman, review, *San Francisco Chronicle*, 23 January 1988.

178. Karl Miller, review, *American Record Guide* (January/February 1992): 144.

179. Rouse, *William Schuman*, 16.

180. Vincent Persichetti, review, *Musical Quarterly* (April 1952): 298–300.

181. Polisi, *American Muse*, 169.

182. Polisi, *American Muse*, 160.

183. Quoted in Polisi, *American Muse*, 169–70.

184. Charles Jones, review, *MLA Notes* (June 1953): 482.

185. Nathan Broder, review, *Musical Quarterly* (October 1955): 553.

186. Edwin Schloss, review, *Philadelphia Inquirer*, 12 January 1963.

187. Elliott Galkin, review, *Baltimore Sun*, 28 March 1963.

188. David Hall, "A Bio-Discography of William Schuman," *Ovation* (August/September 1985): 18.

189. Michael Fleming, review, *St. Paul Pioneer Press Dispatch*, 27 September 1990.

190. Louis Blois, review, *American Record Guide* (May 1984): 43.

191. Miller, "William Schuman at 75," 31.

192. Karl Miller, review, *Classical Net*, 15 October 1997, http://www.classical.net/music/recs/reviews/a/alb00256a.php (accessed 4 February 2010).

193. Butterworth, *The American Symphony*, 124–27.

194. William Bergsma, review, *MLA Notes* (June 1951): 564.

195. Schreiber and Persichetti, *William Schuman*, 116.

196. William Schuman, interviewed by Paul Snook, WRVR-FM (New York), Fall 1969.

197. Schreiber and Persichetti, *William Schuman*, 118–19.

198. Robert Sabin, "Martha Graham Creates Dance with Louisville Orchestra," *Musical America* (15 January 1950): 67.

199. Hans Kuppenheim, "Martha Graham Dances in Louisville Premiere," *Musical Courier* (15 February 1950): 35.

200. William Bergsma, review, *MLA Notes* (June 1951): 564.

201. Richard Franko Goldman, review, *Musical Quarterly* (April 1951): 258–60.

202. David Hall, "A Bio-Discography of William Schuman," 35.

203. William Schuman, *George Washington Bridge* (New York: G. Schirmer, 1950).

204. Mark Lehman, review, *American Record Guide* (November/December 1994), 187.

205. Persichetti, review, *Musical Quarterly* (April 1952): 298.

206. Olin Downes, review, *New York Times*, 29 October 1950.

207. Aaron Copland, review, *Musical Quarterly* (July 1951): 394–95.

208. Quoted in Walter Simmons, LP liner notes, EAV 7RF-7410 (1980).

209. Quoted in Simmons, LP liner notes.

210. Polisi, *American Muse*, 192.

211. Tim Page, CD liner notes, Delos DE-1030 (1994), 8–10.

212. Polisi, *American Muse*, 192ff.

213. Harold C. Schonberg, review, *New York Times*, 5 May 1953.

214. Martin Gardner, ed., *Casey at the Bat* (New York: Dover Publications, 1977), vii.

215. Arthur Berger, review, *New York Herald Tribune*, 5 May 1953.

216. Review, *Time* (18 May 1953): 60.

217. Harold C. Schonberg, review, *New York Times*, 7 May 1955.

218. Paul Hume, review, *MLA Notes* (June 1955): 486.

219. Allen Hughes, review, *New York Times*, 31 August 1967.

220. Leslie Kandell, review, *Musical America* (November 1989): 36.

221. Bernard Holland, review, *New York Times*, 26 June 1989.

222. Harry Haskell, "William Schuman," *New Grove Dictionary of Opera*, ed. Stanley Sadie (New York: Oxford University Press, 1992), IV, 252.

223. Quoted in Polisi, *American Muse*, 321.

224. Polisi, *American Muse*, 163.

225. Nathan Broder, review, *Musical Quarterly* (October 1955): 553.

226. Frederick Sternfeld, review, *MLA Notes* (March 1955): 330.

227. John Proffitt, CD liner notes, Albany TROY276 (1997).

228. Paul Hume, review, *Washington Post*, 21 March 1956.

229. Denis Stevens, review, *Musical Times* (May 1956): 269.

230. Henry Cowell, review, *Musical Quarterly* (July 1956): 386–89.

231. Peter G. Davis, review, *Musical America* (November 1964): 31.

232. Polisi, *American Muse*, 183.

233. Quoted in Polisi, *American Muse*, 79.

234. William Schuman, *New England Triptych* (Philadelphia: Merion Music, 1956).

235. Polisi, *American Muse*, 177.

236. Rose Widder, review, *Musical Courier* (May 1957): 29.

237. Daniel Webster, review, *Philadelphia Inquirer*, 8 July 1987.

238. Paul Driver, review, *Boston Globe*, 1 May 1984.

239. Arthur Trootstwyk, review, *Musical America* (15 November 1956): 10.

240. William Glackin, review, *Sacramento Bee*, 13 November 1990.

241. Polisi, *American Muse*, 179.

242. Polisi, *American Muse*, 189.

243. Quoted in Polisi, *American Muse*, 189.

244. Quoted in Polisi, *American Muse*, 368.

245. Joseph McLellan, review, *Washington Post*, 8 May 1986.

246. Bernard Holland, review, *New York Times*, 17 May 1990.

247. Calum MacDonald, review, *Tempo* (July 1972): 56.

248. Polisi, *American Muse*, 172–74.

249. José Serebrier, CD liner notes, Naxos 8.559083 (2001).

250. Quoted in Joshua Berrett, review, *American Music* (Fall 1991): 337.

251. Review, *Time* (20 February 1950): 46–47.

252. Quoted by Oliver Daniel, "William Schuman" (BMI brochure).

253. Edward Seckerson, review, *Gramophone* (December 1989): 73.

254. Richard Schneider, review, *Stereophile* (May 1990): 181–82.

255. Robert Commanday, review, *San Francisco Chronicle*, 13 November 1992.

256. Berrett, review, *American Music* (Fall 1991), 336.

257. John von Rhein, review, *Chicago Tribune*, 15 October 1989.

258. Richard Dyer, Review, *Boston Globe*, 20 February 1990.

259. David Hall, Review, *Stereo Review* (March 1990): 80.

260. David Denton, Review, *The Strad* (December 1990): 1026.

261. James North, review, *Fanfare* (July/August 1991): 271–72.

262. Roger Dettmer, review, *Classical CD Review*, May 2001, http://www.classicalcdreview.com/wsviolin.htm (accessed 6 February 2010).

263. Rob Barnett, review, *Music Web International*, May 2001, http://www.musicweb-international.com/classrev/2001/May01/schuman.htm (accessed 6 February 2010).

264. Rouse, *William Schuman*, 18.

265. Christopher Rouse, "Schuman and His Generation," *Symphony* (October/November 1985): 74.

266. Oteri, "A Conversation with Joseph W. Polisi."

267. Quoted in Rockwell, "William Schuman."

268. Sheila Keats, LP liner notes, Turnabout TVS-34447 (1971).

269. Winthrop Sargeant, review, *The New Yorker* (10 December 1960): 231–33.

270. Harold C. Schonberg, review, *New York Times*, 1 December 1960.

271. Paul Hume, review, *Washington Post*, 2 December 1960.

272. Leopoldo H. Frias, review, *Musical Courier* (December 1960): 27, 33.

273. Max Harrison, review, *Gramophone* (July 1973): 51.

274. E.R., review, *Music and Letters* (January 1963): 97.

275. Karl Kroeger, review, *MLA Notes* (Summer 1963): 407.

276. Butterworth, *The American Symphony*, 127.

277. Keats, LP liner notes.

278. Polisi, *American Muse*, 197.

279. Polisi, *American Muse*, 290.

280. Hines, "William Schuman Interview," 141.

281. Alan Rich, review, *New York Times*, 29 September 1962.

282. Peter Dickinson, review, *Musical Times* (October 1964): 759.

283. William Schuman, Letter to Edward Downes, 21 August 1962, quoted in Edward Downes, LP liner notes, Columbia MS-6512 (1963).

284. Review, *Time* (12 October 1962): 54.

285. Ross Parmenter, review, *New York Times*, 5 October 1962.

286. Butterworth, *The American Symphony*, 129.

287. Richard Franko Goldman, review, *Musical Quarterly* (January 1963): 91–92.

288. Hugh Ottaway, review, *Musical Times* (October 1965): 786.

289. Daniel Webster, review, *Philadelphia Inquirer*, 22 December 1984.

290. Karl Miller, review, *Classical Net*, 7 November 1997, http://www.classical.net/music/recs/reviews/s/sny63163a.php (accessed 6 February 2010).

291. Mark Lehman, review, *American Record Guide* (January/February 1998): 173.

292. Quoted in Polisi, *American Muse*, 45.

293. Ramey, "William Schuman at Seventy," 21.

294. Polisi, *American Muse*, 257.

295. Robert Evett, review, *Musical Quarterly* (April 1965): 408.

296. M.C., review, *Music and Letters* (April 1967): 184.

297. William Schuman, *Symphony No. 9* (Philadelphia: Merion Music, 1968).

298. Polisi, *American Muse*, 401.

299. Daniel Webster, review, *Philadelphia Inquirer*, 11 January 1969.

300. Ronald Eyer, review, *Newsday*, 15 January 1969.

301. Harold C. Schonberg, review, *New York Times*, 15 January 1969.

302. Louis Blois, review, *American Record Guide* (May 1984): 43.

303. David Hurwitz, review, *Classics Today*, 2005, http://www.classicstoday.com/review.asp?ReviewNum=9046 (accessed 6 February 2010).

304. Roger Dettmer, review, *Classical CD Review*, June 2005, http://classical-cdreview.com/8557543.html (accessed 6 February 2010).

305. Polisi, *American Muse*, 269.

306. Harold C. Schonberg, review, *New York Times*, 4 October 1968.

307. Jon Yungkans, review, *The Flying Inkpot* (1998), http://inkpot.com/classical/sonybarbsternbern.html (accessed 6 February 2010).

308. William Schuman, *In Praise of Shahn* (Philadelphia: Merion Music, 1971).

309. Polisi, *American Muse*, 296.

310. Raymond Ericson, review, *New York Times* (30 January 1970).

311. Richard Swift, review, *MLA Notes* (December 1972): 320.

312. Paul Griffiths, review, *Musical Times* (November 1973): 1149.

313. Yungkans, review.

314. Simon Harris, review, *Music and Letters* (July 1974): 373–74.

315. Phillip Ramey, LP liner notes, Columbia M35101 (1978).

316. Ramey, LP liner notes, Columbia M35101.

317. Ramey, LP liner notes, Columbia M35101.

318. Paul Kresh, review, *Stereo Review* (December 1978): 156.

319. Ben Pernick, review, *Fanfare* (September/October 1978): 105.

320. Michelle Dulak, review, *San Francisco Classical Voice*, 4 June 2002, http://www.sfcv.org/arts_revs/sfsym_6_4_02.php (accessed 6 February 2010).

321. Richard Freed, CD liner notes, RCA Victor 09026–61282–2 (1992).

322. Polisi, *American Muse*, 316.

323. John Rockwell, review, *New York Times*, 22 April 1979.

324. Quoted in Polisi, *American Muse*, 318.

325. Tim Page, review, *New York Times*, 16 December 1985.

326. James Wierzbicki, review, *St. Louis Post Dispatch*, 4 November 1991.

327. Butterworth, *The American Symphony*, 131.

328. William Schuman, *The Young Dead Soldiers* (Philadelphia: Merion Music, 1975).

329. Quoted in Polisi, *American Muse*, 320.

330. Robert Parris, review, *High Fidelity/Musical America* (August 1976): MA-30.

331. Rouse, *William Schuman*, 25.

332. Roger Dettmer, review, *Fanfare* (November/December 1981): 236.

333. Eric Dalheim, review, *American Music* (Spring 1983): 100.

334. Rouse, *William Schuman*, 25.

335. Polisi, *American Muse*, 323.

336. Harold C. Schonberg, review, *New York Times*, 6 November 1978.

337. Joseph McLellan, review, *Washington Post*, 19 May 1983.

338. Dalheim, review, 100.

339. Quoted in Polisi, *American Muse*, 333.

340. Quoted in Polisi, *American Muse*, 333.

341. Harold C. Schonberg, review, *New York Times*, 25 January 1980.

342. Michael Walsh, review, *Time* (24 June 1985): 82.

343. Edward Tatnall Canby, review, *Audio* (December 1985): 110.

344. Niall O'Loughlin, review, *Musical Times* (February 1984): 100.

345. Susan Feder, review, *Musical Times* (November 1983): 705.

346. Leighton Kerner, review, *Village Voice*, 25 February 1980.

347. Stephen Ellis, review, *Fanfare* (January/February 1988): 109.

348. Arnold Rampersad, *The Life of Langston Hughes*, vol. 2: *1941–1967, I Dream a World* (New York: Oxford University Press, 2001), 266.

349. Phillip Ramey, LP liner notes, Nonesuch 79072 (1984).

350. Polisi, *American Muse*, 336.

351. John Rockwell, review, *New York Times*, 29 January 1983.

352. James Wierzbicki, review, *High Fidelity/Musical America* (February 1983): MA 31.

353. Richard Dyer, review, *Boston Globe*, 2 May 1986.

354. Polisi, *American Muse*, 353–54.

355. Polisi, *American Muse*, 354–57.

356. Nan Robertson, "A Musical Collaboration in Homage to America," *New York Times*, 2 January 1986.

357. Richard Wilbur, "On Freedom's Ground," *New and Collected Poems* (Orlando, Fla.: Harvest Books, 1989), 119–22. Reprinted by permission of Houghton Mifflin Harcourt.

358. Polisi, *American Muse*, 359.

359. Oteri, "A Conversation with Joseph W. Polisi."

360. John Rockwell, review, *New York Times*, 2 November 1986.

361. Joseph McLellan, review, *Washington Post*, 18 September 1987.

362. John von Rhein, review, *Chicago Tribune*, 13 November 1987.

363. Peter Dickinson, review, *Gramophone* (August 1994): 68.

364. Mark Lehman, review, *American Record Guide* (November/December 1994): 188.

365. Polisi, *American Muse*, 363–64.

366. J. D. McClatchy, CD liner notes, Delos DE 1030 (1994), 23.

367. Polisi, *American Muse*, 366.

368. Bernard Holland, review, *New York Times*, 26 June 1989.

369. John Rockwell, review, *New York Times*, 16 December 1990.

370. Aaron Copland, upon presenting Schuman with the MacDowell Colony Medal, Summer 1971, quoted by Oliver Daniel, "William Schuman" (BMI brochure).

371. Quoted in Rouse, *William Schuman*, viii.

372. Quoted in Perlis, "A Life Spent on One Musical Path."

373. Peter Jona Korn, "The Symphony in America," in *The Symphony: Elgar to the Present Day*, ed. Robert Simpson (Baltimore, Md.: Penguin Books, 1967), 256.

374. Tim Page, "Schuman Concerto and Tenth Symphony," *New York Times*, 16 December 1985.

375. Rothstein, "A Composer with Many Public Faces."

376. Butterworth, *The American Symphony*, 131.

377. Bruce Lambert, "William Schuman Is Dead at 81."

378. Jerry Dubins, review, *Fanfare* (Sept/Oct 2005): 276.

379. Vivien Schweitzer, review, *New York Times*, 10 October 2009.

380. Steve Smith, review, *New York Times*, 3 April 2010.

381. J. D. McClatchy, "William Schuman: A Reminiscence," *Opera Quarterly* (Fall 1994): 37.

SELECTED BIBLIOGRAPHY

Adams, K. Gary. *William Schuman: A Bio-Bibliography*. Westport, Conn.: Greenwood Press, 1998.

Butterworth, Neil. *The American Symphony*. Brookfield, Vt.: Ashgate, 1998: 116–31.

Copland, Aaron. Review (String Quartet No. 4). *Musical Quarterly* (July 1951): 394–96.

Hines, Robert S. "William Schuman Interview." *College Music Symposium* (Fall 1995): 132–44.

Miller, Karl. "William Schuman at 75: An Appreciation." *Symphony* (June/July 1985): 29ff.

Olmstead, Andrea. *Juilliard: A History.* Urbana: University of Illinois Press, 1999: 142–93.

Oteri, Frank J. "A Conversation with Joseph W. Polisi." *New Music Box.* 11 March 2009. http://www.newmusicbox.org/article.nmbx?id=5903 (accessed 4 February 2010).

Persichetti, Vincent. Review (Symphony No. 6). *Musical Quarterly* (April 1952): 298–301.

Polisi, Joseph W. *American Muse: The Life and Times of William Schuman.* New York: Amadeus Press, 2008.

Ramey, Phillip. "William Schuman at Seventy: A Talk with the Composer." *Ovation* (September 1980): 16–21.

Rothstein, Edward. "A Composer with Many Public Faces." *New York Times,* 3 March 1992.

Rouse, Christopher. *William Schuman: Documentary.* New York: G. Schirmer and Theodore Presser, 1980.

Schonberg, Harold C. "Man to Orchestrate Lincoln Center." *New York Times,* 31 December 1961.

Schreiber, Flora Rheta, and Vincent Persichetti, *William Schuman.* New York: G. Schirmer, 1954.

Swayne, Steve. "William Schuman, World War II, and the Pulitzer Prize." *Musical Quarterly* (Summer/Fall 2006): 273–320.

ESSENTIAL DISCOGRAPHY

Albany TROY566: *Credendum*; Piano Concerto (John McCabe, piano); Symphony No. 4 (Albany Sym. Orch., David Alan Miller, cond.); www.albanyrecords.com/

Delos DE-1030: *The Mighty Casey*; *A Question of Taste* (Juilliard Opera Center Productions, Gerard Schwarz, cond.); www.delosmusic.com/

EMI 5099920661151: Violin Concerto (Robert McDuffie, violin; St. Louis Sym. Orch., Leonard Slatkin, cond.); www.emiclassics.com/

Naxos 8.559254: Symphony No. 4; Symphony No. 9; *Orchestra Song*; *Circus Overture* (Seattle Sym. Orch., Gerard Schwarz, cond.); www.naxos.com/

Naxos 8.559255: Symphony No. 7; Symphony No. 10 (Seattle Sym. Orch., Gerard Schwarz, cond.); www.naxos.com/

Naxos 8.559317: *Judith*; Symphony No. 3; Symphony No. 5 (Seattle Sym. Orch., Gerard Schwarz, cond.); www.naxos.com/

Naxos 8.559625: Symphony No. 6; *Prayer in Time of War*; *New England Triptych* (Seattle Sym. Orch., Gerard Schwarz, cond); www.naxos.com/

Sony Classical SMK-63163: Symphony No. 3; Symphony No. 5; Symphony No. 8 (New York Phil., Leonard Bernstein, cond.); www.sonyclassical.com/

3

Vincent Persichetti

Vincent Persichetti was one of the most widely respected musicians of his generation. A prolific composer, brilliant educator and lecturer, and prodigious pianist, he composed more than 150 works in virtually all genres and for virtually all performing media, while serving for forty years on the faculty of the Juilliard School, many of them as chairman of the Composition Department.

During his lifetime Persichetti influenced the musical lives of thousands of people from all walks of life, and his name came to signify a comprehensive musicianship virtually unparalleled among American composers. Countless young pianists were nurtured on his sonatinas and the *Little Piano Book*, while many other young instrumental students first experienced serious contemporary music through his works for band; church choirs turned to his *Hymns and Responses for the Church Year* as an inexhaustible resource, while many young composers have found his classic textbook *Twentieth Century Harmony* to be an indispensable tool; and among professional soloists and conductors, his sonatas, concertos, and symphonies stood among the masterworks of American music. Throughout his life Persichetti encouraged healthy, creative participation in music at all levels of proficiency while shunning dogmas that advocated one compositional approach at the expense of others.

He was beloved and admired as a teacher and was in great demand as a lecturer, using his comprehensive knowledge of the repertoire, extraordinary gift for improvisation, awe-inspiring piano technique, and mischievous wit to captivate audiences. He immersed himself in all aspects of music with an infectious, childlike enthusiasm devoid of pomposity.

When he was sixty-five he told an interviewer: "I've not yet decided what I'll do with my life. Perhaps I will concertize as a pianist, but, on the other hand, shouldn't I bring audiences some of those neglected orchestral pieces? Then again I'd love to have a larger herb farm, if it weren't for my keen interest in sailing. I know I'd like the life of the Maine lobster fisherman, but my sculpting would keep me on solid ground. I'm too busy with composing to consider what my life's work will be. I suppose, though, at some point I should decide to work for a living."[1]

BIOGRAPHY

Vincent Ludwig Persichetti was born in Philadelphia, Pennsylvania, on 6 June 1915, the son of Vincenzo Ruggiero Persichetti and Martha Buch. Vincenzo, born in a village in the Abruzzi region of Italy, had been brought to the United States at the age of eleven. Employed as a bank clerk, he was described as an intelligent, dignified, and gentle man who was very supportive of his son's musical talent and interests.[2] Vincent's mother had been born in Bonn, Germany, and was brought to the United States as an infant. She was described as a strong woman, whose temperament contrasted with that of her quiet, reserved husband.[3] Her family had settled in Camden, New Jersey, where her father, Ludwig Buch, owned a tavern reportedly frequented by Walt Whitman.[4]

Drawn to music in infancy, young Vincent would sit for hours transfixed by the family's player-piano. Neither of his two younger siblings—a brother, Karl, and a sister, Nina—showed a comparable affinity for music.[5] Vincent spent his childhood in the then-largely Italian-American community of South Philadelphia, where music was taken very seriously—a nurturant environment for a musically talented child. The Persichettis lived six houses away from Berlin-trained Gilbert Combs, president and founder of the Combs Conservatory, a large, well-regarded local music school. As a child Vincent would ply his neighbor with an endless barrage of musical questions. Finally, after much pleading, he was permitted to begin piano lessons at the Combs Conservatory. All of five years old, he was disappointed to learn that he couldn't study with his "friend," the president, but was assigned instead to Warren Stanger, with whom he remained for ten years.[6] He quickly revealed a precocious talent and soon began learning the organ and double-bass as well.

Vincent attended the local public elementary school while pursuing his musical study at the Combs. When he was six, he gave his first public performance at the piano, which was broadcast on one of the Philadelphia radio stations. When he was nine, he was invited to audit the theory classes of Russell King

Miller (1871–1939). He went on to study theory and composition with Miller, whom he later cited as his most influential teacher. He recalled that Miller allowed him to write "contraband" pieces that did not follow academic rules, as long as he also demonstrated his understanding of traditional techniques in his "official" pieces. Even then he "liked bumpy melodic lines and was crazy about music that moved along a zigzag path."[7] However, as he grew older his mischievous musical pranks proved exasperating to Miller, who finally asked him to leave the class when he was fourteen. By this time he had composed his Opp. 1 and 2, as well as much other music that he later rejected.

Vincent attended South Philadelphia High School ("I faked my way through"). By this time he was playing first chair double-bass in the All-Philadelphia High School Orchestra, as well as in other local orchestras.[8] During those years he jumped at any opportunity to play music—especially if he was getting paid for it: weddings, church services, radio performances; he even accompanied a harmonica band. He simply immersed himself in music, studying scores constantly, memorizing the works to be performed weekly by the Philadelphia Orchestra and then attending the concerts to compare his mental realizations with the actual sounds. In this way he began to develop an exhaustive knowledge of the repertoire. "I was unwilling then, and am unable now, to forget anything."[9] It was during this period that he developed a life-long love for the music of Haydn and Schumann, whom he cited as important compositional influences.[10] During his teen years Vincent pursued two other intense interests in addition to music: sailing and art. He attended art school, and sculpture, in particular, remained an important creative outlet for him for the rest of his life. Years later he drew an apt self-portrait in caricature that became a sort of logo that appeared on many of his publications.

When he was sixteen, Vincent was finally accepted as a piano student by his former neighbor Gilbert Combs, continuing with him until the older man's death three years later,[11] at which point he turned to Alberto Jonas ("His ears were sharp, despite his deafness.").[12] At seventeen, the young musician was appointed to the position of organist—and later, choirmaster—at the Arch Street Presbyterian Church. There he developed an astonishing ability to improvise. During church services he would play from memory passages from the many orchestral works he had been voraciously absorbing, combining them with passages of his own. These "arrangements" ranged from Haydn to Verdi and Tchaikovsky, and even Stravinsky.[13]

In 1936, at age twenty-one, Persichetti graduated from the Combs Conservatory, whereupon he accepted an invitation to head the Department of Theory and Composition. The following year he entered the master's program at the Philadelphia Conservatory, pursuing piano study with Olga Samaroff and composition with Paul Nordoff and, at the Curtis Institute, conducting with Fritz Reiner. ("My study with Reiner was a complete joy. . . . [I could never] forget his kindness and gentleness that permeated the surroundings—until the first mistake was made").[14] By this time, Persichetti's fluency at the keyboard—especially his extraordinary sight-reading—astounded not just his peers but seasoned faculty members as well. His proficiency led Reiner to arrange for him to be excused from the ear-training classes of the notoriously demanding Madame Longy, much to her annoyance.[15] While still a graduate student at the Philadelphia Conservatory, he was awarded a diploma from the Curtis Institute.

In 1938, Persichetti applied for a scholarship to continue his piano study with Olga Samaroff. However, he had to share the award with "a beautiful, magnificent" pianist from Kansas, named Dorothea Flanagan (1919–1987).[16] The two quickly became acquainted, and almost immediately she began performing his music, as well as advocating for him in other ways. In 1941 they were married, and the two developed a remarkably successful—if almost symbiotic—partnership. (Their relationship went far beyond mere emotional support and the traditional marital roles: Throughout their life together he depended on her musical judgment, and later described her as "the person who's had the greatest influence of all on my music."[17] In 1960 she completed a doctoral dissertation on his music, and much of her analytic commentary later appeared elsewhere under his own name. He acknowledged this openly when he stated, "One of the finest musicians I have ever known, Dorothea Flanagan . . . is the person who has written my prose and inspired my music."[18]

Although he was gradually building a reputation for musicianship of the highest order, Persichetti's identity as a composer was developing rather slowly. Throughout the 1930s, in the midst of a hectic schedule of study, teaching, and performing, Persichetti composed voluminously. However, he later regarded this work as imitative, part of a search for his own style, and rejected virtually all of it. Commenting on the fruits of the period 1929–1939, which he named retrospectively "the silent decade," he acknowledged, "There was some significant music, but none of it mine."[19]

In 1940 the firm of Elkan-Vogel agreed to publish a piano transcription that Persichetti had made of a Brahms prelude and fugue for organ. This was his first publication, and it initiated a relationship with Elkan-Vogel that was to endure for the rest of his life.

Persichetti was awarded a master's degree from the Philadelphia Conservatory in 1941, and the following year was invited to assume chairmanship of their department of theory and composition, while going on to pursue a doctorate. However, in order to accept this position, which he was to hold until 1962, he had to leave the Combs Conservatory, an affiliation he had maintained from the age of five.

In 1943 Persichetti won his first significant prize in composition: the Juilliard Publication Award, for an orchestral work called *Dance Overture*. The piece attracted the attention of the young choreographer Jerome Robbins, who met with the composer to discuss the possibility of adapting the overture for a dance work about three sailors on leave. Persichetti did not feel that his work was suitable for such a project but suggested instead an unknown twenty-five-year-old composer with whom he was acquainted. (The young composer was Leonard Bernstein, and the result was, of course, *Fancy Free*.)[20]

That summer Persichetti went to Colorado Springs to participate in the city's Fine Arts Festival and to study with Roy Harris—then regarded as one of America's most significant composers. The two worked closely together, and Persichetti was intrigued by the older man's concept of "autogenetic form." The enthusiastic young composer eagerly submitted to Harris page after page of the fruits of his labor. Harris, who produced his own work painstakingly, was reportedly rattled by his student's facility, and asked him to leave after three weeks.[21] However, before he left, Persichetti had completed his Third Piano Sonata, which he performed at the Festival. Interestingly, the notion that Persichetti had been a "student of Harris" has been repeated in print for many years, although their work together was limited to this three-week period.

In March 1944, Persichetti was introduced to Harris-student William Schuman, who had by then achieved national attention for his Third Symphony, championed by Serge Koussevitzky, then conductor of the Boston Symphony Orchestra. This meeting initiated what was to become a most significant relationship for the two composers.[22] This was also the year when Dorothea gave birth to their first child: a daughter, Lauren, who was to become a dancer and choreographer. (A son, Garth, was born two years later.) It was at this time that Persichetti began writing music criticism, first for the noted journal *Modern Music*, then later for the *Musical Quarterly* and *MLA Notes* as well. His reviews were notable for their generally positive, encouraging tone, their lack of stylistic bias, and their remarkable acuity in grasping the composer's intentions and the degree to which these intentions were realized. However, after about ten years, as the demand for his own compositions increased, Persichetti was forced to relinquish this activity.

In the spring of 1945 the thirty-year-old composer was awarded the doctor of musical arts degree from the Philadelphia Conservatory (now the University of the Arts in Philadelphia). That April also marked the first fully professional performance of one of his orchestral works: *Fables*, introduced by the Philadelphia Orchestra and Eugene Ormandy. Meanwhile, word of Persichetti's keyboard prowess had reached Igor Stravinsky, who invited Persichetti to join him in a concert of his works for two pianos.[23]

What may have been the most auspicious and fortuitous development in Persichetti's career thus far took place in 1947. Two years earlier, William Schuman had been named president of the Juilliard School and was in the process of thoroughly revamping the school's curriculum and hiring a faculty to implement his innovations. Perhaps the most significant of these was an approach he called "Literature and Materials of Music," which was intended to integrate the isolated disciplines of theory, ear training, history, and analysis into a systematic, comprehensive study of the repertoire. Learning of Schuman's plans, Olga Samaroff suggested that he consider Persichetti for the faculty. Schuman later recalled that he had realized immediately that Persichetti was an ideal person to help develop the Literature and Materials curriculum and offered him a position, which Persichetti accepted.[24] Schuman had also been impressed by Persichetti's music criticism and asked if his younger colleague would be interested in writing a book on him and his music, to be published by G. Schirmer. Persichetti accepted the challenge and produced a manuscript. Schuman, however, didn't care for the biographical portion, although he was pleased with the section on his music. (He then assigned the biographical portion to another writer, and the book was eventually published in 1954.)

Persichetti as Teacher

Although Persichetti's place in music history will presumably center on his compositions, equally notable during his lifetime was his reputation as a teacher. Not only did hundreds of students reap the benefits of his fifty years as pedagogue, but hundreds—if not thousands—more experienced his unique ability to share his understanding of the history and structure of music in the lecture-recitals he gave throughout the country. Many who knew him felt that Persichetti had compromised his own musical life—that his extraordinary keyboard skills might have enabled him to pursue an international career as a composer-pianist along the lines of Rachmaninoff, had he not devoted so much time and energy to teaching.[25] But his role as educator was of the utmost importance to the identity he shaped for himself. His teaching, his lecture-recitals, and even his own music were the means through which he imparted a principle that he reiterated countless times throughout the entire span of his career: The twentieth century has enriched the language of music with a veritable explosion of new sounds and new techniques. The task of the twentieth-century composer is to master all these materials and approaches, and integrate them into a fluent musical language—a common practice, comparable to the traditional common practice of the eighteenth and nineteenth centuries—that can be drawn upon to produce an infinite range of expression. Clearly Persichetti saw himself as striving to embody this ideal, which he demonstrated through his own creative work and through his prodigious knowledge and skills, aided by a dry, oblique, and often baffling sense of humor.

I recall attending one of Persichetti's lecture-recitals in 1969: He began by discussing the many techniques and approaches that had appeared over the course of the century, illustrating each one at the piano by playing (from memory) representative passages from the literature and identifying each composer, all in his curiously whimsical manner. Then he announced that he would demonstrate how all these techniques might be integrated into a single work. But first he needed a thematic idea. He asked the audience to suggest a series of notes from which he would construct a theme. He then proceeded with an improvisation that introduced the theme and then subjected it to an elaborate development that incorporated complex counterpoint and virtuosic keyboard figurations, illustrating each of the techniques he had previously discussed. The result was an entirely coherent sonata movement of some ten minutes duration, played flawlessly and without faltering or hesitation of any kind.

Persichetti's students include many prominent figures of the subsequent generation, among them Jacob Druckman, Peter Schickele, Thelonius Monk, Steve Reich, Philip Glass, Thomas Pasatieri, Larry Bell, Lowell Liebermann, Einojuhani Rautavaara, Richard Danielpour, Frank Zappa, Joseph Castaldo, Ellen Zwilich, along with many others. Their recollections help to paint a vivid impression of the impact he had on those who came under his influence:

Steve Reich: [Persichetti] was a phenomenal teacher because he had enormous musicianship and he could be a complete chameleon. He could listen to you, look at your score, and he became you. He could improvise pieces in your style. He knew what information you needed at this point in your life today. And that's a great teacher. Because, he has more technique than you have and he can see where you're going, not as a reflection of himself, but as an amplification of yourself. There are precious few people like this and when you find teachers like this they become enormously helpful, because they solve specific problems that you have at a certain period of time.[26]

Larry Bell: Persichetti had already examined a number of my compositions. At my first lesson, he commented, "You have a very advanced technique for your age. So I don't think we should talk about technique." When I asked him what we were going to do, he said, "You're a big fan of Wallace Stevens. Let's talk about his poetry." And that's what we did for the next six months! . . . He had a laconic manner of speech and a dry sense of humor that made it difficult to know whether he was being serious or not. In a way, he almost spoke in poetry—short, terse phrases. In fact, by the end of my second year with him his elliptical manner was starting to get to me. Around that time I asked him if there was anything I should be doing that I wasn't. At that point he turned to the keyboard and played a medley of all the great lyrical themes of Rachmaninoff, Tchaikovsky, that sort of thing, all in an unbroken sequence. Then he said, "I think you could write more of a tune." I'm sure it had something to do with where I was in my own development at the time, but those words made an enormous impact on me, and significantly influenced the direction my work took after that.[27]

Michael White recounted an anecdote recalled by a student, describing a class in which Persichetti was teaching the concept of "hemiola."

In the course of convincing the student[s] to use their ears, he kept running back and forth to the piano. . . . I wrote down all the works he played: a Brahms Intermezzo, a Courante of Bach, a movement from La Mer, a Scarlatti sonata, and another short work of Brahms. By god, he didn't just play a few bars here and there, he did a whole section—talking, singing, and bouncing over to the blackboard all the while!. . . . All the students in that class looked at their neighbors, mouths open, thinking, does this guy know the entire repertoire by heart?

White continued, "Everything he spoke about or played had one purpose: to help the students make essential aural connections to what would otherwise be just intellectual concepts. Anybody could look up the definition of *hemiola* in the *Harvard Dictionary*—but would they really understand? 'You can look at music, talk about music, and read about music until the Second Coming,' he'd say, 'but if you don't have it in your ears, you'll never *get* it.'"[28]

Jan Krzywicki: An older student who was already studying with Persichetti asked me what I was going to bring to my first lesson. I told him, I have the first five minutes of an orchestra piece, to which he said, that's great, you'll get a chance to hear your piece. He explained that Persichetti would be able to play it right through. I was pretty skeptical of this, as the piece started innocently enough with two muted trumpets but soon created a long, large crescendo to fortissimo with lots of things happening. Well, at the lesson I handed the score over to him and he started playing; then as the piece progressed he added the percussion parts by tapping his feet on the floor, and when he couldn't fit the horn parts under his fingers, because there were none left to use, he started singing the horn parts! I really did feel that I heard my orchestra piece that day.[29]
    Joseph Castaldo (student; later, colleague): Vincent was the kind of person that never . . . said an unkind word about anybody. . . . I mean, he'd do it sometimes in such an oblique way that it took you two days to figure out that he did not respect the person he was talking about. . . . He never ridiculed anybody,

but he could make a joke in such a way that you had to realize that there was not a great deal of respect between him and this other person. . . . He was never overtly disparaging of anybody's ability, but if you knew him well, and you read between the lines, you could understand what he was actually saying. . . .

He was the most encyclopedic musician that I have ever met. If someone needed an article on the symphonies of Sibelius, they knew they could call Vincent, and he would have it at his fingertips. And he may not have even been a great admirer of a composer, but he knew the music. And he knew it with great insight. I was always amazed—and other students have told me the same things—at how he could quote from things as he was giving you the lesson. He'd say, "You know, it's like this from Bartók" or this from this, and it relates to this from that, and he'd be playing all these excerpts for you. . . . I was recently at a meeting with George Crumb . . . and there was somebody else at dinner and the guy referred to George's ability to sight-read at the piano . . . and George said, "Listen, I one time watched Vincent Persichetti sight-read at the piano. Nobody—nobody could sight-read the way he did." . . . I mean, Vincent was a highly gifted person, Mozartean in his gifts. . . .

One time, somebody brought in a score . . . still in manuscript, by a composer who has some reputation. Vincent sat down and started sight-reading the score. I was looking over his shoulder, and everything was there as he was doing it. And he got to the point where he started predicting what was going to be on the next page. So we would turn the page and there it was. You know, he so knew the guy's style that he could predict what he was going to be doing. After this has to come this, and then we'd turn the page and there it was. It's a formidable kind of thing. Another thing I saw him do one time, which I was in awe of. [In a lecture] he was talking about good music and bad music. He played some Beethoven sonatas to show what good music was—he'd play a movement or several parts of it—and somebody in the audience . . . popped up with a very interesting question. "Well, you showed us what good music is. Can you play an example of bad music?" . . . I could see Vincent think for just a second and he said, "Oh, yes, I can do that." And he started playing some bad music, and it really was bad music. It took me maybe ten seconds to realize what he was doing was playing a Beethoven sonata backwards. . . . I couldn't believe it, but I could see that that was what he was doing. . . .

The admiration and reverence for his abilities was universal. . . . Not only because he knew so much, but also because he kept it with a wonderful sense of humor. . . . You really enjoyed being in his classes, you wouldn't miss them for death.

And that was another thing about him— . . . it would snow. School [Philadelphia Conservatory] was going to be cancelled. Vincent would put on his boots—to walk down half a mile maybe, to get to his car, start it up, and drive to school to teach—you know, maybe sometimes to people who weren't really in a sense deserving of that kind of effort on his part. But he was so conscientious he would do it. Even during the time of his therapy, when he had cancer, he was driving up to Juilliard to teach. . . .

The wonderful thing about Vincent as a teacher was that he always knew where you were and what to do with you. . . . There was nobody that could come to him who he didn't immediately spot what the gaps were and what was needed. . . . I saw him with younger composers, he would say, "No, this is what you need," and he would write it for them, you see, because the younger composers needed a more firm hand. . . . If a person was more mature, he gave you a hint. And he didn't criticize, he guided you. It was a wonderful ability. He always bolstered people up. He gave a kind of pat on the back that made you want to go home and work. I'm totally indebted to the man. . . .

I remember him saying to me once that the thing he liked to study in music was not . . . the A theme and the B theme, but how Beethoven got from the A theme to the B theme—the music in between, the traveling music, so to speak—how did he get from here to there . . . because he said that revealed more in a composer than the part that he had really kind of labored over. . . . He said the idiosyncrasies of the composer showed up there in the connections, and you see that in his own music. . . .

He loved teaching. . . . He felt the obligation to pass on his knowledge. He loved writing because that was his activity, his soul, so to speak. I don't think he was so crazy about performing. He enjoyed it, but I don't think he wanted to make a life running around the country playing piano. He did enough of that. Vincent loved to show off, and he loved awing people with his ability, his improvisation and things like that. . . .

I had studied with other people before, and when I studied with Vincent, it was a revelation—My God, this is a totally different league. . . . There are musicians, and then there's Vincent Persichetti. There are very few like him.[30]

Some remarks and notes by Persichetti himself help to reveal some of his principles as a teacher:

Analysis is healthy only in an environment of restlessness caused by one's intuitive grasp of a work. Only when a piece increases the pulse rate is it time to search for the architectural bone and muscle. I enjoy tantalizing imperfections and veiled mysteries, but avoid identifying fragments and dissecting them to the point of boredom. I try to keep in touch with the natural force and sweep of the original improvisatory gesture.[31]

Theory teachers make theory teachers who make theory teachers to teach theory. Where's the peck of pickled peppers Peter Piper picked? Where's the sweet bread entire? Where's the heart and pulse? Maybe they are under the harmonic rhythm or in the tangled melodic line. If they are, don't cover them with contrapuntal jargon or chordal tags. Teachers must be careful to avoid excessive repetitions of theoretical observations because they may get to believe what they are saying.[32]

There has always been a need for originality. But a working knowledge of the musical achievements of our forefathers is imperative. One cannot truly understand the style of "now" if one hasn't learned the style of "then." So many composers have no sense of history and no interest in their musical ancestry. They don't know why they're where they are today. . . . My students must connect themselves to living tradition, but must learn to shed encumbrances of all educationally organized platitudes.[33]

Persichetti continued to teach at the Philadelphia Conservatory until 1962. He remained on the Juilliard faculty for forty years, until his death, commuting by car between New York City and Philadelphia.

In 1948, with the additional demands of his new role at Juilliard, Persichetti found it necessary to resign from the position he had held for sixteen years as organist and choirmaster of the Arch Street Presbyterian Church. The following year he and his family purchased Hillhouse, an eighteenth-century farmhouse located in the middle of Philadelphia's Fairmount Park. The family lived there for the rest of Vincent and Dorothea's lives. Today the house is known as "Divertimento," in recognition of the classic work for band that Persichetti composed shortly after the family moved there.

By 1950, although Persichetti—then thirty-five—was continuing to develop an estimable reputation as a teacher of theory and composition, his own music had made relatively little impact on the American compositional scene. Perhaps the most consistent supporter of Persichetti, and the person who did the most to spread his reputation to the music world at large, was William Schuman. Not only did Schuman's invitation to join the Juilliard faculty and help develop the Literature and Materials curriculum show acute perception of Persichetti's gifts, but the latter's presence at Juilliard helped to spread his own reputation. Furthermore, Schuman showed great interest in his younger colleague's creative development and did not hesitate to offer insightful encouragement or constructive criticism of new works as they appeared.[34] And when Schuman accepted an invitation to compose a work as part of the Louisville Orchestra's boldly visionary project to commission, perform, and record new works by American composers, he also suggested Persichetti as a worthy candidate. This resulted in the Serenade No. 5, which was Persichetti's first orchestral commission.

But another work, also written in 1950, was to prove even more consequential: the *Divertimento* for band, introduced in New York City in June of that year by the popular Goldman Band, conducted by the composer. The timing of this work proved fortuitous: There was a growing movement across the country, led simultaneously by several pioneering figures, to transform the concert band—hitherto associated with open-air pops concerts, military marches, and college football games—into a serious artistic medium, capable of stimulating the creative interest of the leading composers of the time. One of these figures was Richard Franko Goldman, who had assumed directorship of the Goldman Band in 1937, upon the retirement of his father, Edwin Franko Goldman, founder of the band. Another was Frederick Fennell, a young percussionist and band conductor on the faculty of the Eastman School of Music. Word had reached him about Persichetti's *Divertimento*, which he conducted at Eastman in 1951. In 1952 Fennell formed the Eastman Symphonic Wind Ensemble. Mercury Records, which had inaugurated a series of recordings featuring the Eastman-Rochester Symphony Orchestra and its conductor Howard Hanson, agreed to include the newly formed Wind Ensemble in its series of recordings. In 1953 Mercury released the ensemble's first recording, "American Concert Band Masterpieces," and included Persichetti's *Divertimento* on the program. This was the first commercial recording of his music, and it precipitated a quantum leap in the composer's reputation. *Divertimento* became a "classic" virtually overnight, prompting requests for more works tailored to this exciting new medium. (Today the *Divertimento* is "standard repertoire" for bands around the world, with hundreds of performances each year.)

Also in 1952, Roy Harris was organizing an International Festival of Contemporary Music, to be held in Pittsburgh later that year. On behalf of the festival, Harris commissioned Persichetti to write a work for two pianos. Instead, he composed Concerto for Piano, Four Hands, and performed it with Dorothea at the festival. They repeated their stunning performance for a recording released two years later as part of Columbia Masterworks' Modern American Music Series. (The work has enjoyed many subsequent recordings, but none has matched the precision, energy, and exuberance of this first performance.)

The Pittsburgh festival was significant also in introducing Persichetti to the music of Luigi Dallapiccola. "Dallapiccola revealed for me a new entrance into the world of serialism. His music was emotionally far removed from that Schoenberg twelve-tone world. A rich and potent essence was always present in this fresh, non-Viennese literature. *The past* was always present. Tension, contrast, tertian remembrances, cadential harmonic groups, color textures, polyphony, and melodic expression all were there. Dallapiccola was one of the major figures who contributed to the nascence of a new era of amalgamation of musical resources."[35]

Commissions began to arrive from auspicious organizations, such as the Koussevitzky Music Foundation, which requested a piano quintet. In 1952 Persichetti was offered a position as music editor with Elkan-Vogel, the firm, located in a suburb of Philadelphia, that had been publishing some of his compositions. He accepted the offer and remained with the company during its absorption in 1972 by the Theodore Presser Company, and eventually served as director of publications until his death.

By the mid 1950s, Persichetti's name and his music were gradually beginning to find their way into the musical life of American communities. This
was not only attributable to the breadth of his musical style but also to the
wide range of constituencies to which his music was addressed (e.g., beginning and intermediate piano students, high school and college band musicians, church choirs, as well as professional orchestras and virtuoso soloists).
In 1954 his Symphony No. 4 was premiered by Eugene Ormandy and the
Philadelphia Orchestra, who recorded the work for Columbia Masterworks
shortly thereafter. In 1955 the *Juilliard Review* published "The Music of Vincent Persichetti," by Robert Evett (1922–1975), a writer and composer who
had studied with Persichetti at Juilliard. The first substantive examination of
his music to appear in print, it is an astute analysis of his compositional style
as of the mid 1950s.[36] By this time Persichetti had written two more pieces
for band, and their popularity was spreading his name widely. (The second
piece, *Psalm*, was recorded on another release by Fennell and the Eastman
Wind Ensemble; the third piece, *Pageant*, was performed some two thousand
times during the 1955–1956 season.[37]) Now Fennell did not hesitate to refer
to him as "the leading composer in the wind band field."[38] In 1956 Persichetti
even appeared on daytime television, where he played one of the anthems
from his *Hymns and Responses*, as a piano duet with the popular song-stylist
and pianist Nat King Cole.[39]

In 1958 Persichetti was awarded a Guggenheim Fellowship that gave him
a one-year reprieve from teaching, enabling him to focus his attention on the
textbook he was working on with Dorothea. By now he was in great demand
as a guest speaker, bringing his unique lecture-recitals to colleges throughout
the country. Patterson states that he made "well over 200 of these appearances
during his career."[40]

In 1960, as part of the requirements for her own doctor of musical arts
degree at the Philadelphia Conservatory, Dorothea Persichetti completed a
monograph, *Vincent Persichetti's Music*, in which she discussed each piece
completed to date. Her comments are astute and informed; the monograph has
been an invaluable source during the preparation of this chapter.

Twentieth-Century Harmony: Creative Aspects and Practice

In 1961 Persichetti's textbook *Twentieth-Century Harmony: Creative Aspects and Practice* was published by W. W. Norton. There is reason to
believe that the book was actually written by Dorothea, although the ideas
and musical examples are clearly Vincent's own.[41] The text is a systematic
presentation of virtually all the harmonic possibilities available to a composer at the second half of the twentieth century. As such, it is an outgrowth

of Persichetti's fundamental principle: the advocacy of a twentieth-century common practice, as stated earlier. He argued that these resources belong within the working vocabulary of the competent contemporary composer. The topics covered are generally arranged in order of increasing complexity, from a listing of scale materials and an overview of triadic harmony to materials associated with atonality and serial harmony. Each topic is covered with a thoroughness that borders on compulsivity, exemplifying a characteristic intellectual predilection that became increasingly prominent in Persichetti's thinking as he grew older: the compiling of comprehensive inventories of materials, which then became resources for further elaboration. (The varied ways that this predilection was manifested were highly idiosyncratic and will be revisited throughout this chapter.) For example, the chapter on scales includes not only the familiar church modes but also synthetic scales such as the "Neapolitan Minor," the "Hungarian Major," the "Double Harmonic," and the "Eight-tone Spanish," as well as many other hypothetical possibilities. This approach is maintained throughout the book. Virtually every conceivable usage within each topic is at least mentioned and usually illustrated by a musical example.

The text is teeming with such examples, each composed by Persichetti specifically to illustrate the point under discussion. An instrumentation is indicated for each one, including some rather baffling choices. For example, in the chapter on quartal harmony, one example is scored for harmonium and another for three saxophones, illustrating an all-inclusiveness that almost seems ostentatious. At the end of each chapter is a list of pieces by other composers that exemplify the devices just discussed. As one might expect, the listing covers the broadest conceivable range of contemporary music, including the works of some two hundred composers.

Also at the end of each chapter is a series of compositional exercises to help students master each usage and incorporate it into their working vocabularies. Perhaps the chief limitation of the book is that it is primarily addressed to composers. There are very few concepts that are useful from the perspective of analysis. Rather, it is an organized presentation of techniques and devices: what functions they serve and in what contexts they are useful.

Twentieth-Century Harmony appeared at a time when musical composition in America was most severely divided among rival stylistic camps, each seeking to discredit and invalidate the others. Hence its militant ecumenism generated considerable controversy. Indeed, its often-quoted opening paragraph proved downright inflammatory: "Any tone can succeed any other tone, any tone can sound simultaneously with any other tone or tones, and any group of tones can be followed by any other group of tones, just as any degree of tension or nuance can occur in any medium under any kind of stress or duration. Successful projection will depend upon the contextual and formal conditions that prevail, and upon the skill and the soul of the composer."[42]Reviewing the book for the *Musical Quarterly*, William Schuman wrote, "The publication of Vincent Persichetti's [*Twentieth-Century Harmony*] is an event of historic importance. Surely this volume will take its place as one of the great books on the art of music." He finds its most striking features to be

> its nonpartisanship and the orientation of every statement and musical example towards an artistic purpose. Persichetti's nonpartisanship should not be misinterpreted as the lack of a point of view. There is a point of view, the essence of which is that in contemporary music it is now possible to examine what composers of this century actually have accomplished and, further, to organize the harmonic materials 20th-century composers have created in terms of objective presentation of the problems, procedures, and solutions.[43]

Peter A. Evans was rather more circumspect, noting, "[I]t is not difficult to foresee the lavish contempt that will be heaped in quite opposed quarters on Vincent Persichetti's book." His chief objection is that the musical examples encourage thinking along the lines of devices rather than ideas. He concedes that "Persichetti's attempts to present true musical situations (rather than merely foisting incipits on the student) will be invaluable to those with unimaginative teachers or with none at all. His ideals of texture and musical rhetoric are far from universally held today, but until there is more convincing evidence that pitch-relations have lost their primacy in the listening experience, so professional a documentation of procedures will shorten many an apprenticeship."[44]

Admittedly, Persichetti might be accused of wishful thinking for his assertion in the foreword that "The music of the first half of the 20th century has produced a harmonic practice that can be defined. . . . Composers have worked instinctively with the ear as their guide, and have arrived at something of a common usage of these materials."[45] However, Peter Wishart seems to find it preposterous. What he gleans from the text is "that you can do exactly what you please, which is a splendid ideal because it is exactly what every good composer has always done." Ultimately he finds it "a frightening book, which will encourage students who use it to think that they know a great deal, whereas most of it is good old fashioned hot air."[46] However, perhaps not surprisingly, the most vicious review came directly from the camp most antipathetic to Persichetti's notion of an all-inclusive common practice: *Perspectives of New Music*. Dripping with disdain, Godfrey Winham states that Persichetti's book aims at "the efficient manufacture of the product [called] 'modern music.'. . . [T]his manufacture consists in seizing handfuls of notes and doodling with them, the only procedural control being that provided by the need for the applicability to the result of adjectives such as 'tempestuous,' 'lyric,' or 'melancholy,' which in turn makes desirable though not absolutely necessary that these handfuls be obtained from specific bins, each containing some general kind of matter such as whole-tone scales, seventh chords, or twelve-tone rows." Incensed by what he perceives as Persichetti's "chief principle of composition. . . that you can do anything, and preferably everything all at once," he deduces from it "that bad music is just as good as good music, provided (perhaps) that it is clear that it is intended to express badness." [47]

Though initially greeted with controversy, *Twentieth-Century Harmony* is still in print today, nearly fifty years after its initial publication. It has served as a systematic resource, embracing a wide range of approaches to modern harmony, for several generations of young composers, and continues to do so.

During the 1960s Persichetti was becoming increasingly recognized nationally as one of America's masters of traditional musical pedagogy. However, as a composer, his reputation continued to rest chiefly on his growing number of works for wind band. He was also recognized for his extraordinary versatility, and most instrumentalists were aware of his contributions for their instruments, but there was little awareness of the full scope of his creative output or of the specific characteristics of his work as a whole. In 1963 he was named chairman of Juilliard's Composition Department, and in 1970 chairman of the Literature and Materials Department. In 1965 he was elected to the National Institute of Arts and Letters, and in 1969 he won a second Guggenheim Fellowship, which enabled him to spend a year in Rome where he worked on his Ninth Symphony, "Janiculum," which was to be introduced in 1971 by Eugene Ormandy and the Philadelphia Orchestra.

It was at about this time when fellow-composer Hugo Weisgall penned the following assessment of Persichetti's stature for a dictionary of contemporary music:

> He has a phenomenal natural musicality, closely resembling Hindemith's. He can improvise entire sonatas, read the most complex scores at sight, and in the classroom quote musical examples covering the entire range of musical literature from memory. Technical fluency is apparent from his earliest works, dated 1929. He has always written in whatever manner suits his particular conception at the time, from freely tonal through quasi-serial music, all with an equally sure hand. . . . The best insight into his style is provided by his own text, *Twentieth Century Harmony*, which is almost a codification of his materials. [48]

In 1970, as part of the inaugural celebration of the new Juilliard School at the Lincoln Center for the Performing Arts, Persichetti conducted the premiere of the composition he later considered his magnum opus: *The Creation*, a large work for vocal soloists, chorus, and orchestra, based on a composite text compiled by the composer from no less than fifty-three different sources.

In 1973 a remarkable incident occurred that briefly brought Persichetti widespread national attention, beyond the world of classical music. This episode, recounted in print many times with numerous inaccuracies, was thoroughly documented by Donald A. Morris, to whose painstaking research I am indebted for this presumably accurate account.[49] In November 1972, Richard Nixon was elected to a second term as president of the United States. The controversial war in Vietnam had been raging, but at this time peace talks were underway, and an end to the conflict seemed near at hand—perhaps even by the time of the inauguration. During the weeks following the election, the Inaugural Committee met to discuss the celebration to take place in January. There was to be a concert on January 19, at which Eugene Ormandy would lead the Philadelphia Orchestra. The committee was considering just what would be on the program. One definite selection was Tchaikovsky's *1812 Overture*. Nixon himself had expressed a preference for the "Battle Hymn of the Republic" and the *Grand Canyon Suite*. There was some discussion of the possibility of an original work to be composed especially for the occasion—a work with narration, along the lines of Copland's *A Lincoln Portrait*. Dimitri Tiomkin was proposed as the composer to be commissioned, and James Stewart and Charlton Heston were suggested as possible narrators. All were staunch supporters of the president. The Roger Wagner Chorale was also considered, as Wagner too was a Nixon loyalist.

On 11 December, the committee met with Ormandy for further discussion of the concert program. In considering whom to approach for an original composition, Ormandy suggested—apparently in this order—Copland, Schuman, Barber, and Persichetti. It is not clear whether all were approached, but for whatever reason, Persichetti was finally selected, and on December 15 was asked to compose a work for narrator and orchestra. It was suggested that the text be drawn from Abraham Lincoln's second inaugural address. The speech included the words, "With malice toward none; with charity for all; . . . let us strive on to finish the work we are in; to bind up the nation's wounds; . . . —to do all which may achieve and cherish a just, and a lasting peace. . . . Fondly do we hope—fervently we pray—that this mighty scourge of war may speedily pass away."

After some hesitation owing to the short notice—after all, the score would have to be completed in about three weeks—Persichetti accepted the challenge and began composing the following day. However, on 13 December, the peace talks had broken down, and several days later Nixon authorized the most intensive bombing of North Vietnam yet undertaken. At about this time, the Inaugural Committee asked Persichetti to substitute the Declaration of Independence for the Lincoln address. As he was quoted in *Newsweek*, "I was told that in view of the intensified bombing the text might embarrass the president." However, Persichetti refused to make the requested change. He was then asked if he couldn't just use "some pretty poem" instead. He declined this as well. At that point, the committee decided to jettison the commission and substituted instead a choral medley of patriotic American songs. However, no one bothered to tell Persichetti of this decision, so he proceeded to finish the work within the time originally allotted. Then on 9 January he received a phone call from Ormandy, who informed him of the program change. Interestingly, Persichetti's reaction was to write a short, courteous letter directly to Nixon, innocently inquiring as to whether the president knew of this decision and gently asking him to intervene, so that his piece could be performed. Persichetti received no response, although White House documents indicate that a graciously apologetic reply was drafted. On January 14, an article appeared on the front page of the *New York Times*, with the headline, "Inaugural-Concert Work Deleted as 'Not in the Spirit,'" and further stories appeared on television and in newspapers and magazines all over the country.

Ironically, the intensified bombing had brought about a resumption of peace talks on 8 January, and on 23 January Nixon announced that an agreement had been reached to end the war. On 25 January the premiere of Persichetti's *A Lincoln Address* took place in St. Louis, with Walter Susskind conducting, and William Warfield as narrator. As a result of the incident and the attendant publicity, the work was subsequently performed by numerous ensembles nationwide. Characteristically, the episode left the composer with no bitterness. "I'm delighted by the work, glad that it's a peace piece, not a war piece. I feel sorry for people who think Lincoln's words are subversive. And I'm overjoyed at the public. All this attention says that the artist is important."[50]

In 1974 Persichetti was awarded a third Guggenheim Fellowship, which he spent in Delphi, Greece, focusing on his next major work. This was to be an opera—his first and only one—an allegory based on the familiar children's story, Chicken Little. He finished the opera, eventually entitled *The Sibyl*, in 1976, but it was not produced until 1985, when it was mounted by the Pennsylvania Opera Theater.

Also in 1974, theorist, organist, and composer Rudy Shackelford (1944–) contacted Persichetti, requesting the opportunity to do an in-depth interview. Initially Persichetti was hesitant, then asked Shackelford to send him a list of questions, which he would answer in writing. Shackelford complied with Persichetti's request, but their correspondence suggests that the latter was decidedly reluctant to provide the sort of penetrating self-revelation that Shackelford was seeking, and he procrastinated for several years before responding.[51] Finally, in 1979, after repeated prodding, Persichetti provided his answers, and the result was published as "Conversation with Vincent Persichetti," in *Perspectives of New Music*.[52] The extensive transcript is probably the most revealing and informative document concerning the composer to have appeared in published form at the time of this writing. However, what is equally revealing, if more than a little perplexing, is the fact that many of Persichetti's responses are taken verbatim from statements made by Dorothea Persichetti in her unpublished 1960 monograph, *Vincent Persichetti's Music*.

In honor of his sixtieth birthday, Arizona State University held a two-week Persichetti Festival in 1975, organized by the composer's former student David Cohen. Resulting from this event were two sets of recordings issued by Arizona State over the next two years: One featured all four of the composer's string quartets; the other comprised his hour-long song cycle *Harmonium*, along with the Piano Quintet. These were excellent performances of important works that had been generally neglected up until that time. And in 1978 Persichetti's English Horn Concerto was awarded the first Kennedy Center Friedheim Award for Excellence in Symphonic Composition.

In 1981 Persichetti developed a fascination with the harpsichord. At a performance of one of his orchestral works that year, he was asked by an acquaintance what he was working on. He responded, with typically epigrammatic verbal whimsy, "I've discovered a new kind of orchestra. It's called a harpsichord. It's a whole new universe."[53] Although he had written a harpsichord sonata in 1951, that had been an isolated instance. But now he returned to the instrument with a vengeance, completing nine more sonatas during the next six years.

Peter Mennin, president of the Juilliard School since 1962, died suddenly in June 1983. The search for a new president began immediately. Persichetti was among the first to be offered the position, but he declined: Administration held no appeal for him.[54] He preferred to continue composing, teaching, and evaluating new works for publication by Theodore Presser.

At the beginning of 1987, Persichetti—a heavy smoker for many years—was diagnosed with lung cancer.[55] Despite rounds of radiation and chemotherapy, he succumbed at Hillhouse in Philadelphia on 14 August of that year. (Dorothea died three months later.) After his death, the following handwritten note was found, dated 16 March 1987, and addressed to "Family and Friends": "Regarding my possible death: I do not want to be kept alive by any severe means once it has been determined that there is no hope that I might live somewhat normally in the future. . . . At death I want my entire body used for medical purposes to help other human beings and/or for research into future medical aid. I do not want a funeral service or procession, or any formal religious gathering. I welcome good vibrations, warm thoughts and spontaneous expressions."

A memorial service was held at the Juilliard School on 5 October 1987. Among those who delivered eulogies were William Schuman and Milton Babbitt. What emerged from the comments of those who spoke was an appreciation of Persichetti's encouragement of healthy, creative participation in music at all levels of sophistication. His works touched the lives of young students and amateurs, as well as professionals of the highest stature. At the time of his death, his name had come to signify musicianship of a comprehensiveness virtually unmatched among his peers.

Following are the impressions of some of those who were close to him or on whose lives he made an impact. In an interview conducted by Donald A. Morris, Persichetti's daughter Lauren recalled that her father

> never spoke to me about his place in history or anything like that. . . . He was interested in what he was writing then, and in performances of pieces he was writing then [or] had just finished, and what he was going to write [next]. That's all that concerned him, as far as I know. . . . [H]e was basically a pretty shy man. . . . He wasn't pompous or anything like that, just very straightforward. A really nice guy. . . .
>
> Fantasy was a big part of his life. I mean, our house was inhabited by all types of little invisible creatures, like Michael Needle. . . . . Well, Michael Needle was a person who lived in our house and he also traveled with my father. . . . And my father would talk to him. I'd hear this loud talking from the bathroom, with the door closed, "No, Michael." And there was Amy Snerd, who lived under the rug and only our cat could see Amy Snerd. There was Rosita Flush, who was in the closets. He loved fantasy, he loved children's stories. . . .
>
> He loved driving. When we would go on these trips, he would drive all day and all night. He would go on for these long stretches and feel very refreshed. . . . He really complained that there was this big problem he had. He had to waste time every day sleeping. Really, he was serious, 'cause it was a waste of time. And he would try to condense the time as much as possible. . . . One thing—he did feel that he wanted to leave a body of work . . . but—he went overboard. . . . I mean, even when I was visiting, like for Christmas vacation, he would work, still work. I've never seen a day when he didn't work. You'd be talking to him, having a conversation, and then all of a sudden you see his foot tapping and you would know that he was working.[56]

Daniel Dorff, who edited Persichetti's new publications at Theodore Presser, quotes him as saying, "I am a very slow writer. I just write all the time. I write sometimes for a six or seven hour stretch."[57]

Persichetti's love of driving was well known to those around him, and the automobile remained his preferred mode of transportation throughout his life. He even liked to compose while driving and dictated to Dorothea much of his Serenade No. 3 for piano trio while they were on their honeymoon. However, a car accident resulted in Dorothea being hospitalized for a minor injury. But this did not end his practice of composing in the car; he simply devised an apparatus to facilitate the process.[58]

In her monograph, Dorothea Persichetti commented,

> The composer is not one who needs insulation from daily living-earning activities in order to find the personal peace in which to write music. He needs time . . . but he does not need isolation. He thrives on activity and is able to withhold enough of himself from non-compositional work which consumes creative energy, to keep part of his mind in constant creative motion. Music can be begun and will continue to develop consciously and subconsciously in the midst of other work, even though the actual writing may not continue for some time. The music is so held in his mind that he does not have to resurrect it when there is time to write. . . . His one obsession is with the lack of time, and the strong feeling that in one lifetime he cannot possibly accomplish everything he wishes. The main thing he wishes is to write a musical literature—not a few good pieces, but a complete twentieth century literature. That this entails more than supplying a long list of opus numbers, he is fully aware. He works at accomplishing this in a number of ways: by consciously excluding wide and tantalizing extra-musical interests; by refusing to keep in his mind anything that seems unimportant, or to spend time on what seems trivial; by caring more about what he must say musically than about anything else, including people, and including himself.[59]

Daniel Dorff recalled that the composer's "cheerful, encouraging, and endearing personality always inspired me. I never heard him say a sour word, even when reviewing unsolicited manuscripts. He never said anything bad about anyone, and many young composers saved the rejection letters he wrote because they cherished his comments about their work."[60] Even the formidably dour fellow-composer Roger Sessions (1896–1985) had kind words for his Juilliard colleague. Sessions biographer Andrea Olmstead recalled an incident that took place in a coffee shop, where she was chatting with the two composers, shortly before the elder's death. After Persichetti stood up to leave the table, Sessions commented, "Mr. Persichetti is pure gold."[61]

MUSIC

The music of Vincent Persichetti stands as eloquent evidence of the composer's conception of a broad working vocabulary, or "common practice," based on a fluent integration of the myriad materials and techniques that appeared during the twentieth century. This all-encompassing embrace set him apart from his peers at a time when partisan antagonism divided American concert music into rival stylistic camps. But it also made his music harder for the listener acquainted with just a handful of his works to grasp and understand. As Evett noted,

> Persichetti is more interested in being himself than in being a symbol. . . . His musical temperament has so many sides that the superficial differences between the extremes of his writing continue to be more immediately noticeable than the technical and esthetic similarities which relate the works to each other. . . . [H]e is a musical Citizen of the World. He has deliberately exchanged the advantages of a single system for the challenges imposed by the critical acceptance of several systems. . . . He has proven that stylistic similarities can be compatible with widely divergent technical means.[62]

Persichetti's vast expressive spectrum, drawing upon musical materials ranging from extreme diatonic simplicity to considerable atonal complexity, together with the extraordinary diversity of media he employed, has made it difficult for many to arrive at a consistent characterization of his work. As composer David Cohen, a former Persichetti student, wrote,

> Because he has attempted to amalgamate much of the musical material available to the contemporary composer, he has sometimes puzzled listeners who enjoy the diatonic accessibility of, for example, some of the works for band, but are disturbed by the thorny complexity of the *Eleventh Piano Sonata*. While he can write works of great simplicity and charm, he also does not hesitate to write works which make unusual demands on both performers and listeners. It is, indeed, the range of expression in the body of his work which is sometimes perplexing to those who know but a few of his works or even those who know many.[63]

More pointedly, his fluent eclecticism often resulted in his being damned with the faint praise that he was merely a virtuoso craftsman whose work lacked an individual personality. But while the attentive listener may detect the influence of composers like Stravinsky, Hindemith, Bartók, Harris, and Copland in some of his music, familiarity with its totality reveals a distinctive personality of its own—a personality characterized by an almost childlike sense of mischief and a pervasive geniality of spirit, reveling in the joy of pure, abstract creativity while remaining in full control of whatever dynamic conflicts may be present within the music. Despite the breadth of his musical language, his overall compositional identity falls among the Neo-Classicists, his mature works favoring pan-diatonic, quartal, and polytonal harmony, lucid contrapuntal textures, and lively, syncopated rhythms in duple meter. But the body of Persichetti's work reaches far beyond the aesthetic parameters that define most of the American Neo-Classicists. In a sense, Persichetti's vocabulary of gestures and figures and the somewhat detached way they unfold and interact form a kind of private language, from which he created his own personal expressive world, a world inhabited by the musical analogues of Michael Needle, Amy Snerd, and Rosita Flush, the characters recalled by Lauren Persichetti in the previous section. Seen in this way, the music begins to appear as a personal metaphor, with cross-references and elaborations of ideas from other pieces winking slyly at the listener, conveying enigmatic allusions that call for a particularly intuitive level of apprehension. All this is carried out with a light touch, free of pomposity or solemnity, yet is far from trivial. The music at times suggests an imaginary world, peopled by a large cast of cartoon-like characters, created by an eccentric master-puppeteer who amuses himself by portraying his own metaphysical vision through the interactions of his puppets. As strange as this reading may appear, it is reinforced by other information discussed in the pages that follow.

The matter of chronological evolution has proven to be another complicating factor in gaining an understanding of Persichetti's body of work: His development as a composer did not follow a conventional linear progression over time, from simple to complex, or from old-fashioned to Modernist. However, it did follow a relatively *un*conventional progression. In one sense, Persichetti arrived at his mature language when he was very young: His Opp. 1 and 2, the Serenade No. 1 for wind dectet and the Serenade No. 2 for piano, are both dated 1929, when he was fourteen. Both pieces comprise very short movements, initiating a proclivity that remained throughout his career. Both display acerbic, polytonal harmony, angular melodic lines, irregular rhythms, and terse, sparse gestures—all general characteristics of his body of work.

Then followed the "silent decade," a period of exploration and experimentation, when he was seeking a musical identity of his own. "[Persichetti] describes it as going beyond the extremes within which he now works: apparently there were some academic studies in the manner of Brahms and experiments in sonority and form that went out into a no-man's land of disorganization."[64] No compositions from that period appear on his list of works. But an examination of the works composed after the "silent decade" suggests that the search for his own personal voice continued all the way up until the 1950s, when he was in his mid-thirties. Many of the pieces from the 1940s are somewhat dry and impersonal in character, and quite chromatic and relatively dissonant in their tonal structure, some even adopting practices associated with twelve-tone composition. His use of these techniques preceded their adoption by many others of his generation. However, a small number of his works from this period embraced the "Americana" sound that dominated American music during the 1940s. It is in the approximately forty works from this decade that the influences of the composers cited earlier are most apparent.

Not until the early 1950s did a unique, unmistakable personal voice appear, although it was anticipated in a work such as the *Pastoral*, Op. 21 (1943), for woodwind quintet. The approximately fifty works composed during the 1950s, while still embracing a broad expressive range, display a consistent and coherent voice that is readily identifiable as Persichetti's. Among them are most of the works for which he is still best known today. It was also during this decade that he composed some of his simplest, most accessible pieces. These are largely tonal, pan-diatonic, or obviously polytonal, with much use of chorale-like material. A particularly distinctive usage that appeared during the 1950s might be termed the "Persichetti 2/4," in which a consistently felt 2/4 meter in fast tempo serves as an organizing structure for brilliant passages bursting with exciting and unpredictable irregularities in accent and pattern. In considering the relatively sudden coalescence of the composer's personal voice, perhaps it is relevant to quote from a letter written by William Schuman, dated 5 September 1950: "Your growing individuality is a source of genuine satisfaction. With the kind of fantastic natural musicianship and facility which you have there is present the danger of these enviable qualities predominating. When this happens (as it has with you on occasion) your works become impersonal because they do not speak of you but of objective procedures. Your new music is becoming personal. In my opinion your contribution as composer will eventually be measured only in these personal terms."[65]

In her monograph, Dorothea Persichetti also noted a change in Persichetti's music from about 1950. In discussing these works, she noted "a breath of fresh air about [them]. The music is buoyant, tender, happy and sometimes clownish. A very likely reason for this is that, in 1949, the composer moved his family from a little colonial house in the center of Philadelphia to a slightly larger one at the outskirts of the town. He would not like to say that surroundings affect musical output, but he could not deny the effect that living on the green hill had, at least indirectly, on his work."[66] Regardless of whether this change of residence is responsible for the coalescence of Persichetti's musical language, there is no question but that such a change did take place at that time.

After 1960–1961 Persichetti continued to integrate newer approaches into his vocabulary. Though most of these pieces reveal their composer's fingerprints, they are not quite as spontaneous and immediate as is the music of the 1950s, hence are less readily accessible.

Persichetti himself identified two temperamental poles underlying his work: a "gracious," amiable spirit, and a "gritty," abrasive one.[67] These two elements infuse his entire output, to one degree or another, in various manifestations. Persichetti's list of works—comprising 167 compositions—is large, but not uncommonly so; many of his contemporaries left larger outputs. It is hoped that the following overview may provide a measure of clarification and coherence.

Persichetti composed nine symphonies. Like both Schuman and Mennin, he withdrew the first two, at least temporarily. However, unlike Schuman and Mennin, his symphonies do not represent the "backbone" of his output—that is, a distillation of the essence of what he had to say. This is partly because the symphony orchestra was not Persichetti's primary medium of expression, and partly because his compositional personality was not organized around large statements. Grandiloquence was antithetical to his nature, although some of his most significant works are large in scale. But while he may have worked with large structures at times, he was inclined toward sparse gestures and epigrammatic forms—indeed, many of his large works are elaborate integrations of diminutive elements. Works for orchestra alone account for only about 7 percent of his output. More representative than the symphonies are his twelve piano sonatas. Works featuring keyboard instruments—piano, harpsichord, and organ—account for some 36 percent of his output. Compositions for band or wind ensemble—still the music for which he is best known—amount to only about 8 percent of his output.

In summary, while Persichetti's body of work does not follow a conventional linear evolution, it does fall into three roughly distinct phases: (1) an early, exploratory phase (1929–1949), when he was still absorbing the techniques of other composers in search of a personal voice; (2) a central, distinctive, personal, and somewhat more consistent phase (1949–1960), when he produced dozens of pieces of varying dimensions, aesthetic purposes, and degrees of difficulty, among which are most of his greatest and best-known works; and (3) a later exploratory phase (1961–1987), when he continued to broaden the range of his language by incorporating into it newer techniques that had attained some currency. During the latter portion of this phase (1971 on), he concentrated on works for small forces; in fact, of his last fifty works, forty are scored for three or fewer instruments.

Before a closer examination of Persichetti's music is undertaken, some of his own comments concerning his compositional identity, as well as his own values and practices, are interesting to consider. "I am my ideal composer. I write my favorite music. I like music to move between soft and prickly bushes."[68]

On his place within the spectrum of American composers of his time: "I've never been a part of an avant garde or any particular camp. What I am, I guess, is an amalgamator—I use everything that's around me. . . . When all of these ideas are synthesized they become the language of the century. I think I'm part of the new renaissance of music."[69]

On pandering vs. being true to oneself: "I tend to amalgamate the sounds around me and press them into the clay of the shaping object. . . . An exciting collection of musical segments creates a newsreel of random shots of unrelated landscapes. I work for completeness in the architecture of all I compose. I avoid sudden flamboyance and momentary pleasure if it does not contribute to the overall design and dramatic purpose. I have no reason to try to please or entertain the listener. I know what I want to say because that thought means something to me. I can find validity in my music only when it is right for me."[70]

On the importance of self-discipline and artistic honesty within his own creative process:

> I concentrate on the idea rather than style. . . . As the music unfolds, I am well aware of the stylistic characteristics but am not intimidated by their presence. I know that expansion and elaboration test the worth of the thematic idea, that comprehensibility depends on memorability. At some point, however, I must stand away from my work and take a synoptic view of the whole. While form-in-time is not quite form-in-space, a musical vision must have an objectively perceptible shape. Only in a con*text* is the meaning of the con*tent* revealed. I prefer to say more about less, than less about more. So I often backtrack and rewrite, continually rejecting elements within a work. If attractive textures don't relate to the harmonic nucleus, they must be discarded. If passages foreign to the basic concept and mood refuse to contribute to the overall concept, the entire work might have to be deleted. Any composer may speak honestly in a work, but that work might fail to communicate because of technical deficiencies or miscalculations. This I can excuse. I certainly cannot tolerate music that's conceived dishonestly. When music is created by a composer who doesn't hear with his *inner ear* what he is writing, then a dishonest collection of sounds results. If a composer doesn't speak as a human being to the listener, he hasn't the right to take up his time.[71]

MOST REPRESENTATIVE, FULLY REALIZED WORKS

Harmonium (1951)
Concerto for Piano, Four Hands (1952)
Little Piano Book (1953)
Symphony No. 5 (1953)
Quintet for Piano and Strings (1954)

Piano Sonata No. 10 (1955)
Hymns and Responses for the Church Year (1955)
Symphony No. 6 (1956)
Emily Dickinson Songs (1957)
Serenade No. 10 (1957)
String Quartet No. 3 (1959)
The Creation (1969)
Symphony No. 9, "Janiculum" (1970)
The Sibyl/Parable XX (1976)

Because chronology is not the primary organizing principle of Persichetti's music, the following overview discusses his work according to genre and performing medium. Within this organization, chronology and the relative importance of different works are addressed. Instances of overlap among categories are treated with an eye toward clarity and usefulness. In the case of such a large and varied output, some pieces are discussed in greater detail than others; as a result, some readers with particular interests may be frustrated that their special area is not treated in sufficient detail. An apology is made to those readers in advance. The purpose here is to articulate the dimensions and broad themes that characterize Persichetti's body of work, so as to highlight those elements that shape his distinctive identity.

Works for Keyboard

Piano Solo

Vincent Persichetti wrote some thirty-five pieces for piano, including twelve sonatas, six sonatinas, a concertino, and a concerto, plus works for two pianos, and piano, four hands as well. The music spans the years 1929 to 1986, and includes pieces for pianists at all levels, from the beginning student to the advanced professional. Perhaps no composer since Scriabin has produced a body of piano music that offers such breadth of meaning, such fluency of articulation, and such richness of invention—not to mention such comprehensive and imaginative use of the instrument's intrinsic resources. Indeed, Persichetti's piano music embodies in microcosm the all-encompassing range of his expression and comprises the most penetrating lens through which to view his formidable output. In view of the significance of this literature, it is baffling that so few of these works have been widely performed.

The following discussion addresses first the sonatas, then the sonatinas, followed by the three serenades involving piano, the pieces suitable for less advanced piano students, and then, in chronological order, individual works for piano solo. Music for two pianists follows; then, finally, the two works for piano and orchestra.

Sonatas for Piano   Piano Sonata No. 1, Op. 3, was the first work Persichetti composed after what he termed, somewhat facetiously, his "silent decade"—the period 1929–1939, when he composed, as he later recalled, "reams of aggressively adolescent, unsophisticated music," which he decided not to include in his catalog of works.[72] He gave the first performance of the sonata himself in May 1939 at the Philadelphia Conservatory, where he was studying composition with Paul Nordoff and piano with Olga Samaroff.

It is a large, often forbidding work in four movements. The first opens with a twelve-tone row and pursues a course that often sounds reminiscent of Schoenberg in its chromatic angularity and contrapuntal complexity, although it does not follow the orthodox Schoenbergian approach. Although it is conceptually dense, the movement reveals a rhythmic and textural lucidity that is typical of Persichetti. The second movement, *Adagio*, is a study in binary vs. ternary meter, as the right hand is largely in 4/4, while the left is largely in 12/8. The movement is melodic in focus, although atonal in effect. The *Adagio* leads directly into a *scherzo*-like *Vivace*. This is the sonata's most accessible movement, and the one that most clearly reveals glimpses of its composer's mature voice, in its light textures, lively rhythmic asymmetries, and sprightly two-voice counterpoint. The finale is a rather weighty *passacaglia*, based on an elaborate, chromatic theme. The movement is developed with considerable contrapuntal sophistication, until it ends with a reminiscence of the sonata's opening. Despite the harshness of much of the harmonic writing, relatively gentle passages offer some respite, while a number of the fuller passages draw upon harmonic gestures suggestive of "cool" jazz.

Reviewing the work shortly after its publication, more than four decades after it was composed, the pianist and American music scholar David Burge wrote that although it is a very early work,

> The hallmarks of [Persichetti's] late style are, nevertheless, already clearly evident: the light, tripping, non-stop figurations in sixteenths and staccato eighths, the mordent-like punctuations (a fast three chord figure of which the first and last chords are the same), the wandering melodies that begin diatonically and then fill in chromatically, the imitative octave passages and the sudden thick chords at the climaxes. Above all, there is the cheery optimism that shines through so much of his music. . . . His musical gifts, as this early work demonstrates, have always been immense; they are matched only by his infectious enthusiasm and good humor. This warmth and irresistible energy come through as much in the four-movement First Sonata as in the much later Twelfth, and if there is a certain naiveté about it all, well, we could all use a little these days.[73]

Robert Evett called Persichetti "the antithesis of the radical composer," noting that he "believes that such devices as the five-one cadence and the note-row are compatible." He points to Persichetti's comfort with "highly chromatic material that clearly stems from note-row procedures and lends itself to note-row analysis, even though it almost never satisfies all the requirements of Schoenbergian discipline."[74] As the composer's adaptation of serial technique plays a role in many of his earlier works, it is appropriate at this point to cite some of his own comments on this approach:

> I first learned about twelve-tone music in my early teens. I was fascinated by the chromatic swirls of the melodic lines and the whirling figures of the rhythmic patterns, but I couldn't understand why the Schoenbergian composers avoided cyclical harmonic ascents and descents, octave color coupling, side-slip parallel structures, and non-chordal embellishment tones. Then I discovered that twelve-tone music didn't have to sound like Schoenberg or Webern, that Berg wrote melody which breathed easily and harmony susceptible to variations in blood pressure.[75]

Piano Sonata No. 2, Op. 6, was another one of five works Persichetti completed in 1939. It is noticeably lighter in texture and mood than the Sonata No. 1, although its overall impact remains dry and somewhat rarefied, suggesting Hindemith rather than Schoenberg.

The first movement, *Moderato*, is largely contrapuntal and reveals Persichetti's fondness for the upper octaves of the piano. The second movement, *Sostenuto*, invokes a dry lyricism, not unlike the analogous movement of the previous sonata. The third movement, *Allegretto*, is *intermezzo*-like, generally atonal in effect, though gently gracious in spirit. The concluding *Allegro* is the densest movement of the work, vigorously developmental throughout but largely genial in spirit, although its ending is surprisingly stern.

Sonata No. 2 was introduced by Dorothea Flanagan in El Dorado, Kansas, in January 1941. She was to become the composer's wife later that year, and had already embarked on her lifelong role as advocate of her husband's music. (The published volume of his piano sonatas bears the inscription, "All of these Sonatas were written for and because of Dorothea Persichetti.")

Piano Sonata No. 3, Op. 22, was composed in the summer of 1943 in Colorado Springs, during the brief period when Persichetti was studying with Roy Harris. The premier performance was given by the composer himself, at the Colorado Springs Fine Arts Festival that August. A marked departure from its two predecessors, it is much easier to perform and much easier to appreciate. Like some of the other works of Persichetti composed during World War II, the sonata creates a distinctly American impression, although no folk or vernacular material is used. Its harmonic language is largely consonant and clearly tonal.

The first movement, "Declaration," begins with a slow, stately introduction in which dotted-note rhythms are prominent. This is followed by a subdued, hymnlike passage that leads to the second section, marked "Resolute." This section develops a bell-like motif in alternation with running scale-like passages, eventually leading to a majestic return of the dotted-note motif. The coda introduces a melodic idea that will reappear significantly later on. The second movement, "Episode," is very slow and presents two gentle melodies in alternation. The movement evokes a poignant sense of nostalgia. The third movement is entitled "Psalm," and suggests the spirit of a patriotic anthem. After a majestic opening, a hymnlike melody is softly introduced, and repeated in varied forms, becoming increasingly fervent. Toward the middle of the movement, a new melody appears, derived from the coda of the first movement, as the anthem continues to build. Despite interruptions, these melodies culminate triumphantly in a peroration suggestive of church bells.

Sonata No. 3 was one of Persichetti's first works to be published, and shortly thereafter it was selected as a required piece for a national piano competition. This, as well as its immediate accessibility, have made it the most popular and most widely performed of Persichetti's piano sonatas.

Reviewing the work upon its publication, John Kirkpatrick wrote, "It is all attractively simple and straightforward music and makes one wish that all of it were as good as the best of it, which is very good and directly appealing. The Declaration starts off with a rousing affirmation in the Copland style but ends in self-assertive clatter. The Episode has a beautiful lyrical wistfulness, but some of it seems to yearn for contrasting timbres. The Psalm is less an inner prayer than an extrovert festival with some unillumined solemnities but a first-rate exciting close."[76]

Piano Sonata No. 3 was first recorded on a program of American music featuring pianist David Allen Wehr, released in 1989.

Piano Sonata No. 4, Op. 36, is the first of six consecutive solo piano works composed by Persichetti in 1949–1950. The Fourth Sonata returns to the "gritty" complexity of the first two, and is the most ambitious and wide-ranging of the early sonatas. It was first performed by the composer in December 1949 at a concert at Columbia University sponsored by the League of Composers. Reviewing the concert, Virgil Thomson found the work to be "suited to the instrument better than almost anything written in America today."[77]

The first movement, which falls into several sections, opens with a broad, bold, declamatory statement of the basic motif from which much of the sonata grows; this motif is then examined from a variety of angles. A gently lilting pastoral section, marked "Intimately," follows, further developing the initial motif. This leads to a brilliant fugue on a stark, angular subject (also based on the initial motif) that spans more than three octaves. David Burge notes an intriguing conceptual similarity between this movement and the opening "Sinfonia" of Bach's Partita No. 2 in C minor.[78] The *intermezzo*-like second movement returns to the gently lilting character of the pastoral passage from the first movement. Another harbinger of Persichetti's later music, this multisectional movement—loosely ternary in design—makes a genial, witty first impression. However, subtle intricacies abound, as closer examination reveals. The finale opens with a reflective, searching introduction bearing the indication, "Plaintively," which leads to the body of the movement, marked "Briskly." This section follows a loose *sonata-allegro* design: The primary material, based on the introductory motif, is playful and highly rhythmic, even percussive at times, while the contrasting, secondary idea is soothing and calm, characterized by quartal harmony.

Burge found the Sonata No. 4 to be "Persichetti's most persuasive and attractive work for solo piano,"[79] while pianist Andor Foldes described it as "a serious, well written work revealing excellent craftsmanship and a thorough knowledge of the instrument for which it was written."[80]

Persichetti's next work, the Piano Sonata No. 5, Op. 37, is more representative of the works to follow during the subsequent decade, when the composer's own distinctive language and individual stylistic approaches began to emerge and take shape. This language was essentially an outgrowth of Neo-Classicism rooted in Stravinsky, as developed by Copland. Its manifestation in Persichetti's piano music is characterized by much two-voice counterpoint, a propensity for the higher end of the piano, pan-diatonic and quartal harmony, and sprightly, highly accented, unpredictably irregular rhythmic syncopations. There is also a great deal of writing in contrary motion, which was to become an almost obsessive focus of attention during Persichetti's later years. Dorothea Persichetti described the Fifth Sonata as "a relaxation from the intensity of the Fourth Sonata. It is a piece of humor and some beauty, and has the sound of being content with itself."[81]

The first movement, *With motion*, has the overall feeling of a *sonata-allegro* design, although there are only a few short motifs, rather than two full-fledged themes. The second movement, *Tenderly*, pursues the same motifs in the context of a lullaby, with a simple, tonal melody, harmonized by gentle polytonal and pan-diatonic dissonances. The third movement, *Briskly*, is *rondo*-like in effect, and is perhaps the sonata's most appealing movement. There is much contrary motion, as well as irresistible, almost jazzy, rhythmic irregularities.

The premiere of the Piano Sonata No. 5 was included in the New York debut recital of pianist Jean Geis, at Town Hall, in March 1951. "In its solid construction, fluency, and avoidance of clichés," wrote Raymond Ericson, "the new Persichetti sonata makes an excellent addition to the piano repertoire."[82] On the other hand, Harold Schonberg found the piece to be "an angular, percussive, fast-moving and very difficult work with about as much cheer as logarithmic tables."[83]

Persichetti's Fifth Piano Sonata was first recorded in 1989 in Belgium by American pianist Jacqueline Herbein, as part of an all-American program called *American Diversions*.

The Sonatas Nos. 6, 7, and 8 were composed in immediate succession in 1950. The Sonata No. 6, Op. 39, comprises four relatively short movements and is an excellent example of Persichetti's "gracious" vein. The first movement is aptly marked *Lightly*. Its opening material is bright, fresh, and airy; the second main idea is a "skipping," dotted-note motif. These two ideas are developed in alternation, in a variant of *sonata-allegro* form. The overall tone of the movement is bright and cheerful; it is light in texture and gesture, and diatonically tonal. The second movement, *Slowly*, is based on a lyrical, diatonically tonal melody, juxtaposed against a rather dissonant harmonization. The movement builds to a climax on a series of massive expanded triads. The third movement bears the unusual marking *Blandly*, with the additional instruction, "with no expression throughout." It is a simple, dance-like *intermezzo*, almost folk-like in character, and follows a consistent 3/8 meter. The final movement is marked *Fast*, and displays the *toccata*-like brilliance of much of the composer's keyboard music, with dazzling, Scarlattian passages running up and down the keyboard in perpetual motion. Dorothea Persichetti noted, "The piece is pianistic to an extraordinary degree and when played freely, is a lark."[84]

Piano Sonata No. 6 was introduced by Joseph Bloch at New York's Town Hall in April 1951. More than one critic at the time noted a resemblance to the music of Hindemith, although greater familiarity with Persichetti's music would readily dispel such an impression. William S. Newman noted that the composer's most recent piano pieces

> depart from the weightier import, the wider-spaced, pan-diatonic harmony, and the rangier lines of his third and fourth piano sonatas. They are more compact and efficient, exhibiting still finer craftsmanship but, to this reviewer, something less in the way of genuine musical communication. The style and technique seem to draw nearer to the more recent Hindemith of the *Unterweisung*, with neutral themes, "axis" tonal relationships, ersatz progressions up and down the scale of tension and relaxation, and synthetic rhythmic schemes. Nonetheless, this music is fun to play and not without its expressive moments, which traits may well mark Persichetti's intended limits in these particular musical communications.[85]

The sonata also reminded Harold Schonberg of Hindemith.[86]

Piano Sonata No. 7, Op. 40, is a short, lightly textured work that "bubbles with good spirits,"[87] and almost anticipates the transparency of the harpsichord works to follow many years later. As in the Fifth Sonata, the first movement, *Moderato*, gives the effect of *sonata-allegro* form, but develops a theme and several short motifs, rather than two contrasting themes. It opens with a simple pentatonic melody, harmonized with gentle dissonances that contradict the overall G-major tonality, and developed delicately in conjunction with gawky little gestural motifs. Dorothea Persichetti wrote, "It has brash rhythms, melodies with funny twists, tunes you can sing and then find suddenly unsingable in the middle of nowhere, droll bass chorales (pompous, but marked 'espressivo'), ridiculous staccato figures, free-for-all fun."[88] The second movement, *Andante*, is based on a descending three-note motif in dotted rhythm, rather like a slow version of a Baroque gigue. It is developed by imitation and inversion, largely in dissonant, two-voice counterpoint. The third movement, *Vivo*, is an extremely fast *rondo*, somewhat suggestive of the *Rondeaux* movement of Bach's C-minor *Partita*. To Dorothea it sounded "like a hop-scotch game played by jitterbugs," with its nervous hocketing effects and irregular accents.[89]

The first performance of the Seventh Sonata was given by Robert Smith at the Philadelphia Conservatory in May 1956.

Each approximately seven minutes in duration, the Seventh and Eighth Sonatas are the shortest of the cycle. Like No. 7, the texture of No. 8 is very transparent, with much two-voice counterpoint. The first movement, *Lightly*, offers the cycle's most readily identifiable example of *sonata-allegro* form. The first theme is characterized by a sputtering motif with an ascending anacrusis that functions rather like a grace note, and spare, terse gestures. It is elaborated with rapid running figurations and sharp, irregular accents. The second theme is related intervallically to the first but is warmly lyrical in character. The second movement, *Quietly*, is very simple on the surface but actually is harmonically complex. Its thematic material bears some affinity with Theme 2 of the first movement. An overall tonality of E prevails but is contradicted by considerable harmonic dissonance. The third movement, *Fast*, is a *rondo* with Neo-Classical figurations and deliberate "wrong-note" effects that immediately suggest Prokofiev. The movement is propelled by off-kilter rhythmic patterns that are, however, pure Persichetti.

The Sonata No. 8, Op. 41, was first performed in March 1956 by Claire Shapiro at the Philadelphia Conservatory. Laurence Rosenthal found in it

a real attempt for clarity, directness, and simplicity. . . . It is a light, charming piece, almost more like a sonatina, being brief, quite compact, and with very extended development. . . . One cannot help observing, however, a tendency to "stylish" American neo-classicism, dryish and economical, meticulous and almost a shade mechanical in its nice precision. This is about the only criticism that can be leveled against the Sonata, for it is expertly and sensitively made, and the dreamy, romantic slow movement and the gay outer ones are all quite fetching. The tunes are delightful throughout.[90]

Sonata No. 9, Op. 58, dates from 1952. Although it is almost as brief as the two previous sonatas, it represents a considerable advance in Persichetti's fluency in shaping his material toward effectively expressive purposes. Compared with No. 9, some of the previous sonatas seem a little contrived, as if their musical materials are being forced into modes of expression for which they are not ideally suited. (This lack of alignment between musical substance and expressive intent—which may be what Rosenthal noted with regard to the Eighth Sonata—is perhaps the chief weakness that may be observed in the works of Persichetti's earlier "exploratory" phase.)

The Ninth Sonata comprises a single movement of about nine minutes' duration, subdivided into four distinct, but closely related sections. The first section, *Moderato*, opens with a fanfare-like motif; after some elaboration, a second idea—a lively, syncopated motif that traverses the interval of a third—is presented and developed. This is the sonata's primary idea. The section concludes with a brief return of the opening motif, in a sort of "rounded binary" design. The contrasting second section, *Allegro agilite*, presents a sweetly innocent melody built from a chain of thirds, against an Alberti-bass accompaniment. As it is elaborated, the primary idea from the first section intrudes for further development. The third section, *Larghetto*, is a warm chorale, harmonized with only the mildest dissonance. As this section concludes, echoes of the second section are heard. The fourth section, *Allegro risoluto*, integrates the work's main musical ideas in a stirring peroration. First a variant of the primary idea from the opening section is developed, followed by a "chorale prelude" treatment of the hymn from the third section, culminating in an apotheosis that unites both these ideas polytonally, eventually confirming the work's overall tonality of F-sharp major.

The Ninth Sonata bears some similarity to the Third in its use of chorale-like material and a general character that is somewhat jubilant; and it is the sonata that most rivals the popularity of No. 3. However, it reveals far greater ease and spontaneity than the earlier work and draws on a much broader array of materials and techniques, resulting in a work of engaging sparkle, vitality, and rhythmic punch, and a range of moods from whimsical to naughty to triumphant. Compared with its immediate predecessors, it is fuller in texture and more complex, both structurally and psychologically, and condenses considerable developmental and expressive substance into a short time span.

Despite the appeal of the Ninth Sonata, some of the material itself has a "clunky" quality. Dorothea's interpretation is that "the piece is a satire, full of much honest beauty but, also, sly derision."[91] It is remarkable that this delightful work had to wait until March 1962 for its first performance, when David Burge introduced it at a convention of the Music Teachers National Association held in Madison, Wisconsin. Burge later described the Sonatas Nos. 5 through 9 as "delightful, relatively short works, characterized by thin textures and modest scope. There are passages of great beauty . . . and of rhythmic and harmonic complexity, but the overall tone of each of these sonatas is somewhat lightweight in comparison to the grander structures of the *Third* and *Fourth Sonatas*. . . . [I]f not highly dramatic in nature, [these works] demonstrated facility, understanding of the piano, and an excellent balance between form and content."[92]

British critic Frank Dawes noted in the work the influence of jazz and characterized the final section as "straight from the shoulder in the modern American way." He concludes that "textures are kept commendably clear, and the sonata is a lightweight, divertimento-type work of no little charm."[93] Although the comments of Burge and Dawes are quite apt, it is important to remember that, as pointed out toward the beginning of this section, in Persichetti's case the characterization of some pieces as "lightweight" and "divertimento-type" does not necessarily mean they are trivial. He certainly composed his share of "weighty" works, but they are not always his most artistically successful efforts; and some of his "lightweight, divertimento-type" compositions are among his most inventive, imaginative, and meticulously constructed pieces.

Although the Sonata No. 9 had to wait ten years for its first performance, it was the first of Persichetti's piano sonatas to be recorded. In 1980 the pianist and populist composer Jackson Berkey included a stunning performance of the Ninth Sonata on a recital program called *The Sunken Cathedral*. Two years later, at the opposite extreme, Soviet pianist Alexander Bakhchiev included a ponderously wrongheaded interpretation of the sonata on an all-Persichetti program released by the Soviet company Melodiya. (Although these Russian performances left much to be desired, this was the first recording ever to be devoted solely to the piano music of Persichetti. It is ironic that this distinction was achieved in the Soviet Union before such a recording was released by an American company.)

Persichetti's Piano Sonata No. 10, Op. 67, was completed in 1955 on a commission from the Juilliard Foundation, for performance at an American Music Festival commemorating the Juilliard School's fiftieth anniversary. (Aaron Copland's *Piano Fantasy*, a work of comparable scope and stature, was completed in 1957 as part of the same celebration.) A highly virtuosic work, it is the longest of the sonatas and is in many ways the consummation of all of the composer's solo piano music written up to that time. Not only is it more technically demanding, but it is also more complex in texture, figuration, harmony, and counterpoint than any of its predecessors, and is possibly the most ambitious statement of the twelve sonatas. Like the Sonata No. 9, it comprises a single movement—in this case some twenty-two minutes in duration—subdivided into four connected sections. It is the least tonal and most consistently dissonant of his piano sonatas composed thus far, and also introduced some instrumental techniques new to his music, such as wide-leaping grace notes, or in many cases, "grace chords," and nonmetered note patterns of gradually increasing rapidity.

The first section, *Adagio*, is stark and improvisatory, with any suggestion of tonality contradicted by polytonal and chromatic complications. The sonata's primary thematic idea is stated at the outset: a stepwise descending line in parallel thirds. This motif is developed in conjunction with several germinal gestures, one of which is a brief *tremolo* figure. Later in the section the sonata's secondary thematic idea is subtly suggested—a chant-like motif that will later grow into a full chorale theme. The second section is a hair-raising, wildly skittish *Presto*, spasmodically nervous in a way that suggests similar moments in the works of William Schuman. Largely focusing on the work's primary thematic idea, it abounds in irregular meters and unpredictable accents, which some commentators have attributed to the influence of jazz. The *Andante* is the sonata's centerpiece—a floridly lyrical melody loosely oriented around F-sharp minor, again based on the descending-scale idea. In a slow 6/8 meter, this section, with its quiet, abstract dignity, almost suggests a slow movement from a Bach suite. As the section proceeds, the incipient chorale motif from the first section is heard, before the florid melody returns with further ornamentation. The concluding *Vivace* falls surprisingly into a clear *sonata-allegro* design, although its articulation belongs to Persichetti's fleetly virtuosic *toccata*-like vein. The primary theme is treated in ascending and descending forms, and in simultaneous rhythmic augmentation and diminution, with reference to its original presentation in parallel thirds. The secondary "chorale" theme is finally stated in full, with richly dissonant harmony. The development section joins the two thematic ideas in a "chorale prelude"–type elaboration. After a recapitulation, the sonata presses forward to a brilliant and triumphant conclusion, which, after much polytonal ambiguity, finally asserts itself in the unusual key of D-sharp major.

Like other extended, multisectional works composed by Persichetti during the mid 1950s (e.g., Concerto for Piano, Four Hands, Symphony No. 5, Piano Quintet, and String Quartet No. 3), the Tenth Sonata represents, in effect, a

summation of modern classicism within the confines of a single tightly structured, fluently coherent composition. These works combine a spirit of spontaneous improvisation with the definitiveness of total premeditation. The result
is highly cerebral music with charm, wit, grace, tenderness, and dynamism.

Joseph Raieff gave the first performance of the Tenth Sonata at the Juilliard School in February 1956 and performed it on subsequent recital programs throughout the United States and Europe. Not surprisingly for a work
so tightly concentrated and dense with substantive detail, the sonata met with
a mixed initial response. Clinton Gray-Fisk found it to be "a long, verbose,
cerebral work devoid of any genuine individuality and containing nothing
either to satisfy the mind or engage the emotions."[94] The critic for *Musical
America* described it as "determinedly dissonant," adding that "the piece
poured forth a niagara of notes so insistently that it defeated its purpose."[95] A
more moderate reaction was expressed by Howard Taubman, who described
the work as "thoughtful and logical in construction and written idiomatically
for the piano, at least in the percussive idiom. But the work did not have much
juice or excitement."[96] Pianist Joseph Bloch, who had given the premiere
of the Sonata No. 6, found the Sonata No. 10 (the latest at the time of his
comment) to be "the finest, as well as the most demanding" of Persichetti's
sonatas. He added, "The interest here, however, is in the stunning sonorities
rather than in any lyric ideas."[97]

Even the knowledgeable and generally sympathetic David Burge found the
Tenth to be "the weakest" of the sonatas, arguing that "its extended length
is not justified by its content. Using the same kinds of pianistic figuration
that had worked so well in pieces of modest dimensions, he prolongs them
over pages and pages of music."[98] However, by 1987 Maurice Hinson had
recognized the work as "one of the very finest contemporary American piano
sonatas."[99] And in 2008, Mark Lehman wrote, "[I]t's clear to me . . . that
Sonata 10, from 1955, is not only (at 22 minutes) the longest of the set, but
also the most immediately impressive. It's one of Persichetti's most important works, and a great American piano sonata, earning a place alongside
the illustrious examples by Barber, Copland, Sessions, Kirchner, Mennin,
Muczynski, and Binkerd."[100]

In 1983 Arizona State University, in conjunction with the Pianists Foundation of America, released a recording of the Tenth Sonata in a stunning
live performance from 1979 by the young pianist James Ruccolo (who died
shortly after the disc was issued). A second recording appeared in 1986, as
part of the first all-Persichetti piano release to be issued in the United States,
featuring Wisconsin-based pianist Ellen Burmeister. Appearing toward the
end of the LP era, neither of these recordings was accorded much attention
nor subsequently released on compact disc.

In the article cited above, pianist Joseph Bloch makes an additional comment that warrants some consideration and reflection:

> I see a sort of kinship between Persichetti and that much misunderstood and underestimated eighteenth century-based composer Clementi. Both men reveal the utmost understanding of the nature of the piano and of piano technic. The piano sonatas of both range from the greatest simplicity to the greatest complexity, incorporating diatonic and chromatic writing, homophony and polyphony, acting almost as catalogues of the styles of their eras; their sonatas invariably feel good under the hand and some movements seem to be composed with that as a primary principle; the music abounds in adroit structural devices; there is always a lively rhythmic interest. On the negative side, both composers, within the framework of their times, seem in spite of their varied elements, rather static harmonically with a resulting lack of direction and climax, and both are generally at their least interesting in slow movements.[101]

Bloch offers an intriguing perspective on Persichetti's sonatas. However, although there is some truth to his observation that the slow movements—at least in some of the sonatas—tend to be less interesting, his comment about "static harmony" and "lack of direction and climax" betrays an orientation rooted in nineteenth-century notions of tonal structure, and a lack of understanding of the Neo-Classical aesthetic. Polytonal and pan-diatonic harmony serve to undermine the grandiosity of organization based on pervasive tonal relationships but without renouncing the local expressive gradient provided by shifts in tonal focus. From this perspective, a sense of "direction" is provided by variations in texture, dynamics, and metrical thrust, while "climax" in the dramatic sense is replaced by accumulations of contrapuntal and rhythmic energy.

Ten years elapsed before Persichetti returned to the piano sonata genre. He composed his Sonata No. 11, Op. 101, in 1965 and dedicated it to his wife, Dorothea, who gave the premiere in December of that year at the Philadelphia Art Alliance. Among the piano sonatas, the work represents a dramatic stylistic departure. It belongs, along with such works as the String Quartet No. 4, among those in which the composer—true to his previously quoted sense of his own identity ("What I am, I guess, is an amalgamator—I use everything that's around me")—attempted to work within what might be called the "serial aesthetic." That is, without following the stringent constraints imposed by Schoenberg's compositional approach, he sought to create a "free serialism" that would embrace the sound world of the post-Webernian dodecaphony that had become pervasive among university-based composers in America, reaching its height during the 1960s: fragmentary, pointillistic gestures and textures, nonmetrical rhythmic flow, harmonic dissonance so consistently extreme that it ceases to function as an expressive variable, an emphasis on the sonority of individual notes, the absence of perceptible tonality, and even the structural discipline of unifying numerological constructs. But Persichetti's intention was to accomplish this while retaining such fundamental traditionalist ideals as expressive coherence and a teleological sense of narrative direction, and while drawing upon the full range of the instrument's capabilities. To this end he broadened his treatment of the piano by incorporating tone clusters, an array of unusual pedal effects, and reverberating overtones produced without striking the keys.

As Michelle Schumann noted in her study of the assimilation of aspects of serialism into the piano music of American Neo-Classicists:

Although Persichetti specifically employs dodecaphonic procedures [in his Piano Sonata No. 11], the sonata does not adhere to any strict serial properties. While Persichetti dutifully presents all twelve tones before moving on to new twelve-tone sets, he does not employ a prescribed, ordered set to preside over an entire movement or even over an entire section. In this way, Persichetti uses a twelve-tone language that is free from the constrictions of serialism yet generally adheres to an overall sense of non-repetition. . . . Throughout, melodic lines and harmonic structures incorporate a steady, although erratic, succession of the twelve tones of the chromatic scale. . . . Yet the intervallic relationships of these twelve tones constantly change, resulting in a language that is basically devoid of any large-scale tonal or serial organization. Instead, Persichetti uses the twelve-tone idiom to exploit properties of tonal freedom and equality without conforming to the pre-ordained rules of serialism. While incorporating an undetermined and inconsistent order of the twelve tones, Persichetti develops a highly experimental dodecaphonic language that is seemingly non-structured and free. The liberated sense of atonality gives the Piano Sonata No. 11 a rather improvisational quality. . . . [O]n the surface, the formal structure of each movement is very free and open. There are no obvious repetitions of thematic materials within the movements or within the piece as a whole. . . . [But] a closer analysis reveals a direct correlation between the twelve-tone organization and formal unity of the piece. [Often] Persichetti aligns occurrences of complete twelve-tone rows with the occurrences of structural phrases to produce a sense of clarity and cohesion to the overall harmonic and formal organization. In this way Persichetti brings together aspects of twelve-tone composition with neo-classical predilection for formal clarity.[102]

Persichetti himself stated,

I would never choose or create a row, to compose. I never begin writing without a dramatic or thematic idea. I often employ a row of twelve or more, or fewer, tones that evolved from a musical utterance. The purpose of serializing after-the-fact is often one of taking inventory of materials. Sound gestures come first, manipulation techniques later. Pitch serialism has helped the composer avoid disparate melodic, harmonic, and contrapuntal devices and irresponsible changes of textures and patterns. It promotes unification, which must be achieved with the basic materials of the work. Serialized dynamics is something else—something alien to structured music.[103]

Just a few minutes shorter in duration than the previous sonata, the Eleventh comprises a single movement subdivided into five sections. But unlike the case with Sonatas Nos. 9 and 10, the sections of No. 11 are tightly elided, rather than distinct. There is an opening *Risoluto*—somewhat declamatory, with intimations of ominous portents, followed by a section marked *Articolato*. Here elements of Persichetti's familiar musical personality can be detected: Although there is no time signature, the section begins clearly in 5/16; the music is light, fleet, and propulsive, linear and contrapuntal, and clearer in texture than the opening. The *Sostenuto* that follows is slow and subdued, leading directly into the fourth section, *Leggero*. This is the highpoint of the sonata—fast, fragmentary, and intricately contrapuntal, culminating in cascading swirls of notes that lead directly to the final *Conclusivo*, which returns to the free, declamatory rhetoric of the opening, before gradually fading away.

Persichetti's Sonata No. 11 was included on Ellen Burmeister's all-Persichetti recording released in 1986.

Late in his career Persichetti became consumed by a device that had always played a fairly prominent role in his developmental arsenal: "mirror-writing," or strict contrary motion. That is, every interval played by one hand is reflected in exact inversion simultaneously by the other, across a central axis. During the late 1970s Persichetti began to apply this technique to entire compositions, initially piano studies and even a *Little Mirror Book* for elementary students. Then, in 1980, he composed a full piano sonata based on this technique: the Sonata No. 12, "Mirror Sonata," Op. 145.

Perhaps in compensation for the stringent discipline and rigorous constraints upon tonality, harmonic dissonance, counterpoint, and texture imposed by strict mirror-writing, the Sonata No. 12 is brief, relative to its two predecessors, and its form follows a clear, straightforward classical design: four distinct movements—the first, a *sonata allegro*; the second, slow and lyrical; the third, a *scherzo* and *trio*, and the fourth, rapid and *rondo*-like. There is also a return to time signatures and a clear sense of metrical rhythm, albeit highly syncopated. Each movement seems to focus on a particular interval or set of intervals, and there is much creative attention paid to touch, articulation, and rhythm; given the constraints, the result proves surprisingly successful in achieving truly expressive, musical values.

The first movement opens with a slow introduction, *Sostenuto*, followed by a rapid exposition, marked *Risoluto*. The first theme emphasizes patterns of triads, while the second focuses on stepwise running figures. A brief return to the introductory material leads into the development section; the recapitulation follows a brief caesura. Another brief return to the introduction is followed by a rapid coda. The second movement, *Amabile*, is a gently lyrical arch-form that emphasizes the intervals of the seventh and the tritone. What is especially interesting is the way a tonality of C-sharp major is established via melodic means, despite harmonic contradictions. The third movement, *Scherzoso*, is light and playful, opening with a running figure, followed by a focus on the interval of the seventh, crisply articulated and rhythmically erratic. The *Trio* section highlights a melody in the outer voices, placed against trill-like patterns in the inner voices, with a central portion based on thirds. This is followed by a *da capo* of the *Scherzoso*. The finale opens with a slow chordal introduction, followed by a vigorous *Brioso* that highlights the octave and the sixth, with much exciting rhythmic activity.

Sonata No. 12 was introduced at St. Mary's College in Notre Dame, Indiana, by Jeffrey Jacob in April 1983. His subsequent recording of the work, released the following year, exhibited a remarkable sensitivity to the distinctive qualities and technical requirements of the composer's approach to writing for the piano.

Persichetti's piano sonatas illustrate the full range of his musical expression. But for the most part they pursue a vein of Neo-Classicism that eschews the dramatic grandeur and virtuosity of the popular piano repertoire. Only Nos. 3, 6, and 9 offer the sort of immediacy that might lead to widespread popularity. And in the final three sonatas the composer explores technical challenges that venture into rarefied sound-worlds not likely to appeal to more than a small, specialized group of sophisticated listeners. However, each of these works is composed with a respect for traditional musical values that becomes apparent once one has penetrated the surface harshness of its musical language.

As noted, some of the piano sonatas found their way individually onto recordings over the years. However, many remained unrecorded until 2008, when New World Records issued a comprehensive set of all twelve in masterly, sympathetic renditions by pianist Geoffrey Burleson, a specialist in American piano music. When this set was released, Blair Sanderson wrote, "[Persichetti's] 12 Piano Sonatas . . . form a consistent body of work typified by intellectual rigor and controlled explorations of forms and counterpoint, though there are many lovely and haunting lyrical passages in these works that give them delicacy and a certain poignancy—still more characteristics that should endear them to new listeners."[104] Reviewing this same release, Mark Lehman, an especially astute commentator on American Neo-Classicism, wrote,

> After several hours with the recordings (both following the scores and just listening) I'm convinced that the necessary time and effort to assimilate Persichetti's sonatas is well spent for anyone seriously interested in the modern piano repertoire. The composer's restless, probing intelligence and magisterial knowledge of the instrument come through in every bar. Not that everything is easy or superficially appealing; Persichetti is often edgy, brittle, choppy, and high-strung. The music is much laced with harmonic clashes, some dulcet and nuanced, others plangent or biting. Textures, though always wonderfully clear, display endless variety; registral, articulative, and dynamic contrasts are used with great freedom and imagination, and can be startling, or subdued. . . . Persichetti manages to be "cool" yet intimate.[105]

And Rob Haskins, writing in the same journal, commented, "Pianists familiar with the classical repertoire will savor Persichetti's sly references to Beethoven, Scarlatti, Mozart, and others—not quotations, but rather artful homages to the composers' sensibilities, feeling for characteristic sonority, and compositional rhetoric. It's hard to imagine any 20th Century composer who has contributed so much to the solo piano repertoire. . . . [T]his release is one of the truly great recordings of Persichetti's music generally, and one of the finest recordings of American piano music that I've ever heard."[106]

Sonatinas for Piano   In addition to his twelve sonatas for piano, Persichetti also composed six sonatinas; they appeared during the early 1950s, when the composer was concentrating most intensively on writing for the piano. The first three sonatinas were composed in 1950 and are rather like miniature versions of the sonatas he was writing at the time. The latter three were composed in immediate succession in 1954 and are easier both to appreciate and to play. In 1991, a set of two tape cassettes was released commercially by Educo Recordings, in which pianist Donald L. Patterson (author of *Vincent Persichetti: A Bio-Bibliography*) was featured in a program of Persichetti's works suitable for elementary and intermediate piano students. All six sonatinas were included on the program.

Persichetti composed the Sonatina No. 1, Op. 38, immediately after the Sonata No. 5. Comprising three tiny movements, it is relatively simple in texture, although its acerbic language does not diverge significantly from that of the Fifth Sonata, with relatively dissonant and often polytonal harmony, fragmentary gestures and sonorities, and attenuated tonality.

Sonatina No. 2, Op. 45, is perhaps the most fully developed and cohesive of the group. It is a single movement, beginning with a slow, stately canon unafraid of dissonant harmonic friction, followed by a brilliant developmental scamper reminiscent of the finale of the Sonata No. 6, completed earlier the same year, with motifs of its own darting in and out of the transparent contrapuntal texture. Eventually, elements of both sections are combined, leading to an exuberant finish in C major. The piece was first performed at New York City's Town Hall by Margaret Barthel in December 1951.

Sonatina No. 3, Op. 47, comprises two movements—the first, gently rolling, with subtle modal shifts; and the second, rhythmically playful and affirmative in character.

Robert Sabin found the first three sonatinas to be "thoroughly modern in harmonic idiom and style, yet their wit, their transparent design, and their clever keyboard devices will attract even conservatively minded pianists. Persichetti is brittle and eclectic in these sonatinas, but he is engagingly polished and concise."[107]

The Sonatinas Nos. 4 through 6 are among Persichetti's pieces that are appropriate for study and performance by elementary-level pianists. They are discussed at greater length in the section of this chapter that addresses the *Little Piano Book* and other pieces for piano students.

Serenades for Piano Over the course of his career, Persichetti composed a series of what he entitled "serenades." There are a total of fifteen serenades for a variety of instrumental media (discussed elsewhere in this chapter). Nos. 2 and 7 are for piano solo, and No. 8 is for piano, four hands. Serenade No. 2, Op. 2 (as well as Serenade No. 1, Op. 1, which is discussed elsewhere in this chapter) is dated 1929, immediately preceding the "silent decade." Originally entitled *Earnest Power, in Three Fantastic Parts*, it was one of the pieces composed "behind the back" of Russell King Miller and contributed to the young composer's expulsion from Miller's theory classes. Its three movements last barely two minutes and are entitled "Tune," "Strum," and "Pluck." Despite their brevity, relative ease of execution, and conceptual levity, these terse, mischievous pieces are quite sophisticated, with plentiful secundal dissonances, rhythmic irregularities, and long stretches of atonality. In fact, these aspects—along with a wryly abbreviated, stylized approach to familiar gestures—make it hard to believe that the piece was not subjected to some revision at a later point. In December 1929, the fourteen-year-old composer performed the Serenade No. 2 at the Combs Conservatory. Reviewing the published score, Andor Foldes found the piece to be "very charming and will definitely make a place for [itself] in the repertoire of many a pianist,"[108] while Henry Harris felt it presented "in capsule form music of rhythmic punch and independence of spirit."[109] Serenade No. 2 is also included on Donald Patterson's recorded program of Persichetti pieces for piano students.

Serenade No. 7, Op. 55, was composed in 1952, immediately preceding the masterly Concerto for Piano, Four Hands. Its six tiny pieces are more accessible than those in Serenade No. 2 and are much easier to play. In addition to appearing on Donald Patterson's recorded program, they are also included on Ellen Burmeister's LP of the Tenth and Eleventh Sonatas.

Serenade No. 8, Op. 62, dates from 1954, is scored for piano, four hands, and is playable by lower intermediate-level students. The four tiny movements of this three-minute work exude a warmth, simplicity, and good humor that belie the sophistication of their construction. Serenade No. 8, along with two other of the composer's works for duo-pianists, was recorded in 1996 by the Moscow-born, America-trained duo Margarita and Olga Malinova. The listener who can perceive the essential unity underlying both the Sonata No. 11 and the Serenades Nos. 7 and 8 will have begun to penetrate the essence of Persichetti. This essential unity is one of the most remarkable and endearing hallmarks of this composer's genius. (Serenades Nos. 7 and 8 are also discussed in the section of this chapter dealing with music for students.)

Music for Piano Students   Among the sizable number of Persichetti's piano pieces suitable for upper-elementary and intermediate-level piano students, perhaps the best known is the *Little Piano Book*, Op. 60, composed in 1953. This group of fourteen easy pieces of uncommon charm and beauty has become a classic of its kind. The composer described it as "a collection of simple pieces written for, or about, friends and relatives and acquaintances. One is a self-portrait. This is my music reduced to its essence; nevertheless these pieces do contain elements found in my larger, more complex works."[110] Dorothea felt that "they may be some of the composer's best music."[111] They were initially introduced by Lauren Persichetti, age ten, at the Philadelphia Conservatory in November 1954. *Little Piano Book* was first recorded by Marga Richter in 1955, as part of a program of piano music for children by living American composers.

Other such works are the slightly more difficult *Variations for an Album*, Op. 32 (1947), premiered by John Kirkpatrick at Baldwin-Wallace College, in October 1947; Serenade No. 7, Op. 55 (1952); *Parades*, Op. 57 (1952), the easiest to play of all Persichetti's piano pieces, premiered by his ten-year-old son Garth at the Philadelphia Conservatory in February 1956; Serenade No. 8, Op. 62 (1954), for piano, four hands; Sonatinas Nos. 4–6, Opp. 63–65 (1954); and *Little Mirror Book*, Op. 139 (1978), the composer's effort to introduce elementary-level pianists to the notion of mirror-writing; even within such a constraint, he was able to create simple pieces of remarkable delicacy and expressivity. Also in 1978 he composed *Four Arabesques*, Op. 141. Perhaps written with Debussy's *Arabesques* in mind, these short pieces are uncharacteristically French in flavor, with much use of whole-tone scales and related synthetic modes. But unlike the sort of nebulous impressionism that was anathema to Persichetti, these pieces are clearly and tightly constructed, with no superfluous, decorative, or purely textural elements.

As stated earlier, an essential aspect of Persichetti's compositional personality was his connection to the inner world of the child. He devoted many of his compositional efforts to capturing this world, often in pieces that are relatively easy to play and hence, manageable by young musicians. When writing music for students, most composers—even those respected as "serious" figures—tend to compromise their natural languages and customary aesthetic approaches. However, in Persichetti's case, such pieces are integral to and aesthetically consistent with the rest of his creative work, revealing musical and psychological sophistication despite their economy of means. The limitation imposed on technical difficulty was just one more constraint of the kind upon which his creativity thrived. These pieces are neither dull exercises nor the sort of trivial "children's music" produced for commercial purposes by the music education industry; they were created with the same attention to expressive and formal details that he devoted to larger, more complex works. Drawing upon polychords and polytonality, modality, dissonant counterpoint, irregular and unusual meters, and even absence of meter, he captured the whimsy, impishness, tenderness, innocence, and silliness of the young personality, as well as its access to a free, nonlinear imagination, with an eloquent precision and delicate beauty that is the province only of an artist whose "inner child" has not been sacrificed to the jadedness of maturity. The fact that many of these pieces provided the thematic material for Persichetti's sole opera *The Sibyl* suggests the importance he placed on them.

Discussing Persichetti's "teaching pieces," Dorothea noted that

the composer vehemently denies that he ever wrote such a thing, maintaining that he writes music, all of which can be taught, but some to students younger than others. The idiom of the large and the small pieces is often the same, and some of the little pieces which seem most simple technically have unexpected subtle and musically sophisticated spots, realized in quarter notes in a five-finger position. . . . [T]he little works are distillations of a musical expression that has undergone clarification to the point of great simplicity. . . . He does not write "down" to attain simplicity. Some of his music is large, and some small; some difficult, and some easy. . . . That the "teaching pieces" . . . are essentially mature, though simple, music accounts for their success with the adult students as well as with children. If they are successful, it is so because they are music, not because they are pedagogy. The composer is almost alone today as one who produces a solid literature of complex and serious music and also writes much music which is both musically and technically satisfying for young and for amateur performers.[112]

All the pieces discussed in this segment except for Serenade No. 8 are included on Donald Patterson's 1991 recording of music by Persichetti suitable for students.

Additional Music for Piano Solo   Reading poetry was one of Persichetti's favorite pastimes; his daughter reports that he rarely read novels or newspapers, or watched television, but often read poetry in his spare time.[113] Dorothea Persichetti also confirmed that his "feeling for words [was] stronger . . . for the sound and feeling of the single word or small, concise groups of words—poetry—than it was for functional words used to portray ideas—novels. . . . The composer is especially comfortable in cozy, succinct small forms."[114] So it is not surprising that poetry often served as a point of departure for his creativity. During the late 1930s and early 1940s, Persichetti composed a series of what he called *Poems for Piano*—a collection of sixteen character pieces, each inspired by a *single line*, laden with imagery, taken from modern poetry—American, for the most part. Though composed when he was still in his twenties, before his mature language had fully crystallized, these brief sketches embrace a boundless array of moods, states of mind, and approaches to piano figuration, achieved with remarkable subtlety and economy of means. Their musical styles range from atonality—even atonal pseudo jazz—to the immediacy of a popular song, yet with virtually no redundancy of either meaning or technique. In describing them Dorothea offered a comment that is apt not only with reference to the *Poems* but to many of Persichetti's other pieces as well: "Some of the *Poems* begin with lush, sensuous melodies but have rather surprisingly nasty-sounding middle sections—or sudden unexpected twists and an abrupt ending. When asked why, the composer said it was like seeing the back of a beautiful girl, and finding when she turned around that she was cross-eyed."[115] Especially memorable are two in particular: No. 10 ("Dust in sunlight and memory in corners," T.S. Eliot) and No. 15 ("And hung like those top jewels of the night," Léonie Adams; Dorothea called this one "the gem of the set"[116]). This latter is one of the composer's most straightforwardly beautiful melodies.

Although they appeared in three volumes, designated Opp. 4, 5 (1939), and 14 (1941), they may be performed as a complete cycle, approximately half an hour in duration, or in smaller groupings; they have also served as the basis for choreography.[117] The pieces in volumes I and II are of intermediate difficulty and very short, while those in volume III are a little more difficult and more elaborate. The *Poems* have achieved some popularity with pianists and piano students, and are played frequently. The complete group was recorded in exquisitely sensitive, deeply comprehending performances by the Argentine-American pianist Mirian Conti in 1998.

Quite a few years had elapsed before Persichetti returned to the solo piano. He composed *Parable XIX* in 1975, on commission from the Southwest Division of the Music Teachers National Association (MTNA), in honor of the American bicentennial. In so doing, he based the work, as indicated in the score, on three American folksongs: "Waillie, Waillie," "Who Will Shoe Your Pretty Little Foot?," and "De Blues Ain' Nothin.'" Such use of preexisting melodies other than his own is uncharacteristic of the composer; furthermore, attempts to blend simple, diatonic folksongs within an angular, dissonant harmonic context are often unsuccessful, as the fragmented treatment tends to destroy the fragile simplicity of the original tune, if not its identity altogether. However, in Persichetti's hands, the folk melodies retain their integrity while they are refracted through a diaphanous haze of dissonance. The result suggests a contemplation of these three folk melodies, vaguely remembered, and improvised in solitude late at night.

Daniel Pollack introduced *Parable XIX* at the MTNA convention in Dallas in March 1976. David Burge described it as

> a ten-minute gem of a work in which there is no attempt to do anything other than write a beautiful, coherent, unpretentious single movement. Elements of the experimental style of the *Eleventh Sonata* remain, and there are occasional glimpses of older compositional trademarks, but what dominates *Parable* is a new kind of improvisational lyricism that is not matched in any of the composer's earlier piano music. Underlining the basically lyric approach are occasional quotations from three folksongs. . . . These tunes flow in and out of the music in the manner of subconscious reminiscences and are rarely very obvious.[118]

Although the work is not difficult technically, controlling the melodies within the surrounding context requires mature musicianship. Nevertheless, Donald Patterson included *Parable XIX* on his recording of the composer's easier piano pieces.

Most of Persichetti's next few piano works grew out of his fascination with mirror-writing. There were the *Reflective Keyboard Studies*, Op. 138 (1978), *Little Mirror Book*, Op. 139 (1978), discussed earlier, *Mirror Etudes*, Op. 143 (1979), and the Piano Sonata No. 12, "Mirror Sonata," Op. 145 (1980), also discussed earlier. The composer stated, "All my life I've kept my fingers in shape by playing a unique kind of mirror music that develops both hands simultaneously."[119] *Reflective Keyboard Studies* comprise three sets of sixteen exercises each. In a prefatory note, Persichetti comments that these exercises are "designed to develop both hands at the same time, giving fingers, wrists, and arms strength and flexibility. This unique species of keyboard technique introduces a kind of finger manipulation that has been neglected throughout the history of keyboard instruments." He explains that his mirror music is based on simultaneous exact inversion around the pivot points of D and G-sharp. When this procedure is followed, "The black and white keys are distributed equally, in graphic reflection between the hands, while corresponding black and white keys are played by corresponding fingers of each hand. The preciseness of reflective keyboard construction causes the fingering of both hands to be the same at all times. . . . D always reflects D, and G-sharp always reflects G-sharp. . . . The most effective fingering for any group of notes in one hand will be the best for the other because of the axial balance of the hand structure."[120] Consumed by this project, he explains, "I couldn't keep these forty-eight studies from blossoming into music: the result was *Mirror Etudes*."[121] The *Reflective Keyboard Studies* help the pianist develop the particular technical skills necessary in learning the *Mirror Etudes* and the Piano Sonata No. 12. Upon their publication, Ruth S. Edwards noted that the *Reflective Keyboard Studies* "contain an overview of contemporary piano technique: scales, arpeggios, octaves, intervals and chords in all possible variety, scope, and range. Their use in technical practice certainly would facilitate mastery of the performance problems of the following etudes but would benefit any pianist's competence."[122]

The *Mirror Etudes* were commissioned by Cameron University in Lawton, Oklahoma, and were introduced there in June 1980 by Virginia Sircy. There is a wealth of musical invention to be found in these seven harmonically severe, largely atonal studies. So fertile was Persichetti's imagination that despite the constraints on creativity imposed by this strict approach, which both limited harmonic construction and permitted counterpoint only *within* each hand, the *Etudes* reveal great variety in mood, articulation, touch, texture, gesture, tempo, and figuration. Clearly defined rhythmic patterns and straightforward meters provide some sense of stability. No. 5, based on a diatonically tonal melody, may even be called "pretty," while several of the faster pieces display an edgy rhythmic drive that proves exciting. In the review just cited, Ruth Edwards continues, "There is no doubting Persichetti's facility and craft in exploring compositional possibilities in the seven *Mirror Etudes*. . . . All of the etudes present a reading and technical challenge. Pedaling, dynamics, and tempo fluctuations are precisely indicated throughout the works to give rhythmic and tonal color and variety."[123] The *Mirror Etudes* were recorded by Texan pianist Frances Renzi in brilliant readings that were released on compact disc in 1997.

In addition to the "mirror music," Persichetti also composed *Three Toccatinas*, Op. 142, in 1979. They were commissioned by the University of Maryland for the 1980 International Piano Festival and Competition, where they were introduced in June of that year. Little *toccatas*, as their title indicates, they display the sort of scurrying, whirlwind, single-line figurations, often divided between the two hands, of which the composer was fond. No. 2, "Grazioso," harks back to the Sonatina No. 6, elaborating one of its motifs into a new piece. The *Toccatinas* call for a gentle touch and generous pedaling, producing an almost impressionistic quality usually avoided by this composer. Of upper-intermediate difficulty, they were included on Donald Patterson's recording of Persichetti's pieces appropriate for students.

Persichetti's last piece for piano solo was *Winter Solstice*, Op. 165. It was completed in 1986, the year before his death. Daniel Dorff, who worked closely with Persichetti as editor during the latter's final years, commented on this work, "I have often wondered whether Persichetti knew he was dying and wrote *Winter Solstice* as his requiem, perhaps another parallel to Mozart. *Winter Solstice* is atypical of Persichetti's piano writing because the language is similar to many of his works except that it is more austere and abstract, perhaps to symbolize winter. The piece uses unusual textural effects, including unattacked notes held by the sostenuto pedal and fluttering of the damper pedal, both techniques Persichetti rarely used."[124] The first public performance of this work is believed to have taken place in Philadelphia in April 1996.

Music for Two Pianists

Persichetti composed his Sonata for Two Pianos, Op. 13, in 1940, in between Piano Sonatas Nos. 2 and 3. In four short movements, the work opens with a rather thorny *Lento*. The longest movement of the work, it is somewhat craggy and forbidding, generally atonal, densely contrapuntal, but always coherent in overall direction. The *Allegretto* that follows is like a highly sophisticated, stylized waltz, also contrapuntally intricate. The *Largo* is rather improvisatory and nebulous in overall shape—chromatic and dissonant, like the first movement; dark and mysterious in effect. The concluding *Vivace* is the most immediately appealing movement, with tremendous, almost jazzlike, rhythmic drive, reveling in its richly complex harmony. Although portions of the piece are a little awkward and ungainly—especially the first movement—it has become something of a staple of its limited repertoire. (Part of its success may be an extension of the popularity of the later Concerto for Piano, Four Hands, one of the composer's unqualified masterpieces.)

The first performance of the Sonata for Two Pianos was given by the composer and his wife at New York City's Town Hall in April 1941. The first recording of the work did not appear until 1974, when a performance by the duo-pianists Yarbrough and Cowan was released. As stated earlier, the 1950s saw the emergence of a clearer, more consistent, and more individual personal voice in Persichetti's music. This was the period when most of his greatest works were composed, and among them was the Concerto for Piano, Four Hands, Op. 56. The Concerto was commissioned by Roy Harris, on behalf of an International Contemporary Music Festival, to be held in Pittsburgh in November 1952. He had heard Persichetti and his wife play the Sonata for Two Pianos and asked for a major work of this kind, and the result was this Concerto for two players at one piano.

The Concerto is the first of a number of works from the 1950s in which Persichetti pursued the concept of a large, single movement subdivided into several—usually five—connected sections, all based on a single thematic idea stated at the outset. (The Tenth Piano Sonata, discussed earlier, is another such work.) This answer to the perennial unity–diversity question seemed to provide the composer with an ideal medium through which to pursue virtually boundless developmental fertility. The Concerto begins with a fourteen-note theme containing eleven different pitches. All the fundamental elements of the work derive from this theme. One in particular is a four-note figure—an ascending minor-third followed by a descending minor-third placed so that the two imply a major-minor triad—that plays a prominent, focal role in unifying the work. The opening *Lento* presents the basic theme and explores its subsidiary elements through a variety of gestures, textures, and rhythmic dynamics, from slow, searching counterpoint, to wild, widely spaced motivic fragments, to pounding chords à la *Petrushka*. The *Andante* highlights smoothly flowing imitative counterpoint that finally stabilizes around a gently diatonic, clearly tonal, almost childlike melody, although its E-flat tonality is contradicted by its largely quartal harmonization. A transition, *Largamente*, in whispered *staccato* mirror-writing, leads to the *Presto*. This is the central and most arresting portion of the work, beginning with running figurations in four-hand octave unison. This section develops with a delightful fluidity of rhythmic energy and is a brilliant example of the "Persichetti 2/4" noted earlier. A gentle *legato* passage in imitative counterpoint that allows the music to "catch its breath" resolves in an unexpected moment of tenderness, before moving on to a lighter passage in irregular meter. A suavely jazzy passage marked *Più mosso* follows, leading to more jaggedly irregular writing that provides an opportunity for much byplay between the two pianists. (As Dorothea Persichetti noted, "It goes without saying that in music of this kind the players are very much in the thing together and should be on friendly terms—the friendlier, the better."[125]) This section finally culminates in a triumphantly triadic passage, followed by swirling figurations, leading to the fourth main section, a reflective *Larghissimo*. This section is brief, chiefly providing an opportunity to restabilize and review some of the elements heard earlier. The fifth section, marked *Coda*, reintroduces the running figurations that began the *Presto* section, but beginning *very* slowly (sixteenth-note = 40). The score indicates a very gradual *accelerando*, which reaches quarter-note = 144 within about thirty measures. This section culminates in a reprise of the simple, childlike melody from the *Andante*, now heard in triumphant triads in the *primo*, against other fragments of the main theme played in octaves in the *secundo*. Other material heard earlier is briefly reviewed, leading to a final, bell-like peroration.

Persichetti's Concerto for Piano, Four Hands is one of the greatest works in the four-hand repertoire, certainly the greatest such work of the twentieth century, displaying a graceful fluency along with a masterfully compressed integration of ideas. Despite its structural complexity, attenuated sense of tonality, and relatively harsh harmonic language, a childlike innocence and ingratiating impishness at the spiritual core of the music comes through. Its emotional tone is wholly free of angst, notwithstanding interactions of considerable tension within the fabric of the music. Not unlike Mozart's "Jupiter" Symphony, the Concerto is a comprehensive tour de force of compositional virtuosity, reveling in the ecstatic delight of the developmental process itself. Dorothea recounts that during one of the rehearsals before the premiere, Roy Harris "stood behind the players and, at the long accelerando, there was a parallel acceleration in his breathing until he was puffing hot gusts on the backs of the players' necks."[126] While noting that it is a very difficult work, she insists that it "sounds more difficult than it actually is. After a brilliant finger passage, a player is allowed recuperative measures of rest before the next; the ostinato figures flow naturally; the scale passages are constructed so as to lie well in the hand, with longer fingers on black keys; and, above all, the infectious rhythms of the piece perk along carrying the performer with them and bringing from him sounds and speeds of which he may not have known he was capable."[127]

The Concerto for Piano, Four Hands, was well received from the outset. Virgil Thomson, who attended the Pittsburgh premiere, found the work "extraordinarily expert in its piano writing. It is difficult; but it sounds, and its figurational ingenuity is vast. Musically the work is prolix and its expressivity diffuse; but the sound of it, moment by moment, is unusually brilliant. Its performance by the composer and Dorothea Persichetti was perfection, the ringing quality of their tone being especially noticeable."[128] Reviewing the initial recording of the work, Nathan Broder wrote, "An innate musicality shines forth from every measure. . . . Unlike many modern works for this instrument, it is very idiomatically written, and despite the mastery of contemporary procedures that may be found here, one senses a basically traditional orientation. . . . It is a brilliantly virtuoso setting of the solidest kind of musical matter."[129] Dorothea quotes a comment about the work by Edward Downes, from a review of a performance in the Music of Our Time series:

"It is poles away from the lush romanticism of Schoenberg, but in its own way just as exciting—for some tastes more so. Its five sections sprawl a bit, but the composer's freshness of invention, his wonderful ear for sheer physical sonorities of the piano and for harmonic combinations, and his rhythmic verve gave the work irresistible appeal."[130]

Vincent and Dorothea Persichetti performed the work many times throughout the country and recorded it for Columbia Masterworks shortly after the premiere; this performance was released in 1955 and was reissued by Columbia in several subsequent editions, remaining on the fringes of availability into the 1970s. Theirs is a rendition of astounding virtuosity and expressive zest, bristling with energy, rhythmic vitality, delicacy, and wit. A second recorded performance, played by the American duo Jean and Kenneth Wentworth, was released in 1979. A third, featuring Alexander Bakhchiev and Elena Sorokina, was issued in the Soviet Union in 1982. The next recording appeared in 1996, played by the Malinova Sisters. A fifth recording was issued the following year, with duo-pianists Margret Elson and Elizabeth Swarthout. In 2003 a sixth recording featured the duo of Georgia and Louise Mangos. While most of these later performances have some commendable qualities, none can match the consummate mastery of the Persichettis' original recording.

Music for Piano and Orchestra

Persichetti composed two works for piano and orchestra: a concertino and a full-length concerto. The two share much in common, although they were written more than twenty years apart. The Concertino, Op. 16, was composed in 1941, one year before the First Symphony. It is a terse, highly compact work that accomplishes considerable developmental elaboration and transformation over the course of a mere ten-minute duration. The Concertino begins with a vigorous, angular, and rather dramatic statement of several motifs from which the work will grow. This is balanced by a lyrical theme that is warmly expansive in tone, though still quite chromatic in structure. The writing for piano here is Romantic in style—quite different from the brittle harshness of so much of the composer's solo piano music. As the work develops, its character shifts back and forth between aggressive angularity and more full-breathed lyricism, until, at the end, the various motivic elements coalesce into a grand, consummatory statement of a theme whose arrival appears to be the destination of all that has preceded it.

The premiere of the Concertino took place in October 1945. Persichetti himself was the soloist, accompanied by the Eastman-Rochester Symposium Orchestra, conducted by Howard Hanson. The work has enjoyed few subsequent performances, for reasons that are hard to fathom, beyond the difficulty of programming short works for piano and orchestra into the excessively rigid structure of the typical symphony concert. The initial critical reactions are a little perplexing. John Kirkpatrick wrote, "As always with this gifted composer, the melodies, patterns, and forms are directly expressive and arresting. If one compares it with the superbly clear *Third Sonata* (1943), its harmony, which is typical 'dissonant counterpoint,' seems a bit irresponsible. But it is so real, whether songful or witty, that it would give a rewarding experience to any efficient group wanting a lively romp."[131] Irving Lowens found it to be a "superior composition" that "contains some characteristically dramatic and eloquent passages in the composer's idiomatic vein but does not, on the whole, appear to be as well integrated as his concise *Third Piano Sonata*,"[132] while Robert Sabin added, "Its clever use of dissonance and brisk rhythmic patterns offset its rather loose development."[133] What is perplexing are the slightly unfavorable comparisons with the highly accessible Piano Sonata No. 3, which, from a more distant perspective, is arguably a less tightly constructed work; also, it is difficult to imagine just what Sabin meant by "rather loose development," as it could hardly be more concise. Dorothea viewed the Concertino as "a rich mixture of chromatic and diatonic materials. Melodies tend to be diatonic and harmonies, chromatic. In performance, it emerges flashy and effective."[134] The Concertino has never been recorded.

More than twenty years later, Persichetti completed his Concerto for Piano and Orchestra, Op. 90—a work eagerly anticipated by those who were following the progression of his pieces for piano solo. Although the Concerto was completed in 1962, it was not performed until August 1964, when Anthony diBonaventura gave the premiere in Hanover, New Hampshire, with the Dartmouth Community Symphony Orchestra, under the direction of Mario diBonaventura, brother of the soloist. The concert was the culmination of Persichetti's two-week stint as composer-in-residence at Dartmouth that summer. The most notable aspect of the new work, in relation to the rest of the composer's output, is its expansiveness. It is more than half an hour in duration, with an opening movement, *Allegro non troppo*, that is nearly half its length. But its expansiveness is not a matter of mere duration: The Concerto embraces the rhetoric of the traditional romantic virtuoso concerto, with the soloist asserting a heroic stance in opposition to the orchestra, dazzling with pyrotechnics, and cajoling with warm lyricism. There is also more attention paid to the evocation of mood than is usually the case with this composer.

Like the Concertino, the first movement of the Concerto—longer than the earlier work in its entirety—varies between a feisty aggressiveness and long-breathed lyricism. Its discursive rhetoric allows the thematic material to develop in a loose, fantasy-like manner, with leisurely excursions through a variety of moods, including passages of uncharacteristic introspectiveness. The second movement, *Andante sostenuto*, is a subdued interlude, more a wistful evocation of vistas reminiscent of Harris or Schuman than an out-pouring of lyrical melody. The vigorous final movement, *Allegro vivace*, opens with a combination of snare drum and bass clarinet that is inescapably Schumanesque. Yet it is also the part of the work that is most characteristic of Persichetti, as well as its most immediately accessible movement. A tour de force of rhythmic agility, the finale accumulates tremendous energy in a fine example of the "Persichetti 2/4," recalling material from the preceding movements before coming to a brilliant conclusion.

Although it did not take place in a metropolitan center, the premiere of Persichetti's Piano Concerto attracted considerable attention and was covered by the major New York critics, whose initial reactions focused on the obvious. Theodore Strongin commented, "It is a brilliant bravura work, sprinkled with moments of unpressured reflectiveness. As a whole, it is spacious in scale, sharp in detail. The first movement is the biggest of the three and the most varied in sound and mood. The second is all soft anticipation of constantly shifting harmonies. In the third, there is again, as in the first, the headlong motor dash that Mr. Persichetti often favors."[135] William Bender noted,

> Its writing is in the assimilative, tonal style familiar to admirers of Mr. Persichetti's music, and it is at once one of his most accessible and enjoyable works. It is a virtuoso concerto that blends contrast and surprise as well as declamation and lyricism in a constantly fresh and convincing way. Though the orchestral scoring is basically contemporary middle-of-the-road, there is a touch of romanticism now and impressionism then, and even a dash of the moderns like Bartok and Prokofiev in the finale. But it has all been fused into one original whole.[136]

A few further performances followed over the ensuing years. Attending a Philadelphia performance, Daniel Webster found the Concerto to be "an immediately endearing piece full of bright pianistic flourishes and lyrical flow. . . . The architecture of the piece insures [*sic*] its coherence, for the essential idea from the opening is used to weld the whole piece together."[137] A performance in Chicago prompted John Von Rhein to observe, "Persichetti is one of the most distinguished voices from what might be termed the muscular-conservative school of American music. His concerto is a splendid work of its kind, thoroughly traditional in its neo-Romantic virtuoso deployment of the keyboard instrument more or less against a massive, drum-laden orchestra, yet full of expertly crafted effects that really *sound*."[138]

But while it elicited respect from critics, the work was not a major success with audiences and did not create an enthusiastic following as did, for example, the Piano Concerto of Samuel Barber, composed the same year. Both works share a similar outward manner. However, the genre arouses certain expectations that, for whatever reason, Persichetti did not fulfill, disappointing those listeners who were led to expect this master of the keyboard to produce a crowd-pleasing virtuoso vehicle. But instead of arresting themes and sentimental melodies, he concentrated on the development of short motifs, the hearty bravura manner concealing a formal structure as logical and unified as the composer's more obviously compact compositions. That is another way that the Concerto resembles the Concertino, but the expectations associated with a ten-minute piece for piano and chamber orchestra are different from those prompted by a full-length concerto. Appealing on a level more cerebral than visceral, the Concerto is almost entirely derived from the intervallic implications of the stentorian five-note motto proclaimed by the horns at the opening. However, this is not to suggest that the work is difficult to understand or endure; rather, it simply does not inspire affection readily. But it does reward persistence; listeners who allow themselves to become familiar enough with the material and its elaboration to follow its course both developmentally and dramatically are likely to find that the Concerto provides an ever-deepening satisfaction.

Persichetti's Piano Concerto did not appear on recording until 1990, when a breathtaking performance by the American pianist Robert Taub was released, accompanied by the Philadelphia Orchestra, conducted by Charles Dutoit. Reviewing the recording for *Fanfare*, James H. North commented, "Persichetti himself was a whiz-bang pianist, which may explain why many of his sonatas are feared finger-breakers; this concerto breaks the pattern, for there is much graceful, simpler writing in it, as well as virtuoso passages. The opening Allegro non troppo builds upon a 'big tune' as well as weaving intricacies around it; contrasting sections are calm, quiet, easygoing. A dreamy Andante sostenuto follows, and the finale, Allegro vivace, is wild and spectacular."[139]

Harpsichord

As noted earlier, during the last years of his life Persichetti developed an intense fascination with the harpsichord. Between 1981 and his death in 1987, he completed twenty-two works, of which twelve are for harpsichord solo, including nine of ten sonatas. The instrument certainly lends itself to the fleet, *toccata*-like figurations and clear, transparent textures favored by the composer. In his quiet, unobtrusive way, free of sensationalism or ostentation, Persichetti left as a legacy what may well be the major contribution to the harpsichord literature of the twentieth century.

However, long before that remarkable—virtually obsessive—flurry of activity, in 1951 Persichetti had written what proved to be the Harpsichord Sonata No. 1, Op. 52. While composing, he worked closely with harpsichordist Fernando Valenti in order to gain a fuller understanding of the instrument's capabilities.[140] It was Valenti who gave the work's premiere in January 1952 at New York City's Town Hall.

Generally warm and playful in character, the Sonata No. 1 is a delightfully genial work in three short movements, each of which begins with an ascending series of three steps, treated rather like on-the-beat grace notes. This three-note stepwise idea, both ascending and descending, serves as the germinal motif of the entire work. The sonata also features some of the chorale-style writing that appears in much of Persichetti's music from the 1950s. The first movement begins with a solemn introduction, *Andante sostenuto*, before proceeding to an exuberantly celebratory *Allegro*, rife with mischievous metrical asymmetries. The contemplative second movement, *Adagio*, features florid, arabesque-like figurations. The third movement begins very slowly, recalling the basic motif, before moving into a lively, high-spirited *Vivace*, based on a repeated-note motif, although the stepwise motif is heard throughout the secondary material. This movement is another excellent example of the "Persichetti 2/4," densely populated with the composer's familiar goofy and gawky chimeras.

Reviewing the Valenti premiere, Russell Kerr complained that "a percussive style was utilized, to the detriment of colorful, expressive media. Constructed with ability, it yet produced a rather dry effect."[141] On the other hand, Jay S. Harrison found the sonata to be

a fanciful, flavorful work. Expressively, it recalls the keyboard suites of J. S. Bach, but its rhythm and harmonic cast are distinctly of our time. Its rhythm, especially, syncopated but not hesitant, accounts for the vigor of the Sonata's movement and the strength of its stride. Melodically, too, the work moves briskly and despite the apparent fragmentariness of its lines, a continuum is set up at the beginning of the piece which thereafter is not for a moment deserted. Best of all, the work is real harpsichord music; those pointed effects for which the instrument is most widely known are collected and husbanded with a master's hand. In sum, we have a new work in which to show pride.[142]

These last points, however, were disputed by Kathleen McIntosh Farr, who commented, "There are many indications that this work was composed at the piano," and proceeded to identify several usages she maintained were difficult or impossible to execute on the instrument.[143] In 1986 the Sonata No. 1 was recorded by American harpsichordist Carole Terry, who successfully managed to navigate these alleged difficulties, offering a brilliant performance.

The Harpsichord Sonatas Nos. 2 through 10 were all written during the period 1981–1987, and their compositional approaches share much in common. Their durations range between seven and thirteen minutes, and most comprise three movements. They embody both the external trappings and the conceptual ideals of Neo-Classicism, especially clarity: Textures are extremely lucid, with much two-voice imitative counterpoint; rhythms are lively and irregular but unambiguous; and motivic relationships are clearly apparent. These sonatas are pure music, devoid of "effects" or evocations of imagery, melodrama, or sensationalism of any kind; rather, they are displays of sheer musical invention, proclaiming the composer's boundless facility. Despite their clarity, the harmonic language is often quite harsh, with much use of the dissonant intervals of the second and the seventh. Although the music is not constructed according to serial principles, tonality is generally transitory, often to a point approaching undetectability, while other dimensions—chiefly rhythm and gesture—contribute to its coherence. But the clear textures found in these works should not be mistaken for simplicity, as the density of motivic relationships and the lack of visceral or emotional appeal results in music that requires repeated exposure before its more ingratiating qualities become evident. And despite the presence of a consistent conceptual logic, they often create an impression of having been improvised. Music like this can easily seem "academic," if viewed apart from the larger context of the composer's body of work and its cumulative impact.

The Harpsichord Sonata No. 2, Op. 146, was composed in 1981. The published score indicates that the work was "commissioned by Michael Needle and Associates for Elaine Comparone," although a glance back at Lauren Persichetti's reminiscence of her father's idiosyncrasies sheds some light on the identity of the commissioning entity. Comparone, who gave the premiere of the four-movement work at the Cleveland Museum in June 1982, followed by further performances elsewhere, recalled that the sonata fit "the hands and fingers perfectly, as does the music of other great keyboardist/composers. I found the falling staccato thirds and rising scales of the opening bars exhilarating. The exuberance of the piece captured me."[144] After sending the composer a tape of the performance, Comparone received a note from him, which said, "Thank you for the reviews, programs, tape. . . . I was not able to write you sooner, because I was writing for the harpsichord. I was not able to attend your concert, because I was writing for the harpsichord. Don't spend too much time on those earlier composers. Get to #3!"[145]

Comparone herself had commissioned the curiously witty, three-movement Sonata No. 3, Op. 149, also completed in 1981, and gave the premiere of this work as well, in Washington, D.C., in October 1982. Sonata No. 3 is perhaps the most immediately engaging of the nine late sonatas.

Persichetti completed three harpsichord sonatas in 1982. The Sonata No. 4, Op. 151, was commissioned by Shippensburg State College for Joan Applegate, who gave the premiere in Shippensburg, Pennsylvania, in April of that year. Reviewing Sonatas Nos. 3 and 4, JoAnn Latorra Smith wrote, "The indication *affabile* in one of these works can be taken as indicative of Persichetti's style—affable, clear, clean. They are very dissonant, but the clarity of his technique contributes significantly to the accessibility of his music. This is not profound music, perhaps even a bit academic, but it is pleasant and makes a good change of pace for a recital program."[146] Mark E. Smith found the same two works to be "highly idiomatic for the instrument, with transparent textures and a wealth of counterpoint. Though these are tonal works, the tonalities are generally not sharply defined."[147]

Persichetti's Harpsichord Sonata No. 5, Op. 152, was commissioned by Arizona State University on behalf of John Metz, who gave the premiere at the Tempe campus in December 1982. The three-movement work introduced the salient appearance of the perfect fifth—a sonority that was to reappear in several of the pieces to follow. Frances Bedford commented, "The composer effectively explores the enormous variety of registration possibilities when he calls for a section in the exposition to be played using only the 4' stop. . . . The Andante movement shows Persichetti at his lyrical best, while the final exhilarating movement returns to a mixture of polyphonic writing, punctuated by some refreshingly dissonant chords. His writing never exceeds the harpsichord's capabilities."[148]

In 1992 a compact disc was released that featured Elaine Comparone in splendid performances of the Harpsichord Sonatas Nos. 2 through 5. In his program notes, composer Bruce Adolphe, who studied with Persichetti, offered some perceptive comments about the music of his former teacher.

> Persichetti's music resembles the man: high-spirited, witty, mercurial, eclectic, spontaneous. In his sleight-of-hand style, melodic figures zip by the ear, always propelling the music forward. But he also had a pensive and nostalgic side. His harmonies linger generously in adagios; he prepares and resolves dissonances with thoughtful care. . . . As a chef loves old recipes for the joy of altering the details, so Persichetti loved the traditional forms. . . . Surrendering to sudden jolts of inspiration, he plays with subtle melodic alterations and improvises joyously.[149]

The Harpsichord Sonata No. 6, Op. 154, was the third of the sonatas to be composed in 1982. It was commissioned by Southern Methodist University on behalf of Larry Palmer, who introduced the work at the dedication of a new harpsichord at Christ Church Cathedral in New Orleans in September 1983. It is similar to the other sonatas, except for the fact that it comprises only one movement: an *Andantino* introduction followed by a faster section, *Allegro con spirito*. At the conclusion of the printed score, the following appears: "Frstrngqt." Those familiar with Persichetti's scores will realize that this "code" indicates a reference to the String Quartet No. 1; and, indeed, the *Allegro* portion is based on the *scherzo* from that early work.

Commissioned by Barbara Harbach, Persichetti completed his Seventh Harpsichord Sonata, Op. 156, in 1983. Harbach gave the first performance in March of that year at Nazareth College in Rochester, New York. Like the other sonatas, this three-movement work is concise, terse, and genial in spirit while wholly abstract in construction, featuring graceful, thin, linear textures idiomatic to the instrument. While the first two movements are quite austere in tone, the finale explodes with an infectious rhythmic vitality. This score too has a cryptic note at the end: "Rgrsns," which is no doubt a reference to composer Roger Sessions, Persichetti's colleague and close friend. Although it may be no more than a private dedication, a more likely explanation is that this sonata borrows a motif from one of Sessions's works. In 1985 Barbara Harbach included the Sonata No. 7 on an LP featuring contemporary harpsichord music, making it the first of Persichetti's harpsichord works to be recorded. The program was reissued on compact disc in 1988.

In 1984 Persichetti completed his Harpsichord Sonata No. 8, Op. 158. Once again, "Michael Needle" is cited as the source of a commission on behalf of Linda Kobler, who introduced the work in November of the following year at the Cathedral of St. John the Divine in New York City. The three-movement work is constructed along much the same lines as the previous sonatas.

Harpsichord Sonata No. 9, Op. 163, followed in 1985, commissioned by the Arcady Music Festival on behalf of Masanobu Ikemiya, best known as a ragtime pianist. Ikemiya gave the premiere in July of the following year at the festival in Mt. Desert Island, Maine. This sonata, also in three movements, is somewhat simpler than its predecessors, both technically and conceptually. Though its linear flow is largely diatonic and much of the harmony is relatively consonant, scale forms change so frequently that there is only a minimal sense of tonal center.

Sonata No. 10 for Harpsichord, Op. 167, was Persichetti's last work, composed during the final months of his life. Daniel Dorff recalls that the editorial staff of the Theodore Presser Company had believed that *Winter Solstice* for piano and the second volume of *Hymns and Responses for the Church Year* were Persichetti's last completed works. "A few months later his wife Dorothea died, and when the house was cleaned out, the *Tenth Harpsichord Sonata* was found in the freezer, wrapped in tin foil."[150] Although again in three movements, this sonata is a radical departure from the others, venturing into the quasi-serial language used, for example, in the Piano Sonata No. 11, with rhythms, textures, figurations, and gestures considerably more complex than in the previous sonatas, and with much less linear counterpoint.

In addition to the ten sonatas, Persichetti composed three other pieces for harpsichord during the 1980s. Each adds to one of his ongoing "series": *Parable XXIV*, Op. 153; *Little Harpsichord Book*, Op. 155; and the Serenade No. 15, Op. 161. *Parable XXIV* was composed in 1982, commissioned by Capital University for Cathy Callis, who introduced it in April of the following year, in Columbus, Ohio, where the university is located. The piece begins with a slow, quite angular introduction, and is followed by a fantasia-like episode that begins canonically in 6/8 and continues with a free development, eventually leading to a recapitulation of the opening sections. Like the sonatas, the music is dissonant and atonal in effect, despite generally diatonic linear material and clear, simple textures.

The *Little Harpsichord Book* was composed in 1983 for the Philadelphia Art Alliance, where it was introduced by Elaine Comparone in October of that year. The collection follows the precedent of the *Little Piano Book* and similar titles by Persichetti, presenting twelve tiny pieces that exhibit modern compositional techniques (including mirror-writing) while providing minimal technical challenges. However, despite their simplicity and unlike the *Little Piano Book*, these pieces—like the sonatas written concurrently—are largely atonal and quite dissonant, and lack the warmth and tenderness of the earlier collection. Nevertheless, there is so little music of this kind in the contemporary harpsichord repertoire, that the *Little Harpsichord Book* has been welcomed enthusiastically by teachers and performers. Frances Bedford exulted, "At last! An engaging set of easy pieces in the modern idiom for the harpsichord player. . . . The variety of moods, character, tessitura and tempos found among these attractive miniatures contributes to the possibility of performing the entire collection of twelve as a unit."[151] Maribeth Gowen commented, "Vincent Persichetti gives us twelve well-etched compositions in his Little Harpsichord Book. They have thin textures and linear writing reminiscent of Baroque harpsichord music. Distinctly Persichetti in style, this diverse group of mostly one-page pieces has been compositionally boiled down to the absolute musical essence. As in much of Persichetti's piano music, all the pieces fit well under the fingers. The pianistic challenge lies in being able to eloquently shape two simultaneous melodic lines."[152]

Serenade No. 15 is the final entry in Persichetti's group of serenades. Composed in 1984, it was commissioned by Larry Palmer, who introduced it in September of the following year in Dallas, Texas. Like so many of the serenades, it consists of five short pieces. It is somewhat less challenging technically than the *Parable*, but a bit more difficult than the *Little Harpsichord Book*. While drawing upon roughly the same freely atonal language, the pieces comprising the Serenade reveal more variety and individual character than either of the other two opuses. In 2000 Barbara Harbach included Persichetti's Serenade No. 15 on a recording of contemporary harpsichord music.

Organ

When one considers the extent of Persichetti's own activities as an organist during the early portion of his career, one may be surprised to discover that he composed only ten works for that instrument. These pieces appeared irregularly throughout the course of his life, from 1940 through 1985. Some of them are substantial and challenging both musically and technically, while others are more incidental and less significant.

The earliest is the Sonatine, Op. 11 (1940), for organ, pedals alone. Comprising three short movements, this is the only one of Persichetti's compositions for the instrument written while he actually served as organist at Philadelphia's Arch Street Presbyterian Church. (Most of what he played during Sunday services were improvisations.) Like many of his works from the 1940s it is highly chromatic and largely atonal in effect, yet relatively lighthearted and playful in character. Dorothea Persichetti's comments on the piece are candid and perceptive: "The *Sonatine* is terse to the point of brusqueness. It flaunts foot virtuosity in the face of no hands . . . and, when played with sureness, sounds brilliant and somewhat glib. The lyric sections have an 'awkwardness,' a left-handedness, which is inherent in the melodic writing, but not in the technique—as if the piece were making fun of its own problems. It is compact, young and a bit fresh."[153] Persichetti himself gave the premiere in November 1940 at the Arch Street Presbyterian Church. The Sonatine was recorded in 1996 by Kyler Brown.

Persichetti's next organ work was the three-movement Sonata, Op. 86, commissioned by the St. Louis chapter of the American Guild of Organists, as part of their fiftieth anniversary celebration. The work's musical language is the "free atonality" found in the composer's many works that inhabit a middle ground between the clear diatonic tonality of the simplest works and the more deliberate atonality of the quasi-serial works. (Rudy Shackelford coined the term "metatonality" to characterize Persichetti's "freely atonal" approach, which he describes as "a reintegration of Schoenbergian and traditionally tonal methods and materials." He elaborates this concept in penetrating detail while also describing the composer's approach to serialism.[154]) The sonata's primary motivic germs are all introduced within the first measure of the introduction, marked *Andante*. The body of the movement is a lilting *Allegro* in 6/8, somewhat reminiscent of the 6/8 portion of the first movement of the Piano Sonata No. 4. The second movement, *Larghetto*, is based on the same motivic elements, treated in a more contemplative fashion. The finale, *Vivace*, is an exuberant *toccata* that presents further transformations of the basic material, and is probably the most effective movement. Somewhat perplexing is the appearance of a number of passages that do not seem especially well suited to the particular qualities of the organ; in particular, the instrument's propensity for thunderous sonorities may obscure textural details and dissonant harmonic relationships—the very elements that provide the focal points of Persichetti's lean, understated style. There are moments when the sheer brute force of the sound—perhaps not intended by the composer—seems on the verge of overwhelming the gentle whimsy and graceful capriciousness at the heart of the music. Also, there is again the sense that the work's harmonic language is more severe than is warranted by its expressive character. One wonders just how the composer—who rarely produced an effect he didn't intend—conceived this juxtaposition of medium and message.[155]

Completed in 1960, Persichetti's Organ Sonata was introduced in December of that year by organist Rudolph Kremer at Washington University in St. Louis. It was recorded by David Craighead in 1981.

Only two years elapsed before Persichetti returned to the organ, this time for a ten-minute fantasy inspired by Psalm 130 ("Out of the depths have I cried O Lord"). Using its Hebrew title, Persichetti explained, "This Psalm in Hebrew, rather than Latin or English, has a sound which seemed closest to my music."[156] *Shima B'koli*, Op. 89, was commissioned by the Lincoln Center for the Performing Arts, for the concert inaugurating Philharmonic Hall's new Aeolian-Skinner organ. This concert took place in December 1962 and featured the world-renowned organist Virgil Fox.

Shima B'koli was one of the first works in which Persichetti explored the quasi-serial style he was to pursue in such works as the Piano Sonata No. 11 (1965).[157] Although he applied the twelve-tone system with considerable flexibility, the piece avoids any overt sense of a tonal center, with wide, pointillistic leaps across registers, wide-ranging chromaticism, and only occasional sense of meter. It is probably the composer's most musically demanding work for the organ. Perhaps the reaction of most listeners is reflected in the comments of Owen Anderson, who described the work thus: "Following a quiet opening, it soon develops into a series of extended, crashing episodes, interspersed with quiet, often contrapuntally developed fragments. On first hearing, it strikes one as being spasmodic and overextended for its thematic material in spite of the great professional skill with which it is assembled."[158] Reviewing the premiere, the distinguished organist Leonard Raver noted that this was one of the first organ works to utilize aspects of the twelve-tone idiom, acknowledging its considerable difficulty for both performers and listeners. However, he concluded by reporting that "Persichetti's Psalm was for me the most challenging and stimulating musical experience of the afternoon."[159] *Shima B'koli* was recorded by organist Kent Tritle and released on compact disc in 1994.

Persichetti's next work for organ was a chorale prelude based on the hymn, "Drop, drop slow tears" (No. 13 in volume I of the *Hymns and Responses for the Church Year*). Based on a text by the seventeenth-century English religious poet Phineas Fletcher, Persichetti's setting centers on F-sharp minor but is harmonized with considerable chromatic freedom. *Chorale Prelude, "Drop, Drop Slow Tears,"* Op. 104, was commissioned by the University of Kentucky, where it was first performed in April 1967 by Haskell Thomson. The work embraces the tradition of the chorale prelude for organ, retaining the wayward, downhearted harmonization of the hymn, while embellishing it with contrapuntal subtleties and onomatopoeic representations of the text. Its expressive coherence and sense of solemn introspection is deeply moving.[160] In a performance by David Craighead, the chorale prelude was included on the 1981 recording that also featured the composer's Organ Sonata.

In 1971 Persichetti was commissioned by the Dallas chapter of the American Guild of Organists to compose a work for their national convention the following year in Fort Worth. The result was his *Parable VI*, Op. 117. It is a substantial piece of some quarter-hour duration and, like *Shima B'koli*, uses the "metatonal" style to which he often resorted during the 1960s and 1970s. Like many entries among his series of *Parables*, the work takes the form of an abstract fantasy in a single movement, based on a small number of generating motifs. Although shaped with the coherent craftsmanship that he applied to all his work, Persichetti's pieces in this vein cannot be expected to appeal to more than a small group of special-interest listeners and musicians. In addition to providing a detailed analysis of the work, Rudy Shackelford proposes a metaphorical interpretation of its "meaning."[161] *Parable VI* was introduced in June 1972 by David Craighead at the convention in Fort Worth.

Two years later Persichetti received another organ commission, this time from organist Leonard Raver, who requested a work for pedals alone. The composer responded with *Do Not Go Gentle*, Op. 132, the title a reference to a poem by Dylan Thomas. This is another uncompromisingly "metatonal" work, although its usefulness as a showpiece for pedal technique has made it popular among organists. Raver gave the first performance in November 1974 at the American Guild of Organists convention in Boston. Reviewing Raver's performance of the New York premiere, Allen Hughes described the piece as "a solemn recitativelike work," adding that "this rather eloquent work owed much of its effect to frequent and telling changes of registration."[162] (Shackelford provides a detailed analysis of this work as well.[163])

Perhaps Persichetti's most fully realized organ work is *Auden Variations*, Op. 136. It was commissioned for Leonard Raver by the Hartt College of Music for its International Contemporary Organ Music Festival in July 1978, when Raver gave the work its premiere. Completed the previous year, it is a set of thirteen variations on the chorale, "Our Father, Whose Creative Will," with a text by W. H. Auden (No. 1 in the first volume of *Hymns and Responses for the Church Year*). It is remarkable that a composer with such fluent mastery of developmental technique was not drawn more often to the theme-with-variations format. The *Auden Variations* is a brilliant example of this mastery, as the triadic but only loosely tonal chorale is subjected to a fascinating exploration. Among the most interesting treatments are a variation based on only the "amen" sequence, canonic variations, including one in which the three voices appear in different rhythmic proportions, some use of contrary motion or "mirror-writing," as well as more traditional variation techniques.[164]

A somewhat similar work, the *Dryden Liturgical Suite*, Op. 144, followed in 1980. Commissioned by the Marilyn Mason Fund at the University of Michigan, the work is based on No. 4 from volume I of the *Hymns and Responses for the Church Year*. The text is taken from John Dryden's poem in three verses, "Creator Spirit, by Whose Aid." However, unlike the *Auden Variations*, the piece comprises five movements, somewhat suggestive of a Baroque suite, in which each movement is identified with a different line of Dryden's poem. But since each verse of the poem is set to the same music, each movement is like an individual chorale prelude on the melody of the hymn. Thus, it combines the notion of a chorale prelude with the concept underlying the *Poems for Piano*, in which each piece was a musical response to a single line of poetry. The harmonic language of the *Dryden Suite* is overall somewhat more acerbic than that used in the *Auden Variations*. The premiere of the *Dryden Liturgical Suite* was given by Marilyn Mason at the national convention of the American Guild of Organists in St. Paul, Minnesota, in June 1980. David Shuler found the work to be "superbly crafted, as is always the case with Persichetti, and the music possesses drive and direction. The organ is used idiomatically throughout the work. The music lays well under the fingers and feet."[165]

Song of David, Op. 148, once again reveals Persichetti's impish sense of humor. The title suggests a reference to the biblical King David, and the score indicates that the work was commissioned for Leonard Raver by "Michael Needle and Associates." However, the reader may recall that Michael Needle was a figment of the composer's vivid imagination. Furthermore, the "David" of the title was David Cohen, a friend and former composition student of Persichetti. At the wedding of David and Dorothy Cohen,

Persichetti used the lovely "Arietta" from his *Little Piano Book* as the basis for a meditative five-minute organ improvisation. In 1981 he concretized his improvisation for publication. Reviewing the work, Raver wrote, "The music is unpretentious, its cantabile lines warmed by introspective counterpoint which builds to a loud middle section climaxed by a brief pedal solo and then returns to the quiet mood of the opening."[166] Raver gave the first public performance of the work in March 1983 at the Church of the Ascension in New York City.

Persichetti's last work for organ was a chorale prelude based on the hymn, "Give Peace, O God" (No. 41 in *Hymns and Responses for the Church Year*, volume II). In this case, both the hymn, with text by Henry W. Baker, and the chorale prelude were commissioned by the Ann Arbor chapter of the American Guild of Organists. The setting of the hymn is solemn and poignant, but its treatment in the chorale prelude is quite harsh and angular, with much attention given to the pedals. *Chorale Prelude, "Give Peace, O God,"* Op. 162, was completed in 1985 and first performed in June of the following year by Donald Williams at the national convention of the American Guild of Organists in Ann Arbor, Michigan. Calvert Shenk found the new work to be the highpoint of the program,[167] while Rudolf Zuiderveld described the chorale prelude as "quite a dramatic, freely virtuosic piece (with a stormy pedal cadenza) concluding in a mysterious calm—brilliantly performed by Donald Williams!"[168]

Works for Orchestra

Symphonies

Like so many other composers, Vincent Persichetti completed nine symphonies. And, like the other composers discussed in this book, he withdrew his first two efforts, at least temporarily. But, as noted earlier, Persichetti's symphonies—unlike those of so many other composers—do not represent the essential core of his output, nor are they necessarily his "best" works, nor was the orchestra his primary medium, as it was for Schuman and Mennin. Nevertheless, these are large, substantive works and are generally representative of Persichetti's compositional concerns during the periods when they were written.

Persichetti composed his first two symphonies during the first six months of 1942, when he was twenty-seven years old.[169] This was three years after Roy Harris completed his celebrated Third Symphony, one year after Schuman had completed *his* Third, and the same year that Mennin composed his (unperformed) Symphony No. 1. Persichetti's own Symphony No. 1, Op. 18,

resembles his chromatic, angular, and "gritty" early works like the Piano Sonata No. 1 (1939) and the Sonata for Two Pianos (1940). The work comprises
a single movement, subdivided into two sections, marked *Lento* and *Andante
con moto*. It opens with a trumpet fanfare that highlights upward and downward leaps of a fifth, in a short-LONG rhythmic pattern. This motif generates
the thematic material of the entire symphony, which is treated contrapuntally
in both sections. With its through-composed design and its avoidance of
classical formal paradigms, the structure of the work reveals the influence
of Harris. Also reminiscent of that composer is an excessive use of unison
writing, as well as some ungainly phraseology. In the first section there is a
passage that anticipates an extremely similar treatment near the beginning of
Persichetti's own Fifth Symphony, while the second section reveals a remarkable instance of borrowing from the finale of Shostakovich's Fifth Symphony
(1937). The work illustrates just how long the composer continued to struggle
in searching for his own voice, especially when writing for the orchestra.

Persichetti's Symphony No. 1 was presented at an informal reading by the
Eastman-Rochester Symposium Orchestra, conducted by Howard Hanson in
October 1947. There is no evidence that it has ever been performed again. By
1960 there had been no second hearing for the work. At that time Dorothea
Persichetti predicted that a revision would be undertaken, but whether this
was ever done is not known.[170] At the time of this writing, the work is not
available for performance.

Persichetti's Symphony No. 2, Op. 19, followed directly on the heels of
its predecessor. By 1960, however, it had never been performed, and there
is no record of its having been performed since then. The work comprises
three lightly scored movements. Dorothea reported that the composer had
played it through at the piano for Harris, who was disappointed by its modest
character, asserting, "A symphony should be like a billboard!" She indicated
that Persichetti intended to rescore the symphony for chamber orchestra, but
whether this was ever done is not known.[171] The work is not currently available for performance.

Persichetti began his Symphony No. 3, Op. 30, during that productive year
of 1942, although he did not complete it until 1946, a period that embraced
his brief term of study with Harris and included such pieces as the *Pastoral*
for woodwind quintet, the Third Piano Sonata, and the Second String Quartet.
A full half-hour in duration, the Third is the longest of Persichetti's symphonies. He described it as a "war symphony," although this is reflected musically only in the first and last movements. The scoring places the piano in a
prominent role within the orchestral texture.

The first of the work's four movements is marked *Somber*, and opens with a
stern, angular melody in the strings, anticipating the opening of his own Fifth

Symphony. As further thematic material is spawned, the movement builds dramatically into a vehement expression of grief. This powerful movement is possibly the most dramatic music ever composed by Persichetti. He seems to have followed Harris's dictum in achieving a large-boned, assertive grandeur, while also adopting the older composer's oratorical posture, as well as his nonclassical approach to form. Though such grandiloquence is quite uncharacteristic of Persichetti's mature mode of expression, it is quite characteristic of the music so many of his colleagues were writing at the time. The roughly contemporaneous works of Roy Harris, William Schuman, and Morton Gould (and perhaps even Samuel Barber's Symphony No. 2) are readily called to mind, although Persichetti's craftsmanship in handling his material is often more agile and proficient than theirs. The high point of the opening is a beautiful melody introduced by the strings and picked up by the trumpet, just before the movement ends in the somber mood in which it began. The second movement, *Spirited*, is a *scherzo*, suggestive of a folk dance, with a gently lyrical middle section. The treatment is pan-diatonic, with a slight nod to Copland. The third movement, *Singing*, is contemplative and sadly wistful, the mood set by a poignant English horn solo, although a dense web of dissonant counterpoint dispels any maudlin tendency. The movement builds to a climax of considerable strength. The martial spirit returns in the finale. Marked *Fast and Brilliant*, the movement is also vigorous and rousing, moving gradually toward a triumphant peroration. Throughout, the distinctive trademarks of Harris and Schuman are ever present, while Persichetti's own fingerprints are hardly to be found. Indeed, virtual paraphrases from Schuman's Third Symphony repeatedly leap out and jar one's attention. In short, Persichetti's Third is much more a reflection of its time and place than it is a harbinger of the direction the composer was to follow in the years to come. The Symphony No. 3 plays much the same role within Persichetti's output—as an isolated work of heroic virility—as Barber's Second Symphony plays in his. Taken on its own terms it is certainly more skillfully wrought than anything Harris ever wrote, but perhaps not as fresh and vital as Schuman's Third.

Persichetti's Third Symphony was first performed by the Philadelphia Orchestra, conducted by Eugene Ormandy in November 1947. Initial critical reaction was peculiar, to say the least; viewed in retrospect, the comments indicate a remarkably limited grasp of the work, not to mention a similarly limited grasp of the English language. Linton Martin was the more favorably inclined, writing, "Arresting originality of idea and idiom of expression in thematic material and treatment, is not a conspicuous quality of the symphony which shows some Russian influence but is not derivative in detail. It shows manifest familiarity with orchestral instrumentation and effects. . . . Diversity of musical moods sustain interest in the progression of the symphony."[172] On the other hand, Elizabeth Emerson Stine commented, "Gratifying as the applause must have been to this hard working young man, he must have known that it came from the strong supporters of the modern school of composition, for comments in the lobby from the older generation were distinctly reminiscent of the day when Stokowski offered the latest offering in dissonances. Knowing his style, this work is exactly what one would expect of Persichetti. Call it atonal or pandiatonic, the effect of unrelated tones remains the same."[173]

Performances of the Symphony No. 3 were extremely sparse over the course of the half century that followed. One performance that took place during the mid 1950s featured the University of Alabama Symphony Orchestra, conducted by Roland Johnson. Reviewing that performance, composer David Ward-Steinman (then a Florida State undergraduate) wrote, "For me, the greatest surprise was in hearing Persichetti's Third Symphony, which was given an electrifying performance. I'm still not certain whether it was really the music or just the performance that made the difference, but at the time I thought this to be the best American symphony I had heard. The Copland Third, Dello Joio 'St. Joan Symphony,' Harris Third, and works of Barber paled in comparison, and they are about the best we have."[174] (Dorothea felt that this performance compared favorably with the Philadelphia Orchestra premiere.[175])

The work's next documented public presentation did not take place until 2003, when it was performed—and recorded—by the Albany Symphony Orchestra under the direction of David Alan Miller. By this time the work's obscurity had made it something of a curiosity among Persichetti enthusiasts, so its first recording, issued in 2005, was received with considerable interest. David Moore commented, "I . . . am very happy to have the opportunity to welcome this first recording of [Persichetti's Third Symphony]. . . . It is indeed an angry work in places, written in 1946 with percussive echoes of war interrupting it; and some demanding work for timpani, particularly in the finale, reminds me of some of William Schuman's embattled endings. . . . [T]here are beautiful feelings of the countryside as well, but . . . the disturbances of the times are more prevalent. It is a strong work and I am most satisfied that it has finally been recorded. . . . . This is an important release."[176]

Only five years elapsed before Persichetti completed his Symphony No. 4, Op. 51, but within that time a remarkable degree of stylistic maturation, not to mention an impression of increased self-confidence, took place, revealing a new and far more individual compositional persona. While not wholly free of trace influences, the symphony displays with effortless mastery what would prove to be a distinctive language that—notwithstanding its great diversity of both form and expression—is coherent, personal, and identifiable from work to work. James H. North has called Persichetti "a twentieth-century Haydn,"[177] and no work exemplifies this more than the Symphony No. 4, in many ways the quintessential Neo-Classical symphony, and one of the composer's most successful orchestral compositions. But Persichetti's Neo-Classicism was more than the mere adoption of a few devices from Stravinsky. Composed at approximately the same time as the ambitious and demanding hour-long song cycle *Harmonium*, the Symphony No. 4 is a work brimming with effervescence and the joyful exhilaration of unfettered musical creativity—a profound expression of the aesthetic ideals represented by Haydn and Mozart at their best, displaying a gentle warmth, as well as an almost childlike playfulness and exuberance. (Composer and former Persichetti-student John Melby recalls that his teacher expressed a great fondness for Beethoven's Symphony No. 4, and filled his own Fourth with subtle references to that work.[178]) There is nary a superfluous, heavy-handed, or rhetorical note in the entire symphony. Virtually devoid of what is generally thought of as "drama," the work, lightly and transparently scored throughout, maintains a placid and moderate level of affect, rarely rising above a *mezzo-forte*. Its most strenuous moments are essentially outbursts of joy.

Like Beethoven's Fourth, Persichetti's Fourth opens with a slow, solemn introduction that proves to be the weightiest music of the entire work, while introducing the primary thematic material. The introduction is followed by a lively *Allegro* in *sonata-allegro* form, which sparkles with a playful, exuberant sense of elation. The second movement, *Andante*, is a tender, gentle, and balletic *rondo*—an impishly wistful and deceptively simple burlesque, its obvious reminiscences of Stravinsky turned to warmer expressive purposes. The third movement, *Allegretto*, is a gracious and whimsical intermezzo, while the finale, *Presto*, is a brilliant whirlwind in perpetual motion, masterfully recalling most of the work's thematic material with a joie de vivre that is irresistibly exhilarating, while providing a delightful showcase for a virtuoso orchestra. In this work, as in the contemporaneous First Harpsichord Sonata, Persichetti had discovered the expressive possibilities of a harmonic language more consonant than his previous norm, as well as more clearly rooted in tonality. He achieved this by employing pure triads—often not tonally related—as well as clearly triadic polychords, while devising motifs based on the interval of the third.

Like its predecessor, Persichetti's Symphony No. 4 was launched by Eugene Ormandy and the Philadelphia Orchestra, this one in December 1954; they made a brilliant, virtuosic recording shortly thereafter. This was its only recorded representation for many years (and was eventually reissued on compact disc in 1998), although additional recordings appeared in 2003 and 2005.

Initial critical reactions to the work seem to suggest some confusion about its remarkably straightforward, unpretentious aesthetic intentions. According to Max de Schauensee, "Inspiration or deep emotion doesn't seem to blow its breath through Mr. Persichetti's symphony. Judging from a single hearing one would say that the composer was more interested in sonorities and combinations of instruments than in any urgent or dire necessity of communicating a message or an attitude."[179] Olin Downes seemed to go out of his way to find fault, complaining, "It is a symphony elaborately planned, but in fact it comes out in bits, skillfully juxtaposed, but not convincingly woven together. The writing is skillful but fussed. The carrying over of thematic material from one movement to another does not remove the impression of patchwork—here a lovely bit of color, there an ingenious contrapuntal detail; yet, in general, the impression of a good deal of ado over little that is essential."[180] Composer-critic Lester Trimble (later to become an eloquent advocate of Persichetti's music) begrudgingly acknowledged that "its four movements are well balanced off against each other in terms of dynamic and tempo character, and the work is, in general, notable for a light-hearted sort of energy." But he seemed to resent the work's light and breezy character, which he confused with superficiality, finding the thematic materials to be

> less impressive than their orchestral treatment, however, and in the scherzo-like 6/8 *Allegro* which follows a rather Tchaikovskian introduction, an air of coyness and superficiality prevails. These qualities are carried over into the second movement, which evolves around a ballet type of theme. The *Allegretto*—again aiming at speedy grace—begins and ends with a Tchaikovskian section and, in its middle, seems a bit "crafted." The final *Presto* is a sort of *perpetuum mobile*, alternating with sections of material restated from previous movements. It, like the other fast movements, is very sleek in its orchestral usage.[181]

Similar reactions appeared as late as 1988, when John Rockwell, a consistent foe of the American traditionalists, wrote, following a performance of the Fourth Symphony in New York, "Persichetti falls victim . . . to a penchant for brisk superficiality, but this is music that epitomizes the strengths as well as the blander weaknesses of the mid-century American symphonic school."[182]

Nevertheless, other critics seemed to grasp the work's intentions immediately. While acknowledging that "harmonically speaking, Persichetti does not do too much skirmishing ahead of the advance guard," Edwin H. Schloss commented, "It is music of considerable originality, vitality and charm, and it is skillfully written."[183] Perhaps the most perceptive assessment was provided by Alfred Frankenstein, who, in reviewing the recording, benefited from multiple hearings. He found the work "an essentially blithe affair; it erupts now and then with a brassy, Sibelian blare to remind us that it is a symphony, but these outbursts do not seriously affect the tonic, zestful, effervescent flow of Persichetti's ideas. It is the kind of music that is written by composers who delight in technical problems and who manage to convey in their music the intellectual and emotional pleasure they derive from finding their solution."[184]

In 1953, two years after its predecessor, Persichetti completed his Symphony No. 5, Op. 61, "Symphony for Strings." One of the composer's masterpieces, this dense, concentrated, and challenging work appeared about the same time as such simple pieces as the *Little Piano Book*, the Serenade No. 8, and the Piano Sonatinas Nos. 4–6. The symphony was one of the many works that had been commissioned by the Louisville Philharmonic Society and is one of the finest to emerge from that ambitious series.

Persichetti's Fifth Symphony differs from the Fourth as radically as the Fourth differs from the Third. It pursues a formal approach similar to that adopted in the Concerto for Piano, Four Hands, composed the previous year, and in the Quintet for Piano and Strings, composed the following year. All three are among the composer's most significant and fully realized works: Each comprises a single, multisectional movement, based entirely on one thematic idea presented at the outset. By this time Persichetti had achieved a fully formed compositional identity. If his Third Symphony was something of an echo of Schuman's Third, his Fifth Symphony leaves Schuman's Fifth (also a symphony for strings, composed in 1943) far behind. It is not simply a matter of accomplishing both unity and diversity: The work's concentrated, tightly focused development of purely musical ideas, articulated with concision, achieves a sense of continuous progression and coherence that exceeds the accomplishment of the elder composer, leaving the listener fully gratified yet eager for an ever-fuller absorption and comprehension of its totality. Interestingly, Persichetti's own program notes refer to the work's single movement as subdivided into five sections,[185] although the structural analysis that appears in Dorothea's monograph identifies six sections.[186]

A generally stern character prevails throughout the work, although there are passages of tenderness, warmth, and exuberance as well. It opens with a fifteen-measure theme played by the violas in unison, severe in tone, and including all twelve chromatic notes within its first five measures. As the composition unfolds, the enormous potential of this theme is explored through a series of linked episodes contrasting in tempo and character, but all intricately related to the opening viola theme. Much of the development within this work is contrapuntal; there are few works in which the composer demonstrates so amply his consummate mastery of this technique. Within the main viola theme, Dorothea identifies two specific motifs that drive the developmental course: (a) a falling seventh followed by an ascending tritone, and (b) a falling third. The presentation of the viola theme, marked *Sostenuto*, builds to a state of intense emotional duress, until it reaches a high C-natural, underlined by an A-major triad in the cellos and basses. This point of great tension is released by slashing contrapuntal lines, largely atonal in effect, that culminate in the first of several violin solos that serve as transitions. A calm passage follows, marked *Piacevole*, which develops the (a) motif contrapuntally and polytonally but in a more relaxed, benign manner.

The energy soon begins to build again through *stretto* passages of imitative counterpoint, eventually attaining another apex of dissonant intensity, which is released with tremendous rhythmic energy at the onset of the second main section, *Allegro agitato*, another representative example of the "Persichetti 2/4." This section focuses chiefly on the (b) motif, with some attention to the (a) motif as well, both of which are developed in vigorous counterpoint. A particularly interesting feature of this section is a return of most of the opening viola theme, now played *Con fuoco*, its rhythm and texture transformed to virtual unrecognizability.

Finally, another stabilizing violin solo leads to the third main section, *Adagio sereno*. In this section, the intervals of the (a) motif are altered to create a more tonal melody, although it is harmonized chromatically and polytonally, while the (b) material is treated more melodically as well. This section offers some of the symphony's most tender, lyrical moments. A passage marked *Andante* follows, beginning with a chromatic line in the solo violin, followed by contrapuntal entrances by other solo strings. This is where Persichetti indicates the beginning of the fourth main section, whereas Dorothea considers the fourth section to begin with what she terms "the chorale," marked *Tranquillo*. This is a transformation of both motifs into a simple diatonic melody, which is examined through a series of different harmonizations. An angular transitional passage brings back the harsh, less tonal language, leading to a surging passage, marked *Molto appassionato*, which is where Dorothea identifies the beginning of the fifth main section. This is interrupted by a return of the diatonic melodic variant.

The return of the surging music leads to an *Allegro agitato*, another "Persichetti 2/4," which is where the composer identifies the beginning of the fifth main section. This is a very active and busy section, which includes a triadic apotheosis of the diatonic melodic motif, a highly jagged developmental passage, followed by an intense, chromatic, contrapuntal treatment of the main motifs, leading to a return of the surging music from the previous section. A passage marked *Vigoroso* continues to increase the level of intensity, toward a passage marked *Severamente*. This is where Dorothea indicates the arrival of a sixth main section. This is, in many ways, the most stunning portion of this otherwise brilliant work: All the foregoing material—the basic motifs and their variants, in both rhythmic augmentation and diminution—is woven into an intricate texture of invertible counterpoint. As the coda is approached, all the various strands are pulled together, until the work finally glides into a smooth landing in C major.

Some writers have spoken of Persichetti's music from the 1950s as a regression into a more consonant, tonal language.[187] But the fact is that compositions like the Symphony for Strings, the Concerto for Piano, Four Hands, and other major works from this period are no less atonal or contrapuntally rigorous than the most challenging pieces of the 1940s, such as the Piano Sonata No. 4 or the *King Lear* Septet. The difference is that the pieces from the 1950s exhibit a gracefulness and ease, a thoroughgoing structural cohesiveness and coherence, and a kinetically invigorating rhythmic sense not always present in the earlier music, which at times seems ungainly and harsh, relative to its apparent expressive content.

Persichetti's Symphony No. 5 had its premiere in August 1954, with Robert Whitney conducting the Louisville Orchestra. It was recorded three months later by these same forces, and issued shortly thereafter on LP. William Mootz described the symphony with remarkable acuity:

> The entire work germinates from a rhapsodic viola melody that appears at the very outset of the piece. Its outer sections fairly bristle with health and exuberant spirits. A serene middle section, in which the composer pits solo instruments against the string family as a whole, is wonderfully rich and full-bodied in sound. This passage is the heart of the work, and is an interlude of arresting beauty from beginning to end. The entire symphony, however, is abstract music of the most forthright sort, and it won enthusiastic support from yesterday's audience.[188]

Dorothea quoted a comment from the demanding composer-critic Arthur Berger, who wrote of the symphony in the *Saturday Review*, "What it lacks in stylistic distinction it makes up in vital musicianship. Persichetti is headed in the direction of the ranks of our best American composers."[189] Reviewing a 1959 performance by the Philadelphia Orchestra, conducted by Eugene Ormandy, Max de Schauensee commented that "the composer had something to say and said it with nobility of thought and the smoothness of technique for which he is noted. The symphony proved a remarkably serious, often beautiful and moving work, which found favor with the large audience."[190]

The Symphony for Strings has proven to be one of Persichetti's most enduring critical successes, although it does not appear frequently on concert programs. The admittedly scrappy Louisville performance remained the work's sole recorded representation until 1990, when a compact disc was issued featuring the Philadelphia Orchestra, conducted by Riccardo Muti.

However, a comparison of these two performances is illuminating: Not even the rich, full-bodied sonority and meticulous precision of one of the world's great string sections can compensate for Muti's meager understanding of the musical dynamics of this work. The result, especially the first of the two *Allegro agitato* sections, sounds dull and routine. The comparison also reveals just what a brilliant musical interpreter Robert Whitney was. Certainly, bringing to life a work with no performance history, no precedent on which to build, is one of the great challenges for an interpreter—a challenge easy to overlook since it is faced infrequently by the more celebrated musical interpreters. Scrappy though the Louisville strings may have been in such a demanding work, Whitney's conception conveys its expressive impetus to an extent that far exceeds Muti's grasp. James H. North attempted to be fair-minded, noting, "Each may be a legitimate view of the symphony, but my heart lies with Louisville." Discussing the work itself, he found it

> an incredibly complex web of harmony and counterpoint, all built from one long opening theme. . . . Rhythms are mostly regular and incessant, in the Persichetti manner, and sonorities are constantly changing, as the five basic lines are sometimes divided, subdivided, and reunited in the course of a few measures. . . . What results is a nineteen-minute intellectual tour de force, but also a potent expression of pure music, knotty in the literal sense of being tightly bound together at every point, in every direction. It is the essence of pure Persichetti.[191]

Fortunately, the Louisville recording was reissued on compact disc in 2005. Reviewing this release, David Lewis described the work as "biting and difficult" but also "dramatically quite coherent, never straying far from its purpose," concluding that it should appeal to listeners who enjoy Bernard Herrmann's music for the film *Psycho*, while speculating that Herrmann may well have had Persichetti's work in mind when he composed that famous score.[192]

It is interesting to observe the inability of many celebrated and respected conductors to understand even a work as clearly rooted in musical tradition as this one, raising serious questions as to their capacity for interpreting music that has not come to them "predigested," as it were. For example, when Carlo Maria Giulini included Persichetti's Fifth on his national tour with the Chicago Symphony during the 1975–1976 season, he deleted the first *Allegro agitato* section altogether, proceeding from the slow introduction directly into the *Adagio sereno*. Such gross disfigurement—done without the composer's permission—clearly proclaims Giulini's utter obliviousness to both the work's formal structure and its dramatic shape. The program notes accompanying these performances made no mention of the fact that what was heard was a total truncation of the symphony.

Persichetti followed his Symphony for Strings with a symphony for wind band. By 1955, he had already written several successful pieces for this medium. That year he was approached by Clark Mitze, the director of bands at Washington University in St. Louis, with a commission for an eight-minute piece. Persichetti accepted the offer, but soon thereafter informed Mitze that the piece "had gotten out of hand" and proposed the idea of a full-length symphony for band.[193] The university accepted his proposal and doubled the commissioning fee. The resulting work has proven to be Persichetti's best known and most often performed symphony by far, and probably his single most widely admired composition as well. An undisputed classic of the symphonic band repertoire, it stands along with its predecessor, the Symphony for Strings, as two of the greatest American symphonies of the mid-twentieth century.

Persichetti completed his Symphony No. 6, Op. 69, in 1956. In it he returned to the Neo-Classicism of his Fourth Symphony but with a somewhat more streamlined and concise approach: The result is a four-movement work of little more than a quarter-hour duration. Like the Fourth, the Sixth begins with a slow, Haydnesque introduction, *Adagio*, that introduces the work's three main motifs: (a) a three-note idea consisting of a falling fifth and a rising sixth; (b) a stepwise ascent, then descent; and (c) a chorale-like motif built on a series of thirds. Following suggestions found in correspondence from Frederick Fennell during the early 1950s,[194] the composer enlarged both the size and the role of the percussion section, as is evident right from the introduction. The first movement is a loose *sonata-allegro* design, although motivic development starts virtually immediately, and there is nothing approaching a literal recapitulation. As the *Allegro* begins, Theme 1, based on motif (b), is introduced rhythmically in the percussion section, before it is picked up by the woodwinds. Soon motif (a) is incorporated into the developmental activity. Motif (c) plays the role of a Theme 2. The *Allegro* proceeds without interruption as the three motifs are developed with a profoundly dynamic energy. Although the motifs are simple and tonal, their development involves considerable polytonal dissonance, all of which contributes to the movement's prevailing character of joyful exuberance. After a large climax, the movement comes to a subdued conclusion. The second movement, *Adagio sostenuto*—the first to be composed—is a touchingly poignant chorale prelude based on a hymn entitled "Round Me Falls the Night," taken from Persichetti's newly completed *Hymns and Responses for the Church Year*. The third movement, *Allegretto*, is a genial *intermezzo* based on a lilting, slightly folk-like melody. (Examination of Persichetti's sketches indicates that this melody was originally intended for inclusion in an early draft of the 1953 work *Pageant*.[195]) There is a central *trio* section of markedly different character, with rapid shifts in rhythm and texture, and greater harmonic dissonance. The finale, *Vivace*, is a classic example of the "Persichetti 2/4." The movement suggests the feeling of a briskly invigorating march in *rondo* form, in which virtually all the symphony's motifs are subjected to intensive, yet seemingly effortless, development, culminating in an exhilarating apotheosis of complex counterpoint, somewhat like the final section of the Fifth Symphony. The work finally concludes on a plangent, strategically scored harmonic sonority containing all twelve notes—a usage that reappeared in a number of Persichetti's subsequent works.

Persichetti's Symphony for Band may be cited as the quintessence of the American Neo-Classical style, constructed with the utmost concision, organic unity, and economy of means and purpose, conveying a sense of revelry in the joyful exercise of compositional virtuosity. A favorite of the young people who comprise most band musicians, the work, with its enthusiasm, warmth, and playfulness, may be said to epitomize youth itself, at its most endearing. Indeed, it is perhaps a more artistically successful composition than the Fourth Symphony, as the hard-edged crispness, freshness, and clarity of winds and percussion is better suited to the composer's musical persona than the richly blended sonority that arises when strings are added to the ensemble. (One may then reasonably ask what makes the Fifth Symphony such a superbly satisfying work. One explanation is that the Fifth is abstract in its focus, rather than a showcase for effects of sonority. There the string section functions as an abstract medium, analogous to the traditional string quartet, successfully communicating the work's motivic development and contrapuntal interplay. This is also why the less-than-perfect ensemble-playing of the Louisville strings doesn't really mar its impact.)

The first performance of Persichetti's Symphony No. 6 took place in April 1956 at the Music Educators National Conference, which met in St. Louis that year. Clark Mitze conducted the Washington University band. The work's reputation spread quickly, and further performances took place throughout the country. Critical comments in response to its first performance in New York City, where the composer himself conducted the Goldman Band, offered cautiously faint praise, while displaying some discomfort with the medium: "The Symphony has a kind of expressivity that is never of the emotional type, but it does possess a candor and a measure of warmth. What its creator is trying to say is anybody's guess. And it is quite possible that he isn't trying to say anything special at all, but merely making what turned out to be fairly palatable music, which he apparently does easily enough."[196] Edward Downes found the music "inviting, with jaunty rhythms not unrelated to jazz in its first and last movements. It has beguiling melodic flow in its slow movement. Its themes are cunningly developed. And it is orchestrated . . . with Mr. Persichetti's customary fine sense of color and balance."[197] Critical appreciation of the work grew as its reputation spread. Less than twenty years later, Lester Trimble expressed himself somewhat more expansively: "The Persichetti Symphony clearly and dynamically presents an American rhythmic and melodic ethos, with instrumentation ranging from one end of the color chart to the other."[198]

The first recording of Persichetti's Symphony No. 6 was an auspicious one: The Eastman Symphonic Wind Ensemble (ESWE), under the guidance of its visionary founder Frederick Fennell, had been pursuing a project directed at the general public to record serious works originally composed for band in performances of professional caliber. Two compositions by Persichetti had already been included in this series. In 1959, the ESWE presented a brilliant performance of the Symphony No. 6, bringing nationwide attention to the work and its composer. This recording has been reissued many times over the years; still available today on compact disc, it continues to be held in high regard. Other recordings quickly followed, many of them featuring college ensembles, with only limited availability to the general public. Patterson's book, published in 1988, lists more than twenty-five different recordings of the work,[199] and more have followed since that date. Among the finest that have been released into the commercial market are another under Fennell's direction, this time featuring the Tokyo Kosei Wind Ensemble; a performance by the Cincinnati Wind Symphony, conducted by Eugene Migliaro Corporon; one by the IUP Wind Ensemble, conducted by Jack Stamp; and one featuring the U.S. Marine Band, conducted by Timothy W. Foley.

Not unrelated to the success of the Sixth Symphony in St. Louis, in 1957 the St. Louis Symphony Orchestra offered Persichetti a commission to write a symphony in commemoration of the orchestra's eightieth anniversary. He responded with the Symphony No. 7, Op. 80, subtitled "Liturgical," completing the work in 1958, in between two other compositions of markedly different character: the Serenade No. 10 for flute and harp and the String Quartet No. 3.

One of Persichetti's distinctive compositional practices, already touched upon, was a propensity to cross-reference aspects of some works within others. This was not simply a matter of devising similar thematic ideas or of the accidental reappearance of a recognizable phrase, but rather, the conscious re-use of ideas from one work for the purpose of developing them in a different way in another. Nothing served him better for this purpose than the *Hymns and Responses for the Church Year*, the first volume of which he completed in 1955. (This collection is discussed in greater detail elsewhere in this chapter.) In composing his Seventh Symphony, subtitled, "Liturgical," Persichetti drew all the thematic material from some fifteen different selections found in this hymnal (and in its sequel, a volume II published posthumously).

Symphony No. 7 comprises five distinct movements, played without interruption. At nine minutes, the first movement, *Lento*, is by far the longest. As it begins, the work's primary thematic idea is gradually introduced—a prayer, "Who Art One God, One Lord" (No. 58 in *Hymns and Responses*, volume II), first played in full by the horn, later joined by trumpet. Serving as a sort of *cantus firmus*, this melody is related motivically to several of the other hymn melodies. Characterized by alternating major and minor thirds, it also creates an "indecisiveness that functions as an harmonic irritant throughout the symphony."[200] Through a sequence of sections varied in mood and attitude, this movement develops the prayer theme in conjunction with several other responses found in the hymnal. However, as it unfolds, much of this section is rather dry and lacks a clear, strong sense of direction. The second movement, *Allegro*, is violently agitated and voraciously developmental, while always remaining under tight emotional control. It is based chiefly on the primary thematic idea—especially the major-minor conflict—combined with the response, "The Lord is in His holy temple" (No. 59 in *Hymns and Responses*, volume II). The *Andante* movement is based largely on the E. E. Cummings Christmas hymn, "purer than purest pure whisper of whisper so" (No. 5 in *Hymns and Responses*, volume I). The tender, tonal lyricism of this melody led Dorothea to describe this section as the "true melodic core and heart of the work."[201] This melody is later combined with the Padraic Colum hymn, "Now in the tomb is laid," and then with the response, "Heaven's light forever shines" (Nos. 12 and 27 in *Hymns and Responses*, volume I). Perhaps the most thrilling portion of the symphony is the *Vivace* that follows. This movement presents a vigorous fugal treatment of Wallace Stevens's Evening response, "We say God and the imagination are one" (No. 26 in *Hymns and Responses*, volume I). (A surprising moment occurs toward the end of this movement, when there is a triumphant octave leap of a major triad with fifth on top—a gesture used so frequently by Schuman in his finales that it is a virtual trademark.)

As in the Fifth and Sixth Symphonies, there is an exhilarating epiphany of developmental brilliance as most of the work's motifs are reviewed contrapuntally, culminating in a bracing polytonal harmonization of the Easter hymn, "The gates of death are broken through" (No. 14 in *Hymns and Responses*, volume I). The symphony ends with a brief, subdued *Adagio*—perhaps the most spiritually inspiring portion of the symphony—based on a sequence of "Amens" from *Hymns and Responses*, volume I. As the work concludes, its elements gradually melt away; as the thirds of the tonic triad drop out, the major-minor conflict is resolved, leaving only a perfect fifth.

Surprising in a work of Persichetti's maturity, the influence of William Schuman is remarkably apparent throughout the symphony. This may be in part because the focus on major-minor conflict results in harmonic usages frequently favored by the older composer; but one also notes the free, nontonal use of triads and even the sort of chattering winds so peculiar to Schuman. Although the hymn melodies themselves are mostly diatonic and tonal, the work's basic harmonic language is freely atonal, as in the Fifth Symphony, while key centers are reaffirmed at structural junctures. During Persichetti's lifetime, a number of commentators found his compositional persona to be "cold"; there are portions of this work where such a characterization may be justified. But perhaps what is most notable about the Liturgical Symphony is that despite its subtitle and its source material, its basic character displays little convincing sense of spirituality, ecstatic or otherwise. Much of it is solemn and severe in tone, and—as with most of the composer's music—largely abstract and formal in its concerns, manipulating its material masterfully but with a cool detachment; indeed, the livelier sections are downright secular in their high-strung dynamic energy. (Interestingly, while religious music forms a not insignificant portion of Persichetti's output, those works tend to be among his most expressively reserved—perhaps, even constrained—compositions, as discussed in the section dealing with his choral music.)

Persichetti's Symphony No. 7 was first performed by the St. Louis Symphony Orchestra, under the direction of Edouard van Remoortel, in October 1959. The work was well received by local critics. Representative comments are these from the *St. Louis Post-Dispatch*:

[T]he superior craftsmanship of the music was reinforced by expressive melodic elements, strong harmonies of varying degrees of dissonance and a steady momentum at all speeds. The composer uses the orchestral medium with apparent ease and sureness of touch. . . . [H]e has synthesized the several features of twentieth century music, but he has also retained a connection with the musical culture of the last 300 years. So Mr. Persichetti shows a deep awareness of human psychology when he carries over elements of traditional musical language into his synthesis. It enables him to set up contrasts between major and minor tonalities and between points of tension and points of repose. By judicious injections of old fashioned triads he can produce an emotional effect that is not limited to a mere acoustical impact. At the same time his language is sufficiently advanced to allow further exploration of combinations that may bring a new realm of values, not yet realized, into a general musical speech.[202]

The first New York performance of the symphony elicited reservations as well as praise from some of the critics. Howard Klein felt that the music "was skillfully set forth and clearly evoked many moods, from the subdued pathos and restraint of the opening *Lento* to a kind of straight-faced gaiety of the two fast sections. . . . Perhaps it was the subtitle that made one yearn for a stronger, more personal statement than what emerged as the work closed. For one's impression at the close was one of unfulfilled promise."[203] John Gruen noted, "Though not particularly religious in character, the symphony moves from slow, broadly conceived hymnal passages, to exhilarating and rhythmically propelled movements, suggesting all the turmoils of fire and brimstone. The composer is never short on ideas, and they spring directly in line with aesthetic consideration. He is never lured by the dazzling possibilities of technique for its own sake, but allows his skill to be put entirely to the service of meaning and intent."[204] Michael Brozen expressed the reservation that the piece "gives no sense of recovering material once it has been stated; the listener is led on to constantly new ground. While original and admirable in itself, this does give the work, on first hearing, a feeling of unfulfillment which closer acquaintance might eradicate. One hopes so, for the piece has much that is distinctive and compelling."[205]

Although the Seventh Symphony has subsequently been performed several times, it did not appear on recording until 2005, when it was issued, along with Nos. 3 and 4, in a performance by the Albany Symphony Orchestra under the direction of David Alan Miller.

Persichetti composed his Symphony No. 8, Op. 106, in 1967, on a commission from the Baldwin-Wallace Conservatory. The work, which appeared around the time he was becoming absorbed in his series of *Parables*, harks back to the Neo-Classicism of the Symphonies Nos. 4 and 6, although here his basic thematic material is considerably more chromatic and his harmonic language more acerbic than in those two earlier works. Its somewhat detached, impersonal character recalls the Seventh Symphony, although its gestural language resembles that found in the earlier symphonies. Also reminiscent of its predecessor is the rather lengthy opening movement, comprising a substantial introduction, *Adagio*, followed by a lively *Allegro grazioso*.

The work's strongly classical manner is clear from the start, with an opening that recalls early Beethoven. The introduction presents the motivic elements that will shape the thematic material of the entire symphony, appearing in different guises in each movement. The most significant of these elements are a descending perfect fourth and an ascending motif outlining a major-seventh, before a return descent. A portentous tone is evoked, as these motifs are explored, developed, and gradually shaped into more elaborate thematic ideas. The ensuing *Allegro* follows a clear *sonata-allegro* design. But instead of the high-spirited exuberance of the respective first movements of Symphonies 4 and 6, this *Allegro grazioso* might be more accurately characterized as gently amiable, its energy relatively subdued and understated, its playfulness rather whimsical in tone. Imitative counterpoint and polytonal harmony both play strong roles in the movement's development before it reaches a quiet, if somewhat impish, repose. The second movement, *Andante sostenuto*, is chiefly an evocation of mood, drawing somewhat on the manner with which Copland sought to evoke feelings of loneliness. The movement unfolds quite slowly, its relatively unresolved, dissonant harmonic language and attenuated sense of tonal center conveying a mood of bleak, searching uneasiness. A stark contrast is provided by the brief third movement, *Allegretto*. This movement suggests the spirit of a *Ländler*, albeit one of boisterous, *giocoso* character, without intimations of either Schubert or Mahler. A trio section pursues a somewhat more lyrical course. The finale, *Vivace*, is the most characteristic and immediately compelling movement of the symphony, the exhilarating vitality of its approach to the "Persichetti 2/4" recalling the respective finales of Symphonies 4 and 6. As in the Symphonies 5, 6, and 7, shortly before the end most of the work's thematic material is reviewed and combined contrapuntally in a tour de force of technical mastery, leading to a decisive conclusion on a twelve-note chord.

Despite the infectious energy of the finale, the Symphony No. 8 is perhaps one of the composer's less artistically successful efforts, resorting to many devices used more effectively and with greater freshness in previous works. It may even be guilty of the charge, frequently leveled unfairly at Persichetti, of exalting technique for its own sake, and lacking convincing expressive content. Like a number of his works from the 1940s, the severity of its harmonic language seems disproportionate to the weight of its expressive content. Although its sense of tonal center is no more attenuated than that of the Fifth Symphony, the musical content and its treatment in that work feel thoroughly integrated and congruent, whereas the austerity of the harmonic language in the later work seems at odds with its intended expressive effect.

Persichetti's Symphony No. 8 was first performed in October 1967 in Berea, Ohio, by the Baldwin-Wallace Conservatory Orchestra, conducted by George Poinar. The work was recorded in 1970 by the Louisville Orchestra under the direction of Jorge Mester. That recording was reissued on compact disc in 2005. Critical response to the symphony was divided. Reviewing the published score together with that of a contemporaneous symphony by Roger Sessions, Richard Swift commented, "At first blush, Vincent Persichetti's Symphony No. 8 seems less consequential than the Sessions work, for its use of the pure color of the instrumental choirs masks with those cool intensities its structural depths and balances that are revealed upon deepening acquaintance."[206] He then goes on to elaborate some of those "structural depths and balances." On the other hand, after a performance of the work in New York City, John Rockwell dismissed it predictably as "an occasionally noisy, occasionally contemplative half-hour of latter-day American symphonic writing, earnestly neo-classical and rather cumbersome in its barrage of percussion."[207]

Persichetti's final symphony is also his most complex and challenging work in that form. The Symphony No. 9, "Sinfonia: Janiculum," Op. 113, was written in 1969–1970, while the composer was in residence in Rome, on the second of his three Guggenheim Fellowships. Eugene Ormandy had selected Persichetti to be the recipient of a commission from the estate of Alexander Hilsberg to compose a work on behalf of the Philadelphia Orchestra, in memory of the late concertmaster and associate conductor. Persichetti composed "Sinfonia: Janiculum" shortly after completing his magnum opus, *The Creation*. Eugene Ormandy conducted the Philadelphia Orchestra in the premiere, which took place in March 1971, and in the work's first recording, which was released later that same year, together with William Schuman's Ninth, "Le Fosse Ardeatine."

Persichetti composed his Ninth Symphony at the Villa Aurelia, now the site of the American Academy in Rome. The villa sits on the summit of the Janiculum, Rome's highest hill. This is the simplest explanation for the work's subtitle. According to program notes by John Briggs, "As the composer worked on his new score at the Villa Aurelia, he could hear the sound of bells from a small church, the Chiesa di San Pietro sul Gianicolo several hundred feet below. The theme of the San Pietro chimes is incorporated into the score." However, Briggs goes on to present a more philosophical interpretation of the work's meaning, but whether these thoughts stem from the composer himself or whether they represent Briggs's own ideas is not clear. It has become axiomatic that music is incapable of expressing philosophical ideas, although for centuries composers have attempted to do just that. These efforts have at times resulted in satisfying musical works, but their philosophical pretensions have served at best only as motivation for the composer. Nevertheless, since Persichetti presumably approved these notes, they are included here for the reader's consideration:

> The symphony is a meditation in music on the meaning of existence. What is the origin of life? What is its beginning, and what is its end? Is the door opening or closing? That is why the composer entitled it *Janiculum*. Janus, the Roman deity for whom both the Janiculum Hill and the month of January were named, was the ancient "god of the gateway." In Roman paintings and sculpture he is depicted as having two faces, looking in opposite directions. Facing two ways Janus symbolizes every beginning and every ending. Looking in opposite directions to right and left, he faces the male and female principles, the active and the passive, the comic and the tragic. . . . The vigorously affirmative conclusion [of the symphony] depicts in music the conviction that the door is opening, not closing, and that man can conquer.[208]

The symphony comprises a single movement subdivided into four continuous sections. The overall musical language is largely atonal, with some use of serial procedures adapted to the composer's needs, although, for the most part, he avoids the sort of fragmentary, pointillistic gestures found in the Piano Sonata No. 11, Harpsichord Sonata No. 10, and *Shima B'koli* for organ. Resembling more closely such works as the *Parable IX* for band, the symphony suggests an abstract narrative conveyed through the continuous development of musical gestures. It is richly orchestrated, with generous use of a large percussion section. However, lacking overt emotional cues, the work may require repeated exposure before the lucidity of its ideas and the depth of its expressive impetus are apparent. The opening section, *Misterioso*, seems to begin from ether, conveying a primordial impression suggestive of the beginning of time. With little discernable sense of meter, it gradually accumulates intensity through long, atonal melodies placed against a highly dissonant harmonic backdrop, until it reaches a state of considerable duress. Consistent with Persichetti's customary process of musical growth, the opening moments introduce source material that will generate most of the work's musical substance. In this case the fundamental element is the interval of the minor-second, in all its permutations: ascending, descending, as major-seventh, minor-ninth (through octave displacement), and so on; its most frequently encountered gesture is a descending minor-second, often repeated. The second section is marked *Allegro articolato*. Its strong sense of pulse and vigorous imitative counterpoint provide a clarity and regularity reminiscent of the composer's earlier work, despite the tenuous sense of tonality. The third section, *Cantabile*, is strongly lyrical, with soaring, highly chromatic melodic lines. After several rapid tempo changes the final section, *Vivace*, settles into a strong rhythmic pulse, with brilliant counterpoint reminiscent of the second section. Considerable excitement is generated as the work develops with an ever-lucid complexity, achieving finality with a powerful eleven-tone chord. Despite its consistently attenuated tonality, the work is structured to begin and end with a tonal anchor of E.

Reviewing the Philadelphia premiere, James Felton seemed to have no trouble grasping the work, writing, "As is usually the case with Persichetti, his new symphony is to be enjoyed in the here and now, apocalyptic visions notwithstanding. Its fragments of theme are woven into a bittersweet tissue of sound, scurrying along and turning light and dark by turn. . . . His symphony is listenable, enjoyable and most palatable. Whether it will stand the test of time is beside the point. The composer writes to be understood in his own time, and once again he has succeeded."[209] Daniel Webster was somewhat less enthusiastic, describing the symphony as "a strongly crafted work of considerable color and range of expression. Single instruments take major roles and there is even a kind of cadenza for the ensemble. . . . What seemed missing was a strong line of direction linking the splendid sections."[210]

Several days later the Philadelphia Orchestra introduced the work to New York audiences. Reviewing that performance, Allen Hughes acknowledged some difficulty in penetrating the symphony's challenging surface, although he blamed the composer, describing it as "rather short on vitality and excitement. . . . The 20-minute work is filled with colorful scoring, but the music seemed more like a compendium of musical remarks and exclamations than a presentation of interesting musical ideas worked out in a compelling manner. This listener had the feeling that throughout the work the composer was searching for a theme that he could get his teeth into and that he never found it."[211] Perhaps the most perceptive and thoughtful reaction was expressed by the composer-critic Lester Trimble, whose review of the recording benefited from the opportunity for multiple hearings. Now far more sympathetic than he was toward the composer's earlier work, he seemed to accept the symphony's philosophical intentions, commenting that it

> has an exceedingly strong rhythmic impulse throughout, and this is especially important in the fast sections. The work does not seem to be one that depends for its primary impulse on formal expressive means. It is rather a through-composed composition, one of very subtle internal organization, with the intent and the impact of a philosophical tone-poem. . . . Persichetti's use of the orchestra . . . blends the sensuous and ideational possibilities of that largest of all instruments, using chromaticism, dissonance, and consonance in ways only a master can, convincing the listener that these musical manipulations are not just sophisticated expertise, but rather a way of postulating a sober philosophical statement. Stimulated by the enigma of the Roman god Janus, whose two faces look in opposite directions, Persichetti has posed himself a number of questions: What is life's beginning, and what is its end? Is the door opening or closing? For the answers I refer you to Persichetti's provocative symphony.[212]

Unfortunately the Philadelphia Orchestra's recording of "Sinfonia: Janiculum" was deleted from the RCA Victor catalog after just a few years; as of this writing, it has never been reissued on compact disc.

Other Works for Orchestra

As previously noted, the symphony orchestra was not Persichetti's primary medium for creative expression. In fact, aside from his nine symphonies, he composed relatively few works for orchestra, and most of them are of lesser significance within his output, although few are trivial, and some have considerable appeal.

In 1942, upon completing his Symphonies Nos. 1 and 2, Persichetti composed *Dance Overture*, Op. 20. With a duration of approximately nine minutes, it is the only light and lively "curtain-raiser" in his orchestral catalog. In its relatively straightforward application of *sonata-allegro* form, this exuberant piece is simple and direct in effect, embracing a pan-diatonic language strongly influenced by the "folksy" evocations of rural Americana developed by Harris and Copland. In this it resembles such other contemporaneous works as the *Pastoral*, Op. 21, for woodwind quintet, and the Piano Sonata No. 3, Op. 22. Perhaps its most notable features are its tightly developmental construction, the elaborate fugue that appears during the development section, and a rather unexpected final cadence.

Persichetti's *Dance Overture* won the 1943 Juilliard Publication Award (predating his association with the Juilliard School). The piece was presented in several informal readings—one by the New York Philharmonic, another by the Eastman-Rochester Symphony Orchestra in 1944. But its first public performance took place in February 1948, when it was played in Tokyo by the Tokyo Symphony Orchestra, under the direction of Hidemaro Konoye.

In 1943 Persichetti completed *Fables*, Op. 23, one of two works he composed for narrator and orchestra. He selected six of Aesop's *Fables*—"The Fox and the Grapes," "The Wolf and the Ass," "The Hare and the Tortoise," "The Cat and the Fox," "A Raven and a Swan," and "The Monkey and the Camel"—although he indicated that the individual movements might be performed in any grouping and in any sequence. He wrote, "The music is an emotional parallel of the ageless tales and the text an integral part of the music; no certain instrument is assigned to any one character, but rather a musical equivalent is given the underlying meaning of the fables."[213] The music again draws upon the composer's simple, diatonic style, although Dorothea Persichetti indicated, "It is not solely for children, nor solely for adults. There are elements of the piece that seem too much for children and others which seem too little for adults. It is clearly scored, contains no Disneyish music-story parallels, is partly for fun and partly 'old fashioned' in its moralism. The stories are some of the very few the composer had read to him as a child. . . . It appears as a somewhat obvious attempt to interest a public. . . . Actually this was not the case. The composer's aim was essentially a search for clarity and direct expression."[214]

The first performance of *Fables* took place in April 1945. Robert Grooters was the narrator, and Eugene Ormandy conducted the Philadelphia Orchestra. Linton Martin found the work to be "deftly scored, apposite and amusing, crisp and compact. While it provides always appropriate setting and commentary for the fables, the music is not too slavishly or insistently pictorial or descriptive. It has pith and point in underscoring and emphasizing the meaning and the moral of each of the fables, and there is engaging diversity of mood. . . . The *Fables* . . . scored quite a popular success."[215]

Persichetti expanded the notion of a musical interpretation of a line of poetry (as in the *Poems for Piano*) in *The Hollow Men*, Op. 25, where he attempted to provide a musical analogue to a larger portion of T. S. Eliot's famous poem of desolation and existential impotence ("This is the way the world ends/Not with a bang but a whimper"). In an interview Persichetti said, "My interest in 'program music' is not one of describing incidents, but of expressing my reactions to incidents. *The Hollow Men* for trumpet and string orchestra is a delicate evocation of T.S. Eliot's lyric poem; it emulates the poet's concentration and simplicity, to create a musical parallel of one's mood just after reading the poem. In the final analysis, programmatic elements in music are irrelevant. Such music is valid only if it can be heard as 'absolute music.'"[216]

Composed in 1944, the eight-minute work is scored for solo trumpet with string orchestra. Despite the use of largely consonant harmony, the strings create a cold, bleak backdrop to the trumpet's expressions of loneliness. The musical language emphasizes the "open" intervals of the fourth and fifth, a usage made familiar by Aaron Copland. In fact, the work's language, scoring, and expressive content cannot help but call to mind Copland's *Quiet City*, composed just four years earlier.

The first performance of *The Hollow Men* took place in Germantown, Pennsylvania, in December 1946. Arthur Bennett Lipkin conducted the Germantown Symphony Orchestra. Although some critics found it an apt reflection of the poem ("Without too obvious an approach, his harmonies suggest the bleakness of the poem, the solo trumpet puncturing the gloom with a gloomy commentary of its own"[217]), others reacted differently ("The reason for the title is not apparent, unless the Eliot poem be taken as a kind of nocturne,"[218] wrote composer-critic Robert. L. Sanders), while Paul Snook felt that "though it is evocative enough in its modestly reflective way, it seems light-years removed from the bitter ironies and grotesque juxtapositions of the classic T. S. Eliot poem which purportedly inspired it."[219] Nevertheless, perhaps because of its ease of execution and the paucity of repertoire for this combination, *The Hollow Men* has become one of Persichetti's most frequently performed works. It was first issued on LP in 1954 in a performance by trumpeter Sidney Baker, with a string orchestra conducted by Izler Solomon, and a number of additional recordings have followed. The string part has been transcribed for piano, as well as organ, and those versions have been recorded repeatedly as well.

Persichetti completed no fewer than eleven works in 1950. Among them were three piano sonatas and three sonatinas. He completed two orchestral works as well, the first in response to a commission from the Louisville Philharmonic Society for a work to be performed by the Louisville Orchestra.

Offered at the recommendation of William Schuman, this was Persichetti's first orchestral commission. The result was the Serenade No. 5, Op. 43. (Persichetti's fifteen serenades for various instrumental combinations are discussed as a group later on in this chapter.) Like most of his serenades, No. 5 comprises six tiny movements, each averaging less than two minutes in duration. Most display the use of polytonality. The movements are entitled "Prelude" (Heavily), "Poem" (Quietly), "Interlude" (Simply), "Capriccio" (Brightly), "Dialogue" (Delicately), and "Burla" (With drive). The work shares much in common with the *Divertimento*, Op. 42, for band, which Persichetti also completed that same year. Each movement is an epigrammatic character-piece; they fall along a spectrum ranging from quietly whimsical to actively playful, somewhat along the lines of the figures found in the work of the painter Paul Klee.

Serenade No. 5 had its premiere in November 1950, when it was presented by the Louisville Orchestra, conducted by Robert Whitney. Whitney later stated, "It is one of the most attractive pieces we have ever commissioned."[220] Dwight Anderson, reviewing the premiere, wrote, "Its six short, contrasting movements have an unlabored eloquence, a quiet wisdom. They form an American 'Children's Corner,' and speak vividly, naively, wittily for us as Debussy spoke for France in his charming Suite."[221] William H. Mootz commented, "The music is concise, frequently lyric, and always unpretentious. The prevailing mood is one of unaffected good humor, and the audience received it warmly."[222]

In 1960 the Louisville Orchestra recorded the work and released it as part of their LP subscription series. That recording was reissued on compact disc in 2005.

The last of Persichetti's works dating from 1950 is a tiny, four-minute orchestral sketch called *Fairy Tale*, Op. 48. Written for a children's concert, the piece suggests the simple, delicate character of a fairy tale but without specifying any narrative content. It is rather like a sonatina for orchestra, opening with a brief English horn solo that leads into a gently wistful, almost Satie-like melody. A lively, playful section follows, with prominent use of the piccolo, before a brief reminiscence of the opening section brings the piece to an end. *Fairy Tale* is a little gem that deserves to be heard more often. It was introduced in March 1951 at a children's concert of the Philadelphia Orchestra, conducted by Alexander Hilsberg.

In 1964 Persichetti composed a short piece for string orchestra, entitled *Introit*, Op. 96, in response to a commission from James Funkhouser on behalf of the Kansas City Youth Symphony. The three-minute piece is solemn, quiet, cool, and contemplative—devoid of any hint of drama. The language is largely triadic, with dissonant counterpoint. Its premiere took place in May

1965. Jack Herriman conducted the Kansas City Youth Symphony. The work was recorded in 1982 in Tel Aviv by members of the Israel Philharmonic, under the direction of David Amos. Initially released on LP, the recording was reissued on compact disc in 1986.

Persichetti returned to the concept underlying the *Poems for Piano* again in 1970, but this time as applied to an orchestral work. The result, commissioned by the New York State School Music Association, is *Night Dances*, Op. 114. Seven lines of modern poetry serve as inspiration for seven short movements, each approximately three minutes in duration. The lines and poets are: (1) "Shadow dancers alive in your blood now" (Carl Sandburg), (2) "Their radiant spirals crease our outer night" (Daniel Hoffman), (3) "Sleep to dreamier sleep be wed" (James Joyce), (4) "The incendiary eve of deaths and entrances" (Dylan Thomas), (5) "The loneliness includes me unawares" (Robert Frost), (6) "Through the black amnesias of heaven" (Sylvia Plath), and (7) "Where at midnight motion stays" (Robert Fitzgerald).

Night Dances followed directly upon the completion of the Symphony No. 9, and the composer considered the two works "companion pieces . . . linked spiritually but subconsciously. . . . These *Night Dances* do have to do with what we all dream in a different reality from that of our waking thoughts. In dreams things appear, bidden or unbidden, as an underside of something made of a fabric that will hold together because it *is* part fantasy. These seven pieces form a crystal created by a melodic pair of dew drops."[223] Put perhaps less poetically, the work is rather like an expansion of the composer's "serenade" concept, while drawing upon a much more rarefied musical language. The "dewdrops" form the interval of a minor-second, which serves as the basis of each dance. While its language is much the same as that used in the Ninth Symphony, *Night Dances* (a title drawn from the Plath poem, *The Night Dancers*) is somewhat more difficult to absorb, largely because of the paucity of the strongly metrical passages that serve as anchors in the symphony. In view of this, whether or not the music bears any tangible relationship to the lines indicated, the poetic images serve the useful function of providing a focus of attention for the listener, who may otherwise find the music to be largely inscrutable. The orchestration is highly varied and colorful, with generous use of percussion, while special effects (e.g., massed string *glissandi*) help to conjure dreamlike sound-images. Although Persichetti never abandoned traditional principles of contrapuntal and motivic development or of the long conceptual line, these character pieces are far removed from traditional romantic notions of musical "expression" based in literal depictions or some form of self-revelation. This is purely abstract expression based on the interplay of gestures, governed by microscopic tensions and releases. Perhaps most readily accessible are the third section, in which the harmonic language is more apparently tonal, and the finale, which reveals some vintage use of the "Persichetti 2/4" (in this case, really 6/8), along with the contrapuntal accumulation of motifs that so often brings his works to "slam-bang" conclusions.

Night Dances was first performed in December 1970 at an annual conference of the New York State School Music Association held in Kiamesha Lake, New York. The New York All-State High School Orchestra was conducted by the composer's longtime advocate, Frederick Fennell. Reviewing the published score, composer-theorist Richard Swift revealed the tortured combination of bias and ignorance, complicated by envy and begrudging admiration, which pervaded so many of the musical judgments made by academicians at the time. He acknowledged that while Persichetti made only "modest use of timbre in association with pitch and interval elements," the result was "by and large, compelling in its contours and textures." However, he did not care for the faster sections, finding "the conventional spinning out of meter and pulse . . . dull and mechanical. The harmonic language is that mixture of modes—whose bittersweet muted clashes seem so French—familiar in Persichetti's musical world." Swift then quotes a remark made in reference to someone else, to the effect that Persichetti displays his limitations as a principle of his style, making it unnecessary to identify them as shortcomings. "But within the language and style that are so personally the composer's own, he has achieved a kind of imaginative clarity that escapes those who attempt the grandiose, the rhetorical or the merely modish."[224]

A recording of *Night Dances*, featuring the Juilliard Orchestra under the direction of James DePreist, was released in 1990. Reviewing that recording, James H. North described the work as an example of Persichetti's "most mysterious, sumptuous vein." All the sections "project a strong aura of night music: of sleep, of dreams, and of darkness. Five are in slow tempos, but the delicate music is often interrupted by sudden bursts of color; each dance contains enormous variety, which replaces the conventional formal arrangement of variety among movements, but the finale is a wild climax. *Night Dances* is the work of a master at the top of his art."[225]

Persichetti's next orchestral work was his second to feature a narrator: *A Lincoln Address*, Op. 124. The story of its having been commissioned for the inauguration of Richard Nixon's second term as president and the subsequent cancellation of that performance was recounted in the first part of this chapter. Although this proved to be the most highly publicized commission—indeed, the most highly publicized event—of the composer's entire career, the piece itself is one of his least consequential. Persichetti always insisted that he did not compose quickly; he attributed his sizable body of work to the fact that he composed during every available moment.[226] So the prospect of completing an orchestral work for performance at such an auspicious occasion within the three weeks that had been allotted for it, including the preparation of the instrumental parts, was daunting, to say the least.

Persichetti decided to meet this challenge by adapting a preexisting work for the purpose at hand. The piece he chose was the Symphony No. 7, "Liturgical," which he simply abridged, reducing the half-hour composition to twelve minutes, over which he superimposed the reading of portions of Abraham Lincoln's second inaugural address, as the Inaugural Committee had originally requested. *A Lincoln Address* begs comparison, of course, with Aaron Copland's beloved *A Lincoln Portrait*, composed in 1942. But few of the passages that Persichetti chose from Lincoln's speech are either as pithy or as poetic as the passages Copland chose from Lincoln's various writings, including *The Gettysburg Address*; nor does Persichetti's music boast the popular appeal of Copland's. Indeed, the fact that a work with explicitly liturgical import could be transformed into a composition suitable for a formal patriotic occasion indicates the power of suggestion in inferring meaning from an abstract piece of music, but it also points to the rather detached, emotionally noncommittal quality of the Seventh Symphony, as noted earlier, which is reflected in this work as well.

The actual premiere of *A Lincoln Address* took place in St. Louis on January 25, 1973. Walter Susskind conducted the St. Louis Symphony Orchestra, and William Warfield served as narrator. Quite a few performances followed, presumably prompted by the work's notoriety; a band arrangement was made, and that has been played numerous times as well. The critical reaction to the piece is interesting, in view of the fact that the source of its musical material was not generally made public. Reviewing the premiere, Hubert Saal wrote, "The twelve-minute work is eloquent in its concern, its warmth and lyricism. The music is not simply a passive accompaniment to the text. . . . Rather it is antiphonal, with the text as a controlling force and the music appropriately responsive and descriptive. When Lincoln describes the anguish and irresolution of war, the orchestra is roused to turbulence and dissonance, turning tremulously nostalgic as the years before the Civil War are evoked, becoming brassy and apocalyptic as hopes for a just and lasting peace are raised."[227] A. DeRhem noted that "the materials typify Persichetti's tastefully conservative style and effectively underscore the quiet optimism of the text. The results are a worthy companion piece to Aaron Copland's *Lincoln Portrait*."[228] Harold Schonberg reviewed the New York premiere, reporting, "The music is conservative, tonal, dignified and heartfelt."[229] Reviewing the same performance, Harriett Johnson commented, "The music is somber in its tonal thought and in the dark color of its orchestration. It is poignant, often moving and beautiful. . . . It is difficult to understand why this Address was not singularly appropriate for the occasion."[230] Reviewing the published score, David Lawton commented, "While the music is continuous, the readings are separated by orchestral interludes which elaborate the mood of the text. In spite of the great changes in character resulting from this procedure, the piece makes a very coherent and unified impression as a whole."[231] Dissenting from the generally positive reactions, Ainslee Cox noted with some justification, "The piece is bound to be played a lot, bringing Persichetti's name to many who might otherwise be unaware of his skills. But it is so weak musically, and even dramatically, that the unknowing listener might question the composer's abilities. Perhaps a text so simple and so strong, yet so un-'poetic,' simply does not need musical enhancement; any music with it is bound to sound either intrusive or bland. This music runs toward the latter."[232]

A Lincoln Address did not appear on recording until 2009, when a performance was released featuring narrator Barry Scott, with the Nashville Symphony Orchestra conducted by Leonard Slatkin. Reviewing this recording, Karl Miller wrote, "The piece has none of the dramatic sweep of the Copland. The text provides the form, more so than any creative impetus of the music. The music merely seems to comment on the text as opposed to there being a true merging of text and music."[233] William Kreindler found it to be "one of the most moving works [on the recording] . . . a wonderful work that should be better known."[234] Christian Carey felt that it was "no match for the Copland in terms of overt appeal, but it features stirring interludes dense with flurried counterpoint and artfully crafted extended tonal harmonies."[235]

Persichetti composed only two full-length concertos for solo instrument with orchestra. The first, his Piano Concerto, is discussed in the section of this chapter dealing with piano music. The second was the Concerto for English Horn and String Orchestra, Op. 137, composed in 1977. The work was commissioned by Francis Goelet on behalf of the New York Philharmonic, for its English horn player, Thomas Stacy.

Persichetti often discussed his pieces as if they were independent entities, with minds of their own. As he grew older, he became bolder about indulging this penchant in public statements. His own program notes for the concerto provide a representative example. In describing the first movement, he wrote, "During the serene opening, the higher strings unveil suggestions of a theme [which will later appear in bolder outline], as the lower strings respond in lyric *pizzicato*. The English horn enters, involving the strings in a search for some thematic footing. The violins discover a deceivingly affable song which the English horn turns into one of complaint. These two dramatic elements persist until the soloist insists upon holding a cadential tone long enough to discourage the entire string orchestra."[236]

The English Horn Concerto comprises three movements. However, tempo changes within the movements tend to lessen the sense of contrast among the movements. As the first, *Con fantasia*, begins, the second violins introduce the work's primary motif, which highlights the interval of a major-sixth. This interval serves as the concerto's fundamental source element. The English horn enters with an expansion of the primary motif, which now also highlights the interval of a minor-third. After some further exploration, a more defined thematic idea is announced by the English horn: a clearly tonal, diatonic melody in which the major-sixth figures prominently. This melody bears a resemblance to the English horn melody ("Daybreak") from Rossini's *William Tell Overture* too strong to be accidental. It also resembles the *Piacevole* passage in the first section of Persichetti's Fifth Symphony. In fact, the shadow of this symphony hovers over the entire concerto. The second movement, *Amabile*, develops a melodic idea that first appeared in the composer's oratorio, *The Creation* (1969). A central section alternates a running figure between the solo instrument and the strings, creating something of a whirring effect. The third movement, *Spiritoso*, brings the interval of a minor-third into focus, integrating its development with that of the other thematic material. Throughout the work Persichetti makes advantageous use of the English horn and its capabilities, with many unaccompanied or minimally accompanied passages that serve as brief quasi cadenzas. Overall, the concerto is more conservative rhythmically, harmonically, and tonally than most of the composer's major works of the 1970s. But its overall character is so pallid and ruminative, its form so lacking in clarity, and its narrative gradient so subtle that most listeners have found it to be a rather colorless, lukewarm effort.

The premiere of Persichetti's English Horn Concerto took place in November 1977. Thomas Stacy was the soloist, and Erich Leinsdorf conducted the New York Philharmonic. Andrew Porter described the work as "dull, 'well-made' stuff."[237] Harold Schonberg noted, "Whatever one's opinion of the actual materials of the concerto, there is no denying that it is more melodious than many works composed these days."[238] Harriett Johnson's verdict was that "While it is skillfully constructed by the prolific composer, it doesn't convey deep or compelling emotion. It skirts the surface more than it probes the heart."[239] Reviewing a subsequent performance, John Rockwell characterized the work as "earnest and well-meaning in a pale Neo-Classical idiom but to my ears fatally bland."[240]

In 1979 the work was released on LP, in a performance featuring Stacy and the New York Philharmonic, conducted by Persichetti himself. Critical reaction to the recording was no more positive. A roundup of reviews quoted Karen Monson's description of the concerto as "of the Friday matinee, music-to-let-your-mind-wander-by variety, full of tunes and mildly dissonant harmonies and virtually devoid of imagination," while Stephen Chakwin complained that it "never goes anywhere from its beginning and turns ever more academic and grey," and Alan Hershowitz found the work "easy enough to listen to, but [it] provides little more than a showcase for Stacy's considerable virtuosity and rich, round tone."[241] Therefore, it is somewhat remarkable that Persichetti's concerto was awarded the first Kennedy Center Friedheim Award in 1978. In 1995 Stacy's recording was reissued on compact disc.

Works for Band

It is through his works for symphonic band and wind ensemble that Vincent Persichetti's name and music is best known today. This is the result of a fortunate confluence of his own creative development with the growth of a musical medium that mushroomed within the high schools and colleges of the United States during the years following World War II: the aggregation of woodwinds, brass, and percussion known as the symphonic or concert band. Some of these groups, led by gifted conductors with high aspirations such as Frederick Fennell (1914–2004), Richard Franko Goldman (1910–1980), and William D. Revelli (1902–1994), attained impressive levels of artistry and technical proficiency, and developed international reputations. As the medium grew, so did its repertoire, filling a voracious, receptive, unjaded appetite for new music among the young musicians of the huge postwar baby boom. Some of the music for this young medium was relatively pedestrian. In order to foster the development of a repertoire commensurate with such high performance standards, the most visionary of these pioneering conductors turned to America's leading composers, encouraging them to contribute challenging new works tailored specifically to the band medium, while shunning its traditional outdoor pops-concert connotations. The result was the appearance of substantial new works—including full-length symphonies. Some of these compositions eventually attained the status of classics, enjoying literally thousands of performances.

Persichetti was arguably the most significant contributor to this rapidly evolving medium. As William Schuman stated in an interview, "Vincent was not an original orchestrator, except when he wrote for band. I felt that his band scoring is the best scoring he did. I liked it very much."[242] As noted earlier, Persichetti's own creative development reached something of a milestone around 1950, when his celebrated breadth of stylistic range crystallized into a very personal language, but before his quest to embrace and incorporate virtually every compositional innovation led him down some less promising paths. Ultimately he produced some fourteen works for band, most of which have entered the active repertoire, and these remain his best-known compositions by far. Four of them date from the 1950s, and they are four of his most frequently performed compositions: *Divertimento*, *Psalm*, *Pageant*, and the Symphony No. 6. In fact, the symphony is perhaps the most fully consummated artistically—as well as one of the most enduringly successful—of the many works for band by a variety of composers that appeared during the 1950s.

Persichetti's first few pieces for the medium represent some of the most warmly ingratiating and readily appealing music he ever wrote. As with the *Little Piano Book*, one encounters the composer's essential creative persona in some of its purest manifestations. The simplest pieces, such as *Psalm* and *Pageant*, have a youthful sweetness and exuberance that are utterly genuine, while displaying meticulous attention to formal values. Indeed, these qualities, along with a sense of mischief and a poignant vein of nostalgia, represent the essence of Persichetti's musical personality, manifest in his most complex work as well. Grasping and appreciating these pieces makes the more challenging, complex works less daunting and helps to reveal the common elements that underlie a body of work so large and varied that it can easily seem overwhelming.

Persichetti took pains to distinguish his own music for band from conventional stereotypes about the medium. In an often-quoted statement, he commented with characteristic whimsy about the misgivings many hold about the band medium:

> I know that composers are often frightened off by the sound of the word "band," because of certain qualities long associated with this medium—rusty trumpets, consumptive flutes, wheezy oboes, disintegrating clarinets, fumbling yet amiable baton wavers, and gum-coated park benches. If you couple these conditions with transfigurations and disfigurations of works originally conceived for orchestra, you create a sound experience that's nearly as excruciating as a sick string quartet playing a dilettante's arrangement of a 19th-century piano sonata. But when composers think of the band as a huge, supple ensemble of winds and percussion, the obnoxious fat drains off and creative ideas flourish.[243]

In 1952, in an effort to create a wind band of unprecedented flexibility and transparency of sound, capable of playing works of high artistic caliber with the virtuoso precision and musicianship of a fine professional orchestra, Frederick Fennell—a young, ambitious faculty member at the Eastman School of Music—formed a smaller group of proficient students and faculty. To distinguish this group from the negative impressions associated with the term "band," Fennell coined the term "wind ensemble." Within just a few years, the Eastman Symphonic Wind Ensemble was making recordings available on the commercial market that illustrated the success of his endeavor while further stimulating the creation of a fine body of repertoire and bringing it to the attention of the general listener.

However, Persichetti became so impressed with this new medium—especially its welcoming attitude toward challenging new works by important living composers—that he preferred to use the term "band," in recognition of its elevation into an artistic medium of the highest order. "He felt that one should no longer apologize for the word."[244] Fennell greatly admired Persichetti's music and encouraged his interest in writing for the new medium, including three of the four works noted above in his recording series for Mercury Records. (More than half a century later, these recordings are still available on compact disc reissues.) Persichetti's pieces for band were ideal showcases for the Eastman Wind Ensemble, while the Ensemble's recordings helped to spread Persichetti's reputation far and wide. During more recent years, many of the finest bands and wind ensembles have devoted entire recordings to various assorted programs drawn from the composer's works in this genre.

Many band works of that era—including some by major figures—sound generic in their relationship to the medium. That is, they might just as well have been scored for most any sort of ensemble—or they sound like music conceived for symphony orchestra, reluctantly transcribed for the medium at hand. But Persichetti's conceptions are essentially wedded to an ensemble of winds and percussion, and could not be rendered by any other without fundamental distortion. Moreover, the most salient qualities of Persichetti's musical personality are naturally suited to the wind ensemble's particular timbral and temperamental strengths—warm chorales, transparent polytonal textures, crisp, dry sonorities, and spunky, syncopated rhythms, along with a pure, boy-soprano-like innocence. He himself stated, "My earliest works were stimulated by the sound of winds."[245] In fact, it is apparent that Persichetti's works for band are more representative of his distinctive musical personality than are his works for orchestra. And his natural and idiomatic way of approaching the medium, once a vehicle for tasteless condescension and compromise, became the model for a whole younger generation of composers interested in writing for band. (Morris offers copious documentation of comments made by conductors and scholars testifying to the enduring significance of Persichetti's contributions to this repertoire.[246])

These pieces may be utilitarian but only in the sense that they were written with an awareness of imminent performance in a variety of different practical contexts. But there is no compromise in standards of taste or quality of workmanship, nor is there a condescending, unconvincing, or insincere moment to be found. Although most of Persichetti's music for band falls along the simpler end of his stylistic spectrum, a late work, *Parable IX*, represents the opposite pole.

This discussion begins with Persichetti's Serenade No. 1, Op. 1. Although it is not, technically, a true band work, it is scored for a wind ensemble of sorts: a dectet of woodwinds and brass. Along the lines of the serenades that would appear later, it consists of tiny movements of varied, contrasting character—five in this case—each about two minutes in duration. Each is based on a short motif presented at the beginning of the first movement. Although it is dated 1929, presumably when the composer was fourteen, it is so sophisticated and displays so many attributes of the mature composer that one cannot help wondering whether perhaps he revised the piece prior to its publication in 1963. As Daniel Dorff noted, the Serenade "uses the same harmonic language, dry and witty phrases, and mastery of form found in most of the music he wrote throughout the century."[247] The serenade bears the strong influence of Stravinsky, with its dry, Neo-Classical approach to sonority, "naughty" dissonances, copious polytonality and pan-diatonic harmony, and tenuous sense of tonality. Particularly Persichettian is the impression that each movement suggests the antics of an imaginary, cartoon-like character.

The first documented public performance of the Serenade No. 1 took place in April 1952 in San Angelo, Texas, by the New York Wind Ensemble. The piece has been recorded several times on noncommercial releases. Its first commercial recording was released in 1979 and featured members of the University of Kansas Symphonic Band, conducted by Robert Foster.

Persichetti's first work for the standard concert band is the *Divertimento*, Op 42. Dorothea Persichetti called it "as happy a work as is to be found in the composer's literature."[248] According to an often quoted account, Persichetti did not initially intend to write a piece for band. He recalled "composing in a log cabin schoolhouse in El Dorado, Kansas, during the summer of 1949. Working with some lovely woodwind figures, accentuated by choirs of aggressive brasses and percussion beating, I soon realized the strings weren't going to enter, and my *Divertimento* began to take shape."[249] There is evidence that some of the material used in the *Divertimento* originated as early as 1946.[250] Completed in 1950, it was the composition that immediately preceded the Serenade No. 5 for orchestra, discussed earlier, and represents much the same concept as that piece, as well as the Serenade No. 1: six tiny movements, averaging less than two minutes apiece, each a miniature character piece. However, the movements are far more graceful than those in the early serenade and are more appealing than the orchestral serenade as well. Although its collective character is light and breezy, an underlying wistfulness hints at a depth barely implied on the surface. The concise eloquence of each movement is extraordinary and far from casual.

Most of the constituent movements are pervaded by polytonality, while the second movement, "Song," is based on a Phrygian melody, and the fourth, "Burlesque," features a jocular tuba solo in the Lydian mode, accompanied by raucous off-beats, framing a taunting central section. The fifth movement, "Soliloquy," is a cornet solo that offers one of the composer's most hauntingly nostalgic melodies. The melody is purely tonal and harmonized triadically, but with unconventional chord connections. *Divertimento* begins and ends in great high spirits. Much of it is diatonic and tonal, but there is also considerable use of dissonant harmony, treated in such a playful and natural way as to be barely noticeable.

The first performance of the *Divertimento* took place in June 1950 in New York City. The composer himself conducted the Goldman Band. The program also included a work by Walter Piston. Miles Kastendieck compared the two pieces: "While Piston went folksy, Persichetti pursued an individual course. . . . The audience was quick to appreciate the difference and applauded the Divertimento enthusiastically."[251] Virgil Thomson was also favorably impressed by the work. Commenting specifically on the "Soliloquy," he noted its "unusual personality and expressive power. Its tune, its harmony and its instrumentation have all of them originality. It makes a mood, sustains it, holds the interest. Neither its sense nor its sound is familiar, and both have a real sweetness."[252] Richard Franko Goldman (whose father Edwin founded the Goldman Band) wrote,

> For all one can say of the composer's debt to Harris or Copland, the music has a personality of its own. Its lack of pretentiousness conceals immense skill and unusual sensibility. Persichetti's exploitation of band timbres and sonorities is highly imaginative, and he has not been afraid to score lightly or to call for unusual combinations of instruments. . . . Persichetti's music is gentle, buoyant, moving and diverting in succession. . . . The Divertimento as a whole is among the most successful works that have been added to the band repertory in many years.[253]

In an article, "New Work for Band," Walter E. Nallin opined that the *Divertimento* "augurs well to become a classic in the repertoire. . . . One cannot praise band literature of this nature too highly."[254]

Frederick Fennell performed Persichetti's *Divertimento* at Eastman in 1951 and urged Persichetti to devote further creative energy to the band medium, and also encouraged the composer to be a bit more adventurous in his percussion scoring, going so far as to make specific suggestions.[255] Meanwhile, Goldman wrote to Persichetti, "Everyone says that [*Divertimento*] is the best new band piece written in the past several years, and I must say that I agree."[256]

The first recording of *Divertimento* was released in 1953 as part of the LP that inaugurated the Eastman Symphonic Wind Ensemble's series of recordings for Mercury Records. Conducted by Frederick Fennell, the record was entitled "American Concert Band Masterpieces." Since then, *Divertimento* has been included on too many fine recordings to enumerate. A representative recent comment terms it "a classic—six short movements mixing hummable tunes, brilliant and sometimes humorous wind orchestration, easily followed rhythmic dislocations, and lyrical sentiment that seems natural and honestly tender."[257]

Persichetti composed *Psalm*, Op. 53, in 1952. A group of band musicians at the University of Louisville had enjoyed playing the *Divertimento* and were favorably impressed by the Louisville Orchestra's performance of the Serenade No. 5. Calling themselves the Pi Kappa Omicron Fraternity, they raised enough money to commission another band work from the composer. The result was *Psalm*, one of the composer's most accessible pieces, featuring diatonic melodies, consonant harmony, simple textures, and an overall feeling of innocent beneficence, all of which make it especially attractive to young musicians. Rapid shifts between instrumental choirs are one of its most notable features. *Psalm* comprises three connected sections: The first introduces a warm, purely consonant chorale played by the clarinet choir, in alternation with the brass; the second section is hymnlike and introduces a bit more motion, while the shifts among instrumental choirs become more active; the third section is a paean of joyful exuberance, highlighting rapid shifts among the choirs of the band. Toward the end, the hymn from the second section returns, bringing the work to a spirited conclusion.

The first performance of *Psalm* took place in May 1952. The composer conducted the University of Louisville Band. In 1954 the piece was included on another of Fennell's recordings with the Eastman Wind Ensemble, a performance that is still available at this writing, on a recording deemed by David Hurwitz "one of the finest band music discs ever made, a true milestone in the history of recordings . . . that absolutely defines the word 'classic.'"[258]

For some reason, the composer's friend and colleague Richard Franko Goldman was initially less taken with this work, noting that "Persichetti's *Psalm* cannot be ranked among its composer's best efforts,"[259] and this verdict seems to have colored the critical consensus about the piece at that time, although such judgments have not hindered its popularity among band musicians. Robert Evett observed that Persichetti "remains one of the most enigmatic and unpredictable composers alive; mostly, perhaps, because the extremes of style which his work embraces show no sign of experimentation, but only of authority." He goes on to comment that *Psalm* "has been one of the most-played of the Persichetti works." He then points perceptively to the similarity between this piece and the third movement of the composer's Third Piano Sonata (also entitled "Psalm").[260] *Psalm* has also been the beneficiary of many fine recorded performances over the years. In 1973 Paul Whear cited it as one of the best band works of the 1950s, which he attributed to its "originality, musical depth, and accessibility."[261] In 2001, Steven Schwartz enthused about its "brilliant, electrifying allegro molto, which at the very end recapitulates themes from throughout the work. It clocks in at a hefty 8 minutes, but it also takes you on a thrill ride. Like a really good roller coaster, it makes you want to ride again as soon as it's over."[262]

Persichetti composed *Pageant*, Op. 59, in 1953, on a commission from Edwin Franko Goldman on behalf of the American Bandmasters Association. It may be viewed as something of a sequel to *Psalm*: The composer's most accessible pieces for band, both present warm chorales followed by lively, exuberant allegros, although it is important to bear in mind that in between these two works appeared the dense and extremely challenging Sonata for Cello Solo, the brilliantly subtle and complex Concerto for Piano, Four Hands, and the Piano Sonata No. 9, among other pieces.

Pageant opens with a three-note motif presented by the French horn. A clarinet choir develops this motif into a warm hymn, elaborated by other instrumental groups in consonant chorale style. This section offers a touching sense of purity and innocence, aptly connoted by the title *Morning Music*, given to an earlier version of the piece. (This early draft also included material that ultimately appeared in the Symphony No. 6.[263]) A brief percussion transition then leads to a march-like "pageant" displaying the "Persichetti 2/4." Festive and celebratory, this section treats two diatonic themes against a polytonal harmonic setting, among which is interwoven the original three-note motif. Motivic fragments are playfully tossed back and forth among the instrumental choirs, leading the work to a stridently jubilant conclusion.

The first performance of *Pageant* took place in March 1953 at the annual convention of the American Bandmasters Association in Miami, Florida. Persichetti again conducted the premiere, this time with the University of Miami Band. Reviewing the first New York performance several months later, Harold Schonberg described the opening section as "conservative, meditative, with a three-note motto threading its way through. There followed a lively, bustling section with a nice out-doorsy quality."[264]

Although there have been many noncommercial recordings, the first generally available recording of *Pageant* did not appear until 1977, when John Paynter conducted a performance by the Northwestern University Symphonic Wind Ensemble. In his review of that release, Peter Frank noted perceptively that "Persichetti may be the most important band composer alive in the country, a composer who takes the wind band entirely seriously and whose whole symphonic style seems to come from his responsivity to the character of the wind ensemble."[265] Many further recordings of the piece have appeared during the subsequent years.

Both *Psalm* and *Pageant* exude a freshness and sincerity that have endeared them to several generations of young musicians, who discover harmonic and contrapuntal dissonance, polytonality, and other Modernist usages within a natural, genial expressive context. Their simple directness conceals a formal sophistication that lends the music strength and durability.

Persichetti's next work for winds was the Symphony No. 6, Op. 69, completed in 1956. One of his greatest works, it is arguably his most significant contribution to the band repertoire. (This work is discussed at length in the section of this chapter dealing with Persichetti's symphonies.)

In 1960 Persichetti was approached by the distinguished band conductor Frank Battisti, who offered the composer a modest commission to write a work suitable for the extraordinary high school band he had been developing in Ithaca, New York. Persichetti accepted the offer, capitalizing on the opportunity to add a piece for wind band to his list of "serenades." The result was the Serenade No. 11, Op. 85, a short piece in five tiny movements. In comparison to the *Divertimento* of 1950, the movements are shorter—averaging a little more than a minute per movement—and the music is considerably easier to play. Also, the expressive character of the later work is more subdued, with less variety among the movements. Perhaps for these reasons, the serenade has never achieved the popularity of the previous works. However, all but the final movement convey with great delicacy and sensitivity a very affecting sense of wistful nostalgia, suggesting a sense of longing for a fondly remembered childhood. The primary motif outlines a triad, creating a largely diatonic thematic framework, and the harmony is clearly tonal and consonant, although enriched by copious use of seventh chords. Other harmonic dissonance occurs through polytonal accompaniments. The texture is consistently light and tender; only the final "Capriccio" introduces a raucous touch. Overall the expressive import of the piece calls to mind the Piano Sonatinas Nos. 4, 5, and 6 of 1954.

The premiere of the Serenade No. 11 took place in April 1961. The composer conducted the Ithaca High School Band. The first commercial recording of the piece appeared in 1969 as part of an all-Persichetti program that featured the Ohio State University Concert Band, conducted by Donald McGinnis. More recent recordings have followed.

Of even more modest dimension are the four *Bagatelles*, Op. 87, commissioned by Dartmouth College and completed in 1961. Although the constituent movements are as concise as those of the serenade, their musical content is considerably more demanding. Barely five minutes in total duration, these tiny pieces are similarly evocative, but their expressive content is less explicit, more cryptic. They are less ingratiatingly tonal and more dissonant harmonically. Morris notes that two-letter symbols appear at the end of each movement. Evidently the composer's daughter identified these as the initials of some of the fantasy characters that inhabited the Persichetti household.[266] For example, "HB" referred to Honey Bear, a stuffed animal that would ride on the composer's dashboard as he drove to his various concert appearances. In light of this revelation, one notes with interest that Persichetti, in discussing his intense childhood involvement with the piano music of Robert Schumann, stated, "It wasn't long before my four personal Eusebian friends, whose initials can be found at the end of each of my *Bagatelles for Band*, came to my aid in most of the Schumann keyboard works I studied with [Gilbert] Combs [Persichetti's piano teacher during his late teens]."[267]

The *Bagatelles* were introduced in May 1961 by the Dartmouth College Band in Hanover, New Hampshire. The composer, whose participation as conductor was increasingly in demand, led the performance. This piece too enjoyed its first commercial recording on Ohio State University's all-Persichetti recording of 1969. Other recordings have followed.

One of the relatively few reviews of the Serenade No. 11 and the *Bagatelles* was unfavorable, written by Cecil Isaac, who stated, "Both are collections of brief movements, in the case of the serenade very brief movements, which are well enough contrasted in spirit but lack any really compelling unity. There is no inexorable law that requires an easy piece to be less adventurous or interesting than a difficult one, and the exceptions to any such generalization are manifold. But that is the way it seems to work out in the present two instances."[268] Perhaps the fact that Isaac's chief area of interest appears to be music prior to the Baroque period accounts for his lack of appreciation of these pieces.

As mentioned earlier, Persichetti's *Hymns and Responses for the Church Year*, in addition to its own intrinsic value, served as a rich source of thematic material for the composer, who increasingly regarded his own output as source material for further creative treatment. One such example is the Chorale Prelude: "So Pure the Star," Op. 91. Composed in 1962 on a commission from Duke University, the piece takes as a point of departure the hymn "Motionless share of thought at last" (No. 7 from *Hymns and Responses*, volume I) and elaborates it into a brief, peacefully contemplative tone poem. Interestingly, a motif set to the words, "At last, our eve," which also fits the words "So pure the star," serves as a means of building to a mild climax. Overall, the harmonic language maintains a somewhat higher level of dissonance relative to the earlier band works. The source of the text is given as "Anonymous," but Morris indicates Persichetti himself as the author.[269]

In December 1962, Persichetti conducted the Duke University Band in the first performance of the Chorale Prelude: "So Pure the Star" in Durham, North Carolina. The work's first appearance on recording was on the Ohio State LP noted above.

Not only did Persichetti treat his compositional output as a source of thematic material: He based his next piece for band—*Masquerade*, Op. 102—on several of the exercises he created for his textbook *Twentieth-Century Harmony*. "The work is a masquerade of my book"[270] In 1965 the composer was offered a commission by the Conservatory of Baldwin-Wallace College. He was given the choice of writing a work for either band, chorus, orchestra, or string quartet.[271] He chose the first option, and the piece he composed proved to be of considerably greater weight and import than his most recent contributions to the medium. Although only twelve minutes in duration, it is extremely concentrated and dense with developmental activity. Describing its gestation from textbook examples, Persichetti recalled, "I [had] composed phrases of music to illustrate specific points, and years later these fragments began haunting me. I realized that certain examples had a thematic kernel in common. . . . [T]hese examples from the harmony book evolved into a set of variations."[272] The cover-page of the full score uses as a backdrop what appears to be a sketch page for the work, with a variety of notations (some of dubious relevance) scribbled across the page. Among the notations are identifications of the exercises on which the piece is based. *Masquerade* consists of an introduction, statement of the theme (based on a minor-third), followed by ten variations and a coda. It is a tour de force of compositional wizardry (the final variation consists of material from the previous variations played simultaneously). Though its language reveals the coolness, attenuated tonality, and relative emotional detachment found in most of his works from the 1960s, *Masquerade* also displays many of the composer's familiar gestures, along with his infectiously lively rhythms, and is scored with great panache.

The premiere of *Masquerade* took place in January 1966 in Berea, Ohio. Persichetti conducted the Baldwin-Wallace Conservatory Band. The success of the performance led to a commission from the same auspices for a new symphony, No. 8, which was completed the following year. The first recording of *Masquerade* appeared in 1969 and featured the Eastman Wind Ensemble, then conducted by Donald Hunsberger. A number of subsequent recordings have included the work. Reviewing the first recording, Donal Henahan complained about the "dated academicism" of all three works on the program (which also included music by Hartley and Dahl). Concerning *Masquerade*, he conceded that "the composer's craftsmanship is beyond cavil."[273] On the other hand, Enos Shupp Jr. found it "a fine work. It is honest music, clearly set forth, with striking effects and a good solid rhythmic movement."[274]

Persichetti next turned his attention to a large work entitled *Celebrations*, Op. 103, which set nine poems of Walt Whitman for chorus and wind ensemble. This piece is discussed in the section treating the composer's choral music.

In November 1963, the Ithaca High School Band was on a concert tour, which was suddenly interrupted by the assassination of President John F. Kennedy. Shortly after their return home the following night, the band decided to commission a work in memory of President Kennedy, and they turned to Persichetti with their request. He accepted the commission, although he was unable to complete the work until 1966. The result was the second of his three chorale preludes for band: "Turn Not Thy Face," Op. 105, which he based on another selection from the *Hymns and Responses for the Church Year*, volume I—this time No. 11, "O Lord, Turn Not Thy Face from Them." A solo flute introduces the chorale melody, from which follows a rhapsodic elaboration of the hymn. The diatonic melody is harmonized with increasing dissonance as it builds to an impassioned climax and then recedes. The overall character of the work is thoughtful and rather stoic.

The premiere of Chorale Prelude: "Turn Not Thy Face" took place in Ithaca, New York, in May 1967. Frank Battisti led the Ithaca High School Band in one of his last concerts with this outstanding ensemble. The piece was first recorded in 1978 on another all-Persichetti band program. This LP featured the University of Kansas Symphonic Band conducted by Robert E. Foster.

In 1971 Persichetti was offered a commission from the Ohio Music Education Association to write a piece for the Ohio Music Educator's Convention the following year. He fulfilled the request with *O Cool Is the Valley*, Op. 118, one of the composer's relatively few instrumental pieces to be directly inspired by a literary work (as opposed to the many pieces prompted by individual lines of poetry). The title was taken from one of the love poems in James Joyce's collection, *Chamber Music*. The poem evokes a calm, hauntingly seductive, pastoral mood, which Persichetti captured with touching immediacy in this six-minute piece. With relatively consonant harmony, amply cushioned with seventh chords, the piece, subtitled "Poem for Band," harks back to the innocent simplicity and poignancy of so many of the composer's works from the 1950s. Perhaps because it appeared relatively late in Persichetti's career, at a time when musical mood-painting was not in fashion, the work has not achieved the currency it deserves. John Paynter described it insightfully as "wonderfully meaningful material, a total contrast to much of the literature for full band, and a mood in which Vincent Persichetti is often at his very most significant."[275]

Persichetti conducted the Bowling Green State University Band in the premiere of *O Cool Is the Valley* in February 1972, in Columbus, Ohio. It first appeared on recording in 1978, when it was included on the all-Persichetti LP featuring the University of Kansas Symphonic Band just mentioned above.

Persichetti's most ambitious, complex, and demanding work for winds is the ninth in his series of *Parables*. Lasting seventeen minutes, the single-movement work is approximately the same duration as the entire Symphony No. 6. *Parable IX*, Op. 121, was commissioned by the Drake University College of Fine Arts to mark the opening of the Fine Arts Center and was completed in 1972.

Parable IX shares much the same language as the Symphony No. 9, "Sinfonia: Janiculum," Op. 113 (1970). After an introductory statement that sets forth some very dissonant textural gestures, the clarinets introduce a lengthy thematic idea that embraces all twelve tones, although there are some repetitions before all twelve are heard. This theme contains gestural ideas, as well as intervallic combinations, all of which serve as the source material for the entire work, while recurring throughout as recognizable unifying elements. Although structured as one continuous, through-composed entity, Morris reports that Persichetti's sketches indicate his own conceptual subdivision of the work into five sections plus coda.[276] As *Parable IX* proceeds, its thematic material pursues an abstract developmental odyssey against a broad canvas of sonic textures. As was true of the Ninth Symphony, the passages in faster tempos are the easiest to grasp and absorb, revealing the clearest connections to Persichetti's more familiar musical language. Percussion instruments play an important structural role; their use is varied and highly active. In the coda, Persichetti recalled much of the earlier material in simultaneous counterpoint—a technique that had served him as far back as the early 1950s.

Works like the band *Parable* and the Ninth Symphony are quite challenging for those accustomed to more traditional musical styles. They demand attentive listening, as their structures are articulated with great concentration. Rather than serving as the foundation of the musical language, tonality is used in these works as a device for a specific purpose. Similarly, metrical rhythm and contrapuntal development, though never abandoned entirely, become part of a repertoire of techniques, along with a language of textures and gestures that many of Persichetti's compositional colleagues were exploring at the time. In such works the composer manipulates all these elements and techniques to achieve varying levels of energy and activity, and varying density and transparency of texture, producing a dynamic but highly abstract narrative structure. Drama is represented grippingly within the music yet without any suggestion of personal autobiography; rather, it unfolds as an autonomous consequence of the inherent properties of the musical material itself. Persichetti's textures are characteristically lucid, so that the concentration of activity never becomes turgid or congested, as is often the case with music that attempts to pack too much into too short a time span. Unlike so much complex music of the 1960s and 1970s, Persichetti's conceptual clarity and his convincing sense of musicality motivate the serious listener to persevere. This is music first and foremost, not ideas translated stillborn into sound; while *Parable IX* may seem initially like a conceptual abstraction, with familiarity its natural sense of vigor and grace becomes increasingly apparent.

The premiere of *Parable IX* took place in Des Moines, Iowa, in April 1973. Don Marcouiller conducted the Drake University Symphonic Wind Ensemble. The work's first recording was that same all-Persichetti program featuring the University of Kansas Symphonic Band, which appeared in 1978. However, it has appeared on several subsequent recordings since then.

A Lincoln Address, Op. 124, and the controversy surrounding it, are discussed in some detail in the biographical portion of this chapter and in the section dealing with Persichetti's orchestral works. In 1973 the composer was approached by Gene Witherspoon, who offered him a commission to transcribe the orchestral work for symphonic band. Persichetti complied with the request—the only time he agreed to such a transcription. *A Lincoln Address*, Op. 124A, was first performed in February 1974 at the convention of the College Band Directors' National Association in Houston, Texas. Tom Slater was the narrator, and Gene Witherspoon conducted the Arkansas Polytechnic College Band.

Persichetti's final composition for band was the Chorale Prelude: "O God Unseen," Op. 160. Like the other two Chorale Preludes for band, it is based on a selection from the *Hymns and Responses for the Church Year*, volume I, in this case, No. 16, "O God, Unseen, yet Ever Near." The piece was commissioned by the North Carolina Bandmasters (Eastern Division) for Herbert Carter and the East Carolina University Wind Ensemble, and was completed in 1984. Somewhat longer than the other two Chorale Preludes, "O God Unseen" begins in the manner of a dirge, as the hymn melody is initially heard in short, detached notes, by the bass and contrabass clarinets, bassoons, and tuba, in a manner suggesting an accompaniment. A countermelody based on the hymn melody, *legato* and somewhat florid, is introduced by the flute and alto clarinet. This and other countermelodies gradually enter, building in intensity and contrapuntal density, and only later does the hymn melody emerge clearly in the foreground. The piece builds to a strong climax before receding, while the dirge-like character continues throughout.

The premiere of Chorale Prelude: "O God Unseen," took place in Winston-Salem, North Carolina, in November 1984. Herbert Carter conducted the East Carolina University Wind Ensemble. The work's initial recording was released in 1994 as part of the first all-Persichetti band program to appear on compact disc. One of the most significant recordings of the composer's music for band, the disc features the winds and percussion of the London Symphony Orchestra, conducted by David Amos. Amos is a dedicated and sympathetic proponent of American traditionalist composers and through this recording made an important contribution toward increased awareness of this portion of the repertoire.

The Serenades

In addition to the traditional genres of symphony, sonata, concerto, and string quartet, there are two others that Persichetti pursued and developed in his own way: the serenade and the parable. "My Serenades," he stated, "are suites of 'love' pieces, usually of the night: small pieces of a certain lyric, under-the-window quality, that had precedence with Mozart and Brahms."[277] Persichetti's serenades, however, reveal remarkably little in common with those of Mozart or Brahms. For Persichetti, the serenade was generally a diverting composition comprising many short—even tiny—character pieces. Most—though not all—represent the more *"grazioso"* side of his compositional personality. He composed fifteen serenades between 1929 and 1984, mostly for single instruments or small chamber ensembles, although No. 5 is scored for full orchestra. Some of them are discussed in the sections where they naturally fell based on their medium; others are yet to be discussed. Following is a complete list of the serenades, in sequence:

Serenade No. 1, Op. 1 (1929) Wind Dectet
Serenade No. 2, Op. 2 (1929) Piano
Serenade No. 3, Op. 17 (1941) Piano Trio
Serenade No. 4, Op. 28 (1945) Violin and Piano
Serenade No. 5, Op. 43 (1950) Orchestra
Serenade No. 6, Op. 44 (1950) Trombone, Viola, and Cello
Serenade No. 7, Op. 55 (1952) Piano
Serenade No. 8, Op. 62 (1954) Piano, Four Hands
Serenade No. 9, Op. 71 (1956) Soprano and Alto Recorders
Serenade No. 10, Op. 79 (1957) Flute and Harp
Serenade No. 11, Op. 85 (1960) Band
Serenade No. 12, Op. 88 (1961) Tuba Solo
Serenade No. 13, Op. 95 (1963) Clarinet Duo
Serenade No. 14, Op. 159 (1984) Oboe Solo
Serenade No. 15, Op. 161 (1984) Harpsichord

The *Parables*

The *Parables* were a project of the latter part of Persichetti's career. There are a total of twenty-five, composed between 1965 and 1986. He described them, in his typically cryptic fashion, as "misstated stories, that avoid a truth in order to tell it. Parables are always 'again,' even when they are new; they're never 'was' or old. The Parables are non-programmatic musical essays. . . . They are always in one movement, almost always about a single germinal idea. Parables convey a meaning indirectly by the use of comparisons or analogies, and they are usually concerned with materials from my other works."[278] Most are very short pieces—often about five minutes long—and fourteen are for unaccompanied monophonic instruments. But there are exceptions: For example, *Parable IX* is a large work for band; *Parable X* is a string quartet; *Parable XX* is an entire opera; *Parable XXIII* is a full-length piano trio. (Interestingly, while the serenades were identified in the more traditional fashion by Arabic numerals, the *Parables* are identified by Roman numerals, a convention adopted by many of the serial composers of the 1960s and 1970s.)

Most of the *Parables* are quite challenging musically and are thoroughly abstract in character. Those for monophonic instruments are essentially exercises in musicianship for the player, rather than—considered realistically—rewarding aesthetic experiences for the listener. They are largely atonal, though not systematically so, but usually conclude having achieved some sense of tonal center. They are tailored meticulously to the technical and expressive qualities of the particular instrument, which they exploit fully, including some modest use of extended techniques. Interpretive and expressive indications are noted generously in the scores. Some of the scores indicate in coded form the sources of material taken from earlier works, reinforcing the notion of a hidden meaning. In a sense, Persichetti's *Parables* are like musical footnotes to the rest of his output, and derive musical significance from that relationship. As with the serenades, some of the *Parables* have been discussed already, and others are addressed in the pages that follow. However, with just a few exceptions, analyses of each of the *Parables*, and comparative studies of the ways that ideas taken from earlier works are treated in later ones, are beyond the scope of this book. Such investigations, though altogether worthwhile, must be left to subsequent scholars. Following is a complete list of the *Parables*:

Parable I, Op. 100 (1965) Flute Solo
Parable II, Op. 108 (1968) Brass Quintet
Parable III, Op. 109 (1968) Oboe Solo
Parable IV, Op. 110 (1969) Bassoon Solo
Parable V, Op. 112 (1969) Carillon
Parable VI, Op. 117 (1971) Organ
Parable VII, Op. 119 (1971) Harp

Parable VIII, Op. 120 (1972) Horn Solo
Parable IX, Op. 121 (1972) Band
Parable X, Op. 122 (1972) String Quartet (No. 4)
Parable XI, Op. 123 (1972) Alto Saxophone Solo
Parable XII, Op. 125 (1973) Piccolo Solo
Parable XIII, Op. 126 (1973) Clarinet Solo
Parable XIV, Op. 127 (1973) Trumpet Solo
Parable XV, Op. 128 (1973) English Horn Solo
Parable XVI, Op. 130 (1974) Viola Solo
Parable XVII, Op. 131 (1974) Doublebass Solo
Parable XVIII, Op. 133 (1975) Trombone Solo
Parable XIX, Op. 134 (1975) Piano
Parable XX, Op. 135 (1976) Opera (*The Sibyl: A Parable of Chicken Little*)
Parable XXI, Op. 140 (1978) Guitar
Parable XXII, Op. 147 (1981) Tuba Solo
Parable XXIII, Op. 150 (1981) Piano Trio
Parable XXIV, Op. 153 (1982) Harpsichord
Parable XXV, Op. 164 (1986) Trumpet Duo

Opera

Although he often expressed a distaste for the traditional operatic repertoire,[279] Persichetti did compose one work that—though far from traditional in many ways—belongs to that genre: *The Sibyl: A Parable of Chicken Little (Parable XX)*, Op. 135. The longest and most elaborate of the *Parables*, the work was commissioned by "a midwestern university."[280] It seems to have been begun in 1974 and completed in short score in 1975. But the commissioning institution evidently was unable to meet the terms of the contract, so the opera sat on the shelf until the early 1980s when the Pennsylvania Opera Theater assumed the remainder of the commission. The work reached its final form in 1984. (Some years earlier Persichetti had hoped the opera might be produced at the Juilliard School, but Peter Mennin rejected the idea, finding the subject matter to be unsuitable.[281])

The work proved to be one of Persichetti's most ambitious efforts, drawing upon much of his previous work. He wrote the libretto himself, basing it on the famous *Jataka* fable said to have originated in Buddhist India.[282] Extant papers indicate that the opera went through many revisions, the composer evidently changing his mind repeatedly about various details. Among the titles he considered for the work were *Little Prophet*, *Sky Gazer*, *Trouble in the Sky*, *One Penny Opera*, and *Hole in the Sky*.[283] At some point he seems to have settled on *Chicken Little*, then changing it shortly before the premiere to *The Sibyl: A Parable of Chicken Little.*[284] The final libretto is structured as one act, subdivided into three connected scenes, with a combined duration of sixty-five to seventy-five minutes. (It appears that Persichetti was not the first composer to base an opera on this unlikely tale: The Polish composer Jerzy Fitelberg [1903–1951] had written an opera called *Henny Penny* in 1949.[285]) Persichetti described his work cryptically as "an ecological opera," adding with characteristic whimsy, "Chicken Little was always a favorite story of mine. I started thinking about it one day; Henny Penny came out of the woods and began walking around, and the text gradually unfolded before me. . . . People and animals are the same to me. Oh, I know people can read and write, but it's still the same thing."[286] (An interesting sidelight: In a letter dated November 1974, composer Dominick Argento informed Persichetti that the latter's Italian name, translated into English, means, roughly, "Chicken Little," which must have delighted him.[287])

The opera is set in the rural south of the United States, during the Great Depression, and is populated by Chicken Little, Henny Penny, Turkey Lurkey, Foxy Loxy, and others. The score calls for a chorus that comments on the proceedings. In keeping with the concept of an allegory, the characters are to be "simply dressed—imaginative makeup with ornaments and hair pieces that identify their type of animal person in an abstract manner." Specific costumes are suggested for the main characters. In one of the earlier drafts, Persichetti specified, "The soloists should have clean, fresh voices. They should sing with warmth and flexibility and all phrases should be shaped freely. There must be no overprojected 'operatic singing,' and no one should hesitate to use a 'pop' voice or speech-oriented sounds."[288] Although this instruction was omitted from the final score, it gives an indication of the composer's thinking regarding the trappings of the "typical opera."

Set during a time of drought, the first scene is entitled "Wishing." The main characters are introduced, except for Chicken Little, who is searching for water. Foxy Loxy reveals his desire for Henny Penny, introducing an ambiguity that persists throughout the opera, in which greed for food and sexual lust are somehow conflated. Eventually, Chicken Little appears. All the characters express longings to be elsewhere, to be what they are not, or to have what is unattainable. A verbal motif, "I wish this were a bayou," set to a distinctive "scotch-snap" rhythm, is heard frequently. Scene Two is entitled "Sky Spell." A pebble falls on Chicken Little's head, and she is convinced that the sky is falling. The others become agitated and set out helter-skelter to tell the king. In an aside, Foxy Loxy sings, "This whole gaggle of beasts are convinced that the end is at hand. The premise of Chicken Little's fable will be repeated time after time. All these poor souls do believe now that the pebble's feathery landing is a signal that the sky is indeed falling. In their

hearts they feel that someday soon the sky *will* fall. They almost wish it."
Donning a magic cloak, Foxy Loxy seizes the opportunity to cast a spell and
leads the group into his cave. The chief object of his desire, Henny Penny,
is wary of him, but he pursues her. ("I want Henny, that ripe red hen, way
inside me.") He tries to catch her, but she eludes his grasp, much to his
frustration. Scene Three is called "Realization." Henny Penny discovers that
what fell on Chicken Little's head was a pebble from the roof of her house
and announces this revelation to the group. Foxy Loxy's spell is broken and
the captives escape from the cave, only to resume their wishing and longing.
Suddenly there is lightning and rain begins to fall, and all begin to dance
gaily. In the uproar Foxy Loxy casts a spell on Chicken Little and leads her
into his cave. Seductively, he sings, "Chicken Little, will you love me tonight?" Entranced, she responds, "My dearest Foxy Loxy. What a beautiful
Boy. Yes, tonight!" She disappears with him into his cave, as she is heard,
pleading, "Please be gentle. You are rough. Don't crush me." A loud moan
is heard, unmistakably indicating her rape and murder. Amidst the ensuing
confusion, Foxy Loxy appears, and proclaims, "The sky *is* falling!" The
opera ends in chaos, as the chorus sings, "Is it the sky or the Fox? Is the sky
the Fox? Or is the Fox the sky?"

The parable seems to point to the propensity of human beings never to be
satisfied with their lot in life, while remaining oblivious to serious dangers in
their midst. This leaves them vulnerable to seduction by a demagogue who
may exploit their trivial concerns while ultimately seizing power over them
for his own ends. Persichetti's reference to "an ecological opera" suggests
that the serious danger he had in mind may have been the destruction of the
environment, while Foxy Loxy may represent the demagogues of politics and
corporate commerce, who play on the fears of the populace and gratify their
petty vanities while enriching themselves and destroying the planet in the
process. As is the case with most parables, this one is open to more than one
interpretation. But there is no mistaking the fact that the typically cheerful,
high-spirited composer has here created a work of dire pessimism.

The musical content of *The Sybil* is wholly derived from previous works of
Persichetti—mostly his simplest, most innocent pieces, making the opera, in
a sense, the apotheosis of the childlike side of his creative persona. By using
material of this kind in creating a nightmarish vision of such scope, Persichetti
also reveals the deep covert connection between his "gracious" and "gritty"
expressive poles. Among the papers with his initial sketches and ideas for the
work are listed the pieces from which he drew its thematic material: "The
Wind Shifts," from *Harmonium*, Op. 50; Serenade No. 7, Op. 55; *Parades*,
Op. 57; *Little Piano Book*, Op. 60; Serenade No. 8, Op. 62; and "The Grass"
from *Emily Dickinson Songs*, Op. 77.[289] There is also a list of the specific mo-

tivic ideas he selected, with sources identified, an analysis of their intervallic interrelationships, and what he called a "composite cantus firmus": a single melodic line comprising an integration of all these motifs.[290] Within the forcefully exuberant five-minute overture to the opera are heard the "Prologue" (*Little Piano Book* [*LPB*]), "Berceuse" (*LPB*), "Sleep" (Serenade No. 7), "Capriccio" (*LPB*), "Canter" (*Parades*), "The Grass," and "Masque" (*LPB*)— some in counterpoint with each other. It is from these and the other motifs noted that the entire work is shaped. Most of the music in Scene One is tuneful and playful in character, contributing to its accessibility and overall appeal. Among the high points are a duet in Scene One ("My balloon") for Ducky Lucky and Piggy Wiggy, based on the lovely "Berceuse" (*LPB*); perhaps most notable of all is Chicken Little's aria "The Swan," which is an adaptation of "The Grass"—one of Persichetti's must touchingly poignant songs—with his own paraphrase of Emily Dickinson's text ("The grass so little has to do,/A sphere of simple green" becomes "The swan has nothing much to do, a tuft of tender white"). In Scenes Two and Three, the musical language becomes somewhat more chromatic and angular, although, in true show-stopper fashion, the Swan aria is reprised as a sextet in the final scene.

The premiere—and, as of this writing, sole—production of *The Sibyl* was given by the Pennsylvania Opera Theater in Philadelphia in April 1985. The conductor was Barbara Silverstein, and the stage director was Grethe Barrett Holby. The part of Chicken Little was taken by Jennifer Ringo, Henny Penny was played by Lynnen Yakes, and Foxy Loxy was played by Harlan Foss. Critical reactions to the work were qualified at best. Daniel Webster commented that the work "is neither a children's opera nor an 'animal opera,' but a serious exploration of how people face—or avoid—serious issues." But he added that *The Sibyl* is not really an opera at all, asserting that it "gains nothing from staging, scenery or action, and the best theatrical efforts of the company do nothing to illuminate or enhance the work." Instead, he found it

> a splendid cantata, composed in taut, symphonic style, that would fit nicely in a program with another of his effective choral works. The score must stand as one of the composer's brightest and most colorful instrumental offerings. It includes at least one finely sculpted aria, but also choral music that speaks clearly and brilliantly. The instrumental score is knit tightly from themes that remain in the ear and that evolve through the work to confirm its architectural solidity. A Persichetti score is generally a model of economy, and this one is especially succinct and expressive.

However, much of the seriousness of the piece seems to have been lost on Webster, who concludes his description: "The final chaotic scene offers a new example of the composer's playful sense of words, for the singers confuse fox and sky, the key words in the threat to the characters." His final verdict: "Unlike children, this is to be heard and not seen."[291]

Other critics were less charitable. Robert Baxter found that the composer "failed to fashion a memorable fusion of music and drama. . . . He does not fill out the characters in his one-act opera with real emotions or make them interact in any meaningful way. His music for all its fine craftsmanship, adds little dramatic dimension to a text that lacks strongly drawn characters and compelling conflict. He has fashioned a score that is more an academic state-ment than a musical drama."[292] Perhaps harshest of all was Will Crutchfield, who found the work to be

> transparently, unpersuasively preachy, burdened not only by a preoccupation with the obvious (we create dramatic, exciting troubles to avoid dealing with nagging real troubles, and so forth), but also by a depressing seriousness about it. The ending is particularly weak. . . . Nor is the music compelling. . . . One senses in "The Sibyl" a desire to be melodic and a desire to be dramatic; the craftsman's observation of certain external characteristics of melodic or dra-matic music is in evidence, but neither melody nor drama is there, not even for a moment. And there is a flaw of conception: Mr. Persichetti never creates the music for the (potentially) charming fairy-tale animal world. He relies on the choice of subject and stage picture to speak for itself, and goes straight (and platitudinously) to the "message."[293]

These unfavorable reviews were digested and regurgitated with some inaccuracy in the *New Grove Dictionary of Opera*, where James P. Cassaro writes, "The work's musical language is essentially atonal. Vocal lines con-tain awkward leaps, and the complex rhythmic patterns often break words apart, compromising proper text declamation. . . . Unfortunately because of hollow characterization and a lack of dramatic tension in both text and music, the work met with little success after its initial performance."[294] There is no gainsaying the fact that the critical response to the opera's sole production was overwhelmingly negative, but the notion that its musical language is atonal is unequivocally false. Nevertheless, others in attendance, including this writer, found the work to be theatrically effective—despite much that is provocative and perplexing—and musically rewarding. Perhaps another pro-duction would be more successful in projecting the opera's theatrical impact, its melodic appeal, and its allegorical implications.

Chamber Music

As might be expected, Vincent Persichetti composed a large and varied array of music for solo instruments and small instrumental combinations. These pieces range from string quartets and other genres associated with the classical tradition, to the serenade for recorder duo, and the *Parables* for individual brass or woodwind instruments, with numerous examples falling somewhere in between. In order to provide some semblance of organization, the following discussion begins with Persichetti's contributions to the primary traditional genres of chamber music: the string quartets, piano quintet, and piano trio, presented in chronological order. The discussion continues with a representative sample of other significant chamber works, proceeding in chronological order.

String Quartets, Piano Quintet, Piano Trio

Central to Persichetti's chamber music are four string quartets that span the period 1939–1972, along with a piano quintet and a piano trio. Fairly evenly spaced throughout his productive life, these works present most facets of his enormous compositional range. However, largely absent from these pieces is the composer's most ingratiating vein: the lively, clearly tonal, largely consonant substyle found in his most popular works, such as the pieces composed during the 1950s for piano and for wind ensemble (although the Quartet No. 2 approaches this to some extent). The aspects of Persichetti's output represented by the quartets, quintet, and trio are found in some of their most austere manifestations; this music does not engulf the listener with sensuous delights. Consequently these are among Persichetti's less frequently heard works.

The String Quartet No. 1, Op. 7, dates from 1939, when the composer was still seeking a distinctive creative voice of his own. Many of his works from this period, such as the Piano Sonata No. 1, Sonata for Violin Solo, and the Sonata for Two Pianos, are quite dissonant harmonically and attenuated tonally—especially as viewed within the context of American music at that time—and the First String Quartet falls into this category as well. Its four short movements last barely fifteen minutes. The first, *Largo*, sets a rather severe tone, reminiscent of both Schoenberg and Hindemith, beginning with a stern twelve-note theme that unfolds fugally. The second movement is a *scherzo*, marked *Allegro molto energico*, in 5/8 meter. Although chromatic in melody and harshly dissonant in harmony, the movement exudes a mercurial energy and maintains considerable textural and rhythmic interest. (Dorothea Persichetti indicated that this movement contains an imitation of the sound made by young turkeys.[295]) The third movement, *Andantino*, is lyrical in gesture, but severe and dry in musical content. The finale, a brief *Vivace*, is the most distinctive movement of the quartet, with a "goofy" motif that seems to evoke the "turkey" notion more obviously than does the *scherzo*.

Although Persichetti was often profound without being acerbic, he was on occasion acerbic without being profound. This is especially true of some of his earlier pieces, when he employed a harmonic language that seems inordinately harsh relative to the expressive content. The First String Quartet, perhaps one of the composer's lesser works, falls victim to this incongruity. Despite its grim, twelve-note opening and its contrapuntal density, it is essentially a lightweight and rather jocular piece.

The Quartet No. 1 was introduced by Philadelphia's Twentieth Century Music Group in February 1942. (The two violinists were Rafael Druian and Broadus Erle, both of whom went on to distinguished careers.) The work was received with limited enthusiasm. The composer and writer Paul Bowles described it as "in the Hindemith tradition" and found it "knowingly wrought and sonorously satisfying. The first movement had the same quality of voluptuous and wistful frustration found in the early Hindemith string works; in fact, there was too much rewriting of the master's music for much originality of expression to come through."[296] Arthur Cohn wrote, "Although extremely derivative, it displayed a tight hand and a purposeful restlessness. The block segmatic unisons and fifths used in building up the second movement, of course stem directly from Hindemith's *Third Quartet*. A better organized top line and a greater usage of the sonorities of the quartet body would improve [Persichetti's] writing."[297]

The String Quartet No. 2, Op. 24, is markedly different from its predecessor. Completed in 1944, it embraces the "Americana" style found in the Piano Sonata No. 3 and the Symphony No. 3, composed at roughly the same time. Its modal, diatonic materials infinitely simpler than those of the First Quartet, it is by far the easiest of the four to approach and is probably the one most often performed. The work comprises three movements. Like the First Quartet, it opens with a slow solo statement of a primary theme, but instead of a twelve-note line, it is a melody in the Dorian mode. Marked *Slow*, the opening movement develops this theme canonically at first, then more freely, drawing upon techniques associated with Roy Harris, such as the latter's adaptation of *organum*. In fact, the Second Quartet, with its "autogenetic" formal designs instead of classical models, is probably the single work of Persichetti in which the influence of Harris is most discernable and pervasive. The second movement, *Moderately fast*, is a *scherzo* that retains the modal flavor, while even betraying a passing whiff of square dance. A *trio* section combines the *scherzo* motif with the first movement theme. The third movement begins *Slow*, with a sustained intensity. This serves as introduction to the body of the movement, marked *Fast*. In 6/8 meter, the music pursues a relentless course, with references to Beethoven's *Grosse Fuge* too obvious to be accidental.

The first performance of Persichetti's Quartet No. 2 was given in August 1945 at the Colorado Springs Fine Arts Festival, where his Third Piano Sonata had been presented so successfully two years earlier. This new premiere was given by the Roth String Quartet. (Dorothea recalled a letter from Persichetti reporting that during one of the rehearsals, "Someone came in breathlessly today with news of an atom bomb. The quartet lit fresh cigarettes and went on with the rehearsal."[298]) Later that year the piece was awarded the Blue Network Prize, as "the most outstanding contemporary work in the field of chamber music."[299] Reviewing the quartet upon its publication some three decades after it was composed, Andrew Frank commented,

> This quartet is an excellent example of Persichetti's ability to make a strong sturdy musical construction, but always relying on an underlying simplicity to give his music a characteristic profile. This is very straightforward music, both rhythmically and melodically, and it looks as though it might be a great deal of fun to play. . . . Even though this quartet was composed thirty years ago, it sounds fresh and energetic today. It may be representational of a certain kind of "American" music rhetoric common in the nineteen-thirties and forties, but it has strength and a great deal of charm.[300]

In 1954 Persichetti composed his Quintet for Piano and Strings, Op. 66, on commission from the Serge Koussevitzky Music Foundation. The work falls among those Persichetti compositions that first appeared during the 1950s in which several sections distinguished by contrasting tempos are integrated into a single movement unified by the continuous development of thematic material stated at the outset—an approach ideally suited to the composer's gift for creating a coherent stylistic entity from diverse expressive elements and for generating a fluent overall design despite many contrasting episodes. These are among the composer's greatest works and include the Concerto for Piano, Four Hands, as well as the Symphony No. 5, the Piano Sonata No. 10 (which followed immediately upon the heels of the Piano Quintet), and the String Quartet No. 3, which is discussed shortly. Persichetti returned to this approach periodically, throughout the rest of his career (e.g. the String Quartet No. 4, and the Piano Trio, *Parable XXIII*).

Dorothea subdivides the Quintet into ten sections, based on the eight-measure entrance of the first violin, which she terms the "germinal material" of the entire work.[301] However, the four opening measures, played by the viola, introduce two motifs that seem even more fundamental to the structure of the composition. These and other motifs introduced within the first minute of the work serve as its source material and permeate its many sections. One motif, comprising rapid scale-like embellishments, does not appear until near the middle of the work. Perceptible tonality is more attenuated than in the

Fifth Symphony, for example, but the Quintet is not consistently atonal. In fact, passages of tonal clarity emerge like brief moments of sunlight during an overcast day. The work is notable for the frequency and number of shifts in tempo and energy level. As is true of most of Persichetti's major chamber works, a brilliant contrapuntal lucidity is maintained throughout, while the rapid sections exhibit a driving, kinetic quality. (There also appears to be a quotation from William Schuman's song, "Orpheus with His Lute" [1944] at m. 574. Persichetti was fond of this song and was responsible for persuading Schuman to develop it into the *Song of Orpheus* for cello and orchestra.) Dorothea hears in the Quintet a pervasive sense of despondency, suggested by one of the motifs, based on a step-wise descent. The work certainly reflects the "gritty" side of the composer's personality, with its harshly dissonant harmonic language and extended periods of aggressiveness. And the lugubrious final section displays a sense of dark resignation. The Piano Quintet is one of Persichetti's finest examples of "absolute music," in which spontaneity and impulsiveness are merged with reason and order in a natural, fluent expression, without recourse to extrinsic references—literary, pictorial, emotional, or otherwise.

The premiere of Persichetti's Piano Quintet was given by the Kroll String Quartet, with the composer at the piano, at the Library of Congress in Washington, D.C., in February 1955. The same forces presented the work in New York City's Town Hall the following January. Although not always the case—as has been documented throughout this chapter—for some reason the merits of the Piano Quintet were recognized immediately. Perhaps attributable to the high quality of the initial performances, or to the composer's own participation in them, or to the auspiciousness of the circumstances of the commission, the critical response was remarkably enthusiastic. Paul Hume wrote after the Washington premiere, "From the beginning one constantly feels this is an exceptionally good piece. The writing is sure though never occupied with display techniques."[302] "Persichetti's new work has earned a place in the permanent repertoire," wrote Samuel L. Singer.[303] Paul Henry Lang felt that he would "have to hear this work at least once more before I can fully grasp its harmonic and formal scheme, both of which are complicated. However, even so I found the quintet thoroughly enjoyable. . . . [Persichetti's] setting is lucid and transparent and abounds in wonderfully eerie sonorities as well as in nice lyric passages. . . . The performance was absolutely first class. . . . Mr. Persichetti, an excellent pianist, proved to be that rarity in modern times, a worthy interpreter of his own music."[304] Edward Downes termed the work "magnificent . . . the high point of the . . . concert. . . . Out of a fullness of technical skill and beguiling musical ideas, [the composer] has produced a long work which seems short. In feeling it is a romantic work, warm, colorful and dramatic."[305] Louis Biancolli noted that "A vigorous gift for idiom and invention pulses through the unbroken span. I thought I detected the influence of Bartok and Alban Berg in places. The rest is wholly Persichetti, a probing, restless mind, sometimes hard to follow but always springing fresh surprises."[306] "It is a work of more than ordinary significance," wrote Rafael Kammerer. "Although romantic in essence, it is modern in texture. Melodically beautiful and harmonically colorful, the Quintet is scored with a fine ear for tonal subtleties. Mr. Persichetti proved to be more than a capable pianist in the performance of his own work."[307] Perhaps the most perceptive remarks were those of Elliot Galkin, who reviewed a Baltimore performance featuring the Juilliard Quartet, with the composer at the piano. "Stylistically Mr. Persichetti's Quintet is a work urbane and sophisticated. His is an eclecticism in which he has been able to absorb many techniques and assimilate them into a personal utterance. . . . He is, in short, a modern neo-classicist."[308]

Yet despite the critical enthusiasm, Persichetti's Piano Quintet did not appear on recording until 1979, when Arizona State University released an LP that included this work in an excellent performance by the New Art String Quartet; once again, the composer was at the piano. Unfortunately, the circulation of this recording was quite limited; it has never been reissued on compact disc.

The String Quartet No. 3, Op. 81, represents a considerable advance over its two predecessors in the genre. It was commissioned by the University of Alabama and completed in 1959, immediately following the Symphony No. 7, "Liturgical." As noted, this quartet exemplifies a structural approach similar to that represented by the Piano Quintet. Among the works of this kind from the 1950s, the Third Quartet is probably the most austere and difficult to penetrate, owing to its twelve-note theme, its often glassy sonorities, and the abstraction of the medium. It comprises seven or eight sections (depending on where the lines are drawn) and is constructed in such a way as to permit an organic integration of both tonal and serial elements.

The work opens, *Adagio*, with a twelve-tone row presented in harmonics by each instrument in succession. The first six notes of the row, however, are diatonic, which prepares the tonal/atonal integration. Most, but not all, of the work's thematic material is derived from this row. As Dorothea Persichetti pointed out (in 1960), "There is more serial writing [in this quartet] than in any of the composer's works."[309] Clearly introductory, the effect of the opening is mysterious and portentous in character. It is followed by an *Allegro molto* of tremendous rhythmic energy and contrapuntal brilliance. As the energy abates toward the end of this section a chorale sequence of eighteen chords is heard. Dorothea notes that the entire work is based on this chorale, the upper line of which comprises the row, though the harmonization is relatively consonant and freely tonal. This duality further allows for the tonal/atonal integration. After the eighteenth chord is reached, the sequence is heard in retrogression. The *Adagio* that follows develops melodically and contrapuntally. There is considerable lyricism in the slow portions of the quartet, but a lyricism of the most abstract, rarefied kind, which may not be accessible to the casual listener. This was described eloquently by David Cohen, a composer who had studied with Persichetti. He commented on this quartet in words that may justly be applied to a number of other works of Persichetti as well: "The emergence of a diatonic melody from untonal surroundings has a different meaning than it would have in a blandly diatonic setting. Such an escape into melody sometimes becomes the expressive center of the longer Persichetti movements. But Persichetti seldom writes tunes. More often he writes the essence of tunes—those phrases and faint refrains that will linger in the memory to remind us of longer melodies which, in fact, we never heard."[310] An exciting section, *Furioso*, follows, leading to a more ambiguous passage, marked *A piacere*. A serial treatment with stark, disjunct gestures elides directly with a brief but beautiful tonal passage, which Dorothea identifies as "the 'heart' of the work," recalling moments from the Fifth Symphony.[311] Rhythmic and contrapuntal energy is revived with a passage marked *Vivo*, before the tonal passage returns, leading to an elaborate canonic passage. This is followed by a vigorous "Persichetti 2/4," marked *Vivace*— simpler in texture, but rhythmically gripping and exhilarating. This extended section finally resolves to a *Lento* that returns to the mysterious cast of the opening, dotted with reminiscences of the foregoing material. Persichetti's Quartet No. 3 is a work of considerable complexity and consummate artistry; a brief commentary can only touch upon highlights.

The String Quartet No. 3 was first performed in April 1959 in Tuscaloosa, Alabama, by the Alabama String Quartet, who toured with the work throughout the United States. Dorothea cites a number of favorable reactions, but without attribution.[312] After a Philadelphia performance by the Walden Quartet, Max de Schauensee described the work as "an admirably constructed, quite moving piece of music."[313]

Persichetti composed the String Quartet No. 4, Op. 122, for the Alard Quartet in 1972, on a commission from the Institute for Arts and Humanistic Studies at Pennsylvania State University. This was a time when the composer was seeking to integrate newer compositional techniques embraced by younger composers into his own broad musical language. It was also a period when Persichetti was intensely involved with his series of *Parables* (*VI* through *XV* were composed between 1971 and 1973); this quartet bears the subtitle, *Parable X*. At the end of the score, the following inscription appears: "Infantavlsonvcsonfoursympianquint," indicating that material from

Infanta Marina, Sonata for Violin Solo, Sonata for Cello Solo, Fourth Symphony, and the Piano Quintet all play a role in the work. However, as David Cohen points out, "One should not make too much of this since the quartet must stand on its own. Knowing the source of the material does nothing to illuminate its use in a complexly intertwined structure. The borrowing might rather be taken as a statement by the composer about the essential unity of his work and as further evidence of his desire to amalgamate diverse materials into a unified whole."[314]

The work is, in a sense, a conceptual expansion of the previous quartet, extending the notion of constant flux within a one-movement design, while relying less completely on linear contrapuntal development and embracing texture and gesture as primary elements, often exhibiting contrapuntal relationships of their own. Though the score subdivides the work into five sections, there are so many additional tempo shifts and other changes of motion that these sections are not readily identifiable aurally. The work opens eerily, *Lento*, with a primary motif introduced by the viola and cello in harmonics doubled at the octave. Two additional motifs are heard immediately in the first and second violins, played *sul tasto*. Although there is no obvious tone row, the impact of the work is consistently atonal, as the individual instruments treat diverse material simultaneously, and rhythmic activity among them often seems unrelated. There is much use of the special string effects that became virtual clichés among the serialists, such as *tremolo* harmonics played *sul ponticello*. As David Cohen noted with acute perspicacity, "The greater contrasts in texture, the simultaneous presentation of different thematic threads and the rich diversity of material contribute to a work which, though it has immediate impact, does not reveal all of its secrets on first hearing. Sometimes the full statement of a theme is preceded by fragmentary anticipations and followed by motivic echoes. There is occasionally the feeling not of transition but of themes coming in and out of focus."[315] Though its rarefied, ethereal sonorities, fragmentary textures, and lack of perceptible tonality may seem somewhat forbidding upon initial acquaintance, this is authentic music-making, albeit at a high level of abstraction and complexity. It is music that truly fulfills the claims of profound expressive depth made on behalf of so many of the atonalists and twelve-toners of the time.

The premiere of String Quartet No. 4 was given by the Alard String Quartet in February 1973 in University Park, Pennsylvania. In light of the comments above, it is interesting to consider the words of James Felton: "Without slipping into electronic or pseudo-electronic masks, this extremely intense and expressive use of four stringed instruments still finds new harmonies and a new formal layout just this side of the traditional brink. . . . Persichetti has grown with his own discoveries and they are nowhere more splendidly on display than in this lovely Quartet."[316]

None of Persichetti's string quartets ever appeared on recording until 1976, when David Cohen produced a beautifully played, intelligently annotated, and handsomely packaged LP set of all four, in brilliant performances by the New Art String Quartet, then in residence at Arizona State University. This set was available to the public at a modest price directly from Arizona State. However, inadequately publicized, these recordings were barely acknowledged by the relevant media and made little impact. Thirty years later, in 2006, a compact disc featuring the four string quartets was released, in equally fine performances by the Lydian String Quartet. Reviewing this recording, the perceptive critic Mark Lehman noted that although Persichetti's musical language "lacks an instantly recognizable individual 'sound,' stints on singable melodies, and often (in his later music) pursues a formal logic too idiosyncratic to allow for easy understanding or appeal . . . [his music] is always vigorous, idiomatic, packed with ideas, and informed by a restless and penetrating musical intelligence." He finds the first two quartets "in form and spirit, essentially neoclassic compositions. Anyone who enjoys the quartets of Piston and early Diamond will have no trouble also enjoying (as I did) this unassuming, well-made, likable music." On the other hand, he describes Nos. 3 and 4 as

"Mid-Century Modern American Eclectic Expressionist" in style, somewhere between the smoother and more sonorous quartets of William Schuman and the more jagged and hyper-intense quartets of Leon Kirchner. At any rate they are far more disjunct and chromatic than Persichetti's first two quartets, entirely dispensing with the vernacular flavor of those earlier efforts. These longer, more ambitious, more violent, more searching and more adventurous works are each cast in a single multi-section movement that evolves unpredictably and with a symphonic scope and complexity that at times seems to be testing the boundaries of what is possible within the limits of chamber music—almost as if they were pen-and-ink blueprints of unwritten but implied full-scale orchestral compositions. . . . I don't have a clue how these works are structured, except to note the obvious fact that both begin and end in slow, quiet, out-of-the-darkness mystery that surrounds a welter of constantly-evolving activity. Nevertheless, however spontaneous-seeming the music, there's always a strong sense of purpose and direction. These recalcitrant, fascinating, and in their own way eloquent quartets will repay the listener willing to give them the time and attention they demand. At every hearing I'm more convinced that they are among the more significant works in this hallowed genre written by an American.[317]

In 1981 Persichetti completed a Piano Trio, *Parable XXIII*, Op. 150. The score bears the dedication, "for the Marlboro Trio," suggesting that the work was commissioned by this group, although it does not appear to have been performed by them. It is the composer's last work of major proportions, written during the period when he was largely preoccupied with the harpsichord. Following along the lines of the String Quartet No. 4, it is a further evolution of Persichetti's concern with integrating wide-ranging development of a minimum of thematic material within a single movement. While it belongs to the series of *Parables*, there is no coded reference in the score to prior works to which there may be allusions. Like his other major chamber works, it is densely textured and highly contrapuntal, making a rather severe initial impression, although its passion and poetry emerge ever more clearly with attentive, repeated listening. The main three-note motif outlines an ascending major-ninth, including a minor-third above the root, and the work exploits these intervals, as well as the major-seventh also embraced within the motif. The structure of this motif has strong tonal tendencies, as well as romantic gestural implications, so that there is a constant sense of yearning, vainly attempting to break through the dissonant contrapuntal web. (At mm. 48–56, between three and four minutes from the beginning, there is a clear example of what David Cohen termed "the essence of tunes—those phrases and faint refrains that will linger in the memory.") The Trio falls into six continuous sections, of markedly different durations. Throughout much of the work the harmonic language is quite dissonant and atonal in effect, but there are frequent passages when intimations of tonality come briefly into focus. The first section, *Gravemente*, fully one third of the work's duration, sets a somber tone of considerable severity while introducing the basic motif as well as a chordal passage for the piano in contrary motion, which plays a recurrent role. This is followed by a vigorous, but much shorter section, marked *Velocemente*. The third section, *Elegantemente*, is shorter still but comprises the most poignantly lyrical, clearly tonal portion of the work. *Tempo Primo* is somewhat recapitulatory of the opening material, treated in dense counterpoint. It is followed by a highly inventive and aptly marked *Capricciosamente*, characterized by brief gestures that shift rapidly. The final section is a somewhat longer *Decisivamente* that brings together most of the myriad ideas and their developmental manifestations into one integrated final statement.

As with the Piano Quintet and the Quartets Nos. 3 and 4, when the Trio finally comes to an end, one has the sense that a coherent narrative has taken place, that an experiential map has been traversed, but one that is so subtle and infinitely nuanced that words are wholly inadequate in capturing it. However, the inescapable reality is that in order to grasp these achievements, the traditionalist listener must suspend his or her appetite for melodic, harmonic, and rhythmic felicities to which he has become accustomed and find enough that is initially provocative and stimulating to justify investing the concentration and intellectual energy necessary in achieving sufficient familiarity with the work to appreciate its rewards. That few are willing to make such an investment is the inevitable fate of music that ventures this far afield from the conventions and expectations of the people whom one is addressing in one's work. (And many Modernists would be quick to point out that Persichetti's explorations of this kind do not diverge from these conventions nearly as far as those of other composers writing at the time.)

The premiere of Persichetti's Piano Trio, *Parable XXIII*, took place at the Juilliard School in January 1982. Hamao Fujiwara was the violinist, James Kreger, the cellist, and the composer was at the piano. The work was recorded in 1991 by the Mirecourt Trio. In his liner notes for the recording, cellist Terry King recounts the events that led to their discovery of this work. The Trio had asked William Schuman for permission to play his early *Chorale and Fugue*. Schuman dismissed the work as juvenilia, but "raved about a new trio he had just heard written by his colleague Vincent Persichetti. He thought it was a special work and that we should play it."[318]

Other Chamber Music

Vincent Persichetti composed more than thirty other works for individual instruments or small groups of instruments, which fall into the general category of chamber music. The following section discusses some of the most important and/or most representative of these compositions.

In 1943 Persichetti composed *Pastoral*, Op. 21, for woodwind quintet. A mere five minutes in duration, this evocatively bucolic work begins with a clearly tonal, diatonic melody presented by the flute and clarinet, before the other instruments enter, gradually enriching the texture as they elaborate the melody with pan-diatonic counterpoint and harmony. Deceptively simple, the melody gradually evolves into other ideas, although their relation to the original melody is always clear, so that its abbreviated return at the end sounds natural and spontaneous. Not only is this composition Persichetti's first clearly tonal, largely diatonic piece—a harbinger of the style found in the band works of the 1950s—it may even be seen as anticipating Samuel Barber's popular *Summer Music*, composed some years later.

Arthur Cohn, a reliably astute commentator despite a propensity for quaint verbiage, observed,

> [Persichetti] does not abjure emotionalism but in taking his place on the creative stage he does not wax overly histrionic. Each work in his large catalog of varied music is in perfect balance, embraces the tonal emancipative doctrine and rhythmic non-symmetrical dogma of the twentieth century. Once a musical

prodigy, Persichetti is a rare example of mature fulfillment. . . . The *Pastoral* is a synthesis of several movements wrapped in one container. The opening Moderato theme is basic to the work as a whole; its free development places it on the periphery of rondo territory. When the principal subject returns toward the end in capsule form it proves its importance and balances the mutational fantasy that has intervened.[319]

The first performance of *Pastoral* was given in April 1945 by the Curtis Woodwind Quintet at the Franklin Institute in Philadelphia. Quickly becoming a staple of the woodwind quintet repertoire, it was first recorded in 1953 by the New Art Wind Quintet. Many recordings have followed, first on LP, more recently on compact disc. Reviewing the work's publication, celebrated French horn player John Barrows described it as "an exemplary piece of writing. From first-hand experience, this reviewer can report that the reaction of the audience is no less favorable than that of the performers."[320] Oliver Daniel wrote, "Although the music travels far from its starting point, the inter-relationship of materials outlines a clear formal path. Toward the end, the principal melody returns in a condensed version to complete the arc created by the piece."[321]

Composed just five years later for a similar ensemble—woodwind quintet plus piano and timpani—*King Lear*, Op. 35, is a very different and far more complex work. It was commissioned by Martha Graham as the musical score for her choreographic work, *Eye of Anguish*, based on Shakespeare's *King Lear*, and intended as a showcase for her former husband Erick Hawkins. Approached by Graham late in 1948—about the same time that she invited William Schuman to collaborate on what was to become *Judith*—Persichetti responded enthusiastically to what was one of the most auspicious compositional opportunities to present itself at that point in his career. Graham presented the composer with a fairly elaborate scenario, which he followed closely, completing the score within six weeks; she then shaped her choreography to his music, later stating that he was one of the few composers with whom she had worked whose score resulted in an exact fit with her conception.[322]

Instrumental works with extramusical reference are almost wholly absent from Persichetti's catalog, except in the most vague and general sense (e.g., *The Hollow Men*), so *King Lear* was a most unusual venture for him. Graham's conception of *King Lear* was highly abstract: As she indicated in her scenario, the subject of her work was to be the "anguish of a soul bound upon a 'wheel of fire'" taking place at

that instant when a being is catapulted by his actions into a madness of storm raging in his own heart. . . .The action is concerned with the purgatorial journey toward awareness. . . . This is not a danced version of the play King Lear with the words omitted. Rather it is the play as myth . . . . I do not want to be rigid

but I do want it to be clear and with a kind of inevitability and passionate sight. .
. . Spiritually Lear rises through the course of the anguish to a wisdom which he
has never before approached, including a sympathetic appreciation of suffering
among the world's unfortunates and a full realization of Cordelia's love.[323]

Despite the similarity of the septet's instrumentation to that of the *Pastoral* just discussed, the music follows a very different course, although some
moments may betray the same hand at work. While the *Pastoral* was largely
diatonic and tonal, the septet is highly angular and dissonant, in Persichetti's
driest, knottiest Neo-Classical manner, displaying the free chromaticism
characteristic of some of his most ambitious works from the 1940s, such
as the Piano Sonata No. 4, which appeared the following year. Graham's
notes are explicit in identifying the character of the feelings she had in mind,
although the scenario itself is quite abstract. Perhaps a more romantically
oriented composer might have focused on the elements of mood and emotion in such a way as to elicit a more empathic response from the audience
(although even a Neo-Romantic like Samuel Barber had drawn upon much
the same angular, hard-edged extreme within his own musical language in
supplying Medea music for Graham's *Cave of the Heart*, in 1945–1946). But
Persichetti's approach is strikingly antimelodramatic, addressing the human
dimensions in the most rarefied way; there is little in this music to suggest
or evoke conventional notions of "anguish" (an emotion rarely suggested in
any work of Persichetti), while the brittle scoring of woodwinds, timpani,
and percussion serves further to mitigate against an empathic response. Not
surprisingly, the piano plays a significant role, and some of the work's most
effective passages are savage moments scored for only piano and timpani. As
a result, although the musical score is a plausible reflection of Martha Graham's choreographic conception, hearing it as an autonomous work, a listener
would be unlikely to discern its expressive intentions.

Persichetti's *King Lear* comprises nine connected sections, closely following Graham's scenario:

I.   *Lear's Dance of Challenge*
II.   *Vision of the Three Daughters*
III.   *Cordelia's Dance of Serenity*
IV.   *Lear's Dance of Grief*
V.   *The Fool and the Philosopher*
VI.   *The Mock Trial*
VII.   *Ensnarement of Lear*
VIII.   *Cordelia's Dance of Grief*
IX.   *Final Union between Lear and Cordelia*

The music is unified by a motif based on the leap upward of a major-seventh (although the exact size of the interval varies somewhat). Persichetti's score bears an inscription that captures the essence of Graham's conception: "The *Eye of Anguish* is the means by which the tragic protagonist achieves insight and self-knowledge, and at the end, redemption."[324]

Eye of Anguish was first presented by the Martha Graham Company in Montclair, New Jersey, in January 1949. Alan Thomas, who had studied composition with Persichetti during this period, recounts an anecdote that reveals a rare instance of the composer's concern with promoting his career: Apparently the composer had learned that the Pulitzer committee would be attending a performance of *Eye of Anguish* in order to evaluate the music.

> [Persichetti] was not very happy with the musical performance [during] the dance run, so he sneaked in and played the piano part on the night the Pulitzer people were there. . . . [H]e really had to sneak in . . . because he was not a member of the union, and that got him into trouble on a number of occasions. [T]he other musicians were . . . delighted to have him come in and play. But he couldn't let anybody know because they would have all gotten in trouble with the union. I was there that night; it was kind of neat. He had disguised himself so nobody would recognize him; he didn't take a bow or anything like that. . . . [H]e would really [have] liked to have won the Pulitzer Prize.[325]

Eye of Anguish was subsequently performed hundreds of times but is not regarded as one of Martha Graham's successes.[326] As an autonomous musical work, Persichetti's septet *King Lear* was recorded by the Albemarle Ensemble in 1993.

As noted earlier, Persichetti's fifteen serenades range from the acerbity of Nos. 1, 2, and 6, to the sweetly benign Nos. 7 and 8. However, perhaps the most fully realized and deeply expressive statement is the Serenade No. 10, Op. 79, for flute and harp. The work was composed in 1957 at the request of flutist Arthur Lora and harpist Edward Vito, who wanted a new piece to perform on their tour of Eastern Europe and Asia. It falls just before the "Liturgical" Symphony in the composer's output, the same year as the lovely Emily Dickinson Songs. Like the latter songs, the Serenade No. 10 emphasizes the composer's "gracious" side, and is an ideal entry point into his musical world. It comprises eight tiny, limpidly ethereal movements, each identified by only a tempo marking, with an average duration of a little more than a minute each. Most are tonal, diatonic, and consonant, although peppered with polytonality, asymmetrical rhythms, and some wandering chromaticism. This was Persichetti's first attempt at writing for the harp, and his treatment draws from the instrument a wealth of evocative effects. The vignettes are varied in their expression, each generating an inner radi-

ance of warmth and love, vividly suggesting a precious image in time and
sound—one might liken them to eight species of magical birds in flight.
The serenade opens with a mysterious *Larghetto*, followed by a dance-like
Allegro comodo, a warmly lyrical *Andante grazioso*, an *Andante cantabile*
with a romantic melody so pretty that it might be a popular tune, a delicate,
fairy-like *Allegretto*, a joyfully sweeping *Scherzando*, an *Adagietto* suggesting sparsely falling raindrops, and concludes with a *Vivo* of whirlwind exuberance. The work evokes the sort of pristine innocence that few composers
have captured since Ravel.

The first performance of the Serenade No. 10 took place in Philadelphia
in March 1957; subsequent performances in Turkey by Lora and Vito drew
outstanding notices.[327] The work was first recorded in 1973, by Samuel Baron
and Ruth Maayani, in a performance that Lester Trimble found to be "excellent," adding that the piece "has absolutely endearing melodic qualities."[328]
That performance has been reissued on compact disc, and many additional
recordings have followed over the years.

In 1960 Persichetti composed *Infanta Marina*, Op. 83, for viola and piano.
Subtitled "Reflections on a Poem by Wallace Stevens," the work was commissioned by the Walter W. Naumburg Foundation. It is based on a song of
rarefied lyricism by the same name, which appears in *Harmonium*, Op. 50,
the mammoth song cycle Persichetti had composed nine years earlier, set to
Stevens's poetry. A motivic fragment from the same song also appears in the
Concerto for Piano, Four Hands, Op. 56. The viola work served in turn as
source material for the String Quartet No. 4, *Parable X*, all of which testifies to the significance of this material to the composer. The chief motivic
elements of the song are a five-note pattern of three ascending steps, which
then descend back to the first note; the descending interval of a third (out-
lined in the previous motif); triadic patterns that juxtapose both major and
minor thirds; and the crucial appearance of a minor-seventh arpeggio. The
viola work expands the song—less than three minutes long—to a veritable
rhapsody of some eleven minutes' duration. It begins with an introduction
for viola solo that hints at some of the motivic material just noted. As the
introduction concludes, the piano enters with the introduction of the song, as
it appears in *Harmonium*, and the viola enters with the vocal line. The song is
thus heard in its entirety, followed by a brief viola cadenza, which then leads
into what is essentially a richly elaborated and at times virtuosic fantasy on
the thematic material.

Infanta Marina was introduced in New York City in March 1961 by violist
Walter Trampler and pianist Lucy Greene. The work was first recorded by
Philip Clark and Bryan Sayer in 1981, and several additional renditions have
appeared since then.

Choral Music

Compositions for chorus hold a significant place in Vincent Persichetti's musical output. However, lacking the immediacy or vivid appeal of many of his works for other media, none of his choral compositions has attained an enduring popularity or become familiar to the public, although a few of the shorter cycles are performed fairly frequently. Of his twenty-one choral works, one is a large-scale oratorio, *The Creation*; four belong to the classic genres of liturgical music; two are hymnals; six are secular works that he numbered as "Cantatas"; the remaining eight are less ambitious and more incidental in nature. As with the chamber music, the following section discusses the most significant of these choral works, in chronological order.

Though not, technically speaking, a "choral work," Persichetti's *Hymns and Responses for the Church Year*, Op. 68, which he completed in 1955, proved to be one of the most important fruits of—as well as stimuli for—his creativity. It is a modern hymnal, intended for use by adventurous church choirs and congregations of all denominations.

Persichetti described himself as a "Judaic-Vedic-Christian" for whom all religious sources were suitable for musical interpretation. "I am a religious person, but not in any formal way. . . . I respect the person and, therefore, whatever he believes I am also touched by and, in a sense, believe in too. . . . I don't really see that there is a difference between a Hindu, Jew, Moslem, Christian, or anything else—except perhaps politically."[329] (It is interesting to note that during the early 1960s, the composer undertook the composition of a Sacred Service for use in Jewish synagogues and temples. He had reached the point of devising thematic material for each section, but, for reasons unknown to me, never completed the project.[330])

When Persichetti composed a work with particular sectarian associations, he totally assumed that spiritual outlook. As a church organist from the age of sixteen, he estimated that by the mid 1950s he had provided music for more than two thousand church services and had become intimately familiar with the standard hymns and anthems. Yet, interestingly enough, he had composed almost no religious music. Then, as he recounted,

Carleton Sprague Smith had mentioned to me a proposed project to assemble an American Hymnbook. . . . Dr. Albert Christ-Janer was in charge of the plan to invite American composers each to contribute a hymn to the collection. I began immediately to make a rough draft of a hymn, and planned to finish it off promptly. But the plan mushroomed. One idea led to others, as new and tempting texts were found. Some became responses, some amens, some hymns—and that season became a day-and-night obsession with music for the church. . . . Some of the texts were those in existing hymnals, but many were by twentieth-century poets.[331]

It was important to Persichetti that the texts be of high literary quality while evoking a direct spiritual experience. As Dorothea Persichetti noted, "Texts for the *Hymns* were drawn from many sources; new and old hymnals, books of poetry and plays. The authors range chronologically from those of the Bible to Peter the Venerable and John Milton, from W. H. Auden and Wallace Stevens to the composer (listed as Anonymous, 20th c.)."[332] Persichetti wanted his music for these pieces to be fresh, yet simple and practical for the congregation to learn and to sing. As with the *Little Piano Book* and some of his other simpler pieces, he aimed for the essence of musical beauty. Dorothea, who discussed each hymn in detail in her monograph, described them as, "in microcosm, distilled versions of the composer's best work, and are the essence of his musical expression. . . . Each piece is a musical entity, complete but compressed. They contain no extra notes; Amens at the ends of the *Hymns* are integral parts of the music and are never to be sung as after-thought. The *Hymn* is usually incomplete harmonically until the Amen has been sounded. Often, the last measure of the *Hymn* rests on a temporary tonic that drops, by way of the Amen, to its final tonal center."[333]

Not only did the *Hymns and Responses* serve their practical devotional function, but they also became significant source material for the composer. As has been indicated earlier, Persichetti regarded his musical output as a resource from which to draw musical ideas for further development or elaboration in other contexts. His use of self-quotation—musical inventories, cross-references, and indices—as a compositional device suggests an archival intellectual bent consistent with the eclecticism so deeply rooted in his nature. Nothing fulfilled this purpose for him more richly than the *Hymns and Responses*. "This collection contains a distilled thematic substance so potent it seems impossible for me to keep larger works from growing out of these yeasty cells."[334] There is no need to enumerate here the many works that drew upon the hymnal for their thematic material, as they have been noted amply throughout this chapter.

Although not necessarily intended for performance from beginning to end as a single work, the *Hymns and Responses* have been done that way. The first such performance was given in October 1956 by the choir of the First Presbyterian Church of Philadelphia, conducted by Alexander McCurdy. The publication of the hymnal that year was marked by an article in *Time* magazine,[335] which helped to alert churches throughout the country to its appearance, and the first printing sold out quickly. Critics also welcomed the appearance of the *Hymns and Responses*. After lamenting the dearth of recent hymnals of high musical quality, Mark Siebert commented,

> Vincent Persichetti has made a contribution that should rightfully do much to remedy the situation. . . . [T]here now exists a body of singable hymns in a con-

temporary vein that could be incorporated in future hymnals. . . . The inclusion of twenty-two items of service material vastly increases the usefulness of the collection. Thus the hesitation of a congregation might be dispelled gradually by introduction of this unusual style by the choir. The composer has wisely included responses useful in non-liturgical churches as well as settings of the Kyrie, Sanctus, Agnus and Gloria Tibi.[336]

Toward the very end of his life, Persichetti was preparing a second volume of *Hymns and Responses*. Evidently many of the forty pieces in this collection were composed years earlier, some in response to individual commissions. The composer's manuscript was edited by Daniel Dorff and Tamara Brooks, and was published posthumously as Op. 166 in 1991. Dorff notes that volume II "was a back-burner project for decades, but it became his daily work in his last months."[337] As with the first volume, many of the entries appear in other works by the composer. However, unlike the case of volume I, some of these pieces seem to have appeared first in other works and were subsequently "retrofitted" as hymns for this collection.

The 1960s was a decade of choral concentration for Persichetti. Of the thirty works he wrote during that period, nine featured the chorus. In 1959, he accepted a commission from the Collegiate Chorale to compose a setting of the Roman Catholic Mass. Completed the following year, the *Mass*, Op. 84, is, in many ways, a highly traditional work, scored for mixed choir *a cappella*, its Renaissance heritage reflected in the use of a Gregorian chant, *Kyrie Deus Sempiterne*, as a *cantus firmus* that underlies each section, and in its reliance on imitative counterpoint as its chief developmental technique. There are no time signatures, and the irregular, constantly changing phrase lengths further reinforce the Gregorian connection. Yet the work does not inspire the sense of rapture that the composer's sixteenth-century antecedents strove to achieve. The Phrygian implications of the Gregorian theme give the work a generally dark color and the extensive use of quartal harmony produces a reserved coolness of mood. Modal consistency is promptly dispelled by considerable chromaticism, especially in the inner voices, making harmonic clarity difficult for even a highly proficient choir to achieve. A general tone of detached introspection is maintained until the final *Agnus Dei*, an ardent plea for peace that rises to moments of plaintive passion.

The first performance of Persichetti's *Mass* was given at Carnegie Hall in April 1961. Mark Orton conducted the Collegiate Chorale. Persichetti's stature was at its zenith at this time, and reviews were generally respectful, if somewhat reserved. "Within his given framework he retains his own personal style with honesty and inventiveness," wrote John Ardoin. "There is a little too much texture (all four parts are going most of the time). . . . But it is, for the most part, a handsome piece and highly idiomatic."[338] Allen Hughes found it to be "an estimable brief work, rather meditative in nature and gently flavored with the modality of plainsong and Renaissance polyphony. In short, it is churchly in sound, though contemporary."[339] Perhaps the most penetrating comments were those of Francis Perkins, who noted that the *Mass* is

> eminently suitable for the church, but also rewarding for a concert-hall audience. . . . Persichetti does not seek to focus attention on his musical personality or on his skill in writing for chorus, but yet this Mass is individual in style, and his knowledge of the choral medium is not disguised by its essential objectivity. . . . The Mass is not only essentially appropriate in its general atmosphere, but also in its projection of the liturgical text, which is carried along without either haste or lingering. . . . Persichetti's idiom here is contemporary. . . . But the music is not attached to this or to any other period, and in this sense it has a timeless quality which corresponds to that of the Mass itself. . . . [T]he music does not suggest an obviously Gregorian style in polyphonic terms, although the spirit of Gregorian chant is apparent in the curving flow of the music, and in a certain correspondence of atmosphere with that of the basic ritual music of the church. While reflecting the emotion as well as the verbal line of the text, it does so in a contemplative rather than an overtly emotional way. Its expressive depth is meditative rather than dramatic; there are no purple patches, no proclamative outbursts or effect-seeking sudden dynamic contrasts.[340]

In 1983 Persichetti's *Mass* was recorded by the Mendelssohn Club of Philadelphia, under the direction of Tamara Brooks. This release too was received with respectful reserve. After commenting in general that the composer "displays predictable expertise, if rather limited imagination, in his choral compositions," John Barker adds that in the *Mass*, "the severe counterpoint is a bit like how-Palestrina-would-have-done-it-if-he-had-been-born-in-twentieth-century-Philadelphia."[341] Lee Passarella noted that "while its sonorities are clearly modern, it stands at a remove from most music of its era. . . . Persichetti's art seems somewhat aloof and uninvolving, though some will find this objectivity a part of the music's attraction."[342]

Just a few years later, Persichetti was offered another commission from the Collegiate Chorale. The result, *Stabat Mater*, Op. 92, for chorus and small orchestra, was completed in 1963. This work resembles the *Mass* in character and musical language but expanded to a larger canvas. Based on a Locrian-flavored motif presented at the outset, which generates most of the music that follows, it maintains a dark coloration throughout, in keeping with the familiar, mournful thirteenth-century poem by Jacopone da Todi that serves as its text. The work's five sections last just less than half an hour. The musical language is highly chromatic but tonal, the harmony maintaining a high level of dissonance. Adding to its austere tone, the tempo of the work is slow throughout, except for the beginning of the final movement. Persichetti accompanied the original Latin text with his own translation into English, so that the composition may be performed in either language. Also like the *Mass*, the *Stabat Mater* eschews any hint of theatricality or melodrama, maintaining a tone of reflective sobriety.

The premiere of the *Stabat Mater* took place at Carnegie Hall in May 1964. This time the Collegiate Chorale was conducted by Abraham Kaplan. Once again, the response of the audience and many of the critics was respectful but reserved. Wriston Locklair felt that the work "made a strong impression at this initial hearing. Almost completely tonal, reflective and subdued in color and seldom rising to a crescendo, its harmonic textures are pure and skillfully interwoven among the four choral voices."[343] Theodore Strongin described it as "a sinewy work that repeatedly creates tension at the end of one phrase in order to propel it on to the next. It uses more or less conventional harmonic language in a way that shows that, in Mr. Persichetti's case conventional harmonic language is not all used up."[344]

However, composer Hugo Weisgall was more enthusiastic about the work:

In view of Mr. Persichetti's past achievements it is no surprise that this music is expertly wrought. The choral writing is fluent and thoroughly vocal throughout; the orchestra provides not only the necessary support and accompaniment, but plays its own distinctive role. . . . The challenge is the work itself—its formal organization, its single pervading mood, its restrained lyricism pitted against its dramatic austerity. The most remarkable feature of the *Stabat Mater*, both in performance and in retrospect, is that it is constructed almost entirely of slow movements . . . [yet] the work does not bog down or become monotonous, nor do the different sections lack variety. This itself is a major achievement. Perhaps equally impressive is the quality of restraint that characterizes the whole piece. The composer consistently avoids using any striking or obvious theatrical effects; the drama of the suffering Mother is portrayed with great containment, and the work has a quality of austerity not too frequently encountered. It is only in the opening part of the last movement that the composer lets loose with some of his characteristic rhythmic devices. . . . What remains to be added is that whatever combination of musical ideas and emotions prompted Mr. Persichetti to write this kind of work, it has resulted in music that comes across in performance as a moving experience. It also seems to demonstrate that a purely musical challenge, such as constructing a large piece of slow music, is still a viable procedure for the composer today.[345]

Concurrently with the *Stabat Mater*, Persichetti was working on another sacred choral work with orchestra, which he also completed in 1963: *Te Deum*, Op. 93, a commission from the Pennsylvania Music Educators Association. It was introduced at the Music Educators National Conference in Philadelphia in March 1964. Allen Flock conducted the Pennsylvania All-State Chorus and Orchestra.

In comparison to the two works just discussed, this fifteen-minute piece is far more extroverted in character, with a ruggedly unsentimental vigor that is distinctly American, yet without recourse to any of the clichés of musical Americana. Though largely homophonic, with much unison choral writing, its contrapuntal passages are clear and straightforward, suggesting a connection more to Handel than to Palestrina. Utilizing an English text, it is more clearly tonal and less dissonant than the two preceding works, though there is a generous use of polychordal harmony. However, like them it is based on a *cantus firmus*—Phrygian in this case—that permeates the work. The overall shape suggests a ternary design, preceded by a slow introduction, with a vigorous A-section, a more subdued, highly developmental, and often quite lyrical B-section, followed by a modified return of the A-section that comes to a jubilantly affirmative conclusion. Although its greater simplicity is doubtless attributable to its having been tailored to student performers, it is highly likely that most listeners would find this to be the composer's most effective sacred choral work.

Following on the heels of the *Te Deum* and completed the same year was the *Spring Cantata*, Op. 94, a short secular cycle setting poetry by E. E. Cummings, for three-part women's chorus with piano. Also identified as Cantata No. 1, the work was commissioned by the Wheelock College Glee Club, who gave its first performance in Boston in August 1964, under the leadership of Leo Collins.

Cummings (1894–1962) was one of Persichetti's favorite poets, and he had already set a number of his poems in small, casual groupings. The composer seemed to find in this poet something of a kindred spirit, especially in his verbal playfulness and impish sense of humor, which often camouflaged serious ideas. In contrast to the austerity of his religious choral works, the Cummings settings are typically lighthearted and whimsical; the music is spare and simple in texture, but, as is so often the case with Persichetti, the apparent simplicity is deceptive, as the musical details are purposefully conceived and meticulously constructed. The harmonic language is freely tonal, though not necessarily consonant; the vocal lines are generally straightforward and simple, if not always diatonic, while the piano contributes more dissonant elements. *Spring Cantata* comprises settings of four poems, each of which captures an image associated with spring: "trees," "if the green," "Spring is like a perhaps hand," and "in Just-spring."

Persichetti composed his *Winter Cantata*, Op. 97, also designated Cantata No. 2, in 1964. In view of his attraction to verbal and musical parsimony, and to brief, essential images with broad reference, it seemed inevitable that the composer would have been drawn to that most parsimonious of poetic forms, the Japanese haiku. Responding to a commission from the Emma Willard School in Troy, New York, Persichetti turned to Harold Stewart's book of haiku in controversial English "verse translations," *A Net of Fireflies*, which his daughter had recently given him.[346] *Winter Cantata* is scored for women's chorus, flute, and marimba, and comprises twelve short movements. Without any obvious references, the music evokes a Japanese spirit, largely as a result of its own delicate, highly concentrated gestures. The coolness of the flute and the brittleness of the marimba evoke the winter moods and images of the poems. The main unifying musical motifs are a chord based on the first five steps of the Phrygian mode, which appears at the outset of the work, and a minor-seventh *arpeggio* that increases in importance as the work proceeds. There are also subtle motivic links that connect each movement to the next. Within the overall unity of mood and subject matter there is great contrast and variety in gesture and articulation. The Epilogue, a compositional tour de force typical of Persichetti, consists of word groups and associated musical motifs drawn in sequence from all the preceding movements and woven into a coherent poetic and musical entity, an appropriate "index" to the entire work.

The premiere of *Winter Cantata* was given in April 1965 by the Emma Willard Choir, conducted by Russell Locke in Troy, New York. It was recorded in 1983 by the Mendelssohn Club of Philadelphia under the direction of Tamara Brooks. Both the *Spring Cantata* and *the Winter Cantata* have become popular mainstays of the women's choral repertoire.

Cantata No. 3 is *Celebrations*, Op. 103, commissioned for chorus and wind ensemble by Wisconsin State University at River Falls (now University of Wisconsin-River Falls), and completed in 1966. In nine sections, the work draws its text from Walt Whitman's *Leaves of Grass*, long a favorite resource for American (and English) composers. However, Persichetti had been avoiding Whitman. "As a young man, I was seriously put off by those gross settings of Whitman by some loud American composers. It wasn't until 1966 that I quietly (and all by myself) found the poem 'On the Beach at Night.' This was *my* Whitman."[347] Now he became excited about Whitman and, halfway through setting that poem, put it aside to write *Celebrations*. Not surprisingly, his settings are notably light in texture and lithe and brightly affirmative in character, with none of the brash grandiosity or heavy-handed fervor that this poet has evoked from so many composers. The choral writing is quite simple, with much unison and homophonic texture, and only a smattering of imitative counterpoint, and the prosody is largely syllabic, emphasizing the plainspoken naturalness of the texts. The scoring for small wind ensemble is extremely light and almost always subordinate to the voices. The musical language is largely diatonic, although frequent modal shifts minimize the sense of tonal center. However, there is a pervasive blandness of affect, with little of the soaring lyricism or rhythmic excitement that suffused and intensified the composer's band pieces of the 1950s. But as one of the few original works for chorus and wind ensemble, it is performed with some frequency.

Celebrations was introduced by the Wisconsin State University-River Falls Concert Choir and Wind Ensemble, under the direction of Donald Nitz in November 1966. A handsome performance of the work was released on compact disc in 1995, featuring the Indiana University of Pennsylvania Chorale and Wind Ensemble, under the direction of Jack Stamp.

Having completed *Celebrations*, Persichetti returned to his setting of "On the Beach at Night," which had been commissioned for the Crane Chorus and Orchestra of the State University of New York (SUNY) at Potsdam. Persichetti completed the work in 1967 and conducted the premiere himself at SUNY/Potsdam, in May 1968. This became his Cantata No. 4, which he entitled *The Pleiades*, Op. 107. "I called it *The Pleiades*, because I feared mispronunciations of the word 'beach'!"[348] (The Pleiades is a cluster of stars in the constellation *Taurus*.)

The setting of this poem is notably different from those in *Celebrations*: In contrast to those simple, terse settings, here the composer expanded the poem—of modest dimensions—to major proportions, through repetition and contrapuntal extension of both words and lines, even introducing interpolations that enhanced his own interpretation of Whitman's poem but without resorting to the "gross loudness" to which he objected in others' settings of this poet's work. Scored for mixed chorus and strings, with a prominent trumpet *obbligato*, the twenty-five-minute cantata treats Whitman's poem as a profound hymn to the essence of eternity, perhaps to God. The musical language is highly dissonant and largely atonal; the primary motifs involve a series of descending scale-steps, with prominent use of the tritone and the interval of the minor-ninth. However, embedded within the largely dissonant harmonic context are those moments of precious consonance (e.g., the music that accompanies the line, "They are immortal—all those stars, both silvery and golden, shall shine out again," which can easily be overlooked at first hearing). The role of the trumpet *obbligato* remains unexplained: Perhaps, like the trumpet solo reiterated in Ives's *Unanswered Question*, it represents the mystery of eternity. The trumpet's music is highly chromatic and improvisatory—almost jazz-like—in character, and seems, if not unrelated to the musical substance of the actual setting, rather like spontaneous commentary on it, interspersed throughout, somewhat like cadenzas. The work finally ends with an extended trumpet cadenza, heard against the backdrop of a single chord in the chorus and strings—an E major-minor chord, eventually joined on the bottom by a C—sustained as if for eternity. (It is this same sustained, Schuman-like chord that opens the work.)

Tim Page, reviewing a performance of *The Pleiades*, commented, "Mr. Persichetti's music has a hard, neo-classical surface. His work, although expressive, is rarely evocative in any coloristic sense of the word."[349]

Page's comment raises once again the issue of those works of Persichetti that are constructed with exquisite attention to subtleties of musical expression and narrative coherence yet maintain a consistently severe demeanor, lacking sufficiently poignant and memorable turns of phrase that might elicit a visceral response from the listener. This, indeed, is the recurrent complaint—noted throughout this chapter—that represents the chief criticism leveled against the music of Persichetti, and will arise again with regard to *The Creation*. A relevant question is whether this austerity, or "coldness," pervades a large portion of the composer's work or merely a small number of lesser—or perhaps more demanding—efforts. This issue is complicated by the fact that many pieces that appear to lack expressive warmth on initial acquaintance gradually "blossom" for the listener as they become more familiar. But one may then ask, with some justification: If there is nothing that compels one's attention initially, why would one return for more? This, of course, is the enduring challenge faced by Modernist approaches to musical composition since their first appearances early in the twentieth century, and continues to remain unresolved.

The following year Persichetti consummated his intense focus on major choral works with the completion of what he subsequently referred to as his "*chef d'oeuvre*," *The Creation*, Op. 111.[350] The work was commissioned by the Juilliard School for its opening year at Lincoln Center and was composed during the period that his series of *Parables* was getting underway, and shortly before his Symphony No. 9, "Janiculum" was completed. Scored for soprano, alto, tenor, and baritone soloists, mixed chorus, and symphony orchestra, the work lasts more than an hour and utilizes a text compiled by the composer himself. *The Creation* epitomizes the composer's all-embracing worldview, reflected in those provocative opening lines of *Twentieth-Century Harmony* ("Any tone can succeed any other tone"), and applied here with regard to the sources of its text, its religious inspiration, and its musical materials and construction.

An investigation of Persichetti's preliminary plans, diagrams, and sketches, as well as the statements he made around the time he composed the work, reveal the near-obsessive attention he devoted to creating a composite text from myriad far-ranging sources. One may speculate that he seemed to place as much importance on—and took as much pride in—the text of *The Creation* as in the music. He compiled this convincingly coherent scenario from some fifty-three different mythological, scientific, poetic and biblical writings. In recognition of this remarkable achievement of "amalgamation" (one of the composer's favorite words), these sources are enumerated here, alphabetically: Altaian, Amos, Apache, Aztec, Bhagavad Gita, Brihadaranyaka, Canaanite, Dead Sea Scrolls, Ecclesiastes, Exodus, Fagatauan, Genesis, Haiku, Hebrews, Hittite, Inca, Iranian, Irish, Isaiah, Job, John, Kalawao, Kojiki, Madagascan, Maori, Navaho, Nihongi, Olympian, Omaha, Papago, Pelasgian, Pima, Psalms, Quechua, Revelation, Romans, Samuel, Sanskrit, Seven Tablets, Siberian, Sioux, Sumerian, Tahitian, Toltec, Torah, Vitoto, Vahitahian, Vedic, Wapokomo, Xinca, Yapese, Zen, and Zuni. "[All these texts] had one thing in common: an awareness and a belief in some force that is above all."[351] Although the biblical story from Genesis provides a familiar overall structure, the supplementary material offers commentary from a most unusual range of perspectives.

In a letter to a choral director, Persichetti wrote,

The Creation started maybe twenty years ago [1957] but I am aware of five years of intense research all over the country—at libraries in towns and colleges that I would pass while on tour. Many of the texts are paraphrased because I did not want to hamper my musical ideas. Music came with texts as I recalled them. When I began writing, I selected texts as I got musical ideas. But at this point I had thousands of text excerpts and I used only a small number of them. I seemed to write everything at once—I certainly had no set libretto nor set musical scheme when I started.[352]

As he developed his concept, he began to shape the work according to the following schema[353]:

(Void)	Prologue	Darkness	Void–Slow
(Light)	Day 1	Day and Night	Dark–Slow
(Heaven)	Day 2	Divide the Waters	Heavy (Maestoso)
(Fruit-Seed)	Day 3	Dry Land	Flowing (Grazioso)
(Measure; Years)	Day 4	Sun and Moon	(Seasons) Allegro, *f*
(Living Creatures)	Day 5	Multiply (Sea and Air)	3/4, Wild
(Image)	Day 6	Man over Beast	Liquid
(Rest)	Day 7	Sanctified	Choral
(Soul)	Epilogue	A Living Soul	Drive to end

Elements of this schema were eventually modified, and the work, as it finally stands, falls into seven sections, as follows:

I.   Darkness and Light (baritone, soprano, and chorus): *Misterioso*
II.   Let There Be a Firmament (alto, tenor, and chorus): *Allegro*

III.   I Will Multiply Your Seed (soprano, tenor, baritone, and chorus): *Teneramente*
IV.   Lights for Seasons (baritone, alto, soprano, and chorus): *Vivace*
V.   Of Sea and Air (alto, tenor, soprano, and chorus): *Con spirito*
VI.   After His Kind (tenor, alto, baritone, soprano, and chorus): *Andantino*
VII. Behold His Glory (baritone, soprano, alto, tenor, and chorus): *Sereno*

The Creation begins with an evocation of "the void," while the primary motif—three notes each a half-step apart—is introduced. These three notes, in all their permutations, generate most of the work's thematic material, beginning as tone clusters but gradually expanding to include larger intervals. A number of characteristic motifs are generated, and these recur throughout, unifying the work. As Barham points out, some fundamental motifs are treated serially, but only as a means to an end *within* the larger structure, rather than as a governing agent of the larger structure.[354] The musical language of *The Creation* is much the same as that used in Persichetti's other major choral works from the 1960s except, understandably in view of its scope, more elaborate and complex. Its overall character is rather severe and largely atonal in effect, with dense, highly dissonant polyphony and cluster-based harmonic structures for the chorus, and declamatory vocal lines that are often quite angular. Tonal regions are identifiable conceptually if not aurally, although consonant, diatonic passages occasionally emerge naturally, rather like oases of sweet, simple beauty; but these are easily overlooked in an underrehearsed performance.

The foregoing factors all militate against a casual, facile reception of the work by a general audience. The difficulty of effectively mastering the challenges faced by soloists, chorus, and orchestra in performance only compounds the challenge to an audience in grasping the work at first hearing. Although contrasts in tempo, dynamics, texture, and tonality are built into the structure (V., perhaps the most immediately accessible section, even features the "Persichetti 2/4"), as are climactic high points, the work's enormous difficulty, given limited rehearsal time, results in a general flattening out of these contrasts, while many subtleties of harmonic and contrapuntal detail are lost in imprecisions of pitch. For these reasons the overall impact in actual performance can be a harsh, gray monotony. Thus it is likely that the generally favorable reviews garnered by its first performances are attributable to the high esteem in which the composer was generally held at the time rather than to an authentic audience response. On the other hand, a proficient, well-rehearsed recorded performance, offering the opportunity for repeated listening and study, may well reveal *The Creation* to be a masterpiece. Persichetti may indeed have accomplished an astonishing feat of creative vision, in tailoring a text according to his own personal and idiosyncratic perspective and setting it musically with recourse to the full range of his tremendous wealth of compositional technique, in addressing one of the primal metaphysical enigmas of existence.

But one might also note that large, "serious" statements did not always evoke Persichetti's most vividly compelling creative responses. Such formidable utterances often seemed to inhibit him, suppressing the more colorful, personal, and "human" sides of his musical personality. Works such as the song cycle *Harmonium*, the Symphony No. 9, "Janiculum," and *The Creation* are profound masterpieces of a very elevated order of musical expression, requiring proficient, highly committed performances, and attentive, sympathetic listeners.

The premiere of *The Creation* took place in April 1970 at Lincoln Center's Alice Tully Hall. The composer conducted the Juilliard Orchestra and Chorus. The vocal soloists were Patricia Wells, soprano; Joy Blackett, alto; Robert Jones, tenor; and Robert Shiesley, baritone. The work was presented two days later by the same forces in Philadelphia's Academy of Music. As noted, the critical response was largely positive. Covering the premiere for the *New York Times*, Raymond Ericson wrote,

> Although not much fanfare attended its first presentation, the work proved to be unusually fine, much of it possessing great eloquence and beauty. As befits its subject, the work is of major proportions, lasting over an hour. . . . The result is contemporary, larger in dimension and implication than the terse biblical story, and mystical. The composer . . . is able to express his self-chosen text in musical terms exactly as he wishes and has thus been able to capture much of its mysticism. The music is conceived in a near-symphonic pattern, moving from introductory descriptions of the original void through two dramatic movements, an extremely beautiful slow movement, and two scherzo-like sections to a long finale. For all the drama in it, the score is basically lyrical, much of which stems from Mr. Persichetti's handling of the words. The contrasting kinds of melodies, which are usually made up of small chromatic figurations for the chorus and of large-intervalled melodies for the soloists, are always affecting, often poignant. Throughout the score there are so many felicitous passages. . . . And the work ends with a kind of mysterious indecisiveness, as if the Creation itself holds only a mysterious meaning. The composer's musical means are traditional but often of heavy harmonic density, which may put some listeners off, but which provide the score's strength. It is also very difficult to perform.[355]

On the other hand, perhaps more candid is Max de Schauensee's reaction to the Philadelphia performance: "I would say that the big composition is homogeneous to a point which finally spreads a certain amount of tedium. In other words, the work's unflagging consistency of form is also in a way its undoing.

The workmanship proves first-class, as solos and choruses are masterfully integrated in the vast conception. . . . I doubt that this is a work that one could ever love (though that even may be possible), but it is a work worthy of respect and I, for one, would be glad, even curious to hear it again."[356] Samuel Singer added, "The composer is never trite. There is no outburst at 'there was light,' for instance, nor at the final magnifying of God's name 'throughout creation.' Persichetti accompanies his text with incisive orchestral comments, beginning when sound arises out of nothingness to depict effectively the Void before Creation. The composer uses precise colors in his scoring."[357]

Perhaps more thoughtful are the comments of Elwyn A. Wienandt, who had the advantages of greater time and the opportunity to study the published score:

> The impact of Persichetti's oratorio, *The Creation*, is not that of a biblical work, even though the title alone might lead one to expect it to be. . . . Despite the widely different versions of a common story, the libretto reads convincingly, a tribute to the composer's selection of text segments and a demonstration of the universality of the creation legend. The division of the work into seven sections holds the emphasis more strongly in the sphere of our commonly known source than in the exotic fables derived from other cultures. This variety of sources results not only in a text of sharp imagery, but the restrictions of time force these images to be used in rapid, almost kaleidoscopic, fashion. As the composer deals with these sections musically, they become cells of tonal imagery, passing successively from section to section without easily perceived relationship. A stentorian pronouncement in unison or in forceful parallel chords may be followed by a brief leaping solo and a choral phrase of repeated clusters made of three or more semitones. Rapid change of texture and materials is found throughout the work. . . . [T]he material flows back and forth from soloists to chorus without lengthy orchestral interludes.[358]

After *The Creation*, Persichetti composed two more works in his series of "cantatas," both based on the poetry of E. E. Cummings. The Cantata No. 5, *Glad and Very*, Op. 129, dates from 1974 and was commissioned by the Huntington Choir of Long Island, New York. It is scored for two-part men's and/or women's choir and piano. For this group five poems were selected: "little man," "i am so glad and very," "maybe god," "jake hates all the girls," and "a politician." Although many of the composer's major works from the preceding decade were rather dry and severe in character, harsh in their musical language, and complex in construction, these settings reflect much the same treatment as those in the *Spring Cantata* of 1963 and are similarly spare, simple, and light on the surface, with clever subtleties that emerge with deeper acquaintance. The premiere of *Glad and Very* took place in December 1974, in Huntington, New York. Andrew E. Householder conducted the Huntington Choir.

Flower Songs, Op. 157, was Persichetti's final work for chorus, and was designated as Cantata No. 6. Scored for mixed chorus and string orchestra, it was completed in 1983, on commission from Michael Korn and the Philadelphia Singers. The composer had not written for chorus in almost a decade, and this final contribution was something of a farewell to the medium, as well as to E. E. Cummings, whose poetry he had set so often. The seven poems selected for this group were drawn from throughout the poet's career, but all share the flower as a central metaphor. Like Persichetti's other Cummings settings, these are gracious and delightful, exhibiting the lively exuberance missing from his more "serious" choral settings. Also like them, the musical language reveals a simplicity of texture and line, with largely consonant, tonal harmony but with no less care and attention to detail than in his more challenging works. On first hearing they may appear to be—though attractive and accessible—simple and perhaps somewhat routine; however, closer inspection reveals that virtually nothing about them is routine or accidental. Every articulation, every rhythmic irregularity is carefully calculated. The third song, "Early Flowers," incorporates in disguised form the same hymn ("Round me falls the night") from *Hymns and Responses*, volume I, used in the second movement of the composer's Symphony No. 6.

The *Flower Songs* were introduced at the Academy of Music by the Philadelphia Singers, conducted by Michael Korn, in April 1984. Reviewing this performance, Daniel Webster expressed a reaction similar to that noted above: "the chorus moved in apparently conventional ways. But Persichetti's way with conventional processes is never ordinary, and the singing rang with inner tensions and unforeseen resolutions. The rhythmic cleverness of Cummings was reflected in Persichetti's settings."[359] Reviewing a subsequent performance later the same year, Allen Hughes described the cycle as "gentle, airy and clear."[360]

In 2006 a magnificent performance of *Flower Songs* was released on a recording that featured the University of Texas Chamber Singers and Chamber Orchestra, under the direction of James Morrow. Reviewing that recording, Chris Mullins found the songs to be "an absolute delight. Persichetti tends to lay a mist-like instrumental fabric under the vocal line, so that the words come through distinctly. As all the works center on floral imagery, the pastel colors of the scoring feel appropriate."[361] On the other hand, David Vernier noted that "although the music is certainly expertly crafted and beautifully scored (there are many very nice choral moments), the angular melodies and often ambiguous harmonic context eventually tires the ear and sets your attention adrift."[362]

At the time of his death, Persichetti had begun another work for chorus and orchestra. It would have been his *Parable XXVI: Emily—A Parable of Death*, based on poems of Emily Dickinson.

Vocal Music

Vincent Persichetti's contribution to the art song repertoire was small, relative to his output in other genres, thought not insignificant. But the fact that this portion of his output has enjoyed few publications, performances, or recordings has created an impression that it is smaller than it really is. Dorothea Persichetti noted that although Persichetti had composed many songs over the years, not until 1945, when he was thirty, did he feel that any were worth including among his definitive oeuvre. She offered the remarkable insight that "verbal communication had always been a real problem" for the composer, "one that natural shyness did not improve. Lack of an easy command of language made [him] impatient with the whole process of speech—his own was so machine-gun quick and monosyllabic that one wonders what his first efforts in a classroom were like. . . . He was also, perhaps, too uncritical about poetry used for texts. If a poem were really good and beautiful, it seemed that it should not be touched; but a lesser one used for the song expression to which he felt drawn, was inadequate."[363]

A few songs from the 1940s appear on his work list. Then came the mammoth, hour-long cycle *Harmonium* in 1951—a true breakthrough work. Quite a few small song-groups appeared in 1957. Then, in 1970, Persichetti composed *A Net of Fireflies*, settings of seventeen haiku. The following discussion begins with *Harmonium*, proceeds with a general overview of the small song-groups, and concludes with the haiku cycle.

By far the most significant of Persichetti's vocal works is the hour-long song cycle *Harmonium*, Op. 50, based on the eponymous collection of verse, published in 1923, by the Pulitzer Prize-winning poet Wallace Stevens (1879–1955). In shaping what was his most ambitious work thus far, the composer selected twenty of the eighty-five poems, rearranging their sequence, and setting them for soprano and piano. He worked on the cycle concurrently with his Symphony No. 4—a composition of strikingly different character.

According to the composer's account,

> During one of my university visits, I happened to be relaxing in the faculty lounge, where several English professors were discussing an interpretation of a poem called "Domination of Black" by Wallace Stevens, one of our great poets. It struck me that I had just as much right to my idea of what the poem should say, and was justified in expressing my reaction in *my* medium—music. I realized that poetry is, in reality, a distilled concept, full of implications which may be interpreted in more than one way. And I felt a strong urge to begin seeing

Stevens' book *Harmonium* as a song cycle. This is how I as a composer, found my way into the vocal medium.

I set nineteen poems; the twentieth and last poem of the cycle was to be "Thirteen Ways of Looking at a Blackbird." In this poem, I discovered that all of the previous nineteen were related musically and poetically, in one way or another. And so the last song is a large structure, containing musical materials of the preceding songs. When I wrote to Stevens about this, he replied that he hadn't been aware of these connections and gave me his full approval. I was so taken with his poetry, and he with my writing music for it, that we discussed the possibility of doing an opera together . . . but he died before this could be realized.[364]

Persichetti's attraction to the works of the Pennsylvania-born Wallace Stevens is not surprising, as the poet's economy of means, his ability to express the most serious thoughts with a light touch, and the elusiveness he achieved through oblique and paradoxical references are traits that apply with equal accuracy to Persichetti's creative work. As he expressed it, "I have always loved Wallace Stevens' poetry, probably because he will state facts in the opposite direction in order to make a truth in another direction."[365] This affinity is further underlined by the comments of leading scholars regarding Stevens's poetry. For example, Mark Van Doren noted Stevens's "delicately enunciated melody, his economy, his clipped cleanliness of line, his gentle excellence," adding that the poet's wit "is tentative, perverse, and superfine; and it will never be popular."[366] Others have identified two sides to Stevens's work: the sensuous and the metaphysical, while Robert Rehder found in Stevens's poetry "many moments rich in beauty, but he does not want them to be too sweet and resists 'the bawds of euphony'."[367] Stevens's lines, "The poem must resist the intelligence/Almost successfully"[368] might almost have been written by Persichetti himself. Unfortunately, Stevens died before he could hear a performance of the composer's cycle, *Harmonium*.

As a result of this affinity between poet and composer, Stevens's words and Persichetti's music are wedded with virtually no distortion or accommodation. The songs abound, as do the poems, with subtle interrelationships; some songs offer relief, while others serve important structural functions as points of summation. On the whole, the textures of the piano part are remarkably spare and uncomplicated; the melodic lines, too, are generally straightforward. The complexity of the work lies in the relationships among the songs, and in the connections between the poems and the music. The treatment of tonality varies between angular atonality and diatonic simplicity, and many of the songs do exhibit the wide leaps, attenuated tonal anchorage, and dissonant accompaniments that typically alienate more traditionally minded music-lovers. But, as with so many of Persichetti's most challenging works, those listeners patient enough to familiarize themselves with the music will find that many of the sparse textures and angular melodic lines gradually suggest more mellifluous implications, which the imagination supplies intuitively, finally revealing a coherent artistic conception within which all the details fall into place.

In her monograph, Dorothea Persichetti devoted considerable attention to *Harmonium*:

> The poems are generally unrelated in idea and have no connection of subjects; but there are words and sounds that appear and reappear, giving the poems an inherent unity. The music enlarges this relationship and through the metamorphosis by which they also become music, the words are expanded and projected. Here is a total integration—a prism of reference and cross-reference of words and music, growing into a single, but composite, entity. . . . There is not only an internal relationship of words and music, but the songs themselves are completely of and in one another.[369]

The first song, "Valley Candle," introduces most of the musical motifs of the entire cycle. This and the six songs that follow comprise the first subgroup. These songs grow out of one another, each focusing on elements from the previous ones. The eighth song, "Six Significant Landscapes," serves as a kind of cumulative consolidation of the first seven while launching the subgroup to follow. They proceed in a similar fashion to the first subgroup. The seventeenth song, "Domination of Black," is a *passacaglia* on a twelve-note theme and is another point of cumulative consolidation. The final song, "Thirteen Ways of Looking at a Blackbird," is by far the longest and most involved of the songs, occupying more than 20 percent of the total duration of the cycle. A compositional tour de force, this song is a summary of the entire work, integrating musical material from all the preceding songs.[370]

In order to demonstrate these relationships, Dorothea not only charted the overall structure of the cycle, as described above, but also traced the derivation of musical material from earlier songs to later ones, and even verbal relationships among the songs that the composer highlighted through related treatments.[371] However, she cautions, "The construction of the cycle is so inventive that an analysis of it may put an improper emphasis on the form rather than the content of the music. . . . This is effective music, varied and satisfying, from a purely aural standpoint, and the relationship of its material gives the work an underlying solidity and reason."[372]

Clearly there is far more intricacy and depth to *Harmonium* than one can plumb within the context of this study. However, before moving on, it is revealing to include a portion of Persichetti's own comments on the cycle, taken from introductory remarks he made prior to a performance at Arizona State University in September 1979. These comments provide a glimpse of the elusive, oblique way that the composer expressed himself verbally, while offering some insight into the way he thought about the connections between words and music. Discussing the second subgroup of songs, he said,

> The next song is called "In the Clear Season of Grapes." . . . Then comes "Tea," a self-contained song, all by itself, and it serves as kind of an oasis. You need places to contemplate a little bit, and it's built from the former songs. However, "The Snow Man" gives you another breather because it's a kind of capriccio ("One must have a mind of winter . . ." is what Wallace Stevens is talking about), and the piano picks up the figure, a motor rhythm against the lyric soprano. Then we get to another of those more congealed songs, "Tattoo," which talks about "And in the edges of the snow." The music from that takes over the whole end of the cycle. So that we could have stopped with "Tattoo," only there's so much more to say that we finally wind up with that later. The next four songs are temporary pauses gathering miscellaneous kernels, melodic kernels, literary kernels, harmonic bits for something to get together. And that's the "Domination of Black," the second cumulative song. All of this material is put down at the bottom of the piano somewhere in a melody that's a kind of passacaglia with variations. So "Domination of Black" in gathering this begins to complain about certain things. And there is what I call a peacock complaint. Stevens refers to peacock, the music makes certain oblique relationships with melody and harmony giving you a nasty outlook. I don't know how well you know peacocks, but it's a peacock sound and we're not necessarily talking about a peacock—it could be this kind of thing you have with a best friend who frightened you suddenly—I don't know; it could be.[373]

The first performance of *Harmonium* took place in January 1952 at the Museum of Modern Art in New York City. The soprano was Hilda Rainer, and the composer was at the piano. Perhaps not surprisingly for a work this ambitious and complex, by a composer as yet largely unknown, the premiere was not well received by the press. Even a listener as sophisticated as composer-critic Arthur Berger was clearly baffled by the work, as can be discerned underneath a protective layer of arrogance. After complaining that the thirty-six-year-old composer's choice of style is "still indeterminate," he wrote, "'Harmonium' is uniform in mood almost to an anesthetizing degree" and a "song marathon to try almost anyone's patience. . . . The cycle not only exceeded an hour's length, but there were song cycles within song cycles. Not only was much of the ideational matter odd for singing, the poems selected did not make much sense as a cycle. The composer has a few serviceable songs. . . . But it was presumptuous of him to think he had an hour's music when there was so little arresting melodic inspiration."[374]

A subsequent Philadelphia performance, featuring soprano Jan De-Gaetani, preceded by an introductory talk by poetry scholar John Ciardi, continued to confound some critics. Eugene Moore expressed admiration for Persichetti's skill, but found the music to be "ultra-modern . . . with intervals and chords as yet unfamiliar to most ears. His imagination has produced settings as far from the path of the traditionalist as was his poet's. The overall result is a song cycle of interest at this stage primarily to the professionals of the arts."[375] Reviewing the same performance with somewhat more insight, Samuel Singer noted, "The soloist has no easy time of it, for there are killingly awkward intervals and often the time changes in every measure. Nor must one forget the audience. The surrealist poems of Stevens need concentration when reading them; hearing them is even harder. . . . Persichetti's music for soprano and piano is unified. It expands on both words and sounds in the poems and the song cycle is indeed 'cyclical.'"[376] The following year DeGaetani and Persichetti performed the work in Washington, D.C. Ten years after its premiere, the composer was now a recognized figure. Paul Hume's reaction stands in considerable contrast to the previous notices:

> Persichetti is widely honored today both as a composer of great expressive power and as a pianist of uncommon ability. His song settings are . . . eminently singable. They have certain recurring gestures that singers find grateful. . . . But always the line, and its shaping with words, is something that can be sung with vocal beauty. . . . The piano's music is of complexity unmatched in the entire realm of song cycles, demanding genuine virtuosity both in comprehension and understanding. . . . With the composer serving brilliantly as his own pianist, the performance had a satisfying emotional impact.[377]

Perhaps not surprisingly, reviewers of the published score revealed a deeper understanding of the work than those called upon to comment after a single hearing.

> Wallace Stevens is as famous for his lyricism as for his subtlety, and Persichetti has dealt with the Stevens texts with superb and musicianly authority. The words fit the music and the music fits the voice. That is not to say the vocal writing is easy, but it is written with full knowledge of the voice and its technical problems. The keyboard parts are uncommonly fresh and beautifully varied. The idiom is astringent, spare and clear, though strangely enough not very personal. . . . The whole work apparently lasts about an hour, though it would be hard indeed to take at one sitting. Many different combinations of songs can be drawn from the cycle—groups of four or five—and I believe Persichetti can be thus revealed as one of the most distinguished vocal writers in America today. The words and the music are laden with qualities of intelligence, wit, and grace, in measure sufficient to hold the attention of serious musicians, though not perhaps for an hour at a time.[378]

Ivor Keys credited the composer for an

assured technique and a fine ear for the rhythms and linked meanings of the words. The subtle correspondences of some passages with others in different songs, brought to a logical and satisfying conclusion in the recapitulatory final song, together with the excellent characterization of the economical piano part, are proof enough that Persichetti knows his business. Yet in reading this long work one found oneself wishing that the music, and in particular the vocal line, were less of a handmaid, however dexterous. Of artistry there is much, of song in the crude sense little. When the voice is allowed to leave its studied declamation, as in the largely canonic no. 19, the effect is of a beautiful flowering, and in no. 17 the composer shows a fine ability to sustain a large design.[379]

After making an intensive study of the score, J. Katts wrote, "I hope I do not sound excessive when I say that Philadelphia's Persichetti's *Harmonium* is by far the best cycle of songs yet to be written by an American and on a par with the greatest cycles in all literature. . . . Whatever may have been the public estimate of Persichetti's work in the past, let it be said now that with *Harmonium*, to paraphrase Stevens, he is much taller, that he reaches right up to the sun."[380]

Just as no informed discussion of American piano music can ignore Persichetti's contribution to the repertoire, no consideration of serious American art song literature can overlook the comprehensive mastery represented by *Harmonium*. This vast work has had but one complete recording as of this writing: The 1979 performance featuring soprano Darleen Kliewer and pianist Lois McLeod at Arizona State University was released the following year in a handsome, thoroughly annotated, if minimally circulated, set of LPs. In addition, several recordings of individual songs from the cycle have appeared along the way.

As noted earlier, Persichetti had composed a few song settings during the 1940s: of two brief Cummings poems, two tiny Chinese poems in translation, and, immediately preceding *Harmonium*, three settings of seventeenth-century English poetry. Then, in 1957, in between his Sixth and Seventh Symphonies, he composed some seventeen song settings, grouped by poet. His Opp. 72–77 comprise four songs to poetry of Sara Teasdale, two of Carl Sandburg, three of James Joyce, two of Hilaire Belloc, two of Robert Frost, and four of Emily Dickinson. In contrast to the cryptic Stevens poetry of *Harmonium*, the texts he chose for these songs are largely short, simple, lyric poetry. Many of the poems are well known and are often set by beginning composers. Persichetti's musical settings are appropriately short, simple, and largely diatonic, capturing unerringly the essence of meaning inherent in each poem. It is unfortunate that they are so little known—a number of them remain unpublished—as they would be ideally suited for many recital programs.

Perhaps the most successful of these song groups are the Dickinson settings: "Out of the morning," "I'm nobody," "When the hills do," and "The grass." These songs feature some of the composer's most precious evocations of childlike innocence, while the first and last present melodies of exquisite poignancy. (The setting of "The grass," with paraphrased text, appears prominently in the opera, *The Sibyl*.) So unpretentious are these settings that they could be rendered effectively by an untrained voice. John Koopman describes them as "superb musical settings of the quintessential American poet, and it is impossible to imagine a more approachable and useful set of teaching songs for undergraduate students." He notes that Persichetti's "sensibilities favored the gentle lyricism and deeply contemplative elements of Dickinson's poetry, and his delicate and introspective musical settings mirrored this. . . . These are at once likable and substantive songs that have been fashioned with minimal vocal requirements, high poetic qualities and limited accompaniment demands."[381]

For his last solo vocal work, commissioned by mezzo-soprano Carolyn Reyer, Persichetti returned to the volume of haiku in English translation from which he had drawn the texts for his *Winter Cantata* in 1964. Selecting seventeen of the poems, he created a cycle that he named (after the title of the Harold Stewart volume), *A Net of Fireflies*, Op. 115, completing the work in 1970. Persichetti matched the almost synaesthetic verbal economy of the poetry with music of comparable pith and concision, the piano often responding to the voice as if in a terse dialogue. But however meticulously apt the match of music to text, these terse, angular vocal lines and wispy piano accompaniments offer little of the conventional lyricism that most listeners expect from vocal music; in order to be grasped, these songs require a listener's full attention.

For the foregoing reasons perhaps it is not surprising that *A Net of Fireflies* was not well received when it was introduced by Carolyn Reyer at Alice Tully Hall in New York City, in May 1971. Allen Hughes objected to the composer's repetition of words, as violating the whole haiku principle, while evidently the mezzo-soprano's own limitations only compounded the disappointment.[382] A. DeRhem reported that the cycle "is a setting of seventeen very enchanting haikus, not one of which was able to inspire a memorable musical phrase from the composer," adding that Reyer is "a rudimentary stylist," who "needs further schooling."[383]

CONCLUSION

Vincent Persichetti's death on 14 August 1987 did not come as a surprise to the Juilliard community or to the surrounding musical community, as he had been undergoing treatment for lung cancer for almost a year. His obituary in the *New York Times* summed up his compositional identity thus: "Mr. Persichetti's esthetic was essentially conservative, a distinctive blend of Classical, Romantic and Modernist elements, contrapuntal, rhythmically charged and expertly scored. Although the composer modestly insisted that there were only two main strains in his work—one graceful and the other gritty—his musical imagination was in fact multifaceted and highly virtuosic."[384]

About a month after the composer's death, I received a phone call from Dorothea Persichetti, who stated, "I have a manuscript I'm going to send you. Something my husband wrote from memory. He loved doing this sort of thing, and he would have wanted you to have this."[385] The manuscript was received several days later. It was entitled *The Magic Chain*, and under the title appears the following code: "(Modapolyrowtunal)," and under that, in smaller letters, "(roe)." The "composition" is written on a grand staff, as if for piano, but no instrumentation is indicated; it is undated and there is no opus number. What follows, for thirty-nine pages, is a series of 207 musical examples from the literature, each a few measures long, each identified by name, and each elided with the next, so that the entirety can theoretically be played seamlessly from beginning to end. The examples follow no apparent order and range from Wagner's *Parsifal* through Hindemith's Third String Quartet, from Schoenberg's *Pierrot Lunaire* to Hanson's "Romantic" Symphony, from Varèse's *Octandre* to Verdi's *La Traviata*, from Gershwin's *An American in Paris* to Reich's *Piano Phase*. What was the point of it? An activity done for his own amusement? It was probably not intended as a work to be performed (although a duration of forty-five minutes is indicated).[386] When it was described to former Persichetti student Larry Bell, he remarked, "It sounds like the sort of thing he used to love to improvise for his students."[387]

At the time of his death, although he was a beloved figure among those with whom he was in regular contact—chiefly his colleagues, students, and former students—Persichetti's national stature rested chiefly on two areas of accomplishment: (1) his reputation as a teacher of composition, spread by his many distinguished students and enhanced by the dozens of lecture-recitals he had given at colleges throughout the country, as well as by the circulation of numerous anecdotes illustrating his feats of sight-reading and musical memory; (2) his fourteen works for concert band, most of which are perennial favorites and securely ensconced as classics of the genre. Their popularity seems undiminished within their musical subculture, and they are performed regularly and have been recorded many times. However, this distinction has perhaps been a mixed blessing. Despite decades of ongoing effort to elevate its image within the music profession, the band subculture remains something of a stepchild, regarded with some condescension by the academic community, as well as by the professional music world, which centers on internationally renowned soloists, jet-set conductors, and their symphony orchestras in the major cities. Therefore, the often-encountered characterization of Persichetti as "a fine composer of band music" comes across as faint praise indeed.

As for the rest of his considerable output, not only has very little of it been heard with enough frequency for it to have achieved an identity in the minds of musicians and listeners, but his enormous stylistic range has made this task especially difficult: The random half-dozen or so pieces one might have encountered are typically too diverse stylistically, and perhaps too difficult to assimilate quickly, so that one frequently encounters such characterizations as "an American Hindemith," "impeccable craftsmanship but no personality," "a minor figure, overshadowed by the likes of Copland and Harris," and so forth. Furthermore, during the last decades of his life, Persichetti's refusal to adopt serialism as dogma placed him among "the old guard" in the minds of "new music" advocates, while more traditional listeners found in the harsh, atonal language of much of his later work little to distinguish it from that of the serialists.

The foregoing remained the prevailing view of Persichetti for the two decades following his death. During this period, little of his music was performed or recorded (aside from the band works), so that the dismissive verdicts noted above became more firmly entrenched. However, the recent appearance of a number of significant recordings—the Albany Symphony Orchestra's recording, conducted by David Alan Miller, of Symphonies Nos. 3, 4, and 7 (released in 2005), the Lydian Quartet's recording of the four string quartets in 2006, and Geoffrey Burleson's recording of the twelve piano sonatas in 2008—perhaps suggest the beginning of a revival of interest in the music of Persichetti.

The release of the piano sonatas prompted several commentaries that warrant consideration at this juncture, for the perspectives they reveal:

> Vincent Persichetti's reputation as a composer, theorist, and educator has seemingly grown in inverse proportion to the dwindling number of recordings of his music that have appeared since his death in 1987; this paradox suggests that his works are perhaps more respected than enjoyed, or at any rate, that they have somewhat fallen out of fashion. This is peculiar, since much of Persichetti's oeuvre is quite tonal, only mildly dissonant, melodious, and fully approachable, and should appeal to a wider audience, especially considering the change to more conservative tastes at the turn of the century. However, there are qualities in his music that may explain its unfair neglect. Its cerebral nature and strong neo-Classical orientation may partly be to blame, and the dry, academic quality that pervades even his most accessible music can make Persichetti seem too much like Paul Hindemith, another great composer whose works are similarly underappreciated.[388]

Rob Haskins wrote,

I've loved Vincent Persichetti's music since I was 16, when I sight-read movements from his Divertimento with my high school band. Then, as now, I was
excited by the rhythmic vitality of his music, its playfulness, its heart, and its
inventiveness. Persichetti's wide-ranging harmonic style could embrace chords
containing all 12 notes of the chromatic scale, but in the main he preferred to
anchor his music in recognizable complexes of combined triads. Little did I
know that he was widely considered to be a kind of reactionary conservative,
a brilliant pedagogue . . . whose music was more workmanlike than inspired. I
heartily disagree with this view.[389]

The following was written by contemporary music commentator and composer Frank J. Oteri, and is entitled "Vincent Who?"

One of the first composers I became excited about when I first began paying
attention to this whole world of contemporary composition was Vincent Persichetti (1915–1987). A friend of mine studying piano showed me a copy of the
score of Persichetti's *Little Piano Book* and I was immediately captivated: Here
was music with some of the weird harmonies I couldn't get out of my head since
first encountering *The Rite of Spring* and Bartók's Third Piano Concerto. . . .
But this was also music that I could look at and play through without too much
agony. I slowly accumulated as much of his solo piano music as I could find in
various music shops—the poems for piano, the sonatinas, and the sonatas. . . .
   As I became more and more of a record collector, it soon became apparent
to me that my Persichetti infatuation was not shared by folks who produced
records. I found an LP with his ninth symphony with the Philadelphia Orchestra
conducted by Eugene Ormandy which was pretty interesting, but that meant
there were at least eight others. Where were they? And the piano music? I
particularly wanted to hear those sonatas which my limited manual dexterity
prevented me from being able to play for myself. Nothing.
   Persichetti died more than twenty years ago, and my musical passions went
many other places since then. But in the last couple of years I've been noticing,
quite out of the blue, the seeds of a Persichetti renaissance through many different recording projects on as many labels. . . .
   Finally getting to hear all of these pieces after a wait of nearly a quarter century is like re-establishing contact with an old acquaintance you deeply admired
but only partially knew. And many lessons to be learnt from both the pieces I
attempted to play and the ones I was always too afraid to go near; some are obvious, some less so. . . . There are gestures in the first sonata that anticipate both
Barber and Carter's monumental piano sonatas from the late '40s. Persichetti
wrote his in 1939 and followed it with 11 more.
   But all this has made me ponder: Why has it taken so long for most of this
music to show up on CD? In an email correspondence I've begun with [Geof-

frey] Burleson after hearing his recordings of the sonatas, he admitted that he was mystified when he realized that his cycle was the first one anyone ever attempted on a recording. And there are plenty of other important compositions of his that have yet to be recorded commercially. Yet Persichetti certainly had big time credentials: he taught at Juilliard and Curtis [*sic*]—there's even a plaque about him in Philadelphia outside the school—and his 20th-century harmony textbook was required reading for generations of music students. He composed a vast body of music in virtually every medium and many of his works seem tailor-made for performances by conservatory students.

But beyond Persichetti's own music, which contains many other gems awaiting recording premieres, the whole issue of the neglect of his music raises even bigger questions about how music becomes part of history and how it gets disseminated to audiences. What causes a composer's music to come back into fashion after years of inactivity? What kind of thing can be done to make the listening audience more aware of the music of a lesser-known composer after his or her death? What other mid-century American composers are sorely in need of a revival?[390]

While the more conservative traditionalists, the Neo-Romantics, have begun to win favor among reviewers and listeners since the early 1990s, prompting ambitious recording projects and critical reassessments, this expanded interest has not extended to the Modern Traditionalists. Even today, much of the music of Persichetti is difficult for general listeners to appreciate, a point that has been emphasized throughout this chapter.

It is indeed difficult to capture the essence of a figure as complex as Vincent Persichetti. Perhaps the most apt epitaph is a comment that appears in the liner notes of the Albany recording of the Symphonies Nos. 3, 4, and 7: "In the concert hall he could weave musical tapestries of dark, dense fiber or sparkling filigree. In the classroom he could appreciate and inspire budding composers of the most wide-ranging stylistic leanings. And in the world at large, radiating an almost cosmic bonhomie, he could cheerfully declare his love for his wife, daughter and son in the same breath as his love for a family of raccoons or ducks or the sun and moon."[391]

NOTES

1. Rudy Shackelford, "Conversation with Vincent Persichetti," *Perspectives of New Music* (Fall/Winter 1981–Spring/Summer 1982): 110–11.

2. Donald A. Morris, "The Life of Vincent Persichetti, with Emphasis on His Works for Band" (PhD diss., Florida State University, 1991), 14.

3. Donald L. Patterson and Janet L. Patterson, *Vincent Persichetti: A Bio-Bibliography* (Westport, Conn.: Greenwood Press, 1988), 3.

4. Shackelford, "Conversation with Persichetti," 104.

5. Morris, "Life of Persichetti," 15.

6. Patterson and Patterson, *Vincent Persichetti*, 4.

7. Shackelford, "Conversation," 106.

8. Morris, "Life of Persichetti," 27.

9. Shackelford, "Conversation," 106.

10. Shackelford, "Conversation," 109.

11. Morris, "Life of Persichetti," 30.

12. Shackelford, "Conversation," 108.

13. Morris, "Life of Persichetti," 34–35.

14. Shackelford, "Conversation," 109.

15. Shackelford, "Conversation," 110.

16. Shackelford, "Conversation," 110.

17. Shackelford, "Conversation," 110.

18. Quoted in LP liner notes, Golden Crest ATH-5055 (1978).

19. Shackelford, "Conversation," 111.

20. Shackelford, "Conversation," 121.

21. Morris, "Life of Persichetti," 60–61.

22. Letter from William Schuman to Vincent Persichetti, 21 March 1944; Persichetti Archive at New York Public Library, JPB 90–77, Box 15, Folder 1.

23. Morris, "Life of Persichetti," 69.

24. Morris, "Life of Persichetti," 74–75.

25. Morris, "Life of Persichetti," 77.

26. Andrea Olmstead, *Juilliard: A History* (Urbana: University of Illinois Press, 1999), 251.

27. Larry Bell, interviewed by Walter Simmons, 8 February 2007.

28. Michael White, "Vincent Persichetti: Portrait of a Teacher," *Juilliard Journal* (May 1993): 8.

29. Quoted in Peter Burwasser, review, *Fanfare* (Sept/Oct 2008): 215.

30. Joseph Castaldo, interviewed by Donald A. Morris, 14 March 1989.

31. Shackelford, "Conversation," 129.

32. Vincent Persichetti, undated scrap of paper; Persichetti Archive at New York Public Library, JPB 90–77, Box 2, Folder 14.

33. Shackelford, "Conversation," 129–30.

34. William Schuman, letters to Vincent Persichetti; Persichetti Archive at New York Public Library, JPB 90–77, Box 15.

35. Shackelford, "Conversation," 123.

36. Robert Evett, "The Music of Vincent Persichetti," *Juilliard Review* (Spring 1955): 15–26.

37. Patterson and Patterson, *Vincent Persichetti*, 13.

38. Frederick Fennell, letter to Vincent Persichetti, 21 December 1956; Persichetti Archive at New York Public Library, JPB 90–77, Box 9, Folder 11.

39. Morris, "Life of Persichetti," 100.

40. Patterson and Patterson, *Vincent Persichetti*, 16.

41. Lauren Persichetti and Howard Harris, interviewed by Donald A. Morris, 20 March 1989.

42. Vincent Persichetti, *Twentieth-Century Harmony: Creative Aspects and Practice* (New York: W. W. Norton, 1961), 13.

43. William Schuman, "The Compleat Musician: Vincent Persichetti and Twentieth-Century Harmony," *Musical Quarterly* (July 1961): 379.

44. Peter A. Evans, review, *Music and Letters* (1963): 77–79.

45. Persichetti, *Twentieth-Century Harmony*, 9.

46. Peter Wishart, review, *Tempo* (Summer 1963): 19–20.

47. Godfrey Winham, review, *Perspectives of New Music* (Spring 1963): 145–46.

48. Hugo Weisgall, "Vincent Persichetti," in *Dictionary of Contemporary Music*, ed. John Vinton (New York: E.P. Dutton, 1974), 570.

49. Morris, "Life of Persichetti," 129–43.

50. *Newsweek*, 12 February 1973, 94.

51. Correspondence between Rudy Shackelford and Vincent Persichetti; Persichetti Archive at New York Public Library, JPB 90–77, Box 15, Folders 13–14.

52. Shackelford, "Conversation," 104–33.

53. Persichetti, conversation with Walter Simmons, 30 November 1981.

54. Olmstead, *Juilliard*, 267.

55. Morris, "Life of Persichetti," 152.

56. Lauren Persichetti, interviewed by Donald A. Morris, 20 March 1989.

57. Daniel Dorff, "Vincent Persichetti's Editor Recalls the Man behind the Notes," *Instrumentalist* (May 2003): 33.

58. Dorothea Persichetti, *Vincent Persichetti's Music* (unpublished monograph, May 1960), 30; Persichetti Archive at New York Public Library, JPB 90–77, Box 103, Folders 17–18.

59. D. Persichetti, *Vincent Persichetti's Music*, 209–10.

60. Dorff, "Persichetti's Editor," 30.

61. Andrea Olmstead, interviewed by Walter Simmons, 8 February 2007.

62. Evett, "Music of Persichetti," 25–26.

63. David Cohen, LP liner notes, Arizona State JMP-102679 (1979).

64. Evett, "Music of Persichetti," 17.

65. William Schuman, letter to Vincent Persichetti, 5 September 1950; Persichetti Archive at New York Public Library, JPB 90–77, Box 15, Folder 1.

66. D. Persichetti, *Vincent Persichetti's Music*, 99.

67. Shackelford, "Conversation," 112–13.

68. Persichetti, undated scrap of paper; Persichetti Archive at New York Public Library, JPB 90–77, Box 2, Folder 14.

69. Quoted in David M. Rubin, "Vincent Persichetti," *ASCAP in Action* (Spring 1980): 12.

70. Quoted in David Ewen, *American Composers: A Biographical Dictionary* (New York: G. P. Putnam's Sons, 1982), 505–06.

71. Shackelford, "Conversation," 114.

72. Shackelford, "Conversation," 111.

73. David Burge, review, *MLA Notes* (September 1983): 169.

74. Evett, "Music of Persichetti," 15–17.

75. Shackelford, "Conversation," 122.

76. John Kirkpatrick, review, *MLA Notes* (September 1946): 381–82.

77. Virgil Thomson, quoted in D. Persichetti, *Vincent Persichetti's Music*, 75.

78. David Burge, "Contemporary Piano: Persichetti's Fourth Sonata," *Contemporary Keyboard* (April 1981): 48.

79. Burge, "Persichetti's Fourth Sonata," 48.

80. Andor Foldes, review, *MLA Notes* (June 1952): 495.

81. D. Persichetti, *Vincent Persichetti's Music*, 78.

82. Raymond Ericson, review, *Musical America* (March 1951): 28.

83. Harold C. Schonberg, review, *New York Times*, 12 March 1951.

84. D. Persichetti, *Vincent Persichetti's Music*, 81.

85. William S. Newman, review, *MLA Notes* (March 1954): 281.

86. Harold C. Schonberg, review, *New York Times*, 27 April 1951.

87. D. Persichetti, *Vincent Persichetti's Music*, 83.

88. D. Persichetti, *Vincent Persichetti's Music*, 83.

89. D. Persichetti, *Vincent Persichetti's Music*, 83.

90. Laurence Rosenthal, review, *MLA Notes* (March 1956): 354.

91. D. Persichetti, *Vincent Persichetti's Music*, 134.

92. David Burge, "Contemporary Piano: Persichetti's Eleventh Sonata," *Contemporary Keyboard* (May 1981): 52.

93. Frank Dawes, review, *Musical Times* (January 1964): 46–47.

94. Clinton Gray-Fisk, review, *Musical Opinion* (September 1956), 703.

95. A.J.E., review, *Musical America* (March 1956): 37.

96. Howard Taubman, review, *New York Times*, 21 February 1956.

97. Joseph Bloch, "Some American Piano Sonatas," *Juilliard Review* (Fall 1956): 13.

98. Burge, "Persichetti's Eleventh Sonata," 52.

99. Maurice Hinson, *Guide to the Pianists Repertoire*, 2nd ed. (Bloomington: Indiana University Press, 1987), 551.

100. Mark Lehman, review, *American Record Guide* (May/June 2008): 165.

101. Joseph Bloch, "Some American Piano Sonatas," *Juilliard Review* (Fall 1956): 13.

102. Michelle Schumann, "Eclecticism and the American Piano Sonata: The Assimilation of Neoclassicism and the Twelve-Tone Technique in the Piano Sonatas of Roger Sessions, Vincent Persichetti, and Ross Lee Finney" (DMA diss., University of Texas at Austin, 2003), 108–9.

103. Shackelford, "Conversation," 123.

104. Blair Sanderson, review, *AllMusic.com*, 2008, www.allmusic.com/cg/amg.dll?p=amg&sql=43:165572 (accessed 15 February 2010).

105. Mark Lehman, review, *American Record Guide* (May/June 2008): 164–65.

106. Rob Haskins, review, *American Record Guide* (July/August 2008): 149–50.

107. Robert Sabin, review, *Musical America* (15 December 1953), 24.

108. Andor Foldes, review, *MLA Notes* (June 1952): 495.

109. Henry Harris, review, *Musical Courier* (1 March 1952): 33.

110. Shackelford, "Conversation," 112.

111. D. Persichetti, *Vincent Persichetti's Music*, 141.

112. D. Persichetti, *Vincent Persichetti's Music*, 122–23.

113. Morris, "Life of Persichetti," 99.

114. D. Persichetti, *Vincent Persichetti's Music*, 8–9.

115. D. Persichetti, *Vincent Persichetti's Music*, 10.

116. D. Persichetti, *Vincent Persichetti's Music*, 25.

117. D. Persichetti, *Vincent Persichetti's Music*, 10.

118. Burge, "Persichetti's Eleventh Sonata," 52.

119. Shackelford, "Conversation," 112.

120. Vincent Persichetti, *Reflective Keyboard Studies* (Bryn Mawr, Penn.: Elkan-Vogel, 1981), 2.

121. Shackelford, "Conversation," 112.

122. Ruth S. Edwards, review, *MLA Notes* (September 1983): 173.

123. Edwards, review, 173.

124. Dorff, "Persichetti's Editor," 32.

125. D. Persichetti, *Vincent Persichetti's Music*, 128.

126. D. Persichetti, *Vincent Persichetti's Music*, 126.

127. D. Persichetti, *Vincent Persichetti's Music*, 126.

128. Virgil Thomson, *Music Reviewed 1940–1954* (New York: Random House, 1967), 358.

129. Nathan Broder, review, *Musical Quarterly* (October 1955): 553.

130. Quoted in D. Persichetti, *Vincent Persichetti's Music*, 127.

131. John Kirkpatrick, review, *MLA Notes* (December 1948): 179.

132. Irving Lowens, review, *Musicology* (April 1949): 322.

133. Robert Sabin, review, *Musical America* (February 1949): 293.

134. D. Persichetti, *Vincent Persichetti's Music*, 28.

135. Theodore Strongin, review, *New York Times*, 3 August 1964.

136. William Bender, review, *New York Herald Tribune*, 3 August 1964.

137. Daniel Webster, review, *Philadelphia Inquirer*, 8 December 1979.

138. John von Rhein, review, *Chicago Tribune*, 28 May 1982.

139. James H. North, review, *Fanfare* (November/December 1990): 310.

140. D. Persichetti, *Vincent Persichetti's Music*, 115.

141. Russell Kerr, review, *Musical Courier* (1 February 1952): 24.

142. Jay S. Harrison, review, *New York Herald Tribune*, 11 January 1952.

143. Kathleen McIntosh Farr, review, *MLA Notes* (December 1975): 398.

144. Elaine Comparone, CD liner notes, Laurel LR-838 (1992), 8.

145. Comparone, CD liner notes, 9.

146. JoAnn Latorra Smith, review, *American Music Teacher* (January 1986): 47.

147. Mark E. Smith, review, *MLA Notes* (September 1985): 161.

148. Frances Bedford, review, *American Music Teacher* (June/July 1986): 46–47.

149. Bruce Adolphe, CD liner notes, Laurel LR-838 (1992), 5.

150. Dorff, "Persichetti's Editor," 32–33.

151. Bedford, review, 46.

152. Maribeth Gowen, review, *Piano Quarterly* (Spring 1985): 9.

153. D. Persichetti, *Vincent Persichetti's Music*, 20.

154. Rudy Shackelford, "Vincent Persichetti's Shimah B'koli [Psalm 130] for Organ—An Analysis," *Diapason* (September 1975): 3ff.

155. Rudy Shackelford, "Vincent Persichetti's Sonata for Organ and Sonatine for Organ, Pedals Alone—An Analysis," *Diapason* (May 1974): 4–7; (June 1974): 4–7.

156. Quoted in Shackelford, "Persichetti's Shimah B'koli," 3.

157. Shackelford, "Persichetti's Shimah B'koli," 3ff.

158. Owen Anderson, review, *Music Journal* (February 1963): 98.

159. Leonard Raver, review, *American Organist* (February 1963): 14ff.

160. Rudy Shackelford, "Vincent Persichetti's Hymn and Chorale Prelude 'Drop, Drop Slow Tears'—An Analysis," *Diapason* (September 1973): 3–6.

161. Rudy Shackelford, "Notes on the Recent Organ Music of Vincent Persichetti," *Diapason* (November 1976): 5–9.

162. Allen Hughes, review, *New York Times*, 9 February 1976.

163. Shackelford, "Recent Organ Music," 5–9.

164. Rudy Shackelford, "Vincent Persichetti's Auden Variations—An Analysis," *Diapason* (October 1979): 12ff.

165. David Shuler, review, *MLA Notes* (June 1982): 944–946.

166. Leonard Raver, review, *MLA Notes* (September 1984): 177.

167. Calvert Shenk, review, *American Organist* (August 1986): 39–40.

168. Rudolf Zuiderveld, review, *Diapason* (October 1986): 13.

169. D. Persichetti, *Vincent Persichetti's Music*, 54.

170. D. Persichetti, *Vincent Persichetti's Music*, 31.

171. D. Persichetti, *Vincent Persichetti's Music*, 32.

172. Linton Martin, review, *Philadelphia Inquirer*, 22 November 1947.

173. Elizabeth Emerson Stine, review, *Philadelphia Evening Bulletin*, 22 November 1947.

174. David Ward-Steinman, review, *Florida Flambeau*, 27 April 1956.

175. D. Persichetti, *Vincent Persichetti's Music*, 204.

176. David Moore, review, *American Record Guide* (January/February 2006): 168.

177. James H. North, review, *Fanfare* (September/October 1994): 284.

178. John Melby, conversation with Carson Cooman, 30 March 2008.

179. Max de Schauensee, review, *Philadelphia Evening Bulletin*, 18 December 1954.

180. Olin Downes, review, *New York Times*, 29 December 1954.

181. Lester Trimble, review, *Musical Quarterly* (April 1957): 278.

182. John Rockwell, review, *New York Times*, 24 April 1988.

183. Edwin H. Schloss, review, *Philadelphia Inquirer*, 18 December 1954.

184. Alfred Frankenstein, review, *Records in Review*, Vol. 3 (Great Barrington, Mass.: Wyeth Press, 1957), 153.

185. Vincent Persichetti, CD liner notes, First Edition FECD-0034 (2005).

186. D. Persichetti, *Vincent Persichetti's Music*, 145–49.

187. Moore, review, 168.

188. William Mootz, review, *Louisville Courier-Journal*, 29 August 1954.

189. D. Persichetti, *Vincent Persichetti's Music*, 150.

190. Max de Schauensee, review, *Musical America* (1 November 1959): 5.

191. James H. North, review, *Fanfare* (November/December 1990): 310.

192. David Lewis, review, *Allmusic.com*, 2006, www.allmusic.com/cg/amg. dll?p=amg&sql=43:124011 (18 February 2010).

193. Donald Morris, "Persichetti Rediscovered: The Manuscripts of Vincent Persichetti's Band Works," *Journal of Band Research* (Autumn 1992): 24.

194. Frederick Fennell, letters to Vincent Persichetti; Persichetti Archive at New York Public Library, JPB 90–77, Box 9, Folder 11.

195. Morris, "Persichetti Rediscovered," 26–27.

196. R. B., review, *New York Herald Tribune*, 2 August 1956.

197. Edward Downes, review, *New York Times*, 3 August 1956.

198. Lester Trimble, review, *Stereo Review* (March 1973): 130.

199. Patterson and Patterson, *Vincent Persichetti*, 125–27.

200. D. Persichetti, *Vincent Persichetti's Music*, 199.

201. D. Persichetti, *Vincent Persichetti's Music*, 201.

202. Thomas B. Sherman, review, *St. Louis Post-Dispatch*, 25 October 1959.

203. Howard Klein, review, *New York Times*, 10 November 1962.

204. John Gruen, review, *New York Herald Tribune*, 10 November 1962.

205. Michael Brozen, review, *Musical America* (January 1963): 109.

206. Richard Swift, review, *MLA Notes* (December 1976): 407.

207. John Rockwell, review, *New York Times*, 9 February 1986.

208. John Briggs, LP liner notes, RCA LSC-3212 (1971).

209. James Felton, review, *Philadelphia Bulletin*, 6 March 1971.

210. Daniel Webster, review, *Philadelphia Inquirer*, 6 March 1971.

211. Allen Hughes, review, *New York Times*, 11 March 1971.

212. Lester Trimble, review, *Stereo Review* (April 1972): 70–71.

213. Vincent Persichetti, quoted in Philadelphia Orchestra program notes (21 April 1945).

214. D. Persichetti, *Vincent Persichetti's Music*, 41–42.

215. Linton Martin, review, *Philadelphia Inquirer*, 21 April 1945.

216. Shackelford, "Conversation," 124–25.

217. Review, *Musical Courier*, 15 February 1949.

218. Robert L. Sanders, review, *MLA Notes* (June 1969): 489.

219. Paul Snook, review, *Fanfare* (March/April 1978): 38.

220. Quoted in D. Persichetti, *Vincent Persichetti's Music*, 91.

221. Dwight Anderson, review, *Louisville Courier-Journal*, 16 November 1950.

222. William H. Mootz, review, *Musical America* (1 January 1951): 6.

223. Vincent Persichetti, quoted in CD liner notes, New World 80396–2 (1990), 7.

224. Richard Swift, review, *MLA Notes* (September 1973): 157.

225. James H. North, review, *Fanfare* (March/April 1991): 321–22.

226. Vincent Persichetti, conversation with Walter Simmons, 10 June 1982.

227. Hubert Saal, review, *Newsweek* (12 February 1973): 94.

228. A. DeRhem, review, *High Fidelity/Musical America* (June 1973): MA-31.

229. Harold C. Schonberg, review, *New York Times*, 3 February 1973.

230. Harriett Johnson, review, *New York Post*, 2 February 1973.

231. David Lawton, review, *MLA Notes* (September 1975): 136.

232. Ainslee Cox, review, *Music Journal* (April 1973): 46.

233. Karl Miller, review, *Classical Net*, 2009, www.classical.net/music/recs/reviews/n/nxs59373a.php (accessed 24 February 2010).

234. William Kreindler, review, *Music Web International*, 2009, www.musicweb-international.com/classrev/2009/May09/Lincoln_portraits_8559373.htm (accessed 24 February 2010).

235. Christian Carey, review, *Sequenza 21*, 2009, www.sequenza21.com/cdreviews/2009/07/abraham-lincoln-portraits-on-naxos (accessed 24 February 2010).

236. Vincent Persichetti, quoted in CD liner notes, New World 80489–2 (1995), 4.

237. Andrew Porter, *Music of Three More Seasons, 1977–1980* (New York: Alfred Knopf, 1981), 58.

238. Harold C. Schonberg, review, *New York Times*, 18 November 1977.

239. Harriett Johnson, review, *New York Post*, 18 November 1977.

240. John Rockwell, review, *New York Times*, 18 February 1987.

241. Reviews, *Ovation* (September 1981): 36.

242. William Schuman, interviewed by Jack Stamp, 5 March 1990, Klavier L11155 (2005).

243. Shackelford, "Conversation," 120.

244. D. Persichetti, *Vincent Persichetti's Music*, 181.

245. Shackelford, "Conversation," 119.

246. Morris, "Life of Persichetti," chapter 6.

247. Dorff, "Persichetti's Editor," 30.

248. D. Persichetti, *Vincent Persichetti's Music*, 87.

249. Shackelford, "Conversation," 119–20.

250. Morris, "Life of Persichetti," 185.

251. Miles Kastendieck, review, *New York Journal-American*, 17 June 1950.

252. Virgil Thomson, review, *New York Herald Tribune*, 17 June 1950.

253. Richard Franko Goldman, review, *Musical Quarterly* (October 1950): 595.

254. Walter E. Nallin, "New Work for Band," *Symphony* (January 1952): 13.

255. Frederick Fennell, letter to Vincent Persichetti, 5 April 1951; Persichetti Archive at New York Public Library, JPB 90–77, Box 9, Folder 11.

256. Richard Franko Goldman, letter to Vincent Persichetti, 29 June 1951; Persichetti Archive at New York Public Library, JPB 90–77, Box 10, Folder 3.

257. Stephen Ellis, review, *Fanfare* (November/December 2003): 266.

258. David Hurwitz, review, *Classics Today*, http://www.classicstoday.com/review.asp?ReviewNum=154 (accessed 26 February 2010).

259. Richard Franko Goldman, review, *Musical Quarterly* (July 1955): 407.

260. Robert Evett, review, *MLA Notes* (December 1955): 147–48.

261. Paul Whear, quoted in Morris, "Life of Persichetti," 194.

262. Steven Schwartz, review, *Classical Net*, 2001, www.classical.net/music/recs/reviews/m/mrc62960b.html (accessed 26 February 2010).

263. Morris, "Life of Persichetti," 205.

264. Harold C. Schonberg, review, *New York Times*, 20 June 1953.

265. Peter Frank, review, *Fanfare* (March/April 1978): 91.

266. Morris, "Life of Persichetti," 209–10.

267. Shackelford, "Conversation," 108.

268. Cecil Isaac, review, *MLA Notes* (Spring 1965): 1102.

269. Morris, "Life of Persichetti," 210.

270. Shackelford, "Conversation," 128.

271. Morris, "Life of Persichetti," 212.

272. Shackelford, "Conversation," 128.

273. Donal Henahan, review, *Musical Quarterly* (July 1969): 425.

274. Enos Shupp, Jr., review, *The New Records* (May 1969): 14.

275. John Paynter, "New Music Reviews," *Instrumentalist* (August 1973): 70.

276. Morris, "Life of Persichetti," 225.

277. Shackelford, "Conversation," 113.

278. Shackelford, "Conversation," 113.

279. Conversation between Vincent Persichetti and Walter Simmons, 22 February 1977.

280. Shackelford, "Conversation," 122.

281. Peter Mennin, Letter to Vincent Persichetti, 10 January 1975; Persichetti Archive at New York Public Library, JPB 90–77, Box 12, Folder 23.

282. Jan Thornhill, *The Rumor: A Jataka Tale from India* (Toronto: Maple Tree Press, 2005).

283. Vincent Persichetti papers; Persichetti Archive at New York Public Library, JPB 90–77, Boxes 70–72.

284. Persichetti papers; Persichetti Archive at New York Public Library, JPB 90–77, Box 72.

285. Fritz Jahoda, letter to Vincent Persichetti, 17 May 1981; Persichetti Archive at New York Public Library, JPB 90–77, Box 15, Folder19.

286. Vincent Persichetti, interview on WFLN Philadelphia, April 1985.

287. Dominick Argento, letter to Vincent Persichetti, November 1974; Persichetti Archive at New York Public Library, JPB 90–77, Box 9, Folder 9.

288. Persichetti papers; Persichetti Archive at New York Public Library, JPB 90–77, Box 70, Folder 1.

289. Persichetti papers; Persichetti Archive at New York Public Library, JPB 90–77, Box 70, Folder 1.

290. Persichetti papers; Persichetti Archive at New York Public Library, JPB 90–77, Box 72, Folder 2.

291. Daniel Webster, review, *Philadelphia Inquirer*, 16 April 1985.

292. Robert Baxter, review, *Opera* (November 1985): 1293–94.

293. Will Crutchfield, review, *New York Times*, 21 April 1985.

294. James P. Cassaro, "Vincent Persichetti," *New Grove Dictionary of Opera*, ed. Stanley Sadie (New York: Oxford University Press, 1992), 3: 971.

295. D. Persichetti, *Vincent Persichetti's Music*, 13.

296. Paul Bowles, review, *New York Herald Tribune*, 15 March 1943.

297. Arthur Cohn, review, *Modern Music* (March-April 1942): 189.

298. D. Persichetti, *Vincent Persichetti's Music*, 44.

299. D. Persichetti, *Vincent Persichetti's Music*, 44.

300. Andrew Frank, review, *MLA Notes* (September 1975): 142.

301. D. Persichetti, *Vincent Persichetti's Music*, 159.

302. Paul Hume, *Washington Post and Times Herald*, 5 February 1955.

303. Samuel L. Singer, review, *Philadelphia Inquirer*, 19 November 1955.

304. Paul Henry Lang, review, *New York Herald Tribune*, 10 January 1956.

305. Edward Downes, review, *New York Times*, 10 January 1956.

306. Louis Biancolli, review, *New York World-Telegram and Sun*, 10 January 1956.

307. Rafael Kammerer, review, *Musical America* (15 January 1956).

308. Elliot Galkin, review, *Baltimore Sun*, 10 December 1962.

309. D. Persichetti, *Vincent Persichetti's Music*, 206.

310. David Cohen, LP liner notes, Arizona State University ASU-1976-ARA (1976).

311. D. Persichetti, *Vincent Persichetti's Music*, 207.

312. D. Persichetti, *Vincent Persichetti's Music*, 205–06.

313. Max deSchauensee, review, *Musical America* (15 December 1959).

314. David Cohen, LP liner notes, Arizona State University ASU-1976-ARA (1976).

315. David Cohen, LP liner notes, Arizona State University ASU-1976-ARA (1976).

316. James Felton, review, *Philadelphia Evening Bulletin*, 9 October 1973.

317. Mark Lehman, review, *American Record Guide* (May/June 2007): 139–40.

318. Terry King, CD liner notes, Music & Arts CD-686 (1991).

319. Arthur Cohn, program notes, quoted in D. Persichetti, *Vincent Persichetti's Music*, 36–37.

320. John Barrows, review, *MLA Notes* (December 1952): 146.

321. Oliver Daniel, review, *Bulletin of the American Composers Alliance*, 4, no. 2 (1954): 21.

322. D. Persichetti, *Vincent Persichetti's Music*, 64.

323. Martha Graham, quoted in D. Persichetti, *Vincent Persichetti's Music*, 64–68.

324. Vincent Persichetti, *King Lear* (Bryn Mawr, Penn.: Elkan-Vogel, 1948).

325. Alan Thomas, quoted in Morris, "Life of Persichetti," III, 28.

326. Clive Barnes, review, *Dance* (1 November 1994).

327. D. Persichetti, *Vincent Persichetti's Music*, 194.

328. Lester Trimble, review, *Stereo Review* (July 1973): 114.

329. Shackelford, "Conversation," 115.

330. Persichetti papers; Persichetti Archive at New York Public Library, JPB 90–77, Box 88.

331. Shackelford, "Conversation," 116.

332. D. Persichetti, *Vincent Persichetti's Music*, 166.

333. D. Persichetti, *Vincent Persichetti's Music*, 166–67.

334. Shackelford, "Conversation," 116.

335. "Religion: Words and Music," *Time* (6 August 1956).

336. Mark Siebert, review, *MLA Notes* (September 1957): 619.

337. Dorff, "Persichetti's Editor," 32.

338. John Ardoin, review, *Musical America* (June 1961): 55.

339. Allen Hughes, review, *New York Times*, 21 April 1961.

340. Francis Perkins, review, *Musical Quarterly* (October 1961): 526–27.

341. John Barker, review, *American Record Guide* (September 1984): 32–33.

342. Lee Passarella, review, *The New Records* (July 1984): 9.

343. Wriston Locklair, review, *New York Herald Tribune*, 2 May 1964.

344. Theodore Strongin, review, *New York Times*, 2 May 1964.

345. Hugo Weisgall, review, *Musical Quarterly* (July 1964): 379–81.

346. Harold Stewart, *A Net of Fireflies* (Rutland, Vt.: Charles E. Tuttle, 1960).

347. Shackelford, "Conversation," 119.

348. Shackelford, "Conversation," 119.

349. Tim Page, review, *New York Times*, 1 November 1985.

350. Shackelford, "Conversation," 117.

351. Robert Page, "In Quest of Answers: An Interview with Vincent Persichetti," *Choral Journal* (November 1973), 5.

352. Vincent Persichetti, Letter quoted in Terry Barham, "A Macroanalytic View of Vincent Persichetti's The Creation, Op. 111," *The Choral Journal* (March 1984): 6.

353. Persichetti papers; Persichetti Archive at New York Public Library, JPB 90–77, Box 59, Folders 14–16.

354. Barham, "A Macroanalytic View," 9.

355. Raymond Ericson, review, *New York Times*, 18 April 1970.

356. Max deSchauensee, review, *Philadelphia Evening Bulletin*, 20 April 1970.

357. Samuel Singer, review, *Philadelphia Inquirer*, 20 April 1970.

358. Elwyn A. Wienandt, review, *MLA Notes* (June 1971): 807–8.

359. Daniel Webster, review, *Philadelphia Inquirer*, 21 April 1984.

360. Allen Hughes, review, *New York Times*, 16 December 1984.

361. Chris Mullen, "American Choral Music," *Opera Today*, 3 May 2007, www.operatoday.com/content/2007/05/american_choral.php (accessed 6 March 2010).

362. David Vernier, review, *Classics Today*, 14 June 2007, www.classicstoday.com/review.asp?ReviewNum=11034 (accessed 6 March 2010).

363. D. Persichetti, *Vincent Persichetti's Music*, 48.

364. Shackelford, "Conversation," 119.

365. Vincent Persichetti, LP liner notes, Arizona State University JMP-102679 (1979).

366. Mark Van Doren, "Poets and Wits," *Nation* (October 1923): 400–401.

367. Robert Rehder, "Stevens and Harmonium," in *The Cambridge Companion to Wallace Stevens*, ed. John N. Serio (New York: Cambridge University Press, 2007), 27.

368. Wallace Stevens, *Collected Poetry and Prose* (New York: Library of America, 1997), 306.

369. D. Persichetti, *Vincent Persichetti's Music*, 102–3.

370. D. Persichetti, *Vincent Persichetti's Music*, 104–5.

371. D. Persichetti, *Vincent Persichetti's Music*, 105–10.

372. D. Persichetti, Vincent Persichetti's Music, 103.

373. Vincent Persichetti, LP liner notes, Arizona State University JMP-102679 (1979).

374. Arthur Berger, review, *New York Herald Tribune*, 21 January 1952.

375. Eugene Moore, review, *Philadelphia Evening Bulletin*, 16 January 1961.

376. Samuel Singer, review, *Philadelphia Inquirer*, 16 January 1961.

377. Paul Hume, review, *Washington Post*, 14 May 1962.

378. John Edmunds, review, *MLA Notes* (June 1960): 484–85.

379. Ivor Keys, review, *Music and Letters* (April 1961): 189–90.

380. J. Katts, review, *The Jewish Exponent*, 8 May 1959.

381. John Koopman, "Emily Dickinson Songs, by Vincent Persichetti," *Unsung Songs*, 1999, www.lawrence.edu/fast/koopmajo/persichetti.html (accessed 6 March 2010).

382. Allen Hughes, review, *New York Times*, 14 May 1971.

383. A. DeRhem, review, *High Fidelity/Musical America* (August 1971).

384. Obituary, *New York Times*, 15 August 1987.

385. Dorothea Persichetti, telephone call to Walter Simmons, 19 September 1987.

386. Vincent Persichetti, *The Magic Chain*, Persichetti papers; Persichetti Archive at New York Public Library, JPB 90–77, Box 87.

387. Larry Bell, interviewed by Walter Simmons, 8 February 2007.

388. Blair Sanderson, "Vincent Persichetti: Complete Piano Sonatas," *All Music Guide*, 2008, www.allmusic.com/cg/amg.dll?p=amg&sql=43:165572 (accessed 6 March 2010).

389. Rob Haskins, review, *American Record Guide* (July/August 2008): 149.

390. Frank J. Oteri, "Vincent Who?" *New Music Box*, 19 February 2008, http://newmusicbox.org/chatter/chatter.nmbx?id=5464 (accessed 6 March 2010).

391. Ray Bono, CD liner notes, Albany TROY771/72 (2005).

SELECTED BIBLIOGRAPHY

Morris, Donald A. "Persichetti Rediscovered: The Manuscripts of Vincent Persichetti's Band Works, Part One." *Journal of Band Research* (Autumn 1992): 21–30.

Morris, Donald A. "The Life of Vincent Persichetti, with Emphasis on his Works for Band." PhD diss., Florida State University, 1991.

Patterson, Donald L., and Janet L. Patterson. *Vincent Persichetti: A Bio-Bibliography*. Westport, Conn.: Greenwood Press, 1988.

Persichetti, Dorothea. *Vincent Persichetti's Music*. Unpublished Monograph, May 1960; Persichetti Archive at New York Public Library, JPB 90–77, Box 103, Folders 17–18.

Persichetti, Vincent. *Twentieth-Century Harmony: Creative Aspects and Practice*. New York: W. W. Norton, 1961.

Schuman, William. "The Compleat Musician: Vincent Persichetti and Twentieth-Century Harmony." *Musical Quarterly* (July 1961): 379–85.

Shackelford, Rudy. "Conversation with Vincent Persichetti." *Perspectives of New Music* (Fall/Winter 1981-Spring/Summer 1982): 104–133.

Shackelford, Rudy. "Vincent Persichetti's Shimah B'koli [Psalm 130] for Organ—An Analysis." *The Diapason* (September 1975): 3ff.

ESSENTIAL DISCOGRAPHY

Albany TROY771/72: Symphony No. 3; Symphony No. 4; Symphony No. 7 (Albany Sym. Orch., David Alan Miller, cond.); www.albanyrecords.com/

Cedille CDR-900000 069: Concerto for Piano, Four Hands; Sonata for Two Pianos (Georgia and Louise Mangos, pianists); www.cedillerecords.org/

Centaur CRC-2833: String Quartets Nos. 1–4 (Lydian String Quartet); www.centaurrecords.com/

First Edition FECD-0034: Symphony No. 5; Symphony No. 8; Serenade No. 5 (Louisville Orch., Robert Whitney, Jorge Mester, conds.); www.firsteditionmusic.com/

Laurel 838: Harpsichord Sonatas Nos. 2–5 (Elaine Comparone, harpsichord); www.laurelrecord.com/

Naxos 8.570123: Divertimento; *Psalm*; Chorale Prelude: "O God Unseen"; *Pageant*; *Masquerade*; *O Cool is the Valley*; *Parable IX* (London Symphony Winds, David Amos, cond.); www.naxos.com/

Naxos 8.570243: Symphony No. 6 (United States Marine Band, Timothy W. Foley, cond.); www.naxos.com/

New World NW-370–2: Piano Concerto (Robert Taub, piano); Symphony No. 5 (Philadelphia Orch., Charles Dutoit, Riccardo Muti, conds.); www.newworldrecords.org/

New World 80677: Piano Sonatas Nos. 1–12 (Geoffrey Burleson, piano); www.newworldrecords.org/

Phoenix PHCD-141: Serenade No. 10 (Samuel Baron, flute; Ruth Maayani, harp); www.phoenixcd.com/

4

Peter Mennin

The career of Peter Mennin is remarkable for its consistent sense of purpose. In personal statements made during his maturity, he gave verbal expression to some of the principles that defined his aesthetic creed and guided his creative life (edited and condensed here for the purpose of succinctness): "Individuality is an inevitable precondition for music of lasting value. By this I mean a strong musical thrust, unconcerned with convention, but, rather, with the drive of the composer's musical ideas; it is having one's own voice. The only thing that lasts is what one human being can bring that is peculiarly his own and not anyone else's. A major composer always brings a visceral reaction, a physical involvement. Unless compositional technique reflects a creative impulse, a creative drive, it doesn't mean anything."[1]

Mennin completed his Third Symphony, which also served as his doctoral dissertation, on his twenty-third birthday. It was introduced later that year by the New York Philharmonic, before it had even been accepted by his doctoral committee. The following year he joined the Juilliard composition faculty. By the time he reached the age of thirty, he had completed six symphonies and was recognized as one of the most promising young composers on the American scene. At thirty-five he was appointed to head the Peabody Conservatory; four years later he accepted the position of president of the Juilliard School, a post he held for twenty-one years, until his untimely death at age sixty. Mennin's output is relatively small, amounting to barely thirty works, but his catalog is notably devoid of music of frivolous or diverting character. Each work follows the last along a continuum of increasing emotional intensity and structural complexity. By the time of his death, Mennin was regarded as a member of "the Establishment," and his reputation as an administrator had displaced his identity as a composer. Yet his body of creative work, notable for its strong personal voice, consistency of vision, seriousness of purpose, and impeccable workmanship, has largely fallen from view.

BIOGRAPHY

Peter Mennin (originally Mennini) was born on 17 May 1923, in Erie, Pennsylvania, located in the northwest corner of the state. His father, Attilio Mennini, a restaurateur, and his mother, Amelia Benacci, were avid music lovers. His father amassed an impressive record collection, and music played a central role within the family household. The family was not religious and had renounced their Roman Catholic heritage while the children were still young. Peter had an older brother, Louis (1920–2000), who also became a composer, and kept the original family name.

Peter's formal study of music began when he was five and was introduced to a local teacher named Tito Spampani, who insisted that the boy study *solfeggio* before taking up an instrument. (*Solfeggio*—or *solfege*—is the traditional European approach to sight-singing and ear-training—a discipline that Mennin reinstated into the Juilliard curriculum many years later.) After a year, he began studying the piano, and at seven, began to compose. Spampani immersed his young student in the music of Verdi and Beethoven, and their works formed the foundation of Mennin's conception of the repertoire. When he was eleven, he made his first attempt at writing a symphony. More practically, he and his brother formed an accordion duo, "The Mennini Brothers," and performed at local showcases. Not surprisingly for brothers pursuing the same field of endeavor, rivalries developed between them, resulting in some estrangement during the years that followed. During his high school years in Erie, Peter earned spending money by working for a sign painter, thereby developing the meticulous penmanship found in his musical manuscripts. He also developed skill in archery, which he taught to other youngsters during the summers. Fascinated by aviation, he learned to pilot an airplane when he was sixteen—before he had learned to drive a car![2]

Peter Mennini graduated from high school in 1940, whereupon he entered the Oberlin College Conservatory, studying composition with Normand Lockwood (1906–2002). However, Lockwood had studied with Nadia Boulanger in Paris, and the independent-minded young Mennini found his Franco-American perspective inimical to his own aesthetic orientation. "We did not hit it off too well," he later stated, adding, "That doesn't mean I didn't learn from him; I learned very much about how to be a little bit more specific in my own terms."[3] In 1942, after two years at Oberlin, during which time he had completed a forty-five-minute Symphony No. 1, he left to join the Army Air Corps. Since he already knew how to fly a plane, he was promptly accepted into Officer Candidate School, reaching the rank of lieutenant before it was discovered that he was extremely near-sighted. He was honorably discharged in 1943 and took a job in a paper factory as his contribution to the war effort.

In 1944 the twenty-one-year-old Mennini decided to resume his education, so one Sunday in October, with his compositions in tow, he boarded a train to New York City. However, having heard about the Eastman School's policy of performing student works, he decided to take advantage of the train's stop at Rochester and made a side visit, appearing at the home of the school's director, Howard Hanson (1896–1981). Hanson welcomed him graciously and, after examining the young composer's manuscripts, offered him a tuition scholarship if he enrolled at Eastman. Mennini decided to accept Hanson's offer.[4]

While at Eastman, the young composer worked under Hanson and his close associate Bernard Rogers (1893–1968). However, the self-described "renegade" resisted much of what the Eastman faculty attempted to offer him. He later recalled, "Howard Hanson's music was very different from mine, and he never expressed any particular liking for my music; but at the same time he was a very big help to me. . . . I've learned from a number of people, I think, in spite of whether I've liked or disliked them. As a matter of fact I think you do not learn properly from a teacher whose music you have enormous admiration for."[5] It was at Eastman that he met a young violinist from Iowa named Georganne Bairnson, whom he was to marry upon completing his formal education. It was also during this period that he decided to shorten his name to "Mennin," ostensibly to avoid confusion with his brother,[6] who was also studying at the school, although others have speculated that an additional motive may have been to avoid an instant ethnic identification. While at Eastman he composed a Symphony No. 2, and a Concertino for Flute, Strings, and Percussion, earning his bachelor's and master's degrees in 1945. Though he later withdrew the work, the Symphony No. 2 brought considerable attention to the young composer that year. The first movement, *Symphonic Allegro*, won the first Gershwin Memorial Prize. Then, after Leonard Bernstein conducted a complete performance in March 1945, the symphony was awarded the Bearns Prize by Columbia University.

As part of the requirements for his PhD, Mennin completed his Symphony No. 3, already revealing the predilection for large forms that was to characterize his mature output. That summer he studied conducting at Tanglewood with Serge Koussevitzky. In 1947 Mennin was awarded his doctoral degree.

However, his new symphony had already been performed by the New York Philharmonic, under the direction of its associate conductor Walter Hendl, before it had even been accepted by the Eastman doctoral committee, much to Howard Hanson's annoyance. (Hendl [1917–2007] was to become an ardent advocate of Mennin's music.) Upon being awarded his doctorate, Mennin accepted an invitation from William Schuman to join the newly revamped composition faculty at the Juilliard School. It was also in 1947 that the composer and Georganne were married.

The auspicious premiere of the twenty-three-year-old's symphony catapulted him to national prominence, and further performances of the work soon followed. Attending the premiere, Louis Biancolli wrote, "I think this boy will bear watching—and hearing. Peter Mennin has lots to say and his own punchy way of saying it."[7] This and similar comments from other critics quickly brought Mennin to the forefront among promising young American composers.

The eleven years Mennin spent on the Juilliard composition faculty were highly fruitful: He composed more than a dozen works—including three more symphonies; altogether, about a third of his entire output—during that period. Many were commissioned by leading arts organizations, such as the Collegiate Chorale (Symphony No. 4), League of Composers (*Canzona*), the Koussevitzky Foundation (String Quartet No. 2), the Dallas Symphony (Symphony No. 5), the Erie Philharmonic (Concertato, "Moby Dick"), the Louisville Orchestra (Symphony No. 6), the Juilliard Musical Foundation (Cello Concerto), the Elizabeth Sprague Coolidge Foundation (*Sonata Concertante*), and the Cleveland Orchestra (Piano Concerto). In order to fit composition into his busy schedule, he developed the habit of writing early in the morning or late at night. He worked away from the piano, writing directly onto the full score, in his impeccable hand. Many of his major works won awards and were performed repeatedly by America's leading conductors and orchestras, and quite a few were recorded as well—and this was all before he reached the age of thirty-five.

During the 1950s, Mennin's reputation soared. The *Juilliard Review* published an analytical study, "The Music of Peter Mennin," by Walter Hendl, who concluded by stating, "There is no doubt in my mind that [Mennin's music] is, and will continue to be, one of the dominant expressions of the creative activity of our times."[8] In 1956 he won a Guggenheim Award and a Fulbright Fellowship, which enabled him to live and work in Europe until the beginning of 1958. In an essay, "The Symphony in America," German-American composer and musicologist Peter Jona Korn (1922–1998) cited Mennin as "America's outstanding younger symphonist."[9] *Life* Magazine featured a spread (with photographs by Gordon Parks) highlighting nine American composers who "stand out" as the most prominent at the time. The first page featured Mennin, the youngest of the group, "a fast-moving symphonist." Neither William Schuman nor Vincent Persichetti was mentioned in the article. (The eight other composers were Alan Hovhaness, Samuel Barber, Leonard Bernstein, Aaron Copland, Roger Sessions, Robert Kurka, Harold Shapero, and Leon Kirchner.[10]) Some have speculated that Schuman's antagonism toward Mennin may have emanated from this article, although it may have been exacerbated by subsequent developments as well.[11]

However, despite his undisputable success, Mennin felt that teaching composition was draining his own creative energy. He began to consider administrative work, which he found less demanding. In 1958, he accepted the position of director of the Peabody Conservatory in Baltimore. But in the autumn of 1958, before assuming his new post, he traveled to the Soviet Union, participating in the first cultural exchange of composers with our erstwhile enemy. Arriving at Peabody, he took on the duties and responsibilities of his new position. Among his accomplishments were instituting the Peabody Art Theatre, which presented lesser-known operas while providing intensive training for young opera singers, and persuading the Ford Foundation to contribute $400,000 to help fund an American Conductors Project; he also reduced the number of courses in music pedagogy, to lessen the school's emphasis on the training of music teachers. During his years at Peabody, Mennin struggled to maintain his compositional activity. He also worked intensively on an opera based on Marguerite Hood's novel *The Island Women*. Although he composed a sizable portion of the work, he was unable to find the concentrated blocks of time necessary for such a project and eventually abandoned it. This was also the period when Mennin's daughter Felicia (1958) and son Mark (1960) were born.

In 1961 William Schuman announced his decision to resign as president of the Juilliard School in order to assume the presidency of the Lincoln Center for the Performing Arts, the huge complex of concert halls and related facilities then in its initial stages. Schuman proposed a number of possible candidates as his successor at Juilliard—William Bergsma, Vincent Persichetti, Hugo Weisgall—but the board of directors reached a compromise and decided to offer the position to Mennin. Although he had already turned down the presidencies of the Oberlin Conservatory, Eastman School, and Curtis Institute, he decided to take on the challenge of Juilliard, which was expected to move from its "uptown" location near Columbia University into the new Lincoln Center complex in midtown Manhattan. Once Mennin was installed as the new president, Schuman had no further connection with the school for the duration of Mennin's tenure.[12] However, his appointment precipitated "hard feelings" between the two men that the following years only exacerbated.

Having had the experience of directing a conservatory at Peabody, a position that also afforded him the opportunity to visit music schools throughout the world, Mennin had developed an idea of how a first-class music school should operate—a view that was very much an outgrowth of his own temperament and values. His was not a democratic or populist approach, a something-for-everyone approach, or one that offered a short cut to success. During a period when educational orthodoxy was under severe attack, Mennin upheld traditional standards of excellence, rejecting "the American tendency to look for an easy way. *There is no easy way.*"[13] Mennin wanted to restore an atmosphere of diligent hard work that he felt had been lost during the later Schuman years. In the process he did away with the controversial Literature and Materials (L&M) approach, which had become lax and overly indulgent of the idiosyncratic inclinations of each individual instructor. As his wife later recalled, "Peter's Juilliard was for the deeply committed, highly talented person who needed to spend their student years concentrating on honing their talents to the highest possible point."[14] As he explained, "Our country tries to sugarcoat education, to make everything seem easy. Very often we try to make a human being so well-rounded that he emerges as a professional in nothing."[15]

Mennin was described as an unabashed elitist, a loner who had little need for the approval or reassurance of others.[16] A revealing comment he made about compositional "movements" is suggestive of the way he saw his role at Juilliard: "I don't think any real composer ever aligns himself with a group. I think groups are silly. A composer has to travel alone. You cannot have expression in common. It becomes a compromise, and a real composer does not compromise."[17] But even his critics were forced to acknowledge that Mennin's elitist tendencies helped to build Juilliard's reputation as one of the world's foremost conservatories.[18] He sought to insulate the school from the turbulent social issues of the day, resisting efforts of the faculty to unionize, refusing to involve Juilliard in political protests during the Vietnam War years, resisting efforts to incorporate jazz into the curriculum and reinstating *solfeggio* as the foundation of ear-training. On the other hand, he did bring to the composition faculty such nontraditionalists as Roger Sessions, Elliott Carter, and Luciano Berio. Perhaps Mennin's most challenging accomplishment as Juilliard's president was supervising the school's move in 1969 into the Lincoln Center complex. During those years he had to devote much time and energy to fund-raising, which often placed him in direct competition with William Schuman, who was vying for the same money on behalf of Lincoln Center. Mennin's surprising success at attracting benefactors created considerable tension between the two men. Schuman's resentment of his successor extended to his taking an active role in 1971 in unseating Mennin from the presidency of the Naumburg Foundation, a position he had held since 1964.[19]

During his twenty-one years as Juilliard's president, Mennin expanded and developed the school's curriculum with a number of innovative programs. One was the Young Conductors Program, which numbered among its alumni Leonard Slatkin, Dennis Russell Davies, James Levine, and James Conlon. He also instituted a new Drama Division, a Dance Division, the Young Playwrights Program, the American Opera Center, the Juilliard Theater Center, the Visiting Artists Program, the Contemporary Music Festival, and a doctoral program. However, he was not able to maintain his own compositional productivity at the level he had hoped. During those twenty-one years he composed only nine works, although most of these were major statements of considerable substance. But his reputation as president of the nation's foremost conservatory began to supersede his identity as a composer. His own works were regarded as representative of an outmoded approach to composition and were received somewhat indulgently as the products of an administrator's leisure time. The Juilliard students were largely ignorant of his accomplishments as a composer and less than charitable in their reactions to his music.

In 1981, commentator David Owens—a champion of traditional compositional approaches and a longtime admirer of Mennin's music—conducted an extensive and probing interview with the composer, which was published in the *Christian Science Monitor*. In it Mennin discussed the principles and beliefs that formed his philosophy as both a composer and a musical educator and administrator.[20]

Mennin was characterized by many as secretive in the extreme.[21] Some connected this quality with his shrewdness as an administrator, while others viewed it as paranoia. In 1982 he was diagnosed with pancreatic cancer. For whatever reason, he decided to keep his illness a secret for some time, even from those who were quite close to him—initially including his wife and children. Others—his mother, his brother, his colleagues—did not learn about his illness until after he died. His wife believed that he was so determined to complete his final work—a flute concerto—as well as a number of ongoing projects at Juilliard, that he sought to avoid the distractions of well-intentioned associates. He continued to fulfill his responsibilities at Juilliard until the week he died, on 17 June 1983, just one month after his sixtieth birthday. His death therefore came as a tremendous shock to most of those close to him, including his colleagues at Juilliard. He left sealed letters of farewell to his mother, his wife, and his children.[22]

The combination of his personal aloofness and sense of privacy, his well-tailored, conservative appearance, the institutional positions he held, and the high-mindedness of his viewpoints led many who came in contact with him to regard Mennin as a rather humorless and unapproachable musical administrator. Few people knew that he counted as one of his closest personal friends the conductor George Szell (whose persona was equally unapproachable and severe). Szell conducted many of Mennin's major works, a number of which he was responsible for commissioning. In fact, Szell personally provided the funding to commission Mennin's Seventh Symphony. "I felt that he was one of the most loyal friends I ever had," he later reflected.[23] Georganne Mennin recounted how Szell and her husband would stay up until all hours of the morning, playing short fragments of music for each other on the piano, challenging the other to "guess the piece."[24]

Mennin's sense of privacy was so contagious that it seemed to exert its power even posthumously. Students and colleagues have been disinclined to discuss their recollections, while those who have, have done so only on the condition of anonymity. The impression of the man that emerges is of a brilliant teacher, with a profound understanding of musical structure and an ability similar to Persichetti's to assess the strengths and weaknesses of an unfamiliar score after only a few moments' perusal. But he is also said to have been strongly opinionated, and resisted teaching more Modernist techniques, such as serialism. His aloofness was displayed in a refusal to discuss himself or his music with his students, while his all-consuming absorption in his own compositions led him to be somewhat absent-minded in his teaching and uninterested in his students' accomplishments. He was considered to be ambitious but highly industrious. As an administrator, he tended to isolate himself and resisted the input of others.

During his Juilliard years, the American symphonic school to which Mennin and the other composers discussed in this volume belonged had fallen out of favor. Finding self-promotion to be repugnant, Mennin did little to encourage performances of his own music, at Juilliard or elsewhere. Hence at the time of his death, his reputation rested much more on his stern stewardship of the school than on his musical compositions. When an interviewer asked him whether he was in contact with the small but devoted coterie of music lovers who knew virtually his entire output and eagerly awaited the appearance of each new work, he replied that he was utterly unaware of any such enthusiasts.[25] However, he affirmed his faith in the judgment of posterity and was confident that if his works had merit they would survive. At the memorial service that took place on 25 October 1983, Vincent Persichetti described Mennin as "an aristocrat on his own terms" and noted that "his latest work was always, in my opinion, more focused and telling than the one before it."[26]

MUSIC

Peter Mennin's career as a musical administrator, compounded by his cool, businesslike demeanor, belied for many his profound dedication to his own creative work. During his years as president of Juilliard his works were often glibly dismissed by critics, whose comments revealed a greater familiarity with his "image" than with his actual music. One critic reportedly described Mennin's symphonies as tasteful, three-piece-suit commissions. Even the *New York Times*' Harold Schonberg wrote, "There is no deep message to this music. . . . What it does is produce attractive sounds in a well-ordered manner."[27] But few with more than a passing acquaintance with Mennin's music would use such terms to describe it. They are more likely to note its expressive power, its individual voice, and its single-minded sense of purpose. Mennin's music is thoroughly devoid of frivolity, coloristic effects, or romantic sentiment, but it is not dispassionately intellectual either. His output of barely thirty works comprises large, absolute forms almost exclusively, of which nine are symphonies. ("I love to write a symphony. I need to write in large forms; I like a big canvas. A symphony is not something that can be tossed off over a weekend. It is cultivated by those who believe in it."[28])

Although his mature compositional career spanned almost four decades, his works do not fall into discrete style-periods. Rather, his output is remarkable for its continuous chronological development along a powerful—if rather narrow—continuum. That is, his chief compositional concerns, which formed the basis of his style, were apparent quite early and continued to evolve throughout his career; listening to each work in chronological succession reveals few if any abrupt shifts in style. However, if one compares, say, the Third Symphony, which evinces a sense of confident determination, with the Ninth, composed thirty-five years later, with its almost unbearably concentrated spasms of febrile delirium, and then traces the steps in between, one cannot help but perceive a continuous process of compression and increasing intensification of expression. In its unswerving quest to pursue and refine a particularly focused expressive goal, Mennin's output somewhat resembles that of Anton Bruckner. Over the course of decades, the linear aspect of Mennin's music became increasingly chromatic, the harmony increasingly dissonant, and the rhythm increasingly irregular. His body of work thus stands as an inexorable progression, each entry grimmer, harsher, and more severe than the last. Yet the essential characteristics, discernible in the earliest works, remain present throughout.

Mennin acknowledged no conscious influences on his compositional style, other than the polyphonic choral works of the Renaissance. However, some listeners have heard in his earlier works the contrapuntal energy of Hindemith, as well as something of the lofty grandeur of the Vaughan Williams symphonies (the Fourth, in particular). Whether these are influences or indications of a coincidental kinship is a moot point. The most salient characteristic of Mennin's mature symphonic style is the approach he adapted from Renaissance choral music: a continuous unfolding of polyphonic lines through imitative counterpoint, rather than the more conventional dialectical opposition and integration of contrasting themes. Indeed, Mennin emphasized counterpoint above all other elements, almost to the point of obsession, with much use of imitation, canon, ground bass, *ostinato, stretto, cantus firmus*, and the like. This approach is readily apparent in the noble, full-breathed lyricism of Mennin's slow movements. But its application in faster music creates an effect vastly different from the serene spirituality of the sixteenth-century masters: A bustling undercurrent of rapid activity creates a constant sense of nervous energy, while strongly felt bass lines carry the music along with unswerving determination. The imitative counterpoint often occurs in rhythmic augmentation and diminution, so that the same material may be treated canonically at three or four different speeds at once. Mennin's thematic motifs display a certain characteristic gesture: boldly assertive, with a syncopated thrust that ends in a "Scotch snap." But it is largely his irregular, highly accented rhythmic drive that marks Mennin's music as identifiably "American." It is interesting, in this connection, to consider an observation that appeared in the Carnegie Hall program notes accompanying a Mennin performance: "In an interview a few years ago, Leonard Bernstein commented that three of the most striking qualities in much American music were the hectic, the lonely, and the athletic. Every creative artist, of course, has his loneliness, at least his alone-ness; Peter Mennin may be no exception. There is no question, however, that the first and third qualities Bernstein mentioned are amply in evidence in the emotional and technical idiom of Mennin's music."[29]

Like Schuman's, Mennin's music is not meaningfully aligned with either the classical or romantic aesthetic poles, but belongs among that of the Modern Traditionalists, as defined in the Introduction. But whereas Schuman's music (and Persichetti's) is thoroughly American in its sources and frame of reference, Mennin's—despite its athletic, syncopated approach to rhythm—is much more European in its aesthetic orientation. Its roots lie not only in the polyphonic choral music of the Renaissance but also in the counterpoint of J. S. Bach and in the metaphysical drama of Beethoven, as carried on by such later northern European symphonists as Carl Nielsen, Edmund Rubbra, Vagn Holmboe, and Robert Simpson. It is a form of expression that strives for neither the perfection, balance, or beauty of the Apollonian classical ideal, nor for the intimate confession of personal feeling and emotion so beloved of the Romantics. The works of these composers develop abstract ideas logically and coherently while seeming to allude to or address profound existential issues in an individual way, without recourse to extramusical references, but as if from a lofty, somewhat depersonalized perspective. It is an approach shared by few other American composers. Indeed, Mennin's music shares more of an affinity with that of Europeans like Edmund Rubbra (1901–1986) and Vagn Holmboe (1909–1996) in particular than with any other American composers. (Yet when an interviewer asked Mennin whether he was familiar with the work of these two composers, he seemed somewhat intrigued but stated that he was not familiar with that of either composer.[30]) Nevertheless, despite these affinities, there is no mistaking Mennin's own individual creative personality, apparent throughout his body of work and characterized by the quest to depict an intense inner drama through thoroughly abstract means. His mature compositions seem to reflect the sober contemplation of ferocious conflict among wild, massive forces in ceaseless turbulence, escalating in intensity toward cataclysmic explosions of almost manic brutality—all articulated through clear musical logic and meticulous craftsmanship. (He commented, "I am concerned with having an unassailable technique." "Music reflects the soul of the composer," he believed, "and there is such a thing as soul. Music must have drama."[31])

Those who question why a listener might be drawn to music of such unremitting turbulence are reminded of the sense of inevitability and cathartic exaltation engendered by works like the Third and Fifth Symphonies of Beethoven, which pursue similar means to similar ends. Mennin's slow movements, on the other hand, reveal a Bach-like dignity and a sense of deep feeling, eloquently expressed. Perhaps the most legitimate criticism that can be leveled against Mennin's music is the charge of monotony—that its consistent preoccupation with creating inexhaustible musical avalanches, interrupted only by solemn, doleful *adagios*, may strike some listeners as indicative of a narrow expressive range, lacking in variety and relief. (In this regard, his compositional personality may be seen as the antithesis of Persichetti's.) There is truth to those criticisms, and one can hardly imagine living on an exclusive musical diet of Mennin. But few indeed are the composers whose works form a balanced diet on which one might subsist exclusively.

Mennin thought a great deal about aesthetic issues, and his prominent position gave him ample opportunity to voice his views on musical composition and on life as an artist. His beliefs were remarkably consistent with each other, with the personality that emerges from his music, and with the principles he implemented at Juilliard, and he expressed himself verbally on these matters with the same kind of unequivocal confidence and sobriety that one finds in his music. It seems appropriate to include a sample of these statements, some of which have been edited for greater concision:

At the very bottom, you have to ask yourself: "Why am I writing, painting, composing—creating—in the first place?" It's really to express something that you feel deeply within yourself. Then you need to find the means of expression in order to do that. The hardest thing in the world is to look inside yourself, because you must then ask, "Does this mean anything?" But unless compositional technique reflects a creative impulse, a creative drive, it doesn't mean anything. And the substance has to be your own. The means you can learn; the substance you can't. You either have it or you don't. The value of a teacher lies in his ability to encourage a young composer to believe in himself and in what he has to say. If something is terribly important to the composer, and he does express it well, and he has something to say, I don't think he can *avoid* being accessible— sooner or later (for an audience isn't always going to get it right away). If the notes, on the other hand, don't arouse the listener, they don't mean anything, and the listener will be bored.[32]

Great art is a matter of great individuality. Too often in recent decades the characteristics of music that give it individuality and personality have been ignored. That's why there are so many pieces today whose sections could be interchanged, and you wouldn't know the difference. It becomes neutral, and I can't stand neutral music. There's not enough individuality around. But in the realm of art, without it permanence is impossible. The only thing that lasts is what one human being can bring that is peculiarly his own and not anyone else's.[33]

The long, singing line is something I have always believed in, to this very moment. Though certain things in my music have changed a little bit, the long line hasn't. I think it's one of the reasons why one writes music.[34]

I immediately distrust any composer who tells me that he writes according to a system. Because that tells me he needs the security of a system instead of the security of his innards. Any system is a kind of a security blanket.[35]

I am not one of those people who have negative feelings about forms like opera or the symphony. I think outlets of expression are there for somebody to come along and do something positive with them. In the process, they may be changed, but I think history is just a matter of slow evolution. To me, there should be no really sharp break between periods.[36]

My wish is that concertgoers, musicians, everybody, would not be concerned with what is ahead of the times, behind the times, or anything like that. They should listen in music for that which arouses them viscerally, as well as intellectually. Without that, they'll be bored. That's the difference between a major composer and a minor one. A major composer always brings a visceral reaction, a physical involvement. You can't resist that. The brain provides the composer with the means for developing his work, for knowing what to do, but it's his guts that tell him what the basic idea should be.[37]

Once I've written what I believe in, the more people that enjoy it, the happier I am. But I will not pay the price of lowering my own sights in order to achieve that.[38]

I am not the revering type. I revere pieces, not people.[39]

MOST REPRESENTATIVE, FULLY REALIZED WORKS

Symphony No. 3 (1946)
Symphony No. 4, "The Cycle" (1947)
Symphony No. 5 (1950)
Symphony No. 6 (1953)
Sonata Concertante (1956)
Concerto for Piano and Orchestra (1957)
Symphony No. 7 (1963)
Cantata de Virtute, "Pied Piper of Hamelin" (1969)
Symphony No. 8 (1973)
Symphony No. 9 (1981)

During the years he was studying with Normand Lockwood at Oberlin (1940–1942) Mennin (still Mennini) completed a piano sonata movement, several vocal settings—solo and choral—a string quartet, an organ sonata, and his Symphony No. 1. Of them, only a short choral *Alleluia* (in both two-part and four-part versions) was authorized by the composer for public performance. Most of these early works reflect only embryonic hints of the composer's mature style, chiefly in their propensity for contrapuntal development and their serious-minded commitment to abstraction and structural autonomy.

The Symphony No. 1, which has never been performed, is an extended work in four movements, nearly an hour in duration. An examination of the full score reveals an accomplishment of considerable sophistication for a nineteen-year-old composer, displaying many of the features that were to characterize his mature output. The first movement, *Adagio, quasi lento*, is slow and highly contrapuntal, and rather thickly scored, with a vehement assertiveness that anticipates Mennin's later works. This movement leads directly into the second, *Moderato; Presto*. After a sober introduction, the movement takes flight, serving as something of a *scherzo* and building momentum through a relentless onslaught of triplets in a manner suggesting Roy Harris. In the third movement, *Adagio*, the counterpoint is simpler and less dense than in the first movement, although it builds to a massive climax. The finale is marked *Allegro deciso*, a designation of the sort Mennin was to use frequently. In this movement especially, a number of traits that were to characterize his mature work are identifiable: syncopated lines in constant contrapuntal development, and even the nervous undercurrent of rapid *ostinato* patterns are found here. In an interview in 1982, Mennin was asked whether he would ever authorize a performance of this early symphony. He laughed, commenting that at the time his level of ambition exceeded his craftsmanship and critical judgment; he felt that the work was best left alone.[40]

Somewhat more mature is the Symphony No. 2 that Mennin composed in 1944–1945 while studying at Eastman. It was performed there under Howard Hanson's direction, and then by an orchestra consisting largely of members of the New York Philharmonic, under the direction of Leonard Bernstein, in March 1945. As mentioned earlier, the work's opening *Allegro deciso* won the first Gershwin Memorial Award, while the entire work was awarded Columbia University's prestigious Bearns Prize. It is noteworthy that despite the symphony's success, the highly self-critical composer decided to withdraw it from further public performance (although it is equally noteworthy that shortly before his death, Mennin lifted the ban on performances of this work).

What is most remarkable about Mennin's Second Symphony is that, rather like Persichetti's Third Symphony, composed at the same time, it reflects the state of American symphonic music of the time more than it reveals the incipient compositional identity of the young composer. As such it may be viewed as a highly sophisticated piece of juvenilia. The mid 1940s constituted a most auspicious period for the American symphonic genre, spurred partly by patriotic wartime sentiments but also as a result of the convergence of a gifted group of composers who were attaining compositional maturity, and seized upon the symphonic genre as an appropriate medium through which to develop their most serious abstract musical ideas while attempting to forge a national repertoire comparable in stature to that of their European forebears. Dating from the same period as Mennin's Second were such symphonies as Harris's Fifth and Sixth, Schuman's Fifth, Piston's Second, Copland's Third, and Barber's Second. In his Second Symphony, Mennin, the youngest of this group, clearly displays the recognizably American surface "sound" of these other composers in his basic thematic materials, although the actual developmental processes he used were those he was to pursue and refine throughout his compositional career.

The work comprises three substantial movements, in a fast-slow-fast sequence. Despite its reminiscences of other American composers, the first movement, *Allegro deciso*, reveals Mennin's distinctive compulsion for constant contrapuntal and rhythmic activity. The second movement, *Andante moderato*, also treats material whose contours are more "generically American" than personal and distinctive and, on the whole, lacks the emotional weight of his subsequent slow movements. The third movement, *Allegro vigoroso*, returns to the character of the opening and, again, displays qualities—especially in its basic materials—that might be described as typical of its time and place.

Also dating from Mennin's Eastman years is the Concertino for Flute, Strings, and Percussion, completed in 1945. The composer later recalled, "I was still a student at the time, so you can imagine how thrilled I was when

Howard Hanson asked me to write a piece for the American Composers series to be performed by the Rochester Orchestra."[41] Although more concise,
this work shares much in common with the Second Symphony, particularly
in its use of materials reminiscent of Harris and Schuman. The Concertino
comprises two movements, the first slow, the second fast. It opens with muted
strings in free counterpoint until the flute enters, when the treatment becomes
more homophonic. The movement ends with a reference to the opening. The
second movement, *Presto*, begins with a snare-drum passage that prompts
an unmistakable association with the final section of Schuman's Third Symphony (1941). Largely in 12/8 meter throughout, this section develops rapid
conjoint lines in triplets. A slower section appears toward the end, suggesting
the opening movement, before an abbreviated return of the *Presto* material
brings the ten-minute work to its conclusion. Returning to the composer's
own comments, "At the time, the flute and the snare drum seemed to me to be
both an unusual and a natural combination. The idea of the two instruments
answering each other in a conversation is the basic premise of the work. That
idea is born in the Larghetto introduction and is more fully developed in the
second [Presto] movement."[42] What is perhaps most striking about the Concertino from the perspective of Mennin's later works, is its generally mild,
subdued character, maintained throughout. The work was first performed in
April 1945 by flutists Joseph Mariano and Allen Jensen with the Eastman-
Rochester Symphony Orchestra conducted by Howard Hanson.

The first work in which Mennin's compositional identity is clearly apparent is the *Folk Overture*, completed in July 1945. It was first performed in
November of that year, by the National Symphony Orchestra of Washington,
D.C., conducted by Hans Kindler. At the time Mennin stated that the piece—a
free development of three short motifs—did not use actual folk tunes, but
rather, he sought "to use creatively elements, both rhythmic and melodic, that
lie in them." This effort is reflected clearly in the robust syncopations of the
main motifs, which are unmistakably "American" in character, but this was to
be Mennin's sole explicitly "national" piece, as he found folk elements "too
confining."[43] Although its vigorous kinetic energy, strongly rooted in diatonic
modality and propelled by lively, syncopated, strongly accented rhythms,
link it to the American mainstream of the time, and occasional moments still
suggest vague traces of Harris and Schuman, a number of traits central to
Mennin's own style can be found: Like other works of his early maturity, the
piece displays a brisk sense of self-confidence; one of the motifs is colored
by the rarely used Locrian mode (the flattened fifth step here perhaps suggestive of the "blues"); the "Scotch snap" rhythmic pattern appears; motivic
development occurs against a continuous nervous undercurrent of syncopated
counterpoint; and the highly accented foreground counterpoint makes aggres-

sive use of canonic imitation and *stretto*. The overall character of the piece is relatively dry and free of personal affect—an almost mechanical display of contrapuntal developmental devices. *Folk Overture* first appeared on recording in 1989 in a performance featuring the Columbus Symphony Orchestra, conducted by Christian Badea.

The work that really launched Mennin's national reputation and almost instantly catapulted him to the forefront of American composers was his Symphony No. 3. As stated earlier, Mennin completed the work on his twenty-third birthday, in May 1946, and it was given its first performance in February 1947 by the New York Philharmonic, conducted by its assistant conductor Walter Hendl. (It is difficult to imagine the work of a twenty-three-year-old being introduced by a major American symphony orchestra today.) Further performances by many of the nation's foremost orchestras soon followed, and a brilliant reading of the symphony was recorded by the New York Philharmonic under the direction of Dimitri Mitropoulos in 1955.

The Symphony No. 3 is the first major work of Mennin's early maturity, and it sets forth many of principles that would underlie and characterize his subsequent works. Like its predecessor and the three symphonies that followed, it is cast in a three-movement fast-slow-fast design. Again one is struck by the constant flow of imitative counterpoint. The symphony's brash assertiveness and strongly accented rhythmic syncopation link the work with those of other American composers of the time, but other reminiscences of their styles and more obvious "Americanisms" are no longer apparent. In fact, many commentators have likened the work, with its forceful statements, strong, vigorous bass lines, and noble, elevated lyricism, to Vaughan Williams' Fourth Symphony (1934).

The first movement, *Allegro robusto*, quickly introduces three motifs, all related intervallically. These motifs, through subtle organic metamorphoses, serve as the thematic basis of the entire work. The first movement attempts to follow *sonata-allegro* form, although Mennin largely abandoned this format in his later symphonies. The music is remarkably forceful in its articulation and phraseology, proclaiming an attitude of confidence and positive determination. A strong rhythmic pulse serves as a constant, to enhance the syncopated effect of the contrapuntal lines. The tonality is largely diatonic, but with prominent major-minor ambiguity. The second theme of the movement illustrates the kind of long melodic line that remained a constant feature of Mennin's music throughout his career.

The second movement, *Andante moderato*, is a prototype for the slow movements of nearly all of Mennin's symphonies. Like the interweaving lines of the Renaissance polyphonists, Mennin's long melodies unfold smoothly, with a metrical freedom unencumbered by bar lines. The movement displays a bleak yet lofty perspective, which distinguishes it from most of the music of his peers, while revealing an emotional depth and complexity remarkable in the work of a twenty-three-year-old.

The third movement, *Allegro assai*, springs forth with tremendous energy and vigor, its primary lines propelled with strongly accented rhythmic syncopations, while a rapid undercurrent of canonic *ostinati* in differing rhythmic proportion creates a constant sense of restlessness. The movement gradually works toward a resounding peroration, its emerging sense of triumph concluding the work with an exaltation that reaffirms an American identity.

The premiere of Mennin's Third Symphony was greeted in the New York press by somewhat guarded enthusiasm. Olin Downes concluded his notice, "The writing is naturally that of a composer who is gradually finding himself, but it has direction and objective, and it is a conspicuous advance in clarification over earlier works of Mr. Mennin that we have heard. This vigorous symphony excited the audience."[44] As noted earlier, Louis Biancolli was impressed by the young composer's individuality and potential for significant growth, adding, "When in the mood he knows how to make an orchestra sing."[45] Both critics, however, felt that the finale was overly long.

Less than two years later, Richard Franko Goldman noted that "the Symphony has had an unusually large number of performances, in New York and elsewhere." Having had the opportunity to study the published score, he commented thoughtfully and at some length:

> Mennin obviously has extraordinary gifts and immense facility. As long as this technical command and fluency remain at the service of his taste and talent, we may expect great things. The Third Symphony impresses by its evidence of real melodic inventiveness and by its management of long lines in a contrapuntal texture that is both learned and complex without seeming labored or contrived. . . . Mennin has already indicated that he is developing an idiom of his own. . . . One feels spontaneity and life in the music rather than cleverness; although the cleverness is formidable, it never makes one feel that it is displayed as an end in itself.[46]

At approximately the same time, the reliably open-minded composer-critic Henry Cowell concluded his review of the score, "The general impression is of a conservative, delicately original work, musical, feelingful, performable, enjoyable. There have been several performances already, and more can certainly be expected."[47] When the recording of the work was issued several years later, the often-disdainful Modernist composer-critic Arthur Berger expressed some resentment of Mennin's early success, of "how much easier Mennin's battle for recognition is" when compared to that of less-conservative composers. He found the young man's "forthright, spontaneous, vigorous manner" to "betray his youth." But Berger grudgingly conceded that "however unadventurous Mennin may be, his talents are considerable. We may only hope that now that he has passed thirty he may exploit his musical drive and exceptional technique for the discovery of new and more interesting qualities."[48]

Although the Mitropoulos recording was reissued several times on different labels, so that it remained in print for most of the following decades, the Third Symphony was not actually re-recorded until 1997, when American-music advocate Gerard Schwarz and the Seattle Symphony released an all-Mennin compact disc. In his review of this new recording, David Hall looked back upon the symphony as one of Mennin's best, "with an opening movement that packs a wallop comparable to the opening of the Vaughan Williams Fourth Symphony. A splendid long line is sustained throughout the slow movement, and a relentless drive manifests itself in the finale."[49]

Following the Third Symphony, Mennin turned his attention to several shorter pieces in which he seemed to concentrate on developing and refining the essential techniques set forth in the larger work. Before the end of 1946 he had composed a *Fantasia* for string orchestra—a two-part work, somewhat more subdued than the symphony. Like most of his music from the 1940s, the melodic lines are largely diatonic, but inflected according to the darker modes. The titles of its two sections, "Canzona" and "Toccata," are—like many of Mennin's titles—direct references to instrumental forms in active use during the early seventeenth century. The slow "Canzona" develops a solemn motif through imitative counterpoint, very much in the Renaissance manner. About a third of the way through, the second violins introduce another motif, which is developed in a similar fashion. A climax is reached as the two ideas are brought together contrapuntally, after which the music comes to a quiet close. Though its form parallels that of the "Canzona," the lively "Toccata" offers a vivid contrast in mood. A vigorous, strongly accented theme is presented in unison, then immediately subjected to a contrapuntal development in which its syncopated aspects are emphasized. A second idea—nervous and even more syncopated—is introduced and developed in a similar fashion to the first. The two ideas are then both developed together—at times simultaneously. Despite the music's emphasis on purely abstract matters, frequent shifts in loudness and in textural density maintain a dynamic tension, until the work reaches a decisive conclusion. The *Fantasia* can be especially illuminating to listeners new to Mennin's music because it displays, simply and clearly, virtually all the principles upon which most of his later works are constructed. The *Fantasia* was first performed in January 1948, again by the New York Philharmonic under the direction of Walter Hendl.

The premiere of Mennin's *Fantasia* did not engender much enthusiasm among New York City critics. The *New York Times* critic noted, "Mr. Mennin's work was one of clear outlines, sweet, simple melodies treated canonically, with a mind to the possibilities of massed sonorities in the high register. The first movement . . . tended to wander in its middle section, but soon got back on the track for an effective ending. The fast movement was a conventional treatment of a jagged theme."[50] Even less charitable was the critic for the *New York Herald Tribune*, who felt that "its slow and fast movements made a static impression; for the composer's skill in handling his thematic material, in itself not very interesting, does not seem to have progressed beyond that of the average student."[51]

The *Fantasia* drew little attention during the years that followed and never appeared on recording until 1997, when another all-Mennin CD appeared, with David Alan Miller conducting the Albany Symphony Orchestra. Although the critical response to this recording was highly favorable, there was little mention of this nine-minute work.

In early 1947 Mennin completed a five-minute *Sinfonia* for chamber orchestra, commissioned by the Rochester radio station, WHAM. In one section, marked *Allegro vivo*, this piece introduces three short motifs, the first, determined and syncopated; the second, more lyrical, like an "answer" to the first; and the third, a longer, more flowing line. These three ideas are developed contrapuntally, against a syncopated undercurrent of canonic *ostinati* in the lower strings. The piece unfolds in a continuous motoric flow, which builds in contrapuntal complexity, until the elements finally come together for an emphatic conclusion.

Although in retrospect pieces like the *Fantasia* and *Sinfonia* seem like studies—efforts by Mennin to clarify and codify the features of a style that was to prove unique among his peers—it is apparent that, at the time, few commentators discerned the factors that distinguished his music from that of other young composers then writing. For example, the *New York Times* critic described the *Sinfonia* as "a one-movement work in the athletic neo-Classic style now common. It is neatly composed but not very personal; and its tunes, though frank, are not sharply expressive. It is a presentable work without much character. Mr. Mennin shows himself in it . . . as a well prepared composer but not yet an original one. His developments are still weak from overdependence on the formulas of the conservatory."[52]

Also in 1947 the twenty-four-year-old composer joined the Juilliard faculty, while beginning his Symphony No. 4, although he was not to complete it until November of the following year. Commissioned by the Collegiate Chorale, this work is unique among Mennin's symphonies in bearing a subtitle, "The Cycle," and in its use of a mixed chorus together with the symphony orchestra. The premiere of the symphony took place in New York City's Carnegie Hall in March 1949, with the Collegiate Chorale and members of the New York Philharmonic conducted by "the mop-haired young conductor Robert Shaw."[53] Perhaps most interesting is the fact that Mennin wrote the text for the work himself, expressly for this purpose:

> I The dark sea is a tide of flowing waters,
> And in its vasty depth we view eternity.
> Look where the start hurls from its flaming rest
> And eyeless worlds are suppliant yet.
> They act not from random thought,
> But from old wounds and maturing Time,
> With sounds that pierce the marrow
> With savage songs of exultation.
> II Come back to the earth again and feel her roots.
> Man forgets.
> The dark waters remember ancient conflicts and are silent.
> Return to earth.
> III Time passing, waters flowing,
> The great cycle begins once more,
> Washing stains away.
> With dark and tragic destiny
> Do all things return to dust.
> Stirring fills the air.
> Sounds of deliverance
> Cancel the past rages.
> Still rising does the waiting earth
> Sublimely sing,
> Embracing all of man.[54]

Mennin's text has been subject to harsh criticism over the years. (Virgil Thomson described it as "without literary value,"[55] while Ivor Keys found it to be "portentous, indeed bombastic."[56] Cecil Smith observed snidely, "I do not think Mr. Mennin's poetry will find its way into many anthologies."[57]) However, taking potshots at the text deflects attention away from its value in illuminating the composer's own view of the "meaning" of his work. After all, not only is Mennin's body of work largely abstract, but he was consistently averse to discussing its "meaning" in program notes and the like (although, as has been demonstrated, he had much to say about musical composition in general). As a result, some commentators have treated his music as devoid of extramusical meaning, while others have attempted to read into it their own interpretations. But the patently philosophical text of "The Cycle" is a rare opportunity to gain through his own words some insight into the emerging character of the expressive language the composer was forging. The first section presents symbols of eternity: the immensity of the ocean, the passage of infinite time, and the expression of primordial emotion. The second section juxtaposes finite, flawed Man against the infinite "dark waters." There are harsh images: "old wounds," "savage songs," "ancient conflicts." The third section points to the cyclical nature of life's "dark and tragic destiny": All of mankind is subsumed within the eternal cycle of disintegration and rebirth, depicted with a kind of impersonal, metaphysical exultation devoid of any the-istically based teleology. In his text Mennin thus provides a clue to the cosmic fatalism he was striving to suggest in much, if not all, of his work to follow.

Initially, the first movement, *Allegro energico*, seems very similar to the *Sinfonia* just discussed, and to the first movement of the Third Symphony. However, a closer examination reveals that instead of the vigorous optimism of the latter work, there is a feeling of grimness, with more biting gestures and snappier rhythms. The sense of grimness is partly the result of the work's basis in the Locrian mode. (The Locrian mode is the scale formed by playing the "white keys" from B to B. Hence, not only is the second step lowered, as with the Phrygian mode, but the fifth step is as well, with the result that the tonic chord is a diminished triad. For this reason the Locrian mode was rarely used during the common-practice period. In his works from the late 1940s and early 1950s, Mennin frequently used both the Phrygian and Locrian modes—the two that are darkest in character.) In this work Mennin treats the chorus as just another element—albeit one that is generally more sustained in function—within the contrapuntal fabric.

The second movement, *Andante Arioso*, is slow and stately, in a manner that more than once calls to mind Stravinsky's *Symphony of Psalms*. It is still highly contrapuntal, with frequently changing meters and long passages when the chorus sings without accompaniment.

The third movement, *Pronunziato; Allegro deciso*, returns to the opening spirit, as the chorus asserts its lines with determination, while the orchestra maintains its vigorous rhythmic interplay, against a nervous backdrop of ir-regularly grouped *ostinato* patterns. As the movement approaches the end, a sense of triumph begins to emerge, finally arriving at a major cadence in A. Like Schuman, Mennin often seemed compelled to conclude his works with a triumphalism that frequently seems unwarranted by the turbulence that precedes it.

The premiere of Mennin's Fourth generated a generally positive reaction as a piece of music. Virgil Thomson characterized the work as "vigorous, athletic, tonic and not at all tedious." He chided the composer for "[plug-ging] his material unmercifully" and complained that it was often difficult to discern the words sung by the chorus. He described the use of *ostinato* in the third movement as "close to boogie woogie, though the superstructure consists rather of rhythmic permutations than of syncopated melody." Yet despite "these crudities," Thomson grudgingly acknowledged that "the work is still vigorous and pleasing." He then went on to elaborate,

> It has a clear and simple feeling content, a clear rhetoric and a sustained energy, even in the slow movement, that are the mark of a strong musical mind and a solid workman. The symphony's force lies, however, in its treatment of the choir as a section of the orchestra capable of rivalry with the instrumental body in loudness and in musical interest. I don't think I have ever heard a choral symphony in which the vocal and instrumental forces were so well equilibrated in the whole expressive achievement. He has really composed them, conceived them as co-operating toward a single end, like a navy and an air force. He has resolved a hitherto unsolved problem and created by that fact a musical work of genuine originality. He is twenty-five years old. Draw your own conclusions about his future.[58]

Thomson's reaction was confirmed by Noel Straus, who praised the "undeniable rhythmic strength in its corner movements and a goodly amount of genuine power throughout. There was true intensity in the slow movement and the double fugue at the end over an orchestral ostinato made known much facility in the use of dissonant counterpoint."[59]

Most of the reviews from the time of the premiere mention Mennin's age, and a certain resentful envy can be discerned in many of the comments. For example, in his review of the vocal score of the symphony, which was published just a few months after the work's premiere, Cecil Smith complains about its designation as a "symphony," insisting that it is no more than "a typical choral-orchestral setting of a text."[60] In his subsequent discussion, however, he acknowledges that "nobody has written yet" an "ideal choral symphony. . . . Beethoven was certainly not altogether successful in the Ninth Symphony."[61] So, having made clear the standards to which he holds the composer, he continues, "It is not to be expected, perhaps, that a twenty-five-year-old composer would succeed where others have invariably failed." Smith then, predictably perhaps, proceeds to damn with faint praise:

> [Mennin has composed] a continuity in the orchestra, of more or less symphonic character—expounding, developing, and summing up his themes in fairly orthodox fashion. Upon this virtually unceasing orchestral commentary, he has superposed choral passages most of the time, nearly always giving them their own separate thematic material, and letting the orchestra serve as a running accompaniment to the voices. . . . *The Cycle* in many aspects is a highly competent work. Mr. Mennin's command of the placement and spacing of choral voices is, in an elementary way, quite assured, though he does not attain much variety of effect. The music has real momentum, and keeps legitimately busy all the time, never resorting to mere filler.[62]

In his review of the symphony, Ivor Keys identified what is perhaps the most justifiable focus of criticism in Mennin's music, stating that a "tendency to monotony is the greatest weakness of the work," caused by the "almost unrelieved contrapuntal style." Yet despite this criticism, Keys acknowledged Mennin to be "a master of counterpoint, shown here at its best in the orchestral part of the second movement, which reminds one of Rubbra in its constructive power."[63]

The Fourth Symphony was recorded during the early 1970s by Abraham Kaplan and the Camerata Singers and Symphony Orchestra. That recording was reissued on compact disc in 1989. It is fascinating to compare a reaction to this work from the perspective of nearly half a century later, and after the composer's death. Writing for the *Classical Net*, Robert Cummings began by asserting that "Mennin and [David] Diamond are the greatest American symphonists, their chief competition coming from Sessions and Schuman." He continued, "The choral Fourth Symphony by Mennin . . . may not quite be on the level of his dark and profound Seventh, for example, but it is still a strong and quite compelling work. It sounds close in its expressive language and mood to the Third." Cummings then credits the performers with "a knowing grasp on Mennin's stormy, austere style."[64]

Also completed in 1948 were Mennin's settings of Four Chinese Poems for mixed chorus *a cappella*. He selected four spare, enigmatic poems from the works of the writer, scholar, and socialist thinker Kiang Kang-Hu (1883–c.1950), in English translations by Witter Bynner: "In the quiet night," "A song of the palace," "Crossing the Han River," and "The gold threaded robe." Making no attempt to evoke associations with China, the musical settings sound somewhat more conventional than Mennin's orchestral works, yet the songs display most of the same features as his larger works: polyphonic textures, modal—largely Phrygian—lines, and even (in "A Song of the Palace") the use of a rapid *ostinato* as an undercurrent to a slower-moving melodic line.

The Four Chinese Poems were followed the next year by more choral settings: this time, two pieces for three-part women's choir. The texts are "Tumbling Hair," by E. E. Cummings, and "Bought Locks," an English translation (by Sir John Harrington) of a first-century Latin poem of the same name. Although Mennin's reputation rests chiefly on his large symphonic works, these brief *a cappella* settings are meticulous in their concise expressiveness and are consistently well-received whenever they are performed.

In 1949 Mennin composed a group of piano pieces he seems to have tentatively entitled *Partita* but later settled simply on *Five Piano Pieces*. *Partita* would have implied a connection to the notion of the Baroque suite, which the individual movement titles still suggest: "Prelude," "Aria," "Variation-Canzona," "Canto," and "Toccata." (As suggested earlier, Mennin had a predilection for titles associated with the early Baroque, which offers a clue to the way he saw his own compositional identity.) The pieces comprising the "suite," whose individual durations average just under three minutes, follow the composer's general procedures at this point in his creative development, although their impact is somewhat less distinctive than that left by his larger works. As one might expect, the odd-numbered movements are torrential perpetual-motion affairs—*toccata*-like, despite their different titles—largely in two voices, with irregularly grouped patterns and phrases, and prominent use of *ostinato* in the third movement. The two even-numbered movements are slow and somber, with long-breathed lyricism, and build to powerful climaxes. The fourth movement in particular has some harmonic usages that recall the language of Roy Harris. Several of the movements are written in the Phrygian mode.

Five Piano Pieces was given its first performance by Grant Johannesen in New York City in March 1950. Francis D. Perkins found it to be a "pianistically very effective contribution," although he found the "momentum and energy" of the fast movements to be "somewhat iterative and relentless" by the end.[65] When the score was published the following year, Eastman faculty member and composer Burrill Phillips wrote,

> There is absolutely no excess pianistic baggage in the *Five Piano Pieces* by Peter Mennin. He has found for himself a fine keyboard language—eloquent and forceful. His orchestral music has accustomed us to his preferences: live rhythms, long melodic lines, polyphonic devices including canons and ostinati. The same are to be found here, but with the difference of greater compression and intensity. If there is a flaw, it is perhaps due to a certain sameness in essential motives in the three fast movements; but the music altogether maintains an elevated character and its effectiveness on the concert stage is assured.[66]

Despite the confidence expressed by the reviewer, not to mention the work's meticulous craftsmanship, general appeal, and relative practicality, Mennin's *Five Piano Pieces* have not made much headway into the repertoire of American piano music. There has been only one commercial recording, an LP issued in 1985 featuring pianist Lydia Walton Ignacio. In 1999 Wayne Richard Pierce produced an orchestration of the *Piano Pieces* as part of his dissertation at the University of Connecticut.[67]

Also dating from 1949 is a cantata entitled *The Christmas Story*. The work was commissioned by the Protestant Radio Commission for broadcast performance on radio station WABC in New York, by the newly formed Robert Shaw Chorale and a chamber orchestra under Shaw's direction. The premier performance was broadcast on Christmas Eve 1949. The cantata comprises nine sections based on familiar Christmas texts and lasts some twenty-five minutes. It is scored for soprano and tenor soli (used sparingly), mixed chorus, and a small orchestra comprising brass quartet, timpani, and strings.

During the years following its initial broadcast, *The Christmas Story* enjoyed a number of public performances, and these were reasonably well received. After a New York City performance by the Interracial Fellowship Chorus, under the direction of Harold Aks, in December 1951, Francis D. Perkins derived "an impression of devotion and often of expressive persuasion. . . . The choral writing had its polyphonic measures, but these did not run to complexity; despite some cogent themes, there might have been somewhat more melodic variety. Narrative passages were flexibly set, but their pace was rather deliberate. The work as a whole had dignity and sincerity, and scored warm applause."[68] Reviewing the same performance, the critic for the *New York Times* wrote, "The music is knowingly composed for voices in effective counterpoint and clear-cut rhythms that showed little apparent attempt either to follow slavishly the emotional content of the words or to develop original musical techniques. Its sound was usually rich in texture, resembling Vaughan Williams more than any other composer, but with poignant touches of Stravinsky-like dissonance and accompaniment figures. Its final movement grew most effectively to a bright, almost ecstatic climax."[69]

Over the course of the decades following its initial presentations, further performances of *The Christmas Story* have been infrequent, and it has never been recorded commercially, despite the generally favorable critical reactions. The work is uncharacteristic of Mennin's output in its extramusical reference, and this aspect distinguishes the work in a number of ways. On the one hand, the composer seems to have approached the project more as a novel application of his compositional principles and practices than as a sacred work for holiday celebration. Hence it is much closer in style to the previous year's Fourth Symphony than to the approach taken in any of the myriad works by other composers based on the same text intended for perennial performance during the holiday period. On the other hand, the cantata seems somewhat constrained in its expression, as if the composer were deliberately avoiding the conventional Yuletide clichés while also attempting to steer clear of the somewhat grim, severe direction toward which his creative voice seemed to be heading. The result is perhaps one of his least successful efforts—reserved, if not almost neutral, in its expressive impact and rather unconvincing in its strained attempt to achieve a sense of affirmation and exaltation. For example, the rousing choral-orchestral "Glory to God" seems like little more than a routine application of the composer's familiar contrapuntal practices to material rooted in the mundane Ionian mode (i.e., major scale), as opposed to the darker modes Mennin ordinarily preferred, rather than a sincere expression of spiritual joy. One suspects that the twenty-six-year-old composer saw this auspicious commission as too promising to pass up as an opportunity for widespread exposure.

A much more successful work is Mennin's Symphony No. 5, completed in 1950 on a commission from the Dallas Symphony Orchestra and its conductor Walter Hendl, who gave the first performance in April of that year. Like its two predecessors, the Fifth is a three-movement work in a fast-slow-fast format. In a general sense, aside from the choral factor, this symphony is remarkably similar to No. 4 in scope, style, character, and technique. Yet there are slight differences as well: The Fifth is a bit more propulsive, as syncopated, clearly articulated motifs reveal an increased rhythmic irregularity, with constantly shifting accents and pattern lengths, while its transparent scoring permits the counterpoint to be heard with greater clarity. The work is somewhat less stable tonally: Yet while it moves more freely from one key to another, the melodic structure is still largely diatonic—usually modal. Although homophonic passages are few—usually at major structural divisions—they, along with the harmonic results of the polyphony, reveal quartal structures, polychords, and pantriadicism.[70] Describing the work in one of the commentaries Mennin became increasingly reluctant to provide, he might as well have been discussing any of his recent works when he stated, "Each of the movements has its own basic character, and achieves contrast within itself through the musical materials and textures rather than from changes in tempo. This is not unlike the principle that guided composers of the Renaissance. The basic aim of this work is expressivity. Therefore, there is a great emphasis placed on the broad melodic line, and little use of color for color's sake. . . . [T]he work as a whole is direct, assertive and terse in communication."[71]

The first movement, *Con Vigore*, is based primarily on three motifs, all heard within the opening moments: The first is a fanfare-like idea introduced by the woodwinds; the second, presented by the whole orchestra, is an emphatic theme whose first seven notes reveal an expanding sequence of intervals, outlining a wedge shape; the third is a syncopated motif introduced by the horns. A rhythmic figure of two sixteenth-notes followed by an eighth-note (and its reverse) appears within these ideas and recurs throughout the work. The movement proceeds to develop this material with tremendous energy and forcefulness. Although the meter remains 3/4 throughout, highly accented rhythmic irregularities are subsumed within that meter and give the music an "American" sound, despite the use of centuries-old contrapuntal techniques.

The second movement, *Canto*, displays a poignant solemnity that calls to mind some of Bach's most serious slow movements. The oboe spins a long-breathed melody—one of Mennin's most beautiful—over sustained chords in the strings. Soon the oboe is joined by a flute, before the melody is passed on to the strings. A second idea is presented by the flute and clarinet, and both are developed together with somewhat greater contrapuntal complexity than in previous works, as the movement grows to a climax of considerable breadth, after which the music comes to a quiet close.

The third movement, *Allegro Tempestuoso*, returns to the spirit of the first. Two motifs—closely related to each other—are presented at the outset, both built on the Locrian mode. As the development proceeds, two other ideas are introduced into the crystal-clear polyphony. Driven by syncopated rhythms, rushing patterns, and various canonic devices, the energy of the music intensifies, only occasionally ebbing to "catch its breath," so to speak, until it finally reaches a decisive and victorious conclusion. Frank J. Oteri calls this movement "an exciting non-stop roller-coaster ride of interlocking voices propelled by throbbing timpani."[72] A transcription of this movement for symphonic band was made by Frank Bencriscutto and has enjoyed numerous performances.

Reviewing a broadcast of the Dallas premiere, Jay S. Harrison had a mixed reaction to Mennin's Fifth Symphony. He found it to be "a ripe and forceful work." The first movement's "expressive meaning seems rooted in its rapid-fire propulsion and its sweep and litheness derive straightway from the brisk-ness of its stride." However, he found the second movement "sweet and glib and commonplace." Harrison noted reminiscences of Hindemith in both outer movements, but felt that Mennin "has absorbed his influences completely and has given to his leaping and disjunct melodic line a thoroughly original (if somewhat brittle) cast." He concluded that the symphony is "a heady and vigorous brew. . . . Moreover, it is a full-fledged symphony."[73]

Shortly thereafter, Charles Munch and the Boston Symphony Orchestra introduced the work to New York audiences. Composer-critic Arthur Berger, whose rather begrudging comments regarding the 1955 recording of the Third Symphony have already been quoted, penned his initial reaction to the Fifth Symphony four years earlier. At that time his comments were less guarded: "Mennin is a composer, a real composer, and one of fluency and force. Let there be no doubt about it. With five symphonies at the age of twenty-seven, he forces us to take account of this as a fact." However his enthusiasm was not without some reservation:

[Mennin's] knack of keeping the music moving at all costs would be so much more compelling if he paused in the composing process to make all the to-do concern itself with more striking material. . . . The music is rhythmically alive, but the rhythms fall into a category of set formulae. The climaxes may be antici-pated. This may be Mr. Mennin's way of developing his extraordinary facility, and it may take him a few more symphonies to develop something in the way of unusual interest and arresting detail. The work and its textures are, however, well integrated and indicate decided growth.[74]

Howard Taubman was somewhat more generous in his praise, endorsing what he inferred to be Mennin's attitude toward composition:

> He sails in and composes. There is a sense of confidence in his music. Not yet 30 and the author of five symphonies, he looks as though he is going to be prolific. . . . The Fifth Symphony has a young man's energy. It has drive, gusto and a fine assurance that it is expressing the author's feelings. . . . The encouraging thing about Mr. Mennin's symphony is that it has an unmistakable profile of its own. It bespeaks a talent for the orchestra. In the busy passages of the first and third movements, Mr. Mennin shows that he can keep the whole apparatus going lickety-split in the most natural way. In the slow movement he indicates that he can sing, perhaps fulsomely at times and with sustained feeling at others, but sing he can. And that is what counts. Mr. Mennin's style may undergo changes, but the main thing is basic—he is a composer.[75]

One wonders what is meant by the seemingly fatuous remark made by both New York critics that Mennin "is a composer, a real composer." Both commentators seemed to perceive a sense of authenticity and naturalness perhaps missing from much of the new music they encountered.

As was so often the case, the most wise, thoughtful, and perspicacious remarks came from Henry Cowell:

> The symphony's three movements . . . are thoroughly integrated in style and interrelated through use of the same thematic material both melodically and rhythmically. . . . [O]ne is left with an impression of greater cohesion than is to be found in most other contemporary symphonies. . . . Mennin . . . is fond of a long, flowing melodic line, with no picayunish interruptions to spoil the steady stream. . . . This is true not only of Mennin's second movement, where it might be expected, but even of the last movement, whose rhythm is somewhat spluttering and explosive. The melodic line's long-limbedness is apparent here in spite of a rhythmic character that in many composers' hands would sound scrappy and even allow the movement to fall to pieces. Moreover, there is a tendency for Mennin's instrumentation, as well as his composition, to be constructed in a large, general, sweeping fashion. . . .
>
> One is grateful . . . for the constant use of a genuine polyphony—counterpoint that does not rest primarily on chord successions, but in which harmonic feeling is established by the association of melodies. The melodies themselves are diatonic in nature, but make eventual use of all the resources of the chromatic scale. . . . [T]here is little tonic-dominant-tonic key sense, but instead we have here a modern revival of the ecclesiastical modes, with rapid changes from one to another. There is almost no direct chromaticism.
>
> One gathers that neither key, mode, nor atonality is a main point of interest to the composer, whose style draws on all these elements without seeming to care particularly about any of them. The vertical relation of simultaneous melodies is

more likely to be concordant than dissonant; and dissonances, when they appear, are more likely to be mild than sharp. . . .

It is obviously the relation of contrasting melodic outlines that is the crux of the matter to Mennin, not the particular intervals formed. . . .

From one point of view one might complain that Mennin's symphony offers too little obvious variety; that the melodies tend to wander in such a manner that they do not give a satisfactory sense of fulfillment when they finally come to a cadence; or that some of the rhythmic figures . . . have become clichés, too frequently used not only by Mennin but by most of his confrères. Against these minor complaints, however, stands the fact that Mennin's Fifth Symphony maintains a convincing feeling of dignity, musicality, skill, unity, and melodic breadth.[76]

In 1961, Robert Whitney and the Louisville Orchestra offered the first recording of Mennin's Symphony No. 5. The following year a more polished reading was released, this one featuring the Eastman-Rochester Symphony Orchestra conducted by Howard Hanson. Both these performances have since been reissued on compact disc. Then, in 1997, a third recording appeared, with David Alan Miller conducting the Albany Symphony Orchestra. These more recent releases provided the opportunity for commentary on a work then nearly half a century old. For example, Howard Dicus described Mennin's Fifth as "one of the most powerful tonal symphonies of the 20th century," calling the finale "one of the most exciting final movements in the entire classical repertory."[77] Similarly, Karl Miller called the symphony "a superb work. The last movement in particular is an orchestral tour de force. The writing is brilliant, engaging, with a clear sense of form that makes the logic of the piece clear."[78] David Raymond wrote, "Certainly few other American composers can build up such a head of steam in an Allegro movement as Mennin does, egged on by an impressive arsenal of contrapuntal devices." He added, "[A]ll that elegant abstraction is offset by a truly beautiful slow movement . . . that has an elevated gravity worthy of Bach."[79]

In 1950, the same year that he completed his Symphony No. 5, Mennin received a commission from Edwin Franko Goldman, via the League of Composers, as part of Goldman's vigorous campaign to encourage leading American composers to write works for symphonic wind band. The following year Mennin complied with a short work entitled *Canzona*, one of his favorite designations. Although the use of this term to characterize a work for winds and brass immediately calls to mind the music of Giovanni Gabrieli, this association has led commentators to attribute to the piece the antiphonal techniques pioneered by the early Baroque master. However, this is not what Mennin had in mind. In fact the work is an extremely compact application of the composer's increasingly familiar developmental principles.

A five-minute piece in a loosely ternary form, *Canzona* opens with a brisk, declamatory motif in polychords, after which the main theme is introduced, a vigorous modal idea accompanied by a bustling, syncopated undercurrent. These melodic and rhythmic motifs are developed with brilliant lucidity via intricate, but always aurally transparent, contrapuntal procedures. There is a brief central section in which the oboe introduces a longer, more lyrical melodic line. This is soon combined with the other, shorter motifs. Then there is an altered return of the opening material, including a brilliant passage in which the main motif is combined canonically with rhythmically augmented and diminished versions of itself. All is propelled forward with sober determination. A masterpiece of concision, *Canzona* packs considerable density of musical substance into its brief duration. The work was first performed by the Goldman Band, conducted by Edwin Franko Goldman, in June 1951 in New York City, and was recorded three years later by the Eastman Symphonic Wind Ensemble, under the direction of Frederick Fennell. Although it proved to be the composer's only contribution to the medium, *Canzona* has since been recorded many times and is recognized today as one of the classics of the American wind ensemble repertoire, appearing frequently on programs of serious music for band.

The other work that Mennin completed in 1951 was his String Quartet No. 2, commissioned by the Koussevitzky Music Foundation. (Mennin's String Quartet No. 1, written in 1941, while he was studying at Oberlin, was later withdrawn.) The Second Quartet marked a new level of expressive intensity for the composer. Although his basic developmental principles and procedures remained essentially unchanged, his music began to reflect increased grimness and sobriety, with contrapuntal activity of unremitting agitation, and with a harmonic language harsher than in anything he had written previously. There is also greater chromatic freedom, with passages approaching atonality, although strong tonal centers are asserted at major structural junctures.

This new harshness is immediately evident in the slashing dissonances that open the quartet's first movement, *Allegro ardentamente*. Several motifs are introduced and promptly subjected to contrapuntal elaboration at a rapid tempo, which, together with irregular yet emphatic rhythmic patterns, produce a sense of great turmoil but also of grim determination. Although this frenzied course is interrupted several times by references to the opening motif, there is no emotional relief until the tempo suddenly changes to *Andante* approximately midway through the movement. Similar and related motivic ideas are developed in a solemn contrapuntal manner, until the movement comes to a quiet close.

The second movement, *Prestissimo*, though conceptually a *scherzo*, maintains the grimly nervous character, in a rapid *perpetuum mobile* out of which grow several motifs subjected to contrapuntal and rhythmic elaboration. The movement avoids a sense of redundancy with the opening portion of the first movement by maintaining a lighter texture, while the articulation is muted and *sotto voce* throughout, until it reaches an abrupt conclusion.

The third movement, *Adagio semplice*, opens with a somber, moderately dissonant harmonic sequence, followed by the unfolding of an angular melodic line by the violin. This material is developed contrapuntally to a dissonant climax, producing a notably drier expressive effect than found in Mennin's previous slow movements.

The finale, *Allegro focosamente*, returns to the agitated character of the opening movement, as a series of angular, rhythmically irregular motifs is introduced into the swirling, *perpetuum mobile* texture and developed energetically. The movement accumulates increased momentum in an even faster coda, before the quartet settles into a decisive final cadence on an open fifth.

Mennin's Quartet No. 2 was introduced by the Juilliard String Quartet in February 1952 at the Museum of Modern Art in New York City. Apparently the work did not make an especially favorable impression on the New York critics. The reviewer for the *New York Times* commented, "Mr. Mennin's work represents this young composer's impressive energy, inventiveness and know-how. At all times his work was polished to a gleam and its workmanship . . . was thorough." However, he voices a reservation that is not unjustified: "One often feels that this composer makes his music work too hard, and last night was no exception. If there had been more light let in, more breathing space, the effect might have been more personal and the profile sharper."[80] On the other hand, after acknowledging evidence of "a young man's vitality," Virgil Thomson adds with a transparent condescension that smacks of "sour grapes," "It has brilliance in the sound and much skill in the note-handling, but essentially it is a quite simple piece . . . that requires little effort in the listener and that, for all its careful workmanship, is a bit thin of thought, monotonous of sound."[81]

On the other hand, in his capacity as critic for the *Musical Quarterly*, Vincent Persichetti seemed to confront the work more directly and with less self-protective qualification when he wrote, "Mennin writes music. There is nothing extra-musical to cloud the issue. It is straight music by a gifted, facile, and energetic young man with taste and talent. His Second String Quartet has contrapuntal architecture and overwhelming rhythmic drive. The blinding virtuosity is wholly remarkable; it has harmonic and formal shape and never succumbs to trickery. The rustling 'sotto voce' Scherzo is a delight. Derivativeness is never a stimulant to Mennin. He has plenty of ideas and the fortitude to send them over their uncompromising formal tracks."[82]

A brilliant performance of Mennin's Quartet No. 2 by the Juilliard Quartet was released in 1954. This recording has never been reissued on compact disc. Some twenty years later a far less polished reading of the work by the Kohon Quartet was released as part of an anthology of American string quartets composed between 1900 and 1950 (or, more accurately, 1951). That compendium was reissued on CD in 1995.

In many ways the 1950s represent Mennin's most fertile and characteristic period. By this time he had developed and refined his compositional approach into a highly personal language—one that was consistent in its aesthetic values and uniquely and unmistakeably his own. He had shed the trappings of the generic "American symphonic school," as well as the reminiscences of Vaughan Williams' Fourth Symphony, while abandoning any pretense at expressive "balance." His works now reflected the obsessive turbulence and explosiveness described earlier in the general discussion of Mennin's compositional style. The melodic structure is still fundamentally modal and diatonic but is elaborated with considerable chromatic freedom. Slow movements continue to loom as solemn oases of grave contemplation.

Although this rather subtle shift toward a harsher mode of expression was initially observed in the Second String Quartet, its first orchestral appearance was in the *Concertato, "Moby Dick."* This work, completed in 1952 on a commission from the Erie Philharmonic and its conductor Fritz Mahler, and introduced by them in October of that year, has become Mennin's most frequently performed orchestral composition. Its popularity can probably be attributed to two factors: The work embodies Mennin's full symphonic manner within a concise ten-minute duration; and it is virtually unique in this resolutely abstract composer's orchestral canon in drawing upon an extramusical reference. The composer insisted that *Concertato, "Moby Dick"* is "a dramatic work for orchestra motivated by the Melville novel, rather than following a specific programmatic outline. The piece depicts the emotional impact of the novel as a whole rather than musically describing isolated incidents occurring in the novel."[83] Listeners unfamiliar with the body of Mennin's work are invariably struck by the effectiveness of the *Concertato* in capturing the spirit of Melville's novel. Yet, in truth, its style does not deviate one iota from that found in Mennin's totally abstract works from the same period. Mennin greatly admired Melville's novel and seriously considered it as the subject of an opera. Indeed, the novel's driving motive—an obsessive and unswerving determination to overcome a seemingly invincible adversary—is one way of verbally encapsulating the emotional theme that seems tacitly to underlie Mennin's work in general. That the character of his music in general so closely parallels that of Melville's novel points to the affinity felt by the composer for *Moby Dick*.

Concertato, "Moby Dick" falls into two sections—the first only half as long as the second. A bleak, portentous *Adagio* introduces the main motif in the strings, elaborated by a solo in the flute. This is developed through gradually intensifying counterpoint to a massive climax, at which point the *Allegro* is unleashed, based on two motifs, both related to the material from the introduction: one, a spunky figure first heard in the upper woodwinds, followed immediately by the second, a more flowing line presented by the violins. This section may be seen as a deeper, darker elaboration of the approach applied in the *Canzona* of the previous year—specifically, the contrapuntal development of several motifs in instrumental "layers," distinguished through simultaneous rhythmic augmentation and diminution. The thematic material is developed with a tremendous concentration of energy to new heights of emotional intensity, before achieving its grimly triumphant resolution.

Several weeks after its Pennsylvania premiere, the Juilliard Orchestra, conducted by Jean Morel, introduced New York audiences to *Concertato, "Moby Dick."* William Bender commented, "Mr. Mennin has created a solid, tightly wrought score of power and intensity. The composer's handling of his musical materials is fluent. His orchestra glows with bright, unexpected colors. The score is economical; it has its say concisely and is done."[84] Jay S. Harrison, however, was somewhat less impressed. In his reaction—as in that of Virgil Thomson to the Quartet No. 2—one notes a sense of insecurity, as if the critic is wary of being "taken in" by something that might sound better than it may actually prove to be. Harrison describes the work as

> a bustling, energetic and cat-footed piece. It is not, however, any more than this, for the composer of late has fallen into the dangerous habit of making a stunning orchestral sound without, at the same time, underpinning it with an equivalent musical meaning. He writes notes, many of them and superbly, but their layout and general character do not strike sparks nor live long in the memory. Last night, for example, Mr. Mennin offered his audience a diatonic, virtuoso display piece centered, after the opening, on a torrential and intricate orchestral design. Woodwinds flew, brasses snorted and string soared; but when they had done, they had left no mark. In sum, the "Concertato for Orchestra" is glib music, slick as pane glass. And one can easily see through it.[85]

One of the most perceptive and informed reactions was again penned by Richard Franko Goldman, writing in the *Musical Quarterly* without the urgency of a newspaper deadline:

> The *Concertato* . . . will not strike the listener as being vastly different in character from Mennin's Third or Fifth Symphonies, the vein of which it quite obviously continues. The interesting and admirable qualities of Mennin's work over

the last several years are all here; the unmistakable personality, distinctive technique, and refinement of thought are little changed, and not the less welcome
for that. In Mennin one recognizes a composer whose style is formed. There is
no longer the slightest question of skill, consistency, originality, or authenticity.
For a composer [not yet thirty years old] this is no mean attainment.

   The core of Mennin's technique and style remains that complete absorption of
technique, esthetic, and rationale found in "early" contrapuntal forms. Mennin
does not imitate the external or "analyzable" aspects of canzonas or ricercare; . . .
Mennin's fluency, assuredness, and above all, his clarity, can come only from
within: from a conversance that is both reasoned and instinctive, and without a
trace of self-consciousness. There is no hesitation in his work, and there are no in-
congruities. . . . One is aware of intellectual ease, not of intellectual inhibition. . .

   The *Concertato* has verve, elegance, succinctness; it moves easily to a sense
of completion and fulfillment. . . . Despite the elaborateness of the contrapuntal
texture, and the subtlety of the melodic variation, the transparency of the large
structure is remarkable. Sections are clearly defined, with consummate grace in
all the transitions, and the proportions are beautifully calculated and satisfying.

Goldman then concludes with cautionary words that point to a legitimate
concern about Mennin's development as a composer from the vantage point
of 1953: "There seems at the moment the slightest danger that Mennin, having evolved distinctively, may tend to repetition of his own ideas. [His recent
works] have not only family kinship of design and technique, but occasionally
striking similarities in thematic material. They are all, individually, works of
beauty and viability. Taken together, they represent an impressive phase of
what one hopes and expects will be Mennin's continuing evolution."[86]

By this time the reader may have noticed that though Mennin was hailed
by leading critics during the 1940s as a major compositional talent freshly
having arrived on the scene, by the early 1950s the general critical attitude
was beginning to shift from one of enthusiastic welcome to one of blasé
skepticism, notwithstanding the continued advocacy of some, such as Richard
Franko Goldman and Walter Hendl. One begins to sense a patronizing tone
among the New York newspaper critics, conceptualizing Mennin's music as
"slick" and "glib," as if its developmental processes demonstrate "facility"
rather than other, "deeper" qualities. One may interpret this as the difference
between heralding that which is new versus questioning the legitimacy of
that which has become successful; or perhaps it represents the beginning of a
general loss of interest in the "American Symphonic School." Or there may
be a more personal explanation: Perhaps there was some resentment of Mennin's apparent ease in composing large-scale works, as if five symphonies
by the age of twenty-seven seemed like "too much," and nothing that comes
this easy can be that good. Maybe this resentment was exacerbated by the

fact that the country's most highly regarded orchestras and conductors were presenting the young man's work in the most auspicious venues.

Or perhaps there was a misunderstanding of Mennin's aesthetic aspirations in the first place: Initially he was seen as one of the most promising of a new crop of American Neo-Classicists. But Mennin was never truly a Neo-Classicist, and as his language evolved, this became increasingly clear. But if he wasn't a Neo-Classicist, what was he? This question was difficult to answer for those whose familiarity with his output—then incomplete, of course—was limited. So they criticized the music for not being what they expected it to be. Whatever the explanation, this attitude gradually took hold as a general position among mainstream critics, lapsing into a scornful dismissal that seemed to harden during the remainder of Mennin's life. This view was, however, in marked contrast to the positions expressed in publications directed toward more serious listeners, which began to appear toward the late 1970s and eventually mushroomed with the advent of the Internet. No one who peruses the critical comments collected here can fail to note the shift in comprehension of Mennin's aesthetic aims that began to take place during the last few years of his life.

Shortly after its initial performances, *Concertato, "Moby Dick"* was recorded by the Vienna Symphony Orchestra under the direction of Hans Swarowsky. Although the performance was mediocre and the recording primitive, it was reissued during the mid 1960s on the Desto label. The work was not recorded again until 1996, on an all-Mennin CD that featured Gerard Schwarz conducting the Seattle Symphony Orchestra. Just a few months later, another all-Mennin disc appeared, with David Alan Miller conducting the Albany Symphony Orchestra. This recording also included *Concertato, "Moby Dick"* in what is perhaps its finest recorded performance to date. Then, in 1999, as part of a deluxe ten-CD special edition, the New York Philharmonic released a live-concert broadcast of the *Concertato* in a surprisingly uninspired performance from January 1963, conducted by Leonard Bernstein.

Once again it is interesting to consider the critical response to the work from this much later vantage point. Commenting on the Schwarz/Seattle performance, Steven Schwartz points out that

> Mennin's work succeeds . . . largely because he avoids programmatic depiction. Mennin isn't a theater or illustrative composer. He seems fascinated by the logic of symphonic argument. His works unfold . . . by "continual variation" and by resorting to a contrapuntal dramatic conflict among themes. The method can have considerable hold on a listener—leading one firmly through the twists of an idea. . . . Don't look for "sea music" or Ahab's obsessive brooding. The "Moby Dick" reference always struck me as a half-apology.

After a slow passage that introduces the musical material, the *Concertato* comes across as a vigorous, rhythmically insistent work. Any links to Melville remain with the composer.[87]

In January 1996, Leonard Slatkin, long a champion of the *Concertato*, featured the work on one of his New York programs with the St. Louis Symphony Orchestra. Considering the piece alongside a piece by Luciano Berio also presented by the orchestra, Alex Ross commented, "Mennin's 1952 Concertato for Orchestra ought to have seemed old-fashioned next to the Berio, but it actually sounded more fresh. It is a rollicking 10-minute overture, faintly inspired by 'Moby Dick.' Despite echoes of Shostakovich, Vaughan Williams and Hindemith, it establishes its own austerely vigorous voice and provides brilliant display for a crack ensemble like the St. Louis. Mennin's nine symphonies deserve a second look."[88] On the other hand, Herbert Kupferberg cluelessly commented that the work "proved to be a well-made 10-minute seascape, whose waves of sound displayed the admirable virtuosity of the orchestra's [string section]."[89]

Upon completing the *Concertato*, Mennin turned his attention to a commission from the Louisville Orchestra and its conductor Robert Whitney, composing his Symphony No. 6, the symphonic culmination of this stage in his development. For a composer at age thirty, the work demonstrates an extraordinary level of emotional maturity and compositional sophistication and mastery; it stands among the Sixth Symphony of Piston, the *Sinfonia Breve* of Bloch, the Fourth of Giannini, and the Fifth and Sixth of Persichetti as the greatest American symphonies of the 1950s. All Mennin's symphonies up through No. 5 might be characterized as vigorous and determined. Some might find them grim, others simply firm and resolute. In the Sixth Symphony, on the other hand, the mood is more severe, its energy not merely assertive but manic and driven. Here Mennin presses his customary developmental processes and principles toward more intense and complex levels of elaboration. Rhythm has become increasingly irregular, and the harmonic consequences of contrapuntal voice-leading are increasingly dissonant. Much of the dissonance, however, is imposed upon triadic harmonic structures—largely minor in modal quality—with the addition of minor-ninths, major-minor juxtapositions, and unresolved *appoggiaturas*, as well as arising from bass lines that conflict with otherwise triadic structures. The tonality is no longer obviously modal or diatonic but freely chromatic, and tonal centers are touched upon more briefly and incidentally, generally serving as an anchor when themes are introduced, climaxes attained, and sections concluded. Yet the characteristic shapes of the motifs and gestures are consistent with those in his previous works. But what is perhaps more important is that, with the

Sixth Symphony, Mennin has clearly parted company with the exuberant, confident, optimistic "American Symphonic School"; in fact, he has clearly diverged from the canons of traditional aesthetics, from notions of balance, symmetry, and restraint, and critical comments increasingly display a lack of sympathy with or understanding of this divergence. Mennin's music has become possessed by a single-minded, almost demonic quest either to overcome some formidable if undefined existential adversary, or perhaps simply to depict the ruthless forces of nature in ceaseless tumult, as suggested by the text of "The Cycle."

The work begins with a slow, solemn introduction, *Maestoso*, that presents three related motifs that will figure significantly throughout the work. The first is a descending line presented at the outset by the violins; the second follows on its heels in the cellos and basses; an important variant of the first is heard immediately in the clarinet and bassoon; and the third is played by the violins, in counterpoint with the preceding motifs in the other strings. The body of the movement, *Allegro*, then begins, introducing what serves as its main theme—a long, irregular line played softly but with suppressed urgency by the strings. This theme drives the movement through its breakneck course, ever-increasing in intensity, and interacting in continual development with the three motifs from the introduction. When the level of intensity seems to have reached the breaking point, the music comes finally to a guarded, temporary repose.

The second movement, "Grave," is similar in character to the corresponding movement of the Fifth Symphony—solemn and reflective, yet intensely lyrical at times—though the harmonic language, embracing a greater degree of dissonance, permits a darker, grimmer expressive dimension. Frank Oteri describes the movement as "almost dirge-like in its emotionally restrained starkness."[90] Based largely on the motifs from the first movement, the *Grave* culminates in two climaxes before ending in the somber mood heard at the beginning.

The third movement, *Allegro vivace*, functions as both *scherzo* and finale. It opens with a theme that was first heard in the violins toward the beginning of the second movement, though clearly derived from the main theme of the first movement. This is developed in whirlwind fashion, as familiar motifs are tossed around, building to a massive canonic treatment that then subsides into a quiet, peaceful interlude, *Adagio sostenuto*. Not quiet for long, this too builds to a climax that ushers in the final section, *Allegro vivace*, with a rapid diminution of the *scherzo* theme. The energy builds and recedes, as most of the material of the symphony finds its way into the seething developmental cauldron, hurtling headlong with an ever-increasing frenzy. After much turbulence a tonal goal perceived in the distance comes gradually into clearer focus, as the symphony reaches its triumphant conclusion on a *tierce de*

Picardie in A major. (Like Schuman's, Mennin's propensity for triumphant endings became increasingly incongruous as his overall harmonic language grew more dissonant and less clearly tonal.)

By far the strongest of his symphonies to date, Mennin's Sixth was given its premiere by Robert Whitney and the Louisville Orchestra in Louisville, Kentucky, in November 1953. In keeping with its policy, the orchestra recorded the work two months after the premiere, for release in 1954 as part of the Louisville Orchestra series of newly commissioned works. This recording was reissued on compact disc in 2003.

Mennin's Symphony No. 6 was introduced to New York audiences in February 1955 by the New York Philharmonic, conducted by Dimitri Mitropoulos. Olin Downes described it as "a busy and lively symphony, full of zip and elan; the work of a young man of 32, who has enough and to spare of the yeast of his years." However, he continued,

> The form is in the broad sense of the word traditional, but the ideas propounded in the introduction are originally treated in the pages and movements that follow. The structural scheme is elaborately worked out. The most brilliant movement and the one that rushes most spontaneously to its conclusion is the first. The second is more reflectively composed, and could be analyzed interestingly throughout its length. The finale is the corollary of the opening movement, brilliant, fugacious, and mostly loud. This characteristic is found elsewhere and too often in the symphony, which needs more of dynamic contrast, more of balance and poise as well as excitement.[91]

But Mennin was no Neo-Classicist; balance and poise were not his goals. It is clear that in this work, and in those that followed, he was seeking to expand and extend his expressive power in the particular directions that were his foci of interest, regardless of the palatability of the result, rather than produce a well-mannered symphonic statement, although this fact had yet to be recognized by the commentators of the time.

Paul Henry Lang similarly displayed some remarkably shallow and conventional thinking in characterizing Mennin's Sixth as "a young man's music—confident and optimistic. Mr. Mennin knows the metier and handles his material with facility and fluency." However, he does penetrate more deeply when he continues,

> His contrapuntal technique seems to be the result of a natural bent; it is not the "barbed wire" variety, nor is it a device, rather an idiom. Another attractive feature of this music is its avoidance of little diversionary effects. The symphony is hard and lean. Only primary colors are used in the orchestra but the large patches thus created are pretty well ordered. The dynamic scheme is just

as simple—relentless mounting toward a climax. The first movement impressed me as a strong piece even though austere. Simplicity and sustained melodic writing characterize the second movement. Again the colors were stark except for a little poetic pleading by the oboe, but after a while the big climaxes were back and the movement did not afford a good contrast to the preceding one. The intensity of mood and sound continued unabated in the last movement.

Lang too seems to long for something more conventionally balanced, as he concludes rather patronizingly, "This gifted young composer has plenty of good ideas and can write nicely drawn lines, but he always wants to get there fustest with the mostest of instruments, and by the end I longed for a little relaxation. Still, there is good reason to believe that eventually Mr. Mennin will discover that drums, cymbals, and other noise makers should be kept in a safe deposit box until needed for exceptional occasions."[92]

Irving Kolodin begins his notice by expressing some amazement that Mennin has "already written six symphonies worth performance by our major orchestras. But the sixth . . . is such a plausible piece of music, with so well-shaped a structure, so well-filled in a facade, that one can't either ignore the facts or dispose of them lightly." Acknowledging minimal prior familiarity with Mennin's music, Kolodin asserts that the work

> certainly defines him as possessing the craftsmanship required to manage the checks and balances of symphonic design on a sizable scale. He plays his hand expertly, always with a few musical cards in reserve to throw in when needed. His sense of form is compact, his writing for the orchestra sinewy. . . . The content, however, is another and more elusive thing. The inevitable second-time round will tell more about it, though I admit some present doubts relating to Mennin's tendency to such extremes as meditation and expostulation. Could I remember a little touch of lightness here, a bit of gauche sentiment there, I would have more hope of discovering something momentous in it on future hearings. As of now Mennin strikes me as fully capable of plotting the kind of work he has set his heart on writing. Now, however, he must convince us what it is in his heart he wants to say. Design of itself is a major absorption of modern life, but art cannot live by blueprints alone.[93]

All three of these critics, each in his own way, were conveying discomfort with Mennin's evolution toward an expressive extremism, rather than providing the neat symphonic packages expected of someone presumed to be a Neo-Classically oriented academic traditionalist.

After the Louisville recording of the Sixth Symphony in 1954, no other recording of the work was to appear for more than forty years. *Fanfare* offers a feature called "Classical Hall of Fame," in which critics select recordings from the past that warrant special merit though they may have been overlooked when they first appeared. In 1978, the encyclopedically knowledgable critic Paul Snook nominated the Louisville recording of Mennin's Sixth for this "Classical Hall of Fame." His commentary, remarkable for its breadth of perspective, stands in marked contrast to the notices quoted above, while remaining one of the most eloquent reflections on Mennin's music ever to appear in print.

> When Peter Mennin burst like a meteor upon the music scene with his Third Symphony in 1946 . . . he arrived fresh from his studies at Eastman-Rochester with a bold and already fully-developed style—combining elements of Harris, Schuman, Barber, and Vaughan Williams—which was determinedly symphonic in scope and instantly recognizable as his own. . . . In less than ten years, and during his twenties at that, he was to produce in quick succession a quartet of symphonies which remain unsurpassed for their seriousness of argument, compactness of form, and ferocious kinetic charge. The Sixth is the crowning summation of this prodigious spurt of youthful inspiration. . . . [T]he entire material of this work . . . is derived from a single motif of a few notes, a darkly heroic and defiant gesture full of both the menace and majesty which are typical Mennin preoccupations. This bare germinal motif, which is the source not only of all the thematic development but most of the accompanying rhythmic and harmonic figuration, as well, is cumulatively elaborated with tremendous fertility and authority—now elongated into a grave, sustained *cantilena*, then suddenly collapsed and accelerated into a propulsive, headlong plunge, always obstinately returning to the same ground again and again. In this way Mennin achieves the intense degree of integration and compression, of overpowering weightiness and onrushing inevitability that he is after. While conceived in terms of purely abstract musical discourse—constant contrapuntal germination, blocklike antiphonal massing and interplay of instrumental choirs, relentless momentum, unbroken linear continuity, lucidity of texture combined with steadiness of pulse—deep underneath this tightly controlled and fluid surface of sound is a churning, chaotic mass of energy demanding release, of Manichean conflict seeking its ultimate, perhaps annihilating resolution. This is an obsessive, tragic, and metaphysical music, with a narrow range of reference but a deep cutting edge of significance, full of the destructive fury and enigma of American power which lies behind Ahab's quest and what Henry James once called "the imagination of disaster."[94]

In the foregoing commentary, Snook obliquely indicates how the spiritual and emotional core of *Moby Dick* informs a good deal more of Mennin's music than merely the one piece that bears its name.

The second recording of Mennin's Sixth Symphony appeared in 1997 on the Albany Symphony's all-Mennin disc, conducted by David Alan Miller. Commenting on these new readings of Symphonies Nos. 5 and 6, David

Raymond described them as "concise, energetic, and absorbing, with a lack of sensuality and a studied abstractness that are rare, if not unique, in American symphonies."[95] David Hurwitz assured listeners,

> Mennin's music "speaks" emotionally, even if the themes aren't of the conventionally tuneful type. The finale of the Sixth Symphony offers a perfect instance of the composer's ability to create instantly memorable musical ideas whose development makes perfect logical sense and carries the listener along however fast, dissonant, or otherwise complex the surrounding musical fabric. Mennin's achievement has yet to be given the acclaim that it surely deserves, but there's not a note on this disc that falls one millimeter below the highest standards of craftsmanship, sincerity, and inspiration.[96]

In the spring of 1954, Walter Hendl's article, "The Music of Peter Mennin" appeared. Although Hendl's perspective is obviously limited to those works composed up until that time, his comments are remarkable for the aptness of their insight in characterizing the first ten years of Mennin's compositional activity.

> Mennin is a symphonist by nature and intent, and his ideas fall naturally into large units, both as to structure and musical content. . . . [A]ll of Mennin's craft is directed toward achieving the dramatic whole. . . . [O]ne finds little display of tricks or "effects" used for [their own impact]. . . . The vitality, consistency and drive command our attention always. This is music for listeners and performers of high musical intelligence and acute musical understanding. . . . [I]t is the feeling of restrained emotion, with all unessential decoration discarded, that gives Mennin's slow movements their special individuality. The singing qualities of these movements seem to be the antithesis of the enormous propulsion and intensity in some sections of the fast movements. . . . Though Mennin's time signatures usually remain constant, the complete freedom given to melodic lines negates any feeling of bar-line regularity. . . . Quick changes of tonality are accomplished through the use of scale patterns. The total harmonic consequence is not one of an extreme nature or of experimentation for its own sake. . . . [T]his music should be presented with a classic regard for its form, tempo and dynamics. Arbitrary fluctuations of tempo, even *rubato*, or exaggerated gradations of romantic dynamics do not work well here. One should seek, rather, a quiet, intense slow-moving dignity, or a rapid pace of firm rhythm, sharp punctuation and unrelenting vitality. . . . [T]here is no doubt in my mind that [Mennin's music] will continue to be one of the dominant expressions of the creative activity of our times.[97]

Mennin did not complete another work until 1956, when he fulfilled a commission from Juilliard in commemoration of the school's fiftieth anniversary, with a Concerto for Cello and Orchestra. The premiere took place in February 1956, with Leonard Rose as soloist and Jean Morel conducting the Juilliard Orchestra.

Aside from the early Flute Concertino, this was Mennin's first attempt to apply his compositional approach to the concerto genre. (He had begun a violin concerto several years earlier but never finished it, leaving only the slow movement complete in short score.) The first movement, *Allegro moderato*, begins exactly as one might expect his next symphony to begin, with a determined orchestral *tutti* that introduces the work's main motifs—most prominently, a short descending gesture that ends characteristically with a "Scotch snap." (It was probably this motif that prompted Vincent Persichetti to remark impishly, "Did you ever notice the way Mennin works his name into his themes?"[98]) After a brief exposition of the thematic material, the solo cello enters, elaborating on these ideas, and a series of interactions takes place between the soloist and the orchestra as the material is developed. Of course, there is nothing remarkable about this framework: What so compels the listener's attention is the nature of what is expressed via this relatively conventional structure—an intensely gripping, if totally abstract, dramatic scenario utilizing essentially the same harmonic and tonal language as was heard in the Symphony No. 6. Through a series of tempestuous *tutti* episodes, the movement builds to a huge, uniquely Menninian climax, as several motifs are unleashed in forceful counterpoint, from lower brass in rhythmic augmentation to swirling strings in frantic canonic diminution. This climax leads directly to an elaborate and extraordinarily difficult cadenza.

The *Adagio* follows the cadenza without pause. The orchestra introduces the movement's chief thematic idea, and the solo cello elaborates on it with a lofty eloquence, both reflective and passionately expressive, in a soulfully searching soliloquy.

The finale, *Allegro vivace*, a brilliant quasi-*toccata in moto perpetuo*, opens with a tremendous burst of energy. The movement is an exciting showcase for the virtuosity of the soloist, with much rapid byplay between the cello and the ensemble. Overall the concerto is less densely contrapuntal than the composer's norm, in order to prevent the solo instrument from being buried within the orchestral texture.

The Cello Concerto's premiere was immediately preceded by the first performance of Roger Sessions's Piano Concerto. In comparing the two, Howard Taubman commented,

> Mr. Mennin's concerto belongs to a different order of approach. His lyricism, particularly in the slow movement, has more direct appeal. He uses the cello in this movement to advantage, for he is mindful of the fact that it is a rich, singing instrument. The first movement has a good deal of spirit and the writing is

idiomatic for the solo instrument. . . . The final movement of this half-hour work has less to say than the first two. Presumably it justifies itself in that it gives the soloist a lot of difficult music to play. One would guess that this concerto would have a better chance than the Sessions of meeting with the approval of the general symphonic public. All three works were hailed with delight by an audience that obviously had a special curiosity about contemporary music.[99]

Mennin's Cello Concerto did not appear on recording until 1969, when a performance was released featuring the Louisville Orchestra, conducted by Jorge Mester. The soloist on that recording was Janos Starker, who provided a rendition that was nothing short of sensational—passionately expressive during the *cantabile* passages and stunningly agile, yet carefully controlled, during the more rapid portions. This performance set a standard not likely to be exceeded for a long time and argued convincingly for the work as the foremost American cello concerto. The recording was reissued on compact disc in 1992 and then again in 2003.

Also in 1956 Mennin completed his *Sonata Concertante* for violin and piano, commissioned by the Elizabeth Sprague Coolidge Foundation. It was given its premiere by Ruggiero Ricci and Leon Pommers in October of that year at the Library of Congress in Washington, D.C. Three months later Ricci, along with pianist Artur Balsam, performed the work at New York's Carnegie Hall.

Its title indicates that the work is structured as a partnership between the two instruments, rather than as a showcase for the violin with piano accompaniment. The *Sonata Concertante* deviates virtually not at all from the Mennin stylistic prototype at this point in its evolution during the mid 1950s. The first movement begins with a brief introduction marked *Sostenuto*, which solemnly introduces several significant motifs that will recur throughout the work. The body of the movement, *Allegro con brio*, then follows, as these and other motifs are developed through a continuous counterpoint of multiple voices, despite the presence of only two instruments. This counterpoint displays Mennin's characteristic devices, in ever-increasing complexity: terse gestures, canon and other forms of imitation, and strong, actively moving bass lines, grouped into irregular rhythmic patterns that create a constant sense of driving forward with grim determination.

In the second movement, *Adagio semplice*, a freely chromatic, *cantabile* melody softly weaves its way in and around largely consonant, triadic, but tonally unrelated harmonic structures. A movement of great beauty, it ranges in mood between the ethereal and the impassioned.

The third movement, *Allegro con fuoco*, returns to the bleak, driven character and contrapuntal developmental processes of the first movement. However, the motivic ideas in this movement are somewhat more clearly defined, and the rhythmic flow is somewhat more lithe and brisk, in comparison with the opening. In this movement, as in the first, the piano serves chiefly as a contrapuntal voice, hard and brittle in sonority, as it drives the music forward in ever-building intensity to a brusque conclusion.

The Washington, D.C., premiere of the *Sonata Concertante* was attended by Howard Taubman, who wrote, "The Mennin sonata proved to be one of the maturest pieces this talented American has written. It bore some of his expected fingerprints—insistent, propulsive rhythms, a sense of dash and energy and a rugged melodic line. The first movement combined these elements with admirable address. In the second, Mr. Mennin allowed himself to sing spaciously and, what was especially impressive, personally. The final movement seemed to revert to an old habit, motion for motion's sake."[100] Irving Lowens reacted similarly to the sonata, describing it as

> a characteristically propulsive work by this prolific young composer, distinguished by complex rhythms, driving melodic lines, and seemingly inexhaustible energy. In some of his earlier big pieces, Mennin displayed a tendency towards writing mere "busy music," evidently a by-product of his tremendous facility and powerful creative drive, but little of this undisciplined nervous chatter can be found in the *Sonata concertante*. Its three movements are economically constructed despite the fact that they bristle with technical problems for the performers and despite an emotional pitch that borders on frenzy, particularly in the final *Allegro con fuoco*. Mennin has succeeded in achieving a unified effect of concise, purposeful musical thought over and against the handicap of an extraordinarily complicated texture. This sonata is a welcome sign of his maturing art.[101]

Mennin's *Sonata Concertante* did not appear on recording until 1971, when violinist Paul Zukofsky and pianist Gilbert Kalish included it on a recital LP. (This performance was subsequently reissued on compact disc in 2004.) In 1990, another performance, this one with Fredell Lack and Albert Hirsh, was released on CD. Neither of these performances, however, captures the fiery, yet controlled, intensity essential to the character of the work.

Mennin's next work was another concerto, this time featuring the piano. Composed in 1957, Mennin's Piano Concerto was commissioned by the Cleveland Orchestra, in commemoration of its fortieth anniversary, and it proved to be the last work Mennin would compose before undertaking the stewardship of the Peabody Conservatory. The premiere took place in Cleveland, with Eunice Podis as soloist and George Szell conducting, at the end of February 1958. The same forces introduced the work to New York audiences the following week.

Mennin's Piano Concerto requires a soloist with extraordinary stamina, along with virtuosity of an unusual kind. Rather than following the conventional Romantic concept of a concerto, with highly contoured themes of contrasting character and some semblance of an adversarial relationship between soloist and orchestra, Mennin's is more a Baroque concerto gone wild. An ominous *Maestoso* introduction sets the stage for a stern proclamation of the main motif, Phrygian in quality. After some elaboration, the orchestra introduces the *Allegro*, plunging the soloist headlong into a *toccata*-like flood of rapidly motoric passagework, as the primary voice within the largely contrapuntal texture. The solo part is intricately interwoven motivically, but at times alternates with the orchestra in a manner suggestive of a Baroque *ritornello*. The movement proceeds through ever-increasing levels of intensity that peak, recede, then start anew.

As the second movement, marked *Adagio religioso*, opens, the strings create a hushed atmosphere against which the piano slowly spins out an improvisatory soliloquy, similar to the effect evoked in the slow movement of the *Sonata Concertante*. The movement is largely reflective in character, and displays an icy, unearthly beauty, not unlike that conjured by Vaughan Williams in both his Sixth and Seventh Symphonies. This movement contains some of the composer's most profoundly moving passages.

The third movement, *Allegro vivace*, returns to the character of the first, as the pianist is called upon to unleash torrential floods of rapid passagework in frenzied dialogue with the orchestra. Throughout much of this movement, like the first, the piano figurations are designed to produce hard, brittle sonorities. Again as in the *Sonata Concertante*, the thematic material of the third movement is distinguished from that of the first by somewhat greater gestural definition. The energy builds without letup until it reaches a peroration of unequivocal finality on an open fifth in the orchestra.

The work is an amazing feat, both for the composer and for the pianist who takes on the challenge of learning it. Although one might claim with some justification that despite the composer's attempt to distinguish them, there is insufficient differentiation between the first and third movements—which, interestingly, is not true of the Cello Concerto—the Piano Concerto stands as one of Mennin's most imposing achievements. Yet it is clear from perusing the critical commentaries that appeared at the time that the work's initial audiences had difficulty grasping the music's expressive purpose, although this purpose seems fairly evident today, at least in a general sense. Nevertheless, each reviewer indicated some awareness of the work's unusual aspects, but these were regarded more as inadequacies than purposeful choices.

Winthrop Sargeant, generally an astute and independent-minded, but often ultraconservative, commentator, provided a clear illustration of this misunderstanding of the concerto's basic ethos, defended by a superior air of ennui:

Mr. Mennin's concerto turned out to be rather disappointing. Although it is technically a very capable composition—well orchestrated, rhythmically vigorous,
and with a solo part nicely suited to the piano—I could find nothing in it beyond
a display of Mr. Mennin's unquestionable competence in putting a lot of notes
together. He has, in common with many contemporary composers, an individual
style—perhaps it would be more accurate to refer to it as a recipe—that seems to
involve various ingredients of polytonality and eccentric scale structure, and this
makes the concerto, like other works of his that I have heard, as homogeneous
as pea soup. One trouble with styles of this sort is that they are unrelated to any
accepted frame of musical meaning and are apt to stand as a barrier between
the composer and whatever, if anything, he is bent on communicating to his
audience. Another trouble is that they tend to become monotonous, since one's
curiosity about their technical ingredients is soon satisfied and there isn't much
else of interest in them. . . . I am afraid that, after an initial absorption in figuring
out Mr. Mennin's recipe, my reaction to the work was one of boredom.[102]

Howard Taubman similarly, if more benignly, coupled relatively accurate
hearing with misguided interpretation, writing,

Like so much of the extensive body of music written by this composer . . . ,
the concerto is filled with motor energy. Mr. Mennin favors rhythms that drive
forward relentlessly, and the end movements of this score have unflagging momentum. The slow movement, sustained in song, is more reposeful and offers
the needed contrast and breathing space. The concerto emphasizes the growing
command by Mr. Mennin of his direction and means. He manipulates his materials, harmonically, contrapuntally and rhythmically, with enormous gusto. You
have the feeling that here is a man who likes to mold sound and that he works
assiduously at it. What one does not feel, however, is that he is reaching more
deeply and arriving at a distinctive utterance. The concerto is not a marked departure from his symphonies and 'cello concerto, if one's memory serves. But
there is no better remedy than Mr. Mennin's—to keep writing.[103]

Francis D. Perkins also acknowledged the concerto's

inventiveness in its ideas and skill in their treatment and their instrumental in-
vestiture. The piano is definitely the protagonist, but the orchestra is a partner
rather than an accompanist in this well-balanced and often high spirited score.
The idea is melodic tempered with discreet pungency, contemporary in its atmosphere. In the first and third movements, the soloist is called upon for virtuosity,
vigor and a capacity for speed. This last characteristic involves the work's chief
drawback. After the impressive opening with a theme of marked profile, the
pace is too relentlessly rapid for the rest of the first movement. The andante,
indeed, has an appealing meditative and imaginative lyric breadth. But more
relaxing of the pace would be welcome in the swift movements. The shortage

of such relief detracted from the variety inherent in the thematic material and lessened the ultimate effect of the finale's bright animation.[104]

Mennin's Piano Concerto has enjoyed but one recording, issued on LP in 1971. The pianist was the extraordinary British virtuoso John Ogdon, and Mennin's was one of the few American concertos he championed. Widely praised as a proponent of unjustly neglected piano music, Ogdon tears through the work with appropriately headlong abandon. The original release, which also featured the Royal Philharmonic under the direction of Igor Buketoff, was available only briefly, but the performance was reissued on LP in 1980 and then on compact disc in 1997. As breathtaking as Ogdon's performance may be, the orchestra does not match his precision, nor is their coordination optimal (as comparison with an air-check of the Cleveland premiere illustrates). Mennin's Piano Concerto is one of America's greatest in the genre, along with those by Persichetti, Barber, and the third of Flagello, and certainly warrants further attention from soloists searching for a challenge that is intellectually, musically, and technically rewarding.

Mennin completed no new works during his tenure as president of the Peabody Conservatory, although he was no doubt immersed in the composition of several, as three new titles appeared in late 1962 and 1963, shortly after he assumed leadership of the Juilliard School. One of these was a short orchestral work—the first such piece to appear in more than a decade—entitled *Canto*. Commissioned by the Association of Women's Committees for Symphony Orchestras, the piece was introduced in March 1963 by the San Antonio Symphony Orchestra, conducted by Victor Allesandro.

Canto, less than ten minutes in duration, was described by the composer as "a dramatic elegy."[105] It begins portentously, with a somber statement of a wedge-shaped motif in the lower strings, not unlike the motif on which the entire Seventh Symphony—composed concurrently or shortly afterward—would be based, making this something of a "study" for the larger work. As this theme unfolds, dissonant brass chords in irregular rhythm offer tense, bitter punctuation, building gradually to a climax, followed by a sudden silence. The strings introduce a softer, more lyrical idea, which again builds in intensity as it is developed in contrapuntal dialogue with the brass, reaching an even more intense climax. A mournful polyphonic passage in the strings follows, gradually leading to a reminiscence of the opening moments, before the work comes to a grim, bleak conclusion. As Joseph Sagmaster notes most aptly in his commentary accompanying *Canto*'s sole recording, "As in much of Mennin's work, the emphasis here is less on lyrical beauty than on dramatic power, achieved through complex harmony and forceful rhythm."[106]

When *Canto* was introduced to New York audiences two years later by Eugene Ormandy and the Philadelphia Orchestra, Thedore Strongin appreciated "a sense of rightness about its time spans. One thing flows into the other with naturalness. It is not a work that breaks new ground, but it is convincing in its clearly stated terms."[107] Reviewing the same performance, another critic felt that it "may well become an American music classic for its profound feeling and beauty of form,"[108] although more than forty years later, the work has yet to achieve that status. Mennin's *Canto* has been recorded only once—by the Cincinnati Symphony Orchestra, conducted by Max Rudolf, on an LP released in 1971.

With his next work, a piano sonata commissioned by the Ford Foundation on behalf of pianist Claudette Sorel, Mennin's music began to reveal another distinct modification in its materials and their treatment, although not in its aesthetic framework or its actual expressive content. Completed in 1963, the Piano Sonata displays a much harsher, more dissonant harmonic language than found in his previous works, as well as linear writing that is much more freely chromatic. Although each of its three movements is clearly anchored in a tonal center, each is largely atonal throughout its course of development, while the meter changes with virtually every measure.

The first movement, *Poco moderato*, opens with a slow introduction that presents the movement's primary thematic material, which includes several motifs that will figure significantly later in the work as well. One of these motifs, a four-note figure consisting of two descending minor-seconds, is the chief focus of development once the vigorous *Allegro* commences and is transformed several times through octave displacement. As the movement proceeds, the tempo changes a number of times, linear counterpoint becomes highly dissonant, and textures quite dense; the emotional temperature is tense and grim. By the time it reaches its resolute conclusion, a tonal center of C has been affirmed.

The second movement, *Adagio*, displays a deeply searching, improvisatory quality reminiscent of the slow movement of the Piano Concerto. It evolves around a lofty melody of melancholy cast, which eventually builds to a powerful, dissonant climax. Again, despite its highly chromatic linear writing and extremely harsh harmonic language, a tonal center of C-sharp minor clearly frames the movement.

The finale, *Veloce*, is a tremendously propulsive movement in perpetual motion, with a constant figuration, but ever-changing meter, suggesting the general feeling of a *rondo*. Again, although the harmony is quite dissonant, the tonality is clearly B-flat minor. Before it reaches its grimly decisive conclusion, motifs from the first movement make their appearance. Some commentators have remarked on a similarity to the finale of Prokofiev's Seventh

Sonata, while the coda of the movement has provoked comparisons with the corresponding passage in the last movement of Barber's Piano Sonata. However, the aggressive energy and ceaseless drive of this movement are far more characteristic of Mennin's body of work than of Prokofiev's or Barber's.

Mennin's Piano Sonata is an extremely difficult work to render effectively, and few pianists have taken on the challenge. It is one of the few mature works of Mennin that, as of this writing, have never been recorded commercially. Yet it ranks among the sonatas of Persichetti, Flagello, Giannini, Muczynski, and Barber as one of the great American contributions to the genre.

The other work Mennin completed in 1963 was his Symphony No. 7. "Here," writes Harvey Philips, "serenity abuts violence, the calmly beautiful is interrupted by frenetic agitation, the dramatic is brushed aside by ethereal repose."[109] A masterpiece of focused emotional intensity expressed through brilliant musical logic, the symphony was commissioned by George Szell and the Cleveland Orchestra, who gave the world premiere in Cleveland in January 1964. (As stated earlier, it was later revealed that Szell had personally provided the funding for the symphony.)

Mennin had reached the age of forty, and it had been ten years since a new symphony had appeared. The Seventh deviated in many significant ways from those that preceded it. It is the first of Mennin's symphonies to diverge from the standard three-movement form. Like Vincent Persichetti's masterpieces from the 1950s, Mennin's Seventh comprises a single movement subdivided into five sections, achieving a maximum of integration and continuity. (However, the expressive aims of the two composers share little in common.) Though far from being a serial work, the symphony is based on a twelve-note theme, stated solemnly at the beginning, and roughly shaped to outline a symmetrical wedge-like sequence of expanding, then contracting, intervals. As in the Piano Sonata, tonal centers are quite remote, and the level of harmonic dissonance has increased considerably. In place of a simple alternation between fast movements based on frenzied counterpoint and slow movements of solemn, long-breathed, polyphonic lyricism (although they are not absent either), passages of different character appear. And, in addition to Mennin's familiar types of gestures, some new shapes appear—especially an upward-thrusting gesture to which Mennin returned in several of his remaining works. The symphony is subtitled "Variation-Symphony." But rather than a series of consecutive variations, each of its five sections has its own character while pursuing a free development of motivic fragments derived from the basic theme, underscoring the essential fluidity of Mennin's means of symphonic articulation. This material is elaborated continuously, with a focused concentration that never flags for a moment. The five connected sections achieve unprecedented expressive intensity and conceptual unity, despite their starkly contrasting characters. Mennin himself commented about this symphony, "In my work there has always been some element of violence and the element of contrast. Here they come out with a vengeance."[110]

The first section, *Adagio*, is largely expository. The main theme is introduced solemnly, then gradually fragmented into shorter motifs, conveying a sense of breathless anticipation, and building to short climactic outbursts. There is a sudden return to sober contemplation, as motivic fragments are slowly developed contrapuntally. The tempo quickens via shorter note-values, while the tension increases gradually. A motif that will soon assume considerable importance—the upward-thrusting gesture noted above, beginning with a triplet—is introduced, the energy recedes, and the second section is anticipated softly. This section, *Allegro*, is a wildly explosive *scherzo* dominated by the upward-thrusting figure. Motivic fragments are developed through perpetual-motion running lines in the strings, punctuated by hard-bitten fragments in the other sections, developed in vigorous counterpoint. The third section, *Andante*, is much calmer, as the strings, in alternation with woodwinds, unfold a solemn lyricism. However, the calm mood is strained by several passages that threaten to erupt in irate agitation, before the section recedes peacefully. The fourth section, *Moderato*, suggests a *passacaglia*, as the motivic material is developed over solemn, stately reiterations of the main theme in the lower strings. This section too builds in intensity and agitation, leading directly into the final section, *Allegro vivace*. Beginning with an edgy restlessness, this section pulls together most of the motivic fragments that have been heard previously into multiple levels of development. The intensity mounts as the development builds with an almost ecstatic escalation of contrapuntal complexity, until the symphony ends with stern finality on an open fifth—the first of Mennin's symphonies to shun a triumphant major-triad conclusion.

After the Cleveland premiere of Mennin's Seventh Symphony, Szell and his orchestra took the work on tour, presenting it to New York audiences in February 1964. The New York premiere was at best a mixed success with the local critics. William Bender was one of the more sympathetic, finding the work to be "very much of the moderate school of contemporary composition peopled by William Schuman and Paul Creston, as well as Mr. Mennin. It eschews the devices of the avant-garde but shuns much of the past, and it has muscle and bustle but not much genuine emotion. It offers dark, murky scoring (brilliantly achieved) for power, and lonely discord for feeling. It is a virtuoso score that bends the orchestra to its fullest arch."[111]

Ross Parmenter noted that the symphony was "clearly . . . a work Mr. Szell believes in," which he gleaned from "the conviction with which he led it" but also from the number of performances of the work the conductor had programmed during that season. But Parmenter's own reaction was ambivalent:

It began very promisingly, with the dark strings droning in mysterious quiet. Then suddenly the high strings are heard above the continuing drone. Other instruments come in. There are layers and layers of sound and a climax is reached. Then one choir was heard in beautiful unison outcries, while another responded poignantly. One got the sense of wave after wave of increasingly intense sound. But at a certain point this listener's attention began to falter. Though there were contrasts of storm and calm, the texture began to seem uniformly thick. The stops and starts didn't always lead to development. And although the final climax was properly larger than all the others, there seemed to be too many along the way.[112]

Two months after the New York premiere, Szell brought the work back again, this time with the New York Philharmonic. In reviewing the performance, Harold Schonberg, like many critics during the late 1950s and 1960s, acknowledged Mennin's craftsmanship but seemed to misunderstand the work's expressive content, commenting on irrelevancies and decrying the absence of qualities alien to its intent.

In days of old it would have been called "cyclic." Material drawn from the initial statement makes up the substance of the work [subtitled "Variation-Symphony"]. But these variations have nothing to do with old-fashioned variations. The variation comes from transmutation of the initial theme rather than from a varied development of the theme proper. That theme is interesting. Its first 12 notes are equivalent to a tone row. But Mr. Mennin, who does not write 12-tone music, added two more notes to his theme. Could he have been kidding the dodecaphonists? Anyway, the symphony is brisk, busy, energetic, brilliantly scored and even exuberant. At basis, it lacks melodic quality, however. Melodies are present, and Mr. Mennin would probably call the slow section one long melody. But just because a long theme goes up and down does not necessarily make it melodically inventive. Thus, at the end, one could respond to the athletic qualities of the writing and to its workmanship, and to Mr. Szell's superior conducting; but one was not especially moved."[113]

Attending the same performance, John Gruen expressed his dissatisfaction even more pointedly, describing the work as "written along fairly conventional lines, with dense harmonic progressions, propelled by uninspired thematic material that inevitably finds its resolutions in deafening crescendos. The one-movement Symphony received a highly polished performance by the Philharmonic, with Mr. Szell attending to its every phrase with the greatest of care. It might be noted here that the audience gave it a decidedly luke-warm reception."[114]

The most sympathetic—and prescient—of these early reactions was that of Jay S. Harrison, who noted that the work's "whole structure derives from a series of germinal motives which are expanded to create the work's form and design. The awesome opening phrase, for example, serves as the basis for all kinds of thematic derivations which pushes the piece ahead and keeps it spinning like a huge, motorized top. Indeed, the Symphony, in my view, is a bit too busy for its own good." Here Harrison identifies what the other critics may have experienced but perhaps lacked the candor to acknowledge explicitly:

> So many things happen at the same time that tension mounts continually and the ear has no point of release. Further, it is an angry work full of tumultuous climaxes which burst upon the hearing. But there is passion to it always and a sense of grandeur that cannot be denied. Harmonically, it is a mixture of the diatonic and chromatic and is polytonal, though it never loses its sense of key or direction. Instrumentally it leans toward grayness, for all of its frenetic activity tends to neutralize one orchestral line as opposed to another. And yet it is a major work despite its density. There is drama to it and heroism. It is a big statement of a big theme. The Symphony is certainly worthy of a place in the repertory, a place, I venture, it will soon find. And that will be to the advantage of us all.[115]

Mennin's Symphony No. 7 was recorded in 1967 and released on LP the following year in a meticulous but somewhat restrained rendition by the Chicago Symphony Orchestra, conducted by Jean Martinon. However, that recording was accorded remarkably little attention among the reviewing media and was soon deleted from the active catalog. However, it was reissued in 1976 with new and far more detailed, probing program notes by Harvey Philips as part of New World Records' original Recorded Anthology of American Music series. Then, in 1980, CRI reissued the same recording, coupling it on an LP together with John Ogdon's by-then-deleted recording of the Piano Concerto. In 1997, these two works were joined by the original New York Philharmonic recording of Mennin's Symphony No. 3 for release on compact disc.

The second recording of Mennin's Seventh received even less attention in the American press than did the Chicago LP: In 1982 the Soviet record company Melodiya released an LP of the work taken from a live performance featuring the Ukrainian State Symphony Orchestra, conducted by Pavel Kogan (son of violinist Leonid and nephew of pianist Emil Gilels). This is a noteworthy recording, if only for the fact that the work is one of the few American symphonies ever to be recorded by a Soviet orchestra. But beyond that, the Ukrainians attack the music with such intense conviction that the cataclysmic spirit of the work comes through with great force, despite some missed notes and ragged ensemble playing.

In 1996 a third recording of the symphony appeared, this time played by the Seattle Symphony conducted by Gerard Schwarz, as part of his ambitious survey of American orchestral music. Schwarz generally follows the approach taken by Martinon—sober, thin-lipped, and tightly controlled. However, no performance yet released on recording can match the precision and explosive power that George Szell brought to the work in his performances with both the Cleveland Orchestra and the New York Philharmonic, as can be verified by air-checks of those readings.

As has been already observed, the passage of time has brought a more favorable perspective to Mennin's works from the mid 1950s on, than they were accorded initially—at least among those few commentators familiar with the music. Clearly some reconsideration had taken place by the late 1990s when a number of Mennin recordings were issued. Reviewing the Schwarz/Seattle recording, Steven Schwartz offered some informal, chatty comments that are relevant enough to warrant quoting at some length:

> I remember very well the Cleveland premiere, Szell conducting. In those heady days of American culture, stations actually broadcast concerts locally on a regular basis as a civic service, and I heard the work with a high-school buddy over my brand-new FM radio in fabulous monaural sound. It struck me then as somewhere on the furthest shore of Modernism . . . . Even today, after the intricacies of Boulez and Carter and decades of familiarity with the LP of the Chicago [performance] led by Martinon, the symphony doesn't rate as easy listening. Mennin subtitled the work "Variation-Symphony," which immediately sets up certain expectations in the listener's mind. Forget them. Mennin doesn't write variations or even vary the basic cell so much as dips into it to riff on its pieces-parts. The argument is swift and concentrated, the basic motive is long and chromatically complex . . . and Mennin plays nasty games with it, including displacing octaves and turning shapes upside-down and backwards. Mennin refused to provide an analysis, insisting that the listener simply follow the rhetorical structure. If you want to know how Mennin put the symphony together, you really do need a score, sharp pencil, and lots of paper. Just listen: Mennin gave good advice, since even here, the listener has a tough—though ultimately rewarding—row to hoe. . . . Compared to this, the third symphony's an exuberant, straight ahead jog around the park. Whether the source of the commission influenced Mennin or he had moved to this point on his own, I can't say. Whatever, Mennin's music had darkened and, in my opinion, deepened. He had left a successful language behind by this kind of hard exploration, essentially a change from a modal idiom to a chromatic one. . . . Mennin . . . even manages to retain affinities with his younger self, particularly in matters of rhythmic contrapuntal contrast and the magnificent, speedball finale.[116]

Reviewing the same recording of the Seventh, David Hall wrote, "Mennin's command of structure and expressive content is absolute"[117]; Karl Miller noted that the Symphony No. 7 "in the opinion of many, including myself, is one of the finest essays in symphonic form written in the 20th century"[118]; and James H. North characterized the work as "a blockbuster of near-Beethovenian energy and eloquence," adding that it "is one of my candidates for The Great American Symphony."[119] Neil Butterworth felt that the work "represents the peak of [Mennin's] symphonic achievement, a closely argued work of massive integrity. It can rank among the finest of the American symphonic tradition this century."[120] I concur with the views expressed by Hall, Miller, North, and Butterworth: Not only is the Seventh Mennin's greatest symphony, but it stands among the finest American works in the genre, along with Piston's No. 7, Persichetti's No. 5, and Flagello's No. 1.

Mennin's next work was an especially significant one, for a number of reasons: One is that it was the composer's first and only programmatic work since *The Christmas Story*, which he had composed twenty years earlier. Second, it is the lengthiest (approximately forty minutes in duration), largest in scale, and, in many ways, most ambitious work in his entire output. *Cantata de Virtute, "The Pied Piper of Hamelin,"* was commissioned by the Cincinnati May Festival for performance in 1969. The May Festival has been a major cultural event of the American Midwest since it was inaugurated in 1873. The annual festival is dedicated to the presentation of major works for chorus and orchestra, and draws a large audience from the Cincinnati community, while attracting visitors from the surrounding region as well.

The idea of basing such a work on the venerable children's tale came from conductor Max Rudolf. Mennin recounted the way Rudolf's idea of a work based on The Pied Piper took shape in his mind:

> Like most persons, I had usually thought of it as a rather typical pleasant fairy tale for children. I re-read *The Pied Piper* for the first time since childhood and found that in fact it was an austere medieval morality tale. My interest grew, and last summer I found and read earlier source material from which Robert Browning had based his poetic text. This proved rewarding, for as inevitably happens when one goes to the source, one finds variations and nuances which were not part of subsequent adaptations. As time passed, various ideas about using *The Pied Piper* as the basis for a major work began fermenting in my mind until I realized that the medieval subject matter was pertinent to modern problems and pressures. Further thought also convinced me that the text of *The Pied Piper* alone would not be sufficient for the broad-scaled conception that had already been developing subconsciously. This led me to examine other materials which might support the concept I had formed, with the result that I have introduced the Latin text of Psalm 117, two Thirteen Century poems which elaborate the basic conception, and an adaptation of the Missa pro Defunctis. The work is titled CANTATA DE VIRTUTE—a cantata about morality, using the word morality in its broadest sense and meaning. The music is clearly dramatic and,

when the conception demands, theatrical. The work includes sections in which approximate notation had to be devised to achieve the proper crowd effects. Finally, in order to create a total context, several additions to and extensions of the textural material have been made.[121]

Based chiefly on the well-known poem by Robert Browning, *Cantata de Virtute* is scored for narrator, tenor and baritone soloists, children's chorus, mixed choir, and symphony orchestra. The work had its first performance as planned, in May 1969, under the direction of Max Rudolf. The narrator was Cyril Ritchard, the tenor Richard Lewis, and the baritone Ara Berberian. An audience numbering some 3,700 people attended the premiere.

Far from being a "work for children," as Mennin's program notes indicate, *Cantata de Virtute* is a brutal morality tale, recounting a town's failure to honor its obligation to a sorcerer of sorts, who delivered it from a plague, and the vengeance wreaked by that sorcerer on the townspeople in retribution for their failure to honor their agreement with him. The musical language used by Mennin in this work is the same atonal, highly dissonant language found in his recently preceding works, such as the Piano Sonata and the Symphony No. 7. However, despite the severity of its musical language, there is a recurrent motif that accompanies the words "The Pied Piper of Hamelin" that serves as an eerie thematic anchor and faintly suggests a B-flat major harmony. Also, the work ends unambiguously in E-flat major, in praise of God and the triumph of Justice. However, consistent with the body of Mennin's work, the cantata maintains a grim intensity throughout, treating the Piper's ruthless revenge as fair redress for the injustice visited upon him.

Cantata de Virtute must have come as quite a shock to its initial audience, who hadn't known what to expect. Their bewilderment was evident in the verdict of one local critic, who found the work "disappointing." As he heard it, the cantata "has one very big problem from the word 'Go'—unremitting thunder, produced by perpetual percussion. . . . What a splendid opportunity for a composer to reveal a witty melodic line or clever turn of phrase! . . . [B]ut all Mennin did was to compound din with din, and throw in one kitchen sink after another." (Of course, "witty melodic lines" and "clever turns of phrase" had nothing to do with Mennin's conception, nor with his aesthetics in general.) Finally, the critic urged that composers for future commissions be selected carefully, so as to avoid another "steam-rollered mish-mash by a 'big-name' composer."[122] On the other hand, Eleanor Bell found in the work "unfailing imagination. There are no dull stretches, no labored patches. Things move logically from here to there in the most musically satisfying way."[123] Perhaps the most thoughtful comment came from Betty Dietz Krebs, who wrote,

Though he has employed twelve-note motives, the piece is extremely listen-able. A mood-setting if sometimes thickly scored overture treats the clamoring voices as part of the orchestral textures, and out of it evolves a moving Miserere, a children's song of desolation which voices the desperation of the rat-ridden Hamelin. Brief arias for the Mayor and the Piper advance the drama, and the Laudate Dominum with which the combined chorus of adults and children re-joices over the drowning of the rats is a remarkably effective hymn of praise. Perhaps, though, the medieval Song of May which takes the unsuspecting chil-dren merrily into the caverns of the mountainside is one of the highlights of the work. Innocent, beguiling, it is overlaid with a strangely Gothic kind of horror. With it Mennin has achieved stunning results. And the skillful use of the Latin texts, some of them from the Requiem mass, further heightens the drama of his setting of the medieval morality legend.[124]

She adds, however, that the "audience reaction was sharply divided on this version of the Pied Piper story—some openly resented the elimination of the 'happily ever after' ending."

The next production of Mennin's *Cantata de Virtute, "The Pied Piper of Hamelin"* took place in Oakland, California, in February 1972. Harold Farberman conducted, and the narrator was linguistics professor and, later, controversial U.S. senator S. I. Hayakawa. Georganne Mennin recalled how Hayakawa recited the lines of Browning's poem with a droll emphasis on just those "clever turns of phrase" missed by the Cincinnati critic quoted above, in senseless contrast to the character of the music, with disastrous results.[125] There have been no further performances of the work since that time.

In 1970 Mennin completed an orchestral work of approximately fifteen minutes' duration entitled *Sinfonia*, not to be confused with the *Sinfonia* for chamber orchestra of 1947. In many ways, this work was unlike anything Mennin had composed previously, representing a distinct shift into a musi-cal language of atonality, of sound masses, a language largely without clear metrical definition or conventional counterpoint. But if its musical language was relatively new to Mennin, what was not new was the expressive content: In two sections—the first slow, the second fast—the *Sinfonia* opened with a dark, somber soundscape, seething with ominous portents; the second section unleashed an explosion of violence, while maintaining a degree of tension that seemed to press forward toward some hypothetical breaking point.

Sinfonia was introduced in Minneapolis in February 1971 by the Min-nesota Orchestra, conducted by Stanislaw Skrowaczewski. The following month, Skrowaczewski presented the work to New York audiences, with a performance by the New York Philharmonic. Harriett Johnson found it "fas-cinating music in its way" and evocative of "contemporary conflict and vio-lence," and even detected speculation "about the end of the world."[126] Harold

Schonberg, maintaining his customary pose of unflappability, as if nothing could take him by surprise, commented absurdly that Mennin's "lean, somewhat William Schumanesque style has not changed much through the years," and felt that the work "looks back rather than forward." While conceding that "it is a fine work of its kind" and "has that lively resilient sound characteristic of the composer at his best," he added, "There is no deep message to the music; it is not that kind of piece. What it does is produce attractive sounds in a well-organized manner."[127]

However, Mennin must have felt that *Sinfonia* warranted expansion. Withdrawing the work, he incorporated it into a much larger conception, its two sections becoming the first and fourth movements respectively of his Symphony No. 8.

Mennin completed his Symphony No. 8 in 1973. The work is unusual among the composer's symphonies in comprising four, rather than three, movements; also, not since No. 4 had he articulated an extramusical stimulus—in this case, four Biblical references. In describing the work, Mennin wrote that

> the thrust of the Eighth Symphony has a diversity and contrast of musical ideas and of moods, texture, and instrumental relationships, not only between movements, but also within them. The musical vocabulary itself has expanded considerably with certain new dramatic and tone-configuration elements. Each of the four movements was stimulated emotionally by Biblical texts. These emotional-musical reactions are not programmatic in nature. On the contrary, each movement is a personal musical response that unfolds along purely musical lines. The texts allied to each of the movements are:
>
> I.   In the beginning . . . Genesis (*In principio* . . .)
> II. Day of wrath . . . Zephaniah (*Dies Irae* . . .)
> III. Out of the Depths . . . Psalm 130 (*De Profundis Clamavi* . . .)
> IV. Praise ye the Lord . . . Psalm 150 (*Laudate Dominum* . . .)[128]

The first movement evokes a sense of stasis. Its rubric, *In principio*, contributes to its evocation of a barren landscape from before the dawn of time. In this movement, the gradual compression of polyphony, first hinted at in the 1960s, has finally led to the "verticalization" of linear motifs into seething, cluster-like chordal structures—the sound-mass technique associated with Eastern European composers of the time, such as Ligeti and Lutoslawski— orchestrated with uncharacteristic attention to sonority. In the second movement, *Dies irae*, characteristically Menninian motivic fragments swirl wildly in frantic instrumental byplay, as plentiful use of percussion contributes to explosive eruptions. The third movement, *De profundis clamavi*, is characteristic of the composer in its focus on somber linear polyphony, as long melodic lines unfold with an icy beauty, but here devoid of the comfort provided by tonal resolution. The fourth movement conveys a tremendous sense of agitation, its unremitting tension and explosions of violence seemingly at odds with its rubric, *Laudate Dominum*. Not until its final seconds does the work achieve a sense of affirmation, through a most unexpected resolution in F major.

This work—and some of those that followed—raised questions, a number of which were posed at the time of the symphony's premiere by the New York Philharmonic, under the direction of Daniel Barenboim, in November 1974. Many listeners who had exalted Mennin as one of the foremost proponents of traditional compositional values and techniques, and held him in high esteem for his imperviousness to the lure of fashion, wondered whether he had "sold out" to the avant-garde and abandoned those principles, so eloquently articulated, to which he had held steadfast for so long. Yet others (e.g., Harold Schonberg) seemed to hear no stylistic change at all. Others questioned whether the music—especially the fourth movement—bore any discernable expressive correspondence to the Biblical texts supposedly associated with it. And what about that F-major finish: What was the purpose of ending a virtually atonal work with a major triad? Was it effective or just incongruous? Was it a vestigial mannerism or a deliberate statement of some sort? (These same questions arose with regard to William Schuman's similar propensity for concluding even atonal works with major triads.) It is certainly illuminating to compare Mennin's two extramusically inspired symphonies— the Eighth and the Fourth, which had been based on the composer's own poetico-philosophical text. One cannot fail to note the way small, incremental modifications of his musical language as he progressed from one work to the next resulted over the course of twenty-five years in a considerable stylistic metamorphosis. There is no question but that Mennin was continuing to seek and discover new ways of refining and developing his musical language so as to further intensify its expressive impact within the aesthetic framework he had followed throughout his career.

Following the premiere of the Symphony No. 8, Harold Schonberg began his perplexing and remarkably patronizing review by noting the performance as an evocation of "nostalgia." He then went on to describe the work as "a look back to the nineteen-thirties and nineteen-forties. That was when Mr. Mennin's style was formed," adding that "he has never departed far from it." He characterized the work as representing the "busy-busy style of the prewar international school." He then conceded that "Mr. Mennin is, after all, an old pro, and he has achieved some brilliant sounds. . . . And he has put everything together neatly and precisely. Where he fails to convince is in the quality of the materials. Everything sounds a little secondhand; the symphony does not really say very much."[129] It is unlikely that many who attended the performance found Schonberg's comments to bear any relationship to their own listening experiences. The comments of Harriett Johnson, on the other hand, though somewhat less favorable, described her listening experience in a manner far more direct and, perhaps, more honest: "Mennin . . . has become obsessed with sonority at the expense of ideas. . . . Mennin's work isn't aimless. He is an expert craftsman and there is distinct shape in every movement. . . . [T]he most appealing quality of the symphony is its elemental feeling. . . . To me the effect is often even more primitive as if primeval urges are having an outlet through the score. The final 'Allegro vivace' to me doesn't praise the Lord or express joy. Instead, the music is loud, dissonant, unrelenting and ultimately bombastic."[130] Both critics, however, commented that the work was enthusiastically received by the audience.

In 1989 Mennin's Symphony No. 8 was released on an all-Mennin compact disc along with the Symphony No. 9, in brilliant performances featuring the Columbus Symphony Orchestra under the direction of Christian Badea. As has been noted, the passage of years resulted in a shift of perspective in the way Mennin's music was received by critics and commentators. Musicologist Edith Borroff began her review with an apt description of context, before noting that these two symphonies "present an expansion of orchestral language in both internal and external facets—in both idea and the statement of idea, form, and orchestration. Mennin was *maestro assoluto* of orchestral writing at a time when the radicals were taking their business elsewhere. What is so electrifying in these works is: one, that the many new sounds devolve upon meaning and are not mere 'effects' (though strikingly effective); and two, that the works are not just "rhythmic" but *live* in rhythm and texture, which are primary and organic."[131] John Canarina found the recording to be a "splendid release. . . . Gone . . . are the influences of Hindemith, Vaughan Williams and Schuman, and if the slow cello and bass passages in the opening moments recall Bartók, so be it. The important thing is that Mennin was able to forge these influences into a personal style that, in these symphonies especially, combines energy and propulsion with an austere lyricism of great intensity."[132] Bret Johnson observed eloquently that the Eighth Symphony

> shows the composer in somber and austere mood: with its Biblical headings to each movement, the music reveals anguish and pessimism, articulated by dark textures and brooding sonorities. The long expressive passages one associates with Mennin are there, but convulsive *sforzandi* and compressed harmonies interspersed with bleak string monodies suggest similarities of demeanour with Shostakovich's war symphonies. . . . More than any other piece by Mennin, this is a powerful *cri de coeur* in which the composer bares his soul, and his fears and doubts, through a medium of boldly conceived musical language. Only in the final bars does the light of major tonality shine through the clouded skies.[133]

Mennin's next work was commissioned by the Chamber Music Society of Lincoln Center. Entitled *Voices*, it proved to be the most perplexing and controversial work of his career. Completed early in 1976, the work comprises settings of four poems, clearly chosen with great deliberation, scored for soprano and chamber ensemble. Further pursuing an expanded role for percussion instruments, Mennin called for harpsichord, harp, piano, pitched percussion (tubular bells, glockenspiel, vibraphone, antique cymbals, and timpani) and unpitched percussion (bell-plates, suspended cymbals, tam-tams, bongos, tom-toms, and timbales).

In his own commentary, Mennin explained that his intention was

> to conceive musical settings that would bring out and strengthen the mystical and spiritual qualities of the metaphysical images. The basic thrust of these poems is in creating new worlds to see, and new visions that seem invisible to the prosaic eye.
>
> I have long admired the small group of American poets (among them Dickinson, Melville, Whitman, Thoreau and Emerson) who were influenced by the transcendental movement originating in New England. . . . These poets explored with their sharp intelligence their own spiritual potentialities. They made abundantly clear that the human mind and heart is not only able to crawl, but is also capable of soaring. From the beginning it has been the domain of the arts to search out the free spaces of the imagination. The large body of poetic work generally considered as having metaphysical elements provides some of the keenest insights into the realm of creativity.
>
> The choice of poems for this work was subject to the musical images they evoked from the composer. There is a common thread in each of them that made these particular choices inevitable. The instrumentation was chosen for its possibilities to enhance the vocal imagery and varies from poem to poem.[134]

As has been illustrated throughout this chapter, on those few occasions when Mennin turned to poetic texts or other extramusical subject matter, they were always carefully chosen to reverberate with or reinforce the stern cosmic vision and grim view of humanity that seemed to underlie all his work, including those pieces that were, on the surface, purely abstract. His words of praise for the writers touched by Transcendentalism and their visions of the unfettered soaring of the human spirit, though exalted and unexceptionable, ring slightly hollow from this composer. The poems he selected are: "Smoke," by Henry David Thoreau; "Lone Founts," by Herman Melville; "When I Heard the Learn'd Astronomer," by Walt Whitman; and "Much Madness Is Divinest Sense," by Emily Dickinson. The first poem, with its reference to Icarus, certainly illustrates the theme that Mennin articulated. But the three other poems seem to touch upon themes that share more in common with some of the composer's other expressed beliefs than with the "common thread" he identified here. For example, the selection from Melville might be said to reinforce Mennin's statement, "Inevitably, with the passage of time, the revolutions of one generation become the symbols of reaction to the next. . . . Committed composers of integrity . . . write . . . from a sense of personal 'rightness' and avoid ever-changing fads by exploring their own convictions and finding their own way."[135] Whitman's poem might be paraphrased, "We have seen all varieties of musical descriptions, from lengthy, abstruse, and convoluted essays . . . to short and even incoherent statements that confuse complex and major achievements. . . . Long, descriptive procedures merely explain the mechanics of craft and are not of intrinsic value in themselves. . . . Works of true quality eventually affirm that they have been written by persons with creative images of their own. . . . It is the music that must have its own identity and individuality. The quality of directness serves this aim."[136] And Emily Dickinson's brief poem reminds us that "Those following the dictates or conceptions of others may do so unconsciously—for comfort, or self-protection, or from a need of conforming to the group or herd mentality. The price of true independence in the arts has always been a certain amount of discomfort in going it alone in order to retain one's personal integrity."[137]

In short, the collective message of the selected texts seems to reverberate with Mennin's oft-stated exaltation of courageous individuality maintained in the face of constant pressure to conform to transitory fads and fashions. And yet the musical composition he produced was perhaps the single work in his output most vulnerable to accusations of capitulation to such pressures. The four settings require the singer to render angular melismas and vocal lines characterized by wide leaps but notably lacking in tonal reference. The richly varied chamber ensemble provides a wealth of fragmentary instrumental color, but virtually no harmonic support, offering little justification for its presence, other than to advertise the availability of timbral resources whose actual contribution is minimal. The characters of the four individual settings show little variety beyond such obvious, superficial matters as tempo and instrumental color, while a number of novel or relatively unusual techniques make obligatory appearances (e.g., instrumentalists echoing the poetic lines sung by the soprano in disparate whispers). There is no indication as to why the selected texts—most of them a century old—require settings in such an abrasive musical language. Most distressing of all, taken as a whole, little about *Voices* deviates significantly from the sorts of vocal settings produced by dozens of other composers active during the mid 1970s.

The premiere of *Voices* took place in March 1976 at Lincoln Center's Alice Tully Hall. Frederica von Stade was the soprano soloist, and Gerard Schwarz conducted the ensemble. After the performance, members of the audience were heard voicing their astonishment that a composer of such strong principle could have succumbed so shamelessly to prevailing fashions. Donal Henahan acknowledged the work as "a departure from the Mennin works with which one is familiar. Although by most standards he would be considered a conservative composer, Mr. Mennin flirts here with some moderately advanced devices." He concludes his review with the half-heartedness that typically greeted the latest auspicious premiere: "In any event, an often evocative work by Mr. Mennin."[138]

Voices was followed two years later by another group of poetic settings. For this work Mennin returned to the writings of the nineteenth-century American poet Emily Dickinson, for whom he displayed a long-standing fondness. Not only had he selected one of her poems to include in *Voices*, but four settings of her poetry, for soprano and piano, are found among the works of his late teens, which he had subsequently disavowed. Mennin's fondness for Dickinson's poetry seems perhaps somewhat surprising: His love of "a big canvas," of grand themes and large statements, of tumultuous outbursts redolent of masculine power, would seem to be antithetical to the verbal parsimony and minute observations of mundane phenomena characteristic of the reclusive poet from New England. Perhaps it was her way of drawing intimations of the infinite from her intense focus on proximal details that appealed to him.

Mennin composed *Reflections of Emily* through a commission from the National Endowment for the Arts on behalf of the Newark Boys Chorus and its conductor Terence Shook. He dedicated the work to his wife, Georganne, scoring it for treble voices in three parts, accompanied by harp, piano, and percussion ensemble. Somewhat less than half an hour in duration, *Reflections* comprises seven sections. Mennin chose five of Dickinson's poems: "This is my letter to the world"; "'tis so much joy!"; "That I did always love"; "Read, sweet, how others strove"; and "Musicians wrestle everywhere." Following the first three settings is an extended interlude for solo harp, entitled "Cadenza Capricciosa," which is performable as an independent entity. The sixth section is an interlude for solo piano.

What is perhaps most remarkable is that *Reflections of Emily* represents the first instance in Mennin's output that deviates from what has been a consistent and unswerving path in the direction of greater harmonic dissonance, attenuated tonality, and ever-increasing expressive intensity. Following the largely atonal explosiveness of the Eighth Symphony and the unremittingly angular *Voices*, *Reflections of Emily* steps aside somewhat from this relentlessly linear trajectory. The work is not in any way "a step backward" in the direction of his earlier compositions, as much of it—the interludes for harp and piano, in particular—continues to explore the remotest regions of tonality, while other sections (e.g., "'Tis so much joy!") pursue such unconventional practices as alternating between phrases sung and phrases spoken in counterpoint. But *Reflections* is also leavened by passages of striking harmonic consonance (e.g., "That I did always love") and by others that achieve a viscerally felt rhythmic vitality (e.g., "Musicians wrestle everywhere"). The work is unified by a number of recurrent motifs, most noticeably and curiously (but not necessarily significantly) the D–Es–C–H motif used by Dmitri Shostakovich as an autobiographical code in a number of his compositions. This motif appears most prominently in the third, fourth, and sixth sections, although there is no indication that Mennin intended any reference to the Soviet composer.

The premier performance of *Reflections of Emily* took place at Lincoln Center's Alice Tully Hall in New York City, in January 1979. Terence Shook conducted the Newark Boys Chorus, with harpist Grace Paradise, pianist Barbara Chernichowski, and percussionist David Fein. Writing in the *New York Times*, Raymond Ericson described it as

> a sterling work, good enough to have made this listener want to hear it repeated immediately after its first performance. . . . The ambiguities in the Dickinson texts are tantalizing under any circumstances, but Mr. Mennin has given them an added dimension through his music. "This is my letter to the world" is set twice, the second time ending in a kind of anxious cry, after which the last line is echoed with quiet pleading. "'Tis so much joy!" is treated in a fast, breathless manner, with speech juxtaposed on singing, as if the emotion could not be contained in just one mode of expression.

Ericson speculates, not unreasonably, that perhaps the interlude for solo harp "is meant as a portrait of Dickinson as seen through her poetry. The workmanship is everywhere expert, as would be expected from a composer of Mr. Mennin's standing and experience. It was often reward enough to observe the skill with which the words were set and the vocal lines overlaid."[139]

In 1981 Mennin completed his Symphony No. 9, commissioned by the National Symphony Orchestra to mark its fiftieth anniversary. Mstislav Rostropovich conducted the orchestra in the work's first performance, at the Kennedy Center in Washington, D.C., in March 1981. Initially Mennin gave the work a subtitle, *"Sinfonia Capricciosa,"* but subsequently retracted it. Later program notes make no mention of a subtitle. The composer described the symphony as "dramatic." "The first movement is brooding, questioning, and then as elements coalesce, more clearly optimistic; the second movement contains elements of wistfulness and introspection; the third movement is in a different character . . . —severe rather than expansive, but generally self-confident, and at the end strongly affirmative."[140]Mennin's Ninth recalls elements of both the Seventh and Eighth Symphonies. As in the former work, the Ninth opens with a somber statement of the main motif in the lower strings—a wedge-shaped motif free of perceptible tonal center. Also prominent in the first movement, marked *Lento, non troppo*, is an upward-thrusting motif very similar to the main idea of the Seventh Symphony's second section. The overall impact of the movement is, initially, as Mennin notes, "brooding" but soon becomes more actively agitated, with rapidly swirling figurations in the strings and woodwinds, before ending solemnly, as it began. The work—the first movement in particular—resembles the Eighth Symphony in its use of the sound-mass technique and in many passages without perceptible meter. The Ninth, however, exhibits more sustained use of linear counterpoint than did its predecessor. The second movement, *Adagio arioso*, is remarkable for its unabashed lyricism, especially within the context of the two surrounding movements. Although its tonality is quite attenuated, the long, flowing melodic line, supported in homophonic relief by a throbbing chordal accompaniment, creates the impression of a heartfelt elegy. Though it is probably the most "personal" or "intimate"-sounding music Mennin ever wrote, its tone of profound grief borne with dignity is consistent with his aesthetic voice. (It was most appropriate that this movement was selected for performance at the composer's memorial service in 1983.) In the brief third movement, *Presto tumultuoso*, shrieking brass and explosive percussion unleash a paroxysm of wild, frenzied violence. Although the level of harmonic dissonance is quite severe throughout the work, once again the symphony comes to a landing on a unison tonic.

The premiere of Mennin's Symphony No. 9 was reviewed by Nicholas Kenyon. He noted its many similarities to the composer's previous symphony, while finding it to be

> less symphonic in character. . . . There is little in the first movement to suggest the organized conflicts and resolutions of symphonic form; instead, there's pleasantly contrasted material, which is cogently reordered and developed to produce a climax of considerable power (a chorale-like theme on trombones and basses, with babbling figuration whirling around it). The slow movement is a Brucknerian essay in intense melody for the violins and violas singing over divided cellos and then over horns; trilling flutes and dark clarinets give an original color to the sound. The final [movement] uses motifs derived from the first movement; it imitates some of Stravinsky's rhythmic methods to produce a moto perpetuo punctuated by jagged chords and jubilant acclamations in winds and brass.[141]

Mennin's Ninth Symphony was recorded in 1989 by the Columbus Symphony Orchestra conducted by Christian Badea, on the same compact disc that included the Eighth Symphony. In her review of the recording, Edith Borroff described the Ninth as "much like its predecessor in its mainsprings: the first movement . . . begins and ends with contained archings in the low register, with big brass and shimmering strings in the middle; the second . . . presents a contrasting high register with a long-limned violin melody as *primus inter pares*; the finale, *Presto tumultuoso* is everything that directive implies, but it never loses power or dignity."[142] John Canarina found the Ninth to be "an unusually angry score, even for Mennin, especially in its . . . finale. Both symphonies are striking, even stunning works. . . . Mennin was not a great melodist . . . , but he was a great sustainer of moods, such as the elegiac tone of the Ninth Symphony's *Adagio arioso*."[143] Bret Johnson felt that the work had "less emotional intensity than the Eighth but, if the mood of the Eighth is one of anguish and despair, that of the Ninth is one of sad resignation, especially in the slow movement. It also exhibits extensive use of tuned percussion and bells to lend more colour and emphasis, especially in the short last movement, a *moto ostinato* in characteristically energetic Mennin style."[144]

With a commission from the New York Philharmonic, Mennin began working on what was to be his final work, a concerto for flute and orchestra. Sometime in 1982, the composer received a terminal diagnosis of pancreatic cancer. Mennin was determined to complete the work in time for its scheduled premiere during the orchestra's 1983–1984 season. Keeping his illness to himself, he continued to fulfill his duties at Juilliard while working feverishly on the Flute Concerto, finishing the work in February 1983. Mennin died four months later. Although the plan was for the orchestra's solo flutist, Julius Baker, to present the premiere, Baker decided to retire that year, leaving the concerto to his successor, Jeanne Baxtresser. But she suffered a hand injury, forcing a postponement of the work's premiere until May 1988, when the composer would have turned sixty-five. The New York Philharmonic was conducted by Zubin Mehta.

There is, of course, a certain unintended—and not terribly significant—symmetry in the fact that Mennin's compositional career both began and ended with concerted works featuring the flute. More germane is a consideration of the Flute Concerto in light of his other two mature concertos: those featuring cello (1956) and piano (1957). Unlike the conventional three-movement structure of the two earlier works, the Flute Concerto comprises a single movement of some twenty-two minutes' duration. But this single movement embraces many sections in contrasting tempos. Along the lines of his most recent works, the Concerto introduces a variety of percussion instruments that suggest through tone-cluster sonorities most of the work's primary motivic material, soon elaborated by the solo flute. Percussion instruments are featured prominently throughout the work. Though the moment-to-moment impact of the concerto is largely atonal, and the har-

monic language extremely dissonant, an overall tonality of D minor is reaffirmed throughout, most clearly by a somber motif that recurs frequently
in the lower instruments. Utilizing the expanded language characteristic
of his last half-dozen works, the Flute Concerto nevertheless continues to
pursue Mennin's characteristic gestures and distinctive expressive concerns, as it alternates between lugubrious moments of deep introspection
and driving passages of rapid solo passagework in breathtaking alternation
with the orchestra, and often in complex networks of counterpoint. As in
the two concertos from the 1950s, the soloist is given some respite during
ritornello-like interludes that unleash violent orchestral tirades. Notable
also is an elaborate and enormously difficult developmental cadenza, as
well as a contrasting passage in which minor triads, not employed tonally,
are used to accompany the improvisatory questioning of the flute, achieving
a strikingly unearthly beauty somewhat reminiscent of Vaughan Williams
in his masterpiece *Flos Campi*. Quite uncharacteristic of the composer is
his avoidance of the customary triumphant peroration in favor of an understated, almost prosaic, conclusion.

When encountering a work written by a composer in the throes of a terminal illness, it is difficult to prevent those circumstances from influencing
one's impression of that work, although the persona that emerges from Peter
Mennin's many public statements suggests that he would have strongly preferred that his composition be understood apart from any sentimental biographical considerations. Nevertheless, in considering the concerto a number
of questions seem unavoidable: Had he not been facing an immutable deadline, might he have altered the course of the concerto in some way—"second
thoughts" that fate had not permitted? More specifically, is the flute the ideal
medium for the expressive intentions of this work? Again, as in his other late
works, Mennin seemed to be exploring the application of some of his recent
compositional ideas to a variety of media, rather than continuing the relentless push toward greater expressive intensity.

The premiere of Mennin's Flute Concerto was reviewed in the *New York
Times* by Michael Kimmelman, who, perhaps in the spirit of the composer's
avoidance of sentiment, commented that the work "swerves between emotional extremes, with the soloist . . . leading quieter, wispier sections and
the orchestra occasionally drowning her out with crashing, brassy waves
of sound. Mr. Mennin's command of coloristic detail and his penchant for
sweeping, neo-Romantic statements emerged strongly. His editorial judgment did not; the concerto might profitably have been cut."[145] On the other
hand, Bret Johnson described the concerto as "magnificent . . . [Mennin's] supreme musical achievement."[146] The Flute Concerto has not been performed
since its premiere, nor has it been recorded.

CONCLUSION

Having kept his illness a secret from most of his colleagues, Peter Mennin's death at the age of sixty, on 17 June 1983, came as a shock to the music world. Always a useful barometer of one's perceived stature at the time of one's demise, the *New York Times* obituary, written by Bernard Holland, stated, "Mr. Mennin enjoyed a dual reputation—first as a composer of sophisticated, well-made compositions and then as an educator. He was a tall, elegant, reserved man, and in addition to exercising discipline and self-control in his own creative life, he was a tough and effective operator in the difficult, and often political, professional world of music." Most of the obituary concentrated on his contributions as president of Juilliard. In describing his music, Holland noted "its restless sense of tension, but also . . . its high degree of technical skill. In style, it adheres neither to the more conservative elements in 20th-century American music nor to the more advanced methods of the post-World War II period." Holland then continued with "what is probably a representative critical comment on his music,"[147] citing Harold Schonberg's fatuous reaction to the withdrawn *Sinfonia* of 1970, quoted earlier.

The Aspen Music Festival had planned to feature Mennin's works in honor of his sixtieth birthday, during the summer of 1983. Though it proved to be a memorial instead of a celebration, the series of concerts continued as planned. After the obligatory memorial services and pious acknowledgments had run their course, little of Mennin's music was played by the major orchestras. The 1988 premiere of his Flute Concerto drew little attention. As the first major performance of his music at Lincoln Center since his death, Benjamin Folkman's program notes offered a more extensive overview of the composer's career than usual and attempted to characterize his identity as a composer:

Mennin's distinctive musical style, fully formed almost from the beginning of his career, was at once cerebral and hard-driving. By his thirtieth year . . . . several critics had begun to refer to him habitually as "the American Hindemith." It was, however, primarily in his devotion to abstract formal balance and his frequent recourse to elaborate polyphonic passages, especially *fugatos*, that Mennin displayed kinship with the German master. In other respects, the emotional worlds of the two are dissimilar. Hindemith's frequent pastoral episodes, rendered Teutonically homey by a faintly lumbering rhythmic quality, have no analogue whatever in Mennin's work; on the other hand, the glacially slow, chorale-like string passages periodically found in Mennin's scores strike a rarefied note of introspective desolation that is not in Hindemith's gamut. Mennin's motor-rhythms, unlike Hindemith's, feature lively syncopations (albeit somewhat stereotyped) that stamp them as American, and are usually expressions of a frenetic, even merciless euphoria, conveying, as the composer himself observed, "an element of violence." Mennin's harmony, far more astringent than Hindemith's, is perhaps best described as post-tonal. Specific keys are rarely established, and then only through bass-note emphasis. Few unadorned triads are present; most chords are highly chromatic. However, strong dissonances continually resolve, in smooth stepwise fashion, to weaker dissonances (or to consonances) according to the traditional principles of voice-leading: there is no serial agenda. . . . [Mennin's] later works demonstrate continued experimentation and growth. The Seventh Symphony, for example, constitutes a provocative attempt to reconcile the symphonic and variation forms. The Eighth Symphony and the song-cycles of the 1970s display a new concentration on unusual coloristic effects, indicating that Mennin was fully abreast of the avant-garde repertory of these years, surehandedly employing those ultra-modern devices that suited his style while rejecting those that did not. The Flute Concerto clearly shows some of these latter coloristic preoccupations, particularly in its percussion writing.[148]

Folkman's characterization is fairly accurate, and a welcome attempt to address Mennin's overall compositional identity. However, the "American Hindemith" notion is something of a red herring, the only real similarity between the two being a shared propensity for contrapuntal "busyness." But seen in light of the larger import of both composers' bodies of work, this similarity is superficial, and Folkman expends too much effort in attempting to refute it. Furthermore, his description of Mennin's harmony is accurate only insofar as it refers to the minority of his works composed after 1960.

During the mid 1980s an important shift began to occur in the music world, along with the advent of the compact disc. A vast array of previously unrecorded repertoire began to appear in the new medium. Following this development came the Internet, which provided a forum for and linkage among enthusiasts who had previously pursued their specialized interests in isolation. This led to a divergence between those who followed the most celebrated composers, conductors, soloists, and ensembles in ever-more-redundant performances of a stale standard repertoire, and those who sought out unfamiliar repertoire on recordings that featured less well-known performers and were released by small, independent companies whose products were now no less accessible than those released by the major international conglomerates. Both these developments led the way toward a decentralization of musical opinion.

As has been implied throughout the course of this chapter, shortly after the arrival of the compact disc, a modest Mennin revival took place. The year 1989 saw the first recording of Mennin's early *Folk Overture*, along with his Symphonies Nos. 8 and 9, in performances by the Columbus Symphony Orchestra, conducted by Christian Badea. In 1996 came Gerard Schwarz and the Seattle Symphony's recording of the Symphonies Nos. 3 and 7, and *Con-*

certato, "Moby Dick." Two all-Mennin CDs appeared in 1997: one, a reissue of LP-era performances of the Symphonies Nos. 3 and 7, along with the Piano Concerto; the other, a new recording featuring Mennin's Symphonies Nos. 5 and 6, *Concertato, "Moby Dick,"* and the early *Fantasia* for String Orchestra, with David Alan Miller conducting the Albany Symphony Orchestra. And in 2003, the Louisville Orchestra's LP recordings of the Symphonies Nos. 5 and 6, and the Cello Concerto were reissued on compact disc. For a composer with an output of barely thirty works, these recordings offered a fairly substantial representation of Mennin's music, although a number of important works remain unrecorded at this writing.

Of the three composers discussed in this volume, Mennin has enjoyed the least widespread posthumous revival of interest in his work. Lacking the gregarious, high-profile persona of Schuman or the reputation as an endearing pedagogue like Persichetti, not to mention the latter's many enduring classics for wind band, Mennin, with his penchant for secrecy and privacy, and his refusal to engage in public self-promotion, has drifted to the periphery, his compositions largely unknown to all but a few enthusiasts.

But the informed and insightful commentaries of these enthusiasts, disseminated through new forums for sharing reactions to music, and coupled with the greater availability of Mennin's music on recordings, have encouraged the development of a new constituency of interested listeners. "For a major American symphonist whose music is relatively accessible, Peter Mennin has not had an easy time," wrote Jack Sullivan. Citing negative comments from earlier reviews, he continues, "It is hard to reconcile these grumblings with the eloquent, powerful music heard on this disc. . . . [T]he music itself, based on a dignified, constantly unfolding polyphony building toward intense climaxes, is very stirring. . . . I'll never forget a concert performance of [his Seventh Symphony] when I first moved to New York in the early 70s. The steely grandeur and frenzied excitement seemed like the city itself."[149]

Peter Mennin is one of the composers whose music was swept away by the post-war radical imperative, the movement which asserted an absolute change from Romanticism to the New Music. But changes in music are never absolute: the history of music is a choreography of slow, graceful change, in which a superconservative J.S. Bach can be given honor in our musical lives even by those who espouse unrelenting modernism in our own day. It takes time for the members of the vanguard to look back and appreciate the rainbow-scope of music from which a new style emerges. Perhaps that time has come; perhaps we are now ready for the excitement and the joy of savoring that scope.[150]

"Mennin's music shows extraordinary polish and craftsmanship, and follows an unusually straight evolutionary path from his diatonic/modal youth

right through to the more dissonant, violent idiom of his Ninth Symphony .
. . . What never changed, though, was his use of counterpoint to enliven his
musical textures and create an irresistible sense of momentum in both slow
and quick movements."[151] "Mennin was one of the most significant of the
postwar generation of American symphonists. . . . Most of his works are in
large-scale symphonic forms, and his concentrated, intense style derives power from his restless, driving energy. . . . His symphonies charted a pattern of
development always keenly anticipated by his admirers. As he progressed, his
music became ever more dramatic and rhetorical, perhaps reaching its apogee
in the explosive 7 and the dark and brooding 8."[152]

Despite the foregoing remarks by knowledgable specialists, Mennin's
music remains infrequently performed and little known, even among experienced professionals, while mainstream commentators continue to rehash
clichés inherited thirdhand. In October 2005, as part of its centennial celebration, the Juilliard School presented "A Tribute to Peter Mennin," in the form
of a concert devoted to his chamber music. Jeremy Eichler revealed the early
twenty-first-century mainstream view of Mennin and his generation in a review entitled "Honoring an Administrator Who Never Stopped Writing":

> [Mennin] grew up to join the hunt for the great American symphony, placing
> his own nine entries alongside those of composers like Roy Harris, Walter Pis-
> ton, David Diamond and William Schuman, his predecessor at Juilliard. That
> mid-century American symphonic tradition never bore the fruit its champions
> coveted, and it has not aged gracefully in the intervening years. Mennin's
> music is rarely performed these days, let alone given a program all its own.
> . . . [T]his is undeniably clean, solid music—sometimes elegant, always well
> constructed and rhythmically vital. Mennin's harmonic language remained
> conservative; he did not chase after the newest avant-garde techniques, or the
> older ones, for that matter."[153]

But perhaps most revealing are the program notes for that concert by David
Wright, which indicate the thoughtful, honest reaction of a mainstream voice
having come into direct, unmediated contact with the music itself. Wright
indicated that until this assignment he had had little actual familiarity with
Mennin's work. After immersing himself in the music in order to write about
it, he stated,

> I found, through his compositions, that Peter Mennin had one of the most dis-
> tinctive personalities in American concert music. To put it bluntly: Although
> he was known to students and colleagues as a man of great personal charm and
> grace, Peter Mennin composed like a bat out of hell. You can talk about the
> wild visions of Ruggles and Varèse, or about the big-sky sound of Harris and

Schuman, but for sheer propulsive force channeled through tightly-wound counterpoint, there is nothing like an allegro by Mennin. Even his slow movements, pretty as their melodies are, are intensely worked, almost impatient in their urge to get on with it. If you want to hear how a composer steeped in classical technique expresses the "on the go" spirit of America in the mid-20th century, Mennin's music does the job.[154]

NOTES

1. Peter Mennin, quoted in "Peter Mennin: The Composer Draws His Own Profile with Original Prose" (booklet distributed at memorial service at the Aspen Music Festival, August 1983).

2. Georganne Mennin, interviewed by Walter Simmons, 8 March 2006.

3. Mark Carrington, "For the Sake of Art: A Talk with Peter Mennin," *Symphony* (October/November 1983): 40.

4. Georganne Mennin, interviewed by Sharon Zane, 3 December 1992, Lincoln Center Oral History Project.

5. Carrington, "For the Sake of Art," 40.

6. Robert Evett, "Peter Mennin," in *International Cyclopedia of Music and Musicians*, 9th ed., ed. Robert Sabin (New York: Dodd, Mead, 1965), 1332.

7. Louis Biancolli, review, *New York World-Telegram*, 28 February 1947.

8. Walter Hendl, "The Music of Peter Mennin," *Juilliard Review* (Spring 1954): 25.

9. Peter Jona Korn, "The Symphony in America," in *The Symphony: Elgar to the Present Day*, ed. Robert Simpson (Baltimore, Md.: Penguin Books, 1967), 262.

10. "U.S. Composers in a Bright Era," *Life* (21 May 1956): 141–49.

11. G. Mennin, interviewed by Walter Simmons, 21 January 2010.

12. G. Mennin, interviewed by Sharon Zane.

13. Martin Mayer, "Are the Trying Times Just Beginning?" *New York Times*, 28 September 1969, 17ff.

14. G. Mennin, interviewed by Sharon Zane.

15. Harriett Johnson, "Juilliard Has New President," *New York Post*, 13 August 1962.

16. Andrea Olmstead, *Juilliard: A History* (Urbana: University of Illinois Press, 1999), 246.

17. Peter Mennin, "In Celebration of Quality," essay in program book accompanying Juilliard School and New York Philharmonic's first Celebration of Contemporary Music, March 1976, 7.

18. Olmstead, *Juilliard*, 264.

19. Joseph W. Polisi, *American Muse: The Life and Times of William Schuman* (New York: Amadeus Press, 2008), 309.

20. David Owens, "Composer Peter Mennin," *Christian Science Monitor* (29–30 July 1981).

21. Mayer, "Trying Times Just Beginning?"

22. Georganne Mennin, interviewed by Walter Simmons, 20 March 1984.

23. Carrington, "For the Sake of Art," 41.

24. G. Mennin, interviewed by Simmons, 20 March 1984.

25. P. Mennin, interviewed by Walter Simmons, 15 September 1982.

26. Vincent Persichetti, eulogy for Peter Mennin; Persichetti Archive at New York Public Library, JPB 90–77, Box 12, Folder 24.

27. Bernard Holland, "Peter Mennin, Juilliard President and Prolific Composer, Dies at 60," *New York Times*, 18 June 1983.

28. P. Mennin, quoted in Harvey Phillips, LP liner notes, New World NW-258 (1976), 4.

29. Program note, Cleveland Orchestra performance of Mennin's Symphony No. 7, Carnegie Hall, 17 February 1964, 14.

30. P. Mennin, interviewed by Walter Simmons, 15 September 1982.

31. P. Mennin, quoted in Harvey Phillips, LP Liner notes, 3–4.

32. Owens, "Composer Peter Mennin," 29 July 1981, 20.

33. Owens, "Composer Peter Mennin," 30 July 1981, 20.

34. Owens, "Composer Peter Mennin," 30 July 1981, 20.

35. Owens, "Composer Peter Mennin," 30 July 1981, 21.

36. Owens, "Composer Peter Mennin," 30 July 1981, 21.

37. Owens, "Composer Peter Mennin," 29 July 1981, 21.

38. Carrington, "For the Sake of Art," 82.

39. P. Mennin, quoted in Harvey Phillips, LP liner notes, 4.

40. P. Mennin, interviewed by Walter Simmons, 15 September 1982.

41. P. Mennin, quoted in David Wright, "A Tribute to Peter Mennin," program notes, Juilliard School (24 October 2005).

42. P. Mennin, quoted in David Wright, "A Tribute to Peter Mennin."

43. P. Mennin, quoted in Francis D. Perkins, review, *New York Herald Tribune*, 21 January 1946.

44. Olin Downes, review, *New York Times*, 28 February 1947.

45. Louis Biancolli, review, *New York World-Telegram*, 28 February 1947.

46. Richard Franko Goldman, review, *Musical Quarterly* (January 1949): 111–15.

47. Henry Cowell, review, *MLA Notes* (March 1949): 328.

48. Arthur Berger, review, *Saturday Review* (26 February 1955): 58–59.

49. David Hall, review, *Stereo Review* (May 1997): 99.

50. C. H., review, *New York Times*, 18 January 1948.

51. J.D.B., review, *New York Herald Tribune*, 19 January 1948.

52. Unsigned review, *New York Times*, 22 November 1947.

53. "No. 4," *Time* (28 March 1949).

54. P. Mennin, *Symphony No. 4, "The Cycle"* (New York: Carl Fischer, 1948).

55. Virgil Thomson, review, *New York Herald Tribune*, 19 March 1949.

56. Ivor Keys, review, *Music and Letters* (July 1949): 288.

57. Cecil Smith, review, *MLA Notes* (June 1949): 488.

58. Virgil Thomson, review, *New York Herald Tribune*, 19 March 1949.

59. Noel Straus, review, *New York Times*, 19 March 1949.

60. Cecil Smith, review, *MLA Notes* (June 1949): 487.

61. Cecil Smith, review, *MLA Notes* (June 1949): 488.

62. Cecil Smith, review, *MLA Notes* (June 1949): 488.

63. Ivor Keys, review, *Music and Letters* (July 1949): 288.

64. Robert Cummings, review, *Classical Net*, 1998, www.classical.net/music/recs/reviews/p/phx00128a.php (accessed 25 March 2010).

65. Francis D. Perkins, review, *New York Herald Tribune*, 29 March 1950.

66. Burrill Phillips, review, *MLA Notes* (September 1951): 750.

67. Wayne Richard Pierce, "An Orchestral Transcription of Peter Mennin's 'Five Piano Pieces' Based on a Study of His Early Works for Orchestra (1942–1953)." PhD diss., University of Connecticut, 1999. *ETD Collection for University of Connecticut.* Paper AAI9946751.

68. Francis D. Perkins, review, *New York Herald Tribune*, 24 December 1951.

69. C. H., review, *New York Times*, 26 December 1951.

70. David Shaw, "Composition and Analysis of Symphony No. 1 by David Shaw, and Analysis of Symphony No. 5 by Peter Mennin" (PhD diss., University of Northern Colorado, 2004), 72–77.

71. P. Mennin, quoted in Frank J. Oteri, CD liner notes, First Edition Music FECD-0013 (2003).

72. Frank J. Oteri, CD liner notes, First Edition Music FECD-0013 (2003).

73. Jay S. Harrison, review, *New York Times*, 1 January 1951.

74. Arthur Berger, review, *New York Herald Tribune*, 18 January 1951.

75. Howard Taubman, review, *New York Times*, 18 January 1951.

76. Henry Cowell, review, Musical Quarterly (April 1951): 248–50.

77. Howard Dicus, "Clef's Notes," *United Press International*, 17 May 1998.

78. Karl Miller, review, *Classical Net*, 1997, www.classical.net/music/recs/reviews/a/alb00260a.html (accessed 25 March 2010).

79. David Raymond, review, *American Record Guide* (February 1998): 131.

80. C.H., review, *New York Times*, 25 February 1952.

81. Virgil Thomson, review, *New York Herald Tribune*, 25 February 1952.

82. Vincent Persichetti, review, *Musical Quarterly* (July 1954): 476.

83. P. Mennin, quoted in Jim Svejda, CD liner notes, Delos DE-3164 (1996), 7.

84. William Bender, review, *New York Times*, 8 November 1952.

85. Jay S. Harrison, review, *New York Herald Tribune*, 8 November 1952.

86. Richard Franko Goldman, review, *Musical Quarterly* (April 1953): 247–49.

87. Steven Schwartz, review, *Classical Net*, 1998, www.classical.net/music/recs/reviews/d/de103164a.php (accessed 3 April 2010).

88. Alex Ross, review, *New York Times*, 27 January 1996.

89. Herbert Kupferberg, review, *New York Post*, 29 January 1996.

90. Frank J. Oteri, CD liner notes, First Edition Music FECD-0013 (2003).

91. Olin Downes, review, *New York Times*, 18 February 1955.

92. Paul Henry Lang, review, *New York Herald Tribune*, 18 February 1955.

93. Irving Kolodin, review, *Saturday Review* (5 March 1955): 29.

94. Paul Snook, "Classical Hall of Fame," *Fanfare* (July/August 1978): 126.

95. David Raymond, review, *American Record Guide* (February 1998): 131.

96. David Hurwitz, review, *Classics Today*, www.classicstoday.com/review. asp?ReviewNum=3170 (accessed 3 April 2010).

97. Hendl, "The Music of Peter Mennin," 18–25.

98. Vincent Persichetti, conversation with Walter Simmons, 22 January 1979.

99. Howard Taubman, review, *New York Times*, 11 February 1956.

100. Howard Taubman, review, *New York Times*, 20 October 1956.

101. Irving Lowens, review, *Musical Quarterly* (January 1957): 97–98.

102. Winthrop Sargeant, review, *New Yorker* (15 March 1958): 110.

103. Howard Taubman, review, *New York Times*, 8 March 1958.

104. Francis D. Perkins, review, *New York Herald Tribune*, 9 March 1958.

105. P. Mennin, quoted in Joseph Sagmaster, LP liner notes, Decca DL-710168 (1971).

106. Joseph Sagmaster, LP liner notes, Decca DL-710168 (1971).

107. Theodore Strongin, review, *New York Times*, 17 February 1965.

108. Review, *New York World-Telegram and Sun,* quoted in David Wright, program notes, Juilliard Orchestra (23 January 2006).

109. Harvey Philips, LP liner notes, New World NW-258 (1976), 4.

110. Philips, LP liner notes, 4.

111. William Bender, review, *New York Herald Tribune*, 18 February 1964.

112. Ross Parmenter, review, *New York Times*, 18 February 1964.

113. Harold C. Schonberg, review, *New York Times*, 3 April 1964.

114. John Gruen, review, *New York Herald Tribune*, 3 April 1964.

115. Jay S. Harrison, review, *Musical America* (Musical America, May 1964): 29–30.

116. Steven Schwartz, review, *Classical Net*, 1998, www.classical.net/music/recs/reviews/d/de103164a.php (accessed 4 April 2010).

117. David Hall, review, *Stereo Review* (May 1997): 99.

118. Karl Miller, review, *Classical Net*, 16 October 1997, www.classical.net/music/recs/reviews/a/alb00260a.html (accessed 4 April 2010).

119. James H. North, review, *Fanfare* (July/August 1997): 191.

120. Neil Butterworth, *The American Symphony* (Brookfield, Vt.: Ashgate, 1998), 158.

121. P. Mennin, "Cantata de Virtute, The Pied Piper of Hamelin," Cincinnati May Festival program notes (May 1969).

122. Henry Humphreys, review, *Cincinnati Enquirer*, 3 May 1969.

123. Eleanor Bell, review, *Cincinnati Post & Times-Star*, 3 May 1969.

124. Betty Dietz Krebs, review, *High Fidelity/Musical America* (July 1969): 16.

125. G. Mennin, interviewed by Walter Simmons, 11 January 2007.

126. Harriett Johnson, review, *New York Post*, 26 March 1971.

127. Harold C. Schonberg, review, *New York Times*, 27 March 1971.

128. Quoted in program notes, New York Philharmonic (21 November 1974).

129. Harold C. Schonberg, review, *New York Times*, 22 November 1974.

130. Harriett Johnson, review, *New York Post*, 22 November 1974.

131. Edith Borroff, review, *American Music* (Fall 1991): 330–31.

132. John Canarina, review, *Classical* (July 1990): 42–43.

133. Bret Johnson, review, *Tempo* (September 1990): 58.

134. P. Mennin, quoted in program notes, Chamber Music Society of Lincoln Center (28 March 1976).

135. P. Mennin, "In Celebration of Quality," March 1976, 7.

136. P. Mennin, "In Celebration of Quality," March 1976, 7.

137. P. Mennin, "In Celebration of Quality," March 1976, 7.

138. Donal Henahan, review, *New York Times*, 30 March 1976.

139. Raymond Ericson, review, *New York Times*, 24 January 1979.

140. P. Mennin, quoted in program notes, National Symphony Orchestra (10 March 1981).

141. Nicholas Kenyon, review, *New Yorker* (13 April 1981): 148.

142. Edith Borroff, review, *American Music* (Fall 1991): 330–31.

143. John Canarina, review, *Classical* (July 1990): 43.

144. Bret Johnson, review, *Tempo* (September 1990): 58.

145. Michael Kimmelman, review, *New York Times*, 29 May 1988.

146. Bret Johnson, review, *Tempo* (September 1990): 58.

147. Holland, "Peter Mennin."

148. Benjamin Folkman, program notes, New York Philharmonic (27 May 1988), 20B-20C.

149. Jack Sullivan, review, *American Record Guide* (September/October 1997): 173.

150. Edith Borroff, review, *American Music* (Fall 1991): 330.

151. David Hurwitz, review, *Classics Today*, www.classicstoday.com/review. asp?ReviewNum=3170 (accessed 3 April 2010).

152. Bret Johnson, "Peter Mennin," in *Classical Music*, ed. Alexander J. Morin (San Francisco: Backbeat Books, 2002), 582.

153. Jeremy Eichler, "Honoring an Administrator Who Never Stopped Writing," *New York Times*, 26 October 2005.

154. David Wright, program notes, "A Tribute to Peter Mennin," Alice Tully Hall (24 October 2005).

SELECTED BIBLIOGRAPHY

Butterworth, Neil. *The American Symphony*. Brookfield, Vt.: Ashgate, 1998: 156–59.

Carrington, Mark. "For the Sake of Art: A Talk with Peter Mennin." *Symphony* (October/November 1983): 40ff.

Hendl, Walter. "The Music of Peter Mennin." *Juilliard Review* (Spring 1954): 18–25.

Holland, Bernard. "Peter Mennin, Juilliard President and Prolific Composer, Dies at 60." *New York Times*, 18 June 1983.

Mayer, Martin. "Are the Trying Times Just Beginning?" *New York Times*, 28 September 1969, 17ff.

Olmstead, Andrea. *Juilliard: A History*. Urbana: University of Illinois Press, 1999, 241–66.

Owens, David. "Composer Peter Mennin." *Christian Science Monitor* (29–30 July 1981).

Phillips, Harvey. "Symphony No. 7," LP liner notes. New World NW-258 (1976).

ESSENTIAL DISCOGRAPHY

Albany TROY260: Symphony No. 5; Symphony No. 6; Concertato, "Moby Dick"; *Fantasia* for Strings (Albany Sym. Orch., David Alan Miller, cond.); www.albanyrecords.com/

NW 371–2: Symphony No. 8; Symphony No. 9; *Folk Overture* (Columbus Sym. Orch., Christian Badea, cond.); www.newworldrecords.org/

NWCR-741: Symphony No. 3 (NY Phil., Dimitri Mitropoulos, cond.); Symphony No. 7 (Chicago Sym. Orch., Jean Martinon, cond.); Piano Concerto (John Ogdon, piano; Royal Phil. Orch., Igor Buketoff, cond.); www.newworldrecords.org/

Phoenix PHCD-107: Symphony No. 4, "The Cycle" (Camerata Singers, Sym. Orch., Abraham Kaplan, cond.); www.phoenixcd.com/

Index

Pulitzer Prizes, 31–32, 46, 73
A Question of Taste (Schuman), 48,
   154–56
Quintet for Piano and Strings, Op. 66
   (Persichetti), 287–89

Ramey, Phillip, 46, 49
Raver, Leonard, 234–35
Raymond, David, 365, 376–77
RCA recordings of Schuman, 43–44
Rees, Rosalind, 139–40
Reflections of Emily (Mennin), 398–99
Reflective Keyboard Studies Op. 138
   (Persichetti), 219–20
Reich, Steve, 179
Reiner, Fritz, 176
Rich, Alan, 114
Robertson, Nan, 148
Rockwell, John: on Persichetti, 242,
   253, 264; on Schuman, 137–38, 147,
   151, 156
Rodzinski, Artur, 31
Rosenfeld, Paul, 59–60
Rosenthal, Laurence, 205–6
Ross, Alex, 372
Rothstein, Edward, 158
Rouse, Christopher, 45, 70, 75, 108,
   140, 142

Saal, Hubert, 262
Sabin, Robert, 86, 102, 215, 225
Sachs, Joel, 18
Sanders, Robert L., 258
Sarah Lawrence College, 27–28
Sargeant, Winthrop, 381–82
Schauensee, Max de, 242, 245, 310–11
Schirmer, Gustav, 32, 37, 45
Schloss, Edwin H., 242
Schneider, Richard, 106
Schoenberg, Arnold, 1–2, 200–201, 285
Schonberg, Harold: on Mennin, 387,
   392–93, 394–95; on Persichetti, 204,
   262, 264; on Schuman, 39, 94, 104,
   111, 125, 127, 142, 144–45
Schreiber, Flora Rheta, 36

Schubart, Mark, 40
Schumann, Michelle, 211
Schuman, William, *22*; administrative work, 23, 36, 44–47; awards,
   31–32, 46, 48, 67, 73, 156; birth,
   24; on composition, 46, 49, 54–55;
   death, 48; early years, 25–26; family
   life, 35–36, 40–41; health, 25–26,
   48; importance of, 23–24, 49–57,
   156–60; influence on Persichetti,
   250–51; at Juilliard School, 32–35;
   lecture tours, 44; at Lincoln Center,
   38–42; marriage to Frances Prince,
   26, 27–28, 44; memorials, 158–60;
   Mennin's relationship with, 341–43;
   on Persichetti, 187, 196, 265; Persichetti's relationship with, 177–78,
   183; personality, 32, 36–37, 48–49;
   at Sarah Lawrence College, 27–28;
   young adulthood, 26–31
Schuman, works of: comparison to
   Mennin and Persichetti, 12–19; early
   style-period, 60–75; essential discography, 171; exploratory phase, 55,
   57–60; late style-period, 55, 107–56;
   middle style-period, 55, 75–107;
   most representative, fully realized, 56
Schuman, specific works: *Amaryllis*, 120–
   22, 132, 133, 140–41; *American Festival Overture*, 30, 60–62; *American
   Hymn*, 145–47; *Anniversary Fanfare*,
   129; *Carols of Death*, 102–3; *Concerto on Old English Rounds*, 132–35,
   140–41; *Credendum*, 35, 98–100, 129;
   A Free Song, 72–73; *George Washington Bridge*, 87–88; *In Praise of Shahn*,
   128–31, 136; *In Sweet Music*, 140–42;
   Judith, 84–87; *The Lord Has a Child*,
   145; *The Mighty Casey*, 16–17, 45,
   48, 91–96, 140, 154–55; *New England
   Triptych*, 100–102, 159; *Newsreel*, 87;
   Night Journey, 34, 78–80; *On Freedom's Ground*, 47, 147–52; *A Question
   of Taste*, 48, 154–56; *Song of Orpheus*, 113–14, 140–42; String Quartet

About the Author

Walter Simmons is a musicologist and critic who has been intensely interested in twentieth-century music since his early teens. Holding a master's degree in theory and musicology from the Manhattan School of Music, he has contributed to several editions of the *New Grove Dictionary of Music*, *American National Biography*, the *All-Music Guide*, and scores of other publications, including the *American Record Guide* and *Musical America*. In addition, he has been a regular contributor to *Fanfare* for more than thirty years. Simmons has been active as a radio host and producer, a program annotator, lecturer, and teacher, and as a producer of recordings and educational materials about music. He is a recipient of the ASCAP/Deems Taylor Award for music criticism and the National Educational Film Festival Award. In 2004, his book, *Voices in the Wilderness: Six American Neo-Romantic Composers* was published by Scarecrow Press. Hundreds of his writings can be found on his website at http://www.walter-simmons.com.

Made in the USA
Monee, IL
22 May 2020